D0145030

**American Educational
Research Association**

Dear *Review of Research in Education* subscriber,

The copy of the 2009 *Review of Research in Education* ("Risk, Schooling, and Equity") previously mailed to you contained numerous errors, including but not limited to a black-and-white image on the front cover. The *RRE* volume accompanying this letter has been prepared with a correctly printed cover and changes made to the table of contents, the introduction, and numerous chapters. Significant corrections were made to chapters 5 and 8; minor corrections were made to other chapters. Please replace the previously received copy with this copy.

The American Educational Research Association asked SAGE to print this corrected copy for you and all other *RRE* subscribers, so that the 2009 edition meets the expectations of AERA, the editors and contributors, and the readership. AERA incurred no additional cost for this corrected copy.

SAGE apologizes for any inconvenience or confusion these errors might have caused. If you have any questions, please contact SAGE Journals Customer Service at 800-818-7243 or journals@sagepub.com.

REVIEW OF
RESEARCH IN
EDUCATION

Review of Research in Education is published on behalf of the American Educational Research Association by SAGE Publications, Thousand Oaks, CA 91320. Copyright © 2009 by the American Educational Research Association. All rights reserved. No portion of the contents may be reproduced in any form without written permission from the publisher. POSTMASTER: Send address changes to AERA Membership Department, 1430 K St., NW, Suite 1200, Washington, DC 20005.

Member Information: American Educational Research Association (AERA) member inquiries, member renewal requests, changes of address, and membership subscription inquiries should be addressed to the AERA Membership Department, 1430 K St., NW, Suite 1200, Washington, DC 20005; fax 202-238-3250. AERA annual membership dues are $120 (Regular and Affiliate Members), $100 (International Affiliates), and $35 (Graduate and Undergraduate Student Affiliates). **Claims:** Claims for undelivered copies must be made no later than six months following month of publication. Beyond six months and at the request of the American Educational Research Association, the publisher will supply missing copies when losses have been sustained in transit and when the reserve stock permits.

Subscription Information: All non-member subscription inquiries, orders, back-issue requests, claims, and renewals should be addressed to Sage Publications, 2455 Teller Road, Thousand Oaks, CA 91320; telephone (800) 818-SAGE (7243) and (805) 499-0721; fax: (805) 375-1700; e-mail: journals@sagepub.com; http://www.sagepublications.com. **Subscription Price:** Institutions: $148; Individuals: $52. For all customers outside the Americas, please visit http://www.sagepub.co.uk/customercare.nav for information. **Claims:** Claims for undelivered copies must be made no later than six months following month of publication. The publisher will supply missing copies when losses have been sustained in transit and when the reserve stock will permit.

Abstracting and Indexing: This journal is abstracted or indexed in Current Contents: Social & Behavioral Sciences, ERIC (Education Resources Information Center), Scopus, and Social Sciences Citation Index (Web of Science).

Copyright Permission: Permission requests to photocopy or otherwise reproduce copyrighted material owned by the American Educational Research Association should be submitted by accessing the Copyright Clearance Center's Rightslink® service through the journal's website at http://rre.aera.net. Permission may also be requested by contacting the Copyright Clearance Center via its website at http://www.copyright.com, or via e-mail at info@copyright.com.

Advertising and Reprints: Current advertising rates and specifications may be obtained by contacting the advertising coordinator in the Thousand Oaks office at (805) 410-7763 or by sending an e-mail to advertising@sagepub.com. To order reprints, please e-mail reprint@sagepub.com. Acceptance of advertising in this journal in no way implies endorsement of the advertised product or service by SAGE or the journal's affiliated society(ies). No endorsement is intended or implied. SAGE reserves the right to reject any advertising it deems as inappropriate for this journal.

Change of Address: Six weeks' advance notice must be given when notifying of change of address. Please send old address label along with the new address to ensure proper identification. Please specify name of journal.

International Standard Serial Number ISSN 0091-732X
International Standard Book Number ISBN 978-1-4129-7573-5 (Vol. 33, 2009, paper)
Manufactured in the United States of America. First printing, March 2009.
Copyright © 2009 by the American Educational Research Association. All rights reserved.

Printed on acid-free paper

REVIEW OF RESEARCH IN EDUCATION

Risk, Schooling, and Equity

Volume 33, 2009

Vivian L. Gadsden, Editor
University of Pennsylvania

James Earl Davis, Editor
Temple University

Alfredo J. Artiles, Editor
Arizona State University

American Educational Research Association

⑤SAGE

Review of Research in Education
Risk, Schooling, and Equity
Volume 33

EDITORS

VIVIAN L. GADSDEN
University of Pennsylvania

JAMES EARL DAVIS
Temple University

ALFREDO J. ARTILES
Arizona State University

CONTRIBUTORS

KATE T. ANDERSON
National Institute of Education, Singapore

ANGELA E. ARZUBIAGA
Arizona State University

JOHN BAUGH
Washington University, St. Louis

GERALD CAMPANO
Indiana University

LIJUN CHEN
University of Chicago

KRIS D. GUTIÉRREZ
University of California, Los Angeles

LIESEL HIBBERT
University of the Western Cape, South Africa

LORI DIANE HILL
University of Michigan

GLYNDA HULL
New York University

SEAN JOE
University of Michigan

EMANIQUE JOE
University of Michigan

CAROL D. LEE
Northwestern University

JIN SOOK LEE
University of California, Santa Barbara

P. ZITLALI MORALES
University of California, Los Angeles

RAY MCDERMOTT
Stanford University

DANNY C. MARTINEZ
University of California, Los Angeles

SILVIA C. NOGUERÓN
Arizona State University

CARLA O'CONNOR
University of Michigan

INGRID SEYER-OCHI
University of California, Berkeley

JASON D. RALEY
University of California, Santa Barbara

SHANTA R. ROBINSON
University of Michigan

LARRY L. ROWLEY
University of Michigan

CHERYL SMITHGALL
University of Chicago

HOWARD STEVENSON
University of Pennsylvania

AMANDA L. SULLIVAN
Arizona State University

DUANE E. THOMAS
University of Pennsylvania

LALITHA VASUDEVAN
Columbia University

FRED WULCZYN
University of Chicago

JESSICA ZACHER
California State University, Long Beach

EDITORIAL BOARD

ARNETHA BALL
Stanford University

PHILIP BOWMAN
University of Michigan
National Center for Institutional Diversity

DENNIS CULHANE
University of Pennsylvania

MICHAEL CUNNINGHAM
Tulane University

FREDERICK ERICKSON
University of California, Los Angeles

ROBERT FECHO
University of Georgia

SARAH FREEDMAN
University of California, Berkeley

NORMA GONZALEZ
University of Arizona

MARJORIE H. GOODWIN
University of California, Los Angeles

VIOLET J. HARRIS
University of Illinois, Champaign-Urbana

NANCY HORNBERGER
University of Pennsylvania

CYNTHIA HUDLEY
University of California, Santa Barbara

JOANNE LARSON
University of Rochester

RICHARD LERNER
Tufts University

ALLAN LUKE
Queensland University of Technology

RITTY LUKOSE
University of Pennsylvania

HUGH "BUD" MEHAN
University of California, San Diego

PEDRO NOGUERA
New York University

MARJORIE ORELLANA
University of California, Los Angeles

CHARLES PAYNE
University of Chicago

BEN RAMPTON
Kings College, London

JOHN RICKFORD
Stanford University

ROBERT RUEDA
University of Southern California

MARGARET BEALE SPENCER
University of Pennsylvania

DAVID TAKEUCHI
University of Washington

HERVE VARENNE
Teachers College, Columbia Univesity

ARLETTE WILLIS
University of Illinois, Champaign-Urbana

STANTON WORTHAM
University of Pennsylvania

AMERICAN EDUCATIONAL RESEARCH ASSOCIATION
TEL: 202-238-3200 FAX: 202-238-3250
http://www.aera.net/pubs

FELICE J. LEVINE
Executive Director

TODD REITZEL
Director of Publications

BARBARA LEITHAM
Publications Coordinator

Contents

Cover image © Jason Moore. *Hallway to Hope*. Shutterstock Images.

Erratum

Editorial Board (2008). *Review of Education Research, 32*, page iv.
The editorial board listing omitted the name of Geoff Whitty, Institute of Education, University
of London.

Introduction
Risk, Equity, and Schooling: Transforming the Discourse

VIVIAN L. GADSDEN
University of Pennsylvania

JAMES EARL DAVIS
Temple University

ALFREDO J. ARTILES
Arizona State University

The issue of risk is addressed across a range of disciplines but has a particularly tenuous history in relationship to schooling and equity. Rist's (1970) study, written almost 40 years ago, provided a provocative analysis of the ways in which classroom experience mirrored structural hierarchies in society and in which teacher interactions often disadvantage poor students, putting them at risk for school failure. Related analyses, prior to Rist's study and into the present, have reinforced this point. For example, in *Social Theory and Social Structure,* Merton (1957) described a self-fulfilling prophecy effect, that is, when a false definition of a situation evokes a new behavior that then makes the original false conception come true. A decade later, Rosenthal and Jacobson (1968) found that students' performance was consistent with teachers' expectations of those who had been identified as high achievers, irrespective of their actual performance. In other words, once an expectation is set, even if it is not accurate, we tend to act in ways that are consistent with that expectation. Aside from the various caveats raised about this study, the idea of self-fulfilling prophecy calls attention to the ways in which strong beliefs are likely to become enacted in classroom practices and interactions such that students fulfill low expectations and, as a result, are placed at risk. More recently, Steele and Aronson (1995) offered evidence about the roles social contexts of assessment and stereotype threats play in individuals' performance. The common reference to "placing students at

Review of Research in Education
March 2009, Vol. 33, pp. vii–xi
DOI: 10.3102/0091732X08330002
© 2009 AERA. http://rre.aera.net

risk" has been used widely, as institutions, most notably schools, are studied to determine their role in both contributing to students' school difficulty and failure and serving as agents and sites of positive change.

In this volume, we are concerned with the multiple ways that the concept of "risk" has been taken up and inscribed in different discourses, the ways that it is experienced and lived in and out of school, and the potential for reducing the institutional barriers to students' full engagement in school. The past decade brought new ways of thinking about children and youth and critical analysis of factors that result in children and youth being placed at risk (Artiles, Klingner, & Tate, 2006; Rose, 1999). However, the concept of risk is variable, depending on disciplinary understandings; perceptions of students based on race, class, gender, and sexual preference; poverty and hardship that result in social vulnerability; and classroom, school, and structural practices across domains that restrict rather than present opportunity.

The chapters in this volume, written by scholars representing a range of theoretical perspectives and research interests in reference to children and youth, raise questions about current conceptualizations of risk and the transformations that these conceptualizations may portend. We have termed this *framing* here and elsewhere as a reconceptualizing of risk that challenges existing frameworks and urges a recrafting of approaches and thinking that reflect the variability in risk, access, and equity experienced by students. Some of these risks concern the socioeconomic constraints that students and their families face; others concern the racial and ethnic bias to which they are exposed directly and subtly; others are located in the quality of their environments; others are situated in their health status; still others represent the approaches that research, practice, and policies have taken that may inadvertently rewrite rather than effectively eliminate constraints. Throughout the poignant analyses in the chapters, readers will see images of students whom they have studied, taught, or known over the course of their lives. These chapters then ask, through direct and indirect references, questions about the trajectories of these students and the best ways to study them and use research to improve instructional and classroom practices as well as school cultures.

In addition, as the chapters in this volume suggest, few terms have evoked more dissension and concern than the concept of risk and the attendant measures around labeling that are often attached. Recent discussions about the achievement gap are but part of an expansive conceptualization of the barriers and possibilities for students' health, well-being, and success in and out of school. With responses that often take issue with or contest a singular focus on standardized measures, emerging analyses are broadening traditional explanations that center on the implicit "at-riskness" of certain status positions. However, the inherent conceptual and methodological limitations related to conventional notions of risk and risk behaviors for children, adolescents, young adults, and their families are increasingly being challenged by growing bodies of research. Rather than only forming questions about the negative link among risk status; education; and social, economic, and health disparities, researchers such as those who have written in the volume pose informed questions about processes at work that create the impetus for the disparities to exist. They consider the ways in which social locations, too often attributed to risk only, can also serve as potential and potent sites for challenging hierarchies and differences in outcomes.

A theme that runs throughout the chapters is that new ideas of risk as places where expected trajectories are interrupted and new ones developed are finding their way into the literature. Understanding the experience of and response to social location and status can provide insightful commentary on the current state and future conditions of children, youth, and their families. Such work is not limited to how well students perform in school but how they navigate school (i.e., the nature of the experience and processes), with attention to the quality of their lives and the availability and accessibility of options that will contribute to, if not ensure, their success. Work in this area continues to deepen, not only embracing the school lives of students but also examining the nature of their out-of-school experiences and the ways in which their lives are affected by race, gender, class, and difference.

This volume addresses longstanding issues in educational and social science research, practice, and policy: risk and equity within the broad contexts of schooling. Unraveling some of the complexities related to precarious risk status for young people creates an opportunity to rethink and reimagine education and social well-being not only for students labeled as at risk but also for all students. Researchers are uniquely positioned to play a critical role in developing well-conceived models and interventions that are strength focused, community driven, geographically relevant, and sustainable to influence the life chances and outcomes for all students. Knowing how the connections between the everyday significance of social categories (positive and negative) implicate risk and how they are addressed will advance the field. What hopefully will surface from a reconceptualized treatment of risk as we know it, particularly at the intersections of race, social class, gender, and other forms of differences, are new insights and perspectives that inform both how educational research reassesses these conditions and their consequences and how policy and practice, in turn, reflect these new understandings.

As the chapters in this volume suggest, it is the manipulation of the concept of risk that makes many uneasy, not because they do not think that many students are placed in vulnerable situations but because they fear that the rhetoric of risk supersedes any effort to understand the issues that make students vulnerable in school; the social conditions and, often, marginalization that contribute to their vulnerability out of school; and the possibilities that must sit in school and that have the potential to interrupt and erode the conditions that create the vulnerability, hence risk, in the first place. They demonstrate that risks may be examined more generally and include sociodemographic factors such as low socioeconomic status, overcrowding or large family size, low maternal education, limited employment skills by the head of the household, and welfare status. They may refer to *high risk*, which has been used more often in work on infants and young children and in the medical and social sciences, and may refer to illnesses such as HIV/AIDS, obesity, or poor emotional attachment (Rutter, 1993; Spencer, 2006). They may also assert the degree to which a set of circumstances, health conditions, and/or social exigencies influence a child's learning, health and well-being, and quality of life. High-risk contexts and precursors are important to understand because of increased levels of vulnerability in which children and their families are positioned both by controlled choice and uncontrolled placement and by circumstance. Schooling experiences informed by instructional practice, curriculum, and classroom and institutional policy offer potential areas for investigating differential levels of risk for students. Although institutions and social hierarchies may be held responsible for placing children at risk, parents and the choices they make around health and behavior play a role as well, and intergenerational cycles often ensue.

These different perspectives on and attributions to risk highlight compelling issues about who places students at risk and the ways in which not only the concept of risk but also the range of risk, discourses around risk, and the embeddedness of risk in problems such as poverty are examined in educational research. They challenge a curious pattern of unstated expectations by adults of children facing hardship or who are made vulnerable: that they have at their disposal a package of strategies that they can readily access to rise above any adverse circumstance (Gadsden, 2006). This view reduces the creation and implementation of needed support for children such that they are revered for their persistence and resilience—to get along with so little and to be able to withstand hardship—but not necessarily relieved of the weighty responsibilities for self-care and survival. Not unlike Kotlowitz's (1991) suggestion in his popular text *There Are No Children Here*, common images capture only a part of the lives of these children (e.g., the victims of Hurricane Katrina), pointing to the one child who "made it" but still seeking ways to create opportunity for those who do not experience success.

Our original hope in this volume was to attend to as many references to risk in relationship to students as possible—to paint a portrait of how the issues are conceptualized and how they may be reconceptualized. As we write this introduction, we are mindful that the recent presidential election has given those of us in the United States a leader who as a child may have been described in any number of ways that put him at risk: Black, male, child of a single mother, child of an absent father, and variable school performer. The significance of support within family, school, and community counteracted the negative stereotyping that would have limited rather than expanded opportunity for him. In similar but not identical ways, students in schools throughout the United States and the world bring with them a range of strengths and exigencies; they often look to schools and those who are committed to schooling to help abate the problems that they face and secure the potential that they possess.

The analyses in the chapters aim to bring notice to theoretical, epistemological, practical, and policy considerations in the constructions of risk as concept and practice, recognizing the reciprocity between the in-school and out-of-school lives of students. The chapters draw from a range of disciplines and perspectives to examine issues often discussed in educational research (e.g., literacy, schooling, and classroom practices), concerns that are only now emerging (e.g., immigrant students and parents and incarcerated youth), and topics typically relegated to explanatory variables but not objects of our attention (e.g., child neglect and health and well-being). All of the entries for this volume address historical and contemporary issues around risk and educational and social disparities and equity—within schools, in teaching, in families and neighborhoods, and in policy. By examining risk at different levels (e.g., individuals, families, and institutions) and through different lenses, experiences, and identities (e.g., race, gender, class, and sexual orientation), our goal has been to provide a critical look at both the issues and the venues that allow us to understand the problems as well as the opportunities and places for change. At this point in our history, these issues do not simply represent social designations for our thinking but are increasingly urgent sites to (re)conceptualize risk, equity, and schooling and to commit to positive change.

ACKNOWLEDGEMENTS

Much of the early work leading to this volume took place at the Spencer Foundation during the research fellowship of the first author. We are indebted to the Spencer Foundation for its support of this work and to the Spencer and Casey Foundations for their support of a roundtable and national working group focused on (re)conceptualizing risk, access, and equity of schooling and education. The third author acknowledges the support of the Center for Advanced Study in the Behavioral Sciences at Stanford University and the National Center for Culturally Responsive Educational Systems under Grant H326E020003 awarded by the U.S. Department of Education, Office of Special Education Programs. The editors wish to thank editorial assistant, Jie Park, a doctoral candidate in the Graduate School of Education at the University of Pennsylvania, who managed the process with great care and precision. The editors also thank Cleopatra Jacobs and Sue Bickerstaff, also doctoral candidates in the Graduate School of Education at the University of Pennsylvania, for their research assistance and for the goodwill with which they took up our requests for such assistance. Address correspondence to Vivian L. Gadsden at viviang@gse.upenn.edu.

REFERENCES

Artiles, A. J., Klingner, J. K., & Tate, W. F. (Eds.). (2006). Representation of minority students in special education: Complicating traditional explanations. *Educational Researcher, 35*(6), 3–28.

Gadsden, V. L. (2006). Educational equity in post-disaster New Orleans. In E. L. Birch & S. M. Wachter (Eds.), *Rebuilding urban places after disaster: Lessons from Hurricane Katrina* (pp. 201–216). Philadelphia: University of Pennsylvania Press.

Kotlowitz, A. (1991). *There are no children here: The story of two boys growing up in the other America.* New York: Doubleday.

Merton, R. K. (1957). *Social theory and social structure* (Rev. ed.). New York: Free Press.

Rist, R. C. (1970). Student social class and teacher expectations: The self-fulfilling prophecy in ghetto education. *Harvard Educational Review, 40,* 411–451.

Rose, M. (1999). *Possible lives.* New York: Penguin.

Rosenthal, R., & Jacobson, L. (1968). *Pygmalion in the classroom: Teacher expectations and student intellectual development.* New York: Holt, Rinehart & Winston.

Rutter, M. (1993). Resilience: Some conceptual considerations. *Journal of Adolescent Health, 14,* 626–631.

Spencer, M. B. (2006). Phenomenology and ecological systems theory: Development of diverse groups. In W. Damon & R. Lerner (Eds.), *Handbook of child psychology: Vol. 1, Theoretical models of human development* (6th ed., pp. 829–893). New York: John Wiley.

Steele, C. M., & Aronson, J. (1995). Stereotype threat and the intellectual test performance of African-Americans. *Journal of Personality and Social Psychology, 69,* 797–811.

Chapter 1

Who's at Risk in School and What's Race Got to Do With It?

Carla O'Connor
Lori Diane Hill
Shanta R. Robinson
University of Michigan

Who is at risk in school, and what does race have to do with it? In responding to the first part of this question, researchers have relied extensively on quantitative analyses. Historically, such studies have either calculated the "likelihood" of poor educational outcomes (e.g., dropping out of high school and/or course failure) for different demographic categories or documented the underperformance of one demographic category compared to another on a host of academic measures, including grade point average (GPA), high school completion, and, most often, performance on standardized achievement tests. In empirical analyses of this kind, race has often been reduced to a variable, and study after study has demonstrated its reliable and robust correlation with indices of educational achievement and attainment (e.g., Baker, 2001; Fryer & Levitt, 2006; Hedges & Nowell, 1999; Jones, 1988–1989; J. Lee, 2002; Patterson, Kupersmidt, & Vaden, 1990; for a detailed discussion regarding the use of race as a variable, also see O'Connor, Lewis, & Mueller, 2007). Within the discourse of risk, findings from these analyses have been interpreted as "evidence" that particular racial groups are more susceptible to negative or maladaptive educational outcomes than others. Conclusions drawn from these findings also suggest that we can "predict" the chances for academic failure or underachievement based on one's racial group membership (see Natriello, McDill, & Pallas, 1990).

Studies of the extent to which race correlates with educational outcomes and elucidates achievement gaps predate the discourse on risk (which was founded in epidemiological studies). However, the publication of *A Nation at Risk* (National Commission on Excellence in Education, 1983) shepherded the notion of risk and

Review of Research in Education
March 2009, Vol. 33, pp. 1-34
DOI: 10.3102/0091732X08327991
© 2009 AERA. http://rre.aera.net

the "at risk" label into educational and popular discourse (Margonis, 1992; Winfield, 1991).[1] The report argued that our nation was *at risk* in a competitive global economy because of a "rising tide of mediocrity" that was evidenced by a wide variety of achievement data that presumably indicated that the academic performance of U.S. students was abysmal and that they were underperforming relative to a previous generation of students and in international comparisons. In this report, at-risk status was defined as a function of inadequate educational outcomes. Thus, the report provided a logic for assigning at-risk status to members of demographic groups whose educational outcomes were routinely judged inadequate. Consequently, when in ongoing studies of race and achievement racial groups were shown to have poor or depressed educational outcomes (relative to other racial groups), they were subsumed under the at-risk label.[2]

Two years post the publication of a *Nation of Risk,* the publication of the report *Barriers to Excellence: Our Children at Risk* (National Coalition of Advocates for Students, 1985) represented early efforts on the part of educational scholars to highlight the environmental conditions and inequities that placed historically disenfranchised groups at academic risk (Margonis, 1992). Despite these early efforts to elucidate the institutional and structural forces that placed children at risk, at-risk status was commonly reduced to an internalized trait or inherent characteristic and rapidly became synonymous with "minority" status (Freeberg, 1987; Natriello et al., 1990; Swadener, 1995).[3]

Having identified Blacks, Latinos, and, to a lesser extent, Native Americans as at risk for poor or depressed educational outcomes,[4] contemporary researchers have worked to explain what places these populations at educational risk. In most instances, the term *risk* is not explicitly invoked in contemporary studies aimed at explaining the relative underperformance of these groups (e.g., Entwisle & Alexander, 1992; Goldsmith, 2003; Orr, 2003; Roscigno, 2000). Of those studies that do invoke the term, few work to conceptualize risk (offering important exceptions are Catterall, 1998; Lubeck & Garrett, 1990; O'Connor, 2002; Skinner, Bryant, Coffman, & Campbell, 1998). Rather, the term is extended as a status that the reader might take for granted in relation to the populations under study. The purpose of these studies is, nevertheless, aimed at explaining the robust statistical relationships that have been evidenced between race and educational outcomes and have marked some racial groups as being at risk in school and in the popular imagination. Consequently, the notion that these populations are at risk in school is a palatable, albeit often unstated, assumption in contemporary educational discourse.

In this chapter, we analyze the survey literature that statistically defines some racial groups and not others as being at educational risk. We begin by examining how in naming which racial groups are at risk in school, researchers not only aggregate demographic data in ways that mask the variation in achievement that occurs within and across racial groups but also selectively highlight some achievement gaps and indices of underperformance and not others. We then elucidate how such selective analyses both infringe on our ability to make sense of risk as a social category and underestimate the extent to which schools operate such that youth are either placed at educational risk or protected from it. In light of the prospective role of schools, we analyze contemporary research efforts aimed at delineating and interpreting how schools structure achievement through their institutional character and practices and by implication inform the relationship between race and achievement. Toward that end, we review the literature that examines how the resources, racial composition, culture, and organization of schools inform racial gaps in achievement. We also examine the research literature that elucidates how schools and teachers make meaning of race in ways that affect students' educational experiences and by implication their educational outcomes. In concluding our review, we illuminate the complement between these two literature strands and how this complement offers promising directions for future research.

INTERPRETIVE BIAS IN THE DELINEATION AND FRAMING OF WHO IS AT RISK IN SCHOOL

Explorations of how race varies with achievement have highlighted the Black–White achievement gap to the near exclusion of other racial gaps. The early privileging of the Black–White achievement gap, in part, grew out of demographic and political realities. Blacks had historically constituted the non-White majority in the United States, and the civil rights movement, Black power movement, and *Brown v. Board of Education* (1954) decision gave "voice" to the subjugation and contestation of Blacks vis-à-vis Whites in ways that overshadowed the subjugation and political activity of other racial minorities. Survey research reflected these demographic and political realities in that the data sets on which the studies were based were developed or analyzed in the interest of establishing singular comparisons between Blacks and Whites. Alternatively, other racial groups were excluded from these analyses because they were underrepresented demographically or in a given data set and did not constitute a population large enough to pursue robust statistical analyses of their educational outcomes (Kao & Thompson, 2003). Given shifting demographics (i.e., the substantive growth in Latino and Asian American populations based on differential birth rates and patterns of immigration; Ream, 2003), survey efforts aimed at including representative samples of these growing populations, and the increasing call to move beyond the Black–White dichotomy, researchers have begun more systematic documentation of other ethnic/racial gaps in achievement.

For example, researchers have explored Hispanic–White achievement gaps and drawn comparisons between these gaps and Black–White achievement gaps.[5] Analyses of various national longitudinal data sets (e.g., National Educational Longitudinal Study, High School and Beyond, National Longitudinal Survey of Youth) indicate that in the case of test scores, both Black–White and Hispanic–White achievement gaps are substantive and enduring, despite evidence showing that they had narrowed through the 1980s, stabilized, and, according to some evidence, grown during the 1990s (Hedges & Nowell, 1999; J. Lee, 2002). With regard to dropout rates and GPA, the gaps between Blacks and Whites and between Hispanics and Whites also situate Blacks and Hispanics at a statistical disadvantage (Teachman, Paasch, & Carver, 1996; Velez, 1989; Warren, 1996; White & Kaufman, 1997). In the case of the Hispanic–White gaps, however, some researchers have found that the variation in some gaps, particularly those related to dropout rates and GPA, can be explained by controlling for background characteristics (e.g., socioeconomic status [SES], immigrant status, and prior achievement; e.g., Hauser & Anderson, 1991; Kao, Tienda, & Schneider, 1996). However, race-related variables generally retain statistical significance after covariates are incorporated in studies of Black–White achievement gaps, with measures of early school achievement being a departure from this pattern and to be discussed later in this chapter (Fryer & Levitt, 2004, 2006; Kao & Thompson, 2003).

Researchers also have documented achievement gaps between Whites and Asian Americans (e.g., Baker, Keller-Wolff, & Wolf-Wendel, 2000; Ng, Lee, & Pak, 2007; Ngo & Lee, 2007); however, the available data are insufficient for pursuing substantive analysis of how the gaps between Whites and Asian Americans have changed over time. As Kao and Tompson (2003) write, "Due to [Asian Americans'] small population size in the 1970s, similar trend data are not available" for them (p. 420). Recent National Assessment of Educational Progress scores, however, suggest that the achievement of Asian Americans is comparable to that of Whites on some measures and exceeds White performance on others (Kao & Thompson, 2003). In fact, Asian Americans outstrip the performance of Whites on a host of academic measures including enrollment rates in advanced math and science courses, educational attainment, and performance on college entrance exams (C. Chen & Stevenson, 1995; Hirschman & Wong, 1986; Pearce, 2006; Wong, 1990). As is the case for the Black–White and the Hispanic–White achievement gaps, the gaps between Whites and Asians are most apparent at the highest achievement levels (Hedges & Nowell, 1999; Kao & Thompson, 2003). Kao et al. (1996) found that parental background accounted for differences between Asian Americans and Whites in test scores. Alon (2007) found that parental background factors also accounted for the likelihood of graduating from elite postsecondary institutions. In contrast, Kao and Tienda (1995) found that the higher GPA of Asian Americans relative to Whites could not be explained by such covariates. In Thomas' (2004) analysis of racial achievement gaps on the SAT II writing tests, she found that although the average White student performs better than the average minority student on the SAT II writing exam, Asian American and Black students outperformed White students when controlling for academic performance, family background, and high school fixed effects.

With regard to Native Americans, their educational outcomes relative to other racial groups has been less cleanly defined, in part as a consequence of their small population size. The academic status of smaller populations goes largely unaddressed while researchers focus their attention on the academic status of larger populations (Franzak, 2006). Consequently, although Native American student achievement is believed by some researchers to be the most severely compromised of all racial or ethnic groups and warrants substantive study (Lomawaima & McCarty, 2002; Yates, 1987), it remains severely understudied and regularly receives only fleeting mention in the study of achievement gaps. However, the available data indicate that Native Americans tend to be underrepresented at the highest achievement levels (Kao & Thompson, 2003). Although the dropout rates for Native American students are based on specific populations or regions and are neither collected nor reported in a comprehensive database (Deyhle & Swisher, 1997), the available evidence reveals that Native American dropout rates exceed those of Whites and are among the highest compared to other minority groups (Ladson-Billings, 2006a; Teachman et al., 1996; Velez, 1989; Warren, 1996; White & Kaufman, 1997). In addition, Native Americans experience the lowest rate of students who return to complete high school or an equivalent program, once they drop out (Deyhle & Swisher, 1997, p. 128).

Analyses comparing Native Americans and other groups remain marginalized in the discourse on racial achievement gaps. This is true in part because performance differences between Native Americans and other racial groups have been less precisely measured. The discourse on racial achievement gaps also reflects researchers' selective consideration of racial gaps in achievement that are well documented. In particular, Asian–White gaps in academic performance have not generally captured the interest of the research community. As a consequence, these gaps are regularly obscured by discussions of how the achievement of Blacks and Hispanics compares to that of Whites *and* Asians. If researchers were inclined to disentangle the performance of Whites *and* Asians, the more competitive performance of Asian Americans would require them to situate Asian Americans as the group with whom all other racial groups are compared. References to the "achievement gap" would, in turn, position Asian Americans (and not Whites) as the normative group. As such, in the same way that researchers have asked what it is about Blacks and Hispanics that causes them to underperform relative to Whites, they would have to ask what it is about Whites that causes them to underperform relative to Asian Americans. Instead, researchers have been preoccupied with explaining the underperformance of Blacks and secondarily Hispanics relative to Whites. Scholars have previously discussed how the selective treatment of racial gaps in achievement reflects researchers' preoccupation with the pathology of non-Asian minority groups and is founded in and reifies the notion of White supremacy (e.g., Ladson-Billings, 2006b; C. D. Lee, 2006; O'Connor, 2006a). For the purposes of this chapter, we analyze how the selective attention to some gaps and not others constrains analytical efforts to make sense of who is at risk in school and why. To contend with this issue, we must first delineate the extent to which these broad empirical cleavages in race-related achievement mask the heterogeneity in the educational outcomes that exist *within* racial groups.

As noted by Catterall (1998), "Roughly half the students will exceed any group average, many by a considerable margin," but when average achievement and attainment measures are displayed by income level, race, ethnic origin, or language skills, the effect can be to label whole groups of students at-risk rather than identify for attention those who are experiencing actual difficulties in performance or social integration. (p. 304)

Consequently, individual children or subgroups of children who are, in fact, not at risk may be considered at risk simply by their racial classification. The inverse would also be true. Although this is a reasonably intuitive concern, recent research (e.g., Bali & Alvarez, 2004; Fryer & Levitt, 2006; Mickelson, 2001; Morris, 2004; Thomas, 2004) has illuminated the extraordinary variation with which racial groups achieve in school. This research also illuminates the context-specific nature of these achievement outcomes across the life course and institutional settings. It thereby provides a fertile landscape for complicating contemporary considerations of risk as they apply to racial groups.

REFRAMING VARIATION IN ACHIEVEMENT (GAPS) ACROSS THE LIFE COURSE AND GEOGRAPHIC SPACE

If certain minority groups are at risk as a consequence of their lag in educational performance relative to Whites, they do not necessarily begin school at risk. Despite evidence that minority children lag behind Whites in early literacy and numeracy skills and begin school at a decided disadvantage (Brooks-Gunn & Markman, 2005; Burchinal, Campbell, Bryant, Wasik, & Ramey, 1997; Hart & Risley, 1999; J. Lee, Autry, Fox, & Williams, 2008; Zill & West, 2000), there is growing evidence that after controlling for background characteristics minority children enter school equal to or nearly equivalent to Whites in their preparation for school. In the case of Blacks, researchers have found that after controlling for other background characteristics (particularly SES), Black–White differences in achievement are either statistically insignificant or minimal at school entry and in early elementary (Entwisle & Alexander, 1990, 1992; Fryer & Levitt, 2006; Ginsberg & Russell, 1981; Phillips, Crouse, & Ralph, 1998). On some measures Blacks were even shown to outperform Whites after controls were in place (Fryer & Levitt, 2006). Despite evidence of proximal, comparable, or advantaged performance early in the elementary school career, Blacks lose substantial ground as they proceed through school. For example, Entwisle and Alexander (1990) in their Beginning School Study of Baltimore 6-year-olds found that Black and White children were

equivalent in terms of verbal performance and math computational skills at the point of school entry and only a few points apart in reasoning [but] by the end of first grade . . . they differed significantly by race on all three dimensions with socioeconomic status (SES) and other relevant variables taken into account. (p. 465)

Fryer and Levitt (2006) found that "Black children enter school substantially behind their White counterparts in reading and math, but including a small number of covariates erases the gap" (p. 249). By the end of third grade, however, there is a large

Black–White test score gap that cannot be explained by the covariates (Fryer & Levitt, 2006).

Entwisle and Alexander (1990) argue that findings regarding how Blacks lose ground over the course of their schooling careers offer "persuasive evidence that school-based factors play a considerable role in explaining later performance" (p. 465). The same might be said for Latinos, as both Phillips (1998), drawing from a national data set, and Bali and Alvarez (2004), drawing from a data set from a racially diverse district in California, found that achievement gaps between Latinos and Whites emerged after the start of school. Bali and Alvarez also reported that the onset of the Latino–White gap appeared to be delayed, particularly in math, relative to the emergence of Black–White gaps.

The role that schools might play in effecting racial gaps in achievement is further complicated by Fryer and Levitt (2006), who documented different trends for the emergence and development of the Hispanic–White gap. Fryer and Levitt also distinguished these trends from those that marked the Asian–White gap. After controls were in place, they found that at the start of school Hispanics underperformed relative to Whites in both reading and math. As Hispanics progressed through school, their reading performance relative to Whites remained relatively flat through third grade, whereas they gained substantial ground in math relative to Whites. In contrast, Asian Americans begin school at an advantage compared to Whites. Although "the large advantage enjoyed by Asian Americans in the first two years of school" is maintained in math, in reading this advantaged status diminishes by third grade (Fryer & Levitt, 2006, p. 260). The aforementioned findings indicate that racial gaps in achievement are not necessarily consistent as children move through school. This literature demonstrates that during the early years of school, racial gaps may develop where they had not existed previously. They can otherwise grow, close, or even reverse during this same point in time.

The findings of Rumberger and Willms (1992) demonstrate that the dynamic nature of racial gaps in achievement is not limited to periods of the life course but can also vary across geographic space. Collecting data from school districts across the state of California, they found that at the state level, Blacks and Hispanics underperformed in both math and reading relative to Whites. Asian Americans, however, outperformed Whites in math and underperformed relative to Whites in reading. Looking within districts and having controlled for background characteristics, the gaps between Asians and Whites and between Hispanics and Whites were greatly reduced in many districts. These same covariates did not similarly reduce the gaps between Blacks and Whites. Rumberger and Willms also found (although they did not emphasize these findings) that there was substantive variation with regard to how much of the variance was accounted for by student background. For example, in the case of the Asian–White gap, Asian Americans continued to exceed the performance of Whites in math in *some* districts even after controls were in place.

In light of the findings of Fryer and Levitt (2006), we could argue that it is Blacks *and* Asian Americans who are at risk in school as they *both* lose ground over the course of their early academic careers. We also could argue that Blacks, Hispanics, *and* Whites are *all* at risk in school because they all begin school at an academic disadvantage compared to Asian Americans. The findings of Rumberger and Willms (1992) alternatively suggest that Whites are at risk in math, as controlling for other factors does not always explain their underperformance relative to Asian Americans. We might add that Whites are particularly at risk for underachievement in some districts and not others.

In characterizing the at-risk status of racial groups in these alternative ways, it becomes transparent that the designation of risk is not in and of itself a static and durable category. Rather, it is constructed—a consequence of how researchers have opted to disaggregate achievement data and how they subsequently interpret this disaggregation. Moreover, our alternative characterizations of *who* is at risk highlight the extent to which risk is context specific such that no racial group can always be (not) at risk, at all times, across all spaces, and in relation to all subject matters. We might further elucidate risk as a dynamic social phenomenon in light of the variation with which schools shape the educational outcomes of racial groups. In complicating how we make sense of this variation in relation to the discourse on risk, we indicate that risk is not simply a dynamic and constructed social category but a structured social phenomenon.

REFRAMING THE VARIATION IN SCHOOL EFFECTS

The notion that schools might differentially affect the academic performance of racial groups is evidenced in research on African Americans. Namely, scholars have found that the achievement of Black children is more responsive to school effects. Thus, even though Coleman and his colleagues (1966) found that background characteristics trumped school effects, they also found that schooling made a bigger impact on how Black students performed academically. More recently, Mickelson (2001) and Ferguson (1998) offered evidence that the impact of a good teacher may be greater for Black than for White students. In other words, schools appear to be more influential in determining Black than White achievement. The empirical evidence of these differential effects, however, paled in comparison to the demonstrated effect of family background. Consequently, researchers emphasized the extent to which family background outstripped the impact of schools in defining the academic disadvantage Blacks experienced relative to Whites. This finding raises questions: What if we refocused scholarly attention on evidence of Blacks' greater receptivity to school effects, an issue over which we have greater control? Moreover, what if we examined this evidence in concert with the aforementioned evidence that Blacks lose ground early in their academic careers? The fact that Blacks evidence greater receptivity to school effects but nevertheless lose ground over their schooling careers should prompt us to conclude that it is the failure of schools to "add value" that places Black students at academic risk. Reconceptualizing risk in this way would also illuminate "teachers and schools in well-off, high achieving schools that are coasting" (Stewart, 2006, p. 3) in that they are not adding to the achievement of their student body beyond what students bring as a function of home advantage.

These considerations are echoed in the findings of Entwisle and Alexander (1994). In comparing the achievement of Black and White students across "integrated" and "segregated" (read predominantly Black) schools they found the following:

African Americans in integrated schools made less progress in reading comprehension in winter when school was in session than did their counterparts in segregated schools. In summers, however, when they were not in school, the African American children who attended integrated schools gained considerably more than their counterparts who attended segregated schools. White children made about the same progress in reading in integrated and segregated schools in winters and summers, even though the Whites in integrated schools came from more educationally advantaged families. Thus children from both races in integrated schools, who generally came from more educated families, did not make the expected gains in reading comprehension when school was open. In summers, however, students whose parents had more education forged ahead of those whose parents were high school dropouts. (p. 446)

Although these findings also complicate dominant notions regarding the effects of attending predominantly White versus predominantly minority schools (an issue to be taken up later in this chapter), for the purposes of our current discussion these findings "offer evidence of the power of schools to affect cognitive growth positively" (Entwisle & Alexander, 1994, p. 457). That is, schools can produce learning beyond that which might be predicted by background. In failing to exert this power, schools necessarily compromise the academic development of traditionally underserved populations and thus might be evaluated as having placed these populations at academic risk. But schools can also fail to exert their power to produce cognitive growth in relation to those (i.e., Whites and the middle class) who have provided the standard by which we have evaluated the performance of "others," in which case evidence of more competitive performance on the part of Whites and the middle class would not in and of itself confirm the absence of risk. Rather, risk would only be eluded if researchers could attribute evidence of more competitive performance to the work of schools. If the work of schools did not contribute to these competitive outcomes in any measurable way, the learning of these students was also placed at risk as a consequence of what schools failed to do. Under these conditions, risk would be a function of being in a school where no or little value is afforded by school attendance. And both historically disenfranchised *and* privileged groups would find themselves at risk in educational institutions that are unable to grow their achievement in ways that cannot be accounted for by differences in family background.

Determining whether schools "add value" or put at risk children's opportunities to learn by failing to add value requires us to compare and analyze measures of academic gain rather than measures of academic status (also referred to as value-added modeling). Currently, value-added modeling is rife with methodological challenges (Stewart, 2006). Raudenbush (2004) identified the many technical difficulties associated with measuring gains:

Whether and how to adjust for covariates, whether teachers (or schools) should be treated as fixed or random, how to present cumulative effects of teachers or schools, how to model covariation in student responses and teacher effects, whether and how to incorporate multiple cohorts, and how to formulate models that appropriately handle missing data. (p. 121)

Although researchers continue to contend with the methodological challenges associated with developing precise and reliable quantitative indices of the value that schools and teachers add to student achievement, there is already a body of empirical (often but not exclusively ethnographic) research that identifies schools that foster the achievement of minority youth in ways that would not be predicted from racially disaggregated achievement data. We refer to this pattern as the "institutionalized productions of unpredicted academic excellence."

An ethnographic study by Morris (2004) demonstrates how this pattern exists and unfolds. The study was conducted at two elementary schools, "renowned for successfully educating" (p. 69) their predominantly African American and low-income student body.[6] Morris documented the organizational structures and processes that facilitated student achievement and enabled the student body to perform at levels that were competitive with and/or exceeded the outcomes of other schools across the city and state on a host of measures (e.g., standardized test scores, attendance rates, and parental participation). Sizemore (1985, 1988) and Hilliard (2003) documented the administrative practices, teacher beliefs, student–teacher interactions, curricular designs, and instructional routines associated with schools that serve predominantly low-income minority populations and that have far exceeded the educational outcomes that would be predicted in light of the population being served. Delpit (2003) reports on "Sankofa Shule," a public, African-centered charter school in Lansing, Michigan, whose African American students, disproportionately low income, were reading two to four levels above their grade level. They also were able to complete algebra and calculus work in grade school and had outscored the Lansing School District and the state of Michigan on the Michigan Educational Assessment Program, the state accountability test, in 2000 in mathematics and writing (p. 20).

In studying the effect of Catholic schools, researchers have found that Blacks and Latinos are advantaged by their enrollment in Catholic schools and that this effect cannot be reduced to selection bias (Hoffer, Greeley, & Coleman, 1985; Keith & Page, 1985). Researchers have attributed the effect of Catholic schools to their more rigorous academic demands and less stratified academic curriculum. More recent work by Lee and colleagues (1997, 2003) confirms the extent to which rigorous academic standards and a less differentiated and more rigorous curriculum (defined as high "academic press") positively contribute to the academic performance of Black and Hispanic youth and allow them to exceed levels of achievement that would be predicted from their racial status and SES. Other research has found that all students, regardless of where they fall demographically, are capable of academic achievement when administrators, teachers, and staff operate with effective instructional leadership, innovative curriculums, and high expectations for every child (Borko, Wolf, Simone, & Uchiyama, 2003; Reyes, Scribner, & Scribner, 1999).

A study by Hill (2008), which focused on how schools can work to facilitate high educational attainment, further illustrates the potential of schools to produce positive educational outcomes for Black and Latino youth. Using a sample of 188 high schools, Hill identified three strategies (i.e., brokering, clearinghouse, traditional) by which schools organized to facilitate students' transition to college. The strategies reflected distinctions in the availability of college planning resources (e.g., college application assistance, information regarding financial aid options) and how these resources were distributed in light of organizational norms for helping students and families navigate the college planning process. Findings from this study indicate that schools that employ a "brokering" strategy by marrying the availability of abundant college planning resources with norms that promote the equitable distribution of those resources to students and their families positively affected the college enroll-ment for students from all racial groups. However, the study's findings also indicated that the characteristic structures of clearinghouse and traditional schools, which reflect depressed institutionalized commitments to equitably distribute resources for college planning, situated youth of color, especially Latinos, at risk for lower levels of educational attainment. Hill's study is one of a few that has examined how schools' organizational structures, resources, and norms influence the educational attainment process and outcomes of racial groups (also see Stanton-Salazar, 2000). Work on other demographic groups (e.g., low-income students), however, substan-tiates how schools might organize in ways that place students at risk or otherwise expand a social group's opportunities for high and potentially unpredicted levels of educational attainment (McDonough, 1997).

It follows that if more competitive academic outcomes of Black, Latino, and Native American youth can be attributed to the organization and culture of institutions and to the pedagogical practices and routines of teachers, the lower achievement of these groups might also be a function of these same influences. Consequently, the risk for academic underperformance would be a consequence of what happens to children in school and is not a characteristic with which children enter school.

THE IMPLICATIONS FOR THE RECONCEPTUALIZATION OF RISK

The prospective reframings of risk we have thus far offered raise questions about the extent to which the designation of risk is not in and of itself a function of racial group membership but is constructed as a function of other factors not unique to this group: for example, where researchers opt to collect the data (in what school, what district, or what region), how researchers opt to disaggregate the data on the achievement of racial groups, who researchers opt to compare with whom and at what point in their schooling careers, and whether risk is defined in terms of acade-mic gains versus academic status. Our reframings of risk, moreover, elucidate how schools can affect educational outcomes (in statistically predictable and unpre-dictable ways) and by implication determine the at-risk or non-at-risk status of racial groups within and across different educational contexts.

There is a substantive body of literature that offers insight into how the systemic inequalities that mark schools shape the relationship between race and achievement. Much of this literature reflects a long tradition of survey-based analyses aimed at examining how school characteristics affect educational outcomes. There is also a much younger tradition of qualitative scholarship aimed at understanding how schools and teachers make meaning of race via organizational practices and differentially frame the bodies, styles, actions, and interactions of youth in ways that likely contribute to gaps in achievement. We review the findings of these traditions in the interest of uncovering how schools can differentially structure the educational experiences and outcomes of racial groups. We also examine the complement between the traditions as a starting point for better conceptualizing and capturing who is at risk in school, when, and by what mechanisms.

Making Meaning of Institutionalized Productions of Race

In comparison to research efforts aimed at examining the effect of school characteristics, the study of how race is given meaning in school is a reasonably young topic of study. This work, nevertheless, grows out of a longer tradition of examining how race and culture inform differential educational outcomes. In early efforts to define the relationship between and among race, culture, and achievement, culture was defined as the various norms, beliefs, and practices that presumably distinguished the home environments of racial groups (O'Connor, Lewis, & Mueller, 2007). In turn, this literature drew invidious distinctions between the culture of Blacks and Latinos and that of Whites. Having situated Black and Latino culture as deficient relative to that of Whites, researchers argued that it was the culture of Blacks and Latinos that placed them at an academic disadvantage (e.g., Bloom, Whiteman, & Deutsch, 1965; Deutsch, 1964; O. Lewis, 1963; for recent reviews of this literature, also see O'Connor, Lewis, et al., 2007; Tyler et al., 2008).

On the heels of situating Black and Latino culture as both a deficiency and an academic liability, researchers have examined the educational effect of Asian American culture. Here, researchers were interested in explaining the greater academic success of Asian Americans and concluded that the norms, beliefs, and practices of Asian Americans facilitated their more competitive academic outcomes (Slaughter-Defoe, Nakagawa, Takanishi, & Johnson, 1990). Some researchers interpreted these norms, beliefs, and practices as native to Asian Americans or arising from tenets or philosophies (e.g., Confucianism) that were interpreted as authentically Asian (e.g., Connor, 1974, 1975; Masuda, Matsumoto, & Meredith, 1970). As a consequence of these analyses, Asian American culture, in contrast to Black and Latino cultures, was situated as a resource rather than as a deficit.

As an explanatory framework, the discourse of cultural deficiency met with substantive criticism. Critics indicated that it not only conceptualized and captured culture inaccurately but also ostensibly blamed the victims (i.e., Blacks and Latinos) for their underachievement (Gordon, 1965; Valentine, 1968). Offering models of cultural difference and conflict in the place of models of cultural deficiency, critics argued that the culture of Blacks and Latinos (who were imagined as poor) was not deficient relative to that of Whites (who were imagined as middle class) but that they were different from them (Erickson, 1987; Foley, 1991). These models conveyed that these differences made it harder for Black and Latino children to accommodate the norms or expectations of schools and/or schools had failed to take up and build on their cultural repertoires in the interest of facilitating their learning and achievement (e.g., Heath, 1982; Kochman, 1981; Labov, 1982).

Despite early efforts to refocus attention on what happens to children in schools, the perception that Blacks and Latinos *enter into* school with cultural deficiencies and or differences that place them at academic risk still seeps into contemporary educational discourse (C. D. Lee, 2007). Most often, this is a function of John Ogbu's (1987, 2003) cultural ecological theory (CET), which is arguably the most influential theory of our time, given the extent to which it is cited in academic and popular discourse (Jencks & Phillips, 1998; O'Connor, Horvat, & Lewis, 2006). In part, CET is compelling because models of cultural difference and conflict seemed inadequate with regard to explaining the higher achievement of Asian Americans.

Ogbu (1987) argued that if in fact cultural mismatches were at the heart of minority underachievement, why did Asian Americans experience greater academic success even though they too evidenced cultural differences relative to the White middle class? Offering CET in the place of models of cultural difference and conflict, Ogbu maintained that Blacks, Latinos, and Native Americans (based on their involuntary minority status) assessed their oppression as systemic and enduring and developed, in turn, cultural adaptations in which they perceive their identities in opposition to those of White Americans. Simultaneously, interpreting schooling as a White and inequitable domain, non-Asian minorities are said to resist the norms and expectations of school in the interest of maintaining their collective racial identities and their affiliation with and approval of same race peers (Matute-Bianchi, 1986; Ogbu & Matute-Bianchi, 1986; Suarez-Orozco, 1987). The stated tension between native racial identity and high achievement has been of particular focus in the study of Black underachievement as researchers debate the notion of whether Blacks make limited efforts in school out of fear of (being accused) of acting White (Fordham, 1996; Fordham & Ogbu, 1986).

In more recent work on Asian American achievement, select researchers have continued to privilege the ways in which presumably Asian cultural orientations afford Asian Americans an advantage in schools (Caplan, Choy, & Whitmore, 1991; Mordkowitz & Ginsberg, 1987; Pearce, 2006). When underachievement is acknowledged for individual members of this community, it is sometimes attributed to their having broken with Asian culture (Hess et al., 1986; Sue & Okazaki, 1990). In terms of CET, Asian Americans' status as voluntary minorities presumably affords them a mode of cultural adaptation that allows them to perceive racial discrimination as a temporary barrier they can overcome (Ogbu, 1987). They are therefore said to approach school with effort optimism and are willing to accommodate to the norms and expectations of schools in the absence of feeling they have sacrificed their culture or ethnic identities in the process (Ogbu, 1987). Researchers also continue to attribute the high achievement of Asian Americans to their high valuation of schooling, their privileging of academic effort over ability, and the high educational expectations and effective child-rearing practices on the part of their parents (H. B. Chen, 2001; Pearce, 2006). In addition, there is evidence that Asian Americans develop and are embedded in ethnic networks and communities that reinforce and extend these values, expectations, and strategies (Schneider & Lee, 1990).

Like the large body of work that challenges the tenets of CET (e.g., Ainworth-Darnell & Downey, 1998; Carter, 2005; Cook & Ludwig, 1997; Harris, 2006; O'Connor, 1997; Tyson, 2003; Tyson, Darity, & Castellino, 2005), there is a growing body of literature aimed at dispelling the image of Asian Americans as model minorities. Emphasizing the extent to which this stereotype fails to account for the variation in achievement that exists among Asian Americans, this work has both documented and sought explanations for the underachievement of Asian American subgroups, particularly those of South Asian descent (Goyette & Xie, 1999; S. Lee, 1996; S. J. Lee, 2001; Ngo, 2006; Sui, 1996). Baker and colleagues (2000) also drew attention to the fact that west Asian individuals from Iranian, Afghan, and Turkish backgrounds are usually not examined under the rubric "Asian," although both their achievement and educational experiences differ from those of Chinese, Japanese, Korean, Filipino, and Indian students. Baker and colleagues (2000), moreover, drew scholarly attention to whether Asian subgroups have been racialized as White versus non-White and how this process of racialization is likely implicated in how different racial groups experience and achieve in schools. Most often, however, researchers have illuminated the variation in Asian American achievement in the interest of elucidating how the model minority stereotype situates Blacks and Latinos as being both oppositional and responsible for their underachievement while holding Whites, White hegemony, and institutionalized inequalities harmless (S. Lee, 1996, 2005; Ngo & Lee, 2007).

These persistent discussions regarding the cultural differences that distinguish racial groups and explain their relative performance in school suggest that Blacks, Latinos, and Native Americans *enter into* school with cultural orientations that place them at academic risk. On the other hand, Asian Americans for the most part enter into school with cultural orientations and practices that create academic advantage. Like the critics of a previous generation whose work indicated that cultural know-how, practices, and orientations are only rendered deficits or assets in light of how they are taken up and responded to in schools, contemporary critics point out that researchers have underestimated the effect of institutionalized productions of race and racialized inequality. That is, a body of contemporary literature draws our attention to how schools and their agents racialize both students and achievement via micro interactions and organizational processes that structure not only how students experience school but also their likelihood of achieving academic success (Dolby, 2001; A. E. Lewis, 2003a, 2003b; O'Connor, 2001; O'Connor, Lewis, et al., 2007). As indicated by O'Connor, Lewis, et al. (2007) these school-based productions of race not only shape and reify race-related inequities in educational access and opportunity but also ultimately function as institutionalized racism (even if not explicitly labeled as such by the researchers).

Making Meaning of Racial Bodies via Micro-Evaluative Processes

Within this tradition of delineating how schools and their agents racialize students and achievement to produce academic consequences, Ferguson (2000) offered a compelling analysis of why Black boys were more apt to find themselves in school trouble. More precisely, she showed that schooling agents, in making differential meaning of students' transgressions, contributed to the disproportionate rates with which Black boys are disciplined in school. She found that both Black and White boys sought to perform their masculinity by breaking school rules. However, Black boys more often find themselves in trouble because of how their performances are interpreted. When White boys transgressed, school officials presumed that "boys will be boys," attributed "innocence to their wrong doing," and believed that "they must be socialized to fully understand the meaning of their acts" (Ferguson, 2000, p. 80). In contrast, when Black boys transgressed, their acts were "adultified." That is "their transgressions are made to take on a sinister, intentional, fully conscious tone . . . stripped of any element of naïveté" (Ferguson, 2000, p. 83). Having framed them as "not children," the interpreters (most of whom were White and constituted authority in the school setting) were necessarily directed toward treatment "that punishes through example and exclusion rather than through persuasion and edification, as is practiced with the young White males in the school" (Ferguson, 2000, p. 90).

Ferguson's (2000) findings have been echoed to varying degrees in other studies of how teachers make sense of the behaviors of minority youth. For example, in analyzing disciplinary referrals, Skiba (2001) found that in comparison to Whites, Blacks are referred for more subjective and less serious offenses. Skiba noted that "even the most serious of reasons for office referrals among Black students, threat, is dependent on the perception of threat by the staff making the referral" (p. 171). His findings are amplified in light of evidence that White teachers demonstrate fear of even Black male kindergartners (A. E. Lewis, 2003b). In a matched effect survey study of whether White teachers evaluated Black students' behaviors more harshly than Black teachers, Downey and Pribesh (2004) also found that Black students are consistently rated as poorer classroom citizens. However, this pattern did not persist when teachers' race was taken into account. Their findings indicated that when Black and White students are placed with same-race teachers and are similar on other measures, Black students' behavior is rated more favorably than their peers. In other words, the finding that Black students were more negatively evaluated with regard to their classroom behavior was a function of having received negative evaluations from White teachers. Downey and Pribesh offer evidence that these findings are not mere artifacts of Black students behaving more poorly in White teachers' classrooms. Through an experimental study, Neal, McCray, Webb-Johnson, and Bridgest (2003) found that teachers perceived Black students who demonstrated movement styles associated with Black culture (e.g., "strolling" rather than walking in a "standard" fashion) as being more aggressive, lower achieving, and in greater need of special education. The aforementioned studies convey that Blacks and Blackness are likely to be stigmatized or evaluated in ways that enhance Black students' susceptibility to disciplinary sanctions and negative evaluations on the part of teachers. The implications for Black student achievement are palatable though still speculative.

In the interest of drawing a more transparent link between micro-evaluative processes and racial gaps in achievement, Roscigno and Ainsworth-Darnell (1999) examined whether Black students compared to White students received less return for having invested in cultural (e.g., trips to art, science, and history museums and extracurricular involvement in art, music, and dance classes) and educational resources (e.g., the availability of numerous books, a computer, an encyclopedia, an atlas, a calculator, or a daily newspaper in the home) that have been shown to inform achievement. They found that Black students received less return to both their GPAs and their standardized test performance depending on their families' investment in these resources. In the interest of explaining these differential effects, Roscigno and Ainsworth-Darnell added measures of track placement and teacher evaluations of student effort, attentiveness, and homework completion. They found that as a consequence of these additions, significant interactions between race and cultural and household resources declined in magnitude. Thus, the lower returns to achievement after the investment in cultural and educational resources appeared to be partially a function of evaluation at the classroom and school levels.

These findings regarding how micro-evaluative processes might inform racial gaps in achievement are "at best suggestive" (Roscigno & Ainsworth-Darnell, 1999, p. 171). Roscigno and Ainsworth-Darnell (1999) cannot offer direct evidence of teacher bias, as they rely on survey analyses as opposed to classroom observation. Thus, there is no definitive evidence that these differential effects were a function of prejudicial evaluations on the part of teachers. That is, they might also reflect objective differences in how Black students make academic use of their cultural and educational resources. However, when these findings are placed in conversation with the previously cited studies regarding how the behaviors of (or those that are associated with) racial groups are differentially framed by teachers, they assume greater gravity and contribute to our developing conceptualization of the "refraction" as opposed to the "reflection" of social identities.

O'Connor (2001) argues that cultural examinations of achievement gaps have usually highlighted the "reflection" of social identities, or how individuals interpret and subsequently perform their identities in school such that they produce academic consequences; however, more attention must be given to the "refraction" of these identities. "Refraction" is how individuals experience identity and social and educational inequality as a consequence of how others, given their own structured and cultured positions, make sense of and subsequently respond to these individuals and their accordant performances (O'Connor, 2001). Yet, as the discussion in the next section suggests, the very structure of schools can also refract social identities to

frame students' experience in schools in ways that have implications for group differences in achievement.

Making Meaning of Achievement via Racialized Organizational Structures

Researchers offer evidence that a tangible alignment of race and achievement
develops when the curriculum of a high school is hierarchically organized and is also
racially stratified. Black students in such schools are more apt to perceive a divide
between being Black and achieving in school and/or experience tension, ambivalence, and/or peer pressure in relation to pursuing high academic achievement
(Mickelson & Valesco, 2006; O'Connor, Fernandez, & Girard, 2007; Tyson, 2003,
2006; Tyson et al., 2005). In their study of Black high achievers in Charlotte, North
Carolina, Mickelson and Valesco (2006) found that Black high achievers were less
susceptible to peer criticism that they were acting White if they attended high
schools in which Black students were equitably distributed across the academic hierarchy. They note, "In a diverse high school in which critical numbers of minority
students take upper-level classes, acting white was not an issue" (p. 49). Accusations
of acting White in relation to high academic performance were, however, evident in
high schools in which Blacks were disproportionately represented in lower-level
courses and underrepresented at the upper end of their school's academic hierarchy.
Mickelson and Valesco indicated that school opportunity structures "normalize"
where Black students belong (p. 49). In doing so, they also naturalize which social
identities are commensurate with which educational statuses.

Tyson et al. (2005), also conducting their study in North Carolina but extending
their data collection beyond the city of Charlotte, found that in five of the six high
schools they selected for ethnographic study, none of the Black high achievers
"reported problems with Black peers related to high achievement" (p. 591) and, in
fact, reported peer support for their academic efforts. The exception to this finding
was Dalton High School, the school that demonstrated the most severe under-representation of Black students in Advanced Placement and honors courses. Tyson et al.
report that "this rural school with more than 1,700 students was the only school in
which we found evidence of a burden of acting white with respect to achievement"
(p. 593). The high achievers in this school were the only ones who indicated that
they "had been accused of acting white by their Black peers because of their academic behaviors" (p. 594).

O'Connor, Fernandez, et al. (2007) offered commensurate findings in their
ethnographic study of five Black female high achievers who transitioned from a
racially stratified and predominantly White high school to historically Black colleges
and universities (HBCUs). In moving from their high school context where Blacks
were underrepresented in advanced courses and overrepresented in remedial and
lower level courses to an HBCU, these young women reinterpreted how race was
aligned with achievement. As students in their predominantly White high school,
they defined "acting White" in terms of speech (speaking standard English, having

a lilt in your tone, and speaking like a "Valley girl"), dress (e.g., wearing clothes designed by Abercrombie & Fitch), personal style (e.g., carrying themselves hesitantly as opposed to confidently), and the company they kept (i.e., socializing only or primarily with White students). Of these students, all but one also aligned "acting White" or Whiteness with being smart and doing well in school. In contrast, they aligned "acting Black" or Blackness with being less than smart and doing poorly in school. They situated themselves as exceptions to this alignment.

On transitioning to HBCUs, they reconceptualized this alignment such that they no longer perceived Blackness to be in conflict with intelligence and competitive educational outcomes. In the voice of one student during a focus group interview with her close friends in college,

I definitely feel bad for the way I judged [Black] people. But when I came to [HBCU] I thought like I was going to be it in class. And I just thought I was going to be like the smart person in all the classes and that [the other Black people] are going to be dumb. I mean to be honest, that's what I thought. . . . I was used to being the smart girl with all the White kids so I figured that that the Black kids—just from my own ignorance, I just figured they would all just be not so smart because I was smarter than White kids in some of my classes back home. (O'Connor, Fernandez, et al., 2007, p. 203)

The change in this student's perception resulting from her transition to an HBCU stood in stark contrast to the experience of two of her college friends who had participated in the focus group and had attended academically but not racially stratified high schools. One friend noted, "I went to an all-black high school . . . so I was used to intelligent African American people and that was all I was used to. . . . So coming to [HBCU] didn't change my thought process" (O'Connor, Fernandez, et al., 2007, p. 203).

The findings from the aforementioned studies (i.e., Mickelson & Valesco, 2006; O'Connor, Fernandez, et al., 2007; Tyson et al., 2005) elucidate how the perceived conflict between being Black and doing well in school on the part of Black students and their tendency to negatively sanction their Black peers who are academically successful can be functions of the demographics and organization of a school. Consequently, this perception and tendency are not necessarily evident in predominantly Black secondary or postsecondary schools or in racially diverse schools in which racial groups are equitably distributed across the academic hierarchy. In her ethnographic study of two all Black elementary schools, Tyson (2003, 2006) also found no evidence of peer pressure aimed at discouraging Black academic achievement. Tyson documents that it was not high achievement that "caused black students the most distress but low or poor performance" (Tyson, 2006, p. 69), and when Black students experienced stigma as per the evaluations of their peers it was for underachieving (Tyson, 2003, 2006). Tyson (2006) notes,

Schools create and sustain structures that conflate race and achievement, but . . . this fusion has little salience for students until they reach adolescence. Even then, only students who experience institutionally imposed and sustained patterns of achievement by race are likely to grapple with the burden of acting white. (p. 84)

Tyson et al. (2005) point out that "an important and often overlooked consequence of the under-representation experienced by minorities in advanced classes is the perpetuation among both blacks and whites of stereotypes about black intellectual ability and the value of education in the black community" (p. 594). Taken in total, this small but growing body of literature elucidates how schools and their agents (via micro evaluations and racialized organizational structures) can make meaning of and inform the relationship between race and achievement. As we discuss later in this chapter, work of this kind promises to resolve the puzzles that remain unexplained with regard to explaining racial gaps in achievement as per the findings regarding the effects of school characteristics.

MAKING MEANING OF SCHOOL CHARACTERISTICS

To make further sense of how students might be placed at risk as a consequence of what happens to them in school, we can draw on research efforts aimed at understanding the effect of school characteristics. We have already alluded to the effect of academic climate as it has been articulated in relation to how Catholic schools and schools that have a less differentiated and academically rigorous curriculum contribute positively to the academic outcomes for Black and Latino youth. Researchers have otherwise examined the impact of school resources, school racial composition, and the organization of schools. Although some of this work was pursued in the interest of determining whether schools could *compensate* for the presumed disadvantages some children brought with them to school (Hallinan, 2001), as a body this literature can also explain the mechanisms by which schools structure learning opportunities and by implication differential educational outcomes across racial groups.

The Effect of School Resources

The long tradition of examining the impact of school resources began with a focus on material resources (e.g., number of library books and availability of science labs and equipment) and fiscal inequalities (e.g., per pupil expenditure and teacher salaries) (Coleman et al., 1966; Greenwald, Hedges, & Laine, 1996; Hanushek, 1994; Jencks, 1972; Spady, 1973). More recently, attention has focused on the impact of teacher quality. Studies of material inequities demonstrated small effects of school resources on students' achievement and indicated that school resources did not explain racial gaps in achievement (Hallinan, 2001). The academic debates that specifically revolved around whether money mattered, however, elucidated the importance of not simply examining the amount of resources available but also determining how those resources were being used. Therefore, in response to Hanushek's (1994) claim that money did not matter with regard to informing educational outcomes, Hedges, Laine, and Greenwald (1994a, 1994b) demonstrated that the effect of funding was dependent on how money was being applied and that money did matter "somewhere." Later, in a synthesis of data from a wide variety of studies conducted over a period of three decades, Greenwald et al. (1996) found that "school resources are systematically related to student achievement and that these relations are large enough to be educationally important" (p. 384).

According to this research, then, not only did school resources contribute to educational outcomes but their effects also were particularly influential in the case of global measures such as per pupil expenditure. Research in this area has demonstrated that teacher quality was strongly related to student achievement (Nye, Hedges, & Konstantopoulos, 2000; also see Rockoff, 2004; Wayne & Youngs, 2003). However, again, findings such as these typically offered no direct evidence that school resources explained racial gaps in achievement. Researchers generally found no or weak effects when analyzing whether the effects of school resources were differentiated by race (e.g., Nye et al., 2000). More recent work (e.g., Fryer & Levitt, 2004, 2006) indicates that school resources, particularly teacher quality, can account for substantive portions of the gaps in racial achievement. Fryer and Levitt (2006) also find that indices of school resources and teacher quality are, nevertheless, inadequate with regard to explaining why Blacks lose ground relative to Whites when being taught in the same classroom by the same teacher.

The Effect of School Racial Composition

In light of debates over the impact of desegregation and contentions over the warrant for school busing, researchers began exploring how racial composition affected students' educational outcomes (see Hallinan, 2001). Early on, there was evidence that attendance at predominantly White schools boosted the academic achievement of minority students, namely Blacks (e.g., Jencks & Brown, 1975; McPartland, 1969; St. John, 1975). Other research, however, found that the academic benefits to Black students were insignificant or offered inconclusive evidence toward this end (Coleman, 1979; for reviews of this early literature, also see Crain & Mahard, 1978; Spady, 1973).

Contemporary research generally supports the academic benefits of desegregation. After controlling for differences in students' background, V. Lee and Bryk (1989) found that the average mathematics achievement of students in high-concentration minority schools was about 15% lower than in low-concentration minority schools. Also controlling for individual characteristics and family background, Mickelson and Heath (2001) found that the achievement of Black students was depressed by both first-generation (i.e., across school segregation) and second-generation (i.e., within school segregation resulting from tracking) segregation. Moreover, the effects of segregation appeared to be long term in that students who had attended predominantly Black elementary schools experienced lower test scores and track placement than those who had attended racially balanced schools.

In terms of school-level findings, Guryan (2004) found that the Black dropout rate diminished in districts that pursued desegregation plans compared to those that did not. The reduction in dropout rates was greatest in districts that experienced the greatest declines in racial segregation. Borman and her colleagues (2004) found that having controlled for other "known predictors of standardized test performance" (e.g., per pupil expenditure, classroom size, and percentage poverty), school composition predicted school-level performance on standardized tests such that pass rates were lowest in Black segregated schools and higher in integrated and White segregated schools (with no discernable differences regarding the impact of these latter settings).

As suggested by the findings of Borman et al. (2004), contemporary research studies have begun to include *integrated* schools in their analyses (sometimes labeled as *racially balanced* or *diverse* schools), rather than relying on simple comparisons between predominantly Black or minority schools and predominantly White schools (Brown-Jeffy, 2006; Goldsmith, 2003, 2004; Southworth & Mickelson, 2007). These studies paint a more complex picture of the effects of racial composition. Their findings indicate that the educational outcomes of Black and Latino students were compromised in *both* predominantly White and predominantly Black or minority contexts (Southworth & Mickelson, 2007). We are left to ask, why is this the case? Mickelson (2001) argued the following, using the Charlotte, North Carolina, schools as a case example:

> School districts allocate resources unequally and inequitably. In Charlotte, racially isolated Black learning environments are inferior—not because the students are Black but because of the measurable relative impoverishment of their learning environments. This is because of the well documented relationship between the political power of middle class White parents and the differential allocation of high quality educational opportunities. Simply put desegregated learning environments are more resource rich: they have better qualified teachers, more stable teacher and student populations, more academically oriented students, school climates with a stronger academic press, and more adequate material resources including libraries, new and safe physical plants, equipment and technology. (p. 241)

This perspective on the advantages of attending desegregated schools is shared by a number of scholars of desegregation (e.g., Armor, 1995; Orfield, 1997; Wells & Crain, 1994) and illuminates the extent to which predominantly Black and Hispanic schools are under-resourced in ways that impinge on student achievement. This explanation does not, however, explain why Black and Latino students also fare less well in predominantly White settings. Given the logic of the explanation, one would expect that Black students would fare better in predominantly White contexts, as they presumably have more material resources than predominantly Black or minority schools. In addition, Mickelson's reference to desegregated schools having more academically oriented students does not fully hold in light of evidence that Latino and African American students in predominantly minority schools often demonstrate more proschool attitudes (e.g., greater attachment to school, higher aspirations, greater optimism, and greater academic self concept) than do their peers in predominantly White schools (see Johnson, Crosnoe, & Elder, 2001; Massey, Charles, Lundy, & Fischer, 2003).

In a related study, Goldsmith's (2004) findings not only indicated that the beliefs of Blacks and Latinos were more optimistic and proschool in predominantly minority schools (when the schools employed many minority teachers) but also demonstrated that these beliefs reduced the Black–White and Latino–White gaps in achievement. Goldsmith argued that these "findings suggest that teachers and administrators in segregated-white schools need to address how they lower minority students' beliefs" (p. 121). Brown-Jeffy (2006) found that although the performance of all students was depressed in predominantly minority schools, the Black–White achievement gap was largest in schools that were less than 10% Black, Hispanic, and Native American. Brown-Jeffy noted that

while having "too many" Black, Hispanic, or Native American students in the school seems to be detrimental for all student success, having "too few" Black, Hispanic, or Native American students in the school is detrimental to the Black students in attendance. (p. 291)

In light of Brown-Jeffy's (2006) findings, we might alternatively offer that having "too many" White students in a school might be detrimental to the Black students in attendance. As with our previous reconceptualizations of risk, we offer this alternative in the interest of elucidating how the discourse that surrounds research findings can selectively define some groups as "problems" and not others. This alternative phrasing constructs *both* Whites and minorities as prospectively posing a risk to "others." The phrasing selected by Brown-Jeffy, however, excludes the prospect that White students can interfere with the success of "other" students and is consistent with how researchers inadvertently demonize non-Asian minority youth.

Entwisle and Alexander (1992) offer yet another wrinkle with regard to understanding the educational effects of school racial composition. At the elementary school level, Entwisle and Alexander found that the racial mix of schools did not affect the reading or math achievement of White students. However, when schools were in session, Black children in integrated schools gained noticeably less in reading than did their counterparts in predominantly Black schools. These same Black children, however, exceeded the math gains of their Black peers in predominantly Black schools. These findings suggest not only that Blacks may be at a particular risk in integrated schools for fewer academic gains but also that depressed gains are not necessarily universal and may be subject specific.

It is important that the effects of segregation may not be consistent across racial groups. In analyzing National Assessment of Educational Progress data, Goldsmith (2003) found that, in the case of Blacks, attendance at predominantly Black schools generally had no effect on Black test scores. When effects were found, they were negative. Latinos, however, received an academic boost from attending predominantly Latino schools. More precisely, Latino test scores rose as the proportion of Latinos in their school rose.

In the midst of these evolving analyses regarding the complex effects of racial composition, Mickelson (2001) found that the effect of racial composition on achievement (particularly the long-term effects of elementary school segregation) is relatively small in comparison to the effects of track placement and prior achievement, the two most powerful influences on academic outcomes.

The Effect of School Organization

In line with Mickelson's (2001) findings, researchers have explored the effects of tracking as a window into how the organization of schools influences educational outcomes and influences racial gaps in achievement.[7] The research on tracking offers compelling insight into how the organization of schools can affect achievement differentials between racial groups. Researchers have documented the extent to which track placement affects achievement outcomes, with higher track placement predicting more competitive educational outcomes (Hallinan, 1991, 2001; Mickelson, 2001); they also have documented the academic and social processes that influence these correlations. Oakes (2005) provided the seminal study of these processes and enumerated how students in high-track classes benefited from higher teacher expectations and more rigorous academic content and engaging pedagogy. Alternatively, the learning opportunities of students in low-track classes were compromised by low teacher expectations and an emphasis on discipline and classroom management over academic rigor and inspiring instructional practices. With regard to influencing racial gaps in achievement, high-track courses are less readily available in predominantly minority schools (Mickelson, 2001). Moreover, in diverse and predominantly White schools, racial groups are inequitably distributed across tracks. After controlling for a host of background characteristics (e.g., SES, parental education, peer group orientation, and prior achievement), Black and Latino students are typically underrepresented in higher-level tracks and overrepresented in lower-level tracks (Hallinan, 1991; Mickelson, 2001; Oakes, 1994; Southworth & Mickelson, 2007). This same research indicates that Asian Americans and Whites are overrepresented in higher-level tracks and underrepresented in lower-level tracks.

These findings have not gone unchallenged. For example, Lucas (1999) found that an enrollment advantage emerged for Blacks once aspirations, achievement, and course requirements were controlled. The enrollment disadvantage for Latinos relative to Whites also disappeared in light of these covariates. Other researchers similarly offer evidence that once prior achievement and/or other covariates are taken into account, not only may racial differences in ability group assignments disappear but non-Asian minority youth also may demonstrate an advantage with regard to track placement (e.g., Gamoran & Mare, 1989; Hallinan, 1991; Hanson, 1994; Pallas, Entwisle, Alexander, & Stulka, 1994). O'Connor, Lewis, et al. (2007), however, caution that researchers' effort to control for factors such as prior achievement may, in fact, underestimate how previous racial discrimination may have already compromised measures of this kind.

Despite the inconsistency in the literature with regard to whether race influences track placement, researchers generally concur that based on the documented differences in teacher and instructional quality, social climate, and curricular standards, placement in upper-level tracks enhances students' opportunities to learn whereas placement in lower-level tracks impinges on students' opportunities to learn (Hallinan, 1991, 2001; Oakes, 1994, 2005). Consequently, the disproportionate assignment of Blacks and Latinos to lower-level tracks (whether as a consequence of prejudicial or nonprejudicial mechanisms) systematically suppresses these students' educational gains and outcomes, as compared to the systematic educational advantage afforded to Whites and Asian Americans in light of their disproportionate assignment to upper-level tracks.

SCHOOL CHARACTERISTICS IN SUMMARY
AND THE WARRANT FOR MAKING MEANING OF RACE

Taken in total, the findings regarding the effect of school characteristics elucidate various structured mechanisms by which schools shape the educational outcomes of youth and influence racial gaps in achievement. These findings indicate that opportunities to learn are inequitably distributed across racial groups and that Blacks and Latinos are systematically disadvantaged by these inequities. Given how race and class segregation marks U.S. society, Blacks and Latinos are more likely to find themselves in racially isolated schools that suffer with inadequate resources, particularly with regard to access to more rigorous courses and lower quality teachers. For various reasons, however, current evidence indicates that school quality provides a strong but still incomplete explanation of differential achievement outcomes across racial groups for various reasons.

First, Latinos by some measures attend the most under-resourced schools (Crosnoe, 2005; Fryer & Levitt, 2006). Yet there is evidence that instead of losing ground relative to Whites (as has been often documented in the case of Blacks and along select dimensions in the case of Asians), they seem to gain ground relative to Whites over the course of their early schooling careers. Second, the inequitable distribution of resources does not appear to explain the differential effects of attending predominantly White versus racially balanced schools. That is, Black and Hispanic students find their achievement also depressed in predominantly White institutions. Racial gaps in achievement appear to be the largest in predominantly White schools, and when school is in session there is evidence that Black students in integrated schools make fewer academic gains than their peers in predominantly Black schools. Inequitable tracking practices cannot fully explain these differential effects, as racially inequitable tracking also plague racially balanced schools.

These findings, however, are derived from quantitative analyses; thus, they fail to capture *how* educational resources are being taken up in the everyday practice of schools and whether variations in take-up begin to unravel the many puzzles evident in the literature on racial gaps in achievement. Throughout this chapter, we have illuminated how institutionalized productions of race permeate the interactions between students and teachers and are reflected in the organization of schools to frame how students experience school differently. We now argue that this meaning making also likely influences how schools and teachers utilize available resources. The need to explore the institutionalized productions of race in tandem with resource utilization is especially warranted with regard to unpacking the effect of teacher quality.

Nye, Konstantopoulos, and Hedges (2004) found that teacher effects not only were real and of a "magnitude that is consistent with that estimated from previous studies" (p. 253) but also outstripped school effects. However, although several studies (e.g., Ingersoll, 1999, 2005; Roehrig & Kruse, 2005; Rosenfeld & Rosenfeld, 2008) point to a range of issues influencing teacher practices (e.g., teacher mis-assignment, beliefs, organization of the profession), we do not yet understand how years of teaching experience, credentials, and the like shape teachers' instructional practice. In the absence of developing this understanding, we cannot explain why the greatest racial gaps in achievement are sometimes found *within* classrooms (Fryer & Levitt, 2006).

Cohen, Raudenbush, and Ball (2003) argue that conventional educational research proceeds as if educational resources (e.g., school funding, curriculum materials, facilities, teacher quality, the academic and social climate of a school, and teacher quality as a function of credentials and teaching experience) "caused learning" (p. 119). Under this assumption, if educational policy effectively manipulates segregation, ability grouping, academic standards, and the assignment of teachers, we can harness and redistribute resources in ways that promise to alleviate group differences in achievement. Cohen et al., however, explain that it is instruction that mediates the relationship between resources and achievement. They stop short of asking whether and how instructional practice might be, in part, a function of how teachers make meaning of race.

The promise that we might explain racial gaps in achievement by integrating systematic examinations of instruction with how teachers make sense of race was suggested by the work of Ray Rist some 30 years ago. Then, Rist (1970) demonstrated how the individual teacher can apply his or her instructional practice in ways that inequitably distribute opportunities to learn across the students in his or her classroom. His examination of teachers' practice was, however, cursory. The reader received only brief and decontextualized snapshots of "how" teachers "worked." What we do know is that the teachers' instructional work, which for Cohen et al. (2003) consists of "interactions between teachers and students around content in environments" (p. 122), seemed to be enacted in ways that facilitated the learning of some students and compromised the learning of others. What we do not know is what drove the selection of content and/or the teaching materials on which the teachers relied; how they documented and evaluated the backgrounds, identities, and knowledge of their students; and how they assessed the context in which the children lived. Moreover, how were these factors shaped by their prospective class biases, and how did they inform the planning and delivery of their instruction such that they converted class hierarchy into academic hierarchy?

What is compelling and wanting in Ray Rist's study should propel us to integrate the call on the part of Cohen et al. (2003) with the call to unpack how race is given meaning in classrooms to differentially affect the experiences and by implication the educational outcomes of youth. That is, researchers should design studies that would allow us to analyze how, in making meaning of race, teachers come to plan and ultimately deliver instruction in ways that either generate or diminish racial gaps in students' opportunities to learn. That is, how does race shape how teachers make meaning of their students, their content area, and the environment in which they work? How does this meaning making also shape what they define as resources in relation to these students and this content and environment? How do these assessments then figure into their planning and delivery of instruction in ways that promise to exacerbate or diminish racial gaps in achievement? How is the work of individual teachers across individual classrooms compounded within schools to produce school effects?

As suggested by Dreeben and Barr (1987), "decisions" made at the classroom level are necessarily informed by decisions that occur at the school and district levels. Efforts to integrate resource use with analyses of institutionalized productions of race warrant a multilevel interpretation of how teachers enact their practice. An analytical model of this type would likely provide substantive insight into both why gaps in achievement vary across school and classroom contexts and why even in racially homogeneous schools racial groups can underperform or overperform as per statistical predictions. In turn, we would be afforded greater insight into when, why, and under what conditions students of different racial groups are put at risk (or not) in some classrooms and schools and not others.

NOTES

[1]For example, studies of status attainment (e.g., Blau & Duncan, 1967; Haller & Portes, 1973) as well as flagship studies such as those completed by Coleman et al. (1966) and Jencks (1972) had already demonstrated how race affected educational outcomes.

[2]As discussed by Natriello, McDill, and Pallas (1990), these same groups had been previously incorporated under the label of "culturally deprived" and then later "disadvantaged."

[3]Also see O'Connor (2006b) for an analog discussion of how the translation into an internalized trait unfolds in the literature on racial disproportionality in special education placement.

[4]Given their small population size and underrepresentation in large data sets, Native Americans were less frequently designated as "at risk."

[5]In naming the gaps that exist between Whites and descendents of Spanish-speaking nations, researchers have relied on the term *Hispanic*. The authors of this chapter therefore use this term interchangeably with *Latino* to refer to this population.

[6]Fairmont School in St. Louis "had one of the highest student attendance rates in the city and consistently outperformed students in the St. Louis public school system, including magnet schools, on traditional measures such as standardized tests" (Morris, 2004, p. 74). Lincoln school in Atlanta "was one of 11 elementary schools in 1997 selected as a 'Georgia School of Excellence,' based on combination of factors that included student attendance rates, and standardized test scores, the curriculum, and parent participation rates" (Morris, 2004, pp. 74–75).

[7]Researchers have also explored the effects of class size. They have concluded that reducing class size positively affects students' educational outcomes. However, they have debated whether the effects associated with reducing class size are more instrumental in raising the achievement of low-income and minority youth. In their meta-analysis of the research on class size, Nye, Hedges, and Konstantopoulos (2000) concluded that "while there are unambiguous positive effects of small class sizes on both reading and mathematics achievement, there is . . . only weak evidence of differential effects for minority students in reading" (p. 1) and no such differential effects exist in relation to math.

REFERENCES

Ainworth-Darnell, J. W., & Downey, D. B. (1998). Assessing the oppositional culture explanation for racial/ethnic differences in school performance. *American Sociological Review, 63*, 536–553.

Alon, S. (2007). Overlapping disadvantages and the racial/ethnic graduation gap among students attending selective institutions. *Social Science Research, 36*(4), 1475–1498.

Armor, D. J. (1995). *Forced justice: School desegregation and the law.* New York: Oxford University Press.

Baker, B. D. (2001). Gifted children in the current policy and fiscal context of public education: A national snapshot and state-level equity analysis of Texas. *Educational Evaluation and Policy Analysis, 23*(3), 229–250.

Baker, B. D., Keller-Wolff, C., & Wolf-Wendel, L. (2000). Two steps forward, one step back: Race/ethnicity and student achievement in education policy research. *Educational Policy, 14*(4), 511–529.

Bali, V., & Alvarez, R. M. (2004). The race gap in student achievement scores: Longitudinal evidence from a racially diverse school district. *Policy Studies Journal, 32*, 393–415.

Blau, P. M., & Duncan, O. D. (1967). *The American occupational structure*. New York: John Wiley.

Bloom, R., Whiteman, M., & Deutsch, M. (1965). Race and social class as separate factors related to social environment. *American Journal of Sociology, 70*, 305–325.

Borko, H., Wolf, S., Simone, G., & Uchiyama, K. P. (2003). Schools in transition: Reform efforts and school capacity in Washington State. *Educational Evaluation and Policy Analysis, 25*, 171–201.

Borman, K. M., Eitle, T. M., Michael, D., Eitle, D. J., Lee, R., Johnson, L., et al. (2004). Accountability in post desegregation era: The continuing significance of racial segregation in Florida's schools. *American Educational Research Journal, 41*(3), 605–631.

Brooks-Gunn, J., & Markman, L. (2005). The contribution of parenting to ethnic and racial gaps in school readiness. *Future of Children, 15*, 139–168.

Brown v. Board of Education of Topeka, 347 U.S. 483 (1954).

Brown-Jeffy, S. (2006). The race gap in high school reading achievement. Why racial composition still matters. *Race, Gender, and Class, 13*(3-4), 268–294.

Burchinal, M. R., Campbell, F. A., Bryant, D. M., Wasik, B. A., & Ramey, C. T. (1997). Early intervention and mediating processes in cognitive performance of children of low-income African-American families. *Child Development, 68*, 935–954.

Caplan, N., Choy, M. H., & Whitmore, J. K. (1991). *Children of the boat people: A study of educational success*. Ann Arbor: University of Michigan Press.

Carter, P. (2005). *Keepin' it real*. Oxford, UK: Oxford University Press.

Catterall, J. S. (1998). Risk and resilience in student transitions to high school. *American Journal of Education, 106*, 302–333.

Chen, C., & Stevenson, H. W. (1995). Motivation and mathematics achievement: A comparative study of Asian-American, Caucasian-American and East Asian high school students. *Child Development, 66*, 1215–1234.

Chen, H. B. (2001). Parents' attitudes and expectations regarding science education: Comparisons among American, Chinese American and Chinese families. *Adolescence, 36*, 305–314.

Cohen, D. K., Raudenbush, S. W., & Ball, D. L. (2003). Resources, instruction, and research. *Educational Evaluation and Policy Analysis, 25*, 119–142.

Coleman, J. S. (1979). Presentation to the Massachusetts legislature: March 30, 1976. In M. Friedman, R. Meltzer, & C. Miller (Eds.), *New perspectives on school integration* (pp. 111-123). Minneapolis, MN: Fortress Press.

Coleman, J. S., Campbell, E. Q., Hobson, C. J., McPartland, J., Mood, A., Weinfeld, F. D., et al. (1966). *Equality of educational opportunity*. Washington, DC: U.S. Department of Health, Education, and Welfare.

Connor, J. W. (1974). Acculturation and family continuities in three generations of Japanese Americans. *Journal of Marriage and Family, 36*, 159–168.

Connor, J. W. (1975). Changing trends in Japanese academic achievement. *Journal of Ethnic Studies, 2*, 95–98.

Cook, P. J., & Ludwig, J. (1997). Weighing the "burden of acting White": Are there race differences in the attitudes towards education? *Journal of Policy Analysis and Management, 16*, 256–278.

Crain, R. L., & Mahard, R. E. (1978). Desegregation and Black achievement: A review of research. *Law & Contemporary Problems, 42*, 17–56.

Crosnoe, R. (2005). Double disadvantage or signs of resilience: The elementary school contexts of children from Mexican immigrant schools. *American Educational Research Journal, 42*(2), 269–303.

Delpit, L. (2003). 2003 Dewitt Wallace–Reader's Digest Distinguished Lecture—Educators as "seed people" growing a new future. *Educational Researcher, 7*(32), 14–21.

Deutsch, M. (1964). Early social environment: Its influence on school adaptation. In D. Schreiber (Ed.), *The school dropout* (pp. 89–100). Washington, DC: National Education Association.

Deyhle, D., & Swisher, K. (1997). Research in American Indian and Alaska Native education: From assimilation to self-determination. *Review of Research in Education, 22,* 113–194.

Dolby, N. (2001). *Constructing race: Youth, identity and culture in South Africa.* Albany: State University of New York Press.

Downey, D. B., & Pribesh, S. (2004). When race matters: Teachers' evaluations of student classroom behavior. *Sociology of Education, 77*(4), 267–282.

Dreeben, R., & Barr, R. (1987). An organizational analysis of curriculum and instruction. In M. Hallinan (Ed.), *The social organization of schools: New conceptualization of the learning process* (pp. 13–39). New York: Plenum.

Entwisle, D. R., & Alexander, K. L. (1990). Beginning school math competence: Minority and majority comparisons. *Child Development, 61,* 454–471.

Entwisle, D. R., & Alexander, K. L. (1992). Summer setback: Race, poverty, school composition, and mathematics achievement in the first two years of school. *American Sociological Review, 57,* 72–84.

Entwisle, D. R., & Alexander, K. L. (1994). Winter setback: The racial composition of schools and learning to read. *American Sociological Review, 59,* 446–460.

Erickson, F. (1987). Transformation and school success: The politics and culture of educational achievement. *Anthropology and Education Quarterly, 18*(4), 335–356.

Ferguson, A. (2000). *Bad boys: Public schools in the making of black masculinity.* Ann Arbor: University of Michigan.

Ferguson, R. (1998). Teachers' perceptions and expectations and the Black–White test score gap. In C. Jencks & M. Phillips (Eds.), *The Black–White test score gap* (pp. 273–317). Washington, DC: Brookings Institution

Foley, D. E. (1991). Reconsidering anthropological explanations of ethnic school failure. *Anthropology and Education Quarterly, 22*(1), 60–86.

Fordham, S. (1996). *Blacked out: Dilemmas of race, identity and success at Capital High.* Chicago: University of Chicago Press.

Fordham, S., & Ogbu, J. (1986). Black students' school success: Coping with the burden of "acting White." *Urban Review, 18*(3), 176–206.

Franzak, J. K. (2006). Zoom: A review of the literature on marginalized adolescent readers, literacy theory, and policy implications. *Review of Educational Research, 76,* 209–248.

Freeberg, L. (1987, February 22). The risks of labeling kids "at risk." *Baltimore Sun,* p. 5M.

Fryer, R. G., & Levitt, S. D. (2004). Understanding the Black–White test score gap in the first two years of school. *Review of Economics & Statistics, 86*(2), 447–464.

Fryer, R. G., & Levitt, S. D. (2006). The Black–White test score gap though third grade. *American Law & Economics Review, 8*(2), 249–281.

Gamoran, A., & Mare, R. D. (1989). Secondary school tracking and education inequality: Compensation, reinforcement, or neutrality. *American Journal of Sociology, 94,* 1146–1183.

Ginsberg, H. P., & Russell, R. L. (1981). Social class and racial influences on early mathematical thinking. *Monographs of the Society for Research in Child Development, 46*(6), 1–68.

Goldsmith, P. A. (2003). All segregation is not equal: The impact of Latino and Black school composition. *Sociological Perspectives, 46*(1), 83–105.

Goldsmith, P. A. (2004). Schools' racial mix, students' optimism, and the Black–White and Latino–White achievement gaps. *Sociology of Education, 77*(2), 121–147.

Gordon, E. (1965). Characteristics of socially disadvantaged children. *Review of Educational Research, 35*(5), 377-388.

Goyette, K., & Xie, Y. (1999). Educational expectations of Asian American youth. *Sociology of Education, 72*(1), 22–36.

Greenwald, R., Hedges, L. V., & Laine, R. D. (1996). The effect of school resources on student achievement. *Review of Educational Research, 66*(3), 361–396.

Guryan, J. (2004). Desegregation and Black dropout rates. *American Economic Review, 94*(4), 919–943.

Haller, A. O., & Portes, A. (1973). Status attainment processes. *Sociology of Education, 46*(1), 51–91.

Hallinan, M. (1991). School differences in tracking structures and track assignments. *Journal of Research on Adolescence, 1*, 251–275.

Hallinan, M. (2001). Sociological perspectives on Black–White inequalities in American schooling. *Sociology of Education, 74*, 50–70.

Hanson, S. L. (1994). Lost talent: Unrealized educational aspirations and expectations among U.S. youths. *Sociology of Education, 67*, 159–183.

Hanushek, E. (1994). *Making schools work: Improving performance and controlling costs.* Washington, DC: Brookings Institution.

Harris, A. (2006). I (don't) hate school: Revisiting oppositional culture theory of Blacks' resistance to schooling. *Social Forces, 85*(2), 797-834.

Hart, B., & Risley, T. R. (1999). *The social world of children: Learning to talk.* Baltimore: Paul H. Brookes.

Hauser, R. M., & Anderson, D. K. (1991). Post-high school plans and aspirations of Black and White high school seniors: 1976–86. *Sociology of Education, 64*, 263–277.

Heath, S. B. (1982). *Ways with words: Language, life, and work in communities and classrooms.* Cambridge, UK: Cambridge University Press.

Hedges, L. V., Laine, R. D., & Greenwald, R. (1994a). An exchange: Part I: Does money matter? A meta-analysis of studies of the effects of differential school inputs on student outcomes. *Educational Researcher, 23*(3), 5–14.

Hedges, L. V., Laine, R. D., & Greenwald, R. (1994b). Money does matter somewhere: A reply to Hanushek. *Educational Researcher, 23*, 9–10.

Hedges, L., & Nowell, A. (1999). Changes in the Black–White gap in achievement test scores. *Sociology of Education, 72*(2), 111–135.

Hess, R. D., Azuma, H., Kashiwagi, K., Dickson, W. P., Nagano, S., Hollaway, S., et al. (1986). Family influences on school readiness and achievement in Japan and the United States: An overview of a longitudinal study. In H. Stevenson, H. Azuma, & K. Hakuta (Eds.), *Child development and education in Japan* (pp. 147–166). New York: Freeman.

Hill, L. D. (2008). School strategies and the "college-linking" process: Reconsidering the effects of high schools on college enrollment. *Sociology of Education, 81*(1), 53–76.

Hilliard, A. (2003). No mystery: Closing the achievement gap. In T. Perry, C. Steele, & A. Hilliard (Eds.). *Young, gifted and Black: Promoting high achievement among African American students* (pp. 131–165). Boston: Beacon.

Hirschman, C., & Morrison, W. (1986). The extraordinary educational attainment of Asian-Americans: A search for historical evidence and explanations. *Social Forces, 65*, 1–27.

Hoffer, T., Greeley, A. M., & Coleman, J. S. (1985). Achievement growth in public and catholic schools. *Sociology of Education, 58*, 74–97.

Ingersoll, R. M. (1999). The problem of underqualified teachers in American secondary schools. *Educational Researcher, 28*, 26–37.

Ingersoll, R. M. (2005). The problem of underqualified teachers: A sociological perspective. *Sociology of Education, 78*(2), 175–179.

Jencks, C. (1972). *Inequality: A reassessment of the effect of family and schooling in America.* New York: Harper Row.

Jencks, C., & Brown, M. (1975). The effects of desegregation on student achievement: Some new evidence from the equality of educational opportunity survey. *Sociology of Education, 48*, 126–140.

Jencks, C., & Phillips, M. (1998). *The black-white test score gap.* Washington, DC.: Brookings Institution.

Johnson, M. K., Crosnoe, R., & Elder, G. H. (2001). Students' attachment and academic engagement: The role of race and ethnicity. *Sociology of Education, 74*, 318–340.

Jones, L. V. (1988-1989). School achievement trends in mathematics and science, and what can be done to improve them. *Review of Research in Education, 15*, 307–341.

Kao, G., & Thompson, J. S. (2003). Racial and ethnic stratification in education achievement and attainment. *Annual Review of Sociology, 29*, 417–442.

Kao, G., & Tienda, M. (1995). Optimism and achievement: The educational performance of immigrant youth. *Social Science Quarterly, 76*, 1–19.

Kao, G., Tienda, M., & Schneider, B. (1996). Racial and ethnic variation in educational achievement. *Research in Sociology of Education and Socialization, 11*, 263–297.

Keith, T. Z., & Page, E. B. (1985). Do catholic school improve minority achievement? *American Educational Research Journal, 22*(3), 337–349.

Kochman, T. (1981). *Black and White styles in conflict.* Chicago: University of Chicago Press.

Labov, W. (1982). Objectivity and commitment in linguistic science: The case of the Black English Trial in Ann Arbor. *Language and Society, 11*, 165–201.

Ladson-Billings, G. (2006a). From the achievement gap to the education debt: Understanding achievement in U.S. schools. *Educational Researcher, 35*(7), 3–12.

Ladson-Billings, G. (2006b). The meaning of Brown...for now. In A. Ball (Ed.), *With more deliberate speed: Achieving, equity, and excellence in education* (National Society for the Study of Education 2006 yearbook, pp. 298-315). Williston, VT: Blackwell.

Lee, C. D. (2006). Foreword. In E. M. Horvat & C. O'Connor (Eds.), *Beyond the burden of acting White: Reframing the debate on Black student achievement* (pp. ix-xiii). New York: Rowman & Littlefield.

Lee, C. D. (2007). *Culture, literacy, and learning: Taking bloom in the midst of the whirlwind.* New York: Teachers College Press.

Lee, J. (2002). Racial and ethnic achievement gap trends: Reversing the progress toward equity? *Educational Researcher, 31*(1), 3–12.

Lee, J., Autry, M. M., Fox, J., & Williams, C. (2008). Investigating children's mathematics readiness. *Journal of Research in Childhood Education, 22*(3), 316–329.

Lee, S. (1996). *Unraveling the model minority stereotype.* New York: Teachers College Press.

Lee, S. (2005). *Up against Whiteness: Race, school and immigrant youth.* New York: Teachers College Record.

Lee, S. J. (2001). More than "model minorities" or "delinquents": A look at Hmong American high school students. *Harvard Educational Review, 71*(3), 505–528.

Lee, V., & Bryk, A. (1989). A multilevel model of the social distribution of high school achievement. *Sociology of Education, 62*(3), 172–179.

Lee, V. E., & Burkam, D. T. (2003). Dropping out of high school: The role of school organization and structure. *American Educational Research Journal, 40*(2), 353–393.

Lee, V. E., Croninger, R. G., & Smith, J. B. (1997). Course-taking, equity, and mathematics learning: Testing the constrained curriculum hypothesis in U.S. secondary schools. *Educational Evaluation and Policy Analysis, 19*(2), 99–121.

Lewis, A. E. (2003a). Everyday race-making: Navigating racial boundaries in schools. *American Behavioral Scientist, 47*(3), 283–305.

Lewis, A. E. (2003b). *Race in the schoolyard: Reproducing the color line in school.* New Brunswick, NJ: Rutgers University Press.

Lewis, O. (1963). *The children of Sanchez: Autobiography of a Mexican family.* New York: Vintage.

Lomawaima, K. T., & McCarty, T. L. (2002). When tribal sovereignty challenges democracy: American Indian education and the democratic ideal. *American Educational Research Journal, 39*(2), 279–305.

Lubeck, S., & Garrett, P. (1990). The social construction of the "at-risk" child. *British Journal of Sociology of Education, 11*(3), 327–340.

Lucas, S. R. (1999). *Tracking inequality: Stratification and mobility in American high schools.* New York: Teachers College Press.

Margonis, F. (1992). The cooptation of "at-risk": Paradoxes of policy criticism. *Teachers College Record, 94*(2), 343–364.

Massey, D. S., Charles, C. Z., Lundy, G., & Fischer, M. J. (2003). *The source of the river: The social origins of freshman at America's selective colleges and universities.* Princeton, NJ: Princeton University Press.

Masuda, M., Matsumoto, G. H., & Meredith, G. M. (1970). Ethnic identity in three generations of Japanese Americans. *Journal of Social Psychology, 81,* 199–207.

Matute-Bianchi, M. E. (1986). Ethnic identities and patterns of school success and failure among Mexican-decent and Japanese-American students in a California high school: An ethnographic analysis. *American Journal of Education, 95,* 1.

McDonough, P. (1997). *Choosing colleges: How social class and schools structure opportunity.* Albany: State University of New York Press.

McPartland, J. (1969). The relative influence of school and of classroom desegregation on the academic achievement of ninth-grade Negro students. *Journal of Social Issues, 25,* 93–102.

Mickelson, R. A. (2001). Subverting Swann: First- and second-generation segregation in the Charlotte-Mecklenburg schools. *American Educational Research Journal, 38*(2), 215–252.

Mickelson, R. A., & Heath, D. (2001). The effects of segregation on African American high school seniors' academic achievement. *Journal of Negro Education, 66*(4), 566–586.

Mickelson, R., & Valesco, A. E. (2006). Bring it On! Diverse responses to "Acting White" among academically able Black students. In E. M. Horvat & C. O'Connor (Eds.), *Beyond acting White: Reframing the debate on Black student achievement* (pp. 27–56). Lanham, MD: Rowman & Littlefield.

Mordkowitz, E. R., & Ginsberg, H. P. (1987). Early academic socialization of successful Asian-American college students. *Quarterly Newsletter of the Laboratory of Comparative Human Cognition, 9,* 85–91.

Morris, J. E. (2004). Can anything good come from Nazareth? Race, class, and African American schooling and community in the urban south and Midwest. *American Educational Research Journal, 41*(1), 69–112.

National Coalition of Advocates for Students. (1985). *Barriers to excellence: Our children at risk.* Boston: National Coalition of Advocates for Students.

National Commission on Excellence in Education. (1983). *A nation at risk: The imperative for educational reform.* Washington, DC: Government Printing Office.

Natriello, G., McDill, E. L., & Pallas, A. M. (1990). *Schooling disadvantaged children: Racing against catastrophe.* New York: Teachers College Press.

Neal, L. I., McCray, A. D., Webb-Johnson, G., & Bridgest, S. T. (2003). The effects of African American movement styles on teachers' perceptions and reactions. *Journal of Special Education, 37*(1), 49–57.

Ng, J. C., Lee, S. S., & Pak, Y. K. (2007). Contesting the model minority and perpetual foreigner stereotypes: A critical review of literature on Asian Americans in education. *Review of Research in Education, 31*(95), 95–130.

Ngo, B. (2006). Learning from the margins: The education of Southeast and South Asians in context. *Race, Ethnicity and Education, 9*(1), 51–65.

Ngo, B., & Lee, S. J. (2007). Complicating the image of model minority success: A review of Southeast Asian education. *Review of Research in Education, 77*(4), 415–457.

Nye, B. A., Hedges, L. V., & Konstantopoulos, S. (2000). Do the disadvantaged benefit more from small classes? Evidence from the Tennessee class size experiment. *American Journal of Education, 109*(1), 1–26.

Nye, B., Konstantopoulos, S., & Hedges, L. V. (2004). How large are teacher effects? *Evaluation and Policy Analysis, 26*(3), 237–257.

Oakes, J. (1994). More than misapplied technology: A normative and political response to Hallinan on tracking. *Sociology of Education, 67*(2), 84–91.

Oakes, J. (2005). *Keeping track: How schools structure inequality* (3rd ed.). New Haven, CT: Yale University Press.

O'Connor, C. (1997). Dispositions toward (collective) struggle and educational resilience in the inner city: A case analysis of six African-American high school students. *American Educational Research Journal, 34*(4), 593–629.

O'Connor, C. (2001). Making sense of the complexity of social identity in relation to achievement: A sociological challenge in the new millennium. *Sociology of Education, 74*, 159–168.

O'Connor, C. (2002). Black women beating the odds from one generation to the next: How the changing dynamics of constraint and opportunity affect the process of educational resilience. *American Educational Research Journal, 39*(4), 855–903.

O'Connor, C. (2006a). America's preoccupation with Black pathology: An enduring obstacle fifty years post Brown. In A. Ball (Ed.), *With more deliberate speed: Achieving equity and excellence in education* (National Society for the Study of Education 2006 yearbook, pp. 316–336). Williston, VT: Blackwell.

O'Connor, C. (2006b). Race, class, and disproportionality: Reevaluating the relationship between poverty and special education placement. *Educational Researcher, 35*(6), 6–11.

O'Connor, C., Fernandez, S. D., & Girard, B. (2007). The meaning of "Blackness": How Black students differentially align race and achievement across time and space. In A. Fuligni (Ed.), *Contesting stereotypes and creating identities* (pp. 183–208). Thousand Oaks, CA: Sage.

O'Connor, C., Horvat, E. M., & Lewis, A. (2006). Framing the field: Past and future research on the historic underachievement of Black students. In E. Horvat & C. O'Connor (Eds.), *Beyond the burden of acting White: Reframing the debate on Black student achievement* (pp. 1-24). New York: Rowman & Littlefield.

O'Connor, C., Lewis, A., & Mueller, J. (2007). Researching "Black" educational experiences and outcomes: Theoretical and methodological considerations. *Educational Researcher, 36*(9), 541–552.

Ogbu, J. (1987). Variability in minority school performance: A problem in search of an explanation. *Anthropology and Education Quarterly, 18*(4), 312–333.

Ogbu, J. (2003). *Black American students in an affluent suburb: A study of academic disengagement.* Mahwah, NJ: Lawrence Erlbaum.

Ogbu, J., & Matute-Bianchi, M. E. (1986). Understanding sociocultural factors in education: Knowledge, identity and adjustment in school. In C. E. Cortes et al. (Eds.), *Beyond language: Social and cultural factors in schooling language minority students* (pp. 73–142). Sacramento: California State Department of Education.

Orfield, G. (1997). Does desegregation help close the gap? (Testimony of Gary Orfield, March 22, 1996). *Journal of Negro Education, 66*(3), 241–254.

Orr, J. A. (2003). Black–White differences in achievement: The importance of wealth. *Sociology of Education, 76*(4), 281–304.

Pallas, A., Entwisle, D. R., Alexander, K. L., & Stulka, M. F. (1994). Ability group effects: Instructional, social, or institutional? *Sociology of Education, 67*, 27–46.

Patterson, C. J., Kupersmidt, J. B., & Vaden, N. A. (1990). Income level, gender, ethnicity, and household composition as predictors of children's school-based competence. *Child Development, 61*, 485–494.

Pearce, R. R. (2006). Effects of cultural and social structural factors on the achievement of White and Chinese American students at school transition points. *American Educational Research Journal, 43*(1), 75–101.

Phillips, M. (1998). *Early inequalities: The development of ethnic differences in academic achievement during childhood.* Unpublished doctoral dissertation, Northwestern University, Evanston, IL.

Phillips, M., Crouse, J., & Ralph, J. (1998). Does the Black–White test score gap widen after children enter school? In C. Jencks & M. Phillips (Eds.), *The Black–White test score gap* (pp. 229–272). Washington, DC: Brookings Institution.

Raudenbush, S. (2004). What are value-added models estimating and what does it imply for statistical practice? *Journal of Educational and Behavioral Statistics, 29*, 121–129.

Ream, R. K. (2003). Counterfeit social capital and Mexican-American underachievement. *Educational Evaluation and Policy Analysis, 25*(3), 237–262.

Reyes, P., Scribner, J. D., & Scribner, A. P. (Eds.). (1999). *Lessons from high-performing Hispanic schools: Creating learning communities.* New York: Teachers College Press.

Rist, R. (1970). Student social class and teacher expectations: The self-fulfilling prophecy in ghetto education. *Harvard Educational Review, 40*, 411–451.

Rockoff, J. E. (2004). The impact of individual teachers on student achievement: Evidence from panel data. *American Economic Review, 94*(2), 247–252.

Roehrig, G. H., & Kruse, R. A. (2005). The role of teachers' beliefs and knowledge in the adoption of a reform-based curriculum. *School Science and Mathematics, 105*(8), 412–423.

Roscigno, V. J. (2000). Family/school inequality and African-American/Hispanic achievement. *Social Problems, 47*(2), 266–290.

Roscigno, V. J., & Ainsworth-Darnell, J. W. (1999). Race, cultural capital, and educational resources: Persistent inequalities and achievement returns. *Sociology of Education, 72*, 158–178.

Rosenfeld, M., & Rosenfeld, S. (2008). Developing effective teacher beliefs about learners: The role of sensitizing teachers to individual learning differences. *Educational Psychology, 28*(3), 245–272.

Rumberger, R. W., & Willms, J. D. (1992). The impact of racial and ethnic segregation on the achievement gap in California high schools. *Educational Evaluation and Policy Analysis, 14*(4), 377–396.

Schneider, B., & Lee, Y. (1990). A model for academic success: The school success and home environment of East Asian students. *Anthropology and Education Quarterly, 21*(4), 358–377.

Sizemore, B. (1985). Pitfalls and promises of effective schools research. *Journal of Negro Education, 54*(3), 269–288.

Sizemore, B. (1988). The Madison Elementary School: A turnaround case. *Journal of Negro Education, 57*(3), 243–266.

Skiba, R. J. (2001). When is disproportionality discrimination? The overrepresentation of Black students in school suspension. In W. Ayers, B. Dohrn, & R. Ayers (Eds.), *Zero tolerance: Resisting the drive for punishment in schools* (pp. 165–176). New York: New Press.

Skinner, D., Bryant, D., Coffman, J., & Campbell, F. (1998). Creating risk and promise: Children's and teachers' co-constructions in the cultural world of kindergarten. *Elementary School Journal, 98*(4), 297–310.

Slaughter-Defoe, D. T., Nakagawa, K., Takanishi, R., & Johnson, D. J. (1990). Toward cultural/ecological perspectives on schooling and achievement in African- and Asian-American children. *Child Development, 61*(2), 363–384.

Southworth, S., & Mickelson, R. (2007). The interactive effects of race, gender and school composition on track placement. *Social Forces, 86*(2), 497–523.

Spady, W. G. (1973). The impact of school resources on students. In F. N. Kerlinge (Ed.), *Review of research in education* (pp. 135–177). Itasca, IL: Peacock.

St. John, N. (1975). *School desegregation: Outcomes for children.* New York: John Wiley.

Stanton-Salazar, R. (2000). *Manufacturing hope and despair: The school and kin support networks of U.S.-Mexican youth.* New York: Teachers College Press.

Stewart, B. E. (2006). *Value-added modeling: The challenge of measuring educational outcomes.* New York: Carnegie Corporation of New York.

Suarez-Orozco, M. M. (1987). "Becoming somebody": Central American immigrants in U.S. inner-city schools. *Anthropology and Education Quarterly, 18*(4), 287–299.

Sue, S., & Okazaki, S. (1990). Asian-American educational achievements: A phenomenon in search of an explanation. *American Psychologist, 45*(8), 913–920.

Sui, S.-F. (1996). *Asian American students at risk: A literature review.* Baltimore: Center for Research on Children Placed At Risk.

Swadener, E. B. (1995). Children and families "at promise": Deconstructing the discourse of risk. In E. B. Swadener & S. Lubeck (Eds.), *Children and families "at promise": Deconstructing the discourse of risk* (pp. 17–49). Albany: State University of New York Press.

Teachman, J. D., Paasch, K., & Carver, K. (1996). Social capital and dropping out of school early. *Journal of Marriage and Family, 58,* 773–783.

Thomas, K. M. (2004). The SAT II: Minority/majority test-score gaps and what they could mean for college admissions. *Social Science Quarterly, 85*(5), 1318–1385.

Tyler, K. M., Uqdah, A. L., Dillihunt, M. L., Beatty-Hazelbaker, R., Conner, T., Gadson, N., et al. (2008). Cultural discontinuity: Toward a quantitative investigation of a major hypothesis in education. *Educational Researcher, 37*(5), 280–297.

Tyson, K. (2003). Weighing in: Elementary-age students and the debate on attitudes toward school among Black students. *Social Forces, 80*(4), 1157–1189.

Tyson, K. (2006). The making of a burden: Tracing the development of a burden of "acting White" in schools. In E. M. Horvat & C. O'Connor (Eds.), *Beyond acting White: Reframing the debate on Black student achievement* (pp. 57-88). Lanham, MD: Rowman & Littlefield.

Tyson, K., Darity, W., & Castellino, D. (2005). "It's not "a Black thing": Understanding the burden of acting White and other dilemmas of high achievement. *American Sociological Review, 70*(4), 582–605.

Valentine, K. (1968). *Culture and poverty: Critique and counter-proposals.* Chicago: University of Chicago Press.

Velez, W. (1989). High school attrition among Hispanic and non-Hispanic White youth. *Sociology of Education, 62,* 119–133.

Warren, J. R. (1996). Educational inequality among White and Mexican-origin adolescents in the American southwest: 1990. *Sociology of Education, 69*(2), 142–158.

Wayne, A. J., & Youngs, P. (2003). Teacher characteristics and student achievement gains: A review. *Review of Educational Research, 73*(1), 89–122.

Wells, A. S., & Crain, R. L. (1994). Perpetuation theory and the long term effects of desegregation. *Review of Educational Research, 64,* 531–555.

White, M. J., & Kaufman, G. (1997). Language use, social capital and school completion among immigrants and native-born ethnic groups. *Social Science Quarterly, 78*(2), 385–392.

Winfield, L. F. (1991). Resilience, schooling and development in African-American youth: A conceptual framework. *Education and Urban Society, 24*(1), 5–14.

Wong, M. G. (1990). The education of White, Chinese, Filipino, and Japanese students: A look at "high school and beyond." *Sociological Perspectives, 33*(3), 355–374.

Yates, A. (1987). Current status and future directions of research on the American Indian child. *American Journal of Psychiatry, 144*(9), 1135–1142.

Zill, N., & West, J. (2000). *Entering kindergarten: A portrait of American children when they begin school. Findings from the Condition of Education.* Washington, DC: National Center for Education Statistics.

Chapter 2

Child Well-Being: The Intersection of Schools and Child Welfare

Fred Wulczyn
Cheryl Smithgall
Lijun Chen
Chapin Hall Center for Children, University of Chicago

In this chapter, we argue for closer collaboration between public schools and the public child welfare system, on behalf of children placed at risk, with respect to whether they will do as well in school as their abilities suggest they might, all else being equal. The need for closer collaboration is tied to two developments affecting schools and the child welfare system. First, both systems, as the result of relatively recent federal, state, and local initiatives, are focused on accountability as never before. For schools, accountability fostered by the No Child Left Behind act means that educators have to pay closer attention to children placed at risk who may fall behind in school if their educational needs are not addressed. In this context, the overall well-being of children involved in the child welfare system poses particular challenges because the incidence of cognitive, social, and behavioral impairment is substantially higher than the rates found in the general population. From the perspective of the child welfare system, public agencies are starting to look at school success as a measure of child well-being and as an indicator of their own service quality, an expanded view of responsibility that was introduced in the wake of the Adoption and Safe Families Act passed in 1997. As a consequence, advocates are pushing child welfare agencies to consider placing foster children within their own home school districts in an effort to preserve educational continuity and minimize disruption in the children's lives.

In turn, the new wave of accountability has focused attention on the shear magnitude of the dually involved population. According to the most recent national data, of the more than 3 million reports of child maltreatment received annually, about 610,000 school-age children (4- to 17-year-olds) are involved in a substantiated allegation of maltreatment each year, a figure that represents about 70% of all official maltreatment

Review of Research in Education
March 2009, Vol. 33, pp. 35-62
DOI: 10.3102/0091732X08327208
© 2009 AERA. http://rre.aera.net

victims and 1% of the school-age population (U.S. Department of Health and Human Services, 2008). However, the national estimates understate the challenges facing schools in high poverty areas, where rates of maltreatment are often three to four times higher than the rates reported in nonpoor areas (Korbin, Coulton, Chard, Platt-Houston, & Su, 1998; Wulczyn, Barth, Yuan, Harden, & Landsverk, 2005). Moreover, few states or localities view risk from a life-course perspective. In California, where scholars have looked at.cumulative risk, the current estimate is that 38% of all Black children and 20% of all White children have contact with the child welfare system (including reports that are not substantiated) by the time they reach age 7 (Magruder & Shaw, in press). In that involvement with the child welfare system may be a marker for cognitive, social, and behavioral impairments that are directly related to child well-being and school success, the implications of these data for classroom practice, pedagogy, and schooling, more broadly defined, are profound.

To deepen our understanding of how risk and child well-being converge in the context of schools, this chapter focuses on child maltreatment and foster care placement, the principle responsibilities of the child welfare system. Two themes run through our review of the issues: (a) the links among schools, the child welfare system, and the well-being of children and (b) school readiness and educational achievement over the life course. From our reading, scholarship and research that address the problem of maltreatment and foster care tend to view shared concerns through the relatively narrow lens of special education and other special learning needs. Although these are important perspectives, the classroom risks that involvement with the child welfare system implies may not be immediately apparent to teachers and school personnel even though the impact on the child's engagement in school is no less profound. More specifically, several factors converge to put children at risk. For example, children with involvement in the child welfare system typically come from poor, single-parent households; are disproportionately exposed to violence and substance abuse; and, if placed in foster care, are likely to experience changes in their caregiving arrangements, all of which undermine a child's ability to achieve mastery in school. In broadening conceptualizations of risk in the context of practice, we aim to capture the breadth and complexities of how risk is interpreted and how children in school are exposed to, succumb to, or rise above everyday risks.

Our chapter has three primary sections, each of which is intended to reinforce the notion that greater awareness of maltreatment, placement into foster care, and the educational challenges of dually involved children is important to schools and the public child welfare system from their respective policy, practice, and research perspectives. We start with the epidemiology of maltreatment and placement into foster care. Although definitions of maltreatment differ as a matter of public policy (e.g., some states do not recognize educational neglect as a form of maltreatment) and local culture, our use of the term in this chapter draws on the general notion of verified allegations of maltreatment. That is, the state public child welfare agency, having responded to an allegation of maltreatment, has completed an investigation and determined that some form of maltreatment did occur. The research we cite was developed using state administrative data (i.e., maltreatment reports) together with county-level poverty data. These findings, which provide baseline incidence data, reveal both a strong poverty–maltreatment link and persistent developmental influences that pertain to when children are most likely to become involved with the child welfare system. In particular, the data point to children who are younger than 1 year at the time they become involved in the child welfare system. As a group, they frame the developmental perspective needed to understand how schools and the child welfare system relate to each other within a life-course perspective. Although finding the child a safe and stable family is the first job of the child welfare system, forward-thinking child welfare agencies see the challenges and the opportunities that come with a developmental perspective that targets school readiness and accompanying support for children as a way to organize interventions that help students get ready for school and help schools adapt to needs of their students.

In the next section, we review findings that pertain to the well-being of children who encounter the child welfare system in the first year of life. Although children come into contact with the child welfare system at all ages, the developmental perspective that frames our presentation places particular emphasis on early care and learning experiences as a foundation for positive school outcomes (Kolker, Osborne, & Schnurer, 2004). Given the preponderance of children who have contact with the child welfare system prior to their first birthday, it seems particularly relevant that we understand the youngest children as they make their way toward school. To do this, we cite results from the National Survey of Child and Adolescent Well-Being (NSCAW), the nation's first study of a child welfare population to examine child well-being using a national probability sample of children. The study combines cognitive and behavioral measures with information about the involvement of children in the child welfare system over five waves of data collection. By using standardized measures and NSCAW, investigators can assess the home context together with the cognitive and language development of children poised to enter school. When paired with the administrative data, NSCAW findings highlight the educational risks facing a substantial portion of the population at the time they start school.

In the third section of the chapter, we examine the educational trajectories of public school students with a history of involvement with the child welfare system. Again, we adopt a developmental perspective that starts with entry into school and considers whether children involved with the child welfare system are already behind (i.e., old for grade) when they start school. We then consider whether children connected to the child welfare system progress through school at a rate that is comparable to their peers. We do this by asking whether reading scores improve over time. Then we examine school completion rates, given different levels of involvement with the child welfare system. The findings point to the fact that children involved with the child welfare system start school behind their peers, are less likely to progress, and are less likely to graduate. We close this section of the chapter by looking at how child welfare involvement intersects with special education and how the classification of learning disabilities appears to dominate the way in which schools respond to children who are struggling with learning or behavioral problems.

We conclude the chapter by suggesting ways that the fields of child welfare and education, particularly early childhood education, can work together to improve the quality of learning, teaching, and schooling to which children at the greatest risk for maltreatment are exposed. The implications for education as a field and for children's school lives are critical to ensuring optimal opportunities for these children.

EPIDEMIOLOGY OF CHILD MALTREATMENT AND FOSTER CARE PLACEMENT

To build the connection between maltreatment, child development, and school success, we start with the epidemiology of maltreatment in a select group of states by age at initial maltreatment, race, and county poverty level (Wulczyn et al., 2005). These data both reinforce the important links among poverty, race, and maltreatment and expand notions of risk within the context of educational success. The data point to age-specific risks that draw particular attention to children younger than 1 year. From the perspective of early childhood experiences in relation to school success, the large number of child victims younger than 1 year suggests that within highly vulnerable populations, the children who come to school with a history of maltreatment are especially vulnerable.

Substantiated Maltreatment, Poverty, and Race/Ethnicity

Although the rate of maltreatment is an important social indicator, theories of child development suggest that there may be significant differences in who is maltreated that bear the imprint of developmental influences. This is not to suggest that no other factors influence the incidence of maltreatment. Rather, the idea is that within the constellation of factors that influence maltreatment, developmental concerns shape the underlying etiology of and response to maltreatment. As Shonkoff and Phillips (2000) suggested, these developmental influences are present in a range of populations and contexts.

To illustrate this idea, we cite data that show the incidence rate for first-time victims of maltreatment controlling for age, county poverty rate, and race (Wulczyn et al., 2005). The analysis draws on National Child Abuse and Neglects Reporting System (NCANDS) data from four states representing 296 counties, 11,450,000 children younger than 19 years, and 64,000 first-time victims. The analysis begins with a simple description of maltreatment rates by age at onset for single-year age groups and then divides the counties into two groups based on the county's poverty level. Counties with low poverty levels are the counties that fall into the top 20%— that is, counties with child poverty rates (in 1999) between 2.3% and 12.2%. Counties with high poverty rates fall in the bottom quintile, a group that includes counties with poverty rates between 17.6% and 43.6%.[1]

The relationship between age and the risk of substantiated maltreatment is shown in Figure 1. The rate of substantiated maltreatment is highest for infants, defined as

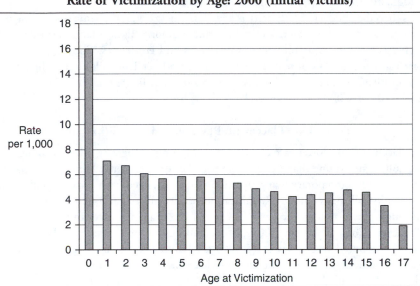

FIGURE 1
Rate of Victimization by Age: 2000 (Initial Victims)

Note. From *Beyond Common Sense: Child Welfare, Child Well-Being, and the Evidence for Policy Reform,* by F. Wulczyn, R. P. Barth, Y-Y. T. Yuan, B. J. Harden, and J. Landsverk, 2005, New Brunswick, NJ: Aldine Transaction. Copyright 2005 by Chapin Hall Center for Children.

children who were younger than 1 at the time of the first substantiated investigation. The rate reported for infants in 2000 was 16 per 1,000, more than twice the rate for 1-year-olds, the group with the next highest rate of maltreatment. Rates of maltreatment decline with age, although small, age-specific exceptions are found in the data. Substantiated maltreatment rates level off around the time children enter school (approximately 6 per 1,000), decline from age 8 through 11 (approximately 4 per 1,000 by age 11), and then rise again from ages 12 through 14.

With respect to the relationship between poverty and maltreatment, the pattern showing the elevated risk of maltreatment for infants exists in both high-poverty and low-poverty counties. In high-poverty counties, the risk of maltreatment for infants is 2.8 times as great as it is for 1-year-olds, the group with the next highest maltreatment rate, and 1.6 times as great in low-poverty counties. For children of all other ages, maltreatment rates are considerably lower, regardless of county poverty level, although there is a persistent pattern of disparity in that maltreatment rates overall are higher in high-poverty counties, as one would expect.

Age-specific disparities in the risk of maltreatment are somewhat more pronounced in high-poverty counties. For example, middle adolescents (14- and 15-year-olds) in high-poverty counties have maltreatment rates that are about 15% as great as those reported for 11- and 12-year-olds. In the low-poverty counties where age-based variation in reported rates of maltreatment is less noticeable, the increase in substanti-ated maltreatment for middle adolescents is unremarkable.

When the child's race/ethnicity is added, the data reveal the same underlying pat-tern of risk. However, the risk of maltreatment among Black infants is substantially higher compared with children of other races and ethnicities. Specifically, among Black infants, the risk of maltreatment is about 50 per 1,000 children, a figure that is equivalent to 5% of Black infants.[2] The comparable figure for White infants is just under 10 per 1,000 (Wulczyn et al., 2005).

Foster Care Placement, Poverty, and Race/Ethnicity

Placement into foster care comes about when public agency officials, along with the courts, determine that a child cannot be kept safely in the home of the parent. Foster care is a temporary living situation that is arranged with the expectation that the family will be reunified. Reunification occurs more than one half of the time, although there are significant differences from state to state and within states (Wulczyn, Chen, & Hislop, 2007). When children cannot be returned home, either they are adopted or custody is given to a relative who agrees to assume custodial responsibilities. Infants are the children least likely to be reunified and the most likely to be adopted.

In this section, we consider placement rates using the same lens used to under-stand maltreatment rates: age, county poverty, and race/ethnicity. Our analysis of age-specific placement risks begins with a baseline placement rate per 1,000 children by age. In Figure 2, the data reveal three distinct patterns that define the relationship between age and the likelihood of placement. These patterns are highly reminiscent of the maltreatment data. The most notable feature is the elevated placement risk for children younger than 1 year. In 2000, almost 10 infant placements per 1,000 chil-dren fell into that age group. This figure is more than 2.5 times the rate reported for 1-year-olds, the group with the next highest likelihood of placement. Second, place-ment rates for children between the ages of 1 and 11 were considerably lower than those reported for infants. Third, the likelihood of placement was higher for adoles-cents than for other children (other than infants). In 2000, the rate of placement for 15-year-olds was 2.8 per 1,000, a full 50% higher than the placement rate reported for 11-year-olds. Placement rates generally rise from age 12 through 15, reaching a peak at age 15.

Age-specific placement rates by county poverty rates reflect the same pattern. Placement rates are significantly higher for infants than for all other children, regard-less of the county poverty rate. The infant placement rate is about 2.8 times higher than the rate for 1-year-olds. After infants, children between birth and 2 years of age face the highest risk, and 14- and 15-year-olds are the group with the next highest likelihood of placement.

Placement rates for Black children by age and county poverty reveal the familiar pattern. Among infants, the risk of placement is uniformly higher, regardless of the county poverty rate. For Hispanic and White children, the data point to similar,

FIGURE 2
Rate of First Admission Into Foster Care by Age at First Admission: 2000

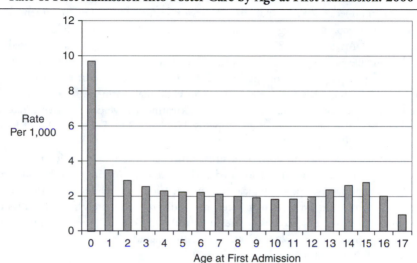

Note. From *Beyond Common Sense: Child Welfare, Child Well-Being, and the Evidence for Policy Reform,* by F. Wulczyn, R. P. Barth, Y-Y. T. Yuan, B. J. Harden, and J. Landsverk, 2005, New Brunswick, NJ: Aldine Transaction. Copyright 2005 by Chapin Hall Center for Children.

age-differentiated risk patterns: Infants living in high-poverty counties are the children most likely to enter placement. Placement rates are significantly higher for Black children compared with Hispanic or White children, regardless of age or the county poverty rate (Wulczyn et al., 2005).

CHILD MALTREATMENT, DEVELOPMENTAL EFFECTS, AND SCHOOL

In this section we interweave maltreatment, child development, and achievement in school. We focus on two issues. First, we review the literature to examine how maltreatment influences child development as a general matter. As we show, maltreatment affects development across multiple domains. We then turn to the specific issue of maltreatment and its impact on outcomes in the educational sphere. To the extent that the literature points to specific risk factors (e.g., parental substance abuse, domestic violence, parent's education, and poverty), these data amplify the notion that children in the child welfare system are exposed to a range of influences known to influence school success adversely.

Correlates of Maltreatment and School Success

Child maltreatment is a complex social problem associated with caregivers' mental impairments, family conflicts, and socioeconomic adversities. Maltreating caregivers and parents are often characterized by psychological impairments such as anxiety and depression (National Research Council, 1993; Wissow, 2001). Caregiver substance abuse often impedes adequate parenting behavior, leading to child maltreatment. Use of drugs and alcohol by pregnant women causes direct harm to the children (Singer et al., 2001). An estimated 8% to 11% of newborn babies are prenatally exposed to alcohol and illegal drugs, although only a proportion of them are identified as victims of child abuse and neglect (Young, Boles, & Otero, 2007). Domestic violence involving the child caregiver is a major risk factor for child maltreatment. Many studies on the overlap of domestic violence and child maltreatment have documented a rate of co-occurrence that approaches 40% (Appel & Holden, 1998; Edleson, 1999; Moore & Florsheim, 2008).

The family's social and economic situation (e.g., poverty, unemployment, and low education of caregivers) is associated with maltreatment both directly and indirectly through parents' psychological well-being. Victims of child maltreatment, as determined by child protection services, come disproportionately from families of low income. As a major ecological stressor, family poverty has long been known to have an adverse effect on parental mental health, including substance abuse (Alder et al., 1994; National Research Council, 1993).

Five domains of children's development are recognized as critical for school success: physical well-being and motor skills, social and emotional development, approaches to learning, language development, and cognition and general knowledge (National Education Goals Panel, 1997). Children lacking in these core competencies are less likely to succeed in school than those who are well prepared (Lewit & Baker, 1994; Shonkoff & Phillips, 2000). According to a report based on the Early Childhood Longitudinal Study, Kindergarten Class of 1998–99 (ECLS-K; Zill & West, 2001), a considerable proportion of kindergarten children experience developmental difficulties, such as having difficulty paying attention for sustained periods (13%) or communicating clearly with others (11%). An earlier study of kindergarteners found that according to teachers' reports, more than one third of the students were not ready for school because they lacked core competencies (Lewit & Baker, 1994).

Differences in developmental status are evident well before school age, and children's experiences in the first few years of their lives have a tremendous impact on their developmental prospects, setting the stage for future academic performance in school and beyond (Entwisle, Alexander, & Olson, 2005). The family and community constitute the major developmental context of a child. The ECLS-K study identified four major risk factors related to the family that compromise children's readiness for school (Zill & West, 2001). Children living in a family on public assistance, living in single-parent homes, having parents with less than high school education, and having a primary language that is not English are described as being less well prepared for school. The effect of the risk is cumulative in that children with more risk factors perform worse in all five domains of development (Pike, Iervolino, Eley, Price, & Plomin, 2006; Stanton-Chapman, Chapman, Kaiser, & Hancock, 2004).

Other studies have found an adverse effect of family poverty and low parental education on the cognitive development and language ability of children before school age (Duncan & Brooks-Gunn, 2000; Mercy & Steelman, 1982; Pike et al., 2006). Furthermore, the adverse effect of early childhood poverty persists through the school years, predicting academic achievement and school completion rates. It is found that only early childhood poverty, not middle childhood or early adolescent poverty, is related to high school dropout rates (Duncan, Brooks-Gunn, Yeung, & Smith, 1998). Obviously children raised in poverty, especially during the first few years of life, have significant disadvantages in preschool competencies, which set them on a trajectory for lower school achievement.

One question is how the home environment, parenting behavior, and poverty intersect to form the context of early child development. For example, research has established that caregiver warmth and cognitive stimulation toward the child as well as physical conditions and learning opportunities of the home are strong mediators between family income and cognitive development of young children (Linver, Brooks-Gunn, & Kohen., 2002; Yeung, Linver, & Brooks-Gunn, 2002). Poverty is associated as well with a number of resources for young children. Children in socioeconomically disadvantaged families have far fewer books and educational toys and receive far less reading from their parents (Adams, 1990; Bradley, Corwyn, Burchinal, McAdoo, & Garcia Coll, 2001; Brooks-Gunn & Duncan, 1997). Moreover, each of the three major indicators of socioeconomic status (family income, parental education, and parental occupation) is associated with school achievement directly and indirectly through better parenting (DeGarmo, Forgatch, & Martinez, 1999).

Developmental Consequences of Maltreatment

Child maltreatment has serious and often long-lasting consequences on the physical, cognitive, emotional, and social development of children. A significant proportion of young children suffering abuse and neglect are found to have physical injuries, health problems, growth delays, and impaired brain functioning (Leslie et al., 2005; Silver et al., 1999). The damaging effect is especially severe for infants and young children because it interrupts and delays their brain development (De Bellis, 2005; De Bellis et al., 2002), with consequences for later performance in school.

Cognitive and language delays are common among maltreated children, exceeding the normal rate found in the general child population (Leslie et al., 2005; Silver et al., 1999; Simpson, Colpe, & Greenspan, 2003; Singer et al., 2001). Although socioeconomic status is associated with developmental delays, some investigators (e.g., Beers & De Bellis, 2002) have found that maltreatment inflicts independent damage on cognitive functioning of children even after socioeconomic status is controlled. A comparative study of maltreated children in foster care with nonmaltreated children with similar socioeconomic status backgrounds indicated that maltreated children have significantly lower scores in visuospatial functioning, language, and general cognitive functioning (Pears & Fisher, 2005). In their comparison of language development among maltreated children and children with comparable demographic and socioeconomic status, Eigsti and Cicchetti

(2004) discovered that both maltreated children and their nonmaltreated peers experienced syntactic delays attributable to their impoverished environments; however, the delays of the maltreated children were more severe than those of the comparison group, indicating that maltreatment exacerbated the language delay.

Maltreated children have been found to have deficits in social–emotional domains, including poor emotional comprehension, heightened arousal to negative emotions, and increased expression of negative emotions (Bennett, Sullivan, & Lewis, 2005; Cicchetti & Curtis, 2005; Pears & Fisher, 2005). Studies have shown that maltreated children are likely to form insecure attachments with caregivers (Barnett, Ganiban, & Cicchetti, 1999) and have poor relationships with peers (see Howe & Parke, 2001).

The developmental impact of early maltreatment is not transient and often has long-term deleterious effects, including inadequate school performance. Studies have shown that children who experienced abuse and neglect are less motivated in school, perform worse in math and English in elementary school, and are more likely to be held back in kindergarten and first grade (Rowe & Eckenrode, 1999). A recent longitudinal study of child aggression indicated that child neglect in the first 2 years of life is a more important precursor of childhood aggression at age 8 than is later neglect or physical abuse at any age (Kotch et al., 2008).

INFANTS AS VICTIMS OF CHILD MALTREATMENT

In this section, we focus on a nationally representative sample of 1,196 children who were involved with the child welfare system in their first year of life. We follow them through age 5 or 6, as they are getting ready for or have just started school. We describe the profiles of these children and their living environments, paying particular attention to risk factors that are present. We also examine the developmental trajectory of these children and assess their school readiness, especially their cognitive and language skills.

The National Survey of Children and Adolescent Well-Being (NSCAW) is a nationally representative survey of more than 5,501 children aged 0 to 14 who were investigated for child maltreatment in 93 designated areas (counties or child welfare jurisdictions) within a 15-month period starting in October 1999. This study is based on a subsample of 1,196 infants, whose median age at the baseline interview was 6 months. These infants were followed up on three more occasions after the baseline survey: at about 22 months, 38 months, and 68 months.[3] Time intervals between two adjacent waves vary for different children, the intervals described above being only the median. As a result, the children's ages at each wave vary. With respect to administrative data presented in the prior section (the incidence of maltreatment and placement in 2000), these survey-based data refer directly to the population of infants identified previously, providing what is in many respects the most comprehensive portrait of the child welfare service population ever assembled.

Profiles of the Infants and Their Living Environments

Table 1 shows the characteristics of infants involved with the child welfare system and the attributes of their family and social contexts. Obviously, with 30% Black and

TABLE 1
Profiles of Children, Caregivers, and Living Environments at Baseline

Characteristics	Unweighted Frequency	Percentage	*SE*
Child gender			
Male	619	49.1	3.2
Female	577	50.9	3.2
Child race/ethnicity			
Black/non-Hispanic	468	29.6	3.0
White/non-Hispanic	410	43.7	3.8
Hispanic	233	21.3	2.3
Other	79	5.4	1.2
Child abuse type			
Physical maltreatment	195	17.9	2.0
Physical neglect didn't provide	492	39.7	2.4
Neglect: no supervision, abandonment	238	27.0	2.6
Emotional, sexual, moral abuse	70	6.6	1.2
Other	89	8.9	1.4
Abuse substantiation indicator			
Not substantiated	350	49.8	3.2
Substantiated	846	50.2	3.2
Child with chronic illness			
No	867	73.9	2.2
Yes	329	26.1	2.2
Caregiver age, years			
<20	145	19.3	2.8
20–25	295	28.0	2.2
26–35	306	23.6	2.2
36–45	249	16.6	1.6
>45	198	12.6	1.7
Caregiver highest degree			
Less than high school	389	37.9	2.3
High school	539	45.6	2.4
High school plus	264	16.5	1.5
Caregiver employment status			
Employed full or part time	566	46.2	2.5
Unemployed or not working	630	53.8	2.5
Family income			
Above poverty line	600	54.9	2.8
Below poverty line	490	45.1	2.8

(continued)

TABLE 1 (continued)

Characteristics	Unweighted Frequency	Percentage	*SE*
Caregiver marital status			
Married	580	47.1	2.8
Divorced or never married	616	52.9	2.8
Number of children in household			
1–4	1050	89.0	2.7
5 or more	146	11.0	1.6
Domestic violence against caregiver in past year			
No	482	58.5	4.2
Yes	245	41.5	4.2
Caregiver arrested in past year			
No	534	69.4	3.8
Yes	216	30.6	3.8
Caregiver neighborhood quality			
No serious problems	953	78.6	2.2
Serious problems	243	21.4	2.2
Caregivers drug/alcohol abuse			
No	646	61.8	2.7
Yes	550	38.2	2.7
Caregiver mental health problem			
No	909	78.2	3.4
Yes	287	21.8	3.4
Poor parenting skills			
No	644	60.4	2.7
Yes	552	39.6	2.7
Low social support			
No	756	71.8	2.3
Yes	440	28.2	2.3
History of abuse/neglect of caregiver			
No	800	67.9	2.1
Yes	396	32.1	2.1
Total	1,196	100	

Note. The frequencies are not weighted, and the percentages are weighted by the sampling weight.

21% Hispanic, minority children are overrepresented compared with the general population. The most common type of maltreatment is physical neglect, followed by neglect (no supervision and abandonment) and physical abuse. One half of the child abuse and neglect investigations are substantiated. However, only 27% of the children are placed in foster care.

With respect to risk factors linked to well-being and school success, the data in Table 1 indicate that infants involved in the child welfare system tend to come from families with low income, low educational achievement, and low employment rates. More than one half of the caregivers were unmarried at the time of the baseline interview; about 40% of the caregivers experienced domestic violence. Mental health problems, crime, and substance use were frequently mentioned. Neighborhood quality, social support, and their own (i.e., the caregivers') history of maltreatment were listed as issues facing families with infants who had been investigated for maltreatment.

Children's Involvement With the Child Welfare System

Although one half of the infants are substantiated victims of maltreatment, many stayed with their parents while receiving various services. At baseline, about 27% of the infants are placed in out-of-home care, mostly in foster homes or with relatives. More than one half of the children in out-of-home care are placed in conventional foster homes, 46% are placed in kinship care, and less than 3% are placed in group home or residential care.

As time goes on, the number of children living in foster care gradually declines, as more permanent family settings are located. By Wave 5 (at about 5 to 6 years old), only 5% of the infants placed in foster care remain in out-of-home care. Most of the children originally placed in foster homes are adopted, while a small percentage return to their parents. Many children placed in foster care experience multiple changes in placement settings. The data indicate that by the time of Wave 5, a child who was placed in foster care at baseline would have experienced an average of two out-of-home placements, and 66% of their short lives would have been spent in out-of-home care.

Developmental Status

With the prevalence of various risk factors and unstable living arrangements, we should expect to see developmental delays within the population. The Bayley Infant Neurodevelopmental Screener (BINS) screens infants aged 3 through 24 months for signs of neurological impairment or developmental delay. The BINS identifies more than 53% of the infants at high risk and 36% at moderate risk for developmental problems. This is much higher than the 14% at high risk for the national normative sample of nonclinical children and similar to the 56% for the normative clinical sample (Aylward, 1995).

In the following, we focus on two developmental domains, cognitive functioning and communication skills that are directly related to school readiness, and track the developmental trajectories of these infants until school age. In the NSCAW survey, cognitive functioning is measured by the cognitive domain of the Battelle Developmental Inventory (BDI) for children younger than 5 years and the Kaufman Brief Intelligence Test (K-BIT) for children older than 4 years. Language development of children is measured for children younger than 5 by the Preschool Language

Scale, third edition (PLS-3), including auditory comprehension and expressive communication. These indicators are standardized normative developmental measures, which facilitate comparison of the sampled children to the national norms.

Notwithstanding how difficult it is to administer developmental assessments of very young children, at the baseline when the children have a median age of 6 months, delays in cognitive development are already in evidence for some children, although delays in linguistic skill are not yet apparent. For cognitive performance, 17% of the infants have very low BDI scores (more than 2 SD below the mean). This is much higher than the 2% expected for a normative sample, demonstrating serious delay in cognitive development for a sizable number of infants involved in child welfare.

At Waves 3 and 4, when the children have a median age of 22 and 38 months, a high proportion of children demonstrate delays in both cognitive functioning and language skills. At about 38 months, more than one half of the children have preschool language scores in the low (35%) and very low (16%) ranges, and nearly one half have low (23%) and very low (21%) cognitive scores as measured with the BDI.

Because BDI scores are not available for most children at Wave 5, the K-BIT score was used to measure their cognitive ability. About 5% of the children have very low K-BIT scores, and an additional 19% are in the low range (within 1 SD and 2 SD below the mean). For language development, because the PLS-3 is not administered to children older than 5 years, only 686 children at Wave 5 have PLS-3 measures. Seventeen percent of these children at Wave 5 have very low scores, comparable to the proportions at Wave 3 and 4. Altogether, more than one third of the children have low or very low scores in language performance.

SCHOOL SUCCESS FOR CHILDREN WITH A CHILD WELFARE HISTORY

In the prior sections, we developed a profile of children investigated for maltreatment in the first year of life. We selected children in the first year of life because of their substantial level of risk relative to children of other ages and because as a group they highlight how risk in the early years relates to whether a child arrives at school ready to learn. The issues that these children face are critical to teachers' and schools' preparedness to receive and support the children. Children investigated for maltreatment in the first year of life face a number of risks that the literature suggests place these children at a significant disadvantage from the perspective of success in school.

The last link in our portrait of children involved in the child welfare system within the context of school examines the population of school children with prior or active involvement in the child welfare system. Whereas in the prior section we looked at children in the child welfare system with an eye toward the day they entered school, the analysis here picks up the story from the school's perspective. Unfortunately, longitudinal data that examine child welfare involvement, school enrollment, and academic success from a national perspective are not widely available in the published literature. As a consequence, we rely on data from the Chicago Public Schools (CPS) that were linked with child maltreatment and foster care placement data, and we use

CPS as a case study of problems faced by both large and small school districts. These data are then used to pinpoint the significant subpopulation of dually involved children and track their academic success. Again, one goal of the discussion is to show how involvement with the child welfare system serves as a marker of academic difficulty.

Measures of Academic Performance

Several different indicators of the academic performance of children in out-of-home care were used in the study: elementary students' scores on the reading section of the Iowa Test of Basic Skills (ITBS), the percentage of elementary students who were at least one grade level behind for their age, and high school dropout rates. These indicators are frequently used in educational research and have been used in studies of the academic performance of children in foster care (Burley & Halpern, 2001; Conger & Rebeck, 2001; Levine, 1999). Where measurement issues or policy factors within CPS may affect the interpretation of findings based on these indicators, we make every effort to state the findings in ways that take these issues into consideration.

Categorization of Students' Experiences

In an effort to better understand how educational experiences vary with respect to different types of involvement with the child welfare system, students must be separated into groups according to the level of their involvement in the child welfare system, either at a point in time or over the period of time covered in the analyses. These groups include the following:

1. Children who attend a CPS school but never experienced a substantiated report of abuse and neglect after 1987 (referred to as "other CPS students")
2. Children who are in foster care
3. Children who were abused and neglected but not placed in out-of-home care
4. Children who were in out-of-home care but have since exited

Starting School

To better understand the academic standing of students involved with the child welfare system when they started first grade, we examined six cohorts of students entering first grade and determined the proportion of those who were already behind their age peers with respect to grade level. Among those students who are in foster care in the year they enter first grade, nearly 10% of students in each of the cohort years are old-for-grade when they enter CPS in first grade, a proportion that is double that of students who have had no involvement with the child welfare system. The proportion of those students who have substantiated reports of abuse or neglect is similar to, although slightly lower than, the proportion of those in care, whereas the proportion among students who spent time in foster care but have since exited more closely approximates, but is slightly higher than, that of students with no involvement.

Focusing on the most recent year of data analyzed (2003), we examined more closely the timing of entry into foster care and entry into the CPS system. Among students in care who entered first grade later than their peers (i.e., those old-for-grade already in first grade), approximately 44% entered foster care at age 6 or older, compared with just 16% of those in foster care who entered first grade at the proper age. This finding suggests that students who experience maltreatment and enter foster care around the same time they are entering school may be particularly susceptible to enrolling in school late and may already be old-for-grade before they are placed in an out-of-home placement.

Are They Keeping Pace With Their Peers?

In an effort to assess changes in academic performance over time, we tracked third-grade through eighth-grade reading achievement test scores for several cohorts of 8-year-olds—those who turned age 8 by September 1994 through those who turned age 8 by September 1998. For these analyses, students were grouped according to their involvement with child and family services over the length of their CPS career, thus providing estimates of how students with different child welfare experiences perform over their elementary school careers. In Table 2, a subset of variables representing students' foster care experiences is presented for three analytic models. (Full model results and a more detailed description of control variables are available in Smithgall, Gladden, Howard, Goerge, & Courtney, 2004).

When no demographic controls were entered, students in care performed more poorly than other CPS students at age 8 and had weaker reading gains (see Model 1 in Table 2). Specifically, students in care who transitioned into a permanent placement between ages 8 and 13 were approximately eight tenths of a year's learning behind other CPS students at age 8. Moreover, their yearly reading gains were 4% of a year's learning behind other CPS students. This means that if the student in care was enrolled in CPS between 8 and 13 years of age, he or she would fall behind other CPS students by almost one fourth of a year's learning. Students who are in care their full academic career in CPS and students who transition from their family into care during their school years are farther behind other CPS students, more than 1 year's learning at age 8, and have yearly growth rates that are 7% to 8% of a year's learning slower.

Once demographic controls are entered (see Model 2 in Table 2), students in care still perform below similar CPS students at age 8, ranging from about one half of a year's learning to about nine tenths of a year's learning, but their reading gains are similar to those (i.e., not statistically different) of other similar CPS students. The one exception to this trend is that students in care during their full careers in CPS have growth rates that are about 4% slower than those of similar CPS students. Over time, students in care fail to close the substantial gap in reading achievement that separates them from other CPS students at age 8 and may fall even farther behind.

In the CPS system, students who scored below average on the ITBS reading test at age 8 tended to improve their reading scores at a faster rate each year, or to have larger reading gains, than students who scored above average on the reading test

TABLE 2
Reading Achievement Trajectories From Third to Eighth Grade

Categories of Students in Foster Care[a]	Model 1: No Statistical Controls	Model 2: Demographic Statistical Controls	Model 3: Demographic Statistical Controls and Performance at Age 8
Reading achievement at age 8 (coefficient divided by average yearly growth age 8–13)			
Students who were always in out-of-home care during their school years	−1.02*	−0.92*	−0.92*
Students who exited care during their school years	−0.81*	−0.62*	−0.62*
Students who entered care during their school years	−1.07*	−0.92*	−0.92*
Students who both entered and exited care during their school years	−0.60*	−0.45*	−0.45*
Yearly growth in reading score (coefficient divided by average yearly growth age 8–13)			
Students who were always in out-of-home care during their school years	−0.077*	−0.040*	−0.068*
Students who exited care during their school years	−0.038*	0.000	−0.017*
Students who entered care during their school years	−0.066*	0.030**	−0.055*
Students who both entered and exited care during their school years	−0.058*	0.026**	−0.038*

a. The reference group was Chicago Public Schools students with no substantiated maltreatment.
*$p < .05$. **$p < .10$.

when they were 8 years old. Taking this into account, Model 3 in Table 2 compares students in care with other CPS students who performed at the same reading level when they were 8 years old. Students in care advance at an annual rate that is about 2% to 7% of a year's learning slower than that of other CPS students. In other words, unlike other low-achieving students in CPS, students in care have reading gains that approximate those of other CPS students, and thus they do not close the reading achievement gap observed at age 8.

Do They Complete Their Primary Education?

Dropping out of high school is an important indicator of both current school performance and future employment prospects and earnings. Three age groups of students—ages 13, 14, and 15—in out-of-home care, in permanent placements, and who had been abused or neglected were followed from September 1998 through September 2003 to track dropout and graduation rates (see Table 3).[4] In all three age groups, the proportion of students in care who dropped out was 50% or more, far exceeding the proportion of other CPS students who drop out. Students in care were much more likely to leave school because of incarceration, with one in ten 15-year-olds in care having been incarcerated. The dropout and incarceration rates contribute to the alarmingly low graduation rates for students in care; only one fifth of 13-year-olds in care and slightly less than 30% of 14-year-olds in care in September 1998 had graduated 5 years later. Students in permanent placement and students who had been abused and neglected graduated at rates slightly better than those of students in out-of-home care but still substantially below the graduation rates for other CPS students.

The large differences in dropout rates between students in care and other CPS students documented above for the 1998 cohort were replicated in more recent cohorts (see Smithgall et al., 2004, Appendix F, for more comprehensive tables detailing the yearly progress of several cohorts of 13- and 14-year-olds). The dropout rates of students in care in their early years in high school have remained relatively stable, whereas the dropout rates of students in permanent placements and other CPS students have shown slight improvements.[5]

A closer examination of the yearly progress of 13-year-olds reveals that around 8% of students in care dropped out of school when they were 14 to 15, or 1 year into high school, and that around 15% dropped out before turning 16, or 2 years into high school. This is much higher than the system averages, 3% and 6%, respectively, and indicates that a sizable number of students in care struggle to make the transition to high school and consequently drop out at an early age. Of the students who were 13 years old and in care between 1998 and 2000 but dropped out of school before age 16, approximately 80% were still in care when they dropped out.

How Do the Education and Child Welfare Systems Address Behavior and Learning Problems?

It is reasonable to hypothesize that school may be one of the first places children exhibit behavior problems, and there are many reasons why children in out-of-home care might be even more likely than their peers to exhibit problematic behaviors. The following factors have been found to be associated with behavior problems among children: non-normative family structure (Hao & Matsueda, in press), trauma (Greenwald, 2002), maltreatment (Eckenrode, Laird, & Doris, 1993; Ethier, Lemelin, & Lacharite, 2002), and poverty (Coley & Chase-Lansdale, 2000; McLeod & Shanahan, 1993). Children in out-of-home care may have several if not all of the

TABLE 3

Graduation and Dropout Rates of Students in the Chicago Public Schools (CPS) Between September 1998 and September 2003

	N	Actively Enrolled, %	Graduated, %	Dropped Out, %	Incarcerated, %
13 years old					
In out-of-home care as of September 1998	761	23	20	50	7
Abused or neglected	1,708	22	29	45	4
Were in care but since exited	747	28	24	44	4
Other CPS students	21,097	20	46	33	2
14 years old					
In out-of-home care as of September 1998	695	9	28	56	8
Abused or neglected	1,701	6	33	56	5
Were in care but since exited	723	8	31	56	5
Other CPS students	21,101	5	57	36	3
15 years old					
In out-of-home care as of September 1998	692	3	32	55	10
Abused or neglected	1,571	3	39	52	6
Were in care but since exited	665	3	39	49	9
Other CPS students	21,672	2	59	36	3

Note. Students who transferred to schools outside of CPS (between 10% and 20% of students) or left CPS for other reasons, such as entering residential care during the 4-year period, were excluded from the analysis.

risk factors cited above. In addition, as Alexander, Entwisle, and Kabbani (2001) suggested, behavior problems at school may indicate that students are disengaged from academics, which is particularly likely to occur if they are struggling academically or if they have experienced multiple education disruptions and/or placements, as is the case for many students in foster care (Smithgall et al., 2004). Finally, the transition into care itself may be considered traumatic and is likely to elevate stress or anxiety levels and potentially increase behavior problems. Thus, identifying the underlying causes of behavior problems among at-risk children in care presents a significant challenge for both the education and child welfare systems.

Special education classifications and services are one way in which the education system attempts to address learning and behavior problems. At the same time, special education services as well as learning disabled (LD) classrooms have received criticism, largely because of inappropriate placement of students who exhibited behavioral problems but not necessarily cognitive problems, particularly in large urban centers and with minority children (Artiles, Klingner, & Tate, 2006). We are aware of the controversies but offer the analysis as one frame that is used to interpret the problems. An analysis of rates of special education classifications for first-grade through eighth-grade CPS students, categorized according to their involvement with the child welfare system, indicates the significant overlap between child welfare involvement and the special education system.

Looking at the academic year ending June 2003, we see that nearly one half (45%) of sixth-grade through eighth-grade students in out-of-home care were classified as disabled. This is much higher than the proportion of other CPS students (16%) and higher than the proportion observed among students who have been abused or neglected or reside in permanent placements (approximately 30%). Younger students in care were much more likely to be classified as disabled than their peers who were not involved with child and family services. About 19% of students in care in first grade were classified as disabled compared with about 7% of other CPS students. An examination of the students' primary diagnosis or special education classification revealed that students in out-of-home care were much more likely to be classified as having an emotional or behavioral disorder (ED) than were other CPS students. The classification of ED indicates that students displayed significant behavioral problems at school. Nearly one fifth of seventh-grade and eighth-grade students in care were diagnosed with an ED, compared with only 1% to 2% of the general CPS population. Even though students in care made up less than 1% of all first through eighth graders, 10% of first through eighth graders classified as having an ED were in out-of-home care. Students in permanent placements and students who were abused and neglected were much more likely to be classified as ED. Combining students in care with students in permanent placement and students who have been abused and neglected reveals that nearly 40% of all first through eighth graders classified as ED in CPS have been abused and neglected and/or placed in care.

Another major special education classification among students in foster care is LD. Approximately 20% of students in care (compared with 12% of other CPS students) are classified as LD by the eighth grade. The percentage of eighth graders in CPS classified as LD increased dramatically over 10 years, from 7.7% in 1993 to 11.5% in 2003.[6]

Although special education provides students with extra resources, its ability to remediate reading difficulties was questioned by a Chicago-based report on grade retention, which found that the reading achievement of retained third and sixth graders subsequently placed in special education deteriorated relative to their own test score trajectories before their placement (Nagaoka & Roderick, 2004). Although the report is not a comprehensive evaluation, its findings highlight the perspective that special education placement should not be viewed as the solution to low achievement. An examination of other methods to remediate reading and general achievement deficiencies of students in care and how to galvanize a wide range of education resources to better address academic problems would be beneficial.

Not only should special education services not be viewed as the solution to low achievement, but they should not be used to address behavioral issues among this population of at-risk children. It is increasingly important that caseworkers, policy-makers, and other child welfare professionals examine closely the extent to which the special education system is the most appropriate response to learning and behavioral problems of children involved with the child welfare system. A detailed analysis of ED classifications among students in foster care revealed a complex set of trends that contribute to the increasingly disproportionate representation of children in care among students with ED classifications (see Smithgall, Gladden, Yang, & Goerge, 2005). Trends occurring at the entry and exit points in both the foster care and special education systems contribute to the overall disproportionate representation of children in care among students with ED classifications.

The issue of responding to the needs of children in care who present with indications of learning difficulties is complex. We do not want to contribute to any further delays in responding to learning disabilities that may have gone undetected prior to entry into care; however, we also want to minimize the likelihood of misclassifications. In the case of learning problems that are related to trauma or other short-term circumstances, a child might benefit from short-term intervention that does not involve a special education classification and labels or restrictive measures. In the case of more chronic behaviors, mechanisms need to be in place to ensure that the child receives timely and high-quality interventions both from the school and from child and family services.

Smithgall and her colleagues (2005) found that in many instances, the aggressive behaviors of children in care were reportedly met with further restrictions or punitive responses, ranging from withdrawal of privileges or enjoyable activities to changes in their living or educational environment. Of significant concern are the reports of workers using warnings of a potential placement move in responding to children's behavioral problems, a practice that, from the child's perspective, essentially amounts to repeated trauma. For children whose behaviors reach the level of an ED classification, many are educated in alternative schools; within the child welfare system, behavior problems at the ED level are associated with increasingly restrictive placement options and sometimes even confinement by means of juvenile detention or hospitalization. As Greenwald (2002) pointed out, whereas the children's initial behaviors may stem from traumatic experiences, responses to those behaviors can have a reinforcing effect, and eventually the pattern of misinterpreted stimuli and increasingly restrictive responses becomes self-perpetuating.

SUMMARY AND DISCUSSION

As noted at the outset of this chapter, 70% of all children reported for maltreatment are between the ages of 4 and 17. With that degree of overlap, it stands to reason that schools and the public child welfare system share an interest in close collaboration. Without collaboration, it is difficult to imagine how child well-being, as measured by school success, will be advanced for dually involved children. That said, tying the rationale for collaboration to the simple fact that most maltreated children are of school age provides little real insight into the nature of risk and what can be done to minimize the impact of maltreatment in school settings and vice versa. Maltreatment affects children across a full range of cognitive, social, and behavioral domains, each of which has bidirectional implications for the manner in which schools and child welfare agencies work together on behalf of children.

In this chapter, we organized our review around a developmental perspective because we believe that it provides a theoretical basis for conceptualizing the problem of at-risk children in the context of schools and the child welfare system. Over the life course of childhood, children are engaged in a series of transitions that mark their developmental trajectories (Elder, 1998). Schools provide the institutional context that shapes key milestones along the way to becoming an adult (e.g., entry into and graduation from school). Schools also play a vital role in transmitting the skills that are the foundation of human capital (Heckman, 2000). Viewing the collaboration between schools and the child welfare in developmental terms raises two obvious questions: Are children who are involved with child welfare system ready to engage in the school experience so that that as each transition approaches, the likelihood of their success is enhanced? Are schools, educators, and child welfare caseworkers prepared to meet the needs of these children?

With respect to early development, children younger than 1 year are a particularly vulnerable group. Infants who have been reported to the child welfare system live in households with fewer adults and fewer economic resources. Their parents report that their neighborhoods are unsafe, domestic violence is common, and substance misuse by their caregivers is high relative to what other children experience. Against this backdrop, it is not surprising to learn that when children are old enough to enter school, those who were involved with the child welfare system during their infancy do so with significant cognitive and language skill delays. When these children do start school, they are more likely to be old-for-grade; their progress in school, as measured by reading scores, tends to lag behind; and those with a history of maltreatment are more likely to drop out rather than graduate. In short, at each transition, children in the child welfare system are among the least likely to move forward.

With respect to what educators are likely to encounter in the classroom, assessment is perhaps the key to understanding how schools can approach the needs of maltreated children. Cicchetti and Toth (2005) provided a useful summary of the psychological and neurobiological sequelae that accompany maltreatment. In particular, difficulties with affect regulation, self-esteem, peer relations, and neuroendocrine regulation are associated with maltreatment, although the extent to which maltreatment influences trajectories is a function of onset in a developmental context and other protective factors with the family and community. Moreover, when discussing the impact of maltreatment, we must remember that children are resilient. Nevertheless, success in school depends on educational approaches that address not only manifest learning difficulties (i.e., special education) but also the social, biological, and behavioral sequelae that affect academic engagement. In the simplest possible terms, maltreated children are less ready to learn (Erickson, Egeland, & Pianta, 1989) and less motivated to become learners (Vondra, Barnett, & Cicchetti, 1989).

How then to address the impact of maltreatment on children through closer collaboration between schools and the public child welfare system? It is clear that more research is needed. There has been increased attention in the research literature to the academic struggles of children in foster care, but few studies have broadened the scope to include children experiencing maltreatment who are not placed in foster care. With respect to how school experiences affect what happens in the child welfare context, there has been even less research. For example, very little is known about the way that struggles with school success foreshadow difficulties at home at some future point. Does the level of school success adversely influence parent–child relationships to the extreme? If so, how and why? To a certain extent, the paucity of research is a function of conceptual and methodological complexities (Stone, 2007). Applying a developmental perspective to untangle bidirectional influences requires linked longitudinal data on both child welfare and educational experiences that is then matched to appropriate statistical techniques that isolate the respective contextual effects. The research also has to capture a broader spectrum of indicators of school success, child safety, family stability, and their interrelationships.

With respect to practice, school interventions that target factors related to teacher–child interactions and teachers' confidence in working with children who misbehave appear to hold promise with respect to fostering positive development among at-risk children (Epstein, Atkins, Cullinan, Kutash, & Weaver, 2008; Hamre & Pianta, 2005; Schiff & BarGil, 2004). However, the need for and value of training that sensitizes a broader array of professionals, including foster parents, caseworkers, and school staff, to the social–emotional dimensions of learning, given what researchers have learned in recent years, are hard to overstate (Fantuzzo et al., 2007). One opportunity for building in such training might be to capitalize on legislatively mandated collaboration and in-service training requirements. For example, the requirements of the Improving Head Start for School Readiness Act of 2007 target an investment in quality training and improved collaboration among programs serving young children. Similarly, licensure and recertification requirements for child welfare staff and foster parents might include training components that infuse a developmental perspective to their education and training. The focus on early childhood cannot come at the expense of other children. The insight offered by the developmental perspective is that children need support at each transition inasmuch as early success begets later success and vice versa (Heckman, 2000).

Policy changes at different operational levels are equally important. On one hand, greater sharing of information is needed between schools and the public child welfare agency, although this is easier said than done. Allegations of maltreatment carry considerable weight for parents and children in the school context. School performance may influence how a child welfare worker thinks about a child's family life. Clearly, the issue of confidentiality has to be addressed in a forthright manner. That said, it is possible to exchange information in ways that protect confidentiality and promote greater awareness of shared responsibilities (Fantuzzo & Perlman, 2007; McNaught, 2005; Smithgall et al., 2004). On the other hand, broader policy prescriptions are equally important. For the child welfare system, a shift away from the residual thinking that emphasizes reaction to problems after they have occurred toward an approach that favors a proactive model of community-level investments is probably necessary if the work with schools is to intensify. The early head start and child welfare initiative funded by the U.S. Department of Health and Human Services offers a useful example of where collaboration may be headed.

Success with at-risk children in a school setting may well depend on how well the child welfare system does its job and vice versa. Professionals within each sector must understand what each contributes to well-being broadly defined. To that end, public accountability framed around broader notions of how well children are doing offers the hope that schools and the child welfare system will come together around a common agenda—helping parents raise the next generation. Failure to do the hard work of collaboration will inevitably leave us with the uncomfortable feeling that we have not done enough to reduce the perils facing at-risk children. Indeed, we may discover that we have only added to the perils, despite our best intentions.

NOTES

[1]We examined rates for all counties, including counties with poverty rates between the top and bottom quintiles. The underlying patterns, as reported here, are largely the same. Notably, regardless of county poverty rate, infants have the highest rate of substantiated maltreatment.

[2]Although the terminology used to designate race differs among the data sources, we use the terms *African American* and *Hispanic*. The coding of "other" races and ethnicities (beyond Hispanic, African American, and White) also varies considerably. Unfortunately, there is insufficient detail in the source data to be more precise.

[3]Because the 12-month follow-up (Wave 2) only collects data from caregivers and caseworkers about case characteristics and service delivery and contains no assessment on child development, this analysis is based on data from the baseline and the 22-month (Wave 3), 38-month (Wave 4), and 68-month (Wave 5) follow-ups.

[4]Groups were followed for 5 years because a substantial number of CPS students fall behind a grade and enter high school late. Also, a significant number of students take 5 years to complete high school. These facts are demonstrated by the finding that 5% of 14-year-olds are still actively enrolled in a CPS high school 5 years later.

[5]Improvements in dropout rates at the beginning of high school have to be viewed cautiously because they may not translate into higher graduation rates if students drop out later in their career.

[6]This increase is partially driven by the implementation of promotional requirements in the third, sixth, and eighth grades (Miller & Gladden, 2002).

REFERENCES

Adams, M. J. (1990). *Beginning to read: Thinking and learning about print.* Cambridge, MA: MIT Press.
Alder, N. E., Boyce, T., Chesney, M. A., Cohen, S., Folkman, S., Kahn, R. L., et al. (1994). Socioeconomic status and health: The challenge of the gradient. *American Psychologist, 49,* 15-24.
Alexander, K. L., Entwisle, D. R., & Kabbani, N. S. (2001). The dropout process in life course perspective: Early risk factors at home and school. *Teachers College Record, 103,* 760-822.

Appel, A. E., & Holden, G. W. (1998). The co-occurrence of spouse and physical child abuse: A review and appraisal. *Journal of Family Psychology, 12*, 578-599.

Artiles, A., Klingner, J. K., & Tate, W. F. (2006). Representation of minority students in special education: Complicating traditional explanations. *Educational Researcher*, 35, 3-5.

Aylward, G. P. (1995). *The Bayley Infant Neurodevelopmental Screener*. San Antonio, TX: Psychological Corporation.

Barnett, D., Ganiban, J., & Cicchetti, D. (1999). Maltreatment, negative expressivity, and the development of type D attachments from 12 to 24 months of age. *Monographs of the Society for Research in Child Development, 64*(3, Serial No. 258), 97-118.

Beers, S. R., & De Bellis, M. D. (2002). Neuropsychological function in children with maltreatment-related posttraumatic stress disorder. *American Journal of Psychiatry, 159*, 483-486.

Bennett, D. S., Sullivan, M. W., & Lewis, M. (2005). Young children's adjustment as a function of maltreatment, shame, and anger. *Child Maltreatment: Journal of the American Professional Society on the Abuse of Children*, 10, 311-323.

Bradley, R. H., Corwyn, R. F., Burchinal, M., McAdoo, H. P., & Garcia Coll, C. (2001). The home environments of children in the United States: Part II. Relations with behavioral development through age thirteen. *Child Development, 72*, 1868-1886.

Brooks-Gunn J., & Duncan, G. (1997). The effects of poverty on children. *The Future of Children, 7*, 55-71.

Burley, M., & Halpern, M. (2001). *Educational attainment of foster youth: Achievement and graduation outcomes for children in state care*. Olympia: Washington State Institute for Public Policy.

Cicchetti, D., & Curtis, W. J. (2005). An event-related potential study of the processing of affective facial expressions in young children who experienced maltreatment during the first year of life. *Development and Psychopathology, 17*, 641-677.

Cicchetti, D., & Toth, S. L. (2005). Child maltreatment. *Annual Review of Clinical Psychology, 1*, 409-438.

Coley, R. L., & Chase-Lansdale, P. L. (2000). Welfare receipt, financial strain, and African-American adolescent functioning. *Social Service Review, 74*, 380-404.

Conger, D., & Rebeck, A. (2001). *How children's foster care experiences affect their education*. New York: Vera Institute of Justice.

De Bellis, M. D. (2005). The psychobiology of neglect. *Child Maltreatment, 10*, 150-172.

De Bellis, M. D., Keshavan, M., Shifflett, H., Iyengar, S., Beers, S. R., Hall, J., & Moritz, G. (2002). Brain structures in pediatric maltreatment-related posttraumatic stress disorder: A sociodemographically matched study. *Biological Psychiatry, 52*, 1066-1078.

DeGarmo, D. S., Forgatch, M. S., & Martinez, C. R. (1999). Parenting of divorced mothers as a link between social status and boys' academic outcomes: Unpacking the effects of socioeconomic status. *Child Development, 7*, 1231-1245.

Duncan, G. J., & Brooks-Gunn, J. (2000). Family poverty, welfare reform and child development. *Child Development, 71*, 188-196.

Duncan, G. J., Brooks-Gunn, J., Yeung, W. J., & Smith, J. R. (1998). How much does childhood poverty affect the life chances of children? *American Sociological Review, 63*, 406-423.

Eckenrode, J., Laird, M., & Doris, J. (1993). School performance and disciplinary problems among abused and neglected children. *Developmental Psychology, 29*, 53-62.

Edleson, J. L. (1999). The overlap between child maltreatment and woman battering. *Violence Against Women, 5*, 134-154.

Eigsti, I., & Cicchetti, D. (2004). The impact of child maltreatment on expressive syntax at 60 months. *Developmental Science, 7*, 88-102.

Elder, G. H. (1998). The life course as developmental theory. *Child Development, 69*, 1-12.

Entwisle, D. R., Alexander, K. L., & Olson, L. S. (2005). First grade and educational attainment by age 22: A new story. *American Journal of Sociology, 110*, 1458-1502.

Epstein, M., Atkins, M., Cullinan, D., Kutash, K., & Weaver, R. (2008). *Reducing behavior problems in the elementary school classroom: A practice guide* (NCEE 2008-012). Washington, DC: National Center for Education Evaluation and Regional Assistance, Institute of Education Sciences, U.S. Department of Education. Retrieved September 29, 2008, from http://ies.ed.gov/ncee/wwc/publications/practiceguides

Erickson, M. F., Egeland, B., & Pianta, R. (1989). The effects of maltreatment on the development of young children. In D. Cicchetti & V. Carlson (Eds.), *Child maltreatment: Theory and research on the causes and consequences of child abuse and neglect* (pp. 647-684). New York: Cambridge University Press.

Ethier, L. S., Lemelin, J. P., & Lacharite, C. (2002). A longitudinal study of the effects of chronic maltreatment on children's behavioral and emotional problems. *Child Abuse & Neglect, 28,* 1265-1278.

Fantuzzo, J., Bulotsky-Shearer, R., McDermot, P. A., McWayne, C., Frye, D., & Perlman, S. (2007). Investigation of dimensions of social-emotional classroom behavior and school readiness for low-income urban preschool children. *School Psychology Review, 36,* 44-62.

Fantuzzo, J., & Perlman, S. (2007). The unique impact of out-of-home placement and the mediating effects of child maltreatment and homelessness on early school success. *Children and Youth Services Review, 29,* 941-960.

Greenwald, R. (2002). The role of trauma in conduct disorder. *Journal of Aggression, Maltreatment & Trauma, 6,* 5-23.

Hamre, B. K., & Pianta, R. C. (2005). Can instructional and emotional support in the first-grade classroom make a difference for children at risk of school failure? *Child Development, 75,* 949-967.

Hao, L., & Matsueda, R. L. (in press). Family dynamics through childhood: A sibling model of behavior problems. *Social Science Research.*

Heckman, J. J. (2000). Policies to foster human capital. *Research in Economics, 54,* 3-56.

Howe, T. R., & Parke, R. D. (2001). Friendship quality and sociometric status: Between-group differences and links to loneliness in severely abuse and nonabused children. *Child Abuse & Neglect, 25,* 585-606.

Kolker, J., Osborne, D., & Schnurer, E. (2004). *Early child care and education: The need for a national policy.* Washington, DC: Center for National Policy.

Korbin, J. E., Coulton, C. J., Chard, S., Platt-Houston, C., & Su, M. (1998). Impoverishment and child maltreatment in African American and European American neighborhoods. *Development and Psychopathology, 10,* 215-233.

Kotch, J. B., Lewis, T., Hussey, J. M., English, D., Thompson, R., Litrownik, A. J., et al. (2008). Importance of early neglect for childhood aggression. Pediatrics, 121, 725-731.

Leslie, L. K., Gordan, J. N., Meneken, L., Premji, K., Michelmore, K. L., & Ganger, W. (2005). The physical, developmental, and mental health needs of young children in child welfare by initial placement type. *Journal of Developmental and Behavioral Pediatrics, 26,* 1-14.

Levine, P. (1999). *Educational attainment and outcomes for children and youth served by the foster care system: A review of the literature.* Seattle, WA: Casey Family Project.

Lewit, E. M., & Baker, L. S. (1994). Child indictors: Race and ethnicity—Changes for children. *The Future of Children, 4,* 134-144.

Linver, M., Brooks-Gunn, J., & Kohen, D. (2002). Family processes as pathways from income to young children's development. *Developmental Psychology, 38,* 719-734.

Magruder, J., & Shaw, T. V. (in press). Children ever in care: An examination of cumulative disproportionality. *Child Welfare.*

McLeod, J. D., & Shanahan, M. (1993). Poverty, parenting, and children's mental health. *American Sociological Review, 58,* 351-366.

McNaught, K. (2005). *Mythbusting: Breaking down confidentiality and decision-making barriers to meet the educational needs of children in foster care.* Chicago: American Bar Association.

Retrieved September 29, 2008, from http://www.abanet.org/child/rclji/education/caseyeducationproject.pdf

Mercy, J. A., & Steelman, L. C. (1982). Familial influence on the intellectual attainment of children. *American Sociological Review, 47*, 532-542.

Miller, S. R., & Gladden, R. (2002). *Changing special education enrollments: Causes and distribution among schools.* Chicago: Consortium on Chicago School Research.

Moore, D. R., & Florsheim, P. (2008). Interpartner conflict and child abuse risk among African American and Latino adolescent parenting couples. *Child Abuse & Neglect, 32,* 463-475.

Nagaoka, J., & Roderick, M. (2004). *Ending social promotion: The effects of retention.* Chicago: Consortium on Chicago School Research.

National Education Goals Panel. (1997). *The National Education Goals report: Building a nation of learners, 1997.* Washington, DC: U.S. Government Printing Office.

National Research Council. (1993). *Understanding child abuse and neglect.* Washington, DC: National Academy Press.

Pears, K., & Fisher, P. A. (2005). Developmental, cognitive, and neuropsychological functioning in preschool-aged foster children: Associations with prior maltreatment and placement history. *Journal of Developmental & Behavioral Pediatrics, 26,* 112-122.

Pike, A., Iervolino, A. C., Eley, T. C., Price, T. S., & Plomin, R. (2006). Environmental risk and young children's cognitive and behavioral development. *International Journal of Behavioral Development, 30,* 55-66.

Rowe, E., & Eckenrode, J. (1999). The timing of academic difficulties among maltreated and nonmaltreated children. *Child Abuse & Neglect, 23,* 813-832.

Schiff, M., & BarGil, B. (2004). Children with behavior problems: Improving elementary school teachers' skills to keep these children in class. *Children and Youth Services Review, 26,* 207-234.

Shonkoff, J. P., & Phillips, D. A. (2000). *From neurons to neighborhoods: The science of early childhood development.* Washington, DC: National Academy Press.

Silver, J., DiLorenzo, P., Zukoski, M., Ross, P. E., Amster, B. J., & Schlegel, D. (1999). Starting young: Improving the health and developmental outcomes of infants and toddlers in the child welfare system. *Child Welfare, 78,* 148-165.

Simpson, G. A., Colpe, L., & Greenspan, S. (2003). Measuring functional developmental delays in infants and young children: Prevalence rates from the NHIS-D. Pediatrics & Perinatal Epidemiology, 17, 68-80.

Singer, L. T., Arendt, R., Minnes, S., Salvator, A., Siegel, C., & Lewis, B. A. (2001). Developing language skills of cocaine-exposed infants. Pediatrics, 107, 1057-1064.

Smithgall, C., Gladden, R. M., Howard, E., Goerge, R., & Courtney, M. E. (2004). *Educational experiences of children in out-of-home care.* Chicago: Chapin Hall Center for Children at the University of Chicago.

Smithgall, C., Gladden, R. M., Yang, D., & Goerge, R. (2005). *Behavior problems and educational disruptions among children in out-of-home care in Chicago.* Chicago: Chapin Hall Center for Children at the University of Chicago.

Stanton-Chapman, T. L., Chapman, D. A., Kaiser, A. P., & Hancock, T. B. (2004). Cumulative risk and low income children's language development. *Topics in Early Childhood Special Education, 24*(4), 124-158.

Stone, S. (2007). Child maltreatment, out-of-home placement and academic vulnerability: A fifteen-year review of evidence and future directions. *Children and Youth Services Review, 29,* 139-161.

U.S. Department of Health and Human Services, Administration of Children, Youth, and Families. (2008). *Child maltreatment 2006.* Washington, DC: U.S. Government Printing Office.

Vondra, J. I., Barnett, D., & Cicchetti, D. (1989). Perceived and actual competence among maltreated and comparison school children. *Development and Psychopathology, 1*, 237-255.

Wissow, L. S. (2001). Ethnicity, income, and parenting contexts of physical punishment in a national sample of families with young children. *Child Maltreatment, 6*, 118-129.

Wulczyn, F., Barth, R. P., Yuan, Y-Y. T., Harden, B. J., & Landsverk, J. (2005). *Beyond common sense: Child welfare, child well-being, and the evidence for policy reform.* New Brunswick, NJ: Aldine Transaction.

Wulczyn, F., Chen, L., & Hislop, K. B. (2007). *Foster care dynamics 2000-2005: A report from the Multistate Foster Care Data Archive.* Chicago: Chapin Hall Center for Children.

Yeung, J., Linver, M., & Brooks-Gunn, J. (2002). How money matters for young children's development: Parental investment and family processes. *Child Development, 73*, 1861-1879.

Young, N. K., Boles, S. M., & Otero, C. (2007). Parental substance use disorders and child maltreatment: Overlap, gaps, and opportunities. *Child Maltreatment, 12*, 137-149.

Zill, N., & West, J. (2001). *Entering kindergarten: A portrait of American children when they begin school: Findings from the Condition of Education 2000* (NCES 2001-035). Washington, DC: U.S. Department of Education, National Center for Education Statistics, U.S. Government Printing Office.

Chapter 3

Historical Evolution of Risk and Equity: Interdisciplinary Issues and Critiques

CAROL D. LEE
Northwestern University

In this chapter I first offer a historical overview on how risk, equity, and schooling have been conceptualized with regard to youth from nondominant groups.[1] I argue that the dominant discourses around these issues have been characterized by deficit assumptions that have been buffered by what were determined to be state of the art theories in psychology, sociology, and human development. These dominant discourses have positioned nondominant communities as passive recipients of structured hegemony and have not reflected the generative sources of resilience and resistance in these communities. Political critiques of the apparent, persistent, and historical educational risks faced by youth from nondominant groups document the structuring of inequality. One inadvertent consequence of the ways we have approached the topic of risks, equity, and schooling has been to position youth from nondominant groups outside the bounds of normative development and to restrict our investigations into isolated silos that separate thinking from emotions, that focus on one site of activity (e.g., the family or the school), and that have a restrictive vision of culture and its influences.

Here, I want to reframe the discussion on risk, equity, and schooling from a reactive perspective in which the fact of vulnerability is viewed as pathological and a problem primarily associated with racial and ethnic minorities and those living in poverty, masking the vulnerability that is also associated with privilege (Spencer, Harpalani, Cassidy, Jacobs, Donde & Goss, 2006). As long as we maintain such a perspective, our science will continue to be viewed as normative even when the samples we study are restricted to the White middle class (Graham, 1992) with little attention to the full ecologies of people's lives (Weisner, 2002); our educational policies and practices will not seek to leverage the full range of repertoires available to all human beings as they navigate what is entailed in learning new things, including learning the

Review of Research in Education
March 2009, Vol. 33, pp. 63-100
DOI: 10.3102/0091732X08328244
© 2009 AERA. http://rre.aera.net

disciplines of the academy (Nasir, Rosebery, Warren, & Lee, 2006). Vulnerability or exposure to risk is endemic to the human species, indeed to all life forms. Thus, a fundamental task of life-course development, including all the tasks associated with learning in schools, is to manage risk in ways that facilitate what we perceive to be positive outcomes across the life course (Spencer, Dupree, & Hartmann, 1997). The nature of the risks we face and the resources available to us to respond to those risks will vary according to the cultural and ecological contexts in which we live. Thus, the examination of exposure to vulnerability and the availability and uptake of protective resources to respond to such vulnerability in the lives of youth from nondominant groups in the United States represent particular cases of a larger and more fundamental set of questions (Lee, Spencer, & Harpalani, 2003). Taking this perspective allows for the possibility, indeed the likelihood, that we can learn more deeply about human learning and development from studies of risk and resilience across the species (Lee, 2008). The discussion in this chapter then intends to highlight the particular ways in which living under contemporary and historical conditions of oppression based on race, ethnicity, language, and class (including important intersections with gender) both structure risks, but also engender cultural repertoires of resilience.

In this chapter, I first offer a historical overview of constructions of risk in the context of schooling for nondominant groups and how communities have organized schooling in ways that support resiliency in the face of these risks. In contrast to the restrictive theories that historically have undergirded the dominant discourses on risk and schooling, I then discuss an expansive orientation to understanding how people learn to respond to risks that is rooted in a cultural and ecological perspective, with examples of programs of research in and about schools that address the inequities in educational outcomes and opportunities. This perspective integrates findings from the learning sciences and human development about adaptive processes that invite multiple access points or pathways through which learning is leveraged and sustained. I conclude the chapter with a discussion of the implications of such an expanded framework for research on educational risks and schooling as well as educational policy. I seek to refocus the conception of risk as an attribute of individuals to the perspective of people using resources and tools to adapt to and cope with exposure to adversity in particular ecological contexts.

HISTORICAL CONSTRUCTIONS OF RISKS AND RESILIENCE IN SCHOOLING FOR YOUTH FROM NONDOMINANT GROUPS

Historically, schooling in the United States has served as a test bed for debates about citizenship (DuBois & Dill, 1911). Fundamental to these debates have been questions about the functions of schooling in a democracy. The idea of the common school has been viewed as a pathway to the cultural, social, political, and economic opportunities that citizenship provides (Tyack, 1974). However, the country has had very contested notions of who is a citizen and who has what rights (Harding, 1981). Conceptions and ascriptions of race have been tightly interwoven with these debates over citizenship and schooling from the beginning of the republic (Ladson-Billings &

Tate, 1995). These conceptions of race have deeply influenced access to schooling, the structure of curricula, and the distribution of resources for education (Hacker, 1992; Hamilton, 1968). It is important to position these conceptions of race as debates because although there has clearly been a dominant hegemonic discourse around race and schooling, there have also been responses within non-White communities that not only have resisted but have offered productive alternatives.

One of the ways that citizenship has been linked to schooling is through access. Segregated public schooling was the legal normative practice in the United States until the 1954 *Brown v. Board of Education* Supreme Court decision and remains the *de facto* practice in many urban school districts today (Ladson-Billings, 2004; Orfield, 1996). This enduring fact of segregated schooling provides a window through which we can view debates over race as it relates to the functions of schooling and evidence of opportunity to learn. Race in the United States has been a shifting category, but racial classifications have always been rooted in Black–White polar distinctions (Mills, 1997). Thus, laws in different states at different points in time have made it legal or illegal for particular racial groups to have access to White schools based on how close to Black they were determined to be on a racial scale. Even the use of the term *racial group* here can be confusing because the criteria for racial classifications have shifted over U.S. history. In 1854, in *People v. Hall,* California defined "Black 'as contradistinguished from white' included 'all races other than the Caucasian,' a decision that legally denied Chinese Americans the right to testify, vote, or otherwise participate in government" (Williamson, Rhodes, & Dunson, 2007) p. 203). Thus, for example, in California in 1863, it was against state law for "Negroes, Mongolians, and Indians" to attend White schools (Wollenberg, 1976) p. 13; cited in Williamson et al., 2007). When the size of the Japanese population in California was small, there were opportunities for them to attend schools with Whites. However, by 1883 and again in 1905, the state expanded the classification of "Mongolian" to include the Japanese and as a consequence assigned Japanese students to the same category as Chinese students (Williamson et al., 2007). After the *Brown v. Board of Education* decision, the 1970 *Cisneros v. Corpus Christi Independent School District* case used the "the Mexican-as-White argument . . . to achieve desegregation by placing Mexican American children in schools with Black children" (Williamson et al., 2007). We find similar examples of segregated schools in urban communities of European immigrants in the opening decades of the 20th century, where many, such as the Irish and Italians, were designated as non-White. Throughout this history, people of African descent were denied equal access to schooling through "the institution of slavery, the equation of Black personhood with property, Black codes, Jim Crow laws, legal decisions, and legislative acts" (Williamson et al., 2007, p. 201).

Thus, access to schooling in any form and racial segregation of schools (both *de jure* and *de facto*) have been blunt instruments for constraining opportunity to learn and as a consequence pathways to social and economic opportunities (Bell, 2004). Foundational to separate schooling have been assumptions about what equity and risk mean. Ironically, a democratic ideal has been invoked over what kind of schooling is appropriate for whom. For purposes of simplicity, I will divide the debate into two orientations. One set of political interests has fundamentally argued the case of deficits in innate ability (Hernstein & Murray, 1994; Sarich & Miele, 2004). The second orientation argues for deficits in cultural practices of families and communities for which schools need to compensate (Deutsch & Brown, 1964). Both orientations conceive equity in opportunity as organizing schooling in ways that allow people to reach their highest potential, with the assumption that such potential has innate limitations, whether cognitive or behavioral. Interestingly, the political interests of both orientations have included politicians as well as scientists (in psychology, education, sociology, and anthropology).

Approaches to the education of youth from nondominant groups in the 19th century through the 1960s had the legal mandates of segregation. The basis for separate schooling is exemplified in the 1908 quotation from the Boston superintendent of schools: "Until very recently [the schools] have offered equal opportunity for all to receive *one kind* of education, but what will make them democratic is to provide opportunity for all to receive education as will fit them *equally well* for their particular life work" (cited in Oakes, 1985, p. 34, and Williamson et al., 2007, p. 197). This statement comes at a time when the field of psychology was propagating the concept of IQ as innate and measurable (Goddard, 1917; Gould, 1981). The leading psychologists of the day—Lewis Terman, Ellwood Cubberley, Henry Goddard, and Edward Thorndike—developed IQ tests (based on the Binet-Simon Intelligence Scale) to scientifically document differences in inherited intellectual abilities between racial, ethnic, and class groups (Goddard, 1920). According to Gould (1981), the psychological community "believed that inherited IQ scores marked people and groups for an inevitable station in life; they assumed that the average differences between groups were largely the products of heredity, despite manifest and profound variation in quality of life" (p. 157). Commercial publishers of the time drew on this "scientific" research and developed assessments that were ubiquitously taken up by school systems across the country. The tests were used to justify low-level curriculum as most appropriate for certain populations. According to Tyack (1974), "Ever since the psychologists had discovered correlations between IQ scores and occupations in the army tests, experts like Terman had repeatedly suggested that data on 'intelligence' be used not only for classifying students into homogeneous groups but also for channeling them into curricula, for occupations could be ranked by the intelligence needed, from professional and business on down to unskilled labor" (pp. 214–215). By the 1930s, criticism was emerging from within the scientific community as well as organized labor. In 1924, the Chicago Federation of Labor issued a report critiquing the use of IQ tests for vocational education (Tyack, 1974). Despite the fact that there were criticisms at the time, the use of IQ tests to train for what were presumed predictable life-course outcomes was common. Tyack offers the example of a school superintendent who found "interesting correlations between ethnicity and ability. The children of immigrants constituted 63 percent of the pupils in the slow track, 36 percent in the normal group and 26 percent in the fast" (p. 211). When parents did not make official protests (although they did object), the superintendent decried, "That's just what you would expect . . . from parents who do not come to the schools and learn what is being done *for their children*" (Tyack, 1974, pp. 211–212). In many respects, the deficit assumptions behind the uses of IQ tests and the racist predictions served as fodder for deficit assumptions this superintendent held about the parents of these children.

So the country moved from the 1872 *Dred Scott v. Sanford* Supreme Court case, which stated that Blacks were "beings of an inferior order, and altogether unfit to associate with the white race, either in social or political relations, and so far inferior that they had no rights which the white man was bound to respect." The scientific progress of the early part of the 20th century recapitulated the condescension by a more vigorous postulation: namely, that democratic ideals of equity could be achieved through the efficiencies of instruments that schools could use to determine the nature of risks that Black and Brown students faced. The rationale was that schools could address the risks that were uncovered in ways the society deemed appropriate. What was deemed acceptable and appropriate was that these youth be in separate schools and be taught a curriculum that would prepare them for their proper, lower stations in life (Muschinske, 1977). Just as Massey and Denton (1993) have argued that concentrations of geographic segregation multiply the negative consequences of neighborhood poverty, so concentrations of segregated schools have historically concentrated low levels of funding, inadequate facilities, low-level curriculum, and lower levels of teacher quality into schools serving predominantly Black and Brown youth (Baron, Tom, & Cooper, 1985; Darling-Hammond, 1987, 1999; Kozol, 1991; National Research Council, 1999; Oakes, 1990).

What is most interesting is that the same fundamental beliefs that fueled second-class schooling until the 1960s has been reappropriated under new guises in the post-*Brown* era. Before the Civil War, the discourse around schooling for African Americans, American Indians, Mexican Americans, Chinese Americans, and Japanese Americans (the dominant non-White groups in the population) was explicitly and overly racist, with virtually no arguments that schooling could or should serve as an instrument for their access to the opportunities of full citizenship. However, after the Civil War and particularly as we moved into the second half of the 20th century, a democratic ideal was being invoked, and the justifications for second-class schooling were made on the basis of deficits in social practices in communities of color. In the first half of the 20th century, the deficits were based on assumptions about innate intelligence, buffered both by the long standing folk beliefs about race that have characterized U.S. history and much of the Western world or by what Charles Mills (1997) calls the "racial contract" as well as by the psychological science of the day. In the second half of the 20th century, the deficits were based on presumptions about social capital in terms of language practices, family socialization, and a culture of low expectations within these very same communities, that is, those identified as non-White (Bernstein, 1970; Jencks, 1972).

These phenomena must be understood in terms of the shifting nature of who, when, and under what circumstances particular populations are legally defined as White or non-White (Guglielmo, 2003; Ignatiev, 1996). By the 1960s, we have the culture of poverty, compensatory education models, and cultural deprivation models as the rationale for policy decisions and educational practices to provide equity in opportunity and address the presumed risks faced by communities of color (Bereiter & Engelmann, 1966; Hess & Shipman, 1965; Labor, 1965). As was the case with the scientific sanctioning of the IQ movement and its uptake in schools in the early half of the 20th century, psychology and sociology as scientific disciplines again provided the conceptual warrants for a new set of practices and policies to address risk and equity in schooling (Carruthers, 1995; Helms, Jernigan, & Mascher, 2005; Muschinske, 1977; Nesbitt, 1998). It is important to note that social science research conventions and strategies are also forms of cultural practices that can be grounded in assumptions that perpetuate deficit views of nondominant communities (Arzubiaga, Artiles, King, & Harris-Murri, 2008).

The construct of social capital has been widely used in conceptualizing risk among youth from nondominant populations and its implications for schooling in the post-*Brown* era. The idea of social capital has been largely associated with the theoretical work of Pierre Bourdieu (1986; Bourdieu & Passeron, 1977) and James Coleman (1988; Coleman et al., 1966). Social capital can include economic, cultural, and social resources available to a person by virtue of networks with which he or she is associated. Economic resources go beyond family income to include intergenerational wealth. Social relationships, in terms of both quality and quantity, give one access to resources. What has been a major point of debate, however, is what resources give a person access to what. From the perspective of child development, the dominant argument has been that language use, child-rearing practices, and social norms associated with the White middle class, along with access to institutions of privilege, represent social capital that provide upward mobility and enhance the likelihood of school success (Brooks-Gunn & Duncan, 1997; Laureau, 2001). Social capital can include intergenerational wealth and knowledge that are valued and provide access in particular contexts. Such knowledge can include norms for how to behave and communicate in particular settings, especially settings that are associated with privilege. Dika and Singh (2002) make useful distinctions between the theorizing of Bourdieu and Coleman:

> Bourdieu sees social capital as a tool of reproduction for the dominant class, whereas Coleman sees social capital as (positive) social control, where trust, information channels, and norms are characteristics of the community. Thus Coleman's work supports the idea that it is the family's responsibility to adopt certain norms to advance children's life chances, whereas Bourdieu's work emphasizes structural constraints and unequal access to institutional resources based on class, gender, and race. (p. 34)

Coleman and his colleagues' focus on the role of family in providing social capital was crystallized in the 1966 publication of *Equality of Educational*

Opportunity, known as the Coleman Report. The Coleman Report stated, "Attributes of other students account for far more variation in the achievement of minority-group children than do any attributes of school facilities and slightly more than do attributes of staff" (Coleman et al., 1966, p. 322). There were two big take-aways from that report. The first is that the risks associated with minority status in terms of family practices outweighed whatever equity in school facilities and staffing could achieve (A. S. Wells, Holme, Revilla, & Atanda, 2004). Second, in the wake of the *Brown* decision and the efforts to desegregate public schools, the Coleman Report reified the idea that being in school with White students from higher socioeconomic status (SES) backgrounds would have a stronger impact on achievement outcomes for minority youth than improving the quality of segregated schools (i.e., the *Plessy v. Ferguson*, separate but equal doctrine). Ladson-Billings (2004) has critiqued the *Brown* decision as inadvertently reifying a negative stereotype of Black self-hatred as a consequence of being in segregated schools. Spencer (2008) has demonstrated that what has been taken as the implications of the Clark doll studies has not been supported by subsequent studies.[2] Subsequent studies have not documented a prevalence of low self-esteem among Black children (Murray & Mandara, 2003).

The Coleman view of social capital represented a critique of family practices that do not fit what is presumed to be a White middle class standard and reified in the normative practices of schooling. Thus, particular family configurations, belief systems, and practices have been presumed to be deficits that place youth from nondominant groups at risk; as a consequence, to achieve equity, schools must develop compensatory programs to address the deficits rooted in family life and language practices.

The deficit orientation toward language practices has included differences in U.S. English dialects largely associated with lower SES as well as English language learners. Researchers in a variety of disciplines from sociolinguistics to sociology of education and child development have claimed that beyond differences in syntax and phonology between dialects, parents and children in low SES families engage in different patterns of questioning, range of speech genres, and vocabulary (Hall & Moats, 1989; Smitherman, 2000; Stotsky, 1999). Drawing on social capital theory, Bernstein (1961, 1975) has distinguished between what he calls restricted versus elaborate codes. Elaborate codes are associated with the language of schooling. Restricted codes involve shared knowledge in which interlocutors need not make shared referents explicit. Elaborate codes involve making explicit referents and relationships in ways that an audience not immediately present could still understand, as in the following example.

Howard's at it again. (Restricted)

I see from the newspaper I am reading that Michael Howard, leader of the Opposition, is once again trying to attack the government from a position of right-wing populism as we discussed a couple of days ago. (Elaborated) (http://www.doceo.co.uk/background/language_codes.htm)

Bernstein argued that low SES families more typically engaged a restricted code whereas middle-class families, by virtue of their social networks, used both a restrictive and an elaborate code; he also argued that academic learning required the elaborated code. Language use was viewed as a window into social reproduction, in part, through access points that curriculum and pedagogic discourse in schools make available. Bernstein (1973) writes: "Curriculum defines what counts as valid knowledge, pedagogy defines what counts as valid transmission of knowledge, and evaluation defines what counts as a valid realization of the knowledge on the part of the taught" (p. 85). Bernstein (1990) was concerned with "the social class assumptions and consequences of forms of pedagogic practice" (p. 63).

Presumed relationships among social class, race/ethnicity, language practices, and academic learning have been defined as a major source of risk hypothesized to explain differences in academic outcomes (Lareau, 2001; Lareau & Horvat, 1999). This issue has served as one of the major arguments since the 1960s and has informed ubiquitous pedagogic practices in Head Start and the expansion of Direct Instruction in schools serving minority youth from low-income communities (Bereiter & Engelmann, 1966). In the early part of the 20th century, the compensatory model of education based on deficit-oriented views of social capital was applied to European immigrants (e.g., Irish, Italians, Germans), many of whom were considered non-White during that period (Ignatiev, 1996; Tyack, 1974).

There are several fundamental problems then with the first and second waves of explanations of educational risk, disproportionately associated with racial/ethnic minorities and low SES status. First, they are based on assumptions of schooling as monolithic and relatively unchanging. Although empirically this is largely true, it is not the case that schools are incapable of change nor that they are not in need of change (The Education Trust, 2000). We have evidence that everyday discourses and the forms of knowledge constructed out of everyday experience can be leveraged to support disciplinary learning (with examples provided in later sections of this chapter). In addition, we have evidence that youth can be socialized to anticipate and respond productively to tensions based on social class distinctions they may encounter in the pedagogy of schooling (Garcia Coll et al., 1996; Phinney & Chavira, 1995).

We have evidence of schools in which achievement is not predicted by race/ethnicity and class (The Education Trust, 2000). We have national school systems in other parts of the world in which differences in achievement based on class are nowhere as large as they are in the United States (Organization for Economic Cooperation and Development, 2004). Rather than continuing the discourse of deficits and its reification by the academy, I propose we consider two bodies of knowledge that can inform an expansive view of learning and human development, with implications for opportunity to learn for youth from nondominant and low SES communities. The first has to do with a historical analysis of the ways in which nondominant communities in the United States have proactively responded to the restrictive policies—in practice and philosophy—of *de jure* segregation and Jim Crow, particularly in African American communities. This is an important analysis that restores the "duality of structure" (in which agency and structure constitute each other) (Giddens, 1976) in a cultural–historical critique of risk.

The second involves a synthesis of research on human learning and development that is rooted in an ecological and cultural focus that recognizes vulnerability as a fundamental part of the human experience. An ecological focus means taking into account the mutual and dynamic relationships among people's participation in a variety of settings (i.e., family, peer social networks, schooling, and other institutional settings such as community organizations and churches) within and across time (both developmental time, in terms of age and maturity, and cultural–historical time, such as being a child of the Great Depression) (Barker & Wright, 1949; Bronfenbrenner & Morris, 1998; Elder, 1985; Spencer, 2006). A cultural focus means taking into account how intergenerational beliefs and practices help to shape people's identities, perceptions, knowledge, and beliefs, including the ways in which cultural knowledge and practices are reshaped and negotiated in face-to-face interactions and historical time (Cole, 1996; Rogoff, 2003; Weisner, 2002).

In the next two sections of this chapter, I offer overviews of the historical data on African American responses to the equity challenges of schooling and then the scientific data from an integrated conception of human learning and development, rooted in an ecological and cultural focus. I conclude with a discussion of the implications of this historical and scientific evidence for an expanded conception and discourse around understanding risk, equity, and schooling.

AFRICAN AMERICAN SCHOOLS UNDER JIM CROW SEGREGATION: 1865–1969

I offer this discussion of African American schools under *de jure* segregation for several reasons. First, the dominant historical and contemporary discourse on what places youth from nondominant groups at risk for inequities in educational outcomes, described in the earlier sections of this chapter, not only has been largely deficit in its orientation but also implicitly assumes that the communities in question are passive recipients of hegemonic laws, discrimination, resource distribution, and stereotypes. This discourse has not acknowledged the protective factors embedded in historical and cultural practices in this community. Second, this dominant discourse does not address the question of what is required for youth from nondominant communities to learn to be productive in a society where they will face low expectations and discriminatory practices in terms of access. I argue that learning not to internalize negative stereotypes, learning how to overcome persistent obstacles, and learning how to navigate tensions that inevitably arise from social class and racial/ethnic distinctions are important outcomes. That is, they are critical for the variety of socializing settings that aim to prepare young people for adulthood, including schools, particularly schools located in communities of persistent intergenerational poverty and concentrations of youth from nondominant groups (Spencer, 1987). This brief commentary on the history of African American schooling offers examples of how schools were organized to address the joint work of academic preparation and preparation for life (see Anderson, 1988; and Siddle-Walker, 1993, 1996, 2000).

Anderson (1988), in a seminal work, documented a variety of ways that African American parents and community members supported Black education between 1866 and 1930: "Founding new schools, providing financial and other support to existing schools, organizing institutions and using existing institutions to support education, petitioning government agencies, convening conventions, participating in demonstrations and school boycotts, and using law suits to achieve educational equity" (Siddle Walker, 2000, p. 258). During the African Holocaust of Enslavement, it was illegal for Blacks to receive any form of formal education. In fact, reading was illegal and could be punished by physical dismemberment. At the end of the Civil War, representatives from the Freedman's Bureau came to the South with the goal of helping the newly emancipated African Americans gain access to schooling. Much to his surprise, John Alvord, national superintendent of schools for the Freedmen's Bureau, discovered that Blacks had already established their own schools—some 500 independent schools and 1,500 of what were called Sabbath Schools, run by churches. These schools were established with the explicit purpose of preparing African Americans to compete in the economic area and to participate in civic activities. Interestingly, some have argued that the efforts of Blacks to establish public schooling contributed substantively to the development of a public school system in the South for all (DuBois & Dill, 1911). In the 1920s and 1930s, there were substantive contributions from White philanthropic institutions such as the Rosenwald Fund to build Black schools in the 1920s and 1930s. However, African Americans contributed more financially than these outside sources (Franklin, 1974). It is important to note that this level of active support for Black schooling and political resistance to second-class schooling was happening at the height of Jim Crow laws and lynching of Blacks. Although evidence of literacy was quite different than today, it is still astounding to witness the rise of literacy rates among African Americans, from an illiteracy rate of almost 70% in 1900 to roughly 25% in 1930 (Bond, 1939).

In contrast to the view of African American segregated schools as inferior, Siddle-Walker offers evidence of institutions that worked with limited resources but accomplished impressive results. The Siddle-Walker (2000) review covers the period from 1935 to 1969. Siddle Walker (2000, p. 254) points to "the caring behaviors of teachers and principals, the support of parents, the forms of institutional support for students, and the high expectations placed upon students by the school and community" (Cecelski, 1994; Foster, 1990; Noblit & Dempsey, 1996). Among the schools whose records have been well documented are Dunbar High School of Washington, D.C., and another Dunbar High School in Little Rock, Arkansas, Booker T. Washington in Atlanta, Frederick Douglas High School in Baltimore, Central High School in Louisville, Kentucky, Beaufort/Queen Street High School in North Carolina, and the Caswell County Training School in North Carolina, among others (Hundley, 1965; Jones, 1981; Siddle-Walker, 1996; Sowell, 1974, 1976). These schools were both elementary and high schools and were located in urban as well as rural areas. Assertions of the success of these schools were based on data from graduation and college attendance rates, institutional accreditation, exemplary teachers, and alumni who went on to make significant contributions. Interview and survey data document that teachers not only insisted that students complete schoolwork but also established working relationships with parents to ensure compliance and focused their attention on the holistic development of the youth. Sowell (1979, p. 36) quotes a principal who said, "You are pushing for them, and dying inside for them, [but] you have to let them know that they have to produce" (cited in Siddle-Walker, 2000, p. 265). There are also stories of teachers who provided clothing and scholarship money for students in need (Siddle-Walker, 2000). As opposed to the prevalence of tracking based on IQ testing in public schools run by predominantly White school boards during this time period, these schools eschewed "the argument about industrial or classical training[;] the schools unabashedly offered both vocational and classical courses and children who took vocational courses also took the classical courses" (Siddle-Walker, 2000, p. 267). Community and school leadership had to be politically savvy to resist constraints imposed by White school boards.

I take several propositions from this history. First, the dominant conceptions of risk based initially on deficit assumptions about innate ability and later on restrictive conceptions of social capital that supports academic learning were not internalized, in this case, by the African American community. Second, there is strong evidence that families and schools, working in tandem, saw as one of their primary goals for children's development learning how to live in what was then an institutionally sanctioned segregated world, while simultaneously resisting and achieving inside it. By learning to live in a segregated world, I do not mean internalizing negative stereotypes and succumbing to low expectations. Rather I mean seizing the day to build community infrastructure, to prepare young people for leadership and political resistance (in part, because young people saw this resistance in the lives of adults in their communities). During the Civil Rights and Black Power movements in the United States, we find a similar concentrated focus on schooling as an instrument for social justice (see Payne & Strickland, 2008, on the freedom schools of that era, including contemporary manifestations). We find similar educational histories in American Indian, Latino, and Asian American communities (Lomawaima, 2004; Nieto, 2000). In other words, communities were redefining what equity in the contexts of schooling looked like and intended to accomplish. These histories were not crafted harmoniously; indeed, they involved internal conflicts and debates (e.g., the debates between W. E. B. DuBois and Booker T. Washington) (DuBois, 1973). It is equally the case that these schools also had many problems. However, these problems do not negate what we can learn from these schools that were achieving against the odds of their times.

In the next section of this chapter, I draw on research in the learning sciences and in human development to argue that the aims of social, emotional, and cognitive development that were intrinsically embedded in the practices of these highly successful African American segregated schools constitute an important element of what is entailed in successful academic learning, of protective factors, or of supports for learning to be resilient in the face of challenge.

RE-ENVISIONING RISK AND EQUITY IN SCHOOLING: CONTRIBUTIONS FROM THE SCIENCES OF HUMAN LEARNING AND DEVELOPMENT WITH A CULTURAL–ECOLOGICAL FOCUS

Our responses to risk in education are influenced by how we conceptualize it and what we determine to be evidence of equity in opportunities and/or outcomes. I have offered evidence of conceptions of risk that are presumed to be the primary purview of youth from nondominant groups and are based on deficit assumptions with regard to these youth and their families. These conceptions of risk are situated largely as traits of people (Gutierrez & Rogoff, 2003). By contrast, Spencer and her colleagues (Spencer, Fegley, & Dupree, 2006; Spencer, Harpalani, et al., 2006) argue for situating risk as an attribute of the challenges to which youth are exposed. I articulate in this section conceptual links between culturally and ecologically based research in the learning sciences, social psychology, and human development which I believe, in coordination, offer a more holistic and generative framework than what has informed our responses to inequities in education in the past.

Spencer (1987, 1999, 2000) cogently illustrates that youth from nondominant groups face multiple challenges. These include the normative challenges of life-course development. As Rogoff (2003, 2002) has documented in cross-cultural comparisons, there are markers of age ranges (i.e., infanthood, early childhood, middle childhood, and adolescence) in which we can expect common constraints and developmental goals. Although the meaning attached to the transition from childhood to adulthood looks different across cultural communities and historical time (Burton, Allison, & Obeidallah, 1995; Phinney, 1990; Spencer, Dobbs, & Swanson, 1988; Super & Harkness, 1986; Weisner, 1984), the biological changes that mark the transition into the possibility of fulfilling adult-like roles pose a common family of challenges for young people. Certainly, in the United States, we find with the onset of adolescence a high salience for peer relationships, for wrestling with sexual identity, and for consolidating psychological construals of the self. These normative tasks of life-course development pose particular challenges for schools.

In Western schools, the transition from home to preschool or kindergarten is a common challenge that directly informs the kind of pedagogy used for children at that age in comparison to high school. At the same time, youth from nondominant groups, especially those also living in persistent intergenerational poverty, face additional challenges above and beyond the normative developmental issues I have described. As Massey (1990) and others (Brooks-Gunn & Duncan, 1997; Duncan & Brooks-Gunn, 1997; McLoyd, 1998) have documented, a concentration of poverty and racial/ethnic segregation compounds exposure to social problems (e.g., neighborhood violence, chronic stress, and harsh discipline practices in school) and a scarcity of resources (e.g., lack of adequate health care, inadequate housing, lack of green space, limited opportunities for extracurricular activities, and transportation challenges). It is more likely that a student will be in a school with a culture of low expectations, fewer curricular resources, teachers who are not well prepared (e.g., years of experience, certification, and relationships with the community in question), significantly less per-pupil funding than their more affluent peers, harsh disciplinary practices, and a nonrigorous curriculum (Darling-Hammond, 1987, 1999; Kozol, 1991; National Research Council, 1999). This young person is also faced with societal stereotypes based on race, ethnicity, immigrant status, and gender (Steele, 2004). Boykin (1986) calls this the triple quandary of race, gender, and class. These ecological conditions are indicators of macro-level policies and belief systems that the young person experiences in daily face-to-face interactions—in the neighborhood and in school. Thus, the developmental challenge for this youth is to manage *both* the normative challenges, for example, of adolescence, and the challenges that he or she faces attributable to societal stigmatization. The work of schooling sits inside this quandary (Lee, 2007).

The idea that youth from nondominant communities face societal challenges and that these challenges should be considered in how we design schooling is not new. In many respects, this fundamental assumption can be found in the use of IQ assessments for tracking and in the various compensatory models we have seen (discussed in earlier sections of this chapter). There is, however, a fundamental difference between what we are offered in a cultural–ecological framework for learning and development and what we have seen from educational sciences in the past. This framework posits that families and communities are agentive—not passive recipients of oppression—and have resources that facilitate youth development. If this were not the case, these communities would literally die out, and only rich people would be left. Our challenge in education is to understand what are pathways to resilience in the face of risk, how these pathways are rooted in the everyday cultural practices of families and communities, and what these pathways mean for the practices of schooling (Lee, 2008). The cultural–ecological framework for learning and development that I glean from a synthesis of cultural and ecological research in the learning sciences, social psychology, and human development proposes that learning is a consequence of dynamic adaptive processes (e.g., people learning to adapt to their environments in ways that lead to productive or nonproductive outcomes over the life course), entailing cognition and emotions, and linked to issues of identity (Lee, 2007; Lee et al., 2003; Nasir et al., 2006; Nasir & Saxe, 2003; Spencer, Fegley et al., 2006; Spencer, Harpalani et al., 2006; Spencer & Markstrom-Adams, 1990).

A simplified version of the argument goes something like this: From the perspective of social psychology, identity has to do with how we see ourselves in relation to others (Flavell & Miller, 1998; Kunda, 1999; McAdams & Pals, 2006). The groups whom we consider affiliations include family, race/ethnicity, gender, nationality, age cohort, and communities of practice (e.g., rappers, basketball players, folks who like to tinker with mechanical things, visual artists). These affiliations are associated with a sense of obligations, rights, beliefs, and valued practices that include ways of using language and expected ways of organizing particular activities. Identity work (e.g., the work we do to negotiate who we think we are) also helps to influence (not determine) goals we set, which in turn influences our motivations to engage or resist (Dai & Sternberg, 2004; Dweck, 1999; Dweck & Legget, 1988; Graham & Golan, 1991). Our identity (or one might say identities as an individual [i.e., personality traits], a member of a racial or ethnic group or a gender group) also influences the perceptions we bring to the settings and activities in which we engage. The perceptions of the setting, the tasks, and the people matter for our goals and motivations (Eccles, O'Neil, & Wigfield, 2005; Weiner, 1985). For example, perceptions of ability as fixed or malleable can influence effort (Dweck, 2002; Dweck & Legget, 1988) and have been associated with broad orientations across historically defined pan-ethnic communities (Graham & Hudley, 2005; Stevenson & Stigler, 1992). This is not a one-way street because people (their messages and our relationships with them) and the social processes embedded in routine practices (like schooling generically or instruction in mathematics or reading specifically) can also work to reshape existing perceptions (e.g., of one's ability, of mathematical problem solving, or of what was imagined in terms of low expectations from teachers). As Spencer (2006) explains in her ecological framework, PVEST (phenomenological variant of ecological systems theory), the relationship between perceptions of risk and the nature of resources influences outcomes. This is the implicit, albeit tacit, theory that informed many of the practices of the segregated African American schools described by Anderson (1988), Siddle-Walker (1996, 2000), and others. Despite living at the height of *de jure* segregation and Jim Crow, these schools were organized to create multiple safety nets for youth (i.e., working relationships between families and schools, caring teachers, a culture of high expectations, and an expansive rather than a restrictive curriculum) with the goal of teaching them not to be beaten down by overt racism and discrimination but to excel in spite of it.

What I am describing as multiple safety nets can be thought of as multiple pathways, each representing a point of access for recruiting psychosocial resources that we use and that we coordinate when we work to accomplish new goals. My aim is to apply this idea of multiple safety nets or multiple pathways to academic learning in the context of schooling. I resist the idea that there is a singular pathway through which academic learning occurs. In our efforts to reform schools, particularly in the past 30 years, we have focused our attention on singular pathways (e.g., cognitive reforms in the teaching of reading, mathematics, and science; relationship building through small school configurations in middle and high school; relevance through multicultural education and culturally responsive pedagogy; and resources through technology-rich programs or community partnerships). Each of these reform efforts that were aimed at achieving equity in educational outcomes for youth from nondominant groups implicitly presumes that the singular rationale undergirding their design will work for the vast majority of young people. And yet few of these programs have persistently strong outcomes (as measured by the very incomplete instruments available to us in terms of standardized assessments) (Ramani, Gilbertson, & Fox, 2007).

The framework offered here proposes that family, school, and informal settings offer supports and constraints that are available to youth for figuring out how to engage life work which, of course, includes the work of schooling. The psychosocial resources that we want to tap with each young person are situated in the relationships among identity, perceptions, emotional states, and goals, which in turn affect effort, persistence, and resilience in the face of challenge. This is true for all youth, indeed all human beings. The specific concern has to do with how these relationships play out with regard to vulnerabilities as a consequence of positioning, that is, in terms of race, ethnicity and class. How does knowledge influence these relationships; how do personal relationships influence them; how does the relevance of tasks influence; and what in the nature of resources, such as technology, can also tap these psychosocial resources? How these relationships (e.g., between identity, perceptions, emotional states, and goals) operate will be influenced by individual differences and perceptions about group membership in terms of family, race/ethnicity, nationality, class, gender, and age cohort.

Figure 1 offers a graphic representation of these pathways or points of access (e.g., knowledge, relationships, relevance, and human and material resources) and the psychosocial resources that need to be tapped to promote learning (e.g., relationships among identity, perceptions, emotional states, and goals). Although this sounds very complicated, I would argue that on a commonsense level, as parents we understand individual differences in our children, the kinds of challenges our African American and Latino boys will likely face as they get closer to adolescence, and approaches to build on the interests or to spark particular interests of our children. These commonsense, everyday efforts to facilitate the development of our children are possible by recognizing salient aspects of their identities, their perceptions of themselves and the tasks that we want them to master, the ways in which their emotional states influence their efforts, and the kinds of guided supports they need to feel competent. We consider the influences of their peers and what is happening in their neighborhood that helps or hinders, but we do all this work with the explicit expectation that we will succeed and that our children are capable. This is work that both middleclass and lower income parents alike do, despite arguments to the contrary. It embodies the principles I have described, a dynamic and adaptive approach to learning that takes the ecological and cultural contexts into account.

In the next section, I offer an abbreviated discussion of the science that informs these propositions about multiple pathways, particularly with regard to youth from nondominant groups. I then go on to discuss their implications for the education of youth from nondominant groups.

WHAT IS THE NEXUS OF IDENTITY, PERCEPTIONS, EMOTIONAL STATES, AND GOALS AND WHAT DOES IT SUGGEST FOR UNDERSTANDING MULTIPLE PATHWAYS?

The argument is that the following are multiple pathways through which organized environments (such as schools) can influence the cycles of identity, perception,

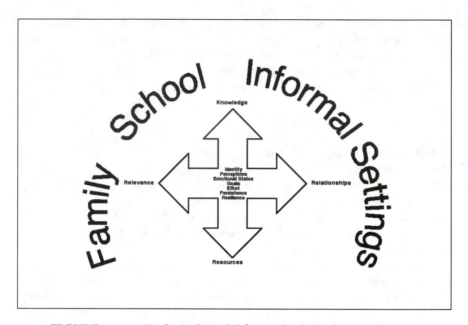

**FIGURE 1   An Ecological Model for Multiple Pathways Through
Which to Access Psychosocial Resources for Learning**

emotional states, goals, effort, and persistence entailed in learning: (a) knowledge, (b) human and material relationships, (c) relevance, (d) resources. In Figure 1, I place these pathways within an ecological context, indicating that youth may experience supports (or for that matter constraints) for any of these pathways through routine experiences in family, school, or informal settings. I argue further that although having congruence across these settings may be ideal, dissonance across settings is not in itself bad (Phelan, Davidson, & Cao, 1991; Piaget, 1952). Where there is dissonance across settings, the challenge is determining where youth learn to make sense of and respond to that dissonance in ways that lead to productive outcomes (Spencer, Fegley, et al., 2006; Spencer, Harpalani, et al., 2006). As in most life circumstances, youth will experience dissonance, unless they live in a highly homogenous community where dissonance is less pronounced, for example, very close-knit religious communities such as the Amish, Mormons, orthodox Jewish, or Muslim communities. For those communities that have historically experienced persistent inequalities in educational outcomes, such dissonance is pervasive. I argue that schools can serve unique and important functions in helping youth to deal with this dissonance.

I will discuss each of these pathways in terms of its implications for academic learning inside schools. I am viewing pathways here as points of access for linking to the internal mechanisms listed inside the four-point arrow in Figure 1. Each pathway has both a cognitive and a socioemotional dimension.

Knowledge Pathways—Socioemotional Dimensions

The knowledge pathway may include subject matter–related knowledge as well as social and emotional knowledge. Social and emotional knowledge concerns knowledge about the social systems in which youth must operate, including knowledge about productive ways of responding to perceptions of vulnerability. Such knowledge is important for all youth. This is exemplified in what Spencer (2006, 2008) calls "masked vulnerability of the privileged," as illustrated in the case of the murders at Columbine High School, recent attacks on college campuses, and the growing rate of suicide among White males. On one hand, knowledge about social systems must be developmentally appropriate; on the other hand, it is important to expand our notions about developmental constraints. We tend to think that young children are not aware of political environments. However, there is evidence to suggest this is not necessarily the case. For example, even young children have intuitive senses of opportunities and constraints that societal norms communicate (Coles, 2000; Spencer, 2008). Although we do not fully understand the limits of such understanding by young children, a recent example from China suggests that such limits may be broader than we expect if we rely solely on evidence from Western industrialized nations such as the United States. In the opening ceremonies of the 2008 Olympics in Beijing, China, Lin Hao, a 9-year-old boy, was featured. He had been buried beneath rubble when his school collapsed during the 2008 earthquake in Sichuan Province, China. He managed to get himself out but then went back into the school to rescue two other classmates. The reason he gave for this act of courage was that he was a school leader and it was his responsibility to do so. We do not know whether this explanation was actually what the boy said or what the government wanted to convey during the Olympics. But we do have evidence of societal-level socialization efforts in which even young children (e.g., between the ages of 6 and 12) have assumed political roles beyond what we would expect them to be capable. We have national examples during the Civil Rights movement of young children integrating public schools at great personal risk, but doing so with courage because of what they understood the political stakes to be (Levine, 1993). Such political engagement can also be psychologically destructive, as in the case of child soldiers in several parts of the world (Garbarino, 2008).

Knowledge of and perceptions about political conditions have been shown to be particularly salient for youth from nondominant groups. As children mature, they are cognitively more attuned to dissonance in their environments, including their experiences of stereotypes and unfairness. For example, in several recent studies, Spencer (2006, 2008) has assessed adolescents' political attitudes using the Political Attitudes Survey–2 in which respondents evaluate statements about the political environment of the country. One of the subscales on this survey assesses respondents' perceptions of equality and fairness in society. Spencer (2008) reports "marginally achieving (C/D) youth perceived higher levels of inequality . . . than high-achieving (A/B) youth " (p. 261).[3] This and other research suggests not only that there is a relationship between political views of equality and fairness and school achievement but that this relationship can be influenced by knowledge of how to resist inequality and evidence that such efforts have yielded some measure of success.

Several studies have shown negative impacts of pre-adolescents' and adolescents' perceptions of being discriminated against on a number of outcomes, including lower self-esteem, depression, anger, and negative attitudes toward school (Fischer & Shaw, 1999; Fisher, Wallace, & Fenton, 2000; Neblett, Philip, Cogburn, & Sellers, 2006; Romero & Roberts, 1998; Simmons et al., 2002; T. T. Wells, 1969; Wong, Eccles, & Sameroff, 2003). Such reports are important because they illustrate the ways that macro-level policies and belief systems are embodied in face-to-face inter-actions, including the prevalence with which they are experienced by youth of color. We do not fully understand what youth learn from the messages about interpreting their experiences with unfairness and discrimination. However, a few studies have found correlations between positive racial socialization and an array of outcomes, including self-concepts, personal efficacy, and higher grades (Bowman & Howard, 1985; Caughy, O'Campo, Randolph, & Nickerson, 2002; Davis, Aronson, & Salinas, 2006; Knight, Cota, & Bernal, 1993; Ou & McAdoo, 1993; Phinney & Chavira, 1995). Messages by parents to children concerning race and ethnicity that focus on mistrust have shown negative outcomes in terms of psychological health, delinquency, and school achievement (Hughes & Chen, 1999; Marshall, 1995; Murray & Mandara, 2003; D. L. Taylor, Biafora, & Warheit, 1994).

Racial socialization typically refers to the messages that parents give to their chil-dren about the salience and experience of race (Hughes, 2003). Such messages include knowledge and beliefs "(a) about cultural heritage and pride, (b) that prepare children for future discrimination, (c) that promote outgroup mistrust, and (d) that emphasize 'racelessness' or similarity among groups" (Mandara, 2006, p. 213; see also Hughes & Chen, 1997, 1999). One can expand such socialization to include ethnic socialization or examine the intersections between race and ethnic socializa-tion. One example of these intersections is the many groups that we refer to as Pan-Latino—joint American Indian, African, and Spanish heritages (e.g., mestizo)—and the associated vulnerabilities positioned by these histories. It is also important to acknowledge that the messages about race come not only from parents but also from other adult caregivers in schools, community organizations, extended family, and social networks as well as the media. For example, studies of segregated African American schools in the South in the pre-*Brown* era (discussed in an earlier section of this chapter) and of African-centered schools in the last 40 years illustrate the embeddedness of racial socialization messages in school cultures (Irvine & Irvine, 1983; Lee, 1994). We have similar examples in American Indian schools as well as institutions such as Korean Schools, Chinese Schools, and Jewish Schools that stu-dents often attend to supplement traditional formal schooling.

One important tenet of a cultural and ecological focus is that cultural communi-ties are patterned but maintain significant variation (Gutierrez & Rogoff, 2003; Rogoff, 2003). This means that socioemotional knowledge about how to respond to discrimination must take into account both the regularity and the variation in people's experiences of discrimination. One example that is not sufficiently studied is the variation within the African American community, variation that goes beyond class distinctions that receive greater attention (Patillo, 1999). African and Caribbean Black immigrants face challenges that are both similar to and different from those of African Americans who trace their family histories back to the African Holocaust of Enslavement (Bashi & McDaniel, 1997). Black immigrants from both groups have higher academic outcomes (e.g., grades, test scores, and college graduation rates) than U.S.-born Blacks (Gibson, 1991; JBHE Foundation, 1999–2000; Rong & Brown, 2001). Depending on immigrant status (i.e., first, second, or third generation) and where they reside (e.g., high Caribbean enclaves in New York City vs. other urban areas where they are less concentrated), people of African descent wrestle between ethnic identities (e.g., Jamaican or Somalian), pan-ethnic identities as Caribbean or African, hyphenated national identity as African-American, and a racial identity as Blacks (Kasinitz, 1992; Waters, 1991, 1994; Zaphir, 1996). Some studies have shown when Caribbean Blacks position themselves, for example, as Caribbean rather than Black American, they may presume some advantages, including the ability to distance themselves from traditional negative stereotypes of Blacks (Foner, 1987; Rong & Brown, 2002; Vickerman, 1999). The point is that the knowledge repertoires about learning to persist in the face of discrimination (e.g., in educational and other settings) are different among different groups of African Americans. This variation has implications for how we think about sources of resilience to perceptions of risk within and across groups (Gibson, 1995; Portes & Rumbaut, 2001; Suarez-Orozco & Qin-Hilliard, 2004; Valenzuela, 1999).

A logical conclusion is that if you are surrounded by conditions that clearly signal inequality and unfairness in opportunity, it is much easier to feel hopeless, including hopeless about the ways that school can help one resist. This is particularly the case if what one experiences repeated failure in school. On the other hand, we have evidence, particularly from the racial socialization literature described above, that knowledge—in this case cultural knowledge—can serve a protective function against the vulnerabilities that racial, ethnic, gender, and class discrimination poses.

Knowledge about how to respond productively to perceptions of vulnerability is an important, in fact, crucial developmental outcome. For youth who face multifold challenges attributable to racism and poverty, perceptions of vulnerability are inescapable. If such youth and their families must wait for structural changes to evolve in society, many youth will be sacrificed. Rather, it is the responsibility of all institutions with which youth have routine and sustained involvement (e.g., family, school, church, and youth organizations) to teach youth how to interpret signals of vulnerability and how to deal with the emotions that such perceptions will inevitably engender. The developmental literature deals with this in terms of concepts such as locus of control and attribution theory (Weiner, 1985). Both focus on the kinds of explanations a person generates about the source of vulnerability. The studies, which have been based largely on White middle-class samples, have argued that an internal locus of control is superior because it embodies the idea that a person has control over his or her vulnerabilities (Graham & Weiner, 1996; Strickland, 1989).

However, other scholars, particularly those studying African American youth, have argued that an external locus of control can be productive for persons living under hegemonic conditions where the explanation is not unduly about weakness in the individual but about attributing the vulnerability to structural forces (Graham, 1994; Graham & Hudley, 2005). Mandara (2006) has created a racial socialization typology that incorporates dimensions of locus of control with dimensions of group pride or racial socialization. Mandara argues that the combined focus on racial/ethnic pride and personal power contributes to positive academic outcomes for African American youth, especially males, over the life course. For youth of color living in low-income communities, it is likely that learning to be flexible and strategic in the deployment of both internal and external loci of control will be important because the contexts of their lives require both. In the social contexts of schooling, particularly schools and school districts with long histories of underachievement, this kind of social and emotional learning (e.g., learning how to "read" problems and how to understand and reroute one's emotional responses) is important because of the many inconsistencies in school and classroom culture that these students are likely to meet across their K–12 schooling. These inconsistencies may be in the form of differences in teacher quality from one grade to another, from one class to another, from one school to another; differences in overall school culture; or differences in the cultures of subject matters, particularly at the high school level.

Knowledge Pathways–Cognitive Dimensions

The knowledge pathway from a cognitive perspective focuses on knowledge of the academic tasks of schooling. Unless students have reason to believe that there are other outlets for learning required academic content (e.g., parents and tutors), they are likely to feel quite vulnerable when asked to solve content area problems and they do not know how. On the other hand, making problem-solving processes explicit and providing guided support while students are engaging in such processes increase the likelihood of success, and success builds confidence (Collins, Brown, & Holum, 1991; Palincsar & Brown, 1984; Rosenshine & Meister, 1994). This issue of making problem solving explicit and visible is not a straightforward process of simply telling a student how to engage a task. The cognitive literature makes a distinction between declarative knowledge (e.g., knowing that something is the case) and procedural knowledge (e.g., knowing how to do something) (Anderson, 1983, 1993). Procedural knowledge is made even more nuanced because the transfer of knowledge from one task to a related task is influenced by the ability of the learner to perceive the most salient features of a new problem and infer its significance to his or her existing knowledge (Schwartz & Nasir, 2004). Thus, teaching generative knowledge, that is, knowledge that allows one to do many things, including new kinds of problems one has never encountered directly, is one hallmark of a high-quality education (Hatano & Inagaki, 1986; Perkins, 1995) or what Perkins calls "generative knowledge." Decades of research in cognitive science supports the foundational role of prior knowledge for new learning (Bransford, Brown, & Cocking, 1999; Rumelhart, 1980; Walker, 1987). One problematic issue for teaching generative knowledge in schools serving minority youth and youth from low-income communities, particularly in schools and districts with long histories of low achievement, is the limitations of traditional educational approaches to understand the points of leverage between everyday knowledge rooted in the routine experiences of these youth and the demands of specialized learning in the content areas. This is ironic, in part, because we do have significant research on the significance of knowledge constructed out of everyday experience; however, this work does not focus on the everyday experiences of youth of color from working-class communities (Alterman, 1999; Baillargeon, 1995; Gardner, 1991; Hatano & Inagaki, 1987; Hutchins, 1995; Lakoff & Nunez, 2000). Although we have many examples of programs of research that examine the points of leverage and have designed school interventions to scaffold such connections, their approaches have not been codified in curricular materials and assessments that are readily available to most teachers and schools, nor have they filtered down into teacher preparation or in-service professional development on a large scale (Atran & Medin, 2008; Ball, 1995; Bang, Medin, & Altran, 2007; Lave, Murtaugh, & de la Rocha, 1984; Medin & Altran, 1999; Nasir, Hand, & Taylor, 2008; Saxe, 1999).

Examples of such programs of research include The Algebra Project in mathematics (Moses, 1994; Moses & Cobb, 2001; Moses, Kamii, Swap, & Howard, 1989) and the Chèche Konnen Project in science (Rosebery, Warren, Ballenger, & Ogonowski, 2005; Rosebery, Warren, & Conant, 1992; Warren, Ballenger, Ogonowski, Rosebery, & Hudicourt-Barnes, 2001) and many programs in bilingual education (Gutiérrez, 2004; Gutierrez, Baquedano-Lopez, & Alvarez, 1999; Gutierrez, Baquedano-Lopez, & Tejeda, 1999; Valdes, 2001, 2002). For illustrative purposes, I will describe the Cultural Modeling Project and its framework to illustrate one way of conceptualizing linkages between the everyday knowledge of students of color living in low-income communities and disciplinary knowledge that is generative (Lee, 1995a, 1995b, 2001, 2004, 2007). The Cultural Modeling Project focuses on African American adolescents and the discipline of response to literature at the high school level. I use this high school example, in part, because conceptualizing links that are subject-matter specific at the level of the secondary school curriculum has been challenging, with interesting differences by subject matter. I also use the Cultural Modeling example because it reinforces an overarching point I have been trying to make in this chapter, namely, that the extent to which we understand and respond in our science to the complexities of the youth who most experience low academic achievement affects the likelihood that we will generate foundational knowledge that expands our fundamental understandings about how people learn. Thus, I see this work as both one of equity and one of science.

Cultural Modeling begins with a careful examination of generative knowledge in a domain, much as Li Ping Ma (1999) has done with regard to mathematical knowledge at the elementary level. It involves identifying what the core concepts are, how concepts are related to one another, and what problem-solving processes typify approaches to the discipline, broadly speaking, and to specific kinds of concepts and problems within the discipline. Building on other bodies of work in literary theory and sociolinguistics, the Cultural Modeling Project has identified a core set of concepts and problem-solving processes in response to literature. From that analysis, building on decades of research in sociolinguistics, the Cultural Modeling Project has identified routine, everyday practices in the linguistic repertoire of speakers of African American English that embody these same core constructs and entail similar problem-solving processes. In addition, we have made similar extrapolations to what youth do with literary tropes in rap lyrics and videos and popular television and movies. By having students analyze how they engage in the tacit reasoning of the everyday practice, we have been able to make explicit and public how to identify problem types and how to tackle such problems in canonical literature. Assessments in the project have shown youth with standardized reading comprehension scores in the bottom quartile achieve high levels of competence in interpreting very complex works of canonical literature. For a more detailed discussion, see Lee (2007). Cultural Modeling is only one of what I will call a family of research in the disciplines of science, math, and literacy education that deconstruct generative relationships between everyday and disciplinary knowledge.

Relevance Pathway in Conjunction With the Cognitive Knowledge Pathway

One of the outcomes I have found in the work on Cultural Modeling has to do with the relevance pathway for knowledge building, captured in Figure 1. I have found that through the examination of what we call "cultural data sets" (e.g., everyday texts that embody a foundational literary construct or type of problem), youth who have been disengaged see the relevance of what we are asking them to do with canonical texts. This is not merely an issue of seeing the relevance of themes within literature to one's own life; rather, it is the understanding that the problem-solving processes and habits of mind that characterize literary reasoning are practices in which they already engage (albeit tacitly and in qualitatively different ways) and which they value. For example, both speakers of African American English and expert readers of canonical literature value the aesthetic dimensions of language play as a worthwhile end in itself, above and beyond the content of the message (Smitherman, 1977).

Dispositions or what Perkins (1992) calls "habits of mind" are a central part of discipline-specific modes of reasoning. For example, one hears mathematicians talk about the elegance of a solution; scientists value the disposition to be inquisitive; and historians value a critical stance toward the construction of stories of the past. These dispositions are perhaps the hardest outcomes we seek to teach. Thus, if we can find places in youth's lives in which they display such dispositions, without the aid of schooling, we have a potentially powerful source of everyday knowledge on which schools can build.

Overall, the relevance pathway has to do with the extent to which the learner sees the significance of the school-related tasks to his or her immediate or long-term goals. The relevance question is captured in the expectancy × value theoretical framework (Eccles et al., 2005; Graham & Weiner, 1996; Wigfield & Eccles, 2002). This framework proposes that effort and persistence are influenced by how much the learner believes that attaining the learning goal is possible (e.g., expectancy) and the value he or she places on achieving the goal. These goal-related values include how important it is to achieve this end, its intrinsic value or lack thereof, its utility in relation to immediate and future goals, and finally the costs entailed in working to achieve those goals. Scholars (Hudley & Graham, 2001; Taylor & Graham, 2007) argue that in this line of research, insufficient attention has been paid to ethnic minority youth. A cultural and ecological focus will consider the influences of a range of factors on youth's perceptions of the attainability, the value, and the costs associated with particular academic tasks at particular points in the life course: societal stereotype (e.g., of Black and Latino males), stereotype threat, school culture (e.g., discipline policies and the impact of district, state, and federal school accountability practices), and neighborhood resources (e.g., availability of libraries, bookstores, and businesses) (Graham, 1994; Graham & Golan, 1991; Graham & Hudley, 2005; Hudley & Graham, 2001; Neblett et al., 2006). For example, working with a sample of African American and Latino youth, Taylor and Graham (2007) found that perceptions of barriers to attaining academic goals increased with age, especially for boys. Others have found similar differences in terms of grades, attitudes toward school, and academic goals based on intersections between race/ethnicity, age, and gender (Cook et al., 1996; Ford, 1992; Kao & Tienda, 1995; Pollard, 1993; Suarez-Orozco & Qin-Hilliard, 2004; Valenzuela, 1999).

Sometimes the relevance pathway indirectly influences goals and academic tasks, another way of achieving task value. We know, for example, that expectations for at least a C average often keep high school athletes attending class and completing classwork (Braddock, Royster, Winfield, & Hawkins, 1991; Broh, 2002). What, then, are the possibilities if the mathematics courses can help the basketball player develop more strategic ways of thinking about statistics or probability as these are embodied in the practice he values (Nasir, 2000) or if the physics class can help the baseball pitcher or football quarterback understand the forces that have an impact on how well he throws (Brown, 2004; Brown & Kloser, 2006). The area of relevance-related pathways linked to content-area learning is severely underdeveloped but offers both interesting opportunities to engage youth who currently see little relevance of their school-related work to their lives and opportunities to gain more nuanced knowledge about naïve concepts and misconceptions.

Relationship Pathway

A third pathway addresses the role of relationships. As I have discussed earlier in this chapter and elsewhere (Lee, 2007), embracing different identities always entails obligations to others. We do many things in life not because we want to do them but because they are expected or because we want to please others with whom we have close personal relationships (Markus & Kitayama, 1991). In addition, relationships are a source of social networking, expanding the range of opportunities and experiences available to us. Many studies of social networking have shown both the positive and negative effects of the nature and density of social networks (Smith-Maddox, 1999; Zimmerman, Bingenheimer, & Notaro, 2002). In the case of teaching, relationships between teachers and students are influenced by students' perceptions of the expectations and evaluations made by teachers. There is a long history of research documenting the prevalence of a culture of low expectations in low-income schools and the narrowing of the curriculum in response to these low expectations (Baron et al., 1985; DeMeis & Turner, 1978; Rist, 1970). Ferguson (2003, 2007) and others have shown, for example, that perceived relationships with teachers are particularly salient for African American youth (Casteel, 1997; Eccles & Wigfield, 1985; Entwisle & Alexander, 1988; Haller, 1985; Jussim, Eccles, & Madon, 1996; Kleinfeld, 1972; Weinstein, 1985). We know anecdotally that in high schools, youth will come to school to visit their friends and will selectively attend classes, based on perceptions of relationships with their teachers.

Resource Pathway

The fourth pathway refers to human and material resources. This can subsume all of the pathways I have discussed, but here it refers to artifacts that can aid knowledge building in ways that reduce the cognitive load and, as a consequence, perhaps decrease vulnerability to failure—or at least provide enough supports such that the learner is more inclined to persist in trying. I offer three brief examples related to learning in school. The first is technology. Although youth across SES groups are generally highly engaged with technology (in comparison with their parents and their teachers, for example), schools with histories of underachievement generally have the least access to new and cutting-edge technologies. Quite simply, Black, Brown, and poor children rarely have ubiquitous access to recent technologies, whether worldwide knowledge access through the Internet, digital technologies that empower sophisticated forms of media production for the average user, software environments that allow users to perceive themselves inside a 3-D environment, or learning technologies in which users can simulate experiments that would otherwise be too costly, for example, using GPS data to infer migration patterns or environmental shifts (Radinsky, Smolin, & Lawless, 2005) or simulating the evolution of an ecosystem such as that of the Galapagos Islands (Reiser et al., 2001). I argue that technology can serve as a resource because for youth at this point in our history technology is inherently enticing (Goldman, 2005) and because it typically provides scaffolds to aid the cognitive load and as a consequence to potentially reduce vulnerability to failure (Edelson & Reiser, 2006; Linn, Shear, Bell, & Slotta, 1999; Pea & Gomez, 1992). Such resources have the potential to integrate knowledge, relevance, and relationship pathways, although this is rarely explicitly the case (Hooper, 1996; Pinkard, 2000; Shaw, 1996).

A second family of resources is connected to the relationships pathway. This includes the array of resources that settings outside of schools make available to youth but that are typically not taken up in any meaningful way by schools, especially related to content-area learning. One example of a program of research that explicitly builds on community-based resources is the Funds of Knowledge Project (FOK) (Gonzalez, 1995; Gonzalez, Moll, & Amanti, 2004; Mercado & Moll, 1997; Moll & Gonzales, 2004; Velez-Ibañez & Greenberg, 2004). The FOK work has taken place primarily in low-income Latino communities, particularly Mexican-descent communities in the Southwest. A central premise of FOK is that embedded in community life are a multitude of practices in which adults are engaged that embody school-relevant knowledge and that by enhancing active relationships between and among teachers, parents, and community residents, school can significantly expand the resources—human and technical—available to help youth in school. The concept "funds of knowledge" has come to refer to the knowledge embedded in everyday practices in the communities with which the researchers have worked. Such knowledge includes carpentry, plumbing, electrical work, sewing, everyday medical knowledge, and linguistic knowledge involved in what Orellana (Orellana, 2009; Orellana & Eksner, 2006; Orellana & Reynolds, 2008; Orellana, Reynolds, Dorner, & Meza, 2003) calls language brokering, among others. In one activity, teachers working in the FOK physically go out into the community, although it is not required that they do, and conduct open-ended ethnographic interviews with parents and community members, the social networks of their students' lives. They then work to develop curriculum that uses these human resources to enhance teaching and learning. Funds of Knowledge integrates the knowledge, relevance, relationship, and resource pathways.

CONCLUSION

In this chapter, I have argued that the persistent achievement gap based on race/ethnicity and class must be understood in its historical context and in the ways in which risk has been explicitly institutionalized and that our approaches to addressing these inequities should be informed by a robust science of learning and development. In many respects, that science has been warped by historical beliefs about race and class, reflected in the uses of IQ to sort and deficit assumptions about social capital. I have argued that a cultural and ecological focus on the ways that identity, perceptions, and emotions influence cognition offers an expanded view of learning and new opportunities for how we envision risk, equity, and schooling. I have tried to apply that proposition with regard to multiple pathways through which schools, in particular, can provide access points to influence the identity processes that help to shape youth's goals, efforts, persistence, and resilience. To understand how these pathways operate to help shape identity processes that support learning, we need coordinated research efforts that consolidate and synthesize across the fields of cognition, human development, and social cognition, minimally. However, such efforts need to be culturally focused and ecologically grounded. We need a cultural focus in order to understand the range of variation in desired goals of development and conditions that optimize learning. We need an ecological focus because it is the immediate level of context, that is, what youth actually experience as they move in and across settings, that most directly affects their development. This includes the routine practices of schooling that constitute a major influence on learning opportunities for youth. To the extent that such practices are characterized by generativity and robust principles of learning, schools have the power to turn around historical trajectories of low achievement. We certainly have many local examples of this power of schools. However, to accomplish such goals, schools must themselves be sufficiently adaptive and capable of providing multiple points of access that are responsive to the contexts of youth's lives. There is an important role for a culturally responsive, ecologically rooted integrated science of learning and development to inform how schools take up this challenge. It is a complex and compelling challenge that should not be taken up without considerable commitment and planfulness—we cannot make up our response as we go. Even with contributions from an expansive science of learning and development, the process of translating theory into practice will require a coordinated, systemic take-up, supported by public policy. This will require coordination that addresses issues of teacher quality (i.e., teacher preparation, certification, and the long-term conditions of teaching that facilitate teaching as a learning profession), assessments, standards, curriculum, and infrastructure needed to support coordinated change across these areas. Such a science of learning and development needs to address the fundamental issues of human vulnerability across populations, taking into account (a) patterned ways of learning to be resilient in the face of risk and (b) the way such patterns of resilience respond to differences in the ecologies of people's lives, including the influences of positionings with regard to the intersections among race, ethnicity, class, and gender.

ACKNOWLEDGMENTS

I thank Frederick Erickson, Charles Payne, and Margaret Beale Spencer for their insightful comments that helped me conceptualize the fundamental argument of the chapter. I also thank Alfredo J. Artiles and Vivian Gadsden for pushing my thinking about the chapter.

NOTES

[1] I alternatively use the terms *nondominant groups* (to emphasize the political positioning of these youth) and *racial and ethnic minorities* (to make clear the racial and ethnic makeup of such groups).

[2] In the studies conducted by Kenneth and Mamie Clark, the fact that the Black children in the studies showed a preference for White dolls was used in the Brown case as evidence of feelings of inferiority based on being in segregated schools. See Spencer (2008) for a review.

[3] C/D and A/B represent grade point averages.

REFERENCES

Alterman, R. (1999). Everyday reasoning. *Mind, Culture, and Activity, 6,* 117–142.

Anderson, J. (1983). *The architecture of cognition.* Cambridge, MA: Harvard University Press.

Anderson, J. (1988). *The education of Blacks in the South, 1860–1935.* Chapel Hill: University of North Carolina Press.

Anderson, J. (1993). *Rules of the mind.* Hillsdale, NJ: Lawrence Erlbaum.

Arzubiaga, A., Artiles, A. J., King, K., & Harris-Murri, N. (2008). Beyond research on cultural minorities: Challenges and implications of research as situated cultural practice. *Exceptional Children, 74,* 309–327.

Atran, S., & Medin, D. L. (2008). *The native mind and the cultural construction of nature.* Cambridge, MA: MIT Press.

Baillargeon, R. (1995). Physical reasoning in infancy. In M. S. Gazzaniga (Ed.), *The cognitive neurosciences* (pp. 181–204). Cambridge, MA: MIT Press.

Ball, A. (1995). Text design patterns in the writing of urban African-American students: Teaching to the strengths of students in multicultural settings. *Urban Education, 30,* 253–289.

Bang, M., Medin, D. L., & Altran, S. (2007). Cultural mosaics and mental models of nature. *Proceedings of the National Academy of Sciences, 104,* 13868–13874.

Barker, R. G., & Wright, H. F. (1949). Psychological ecology and the problem of psychosocial development. *Child Development, 20,* 131–143.

Baron, R., Tom, D. Y. H., & Cooper, H. M. (1985). Social class, race and teacher expectations. In J. B. Dusek (Ed.), *Teacher expectations* (pp. 251-269). Hillsdale, NJ: Lawrence Erlbaum.

Bashi, V., & McDaniel, A. (1997). A theory of immigration and racial stratification. *Journal of Black Studies, 27,* 668–682.

Bell, D. (2004). *Silent covenants: Brown v Board of Education and the unfulfilled hopes for racial reform.* New York: Oxford University Press.

Bereiter, C., & Engelmann, S. (1966). *Teaching disadvantaged children in pre-school.* Englewood Cliffs, NJ: Prentice Hall.

Bernstein, B. (1961). Social class and linguistic development: A theory of social learning. In A. Halsey, J. Floud, & C. Anderson (Eds.), *Education, economy, and society* (pp. 288–314). New York: Free Press.

Bernstein, B. (1970). Social class, language, and socialization. In P. P. Giglioli (Ed.), *Language and social context* (pp. 157–178). Harmondsworth, UK: Penguin.

Bernstein, B. (1973). *Class, codes and control* (Vol. 2). London: Routledge.

Bernstein, B. (1975). *Class, codes and control* (Vol. 3). London: Routledge.

Bernstein, B. (1990). *Class, codes and control* (Vol. 4). London: Routledge.

Bond, H. M. (1939). *Negro education in Alabama: A study in cotton and steel.* Washington, DC: Associated Publishers.

Bourdieu, P. (1986). The forms of capital. In J. Richardson (Ed.), *Handbook of theory and research for the sociology of education* (pp. 241–258). New York: Greenwood.

Bourdieu, P., & Passeron, J. C. (1977). *Reproduction in education, society and culture.* Beverly Hills, CA: Sage.

Bowman, P., & Howard, C. (1985). Race related socialization, motivation and academic achievement: A study of Black youths in three-generation families. *Journal of American Academy of Child Psychiatry, 24,* 134–141.

Boykin, A. W. (1986). The triple quandary and the schooling of Afro-American children. In U. Neisser (Ed.), *The school achievement of minority children* (pp. 57–92). Hillsdale, NJ: Lawrence Erlbaum.

Braddock, J. H., Royster, D. A., Winfield, L. F., & Hawkins, R. (1991). Bouncing back: Sports and academic resilience among African-American males. *Education and Urban Society, 24,* 113–131.

Bransford, J., Brown, A., & Cocking, R. (1999). *How people learn: Brain, mind, experience and school.* Washington, DC: National Academy Press.

Broh, B. A. (2002). Linking extracurricular programming to academic achievement: Who benefits and why? *Sociology of Education, 75,* 69–95.

Bronfenbrenner, U., & Morris, P. A. (1998). The ecology of developmental processes. In W. Damon & R. M. Lerner (Eds.), *Handbook of child psychology: Theoretical models of human development* (5th ed., Vol. 1, pp. 993–1028). New York: John Wiley.

Brooks-Gunn, J., & Duncan, G. (Eds.). (1997). *Neighborhood poverty: Context and consequence for children* (Vol. 1). New York: Russell Sage Foundation.

Brown, B. (2004). Discursive identity: Assimilation into the culture of science and its implications for minority students. *Journal of Research in Science Teaching, 41,* 810–834.

Brown, B., & Kloser, M. (2006, April). *Conceptual continuity & accessing everyday scientific understandings: Cultural studies in science.* Paper presented at the Annual Meeting of the American Educational Research Association, San Francisco, CA.

Burton, L., Allison, K., & Obeidallah, D. (1995). Social context and adolescents: Perspectives on development among inner-city African-American teens. In L. Crockett & A. Crouter (Eds.), *Pathways through adolescence: Individual development in social contexts* (pp. 119-138). Mahwah, NJ: Lawrence Erlbaum.

Carruthers, J. H. (1995). Science and oppression. In D. A. Azibo (Ed.), *African psychology in historical perspective and related commentary.* Trenton, NJ: Africa World Press.

Casteel, C. (1997). Attitudes of African American and Caucasian eighth grade students about praises, rewards, and punishments. *Elementary School Guidance and Counseling, 31,* 262–272.

Caughy, M. O., O'Campo, P. J., Randolph, S. M., & Nickerson, K. (2002). The influence of racial socialization practices on the cognitive and behavioral competence of African American preschoolers. *Child Development, 73,* 1611–1625.

Cecelski, D. (1994). *Along freedom road: Hyda County, North Carolina, and the fate of Black schools in the South.* Chapel Hill: University of North Carolina Press.

Cole, M. (1996). Interacting minds in a life-span perspective: A cultural-historical approach to culture and cognitive development. In P. Baltes & U. Staudinger (Eds.), *Interactive minds* (pp. 59–87). New York: Cambridge University Press.

Coleman, J. (1988). Social capital in the creation of human capital. *American Journal of Sociology, 94*(Suppl.), S95-S120.

Coleman, J. S., Campbell, E. Q., Hobson, C. J., McPartland, F., Mood, A. M., Weinfeld, F. D., et al. (1966). *Equality of educational opportunity.* Washington, DC: U.S. Government Printing Office.

Coles, R. (2000). *The political life of children.* New York: Atlantic Monthly Press.

Collins, A., Brown, J. S., & Holum, A. (1991, Winter). Cognitive apprenticeship: Making thinking visible. *American Educator,* pp. 6–91.

Cook, T. D., Church, M. B., Ajanaku, S., Shadish, W. R., Jr., Kim, J. R., & Cohen, R. (1996). The development of occupational aspirations and expectations among inner-city boys. *Child Development, 67,* 3368–3385.

Dai, D. Y., & Sternberg, R. (2004). *Motivation, emotion, and cognition: Integrative perspectives on intellectual functioning and development.* Mahwah, NJ: Lawrence Erlbaum.

Darling-Hammond, L. (1990). Teacher quality and equality. In J. I. Goodlad & P. Keating (Eds.), *Access to knowledge: The continuing agenda for our nation's schools* (pp. 237-258). New York: College Entrance Examination Board.

Darling-Hammond, L. (1999). *Teacher quality and student achievement: A review of state policy evidence.* Seattle, WA: Center for the Study of Teaching and Policy.

Davis, C., Aronson, J., & Salinas, M. (2006). Shades of threat: Racial identity as a moderator of stereotype threat. *Journal of Black Psychology, 32,* 399–417.

DeMeis, D. K., & Turner, R. R. (1978). Effects of students' race, physical attractiveness and dialect on teachers' evaluations. *Contemporary Educational Psychology, 3,* 77–86.

Deutsch, M., & Brown, B. (1964). Social influences in Negro-White intelligence differences. *Journal of Social Issues, 20,* 24–35.

Dika, S., & Singh, K. (2002). Applications of social capital in educational literature: A critical synthesis. *Review of Educational Research, 72,* 31–60.

DuBois, W. E. B. (1973). *The education of Black people: Ten critiques 1906–1960.* New York: Monthly Review Press.

DuBois, W. E. B., & Dill, A. G. (1911). *The common school and the Negro American.* Atlanta: Atlanta University Press.

Duncan, G., & Brooks-Gunn, J. (1997). Income effects across the life span: Integration and interpretation. In G. Duncan & J. Brooks-Gunn (Eds.), *Consequences of growing up poor* (p. 596-610). New York: Russell Sage Foundation.

Dweck, C. S. (1999). *Self-theories: Their role in motivation, personality and development.* Philadelphia: Psychology Press.

Dweck, C. S. (2002). Beliefs that make smart people dumb. In R. Sternberg (Ed.), *Why smart people can be so stupid* (pp. 24-41). New Haven: Yale University Press.

Dweck, C. S., & Legget, E. (1988). A socio-cognitive approach to motivation and personality. *Psychological Review, 95,* 256–273.

Eccles, J., O'Neil, S., & Wigfield, A. (2005). Ability self-perceptions and subjective task values in adolescents and children. In K. Moore & L. Lippman (Eds.), *What do children need to flourish: Conceptualizing and measuring indicators of positive development* (pp. 237–270). New York: Springer.

Eccles, J., & Wigfield, A. (1985). Teacher expectations and student motivation. In J. B. Dusek (Ed.), *Teacher expectancies* (pp. 185-217). Hillsdale, NJ: Lawrence Erlbaum.

Edelson, D., & Reiser, B. (2006). Making authentic practices accessible to learners: Design challenges and strategies. In K. Sawyer (Ed.), *Cambridge handbook of the learning sciences* (pp. 335–354). New York: Cambridge University Press.

Elder, G. (1985). Household, kinship, and the life course: Perspectives on black families and children. In M. B. Spencer, G. K. Brookins, & W. R. Allen (Eds.), *Beginnings: The social and affective development of black children* (pp. 29–44). Mahwah, NJ: Lawrence Erlbaum.

Entwisle, D. R., & Alexander, K. L. (1988). Factors affecting achievement test scores and marks of Black and White first graders. *Elementary School Journal, 88,* 449–471.

Ferguson, R. (2003). Teachers' perceptions and expectations and the Black-White test score gap. *Urban Education, 38,* 460–507.

Ferguson, R. (2007). *Toward excellence with equity: An emerging vision for closing the achievement gap.* Boston: Harvard Education Press.

Fischer, A. R., & Shaw, C. M. (1999). African Americans' mental health and perceptions of racist discrimination: The moderating effects of racial socialization experiences and self-esteem. *Journal of Counseling Psychology, 46,* 395–407.

Fisher, C. B., Wallace, S. A., & Fenton, R. E. (2000). Discrimination distress during adolescence. *Journal of Youth and Adolescence, 29,* 679–695.

Flavell, J. H., & Miller, P. H. (1998). Social cognition. In W. E. I. C. Damon, D. Kuhn, & R. V. E. Siegler (Eds.), *Handbook of child psychology* (5th ed., Vol. 2, pp. 851–898). New York: John Wiley.

Foner, N. (1987). The Jamaican: Race and ethnicity among migrants in New York City. In N. Foner (Ed.), *New immigrants in New York* (pp. 131–158). New York: Columbia University Press.

Ford, D. (1992). Self-perceptions of underachievement and support for the achievement ideology among early adolescent African-Americans. *Journal of Early Adolescence, 12,* 228–252.

Foster, M. (1990). Constancy, connectedness, and constraints in the lives of African American teachers. *NWSA Journal, 3,* 233–261.

Franklin, J. H. (1974). *From slavery to freedom: A history of Negro Americans.* New York: Knopf.

Garbarino, J. (2008). *Children and the dark side of human experience: Confronting global realities and rethinking child development.* New York: Springer.

Garcia Coll, C., Lamberty, G., Jenkins, R., McAdoo, H. P., Crnic, K., & Wasik, B. H. (1996). An integrative model for the study of developmental competencies in minority children. *Child Development, 67,* 1891–1914.

Gardner, H. (1991). *The unschooled mind: How children think and how schools should teach.* New York: Basic Books.

Gibson, M. A. (1991). Ethnicity, gender and social class: The school adaptation patterns of West Indian youths. In M. A. Gibson & J. U. Ogbu (Eds.), *Minority status and schooling: A comparative study of immigrant and involuntary minorities* (pp. 169–203). New York: Garland.

Gibson, M. A. (1995). Additive acculturation as a strategy for school. In R. G. Rumbaut & W. A. Cornelius (Eds.), *California's immigrant children* (pp. 77–106). San Diego, CA: Center for U.S.-Mexican Studies.

Giddens, Anthony. (1976). *New rules of sociological method: A positive critique of interpretive sociologies.* London: Hutchinson.

Goddard, H. H. (1917). Mental tests and the immigrant. *Journal of Delinquency, 2,* 243–277.

Goddard, H. H. (1920). *Human efficiency and levels of intelligence. Princeton.* Princeton, NJ: Princeton University Press.

Goldman, S. R. (2005). Designing for scalable educational improvement. In C. Dede, J. P. Honan, & L. C. Peters (Eds.), *Scaling-up success: Lessons learned from technology-based educational improvement* (pp. 67–96). San Francisco: Jossey-Bass.

Gonzalez, N. (1995). The funds of knowledge for teaching project. *Practicing Anthropology, 17,* 3–6.

Gonzalez, N., Moll, L., & Amanti, C. (Eds.). (2004). *Funds of knowledge: Theorizing practices in households, communities, and classrooms.* Mahwah, NJ: Lawrence Erlbaum.

Gould, S. J. (1981). *The mismeasure of man.* New York: Norton.

Graham, S. (1992). "Most of the subjects were White and middle class": Trends in published research on African Americans in selected APA journals, 1970–1989. *American Psychologist, 47,* 629–639.

Graham, S. (1994). Motivation in African Americans. *Review of Educational Research, 64,* 55–117.

Graham, S., & Golan, S. (1991). Motivational influences on cognition; Task involvement, ego involvement, and depth of information processing. *Journal of Educational Psychology, 83,* 187–194.

Graham, S., & Hudley, C. (2005). Race and ethnicity in the study of motivation and competence. In A. J. Elliot & C. S. Dweck (Eds.), *Handbook of competence and motivation* (pp. 392–413). New York: Guilford.

Graham, S., & Weiner, B. (1996). Theories and principles of motivation. In D. Berliner & R. Calfee (Eds.), *Handbook of educational psychology* (pp. 63–84). New York: Macmillan.

Guglielmo, T. (2003). *White on arrival: Italians, race, color and power in Chicago, 1890–1945.* New York: Oxford University Press.

Gutiérrez, K. (2004). *Rethinking education policy for English learners.* Washington, DC: Aspen Institute.

Gutierrez, K., Baquedano-Lopez, P., & Alvarez, H. (1999). A cultural-historical approach to collaboration: Building a culture of collaboration through hybrid language practices. *Theory into Practice, 38,* 87–93.

Gutierrez, K., Baquedano-Lopez, P., & Tejeda, C. (1999). Rethinking diversity: Hybridity and hybrid language practices in the Third Space. *Mind, Culture, and Activity, 6,* 286–303.

Gutierrez, K., & Rogoff, B. (2003). Cultural ways of learning: Individual traits or repertoires of practice. *Educational Researcher, 32*(5), 19–25.

Hacker, A. (1992). *Two nations: Black and White, separate, hostile, unequal.* New York: Scribner.

Hall, S., & Moats, L. (Eds.). (1989). *Straight talk about reading: How parents can make a difference during the early years.* Chicago: Contemporary Black Books, McGraw Hill.

Haller, E. J. (1985). Pupil race and elementary school ability grouping: Are teachers biased against Black children? *American Educational Research Journal, 22,* 465–483.

Hamilton, C. V. (1968). Race and education: A search for legitimacy. *Harvard Education Review, 38,* 669–684.

Harding, V. (1981). *There is a river: The Black struggle for freedom in America.* New York: Harcourt Brace Jovanovich.

Hatano, G., & Inagaki, K. (1986). Two courses of expertise. In H. W. Stevenson, H. Azuma, & K. Hakuta (Eds.), *Child development and education in Japan* (pp. 262-272). New York: Freeman.

Hatano, G., & Inagaki, K. (1987). Everyday biology and school biology: How do they interact? *Quarterly Newsletter of the Laboratory of Comparative Human Cognition, 9,* 120–128.

Helms, J. E., Jernigan, M., & Mascher, J. (2005). The meaning of race in psychology and how to change it: A methodological perspective. *American Psychologist, 60,* 27–36.

Hernstein, R., & Murray, C. (1994). *The bell curve: Intelligence and class structure in American life.* New York: Free Press.

Hess, R., & Shipman, V. (1965). Early experience and the socialization of cognitive modes in children. *Child Development, 36,* 869–886.

Hooper, P. K. (1996). "They have their own thoughts": A story of constructivist learning in an alternative African-centered community school. In Y. Kafai & M. Resnick (Eds.), *Constructionism in practice: Designing, thinking, and learning in a digital world* (pp. 241–255). Mahwah, NJ: Lawrence Erlbaum.

Hudley, C., & Graham, S. (2001). Stereotypes of achievement strivings among early adolescents. *Social Psychology of Education, 5,* 201–224.

Hughes, D. (2003). Correlates of African American and Latino parents' messages to children about ethnicity and race: A comparative study of racial socialization. *American Journal of Community Psychology, 31,* 15–33.

Hughes, D., & Chen, L. (1997). When and what parents tell children about race: An examination of race-related socialization among African American families. *Applied Developmental Science, 1,* 200–214.

Hughes, D., & Chen, L. (1999). The nature of parents' race-related communications to children: A developmental perspective. In L. Balter & C. S. Tamis-Lemonda (Eds.), *Child psychology: A handbook of contemporary issues* (pp. 467–490). Philadelphia: Psychology Press.

Hundley, M. G. (1965). *The Dunbar story (1870–1955).* New York: Vantage Press.

Hutchins, E. (1995). *Cognition in the wild.* Cambridge, MA: MIT Press.

Ignatiev, N. (1996). *How the Irish became White.* New York: Routledge.

Irvine, R. W., & Irvine, J. J. (1983). The impact of the desegregation process on the education of Black students: Key variables. *Journal of Negro Education, 52,* 410–422.

JBHE Foundation. (1999–2000). African immigrants in the United States are the nation's most highly educated group. *Journal of Blacks in Higher Education, 26,* 60–61.

Jencks, C. (1972). *Inequality: A reassessment of the effect of family and schooling in America.* New York: Basic Books.

Jones, F. C. (1981). *A traditional model of educational excellence: Dunbar High School of Little Rock, Arkansas.* Washington, DC: Howard University Press.

Jussim, L., Eccles, J., & Madon, S. (1996). Social perception, social stereotypes, and teacher expectations: Accuracy and the quest for the powerful self-fulfilling prophecy. *Advances in Experimental Social Psychology, 26,* 281–387.

Kao, G., & Tienda, M. (1995). Optimism and achievement: The educational performance of immigrant youth. *Social Science Quarterly, 76,* 1–19.

Kasinitz, P. (1992). *Caribbean New York: Black immigrants and the politics of race.* Ithaca, NY: Cornell University Press.

Kleinfeld, J. (1972). The relative importance of teachers and parents in the formation of Negro and White students' academic self-concepts. *Journal of Educational Research, 65,* 211–212.

Knight, G. P., Cota, M. K., & Bernal, M. E. (1993). The socialization of cooperative, competitive, and individualistic preferences among Mexican American children: The mediating role of ethnic identity. *Hispanic Journal of Behavioral Sciences, 15,* 291–300.

Kozol, J. (1991). *Savage inequalities.* New York: HarperCollins.

Kunda, Z. (1999). *Social cognition: making sense of people.* Cambridge, MA: MIT Press.

Labor, U. S. D. o. (1965). *The Negro family: The case for national action.* Washington, DC: U.S. Government Printing Office.

Ladson-Billings, G. (2004). Landing on the wrong note: The price we paid for Brown. *Educational Researcher, 33*(7), 3–13.

Ladson-Billings, G., & Tate, W. (1995). Toward a critical race theory of education. *Teachers College Record, 97,* 47–68.

Lakoff, G., & Nunez, R. (2000). *Where mathematics comes from: How the embodied mind brings mathematics into being.* New York: Basic Books.

Lareau, A. (2001). Linking Bourdieu's concept of capital to the broader field: The case of family-school relationships. In B. J. Biddle (Ed.), *Social class, poverty and education: Policy and practice* (pp. 77–100). New York: Routledge/Falmer.

Lareau, A., & Horvat, E. M. (1999). Moments of social inclusion and exclusion: Race, class and cultural capital in family-school relationships. *Sociology of Education, 72,* 37–53.

Lave, J., Murtaugh, M., & de la Rocha, O. (1984). The dialectic of arithmetic in grocery shopping. In B. Rogoff & J. Lave (Eds.), *Everyday cognition: Its development in social context* (pp. 67–94). Cambridge, MA: Harvard University Press.

Lee, C. D. (1994). The complexities of African centered pedagogy. In M. Shujaa (Ed.), *Too much schooling, too little education: A paradox in African-American life* (pp. 295–318). Trenton, NJ: Africa World Press.

Lee, C. D. (1995a). A culturally based cognitive apprenticeship: Teaching African American high school students' skills in literary interpretation. *Reading Research Quarterly, 30,* 608–631.

Lee, C. D. (1995b). Signifying as a scaffold for literary interpretation. *Journal of Black Psychology, 21,* 357–381.

Lee, C. D. (2001). Is October Brown Chinese: A cultural modeling activity system for under-achieving students. *American Educational Research Journal, 38,* 97–142.

Lee, C. D. (2004). Literacy in the academic disciplines and the needs of adolescent struggling readers. *Voices in Urban Education, 3,* 14–25.

Lee, C. D. (2007). *Culture, literacy and learning: Taking bloom in the midst of the whirlwind.* New York: Teachers College Press.

Lee, C. D. (2008). The centrality of culture to the scientific study of learning and development: How an ecological framework in educational research facilitates civic responsibility. *Educational Researcher, 37,* 267–279.

Lee, C. D., Spencer, M. B., & Harpalani, V. (2003). Every shut eye ain't sleep: Studying how people live culturally. *Educational Researcher, 32*(5), 6–13.

Levine, E. (1993). *Freedom's children: Young civil rights activists tell their own stories.* New York: Putnam Books for Young Readers.

Linn, M. C., Shear, L., Bell, P., & Slotta, J. D. (1999). Connecting school science with real science: A knowledge integration model of partnerships between teachers, scientists, and educators. *Educational Technology Research and Development, 47,* 61–84.

Lomawaima, K. T. (2004). Educating Native Americans. In J. Banks & C. Banks (Eds.), *Handbook of research on multicultural education* (2nd ed., pp. 441–461). San Francisco: Jossey-Bass.

Ma, L. (1999). *Knowing and teaching elementary mathematics.* Mahwah, NJ: Lawrence Erlbaum.

Mandara, J. (2006). The impact of family functioning on African American males' academic achievement: A review and clarification of the empirical literature. *Teachers College Record, 108*, 206–223.

Markus, H., & Kitayama, S. (1991). Culture and the self: Implications for cognition, emotion, and motivation. *Psychological Review, 98*, 224–253.

Marshall, S. (1995). Ethnic socialization of African American children: Implications for parenting, identity development and academic achievement. *Journal of Youth and Adolescence, 24*, 377–396.

Massey, D. (1990). American apartheid: Segregation and the making of the underclass. *American Journal of Sociology, 96*, 329–357.

Massey, D., & Denton, N. (1993). *American apartheid: Segregation and the making of the underclass.* Cambridge, MA: Harvard University Press.

McAdams, D. P., & Pals, J. L. (2006). A new Big Five: Fundamental principles for an integrative science of personality. *American Psychologist,* 204–217.

McLoyd, V. (1998). Children in poverty: Development, public policy and practice. In I. E. Sigel & A. Renninger (Eds.), *Handbook of child psychology: Social, emotional and personality development* (Vol. 4, pp. 135–210). New York: John Wiley.

Medin, D. L., & Altran, S. (Eds.). (1999). *Folk biology.* Cambridge, MA: Bradford.

Mercado, C. I., & Moll, L. (1997). The study of funds of knowledge: Collaborative research in Latino homes. *CENTRO, Journal of the Center for Puerto Rican Studies, 9*, 27–42.

Mills, C. W. (1997). *The racial contract.* Ithaca, NY: Cornell University Press.

Moll, L., & Gonzales, N. (2003). Engaging life: A funds of knowledge approach to multicultural education. In J. Banks & C. A. M. Banks (Eds.), *Handbook of research on multicultural education* (2nd ed., pp. 699-715). New York: Jossey-Bass.

Moses, R. P. (1994). The struggle for citizenship and math/sciences literacy. *Journal of Mathematical Behavior, 13*, 107–111.

Moses, R. P., & Cobb, C. E. (2001). *Radical equations: Math literacy and civil rights.* Boston: Beacon Press.

Moses, R. P., Kamii, M., Swap, S. M., & Howard, J. (1989). The Algebra Project: Organizing in the spirit of Ella. *Harvard Educational Review, 59*, 423–443.

Murray, C. B., & Mandara, J. (2003). An assessment of the relationship between racial socialization, racial identity and self-esteem in African American adolescents. In D. A. Azibo (Ed.), *Africa-centered psychology* (pp. 293–325). Durham, NC: Carolina Academic Press.

Muschinske, D. (1977). The nonwhite as child: G. Stanley Hall on the education of nonwhite peoples. *Journal of the History of the Behavioral Sciences, 13*, 328–336.

Nasir, N. (2000). "Points ain't everything": Emergent goals and average and percent understandings in the play of basketball among African American students. *Anthropology and Education, 31*, 283–305.

Nasir, N., Hand, V., & Taylor, E. (2008). Culture and mathematics in school: Boundaries between "cultural" and "domain" knowledge in the mathematics classroom and beyond. *Review of Research in Education, 32*, 187–240.

Nasir, N., Rosebery, A. S., Warren, B., & Lee, C. D. (2006). Learning as a cultural process: Achieving equity through diversity. In K. Sawyer (Ed.), *Handbook of the learning sciences* (pp. 489-506). New York: Cambridge University Press.

Nasir, N., & Saxe, G. (2003). Emerging tensions and their management in the lives of minority students. *Educational Researcher, 32*(5), 14–18.

National Research Council. (1999). *Equity and adequacy in education finance: Issues and perspectives.* Washington, DC: National Research Council Committee on Education Finance.

Neblett, E. W., Philip, C. L., Cogburn, C. D., & Sellers, R. (2006). African American adolescents' discrimination experiences and academic achievement: Racial socialization as a cultural compensatory and protective factor. *Journal of Black Psychology, 32*, 199–218.

Nesbitt, R. (1998). Race, genetics, and IQ. In C. Jencks & M. Phillips (Eds.), *The Black-White test score gap* (pp. 86-102). Washington, DC: Brookings Institute.

Nieto, S. (2000). *Puerto Rican students in U.S. schools.* Mahwah, NJ: Lawrence Erlbaum.

Noblit, G., & Dempsey, V. (1996). *The social construction of virtue: The moral life of schools.* Albany: State University of New York Press.

Oakes, J. (1985). *Keeping track: How schools structure inequality.* New Haven, CT: Yale University Press.

Oakes, J. (1990). *Multiplying inequalities: The effects of race, social class and teaching.* Santa Monica, CA: Rand.

Orellana, M. (2009). *Translating immigrant childhoods: Children's work as culture and language brokers.* New Brunswick, NJ: Rutgers University Press.

Orellana, M., & Eksner, H. (2006). Power in cultural modeling: Building on the bilingual language practices of immigrant youth in Germany and the United States. *National Reading Conference Yearbook, 55,* 224–234.

Orellana, M., & Reynolds, J. (2008). Cultural modeling: leveraging bilingual skills for school paraphrasing tasks. *Reading Research Quarterly, 43,* 48–65.

Orellana, M., Reynolds, J., Dorner, L., & Meza, M. (2003). In other words: Translating or "para-phrasing" as a family literacy practice in immigrant households. *Reading Research Quarterly, 38,* 12–34.

Orfield, G. E., S. (1996). *Dismantling desegregation: The quiet reversal of Brown v Board of Education.* New York: The New Press.

Organization for Economic Cooperation and Development. (2004). *Learning for tomorrow's world: First results from PISA 2003.* Paris: Author.

Ou, Y., & McAdoo, H. P. (1993). Socialization of Chinese American children. In H. P. McAdoo (Ed.), *Family ethnicity: Strength in diversity* (pp. 245–270). Thousand Oaks, CA: Sage.

Palincsar, A. S., & Brown, A. (1984). Reciprocal teaching of comprehension-fostering and comprehension-monitoring strategies. *Cognition and Instruction, 2,* 73–109.

Patillo, M. (1999). *Black picket fences: Privilege and peril among the Black middle class.* Chicago: University of Chicago Press.

Payne, C., & Strickland, C. (2008). *Teach freedom: Education for liberation in the African-American tradition.* New York: Teachers College Press.

Pea, R. D., & Gomez, L. (1992). Distributed multimedia learning environments. *Interactive Learning Environments, 2,* 73–109.

Perkins, D. (1992). *Smart schools: Better thinking and learning for every child.* New York: Free Press.

Perkins, D. (1995). *Outsmarting IQ: The emerging science of learnable intelligence.* New York: Free Press.

Phelan, P., Davidson, A. L., & Cao, H. T. (1991). Students' multiple worlds: Negotiating the boundaries of family, peer, and school cultures. *Anthropology & Education Quarterly, 22,* 224–250.

Phinney, J. (1990). Ethnic identity in adolescents and adults. *Psychological Bulletin, 108,* 499–514.

Phinney, J., & Chavira, V. (1995). Parental ethnic socialization and adolescent coping with problems related to ethnicity. *Journal of Research on Adolescence, 5,* 31–53.

Piaget, J. (1952). *The origins of intelligence in children* (M. Cook, Trans.). New York: International Universities Press.

Pinkard, N. (1999). Lyric reader: Architecture for creating intrinsically motivating and culturally relevant reading environments. *Interactive Learning Environments, 7*(1), 1-30.

Pollard, S. (1993). Gender, achievement and African American students' perceptions of their school experience. *Educational Psychologist, 28,* 341–356.

Portes, A., & Rumbaut, R. (2001). *Legacies: The story of the immigrant second generation.* New York: Russell Sage Foundation.

Radinsky, J., Smolin, L. I., & Lawless, K. (2005). Collaborative curriculum design as a vehicle for professional development. In C. Vrasidas & G. Glass (Eds.), *Preparing teachers to teach with technology: Current perspectives on applied information technologies* (pp. 369–380). Greenwich, CT: Information Age.

Ramani, A. K., Gilbertson, L., & Fox, M. A. (2007). *Status and trends in the education of racial and ethnic minorities.* Washington, DC: Institute of Education Sciences National Center for Education Statistics.

Reiser, B., Tabak, I., Sandoval, W., Smith, B., Steinmuller, F., & Leone, T. J. (2001). BeGuile: Strategic and conceptual scaffolds for scientific inquiry in biology classrooms. In S. M. Carver & D. Klahr (Eds.), *Cognition and instruction: Twenty five years of progress* (pp. 263-305). Mahwah, NJ: Lawrence Erlbaum.

Rist, R. (1970). Student social class and teacher expectations: The self-fulfilling prophecy in ghetto education. *Harvard Educational Review, 40,* 411–451.

Rogoff, B. (2003). *The cultural nature of human development.* New York: Oxford University Press.

Rogoff, B. (Ed.). (2002). How can we study cultural aspects of human development [Special Issue]. *Human Development, 45.*

Romero, A. J., & Roberts, R. E. (1998). Perception of discrimination and ethno-cultural variables in a diverse group of adolescents. *Journal of Adolescence, 21,* 641–656.

Rong, X. L., & Brown, F. (2001). The effects of immigrant generation and ethnicity on educational attainment among young African and Caribbean Blacks in the United States. *Harvard Educational Review, 7,* 536–565.

Rong, X. L., & Brown, F. (2002). Socialization, culture, and identities of Black immigrant children: What educators need to know and do. *Education and Urban Society, 34,* 247–273.

Rosebery, A. S., Warren, B., Ballenger, C., & Ogonowski, M. (2005). The generative potential of students' everyday knowledge in learning science. In T. Romberg, T. Carpenter, & D. Fae (Eds.), *Understanding mathematics and science matters* (pp. 55-80). Mahwah, NJ: Lawrence Erlbaum.

Rosebery, A. S., Warren, B., & Conant, F. R. (1992). Appropriating scientific discourse: Findings from language minority classrooms. *Journal of Learning Sciences, 2,* 61–94.

Rosenshine, B., & Meister, C. (1994). Reciprocal teaching: A review of the research. *Review of Educational Research, 64,* 479–530.

Rumelhart, D. (1980). Schemata: The building blocks of cognition. In R. Spiro, B. Bruce, & W. Brewer (Eds.), *Theoretical issues in reading comprehension: Perspectives from cognitive psychology, linguistics, artificial intelligence and education* (pp. 33–58). Hillsdale, NJ: Lawrence Erlbaum.

Sarich, V., & Miele, F. (2004). *Race: The reality of human differences.* Cambridge, MA: Westview.

Saxe, G. (1999). Cognition, development and cultural practices. In E. Turiel (Ed.), *Culture and development: New directions in child psychology* (pp. 19-35). San Francisco: Jossey-Bass.

Schwartz, D., & Nasir, N. (2004). Transfer of learning. *Encyclopedia of Education 4,* 1449–1452.

Shaw, A. (1996). Social constructionism and the inner city: Designing environments for social development and urban renewal. In Y. Kafai & M. Resnick (Eds.), *Constructionism in practice: Designing, thinking, and learning in a digital world* (pp. 175–206). Mahwah, NJ: Lawrence Erlbaum.

Siddle-Walker, E. V. (1993). Caswell County Training School, 1933–1969: Relationships between community and school. *Harvard Educational Review, 63,* 161–182.

Siddle-Walker, E. V. (1996). *Their highest potential: An African-American school community in the segregated South.* Chapel Hill: University of North Carolina Press.

Siddle-Walker, E. V. (2000). Valued segregated schools for African American children in the South, 1935–1969: A review of common themes and characteristics. *Review of Educational Research, 70,* 253–285.

Simmons, R. L., Murray, V., McLoyd, V., Lin, K., Cutrona, C., & Conger, R. D. (2002). Discrimination, crime, ethnic identity, and parenting as correlates of depressive symptoms among African American children: A multilevel analysis. *Development and Psychopathology, 14,* 371–393.

Smith-Maddox, R. (1999). The social networks and resources of African American eighth graders: Evidence from the National Education Longitudinal Study of 1988. *Adolescence, 34,* 169–183.

Smitherman, G. (1977). *Talkin and testifyin: The language of Black America.* Boston: Houghton Mifflin.

Smitherman, G. (2000). Ebonics, King, and Oakland: Some folks don't believe fat meat is greasy. In G. Smitherman (Ed.), *Talkin that talk: Language, culture and education in African America* (pp. 150–162). New York: Routledge.

Sowell, T. (1974). Black excellence: The case of Dunbar High School. *Public Interest, 35,* 1–21.

Sowell, T. (1976). Patterns of black excellence. *Public Interest, 43,* 26–58.

Spencer, M. B. (1987). Black children's ethnic identity formation: Risk and resilience in caste like minorities. In J. Phinney & M. Rotheram (Eds.), *Children's ethnic socialization: Pluralism and development* (pp. 103–116). Newbury Park, CA: Sage.

Spencer, M. B. (1999). Social and cultural influences on school adjustment: The application of an identity-focused cultural ecological perspective. *Educational Psychologist, 34,* 43–57.

Spencer, M. B. (2000). Identity, achievement orientation and race: "Lessons learned" about the normative developmental experiences of African American males. In W. H. Watkins, J. H. Lewis, & V. Chou (Eds.), *Race and education: The roles of history and society in educating African American students* (pp. 100-127). Needham Heights, MA: Allyn & Bacon.

Spencer, M. B. (2006). Phenomenology and ecological systems theory: Development of diverse groups. In W. Damon & R. M. Lerner (Eds.), *Handbook of child psychology* (6th ed., Vol. 1, pp. 829–893). New York: John Wiley.

Spencer, M. B. (2008). Lessons learned and opportunities ignored since Brown v. Board of Education: Youth development and the myth of a color-blind society. *Educational Researcher, 37,* 253–266.

Spencer, M. B., Dobbs, B., & Swanson, D. P. (1988). African American adolescents: Adaptational processes and socioeconomic diversity in behavioral outcomes. *Journal of Adolescence, 11,* 117–137.

Spencer, M. B., Dupree, D., & Hartmann, T. (1997). A phenomenological variant of ecological systems theory (PVEST): A self-organization perspective in context. *Development and Psychopathology, 9,* 317–833.

Spencer, M. B., Fegley, S., & Dupree, D. (2006). Investigating and linking social conditions of African-American children and adolescents with emotional well-being. *Ethnicity and Disease, 16,* 63–67.

Spencer, M. B., Harpalani, V., Cassidy, E., Jacobs, C., Donde, S., & Goss, T. N. (2006). Understanding vulnerability and resilience from a normative development perspective: Implications for racially and ethnically diverse youth. In D. Cicchetti & E. Cohen (Eds.), *Handbook of developmental psychopathology* (pp. 627-672). Hoboken, NJ: John Wiley.

Spencer, M. B., & Markstrom-Adams, C. (1990). Identity processes among racial and ethnic minority children in America. *Child Development, 61,* 290–310.

Steele, C. M. (2004). A threat in the air: How stereotypes shape intellectual identity and performance. In J. Banks & C. Banks (Eds.), *Handbook of research on multicultural education* (2nd ed., pp. 682–698). San Francisco: Jossey-Bass.

Stevenson, H. W., & Stigler, J. W. (1992). *The learning gap: Why our schools are failing and what we can learn from Japanese and Chinese education.* New York: Simon & Schuster.

Stotsky, S. (1999). *Losing our language: How multicultural classroom instruction is undermining our children's ability to read, write, and reason.* New York: Free Press.

Strickland, B. (1989). Internal-external control expectancies: From contingency to creativity. *American Psychologist, 44*, 1–12.

Suárez-Orozco, C., & Qin, D. B. (2004). The cultural psychology of academic engagement: Immigrant boys' experiences in U.S. schools. In N. Way & J. Chu (Eds.), *Adolescent boys in context* (pp. 295-317). New York: New York University Press.

Super, C., & Harkness, S. (1986). The developmental niche: A conceptualization at the interface of child and culture. *International Journal of Behavioral Development, 9*, 545–569.

Taylor, A. Z., & Graham, S. (2007). An examination of the relationship between achievement values and perceptions of barriers among low-SES African American and Latino students. *Journal of Educational Psychology, 99*, 52–64.

Taylor, D. L., Biafora, F. A., & Warheit, G. J. (1994). Racial mistrust and disposition to deviance among African American, Haitian, and other Caribbean Island adolescent boys. *Law and Human Behavior, 18*, 291–303.

The Education Trust. (2000, May). *Dispelling the myth . . . over time.* Washington, DC: Author.

Tyack, D. (1974). *The one best system: A history of American urban education.* Cambridge, MA: Harvard University Press.

Valdes, G. (2001). *Learning and not learning English: Latino students in American schools.* New York: Teachers College Press.

Valdes, G. (2002). *Expanding the definitions of giftedness: The case of young interpreters from immigrant countries.* Mahwah, NJ: Lawrence Erlbaum.

Valenzuela, A. (1999). Gender roles and settlement activities among children and their immigrant families. *American Behavioral Scientist, 42*, 720–742.

Velez-Ibañez, C., & Greenberg, J. B. (2004). Formation and transformation of Funds of Knowledge. In N. Gonzales, L. Moll, & C. Amanti (Eds.), *Funds of Knowledge: Theorizing practices in households, communities, and classrooms.* New York: Routledge.

Vickerman, M. (1999). *Crosscurrents: West Indian immigrants and race.* Oxford, UK: Oxford University.

Walker, C. H. (1987). Relative importance of domain knowledge and overall aptitude on acquisition of domain-related knowledge. *Cognition and Instruction, 4*, 25–42.

Warren, B., Ballenger, C., Ogonowski, M., Rosebery, A. S., & Hudicourt-Barnes, J. (2001). Rethinking diversity in learning science: The logic of everyday sense-making. *Journal of Research in Science Teaching, 38*, 529–552.

Waters, M. C. (1991). The role of lineage in identity formation among Black Americans. *Qualitative Sociology, 14*, 57–76.

Waters, M. C. (1994). Ethnic and racial identities of second-generation Black immigrants in New York City. *International Migration Review, 28*, 795–820.

Weiner, B. (1985). An attributional theory of achievement motivation and emotion. *Psychological Review, 92*, 548–573.

Weinstein, R. S. (1985). Student mediation of classroom expectancy effects. In J. B. Dusek (Ed.), *Teacher expectancies* (pp. 329-350). Hillsdale, NJ: Lawrence Erlbaum.

Weisner, T. S. (1984). Ecocultural niches of middle childhood: A cross-cultural perspective. In W. A. Collins (Ed.), *Development during middle childhood: The years from six to twelve* (pp. 335–369). Washington, DC: National Academy of Sciences Press.

Weisner, T. S. (2002). Ecocultural understanding of children's developmental pathways. *Human Development, 174*, 275–281.

Wells, A. S., Holme, J. J., Revilla, A. T., & Atanda, A. K. (2004). How society failed school desegregation policy: Looking past the schools to understand them. *Review of Research in Education, 28*, 47–99.

Wells, T. T. (1969). The effects of discrimination upon motivation and achievement of Black children in urban ghetto schools. *American Behavioral Scientist, 12*, 26–33.

Wigfield, A., & Eccles, J. (2002). The development of competence beliefs, expectancies for success, and achievement values from childhood through adolescence. In A. Wigfield & J. Eccles (Eds.), *Development of achievement motivation* (pp. 92-115). San Diego, CA: Academic Press.

Williamson, J. A., Rhodes, L., & Dunson, M. (2007). A selected history of social justice in education. *Review of Research in Education, 31,* 195–224.

Wollenberg, C. (1976). *All deliberate speed: Segregation and exclusion in California schools, 1855–1975.* Berkeley: University of California Press.

Wong, C. A., Eccles, J., & Sameroff, A. (2003). The influence of ethnic discrimination and ethnic identification on African American adolescents' school and socioemotional adjustment. *Journal of Personality 7,* 1197–1232.

Zaphir, F. (1996). *Haitian immigrants in Black America: A sociological and sociolinguistic portrait.* Westport, CT: Bergin & Garvey.

Zimmerman, M. A., Bingenheimer, J. B., & Notaro, P. C. (2002). Natural mentors and adolescent resiliency: A study with urban youth. *American Journal of Community Psychology, 30,* 221–243.

Chapter 4

Race and Class in a Culture of Risk

RAY MCDERMOTT
Stanford University

JASON D. RALEY
University of California, Santa Barbara

INGRID SEYER-OCHI
University of California, Berkeley

Studies of race, class, and educational risk often proceed in an established but misleading order: First, race is defined as a trait given at birth and turned into trouble by prejudice and unequal conditions; then, class is defined as traits socialized into children with diminished socioeconomic opportunities; finally, risk is treated as the result of children being damaged by racism and class disadvantage. The order shapes an easy but misleading argument: Because race and class inequities suppress normal growth and development, minority and poor children are most at risk of disabilities and school failure. The diagnosis of risk is embedded in cultural preoccupations and circumstances that, because rarely specified, invite a general bias: White, middle-class lives offer children the best of all worlds. The message to educators: Fix the children, and race and class barriers can be overcome one person at a time.[1] By this mainline of reason, to organize classroom activities for access to success, teachers must remediate the effects of race and class on individual children.

This chapter is not a traditional review of the literature but a critical look at the issues of race and class as they are embedded in discourses of risk. Our discussion should complicate the procedures, conclusions, and implications of educational research by treating race and class as social activities: not race and class as what people are, but race and class as what people do to each other. A shadow topic of learning disabilities (LD) receives occasional mention. Race, class, and disability, if treated as traits—we prefer the word *situations*—are statistically related to each other (Artiles, 2003; Artiles, Klinger, & Tate, 2006), and some analysts think they are related causally. We, on the other hand, acknowledge only that the social activities

Review of Research in Education
March 2009, Vol. 33, pp. 101-116
DOI: 10.3102/0091732X08327163
© 2009 AERA. http://rre.aera.net

of noticing or labeling a person as, say, Latino, increase the chances of labeling the same person poor and/or LD. All three labels allow people to be caught or acquired by a collective representation enforced by convention and conversation.[2] Although we emphasize the nuanced production of the race and class labels people use to catch each other, similarities in the logic of race and class talk, on one hand, and disability labeling, on the other, deserve notice.

We offer three studies disrupting easy conceptual ties among race, class, and education in a culture of risk: one on the risks of talking about race in school settings, a second on risky race and class borders between neighborhoods, and a third on building school environments in which students can forcefully confront race and class borders without too much risk. Each study, and so each section of this chapter, begins with situated versions of race and class, seeks analytic methods focused on how people collectively produce success and failure, and finds responsibility for inequalities in ever-emerging situations in which risks, winners, losers, races, and classes are locally produced and ameliorated in varying proportions. Our goal is to display how race and class differences are acted on by people in social relationships with each other, on one hand, but made consequential in risk-embedded situations staged by the wider population, on the other.

Although race and class are two of the most pressing facts in American society, analytically and politically, they are facts more about the whole society than about isolated individuals. Confusion on this point distorts the task facing educators. Research on race and class as traits can divert attention from the risk-loaded activities, experiences, and histories for which the words became salient. One cannot belong to a race, class, or disability group alone; they are all relational terms, and everyone in the culture is somehow involved in their expression. Failure to specify the circumstances of race, class, and disability—as if they could operate on their own, as if environments were mere decorations—ignores the up-close risks and ranks of American culture and obscures the built-in background of actual activities where risk is staged. At play in every race- and class-relevant moment, there are ongoing histories of subjugation, hierarchical structures of opportunity, an incessantly competitive market, and a culture that stages endless rituals of risk along with promises of fleeting achievement—conditions ironically enacted even by good educators trying to make race and class less negatively consequential.

Risk rituals dominate American life, not just for the minority or poor but for everyone. Risk lives in immediate environments, in next-door neighbors, next-seat students, and next-race and next-social class job applicants. Studies that make the life and times of risk a primary analytic fact conceive of race and class as simultaneously the problem, method, and product of skillful practices among people in pressing circumstances. Novelists have delivered the most nuanced portrayals of the ups and downs of race and class practices in capitalist states over the last 2 centuries (for analytic displays, see Kaufmann, 1995; Tratner, 2001), and recent ethnographies of education in and out of school have delivered more analytic versions of the same drama.[3] Together, they tell a story. The story is that when called on, Americans must display inherent worth and ability and/or enforce degradation and disability as strategic moves: up the system for the few, down the system for the rest.[4] Even for the majority who seem set in the same positions their parents occupied a generation before, risk is everywhere. In a culture that promises equality but delivers hierarchy, everyone is risk rich, everyone a victim and a perpetrator. Race and class differences are the traditional (and LD the most recent) resources, weapons, and propped-up consequences in the struggle of all against all. At play in every risky moment: everyone.

RACE AND RISK IN EDUCATION

Inquiries into educational risk usually conceive race as a personal trait consequential for a child's learning. Directly racist accounts theorize outcomes as the effect of biological inheritance: most infamously, racial differences in intelligence. More egalitarian accounts stress how racial minorities suffer diminished access to social and cultural resources, but unless supported by an aggressive political stand, these might just as well be blatantly racist. The first puts educational failure on biology, the second on society, but both use race as a naturally occurring fact, an independent variable, to support the arguments.

Biological anthropologists have been dismissing race as a descriptive category for more than a century (Baker, 1998; Smedley, 2007), but it remains a robust identity tag (for a summary and an American/South African comparison, see Fredrickson, 1997, 2002; Bowker & Star, 1999). Categories of racial classification, from Linnaeus's five (white, black, yellow, red, and other) to 20th-century taxonomies with hundreds of entries, have flimsy borders. Americans achieve rough consistency by isolating a few physical traits and treating them, in proportions convenient to the situation, as markers of racial identity (the same logic applies to the diagnosis of LD). Educational researchers rely on these flimsy categories as units of analysis.[5] A better strategy asks about the social contexts and political uses of racial terms.

First as a teacher, then as a researcher, Mica Pollock (2004) observed students, teachers, administrators, and others using and not using race labels in and about Columbus High. Her achievement: She shows when race is the subject not talked about; that is, she gives enough detail on how school personnel talk to determine when race is the topic at hand even when it is not directly mentioned.[6] For example, although race must be talked about in a district office meeting on achievement gaps, race labels are avoided at school faculty meetings on the disproportionate number of African American students wandering the halls during class or not graduating at year's end. The silences are systematic and reveal a concern for race and rank as dangerous; behavior aimed at altering the plight of students can become new occasions for racism and/or accusations of racism.

The fears are played out against every school's preoccupation with assessment and embarrassment at differential performances across groups, and speakers respond with silences, clichés, or complaints designed to reduce risk. Differential performances across racial groups can be measured and discussed objectively on formal occasions but are addressed as racial by teachers only in informal conversations. Figure 1,

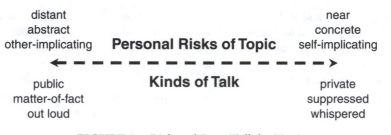

FIGURE 1   Risk and Race Talk by Topic

roughly based on Pollock (2004), shows a general pattern of talk and topic. As long as a topic remains distant and abstract and implicates only those not present, people address race matter-of-factly and out loud. As a topic moves closer to home, refers to local events, and has implications for speakers, race is limited to whisper.

Similarly, the details of race talk depend on whom one is speaking as, to whom one is speaking, and who else might be listening and judging. Figure 2 is stimulated by Pollock's (2004) representation of race and rank in talk about race-relevant topics. Educators and students who share race and rank generally use race labels matter-of-factly. Race talk up and down the hierarchy (e.g., between principal and teacher or between teacher and student) can be difficult, even if it occurs in private; so too is race talk between teachers of different race groups. Sharing neither race nor rank, participants use race labels to fuel accusations across the dividing categories. Students accuse teachers of racial injustice, principals demand reform from teachers, and superintendents assign blame to whole schools for racial differentials in achievement. When pressed, participants can almost always find ways not to talk about race.

Life is never as simple as a 2 × 2 figure or table. Topics shift quickly, and group membership moves around easily among students. By Pollock's stories, people are constantly figuring out who's who in relation to whom, and race talk is moved in and out accordingly. If race talk is an effective strategy for reckoning relative position in a group of speakers, it is because they make it so. Race talk can go badly, even for those trying directly to make it otherwise (Lin, 2007). Depending on who remembers and reports what is said, how, to whom, and under what conditions, race talk can be a little or a big problem, an immediate or a long later problem.[7] Teachers at Columbus find themselves stuttering, pausing, hedging, and complaining. It is difficult to speak truth in race terms. Race in a culture of risk is a resource in the calculation of who wins, who loses, who moves up, who moves on, and who moves to the back. Education is a risky game, and the race card, like the LD card, gets played accordingly.

Recognizing the cultural play of race categories tied to school performance does not make racial problems easy to fix, but it shifts responsibility to the gatekeepers who make racial struggles institutionally consequential (Ladson-Billings, 2006;

	SAME or SIMILAR position	DIFFERENT position
SAME race group	matter-of-fact	uneasy
DIFFERENT race group	uneasy	rare

FIGURE 2   Risk and Race Talk by Relations Among Participants

Morrison, 1992). Analyzing race as a work-a-day construction or fiction does not make race not real. The adjective *real* makes a misleading contrast with preceding or transcending ordinary human activities. Ethnographic studies of the uses and consequences of race in social practice bow to its political reality by locating it at work.[8] Race is never before or outside of current engagements. Race is locally produced for everyone to see, feel, occasionally expose, and mostly keep quiet about, except at times prearranged and tightly scripted enough to not make a difference (as in policy discussions). The unit of analysis is not anyone's race but the high-risk stakes that keep performance differentials and degradation rituals racialized and generally unspoken. Anyone entering an American school has to learn how to talk about race. It is an activity fraught with risk to the extent it overlaps with success, failure, and access to the rewards of the wider society.

CLASS AS RISK IN EDUCATION: FROM POVERTY TO NEIGHBORHOOD

Both race and class identify traits seemingly consequential for a child's educational potential, but they are operated on differently. Race is easy to articulate but often silenced or turned into trouble (the latter sometimes productively so). Class, in contrast, is difficult to articulate; it is a third-person ascription more than a term of self-reference (first person) or address (second person). A simple two-part concept of social class (Marx's owners and workers—with no middle class) has rarely fueled the American imagination, and class warfare looks more like an occasional prizefight put on for ritualized public proclamations.[9]

School failure correlates well with poverty. The situation screams out for explanation but receives mostly accusations: that poor children cannot think straight for the problems on their minds, that their parents have no time to spend or no knowledge to impart, or that people in poor neighborhoods are unmotivated and have little sense of what the world offers. Even studies trying to contradict deprivation theories— studies showing how wonderful the children are—support the usual stereotypes by accepting the dichotomies that frame the arguments: smart/dumb, middle class/poor, enabled/disabled, and so on (McDermott & Varenne, 2006; Wacquant, 2002). Statistics are gathered and predictions made. The correlations hold. New data are tweaked, old explanations reframed, new ones formulated, but not much changes. The bell curve tolls for every new generation of poor children with rarely a mention of those who succeed at the expense of the poor: for example, auto factory executives at the expense of the unemployed or the SAT rich at the expense of the SAT weak. Risk is everywhere responded to by individuals but rarely addressed collectively.

Limiting public knowledge of the poor to school performances hides their capacities and achievements and allows the lazy assumption that an absence of middle-class things (e.g., books, computers, travel, tutors, and coffeehouses) degrades intelligent thought. Because school is demanding, as if the rest of life were not, educators claim authority to sort by ability. A better view appreciates the survival knowledge required of children and parents with little leeway in the dance of social structure. School is not so much harder, as it is well designed to sort. Poverty has become a balance point for individual identity and a measurable determinant of aptitude and ability. Educational and social policy has investigated poverty without a corresponding critique of those who profit and succeed (Katz, 1997; Schram, 1995), and the well-off have successfully avoided detection. The poor now face two problems. One is not having access to material and cultural resources and connections; the other is to be constantly probed and degraded by explanations officially designed to help. This is an old tradition (Ranciere, 2004) but particularly complex in societies claiming democracy. Can educators and researchers address the plight of poor children without making things worse? Answer: not without taking responsibility for their privileged positions in the cycle of competition and risk.

Neighborhoods offer a productive focus for making class visible. The concept of neighborhood is blatantly collective and twice so. Neighborhoods are defined by their borders—both sides of their borders—and survive on the pathways that connect and constrain them.[10] A focus on neighborhoods should remind researchers to examine both sides and to resist the analyses of one kind of person at a time. Across borders, neighborhoods harbor the full round of economic life. Teachers and poor children, for example, generally live on opposite sides of school borders. Neighborhoods are vibrant, alive at the edges—undeniably part of larger structures of production, consumption, and distribution—and organize the full press of current circumstances right down into the vocal cords (Rampton, 2005). Lively, contested, and sometimes profitable border crossings should be a first consideration for policy researchers.

Educational research has focused on isolated children, but homes, stores, and parks animate and constrain their lives. Insight comes with zooming the analytic gaze into the moment-to-moment organization of children's activities, while simultaneously zooming out into the traffic of people, goods, and ideas that shape the sensuous lives of neighborhoods—into their "inhabitus" (Varenne & McDermott, 1998). Analytically, neighborhoods require focus even as they expand one's questions. Examining the local production of risk in a neighborhood requires both a deep description of people's engagements with each other and expansive accounts of the political and economic forces beyond the line of sight or insight available to most participants (Bartlett, Hart, Satterthwaite, de la Barra, & Missair, 1999). Without looking both in and out, porous and vibrant borders can be mistakenly (or politically and thereby invidiously) conceived as rigid, with each side a nowhere to the other. A ghetto label can be used against a people. Looking simultaneously in and out keeps the mutual constitution of borders at the center of analysis.

School achievement is easy to plot by neighborhood variables. The achievement gap is literal. It exists only incidentally in the skill sets of children and more actively in the gaps that divide urban neighborhoods from each other and from suburban and rural areas. In ways various but relentless, every city has major borderlines dividing it into two rough halves (in a big city, many times over). With each border, one side is filled with school failure, the other with school success. Consider MacArthur Boulevard separating the Hills from the Flats in Oakland, the 40-foot rock wall keeping Columbia University's White Upper Westside from Harlem, or the eight-lane highway dividing well-to-do Palo Alto from the struggling minority city of East Palo Alto. These obvious structural barriers are also porous, and because they are porous, they are both defended and carefully crisscrossed by participants on both sides. The specifics vary most immediately by time of day and almost imperceptibly by shifts in real estate demands.

We turn now to San Francisco's six-lane Geary Boulevard sealing off Japantown and Pacific Heights from the Fillmore. Seyer-Ochi (2006) describes the race and class history of San Francisco through a study of one neighborhood as a web of relationships across the surrounding city (in the traditions of Basso, 1996; Hayden, 1996; Nespor, 1997; Rosaldo & Flores, 1997; Zerubavel, 2003). As a long-term teacher and researcher, she worked for 6 years with four students whose lives revealed a network of families, friends, jobs, churches, stores, and gangs with which they had to deal. All four youths and most of their peers were also caught in the web of labeling, sorting, and risk that is special education. Some were directly caught by LD diagnoses, and others were in remedial classes. The risk of disability caught them all.

Her ethnography of neighborhoods shows how, in daily trips to and from school, her students encounter a full run of risky environments that can limit their institutional horizons. After-school jobs and family responsibilities across the city make life complex. Minds do not go to school alone but emerge from put-upon homes, go through competing neighborhoods, and land in schools that impose a competitive structuring of their own. (Thus, LD: a way to do race and class without talking about race and class.) The mind's road to learning is more about roads than minds.

Seyer-Ochi's (2006) ethnographic atlas of space, place, and movement in and around the Fillmore portrays her participants as less risky or personally at risk than as constantly immersed in risky circumstances produced and nurtured by a citywide division of labor, opportunity, debt, crime, and levels of enforcement. She documents the organization of opportunity and risk not just in the Fillmore, but miles away in the halls and classrooms of Jefferson High and along the streets of San Francisco. To outsiders, risk is always everywhere in the Fillmore. To insiders, risk is ever ready across all neighborhoods. Her maps identify key institutions, practices, and actors staging risk rituals. The homicide rate in the Fillmore is among the highest in the city, particularly for young African American males. Media and police surveillance focus on the neighborhood's key corners, most of them known for active drug sales by young men in the service of passersby (many of them outsiders from other neighborhoods). Labels abound—the corners are risky, the youth criminal—but the maps overwhelm the labels with detail. The distribution of key institutions demands an account of their relation to each other and the people involved. As the social network gets better described, the individuals and even the corners begin to recede from view.

Consider the convenience and liquor stores that dot the Fillmore landscape more than in other neighborhoods. They are no mere backdrop for the activities that unfold day and night at the nearby "key corners;" they are full participants. How did they get there, and how are they related to other institutions in the neighborhood and beyond? With no large-scale shopping malls or few food chain stores nearby, the small stores offer necessities to shoppers and possibilities for small-business owners. Many of the stores are situated at the main gates of the low-income housing projects concentrated in the heart of the Fillmore, thanks to an aggressive urban redevelopment plan a half-century ago. The analytic question shifts from who is involved in the stores and key corners to who is not involved. Everyone participates: city planners, housing developers, media, police officers, store owners, delivery truck drivers, drug dealers, residents, students, peers, and the passersby. Risk is staged by all hands.

The neighborhood stage extends across borders into classrooms miles away. It draws all the students at Jefferson into its rituals. Seyer-Ochi (2006) collected city and neighborhood maps from an entire Jefferson senior class. Figure 3 is a telling example drawn by Raisa, a Fillmore student, who sketched San Francisco's primary neighborhoods and defining landmarks. More than 15% of the Jefferson student body commuted from the Fillmore, but Raisa does not note the area on her map. She marks other key neighborhoods, many in risk-laden ways. The Mission (a core Latino community) shows stick figures in a holdup, "Give me your money!" Hunters Point, another African American neighborhood, shows one figure telling another, "Let's do a drive by today!" Race and class are ever at work. Raisa sat every day at Jefferson alongside students from the Fillmore, Mission, and Hunters Point areas. Along with their peers, teachers, and families, the students collectively produced risk and opportunity in their moment-by-moment interactions. Race and class are always getting worked on, worked in, worked out, worked through, worked over, and overworked. This work is in everyone's face—in everyone's face-to-face—and far from random. In the segregated, tracked classrooms at Jefferson, it reproduces the hierarchies of educational access, while across the city, it responds to and re-creates slippery, risky borders and boundaries of neighborhoods.

Anyone crossing neighborhood borders in American cities finds outs out that class, although well patterned, refers to emergent and situated activities presented, manipulated, and enforced across persons in social interaction. Every move is fraught with class relevance on both sides of every border. Although it is no surprise that specific packages of attire and comportment slot children into various levels of hierarchy in schools, it is important, says Seyer-Ochi, to recognize and reorganize the role of all parties to every occasion of academic and social risk.

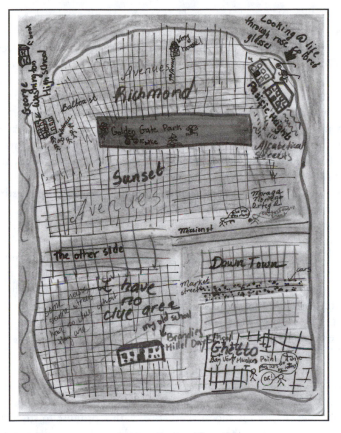

FIGURE 3   Raisa's Map
Source. Seyer (2002).

BEYOND THE USUAL VIEW OF CLASS AND RACE AS RISK

American schools run on risk and competition. It is the first fact for children going to school in a market designed for the few to lord over the many and a culture that makes desires and achievements dependent on the deficits and deficiencies of others (Henry, 1963; Varenne & McDermott, 1998). A too-easy focus on race, class, and LD as traits obscures the invisible demands of the political economy from those who are operating on it, worrying about it, talking about it, strategizing it, and manipulating it from within partial positions and perspectives. Risk is the first consideration; race, class, and now disability, each in its own way, are its tools.

Hierarchies reproduce race and class as resources in risk management. They can be reformed and reorganized but not if focused too quickly on the race or class of analytically isolated individual children. As long as schools pit everyone against everyone else, as long as success is defined at the expense of others being called failures, massive inequalities follow. Race and class problems in school replicate social structural problems so closely that educators should not drop children too quickly into success and failure piles and then explain them as a product of race and class differences.

Raley (2006) offers an alternative situation that keeps risk at bay long enough that race and class can be used to new ends. After 3 years of fieldwork in a small, independent high school, he delivered a close analysis of a single classroom argument on the decision of a prominent African American civil rights lawyer to defend the First Amendment rights of the Ku Klux Klan. It is not an easy task, but the students laugh and shout their way to a direct, earnest, and sustained discussion of how race matters. Popular race labels and racialized talk were the stuff of teases, dares, and parody instead of silence or violence; the students seemed to arrange the argument so they could have something to untangle together. Race was more than the destination for their talk; it was both method and material for finding the way.

What made this discussion possible? Raley had followed the same cohort of students in and out of school. They talked about the school as a "safe" place. By the usual views of race and class, a complementary pair of images come easily to mind. The school is physically safe, offering students shelter from the violence that characterizes their poor, mostly brown community; the school is psychologically safe, sheltering them from the risks that come from being brown and mostly poor. At best, these images are a partial fit. At worst, they obscure the real accomplishment of the school: the necessary articulation of race and class.

In 1976, poorly conceived desegregation policies closed the neighborhood's only public high school, and the children of Bayview's 25,000 residents were placed in high schools scattered throughout the region, often in the lowest tracks. By their own account, the students often felt unwelcomed, and perhaps as many as 65% left school altogether. Pacifica is a local alternative, with a promise to students: Come, and we will do whatever it takes to pave your way into a 4-year college or university. Pacifica's network of adults—that is, teachers (working and retired), administrators, fund-raisers, entrepreneurs, university faculty—struggled to fulfill the promise. They kept the school open all day and many nights, connecting students to mentors and work as interns and finding money to pay for applications and tuitions. The adults were convinced their hard work could open a path for every student, and they refused to sort students into success and failure piles. Structural inequalities and the risks associated with rank were the direct concern of the grown-ups. The structural risks of going to school pushed away from the day-to-day lives of students. They were offered the relative safety of not having to tear each other down, at least not in ways recorded in the principal's office. The specter of failure was softened, and the children were asked to pull up their chairs to work together.

With the risks of being put down, dropped out, or left behind reduced, students were free to take more educationally generative risks. Race and class did not disappear but turned into a risk of a different type. No longer personal markers of shame and risk, race and class became materials for playful discussion. The new risk lived in the spaces occupied by people rather than in their genes. Pacifica's students showed each other how to achieve trusting relations, both momentary and durable. This demanding work was at least educative and, at its best, democratic.

Race and class could be problematic enough to keep students locked out, but the only issue at Pacifica was how to make everyone successful enough to go to college (a task at which they were and continue to be completely successful). The students could talk about race and class forcefully, even aggressively and to the point of confrontation, and then they could compromise, move on, and return to the business of doing school together. Race and class did not seem to scare anyone in this school community. Life outside school remained risk and rank rich, but life in school, even in the midst of heated arguments, was safe. Race and class did not divide; instead, they became points of consideration and engagement.

Respecifying race, class, and LD does not make them go away, but it does reorganize their usual run through our lives. Building situations in which race, class, and LD can be repositioned in school requires also a reorganization of the adults who run the schools. It requires in the long run a reorganization of those who have been profiting from race, class, and even LD (the new upper-class syndrome of choice if it leads to extra time on tests).

Our position stands with Toni Morrison, who critiqued *The Bluest Eye*, her 1969 novel about an African American child badly violated by family and neighbors, for excusing those most responsible for fixing the troubles:

The weight of the novel's inquiry on so delicate and vulnerable a character could smash her and lead readers into the comfort of pitying her rather than into an interrogation of themselves for the smashing. . . . Many readers remain touched but not moved. (Morrison, 1993, p. 211; see Bloom, 1999)

Correlations among race, class, and school performance are real but not as taken. They are not starting places for analysis but products of the work done by everyone in society to handle the risk of being put down, pushed down, cut off, and certified as failures. They are not calls to pity but to self-interrogation and confrontation. The assumption of a natural hierarchy of intelligence correlated with race and class places bets in exactly the wrong place.[11] Race and class are invidious categories when conceived as naturally occurring units for the explanation of school success and failure. Without the reigning assumptions—that schools are working properly and in accord with the biological and social potentials of students—race, class, and the explanation of school achievement can be reformulated. Specifying productive units of analysis in educational research and reform requires a shift in focus: from children and teachers as kinds of persons (by race, class, gender, IQ—whether by genetics, socialization, or whatever combination) and from passive oversocialized persons in kinds of situations (by social structure, social status, economic opportunity) to active persons, creating kinds of persons in situations organized by the wider web of institutions for sorting and socializing a next generation.

NOTES

[1]We use *educator* to refer to those with authority over school policies and practices but realize the term should ultimately include everyone in education, for example, parents, children, test makers, and community gatekeepers (Varenne, 2007). The term must include university researchers, who are, by their privileged position, deeply complicit in current arrangements (Mehan, 2008).

[2]The analytic work used to destabilize notions of race and class can be used to destabilize learning disabilities (LD). No one has to be a racist beyond using American English for racism to be at play in school, no one has to be class biased beyond living where they do to enforce hierarchies of access, and no one has to be LD to be declared broken, special, or in need of extra time. People do not have to be what they are called for the system to work, for the social order works on what people—mostly other people—do. No one in modern rural France claims to believe in witchcraft, but with accusations and denials rampant, people can get caught by a witchcraft complex of gossip, alignment, and condemnation (Favret-Saada, 1984); similarly, everyone entering prisons and halfway houses in the United States gets caught by the loyalty demands put on both inmates and staff by the convict code (Wieder, 1974), and so again, everyone entering American schools, to the extent they are fully organized for half the students to fail, one way or another gets caught by LD (McDermott & Raley, 2008; Mehan, 1993; Varenne & McDermott, 1998).

[3]For a historical summary of failure in American culture, see Sandage (2005); for the rhetoric of saving children, see Levander (2006).

[4]The ethnography of education, in and out of schools, has been coming of age for 50 years (for summary statements, see McDermott, 1997; McDermott & Varenne, 2006; for recent collections, see Bekerman, Burbules, & Silberman-Keller, 2006; Gonzalez, Moll, & Amanti, 2004; Hull, 1997; Singleton, 1999; Varenne, 2007; and for after-school settings, see Cole & the Distributed Literacy Consortium, 2006; Hedegaard & Chaiklin, 2005). Since 1955, George Spindler has edited 11 volumes of papers on anthropology and education; for the latest, see Spindler and Hammond (2006). A word of caution: The word is *ethnography*; the caution is that it refers to well-documented, long engagements with the emergency-filled lives of people interacting with each other. Ethnography is not a simple reporting of what people say in overdetermined interviews or unanalyzed and detail-thin transcripts—as if the world were available for the asking, as if anyone would listen if it were. The difference between good journalism and good ethnography: analyses, methodic and self-conscious enough to reveal the hidden systematics of everyday life (linguistic anthropology offers the best examples; for studies without explicit ties but with great relevance to American education, see Basso, 1996; Conklin, 2007; Frake, 1998; Kuipers, 1998; for studies directed to education, see Viechnicki & Kuipers, 2006; Wortham, 2005; Wortham & Rymes, 2002).

[5]American learning theory builds on behaviorist, psychometric, and cognitive psychology with little attention to social realities—and ignores, unfortunately, indigenous schools of philosophy (Dewey, 1916, 1933; Mead, 1938; see excellent accounts in Bredo, 1997, 2006). Activity and social practice theory, mostly European, with varying relations to Lev Vygotsky and Karl Marx, articulate learning within the constraints and contradictions of social life (Cole 1996; Chaiklin, 2001; Chaiklin, Hedegaard, & Jensen, 1999; Dreier, 2008; Lave, 1988; Lave & McDermott, 2002).

[6]Silence is an important but generally unrecognized resource in social interaction. To say the least (good joke here), silence is hard to describe. The Irish poet, John Montague, has called silence "a hunger strike of the tongue" (personal letter; see McDermott, 1988), but it can serve events with much less purpose. Feminist and minority scholars have examined it most thoroughly, and Samuel Beckett and Harold Pinter are its deepest explorers. Basso's (1979, 1996) accounts of Apache Indians mocking White American speech conventions are a delight. Pollock is interested in the systematic silence that occurs when people together build a road to a topic and then get quiet.

[7]Unspoken racism allows received inequalities to go unchecked. Pollock (2008) has gathered accounts of educators confronting race silence.

[8]A definition of objective reality: "all that is appropriate to, noticeable within, and marked by the self-directed, or practical, actions of collectivities in situations of conflict" (Brown, 1986, p. 15).

[9]Descriptions of class as multilayered are more accurate and account for how class struggle becomes visible only intermittently (Hall, 1997; Wright, 2005). Martin Packer (2001) describes social class highlighted in a school system in economic crisis. First, the children had parents with steady employment. Then, the local automobile factory closed. The children changed classes. They were suddenly at risk. Budgets were tightened. Positions on fault and justice became news. Important people (e.g., local politicians, company apologists, even the governor) argued for back-to-basics classrooms, and the children were asked to solve their own problems. Packer's question: Whose social class alignments acquired the children? In no time, with no change in cognitive skills, the children lost ties to opportunities. Who was not involved in producing their poverty?

[10]For more than 40 years, an emerging literature on ethnic groups has focused on borders, because that is where the action is. All communities, says Gerald Suttles (1973), near the end of the Chicago tradition of urban sociology, exist at their borders; other traditions making the same point at that time include linguistic anthropology (Frake, 1980; Moerman, 1968), cultural geography (Ley, 1974), and British social anthropology widened by Fredrik Barth (1961, 1969). For a contemporary version on "global neighborhoods," see Blommaert, Collins, & Slembrouck, 2005).

[11]Herman Melville thought any seeming intellectual superiority is likely a bad measure of intelligence in practice. His 19th-century voice cries out for a democracy of intelligence:

For be a man's intellectual superiority what it will, it can never assume the practical, available supremacy over other men, without the aid of some sort of external arts and entrenchments, always in themselves, more or less paltry and base. (Melville, 1851/1991, p. 165)

For another 19th-century voice against a hierarchy of false smartness, see the new translation of Abbé Grégoire (1808/1997) and related scholarship from Popkin and Popkin (2000).

ACKNOWLEDGMENTS

We greatly appreciate comments from Alfredo Artiles, Eric Bredo, Shelley Goldman, and Mica Pollock.

REFERENCES

Artiles, A. (2003). Special education's changing identity. *Harvard Educational Review, 75,* 164–202.

Artiles, A., Klinger, J., & Tate, W. (Eds.). (2006). Representation of minority students in special education. *Educational Researcher, 35*(6), 3–28.

Baker, L. (1998). *From savage to Negro.* Berkeley: University of California Press.

Barth, F. (1961). *Nomads of South Persia.* Boston: Little, Brown.

Barth, F. (1969). (Ed.). *Ethnic groups and boundaries: The social organization of cultural difference.* Boston: Little, Brown.

Bartlett, S., Hart, R., Satterthwaite, D., de la Barra, X., & Missair, A. (1999). *Cities for children.* London: Earthscan.

Basso, K. (1979). *Portraits of the White man.* Cambridge, UK: Cambridge University Press.

Basso, K. (1996). *Wisdom sits in places.* Albuquerque: University of New Mexico Press

Bekerman, Z., Burbules, N., & Silberman-Keller, D. (Eds.). (2006). *Learning in places*. New York: Peter Lang.
Blommaert, J., Collins, J., & Slembrouck, S. (2005). Polycentricity and interactional regimes in "global neighborhoods." *Ethnography, 6*, 205–235.
Bloom, H. (Ed.). (1999). *Toni Morrison's The bluest eye*. Philadelphia: Chelsea House.
Bowker, G., & Star, S. (1999). *Sorting things out*. Cambridge, MA: MIT Press.
Bredo, E. (1997). The social construction of learning. In G. Phye (Ed.), *Handbook of academic learning* (pp. 3–45). New York: Academic Press.
Bredo, E. (2006). Philosophies of educational research. In J. Green, G. Camilli, & P. Elmore (Eds.), *Complementary methods in educational research* (pp. 3–31). Washington, DC: American Educational Research Association.
Brown, M. (1986). *The production of society*. Totowa, NJ: Rowman & Littlefield.
Chaiklin, S. (Ed.). (2001). *The theory and practice of cultural–historical psychology*. Aarhus, Denmark: Aarhus University Press.
Chaiklin, S., Hedegaard, M., & Jensen, U. (Eds.). (1999). *Activity theory and social practice*. Aarhus, Denmark: Aarhus University Press.
Cole, M. (1996). *Cultural psychology*. Cambridge, MA: Harvard University Press.
Cole, M., & the Distributed Literacy Consortium. (2006). *The fifth dimension*. New York: Russell Sage.
Conklin, H. C. (2007). *Fine description: Ethnographic and linguistic essays of Harold C. Conklin*. In J. Kuipers & R. McDermott (Eds.), Monograph 56 (pp. 410–427). New Haven, CT: Yale Southeast Asia Studies.
Dewey, J. (1916). *Democracy and education*. New York: Macmillan.
Dewey, J. (1933). The social–economic situation and education. In W. Kirkpatrick (Ed.), *The educational frontier* (pp. 32–72). New York: D. Appleton-Century.
Dreier, O. (2008). *Psychotherapy in everyday life*. Cambridge, UK: Cambridge University Press.
Favret-Saada, J. (1984). *Deadly words*. Cambridge, UK: Cambridge University Press.
Frake, C. O. (1980). The genesis of kinds of people in the Sulu Sea. In A. Dil (Ed.), *Language and cultural description* (pp. 212–232). Stanford, CA: Stanford University Press.
Frake, C. O. (1998). Abu sayyaf: Displays of violence and the proliferation of contested identities among Philippine Muslims. *American Anthropologist, 100*, 41–54.
Fredrickson, G. (2002). *Racism: A short history*. Princeton, NJ: Princeton University Press.
Fredrickson, G. M. (1997). *The comparative imagination: On the history of racism, nationalism, and social movements*. Berkeley: University of California Press.
Gonzalez, N., Moll, L., & Amanti, C. (Eds.). (2004). *Funds of knowledge*. Mahwah, NJ: Lawrence Erlbaum.
Grégoire, H. (1808/1997). *On the cultural achievements of Negroes*. Amherst: University of Massachusetts Press.
Hall, J. R. (Ed.). (1997). *Reworking class*. Ithaca, NY: Cornell University Press.
Hayden, D. (1996). *The power of place: Urban landscapes as public history*. Cambridge, MA: MIT Press.
Hedegaard, M., & Chaiklin, S. (2005). *Radical–local teaching and learning*. Aarhus, Denmark: Aarhus University Press.
Henry, J. (1963). *Culture against man*. New York: Vintage.
Hull, G. (Ed.). (1997). *Changing work, changing workers*. Albany: State University of New York Press.
Katz, M. B. (1997). *Improving poor people*. Princeton, NJ: Princeton University Press.
Kaufmann, D. (1995). *The business of common life*. Baltimore: Johns Hopkins University Press.
Kuipers, J. (1998). *Language, identity, and marginality in Indonesia*. Cambridge, UK: Cambridge University Press.
Ladson-Billings, G. (2006). It's not the culture of poverty. It's the poverty of culture. *Anthropology of Education Quarterly, 37*, 104–109.

Levander, C. (2006). *Cradle of liberty: Race, the child, and national belonging from Thomas Jefferson to W. E. B. DuBois*. Durham, NC: Duke University Press.

Lave, J. (1988). *Cognition in practice*. Cambridge, UK: Cambridge University Press

Lave, J., & McDermott, R. (2002). Estranged labor learning. *Outlines, 4*, 19–48.

Ley, D. (1974). *Black inner-city as a frontier outpost: Images and behavior of a Philadelphia neighborhood*. Washington, DC: American Geographical Society.

Lin, L. J. (2007). (Mis-)education into American racism. *Teachers College Record, 109*, 1725–1746.

McDermott, R. (1988). Inarticulateness. In D. Tannen (Ed.), *Linguistics in context* (pp. 37–68). Norwood, NJ: Ablex.

McDermott, R. (1997). Achieving school failure, 1972–1997. In G. Spindler (Ed.), *Education and cultural process* (3rd ed., pp. 110–135). Prospect Heights, IL: Waveland Press.

McDermott, R., & Raley, J. (2008). The tell-tale body: The constitution of disability in schools. In W. Ayers, T. Quinn, & D. Stoval (Eds.), *Handbook of social justice in education* (pp. 431–445). Mahwah, NJ: Lawrence Erlbaum.

McDermott, R., & Varenne, H. (2006). Reconstructing culture in education research. In G. Spindler & L. Hammond (Eds.), *Innovations in educational ethnography* (pp. 3–30). Mahwah, NJ: Lawrence Erlbaum.

Mead, G. H. (1938). *The philosophy of the act*. Chicago: University of Chicago Press.

Mehan, H. (1993). Beneath the skin and between the ears. In S. Chaiklin & J. Lave (Eds.), *Understanding practice* (pp. 241–269). New York: Cambridge University Press.

Mehan, H. (2008). Engaging the sociological imagination. *Anthropology and Education Quarterly, 38*, 77–91.

Melville, H. (1851/1991). *Moby-Dick*. New York: Everyman's Library.

Moerman, M. (1968). Being Lue: Uses and abuses of ethnic identification. In J. Helm (Ed.), *Essays on the problem of the tribe* (pp. 153–169). Seattle: University of Washington Press.

Morrison, T. (1992). *Playing in the dark: Whiteness and the literary imagination*. New York: Vintage.

Morrison, T. (1993). Afterword. In T. Morrison, *The bluest eye* (pp. 209–216). New York: Plume.

Nespor, J. (1997). *Tangled up in school: Politics, space, bodies, and signs in the educational process*. Mahwah, NJ: Lawrence Erlbaum.

Packer, M. (2001). *Changing classes*. Cambridge, UK: Cambridge University Press.

Pollock, M. (2004). *Colormute: Race talk dilemmas in an American school*. Princeton, NJ: Princeton University Press.

Pollock, M. (Ed.). (2008). *Everyday antiracism: Getting real about race in school*. New York: New Press.

Popkin, J., & Popkin, R. (Eds.). (2000). *The Abbé Grégoire and his world*. Dordrecht, The Netherlands: Kluwer Academic.

Raley, J. (2006). Finding safety in dangerous places. In G. Spindler & L. Hammond (Eds.), *Innovations in educational ethnography* (pp. 87–117). Mahwah, NJ: Lawrence Erlbaum.

Rampton, B. (2005). *Crossing: Language and identity among adolescents*. Manchester, UK: St. Jerome.

Ranciere, J. (2004). *The philosopher and his poor*. Durham, NC: Duke University Press.

Rosaldo, R., & Flores, W. (1997). Identity, conflict, and evolving Latino communities. In W. Flores & R. Benmayor (Eds.), *Latino cultural citizenship* (pp. 57–96). Boston: Beacon.

Sandage, S. (2005). *Born losers: A history of failure in America*. Cambridge, MA: Harvard University Press.

Schram, S. (1995). *Words of welfare*. Minneapolis: University of Minnesota Press.

Seyer-Ochi, I. (2006). Lived landscapes of the Fillmore. In G. Spindler & L. Hammond (Eds.), *Innovations in educational ethnography* (pp. 168–232). Mahwah, NJ: Lawrence Erlbaum.

Singleton, J. (Ed.). (1999). *Learning in unlikely places*. Cambridge, UK: Cambridge University Press.

Smedley, A. (2007). *Race in North America* (3rd ed.). Boulder, CO: Westview.

Spindler, G. & Hammond, L. (Eds.). (2006). *Innovations in educational ethnography*. Mahwah, NJ: Lawrence Erlbaum.

Suttles, G. (1973). *The social construction of communities*. Chicago: University of Chicago Press.

Tratner, M. (2001). *Deficits and desires*. Stanford, CA: Stanford University Press.

Varenne, H. (Ed.) (2007). Alternative anthropological perspectives on education. *Teachers College Record, 109*(7), 1530–1843.

Varenne, H., & McDermott, R. (1998). *Successful failure*. Boulder, CO: Westview.

Viechnicki, G., & Kuipers, J. (2006). "It's all human error": When a school science experiment fails. *Linguistics and Education, 17*, 207–130.

Waquant, L. (2002). Scrutinizing the poor. *American Journal of Sociology, 107*, 1468–1532.

Wieder, D. L. (1974). *Language and social reality*. The Hague, The Netherlands: Mouton.

Wortham, S. (2005). *Learning identity*. Cambridge, UK: Cambridge University Press.

Wortham, S., & Rymes, B. (Eds.). (2002). *Linguistic anthropology of education*. New York: Praeger.

Wright, E. O. (Ed.). (2005). *Approaches to class analysis*. Cambridge, UK: Cambridge University Press.

Zerubavel, E. (2003). *Time maps: Collective memory and the social shape of the past*. Chicago: University of Chicago Press.

Chapter 5

Youth, Risk, and Equity in a Global World

GLYNDA HULL
New York University

JESSICA ZACHER
California State University, Long Beach

LIESEL HIBBERT
University of the Western Cape, South Africa

GIRLS LIKE LAXMI: YOUTH AT RISK IN A GLOBAL WORLD

The uniformed girls sat cross-legged on the carpeted floor of a second-story classroom situated off the inner courtyard of a large private school in a north Indian city. There they studied, read, and wrote, the walls of their schoolroom lined with computers protected by cloth dust covers, its big ceiling fans scarcely disturbing the heavy heat of early March. On this afternoon, they bent over notebooks, writing in fits and starts, stopping to whisper and laugh with each other, then returning to the task at hand, which was a summary of their initial thoughts of what to share about themselves as well as what they would like to ask of youth in the United States and South Africa. "How do boys treat girls there?" one young woman ventured. "What subjects do students study in school?" queried another. They wrote notes and questions in Davangari script, and they chatted with each other and their teacher in Hindi, but they spoke and wrote passably, if haltingly, in English when prompted to interact with their American visitors. These adolescent girls were preparing to participate in an international exchange project with youth in other countries, in effect a multimedia pen pal activity, made prescient and possible by the social networking capabilities of our digital age and our global world (Hull & Nelson, in press).

This scene will strike some readers as commonplace, as unremarkable perhaps, one that is daily duplicated, albeit with local variation, in schools, cities, and countries around the world. And, so it is: Young people attend school, read and write,

Review of Research in Education
March 2009, Vol. 33, pp. 117-159
DOI: 10.3102/0091732X08327746
© 2009 AERA. http://rre.aera.net

engage with mediational technologies, and take part in activities designed in some way to broaden their understandings of other cultures and places. Yet the situations of these particular girls are anything but ordinary, unless as part of "ordinary" we also include poverty, deprivation, and risk—as indeed we should if, as some estimate, approximately 80% or 6 billion of the world's population is "socially and fiscally at risk" (Appadurai, 2000). Take Laxmi,[1] for instance, a girl of 13 who attends the school described above. She rises at 6:00 a.m. each day, then walks, by 6:30 a.m., to a home where she does domestic work for a wage of 700 rupees (US$14) a month. Laxmi's mother died when she was 11; her father, a rickshaw driver, provides no support to their family of six children, and the family is now headed by Laxmi's sister.

After her morning job Laxmi returns home, fetches water from an outdoor communal pump, fills her house's receptacles, and washes dishes and utensils. In the afternoon, she goes to her school, which she attends via scholarship, a scene from which we have just detailed. After school she helps her sister with the evening work at home, then leaves to clean another house, returning late. Laxmi not only longs for a different life but also intends to achieve it through study and hard work; she dreams, in fact, of becoming an artist, and she wistfully remembers seeing a movie once with her aunt, one that engages her imagination about possible futures. Laxmi's material situation, characteristic of the demographics and lifeworlds of her classmates (cf. Sahni, in press), is not uncommon. Nor, of course, does her desire for a good life set her apart. What is uncommon is her access to educational resources that go some distance in positioning her to create it.

This is a chapter for girls like Laxmi, or more properly, and long-windedly, a chapter that selectively reviews those educational literatures that should be relevant to helping us understand and improve the lot and life chances of girls and boys like Laxmi and their equivalents everywhere.[2] We intentionally began this review, which appears in a U.S. journal, with a vignette from India, a country whose linguistic and ethnic diversity, whose international reputation for advances in information technologies, and whose considerable progress and remaining challenges related to taming poverty and offering education to a large proportion of its population are well known. It is our observation that as we conceptualize risk, equity, and schooling inside the U.S.'s geographic borders, we most often do so without taking into account what can be learned from the material facts and ideological points of view of youth in countries, societies, and communities apart from our own, including and especially "transforming" and "developing" nations and their diasporas. We respectfully suggest, and we hope our chapter illustrates, that such a narrow and isolationist view is an anachronistic and unhelpful one. The point of our chapter, however, is not so much to levy a critique against U.S. or more generally "Western" educational policies and interventions in relation to youth—indeed, thoroughgoing critiques abound (e.g., Bottrell, 2007; Finn, 2001; P. Kelly, 2001; Sukarieh & Tannock, 2008)—but to assemble and juxtapose literatures that help us see these issues anew.[3]

Arguably, the most important economic, cultural, and social trend of the past half century continues to be globalization, the radical intensification of flows of capital, people, services, expertise, goods, texts, images, and technologies around the world and across national and regional borders. The nature of globalization's effects, its uneven spread, its accompanying possibilities and injustices, and even the question of whether it is at the end of the day a radically new phenomenon or the continuation of an age-old process continue to be debated vigorously and with feeling (Stiglitz, 2003). In the academy, scholars from a range of fields—history, economics, political science, cultural theory, and anthropology—are challenged to retain or regain their disciplinary footing and perhaps their contemporary relevance in the face of this complex and undeniable phenomenon, a challenge that is engaged sometimes with excitement but almost always with angst (Appadurai, 2000, 2006a; Lukose, 2009). As we explore below in a selective way, educational researchers hailing from a variety of traditions have taken a seat at the globalization table, wanting to understand its implications for, variously, students' skill sets; teachers' preparation; and, more radically, the rethinking of the forms, purposes, and, usefulness of current conceptions of schooling (i.e., Burbules & Torres, 2000; Gee, Hull, & Lankshear, 1996; Luke & Carrington, 2002, 2008; Spring, 2008; Stromquist & Monkman, 2000; Suàrez-Orozco & Qin-Hilliard, 2004; Suàrez-Orozco & Sattin, 2007).

Our particular interests in education in the context of globalization center on notions of risk and at riskness. What is the nature of risk for young people—Laxmi and others—we want to ask, in our determinedly global world? Who becomes at risk, and at risk of what? What are the most important challenges for educators and researchers in this context, and what are our most profound opportunities?

Globalization has an impact on cultures by virtue of processes of imposition, juxtaposition, and interpolation, and the metaphors used to describe its influence often draw on images of interconnection: networks (Castells, 2000, 2004), constellations (Massey, 1998a, 1998b), spaces (Appadurai, 1996), and webs (Appiah, 2005). The philosopher Kwame Anthony Appiah (2005) captures the positive valence of this phenomenon:

Planes and boats and trains, satellites and cables of copper and optic fiber, and the people and things and ideas that travel all of them, are, indeed, bringing us all every more definitively into a single web. And that web is physical, biological, electronic, artistic, literary, musical, linguistic, juridical, religious, economic, familial. (p. 216)

Yet in the post-9/11 era, most would agree that in the United States our propensity for welcoming interconnection has lessened; we think in terms of fissures and chasms between ideologies and cultures while globalizing flows loom large as frightening trends that might engulf us against our will, taking jobs, lifestyles, and lives rather than connecting and enriching us. As Benhabib (2002) notes, "Global integration is proceeding alongside sociocultural disintegration, the resurgence of various separatisms, and international terrorism" (p. viii). In this view, in a globalized world, we are all at risk (cf. Beck, 1986/1992, 2000), not only our youth, and the leading metaphors used to characterize our vulnerability include clashes, attacks, and wars of cultures, faiths, and civilizations.

Helpfully, and hopefully, contemporary political and philosophical theorists have provided ways of thinking about our current world's intensifying conflicts that can help us reframe such debates. Their metaphor of choice is often conversation and dialogue. Benhabib (2002), for example, firmly maintains that deliberative democracy can be sensitive to political and cultural differences, allowing these differences to be voiced, contested, and negotiated. On the other hand, she disavows certain strong versions of multiculturalism whose raisons d'être are supporting identity and difference movements in which the rights of women and children in minority cultures can be compromised (cf. Wikan, 2007). "Practical autonomy, in the moral and political sphere," Benhabib (2002) writes, "is defined as the capacity to exercise choice and agency over the conditions of one's narrative identifications" (p. 16), including identifications within one's own culture as well as outside it. In a complementary way, Sen (2006) celebrates not only the multiplicity of affiliations that make us all "composites" as human beings but also the freedom to decide which identity is important in a given context.

Appiah (2005), too, emphasizes the ties that should bind us, choosing "cosmopolitanism" as a strategy, a challenge, and a means for balancing difference and universality.[4] He writes, "We have obligations to others, obligations that stretch beyond those to whom we are related by the ties of kith and kind, or even the more formal ties of a shared citizenship" (p. xv). Beyond such obligations, Appiah believes that the notion of cosmopolitanism also entails respect for legitimate difference. When those differences result in practices motivated by opposing and alienating values, our most important tool is dialogue. In this worldview, there is no path to walk except one that leads us to explore our moral obligations to "strangers," overcoming our many fears (Appadurai, 2006a), and to construct a global ethic that constantly asks, what is it that we owe to others because we all belong to the human community? Thus, we might ask with him, what do we owe to youth like Laxmi?

In the following review, then, we attempt to situate discussions of at riskness within a discourse of the global, but also, following Benhabib and Appiah, we keep the moral entailments of living in a global society in view and attempt to sort out the implications that may accrue from this stance for future educational research. We look first at how notions of being at risk as a young person have been formed in the United States, influenced through the lenses of the disciplines of psychology and sociology; how resulting notions of risk and their implications seem to have spread internationally; and to what effect. Next, we review recent literature that has examined global youth, a diverse scholarship hailing primarily from cultural studies and anthropology that attempts to describe and theorize the experiences of youth around the world as they confront the challenges of contemporary life. We see an "aesthetic turn" in this scholarship and in the actions and products of youth, and we discuss it here. Although there is much to appreciate in this work, we also note what strike us as blind spots. For instance, this research includes a stimulating exploration of the nexus of youth, popular culture, and globalization, yet it often seems to neglect other important contexts for identity formation and learning, including formal schooling. We conclude with descriptions of promising projects and research related to youth at risk and equity in a global world, including a teacher education effort associated with the school that Laxmi attends.

BOYS LIKE JOSÉ: CONCEIVING RISK IN A GLOBALIZED WORLD

In a fourth-grade classroom in Southern California, a 9-year-old named José worked diligently on any assignment his teacher asked him to complete. José and his brother had immigrated from Mexico with their mother when José was 6, and they had lived in California for 3 years. José estimated that he was "a little bit good" at English, "a little bit good" at reading, and "bad" on his biannual reading benchmarks (Shin, 2004). If test scores are to be taken as measurements of good skills, as they assuredly are in the United States and many other countries, he was accurate in his self-assessment. At the end of third grade, José was labeled "Far Below Basic" by his score on the California Standardized Test (258 out of 600 possible points); he was also, after 3 years of school, still labeled a "beginning" English language learner, based on his end-of-third-grade California English Language Development Test score. He came in with very low "reading benchmark" test scores—he had only achieved "middle of Grade 1" status—and would be a candidate for retention based on reading scores in fifth grade if he did not improve in the fourth grade. José and his peers at "Washington Elementary" were immersed in testing: They took 35 tests per year, approximately one test per school week.

There is little doubt, then, that José had been found to be educationally at risk. His teacher and principal, as well as his school's literacy coach, considered him at risk of failing to read beyond a first-grade level; at risk of retention in fifth grade (one of the "retention years" for low reading scores in California); at risk of failing out of school with continued test score failure; at risk of failure to learn English; at risk, as an expectant middle school student, of failing to acquire the subject-matter foundation needed to succeed in high school; and, looking further down the road, at risk of failing to satisfy California's high school requirements that govern college admission. In the background of José's difficulties with school lay the difficulties, the risk factors, if you will, of being a particular kind of global child, one whose parents had joined the movement of people across any number of national borders in search of jobs, refuge, and futures and who are likely to encounter joblessness, legal trouble, poverty, and health problems along the way (cf. Nazario, 2007).

There is no denying that in the United States identifying and ministering to students who are educationally at risk have long been foci of education and educational research (Deschenes, Cuban, & Tyack, 2001); that such interests intensify in times of crisis (Apple, 2001; Flores, Cousin, & Diaz, 1991); and, as we shall illustrate, that U.S. conceptions of youth at risk have had policy and practice implications that stretch far past our national borders, influencing both developed and developing countries, where conceptions of risk and categories related to adolescence previously differed, were not prominent, or did not exist. As Carnoy (2007) notes in the context of the surprising results of his comparison of schooling outcomes for youth in Cuba, Brazil, and Chile, "The urgency and the ideas about school improvement [in the United States] have spread to developing countries. . . . The mantra is that smarter graduates will make the country more competitive and increase economic growth" (p. 4). Indeed, the policies and sanctions of the No Child Left Behind Act of 2001 can be viewed as the most recent neoliberal interpretation of U.S. longstanding interest and perceived responsibility in this arena (Hursh, 2007). The extent to which the work to ameliorate risk factors has been effective and the extent to which the new stresses and possibilities of globalization render this work of limited utility for youth like José remain to be seen.

A variety of critical accounts provide commentary on the origins of the practice of labeling students educationally at risk in the United States (Cuban, 1989; Hudak & Kihn, 2001; Hull, Rose, Fraser, & Castellano, 1991; Rose, 1989, 1995; Valencia & Solorzano, 1997; Zehm, 1973). There are also deeply critical accounts of a broader sociological and psychological literature, especially in the United States, Great Britain, and Australia, that takes as its aims identifying the "risk factors"—that is, growing up in poverty and being from a single parent household—that contribute to making youth susceptible to "risk behaviors," such as drug use, gang membership, crime, and dropping out of school (Dwyer & Wyn, 2001; France, 2008; Schonert-Reichl, 2000; Swadener & Lubeck, 1995). The critiques of these literatures are diverse, and they often center on the individualistic and deficit-oriented nature of accounts wherein young people are defined solely in terms of, and are blamed for, aberrant behaviors, whereas context-sensitive explanations are given short shrift. In the educational literature, related concerns have been raised about the locus of blame assumed to reside within individual youth, their families, or their cultures (Deschenes et al., 2001; Flores et al., 1991). Ironically, although contextual factors such as poverty have been brought to bear in the risk factor literature, conceptualizations of youth as at risk remain conceptually stunted, a reminder that context can be taken into account in reductive ways.

In this section we consider how the phenomenon of globalization has recently intersected with thinking about and programs and policies for and research on youth and risk (Dolby & Rahman, 2008; Spring, 2008; Suàrez-Orozco, 2007). Both José and Laxmi are growing up in a global world, and, as variously poor, immigrant, female, urban, and brown, they have long been situated, on local and world stages in multiple societies, as disadvantaged. Unhelpful thinking about youth like them in research and policy marches steadily along, adhering to well-worn ideological, methodological, and theoretical paths, despite a changing world. In this regard, we submit that because of their sphere of influence, the United States and other "developed" countries bear a special responsibility to change this situation. Indeed, the U.S.'s determined interest in accountability and testing, which holds José so tightly in its clutches and which arguably has increased rather than lessened his risk of failure, has spread widely (cf. Meier & Wood, 2004; Zacher, 2008).

Several themes emerge from the combined bodies of globalization and risk litera-ture. First and most predominant is evidence that globalization itself is indeed mak-ing at-risk youth more at risk (cf. Katz, 2004) in a variety of ways. However, processes of globalization, it is often observed, are uneven and unpredictable, and for youth at risk there is evidence of the creation, albeit often serendipitously, of previously unavailable potential for mobility. Second, and equally though differently prevalent, is the "skills question." Long a staple in the U.S. policy arsenal, especially in times of economic downturn (viz., *A Nation at Risk*; National Commission on Excellence in Education, 1983), worries (re)surface about the kinds of skills youth do and do not have, their level of preparedness to compete for jobs in global markets, and the lack of preparation they may receive in today's schools for tomorrow's jobs (Nayak, 2003; Stromquist, 2002; Stromquist & Monkman, 2000). A third theme has to do with the export of—and in some cases the imposition of—ideologies and practices around accountability, at riskness, and larger conceptions of teaching and learning. We dis-cuss the implications of research that shows how these Western ideologies are being grafted onto educational institutions in developing and transforming societies through agencies such as the World Bank (Sukarieh & Tannock, 2008).

Increasing the Risks of Risk

It is clear that globalization has complicated notions of at riskness in multiple ways (Schonert-Reichl, 2000). As Appadurai (2006a) explains, our global world is substan-tially different from earlier periods, in part because of changes in the role of capital in the global economy, increases in (electronic) information access, and the increasingly extreme wealth of some individuals, regions, and nation states and extreme poverty of others. These factors, visible or invisible though they may be to those who study youth in different locations in the world, mean that the world is changing and that those who would work with youth who are "growing up global" (Katz, 2004) should take note. Ulrich Beck (1986/1992), writing about the changes brought about by modernity, asserts that we live in a "risk society"; we further note that children and youth are the least capable of defending themselves from potential societal risks. The most negative aspects of globalization—financial instability, increased violence, ethnic cleansing, ter-rorism, child labor, and the sex trade—have increased the kinds of risks to children's safety and security in ways that are almost impossible to calculate, even with the risk factor calculations employed by some sociologists (cf. France, 2008).

According to UNICEF, there are 2.2 billion children in the world; 1.9 billion of these live in developing countries. Of the 2.2 billion children in the world, an esti-mated 1 billion live in poverty, based on assessments of the existence and quality of shelter, water, sanitation, education, information, health, and nutrition (see www.unicef.org). There are numerical "bulges"—large population groups—of youth in many developing countries; in El Salvador, for instance, youth younger than 18 make up half of the population. When combined with the effects of immigration, transna-tionalism, global flows of people, and extremely poor national economies, youth "bulges" make for uncertain futures for youth and adults alike. More and more research shows how the patterns of global migration and immigration leave many poor children at risk (Chavez, 1991)—the left-behind children of Central America are one example. Although fathers and, increasingly, mothers go north for employment as laborers and nannies in America, children are left behind, sometimes for years, to survive financially on remittances sent home (Hondagneu-Sotelo & Avila, 1997; Nazario, 2007). Similar situations are occurring in China, where up to 20 million rural children have been left behind, often with grandparents, while their parents migrate to cities to find work (Xinhua, 2007).

In such situations, economic benefits do accrue, but emotional and social problems engendered by absent adult-age workers are equally problematic for youth and their families in the left-behind communities. The enforcement of immigration law can have unexpected international consequences as well. For example, foreign-born U.S. youth who belonged to gangs in Los Angeles were deported to El Salvador after changes in immigration laws (G. A. G. Vasquez, 2005); when these youth got to El Salvador, a foreign country to them, they were marginalized. The end result was the doubly troubling "deportation of Southern California youth and the transplanting of U.S. gang cultures to El Salvador" (G. A. G. Vasquez, 2005, p. 103). Indeed, one of globalization's less-discussed and more negative effects, some argue, is the increasing transnationalism of gangs (e.g., the Salva Maratrucha, a Nicaraguan gang based partly in Los Angeles; Johnson & Muhlhausen, 2005).

Another way in which processes of globalization are claimed to put at-risk children more at risk is through the global spread of a corporate curricular ethos dispersed purposefully via the World Bank and other international agencies (Kincheloe, 1997) as well as via mediascapes through which images and products are spread. The agencies that feed into this transnational flow do not generally attend to whether youth have the financial wherewithal to make purchases and be capitalist consumers; rather, they seek "to teach the young that consumption can assuage dissatisfaction and that consumption, identity, and pleasure are one," which in turn "reifies the general shift from a society of producers to a society of consumers" (Kenway & Bullen, 2008, p. 21). Countries such as Singapore worry that their youth are "a generation devoid of national roots and patriotism" (Koh, 2008, p. 199) because, as participants in this global corporate culture, they engage in excessive consumption and seem to be becoming too Western. The metaphor of consumption applied to texts, images, and mediascapes is also cause for concern in relation to critical conceptions of reading. That is, there is an important distinction to be made between the consumption of texts and their critical interpretation. The fear is that, in a global, media-saturated world bombarded with information, images, and multimodal representations, youth may become passive consumers rather than active interpreters of texts. For scholars such as Kenway and Bullen (2008), such risks require a "postcritical pedagogy" that young people may use to develop a "critical global political sensibility" (p. 30).

If secular, corporate approaches are seen as a threat to the ideological development of youth, religion also plays an important and complex role in discussions of youth and risk. In the United States, faith-based initiatives have received encouragement through infusions of federal dollars during the past decade, and the efficacy of religiosity and the "faith factor" in "avoiding violence, achieving literacy, promoting employment, and achieving other desirable secular social goals among disadvantaged urban youth and young adults" (DiIulio, 1998) has been hopefully and keenly explored (cf. Larson & Johnson, 1998). There is a long and venerable tradition, for example, in some African American communities of relying on religious faith and practice to protect youth from societal ills and dangers and to inculcate knowledge and skills not provided through formal schooling (cf. Moore, 1991; Moss, 2001; Stanton, 2006). As well, religion governs many coming-of-age rituals that are important for young people the world over, as societies signal the passage of youth into new realms of adult identity and responsibility. In other moments, contexts, and circumstances, however, we are also primed to look with worry on youths' induction into religion. When a given immigrant community's religious rituals appear unacceptably alien, or when religion is used to justify violence or oppression (Wikan, 2007), or when religious beliefs are seen as negatively implicated in educational practice, religion can be viewed as increasing risk as well as a practice, community, and/or belief system that provides refuge (Sarroub, 2002). To be sure, judgments of what constitutes oppression or retrograde educational practice are value laden; we are reminded of Benhabib's (2002) and Appiah's (2005) discussions of the complex dialectic of universalism and local beliefs. There are class-based complexities as well; for example, both radical Islamic and evangelical Christian movements have appealed especially to the poor. What does seem clear is that the likelihood of faith-induced risks and the need for mediation concerning divergent belief systems have intensified with globalization. In a global world, then, the ways that youth negotiate religion—their own and other people's—may both increase and decrease risk.

Finally, to draw some of these issues into focus in a specific study, we highlight the long-term ethnographic work of Katz (2004). Writing about findings from her research projects in Sudan and in New York, Katz argues that children's development and economic development are inseparable and that both are particularly visible and inextricably intertwined in the context of a country in the midst of implementing a specific economic development plan. Following children in the rural town of Howa, Sudan, from the age of 10 (in 1981) through their young adulthood, Katz documents the effects of a rural development agenda on their daily lives and the changes in modes of social reproduction that occurred as the village inhabitants were pressed to change aspects of their livelihoods in the name of agricultural and social progress. She suggests that there are "young people in danger of being excessed by the processes of capitalist globalism" (p. 258) both in the town of Howa and in New York City, where she later continued this research comparatively. Katz describes the displacement of these youth, and the accompanying deskilling and community destabilization in both Sudan and America, as life in "the shards of capitalist modernity" (p. 259). Although some are made more mobile because of processes of globalization—the migrant worker sending reparations home—others are financially or politically immobilized and unable to leave increasingly worsening situations (e.g., the Burmese). These are the youth who are not even at risk of failing to be competitive, as they have not yet made it to the skills-for-competition table.

Skills for Competition

A second theme in educational literature on globalization and risk is a concern about whether youth are acquiring the necessary skills that will allow them to eventually compete in globalized markets (Spring, 2008; Stromquist, 2002; Stromquist & Monkman, 2000). Two international tests—the Programme for International Student Assessment (PISA) and Trends in International Mathematics and Science Study (TIMMS) tests, run by member countries of the Organization for Economic Co-operation and Development (OECD) and the International Association for the Evaluation of Educational Achievement, respectively—exemplify some of the complexities involved. In slightly different ways, PISA and TIMMS measure the performance of students in developed countries on Western standardized literacy and mathematics tests. These tests seek to answer such questions as the following: How well are young adults prepared to meet the challenges of the future? What skills do young adults have that will help them adapt to change in their lives? (ACER, 2003; see http://www.acer.edu.au). These are indeed important questions, and the attempts undertaken by such agencies are laudable for their scope and efforts. Each agency tests in more than 50 countries, a truly global effort. In individual test countries, the comparison of test results can either alleviate or make more dire predictions that youth are less prepared for the future by present schooling methods. They can also offer first steps to models for more equitable achievement. Schleicher's (in press) analysis of the 2006 PISA data shows, for example, how parents in a country such as Finland, with the highest PISA scores, can "rely on high and consistent performance standards across the entire school system" regardless of their own socioeconomic statuses.

There are a variety of critiques, both implicit and forthright, of these testing efforts. What counts as a marketable skill, and how to develop human capital based on those skills, are increasingly debatable, as educators and policymakers attempt to come to terms with the requirements of an information age, knowledge economy, and global world. Like capital itself, Beck (1986/1992) argues, the risks inherent in modernity are unequally distributed. Drawing on Beck's work, Nayak (2003) contends that processes of globalization have made transitions to labor markets more risky for youth, because of both a lack of skills and shifting labor markets and national economies. Various efforts are underway to document and describe those new requirements, including the Partnership for 21st Century Skills (see http://www.21stcenturyskills.org/index.php). Reconceptualizations of such new requirements often emphasize flexibility, global awareness, and collaboration. In Suárez-Orozco and Sattin's (2007) description of what youth will need in regard to these new skills, they write,

The skills, sensibilities, and competencies needed for identifying, analyzing, and solving problems from multiple perspectives will require nurturing students who are curious and cognitively flexible, can tolerate ambiguity, and can synthesize knowledge within and across disciplines. They will need the cultural sophistication to empathize with their peers, who will likely be of different racial, religious, linguistic and social origins. They will need to be able to learn with and from them, to work collaboratively and communicate effectively in groups made up of diverse individuals. An education for globalization should aim at nothing more nor less than to educate "the whole child for the whole world." (p. 19)

To devise instruments to test such skills and dispositions is, of course, a challenge, but to reimagine schools to teach them is a deeper problem still, one that recasts worries about economic competitiveness across a global world to include worries about equity within societies (cf. Grubb & Lazerson, 2006). Suàrez-Orozco and Sattin accompany their description of new skills with the worry that "schools continue to teach sclerotic facts and have no way of coping with the increasing ambiguity, complexity, and linguistic, religious, and ethnic diversity that defines the world" (p. 12).

One scholarly movement that has addressed this fear is the field of "adolescent literacy" (Cassidy, Garrett, & Barrera, 2008). During the past 15 years, its worthy aim has been to redress the pedagogical neglect of teenaged readers and writers by researchers and educators (for early examples, see Alvermann et al., 1996; Alvermann, Hinchman, Moore, Phelps, & Waff, 1998; Finders, 1997; for more recent work, see Alvermann, 2002, in press; Moje, 2002; Moje, Overby, Tysvaer, & Morris, 2008). This work suggests that adolescence in the United States is a period fraught with particular potential risks of failing to acquire the 21st century literacy dispositions, credentials, and practices believed necessary to outfit young people for productive educational and vocational futures. One gap in this research is its overall inattention to global or even international issues (for an exception, see Sarroub, 2005; 2008). On the whole, it remains a relatively Westernized (American [e.g., Morrell, 2002], U.K. [e.g., Brozo, Shiel, & Topping, 2007; Hopper, 2005], and Australian [e.g., Ryan, 2005]) endeavor.

A flash point in debates about the globalization of particular skills, knowledge, and dispositions surrounds the worldwide use, promotion, and teaching of English. To be sure, the ability to communicate across geographies, countries, and cultures, often by means of information technologies and via multiple modalities, has come to the fore as a quintessential need for our times, and such communication is largely and increasingly done in English (McKay, 2002; Pennycook, 2007a, 2007b). Indeed, most national school systems offer instruction in English as a second language (Edge, 2006; Kumaravadivelu, 2006; Spring, 2008). Although the spread of English is viewed unproblematically by some (Crystal, 2003), there is considerable worry that the spread of English as the global language is resulting in the neglect and destruction of indigenous languages, a phenomenon that not only lessens the cultural richness of the planet but also disadvantages numerous children who are not allowed to learn in their home languages (cf. Canagarajah, 1999), making them further at risk as a byproduct.

Take the case of South Africa, a country in which English has been superimposed over all native languages in schools. There is very little literature in native languages: "Particularly in rural areas, but even in peri-urban and urban settings," writes Bloch (2006), "any print that might be abundant is in English or another ex-colonial language" (p. 22). So entrenched is the disempowerment of language and education policy that "a severe form of home-language deprivation is experienced by Xhosa-speaking learners in . . . schools which do not offer isiXhosa as a subject, let alone as a LoLT (Language of Learning and Teaching). Predictably, drop-out and failure rates are high" (Plüddemann, Braam, October, & Wababa, 2004, p. 40). These researchers claim that educational failure and dropout rates in South African schools are directly linked to the absence of the mother tongue as a language of learning in school; several others have also convincingly made the case for the paralyzing effects of the hegemony of English and other colonial languages in Africa (Bloch, 2006). Here we see the risk of putting another generation of South Africans—particularly the "born free" generation (Masland, 2004)—through a system of education in a superimposed language.[5]

On the other hand, the pan-African localization initiative, with Internet localization for African language support and extension, online dictionary development, and other features, is high on the development agenda (Osborn, 2006). Other attempts are also being made to overcome the dearth of the use of the mother tongue as the medium of instruction in the South African education system (Abel, 2001; Arua, 2001; Brock-Utne, Desai, & Qorro, 2004; Watson & Pienaar, 2007). The new national language and education policy prescribes mother-tongue instruction alongside other languages and English (up to sixth grade). Although the policy has been in existence for some time (see Plüddemann et al., 2004), it has not always seemed practical to implement (cf. Bekker, 2003; Dyers, 2004).

Exporting Accountability and At Riskness

The exportation of Western notions of accountability and risk is a third key theme in this literature. The World Bank (2008) has led the charge to empower youth, to focus on their needs and potential skills, in a series of reports. The latest of these suggests that

for a country or a region to be competitive, the education system must be capable of providing two types of services. First, it must be able to produce the broadest possible human capital base. If knowledge is increasingly recognized as key to competitiveness, it follows that, the more people have a fundamental level of instruction, the better. Second, if a country or region's "knowledge" endowment is to be ever elastic and growing, an individual's knowledge base must also continuously change and expand. (p. 86)

There is much to laud in any attempt to make countries "competitive" in a global world in which capital "is faster, more multiplicative, more abstract, and more invasive of national economies than ever in its previous history" (Appadurai, 2006a, p. 36). Without the support of organizations such as OECD and the World Bank, there would be many fewer attempts to ameliorate poverty in non-OECD countries.

However, we mention here two main critiques of the effects of the World Bank's work with youth. First, some argue that the ideology underlying the World Bank's many reports and surveys is geared toward "the incorporation of youth in a global, neoliberal economic system" (Sukarieh & Tannock, 2008, p. 302) instead of toward ensuring that youth are "agents of change, citizens and leaders, participants and activists" (p. 302). Sukarieh and Tannock (2008) assert that such reports put work, work skills, and the development of youth as workers above all else. In a similar analysis of the Mexican government's attempts to import Western assessments, Buenfil (2000) claims that the importance of the marketplace—the future employability of youth in a knowledge economy—subsumes interest in other issues related to education for purposes other than creating competitive workers and increasing human capital.

Second, many argue that such reports and tests, and the models of education on which they are based, are part and parcel of continued attempts to maintain hegemonic, Western notions of what counts as knowledge (Appadurai, 2001, 2006a, 2006b; Hoppers, 2000; Mbembe, 2001). These critics assert that such international reports—including World Bank Development summaries (Buenfil, 2000; Sukarieh & Tannock, 2008)—evaluate non-Western countries based on their own (Westernized) standards and make funding recommendations accordingly. We find that these international reports on youth education, and the attendant efforts to implement Westernized educational systems in developing countries, overlook the educational agendas of those countries themselves. Increasingly, however, those countries are talking back. For instance, Thaman (2007), writing as a citizen of Oceania, characterizes globalization and its influence on values as a serious threat to Pacific Islander cultures.

At the other end of the spectrum from such skill-, test score-, and economy-centric perspectives on risk, Suàrez-Orozco and Sattin (2007) argue that children in both developed and developing countries increasingly find schools boring and irrelevant. Ironically (given the World Bank's emphasis on training youth for productive work lives), Suàrez-Orozco and Sattin also argue that schools are failing to educate an increasing number of immigrants whose work currently fuels, and has the potential to add even more fuel to, the global economy. As a last note, we remind readers that such reports on the state of global education allow us to forget that many children in poorer parts of the "developing" world do not get to attend school at all.

COMING OF AGE IN A GLOBAL WORLD: POSSIBILITIES AS WELL AS RISK

Randy, aka Relix Stylz, is now in his late 20s and thereby is past the age usually ascribed to the category of youth in the United States, but he is not past the designation of youthful in other societies. Most certainly, he is not removed from a deep engagement in youth's cultural forms, especially hip-hop. A warehouse quality control checker who works a swing shift, he is an artist during as much of his nonwork time as he can manage—a writer, musician, performer, rapper, photographer, videographer, and digital storyteller par excellence. The artistry of his multimodal compositions—narrated poems or raps illustrated and extended by images found, taken, or constructed and usually set to his own music—have been chronicled through research (Hull & Katz, 2006; Hull & Nelson, 2005). Now that video can circulate easily on the Internet, his creative work has reached a wide audience, primarily in the United States but increasingly across the world (see www.youtube.com/user/Relixstylz).

His digital stories draw on his experience as a young African American male, offering his critical take on poverty, race, imprisonment, violence, and miseducation and also revealing his belief in hope, love, family, and social justice. His most recent piece, "Absolute," which juxtaposes images of atrocities in Darfur with the plight of African Americans past and present, reveals both his global consciousness and his commitment to local action. Having completed this digital story, he took it to a street corner in his city where most people do not venture and showed it to any youth who had the time to stop, watch, and listen, engaging with them over what they perceived its message to be (Hull & Nelson, in press). Like Laxmi and José, Randy would be considered by most as multiply at risk; indeed, he perseveres financially, hoping to convert his off-work labor into a job in the entertainment sector. And, like many young people who engage with popular cultural forms and new media, he is on the cutting edge of a new global aesthetics and creative practice. In fact, through his biography and his creative work, he prefigures many of the themes found in the literature in the following section on global youth.

In the previous section, we explored some of the ways in which processes associated with globalization are believed to have increased the material, social, and psychological vulnerabilities of young people; how youth have been framed as at risk in our global world; and how these framings are circulated, imposed, and contested. Next, we turn to a different literature on youth culture that is considerably more hopeful, if still wary of the impacts of globalization and the motivations propelling a neoliberal agenda (cf. Best & Kellner, 2003). The same processes of globalization that engender increasing risk for children can also afford some potential changes for the better—for upward social mobility or for destabilizing previously solidified social orders in which youth at risk have had the least possible options. These changes include both the opening up of new financial sources—for instance, the increase in human mobility has certainly led to an increase in the remittances sent home to children in developing countries by their parents (Orozco, 2002)—as well as new educational opportunities and efforts to foster the development of what Appiah (2006) terms cosmopolitan citizens. Studies of global youth culture, as we shall see, and as the vignette of Randy suggests, often emphasize the agency and creativity exhibited by young people in their local social worlds, in relation to and in intersection with global forces, at one and the same time that young people also experience new vulnerabilities via globalization. It is interesting that this literature rarely intersects with the global testing and accountability agenda or risk factor studies or, more generally, educational literature on the "disadvantaged." One aim of our review becomes, then, to juxtapose the insights and blind spots of such literatures that operate in parallel, each of which examines youth, risk, and globalization from particular ideological and disciplinary points of view.

The roots of global youth studies are found in the well-known "Birmingham School" of cultural studies, which began in the United Kingdom at the Centre for Contemporary Cultural Studies (CCCS) and focused on working-class youth. Willis's (1977) *Learning to Labour* is an early and still perhaps the most celebrated example of this kind of work. In his ethnography, Willis documented and theorized the process by which a group of working-class White boys embraced an antischool culture and thereby sealed their own fates, perpetuating their working-class position. Scholars at the CCCS in turn drew their inspiration from the well-known U.S. sociological tradition of ethnography that flourished at the University of Chicago in the 1960s and focused on subcultures, especially among youth, labeled deviant by the mainstream (cf. Hebdige, 1979).

Although these literatures did not use the terminology of "at riskness," they clearly focused on youth who would, in different traditions, be gathered under this label. The virtues and shortcomings of these antecedent literatures have been rehearsed many times. For example, this scholarship is renowned for bringing to light the social reproduction practices and processes of such youth (cf. Skelton & Valentine, 1998) but has been taken to task for the limitations of a class-based analysis that has neglected gender and culture and valorized resistance (cf. Huq, 2006; McRobbie, 1991, 1993). It has been celebrated for calling attention to the importance of popular culture and young people's "symbolic creativity" (Willis, 1990), but it has been pilloried as well for its limited and limiting constructions of subcultures. For thoroughgoing reviews of these founding literatures, as well as the newer work that attempts to redress some of its shortcomings through a theorization of "new ethnicities" (Hall, 1997), see also Bucholtz (2002), Nayak (2003), Rampton (1999), and Turner (1996).

The recent work that we feature below has attempted to move beyond the limitations of the older cultural studies approaches. Even more important for our project, we bring to center stage work that locates itself, and the youth it portrays, in the global moment. Although accounts of youth cultures from the perspective of cultural studies abound, scholarship on young people that is alert to the promise and hazards of globalization is still relatively scarce, as is work that deliberately expands its purview beyond U.S., U.K., or Western perspectives. We agree with Bucholtz (2002), who argues that "a full account of youth as cultural agents . . . must look not only to the U.S., Britain, and other postindustrial societies for evidence of youth cultural practices, but also to young people's cultural innovations in other locations around the world" (p. 539). We would add that those youthful innovations are currently imbricated by the global in ways never before possible for most young people and that youthful agency, long theorized by cultural studies approaches, both draws new life and faces new challenges from unprecedented and unprecedentedly uneven cultural, economic, and technological flows (also see Best & Kellner, 2003).

How do youth, diverse in location, privilege, ideology, and aspiration, experience their coming of age in a global world? What obstacles do they face, and what potentials might empower them? What awarenesses, what habits of mind and body, mediate their encounters with local and global activities? And, for those youth such as Laxmi and José, whose vulnerabilities are more apparent than most because they are thought to be multiply "at risk," what does a global world offer, and what does it portend? How might we usefully interleave such understandings of coming of age in a global world with literatures on education and risk? These are the kinds of questions that we believe could helpfully motivate a global youth studies more responsive to risk as well as promise.

The following review draws primarily from three edited volumes, selected because of their deliberate focus on contemporary research on youth culture situated at the confluence of global and local (cf. Grossberg, 1993). We paid particular attention to empirically based chapters in transnational or non-Western contexts; a focus on these contexts composed the majority of the chapters in two of the three volumes, or approximately 30 chapters and individual studies. Maira and Soep's (2005) *Youthscapes: The Popular, the National, the Global* takes its initial inspiration, as its title suggests, from Appadurai's (1996) notion of "scapes"—ethnoscapes, technoscapes, financescapes, ideoscapes, mediascapes—that are suggestive of the multiple perspectives and dimensions of global cultural flows. Young people's experiences range over all of these, and by appropriating Appadurai's terminology, Maira and Soep call attention to the centrality of youth in global economic, cultural, and social processes. Studies of youth culture and globalization have not often intersected, perhaps because "much work on globalization and transnationalism has tended to focus largely or explicitly on adults, and youth are assumed to be incomplete social actors, or subjects less able to exert agency in the face of globalization" (p. xxii). They set out to redress the balance by calling attention to "the ways young people *themselves* understand or grapple with globalization" (p. xx).

Nilan and Feixa (2006a), editors of *Global Youth? Hybrid Identities, Plural Worlds*, are interested "in the social construction of identity, in young people as creative social actors, in cultural consumption and social movements—the distinctiveness of local youth cultures in a globalized world" (Nilan & Feixa, 2006b, p. 1). They are adamant that the forces of globalization do not merely homogenize youth, destroying local variation and imposing Western values, but rather that cultural interactions result in "hybridizations" whereby both "global cultures are assimilated in the locality, and . . . non-western cultures impact upon the West" (p. 2; cf. Luke & Luke, 2000). They introduce research by non-Western researchers on youth cultures from 11 countries on five continents. Contributors to Dolby and Rizvi's (2008) *Youth Moves: Identities and Education in Global Perspective* focus on multiple meanings of mobility in a global age, or "how youth 'move' within these new geographies of modernity" (p. 5). Such movements include the literal movement of people through travel and immigration and for education; the figurative movement of images, texts, and information constructed, sent, and received through digital technologies; movement through imagination (Appadurai, 2001); and mixtures of literal and figurative movement as diasporic communities are formed and maintained.

These authors are also interested in how youth themselves produce the conditions that will change their futures. Although they pay some attention to schools as important sites for youth, they believe, as do the contributors to the other volumes, that "other sites are also both pedagogical and formative of the increasingly global terrain on which youth find themselves" (p. 6)—including the arenas of work, technology, and consumer culture.

To analyze the chapters in these volumes for what they might tell us about youth who are growing up in a global world, we devised, through open and iterative coding, approximately 20 categories and subcategories related to youth and globalization. They can be summarized as follows: (a) the extent to which globalization is experienced as hegemonic or as having multiple, at times unpredictable impacts, as well as resistances and receptiveness on the part of youth to Western and U.S. influences; (b) "hybrid" practices as the result of global flows and hybridization as a global habit of mind; (c) the process of identity formation for youth, including the creation of and interconnections among transnational, national, and local senses of self; (d) the nature of youth agency in a global world, including manifestations of resistance, young consumers as choosers, and "reflexivity" about global processes; (e) the confluence of popular culture, consumption, and identity in youth culture the world over; (f) an aesthetic turn, the centrality of symbolic creativity in youth culture, manifested in the consumption and production of music, video, language, and fashion, its global influences, local variations, and reliance on digital media and technologies; (g) the creation, reclamation, and reconfiguration of desirable spaces for interaction, consumption, play, and creativity—spaces both literal and metaphorical, actual and digital; and (h) trajectories within and toward education and work, or the lack thereof, including labor around aesthetic practices. These we explain and illustrate below.[6]

Appropriating and Recontextualizing the West

If globalization is a unidirectional force, colonizing, destroying, or homogenizing local cultures (the so-called McDonaldization phenomenon), then we can expect its impacts on youth to be routinely pernicious. But globalization is rarely characterized in this way in the youth culture literature, although many scholars and others express their misgivings and worries over its impacts and implications. References are made, for example, to the destructive hegemony of English (Dallaire, 2006); it is lamented that African American cultural styles define being Black in countries such as Canada (Kelly, 2008); and certain governments, such as France and Singapore, to name only two, adopt policies to protect their languages, prevent brain drain, and control their youths' adoption of Western values and popular cultural styles. But, by and large, when youth cultures are examined, researchers find, first, a range in the degree of uptake of things Western, across youth cultures internationally and even within a given nation state.

A case study of two middle-class Japanese teenagers showed how their peer group embraced Western popular cultural materials via cell phone technologies, enjoying the display of all things cool through "engaging in shared acts of consumption"

(Holden, 2006, p. 87). Nilan (2006), whose research focused on devout middle-class urban Muslim girls in Indonesia, observed the careful consumptive choices these young women made around cosmetics, music, and clothing, including global popular cultural products personalized by Islamist iconography, that were acceptable within religious law. Nilan described their conscious positioning of themselves as anti-Western and anti-American and their selective consumer choices as the "antithesis to Western cultural hegemony" (p. 91). Shahabi (2006) presented data on three types of youth in Iran, demonstrating the variation within youth cultures there, using the categories "conventional," "cosmopolitan," and "radical." Those she termed "cosmopolitan" youth (who were middle and upper class) embraced many things Western and resisted the authority of the religious state, though not necessarily because of political motivations, whereas the "radical" young people were intent on rejecting the same; yet, both were subject to exposure at school to Islamic values.

A second finding across the studies of youth culture that we reviewed, in relation to worries about the hegemony of globalization, is the recontextualizing (Bauman & Briggs, 1990) of ideas, artifacts, and values as well as a pluralism of discourses and cultural forms. Niang (2006), studying Sénégalese "bboys" (or break boys, Bronx boys, bad boys—all synonyms for male participants in hip-hop culture), noticed that their use of African American culture was "much more complex than simple imitation" (p. 168). As others who study the international appropriation of hip-hop have observed (Pennycook, 2003; Spady, Alim, & Meghelli, 2006), local variations and blends abound. Nuttall (2008) examined not only hip-hop practices but also what she termed, following Foucault (2005), the "self-stylization" of mostly middle-class youth associated with post-apartheid "Y" culture in Johannesburg, South Africa. In this context, youth also draw on Black American culture to "rework" it.

Shepler (2005) writes about former child soldiers in Sierra Leone. There "legions of youth with no hopes for education or employment" (p. 119) were conscripted as child combatants and committed atrocities during the war, but postwar they learned to make use of local and global discourses and cultural forms—for example, ideas from NGOs about the helplessness, innocence, and the rights of children; Rambo films and many other circulating popular media products; and local models of forgiveness—to begin finding their ways back into their local communities. To sort out the social and cultural influences on the child soldiers, Shepler argues that "these children are globalized in that they are caught up in sweeping international forces, and they are globalizing in that they are strategic users of global discourses and cultural artifacts" (p. 121). We find Shepler's argument a helpful way to resolve the at times strident tension between the risk literature and the youth studies scholarship. Youth and children are in both subtle and obviously horrific ways vulnerable in our world, but as the examples above begin to suggest, they are also active, inventive, creative beings, busy making what sense of it they can, drawing on the local and global cultural resources to which they have access.

Hybridization: A Global Habit of Mind

The term "hybridity" is ubiquitous in the youth cultures literature and suggests somewhat more concretely how global cultural forms can mix or blend with rather than cannibalize the local. Long used in postcolonial literature (e.g., Bhabha, 1994), it has also been popularized through Bakhtin (1981), who used it in reference to the polyphony of dialects, registers, and languages found within even a single culture. We believe that accounts of hybridity go some distance in the youth cultures literature in illustrating how local youth are creative participants rather than global dupes or victims in processes of cultural production and consumption (cf. Knobel & Lankshear, 2008; Kraidy, 2005). Once more, then, we see global youth studies taking care to characterize youth as more than merely at risk. In the introduction to their edited volume, Nilan and Feixa (2006b) recount in some detail their choice of "hybrid" as a descriptor for "identities" in the title of their book:

On the one hand, hybridization is a process of cultural interactions between the local and global, the hegemonic and the subaltern, the centre and the periphery. On the other hand, hybridization is a process of cultural transactions that reflects how global cultures are assimilated in the locality, and how non-western cultures impact upon the West. (p. 2)

Reports of blendings of musical traditions are common in this literature. Valdivia (2008) mentions "reggeaton" as popular currently among Latina/o youth in the United States but predicts in the fast-moving culture of youth that in another year this blending of Caribbean, Hispanic, and Anglo traditions will be old news, already transformed. (Similarly, youth in Los Angeles who devote themselves to the urban dance form called "krumpin" claim that to miss an evening of practice means to be out of date, so quickly do the moves evolve [see LaChapelle, 2005].) Hybridization also describes processes of ethnic, national, and diasporic identity formation. Butcher and Thomas (2006) studied young people from migrant backgrounds in Sydney, Australia, primarily second-generation Middle Eastern and Asian youth, and found them actively attempting to define themselves at once as contemporary Australians, as connected to their families' cultural backgrounds, and as a part of global youth culture. This sometimes confusing process is captured by a 15-year-old of Lebanese descent, when asked to describe his cultural background: "Well I can't decide what I am. Sometimes I'm like 'what's up bro' and other times I'm like 'g'day mate.' Sometimes I eat woggy food and sometimes I eat meat pies" (p. 64).

Butcher and Thomas (2006) provide several striking examples of staggeringly hybrid identity work among youth who hail, and whose families hail, from different multiple countries, who speak multiple languages, and who partake of multiple traditions. They describe the mixing of cultural forms and identities that they observed among youth as "ingenuous," "inventive" (p. 69), and adaptive, and following Amit-Talai and Wulff (1995) they predict that resulting intercultural skills and dispositions prepare these young people well for poly-ethnic settings of the future. Indeed, one productive reading of the global youth literature could take as its purpose gleaning

concrete examples of the habits of mind, interpretive skills, and interactional strategies and expectations that are gathered under rubrics such as "global awareness" in
lists of 21st century skills (e.g., Partnership for 21st Century Skills; see
http://www.21stcenturyskills.org/index.php). It could be argued, then, that many
contemporary youth, by virtue of necessity, are themselves at work lessening their
own at riskness in our global world. It is important, however, not to romanticize or
overestimate this necessity or to abdicate institutional responsibility for fostering such
valued skills, dispositions, and identities. Petrova (2006), providing a counternarrative, has explored the emergence of contemporary skinhead cultures that "represent
intensely hybrid identity formations" (p. 202); these formations are, by and large,
anything but desirable responses to global exigencies.

Conceptualizing Agency Beyond Resistance

The calling card of early cultural studies work was its sustained interest in theorizing resistance as a quintessential instantiation of youth agency. As has often been
noted, the Birmingham School framed their analyses in reference to postindustrial
Britain and conflicts among social classes. So it was that Willis's (1977) working-
class lads were viewed as putting themselves at risk by contributing to the reproduction of their own working-class status through their rejection of school. Now, of
course, the settings for cultural studies of youth extend far beyond the United
Kingdom to globalizing postcolonial contexts, whereas interpretive frames that rely
only on class-based analyses and that privilege White male experience are considered
less than salutary. An important focus for future theorizations and empirical
research, we believe, is how agency and resistance might be best conceptualized in
relation to global youth (cf. Bucholtz, 2002; Grossberg, 1993; Maira & Soep, 2005)
as well as how these concepts intersect with the understandings of youth at risk.

The studies we reviewed suggest several directions. In general, this scholarship
decouples youth agency from traditional notions of resistance, and at its most con-
vincing it examines youth agency as realized within particular historical, social, economic, and cultural contexts. Youth are generally represented as active, creative, and
productively engaged, almost always in popular cultural worlds rather than school;
often as reflective and strategic, especially in relation to consumption; and more rarely
as politically alert and involved in working toward social change. Even when youth
are obviously vulnerable, and the social, political, and economic dangers of their lives
are clearly in view, at riskness is usually not dwelled on in this literature, nor are institutional, pedagogical, or programmatic interventions generally offered (for an exception, see G. A. G. Vasquez, 2005). This is, no doubt, a disciplinary entailment rather
than a lack of interest; cultural studies scholarship is not customarily called on to provide solutions, and its focus on popular culture has privileged out-of-school and non-
institutional contexts. However, the insights about youth gleaned through global
youth studies seem to us richly informative for classroom inventions and teacher
education and for rethinking conceptions in the educational literature of youth as at

risk or disadvantaged. On the other hand, schools and other educational settings deserve attention, via serious reconceptualizations, not merely as incidental sites for identity development via popular cultural means (cf. Dolby, 2001) but also as genuine venues for learning and for trajectories toward work, career, and citizenship in a globalized world.

The following examples make concrete some of the points about agency, resistance, and risk summarized above. In the context of a globalizing South India, Lukose (2008) examines the "consumer agency" of young women. She uses as an example for analysis the controversial "Miss World" pageant, which liberal and conservative women alike decried (albeit for different reasons), and the choices that young women make around clothing—the selection, for example, of the "churidahs" as a garment of compromise between traditional Indian and Western tastes. Her analysis brings to light unexpected subtleties around consumption, demonstrates that agency does not automatically connote resistance, and calls attention to the importance of understanding consumer agency and other instances of youth cultural practices within historical, political, and economic contexts. Indian girls, she argues, make their choices regarding fashion within a colonial and postcolonial discourse about consumption.

Thus, the act of "choosing" or "selecting," usually in relation to being a consumer, is a thread that runs through studies of global youth culture. Sometimes researchers suggest that this quality of reflexiveness (Giddens, 1991) distinguishes global youth as having a particular kind of postmodern consciousness that can even promote an awareness that tends toward the critical (cf. Lash, 1994; Nilan & Feixa, 2006a). But, of course, this is not automatically the case, as Holden's (2006) study of mobile phone use demonstrates. In this study, youth participated actively, playfully, and optimistically with new technologies but with little awareness of the patterns and significance of their consumptive practices. Figuring out how to position youth to be reflective, a project long valued in critical studies of education, might be reinvigorated by such insights from global youth studies. Echoing Benjamin (2002), Kenway and Bullen (2003, 2008) use the term *cyberflâneur* (also see Featherstone, 1998) to describe a particular kind of youth engagement with and in the global world. Kenway and Bullen (2008) call for a "postcritical pedagogy" that combines being critical of media products with having fun, so that "the earnestness of the critical is balanced with parody, play, and pleasure, and parody, play, and pleasure are understood as political" (p. 23). Such pedagogies include "Reclaim the Streets" parties as well as the design and use of critical political action websites such as www.whirledbank.org (satirizing the World Bank's mission), www.mcspotlight.org (an anti-McDonald's site), and www.globalarcade.org, at which youth can "play arcade games and learn about globalization" (Kenway & Bullen, 2008, p. 23).

Once more, careful contextualizations of global youths' agency, resistance, or seeming lack thereof within historical, political, and social configurations of power, constraint, and opportunity can reenergize our conceptual categories, including our understandings of global and local relationships. Shepler's (2005) study of child soldiers in Sierra Leone is a case in point. As mentioned earlier, these children strategically adopted a variety of global and local discourses, creating a bricolage that combined elements from local and Western cultures, including an international discourse about children's rights that frames children as innocent and deserving of protection. Shepler points out the irony of the former child soldiers being able to express agency by claiming none, an insight that allows her to frame a question that captures the importance of careful contextualizations: Where do we locate youths' power? Sometimes that power seems reduced to practices of consumption, as already discussed, or connected to the stylization of self and other creative practices of meaning making, as we see below; but in Shepler's study, the power came from a shift in subjectivity, from the wielding of force to the assumption of helplessness. What an important reminder, as we contemplate risk and equity in a global world and as we extend our worldviews to include the cosmopolitan and the non-Western, that youthful agency comes in many shapes, sizes, and disguises.

Symbolic Creativity and an Aesthetic Turn

During the past 10 years, there has been what we label an "aesthetic turn" in studies of youth culture, in which accounts of participation in popular cultural forms, especially music and media-related consumption and production, have taken center stage, pushing the older tradition of accounting for the class-based resistance of young people to the side (cf. Bucholtz, 2002; Nayak, 2003).[7] This does not mean that all youth who are so engaged do so without being politically alert or aware. In his study of the hip-hop countercultural youth movement in Dakar, Sénégal, Niang (2006) contends that "the musical and cultural meaning of local rap is constituted in significant critical fields such as inadequate social policy, stultifying social practices, infuriating inequalities, and everyday harsh reality for Africans" (p. 168). However, the road is not smooth, even when one's political vision is clear. The Sénégalese rappers, already members of the majority poor, were sometimes further marginalized by their own communities because of their participation in hip-hop, especially their adoption of distinctive fashion statements such as baggy trousers, and were dismissed as foolish imitators of African American urban youth. Comparing the British Asian underground to French hip-hop, Huq (2006) traces the movement of hip-hop in these countries from the margins to the mainstream, economically but also culturally, as these musical forms receive more acceptance. He makes the point that the music is now international, not American, and that the new hybridized forms belong incontrovertibly to their local contexts and suggest "a decentering of the West" (p. 28). There is, of course, a huge literature on hip-hop worldwide (cf. Condry, 2001 [Japanese B-boys and B-girls]; Durand, 2002 [Francophone hip-hop]; and Ibrahim, 1999 [Canadian Africans adopting hip-hop]).

Our modest point here is that educators interested in youth conventionally viewed as at risk would do well to be mindful of the relationships between youthful agency and music, especially hip-hop, along with other forms of popular culture, for insights about what Huq (2006) terms youths' "productive engagement" (p. 14) and

Muñoz and Marín (2006) similarly describe as "active and creative engagement . . . in the production of meanings" (p. 130). It is surely important to consider why it is that many young people who would be considered at risk in every category, and are mostly if not completely disengaged with school, reveal themselves to be remarkably devoted to and adept at the sophisticated and skillful interpretation and creation of popular cultural forms (cf. Hull & Nelson, 2005; Hull & Schultz, 2002; Kirkland, 2007; Muñoz & Marín, 2006).

We interpret the aesthetic turn among youth not only as a venue on the part of some for engaging in collective politically alert activity but also as the expression of a quintessentially human need to make meaning by engaging in what Willis (1990) termed "symbolic creativity." Through language, visual arts, dance, music, or a multi-modal combination of these (cf. Finnegan, 2002), youth express themselves through performance, the production of artifacts, and the stylization of their bodies. The significance of such creative activity for young people is perhaps lost for some through the negative connotations of *popular* in popular culture (cf. Bucholtz, 2002; Willis, 1990). However, we can begin to appreciate its role by acknowledging its connection to the active construction of a self. The aesthetic activities of youth, we and others submit (cf. Muñoz & Marín, 2006), join palpably the pleasures of making meaning with the pleasures of constructing and enacting a self. This is quite a potent combination. In their study of music in Columbian youth cultures, Muñoz and Marín (2006) assert that participation in an artistic process, such as music making, "leads young people towards self-creation, to the production of new subjectivities—to the search for, and generation of, *something else* in the domains of ethics, politics, art and forms of knowledge converted into praxis" (p. 132). They describe what they term the "motor forces of creation" (p. 132) that drive or liberate creativity in youth cultures. One example is the ethos of DIY, or "do it yourself," which encourages young people to believe that "anyone can," including them. Another example is the importance of searching for one's own style and making one's own mark within a culture, a hip-hop mantra.

Included as well among youths' aesthetically alert practices, also long noted by researchers (cf. Willis, 1990), are self-stylizations—the cultivation of a look, a style, a language, a set of tastes and preferences—meant and used to signal membership and establish group boundaries as well as to set oneself apart individually. In her book-length ethnography, Dolby (2001) demonstrates how "coloured," Black, White, and Indian youth enacted racial categories in a post-apartheid South African school through choices in clothing, music, and place. Although the site for her study was a school, she observes that "formal schooling is increasingly marginalized and disconnected from the pulse of students' lives" (p. 9), and she argues instead that "the global context of popular culture emerges as a critical site for the negotiation of race: for the marking of racialized borders, and for their subsequent displacement an rearrangement" (p. 9). Dolby thereby joins symbolic creativity and race. A major finding from her study is that global popular culture—specifically, the selection and combination of global commodities and preferences and their use and signification in a South African post-apartheid context—has become racialized: "Race is defined and determined," Dolby writes, "through attachments to particular aspects of popular culture," and "popular culture is foregrounded as a terrain of struggle, from the school fashion show, to the music played at school events such as dances to school sports" (p. 15).

Also writing about the "born-free" generation of South Africa (Masland, 2004), those first to come of age post-apartheid, Nuttall (2008) describes "Y Culture," known too as *Loxion Kulcha.* "Y" comes from a radio station called "YFM," set up in 1996, 2 years after the democratic transition, as dedicated airspace for South African youth. This station played and popularized *kwaito,* a local music form that gained international popularity; a hip magazine; and a fashion label, "Loxicon Kulcha." The language play in the latter—"loxicon" is a text-message-type spelling of "location," which is also a synonym for "township," and "kulcha" is a humorous spelling of "culture"—signifies a remix, the infusion of the township, long isolated from the central city, into a previously White preserve. Nuttall also analyzes a set of advertisements appearing in magazines and on billboards that similarly, but in an edgier way, take up issues related to South Africa's racial history and, through irony and parody, redraw race in relation to style and class. For example, one advertisement for sports shoes showed several Black and White young people, all dressed in white sports gear, lounging next to a street sign that reads "Whites only," while a policeman arrests a man who is not dressed in white. The image plays on the apartheid practice of arresting Africans who did not have passes to authorize their presence in a locale and suggests that the crime of the current moment is a fashion faux pas—in effect, that style trumps race.

Nuttall (2008) argues, then, that within such youth cultural forms "selfhood and subjectivity are presented less as inscriptions of broader institutional and political forces than as an increased self-consciousness about the fashioning of human identity as a manipulable artful process" (p. 151). The body as canvas, language as play and wit, the production of aesthetic distinctions that mark one as cool, as knowledgeable: These are Foucault's technologies of the self (Martin, Gutman, & Hutton, 1987) and youths' modus operandi at the current historical moment. In Nuttall's words, "To be in Johannesburg today is to feel the immense coincidence of the end of apartheid and the rise of globalization, new media cultures and cultures of consumption" (p. 153). Such creative practices around self-fashioning do not, of course, obviate the racialized oppression that endures in South Africa post-apartheid.

The aesthetic turn is increasingly mediated and amplified by digital and electronic technologies that themselves sometimes become an extension of the bodies of global youth—mobile phones, iPods, and, formerly, boom boxes. And now, more and more routinely for some youth across the world, access to multimedia tools for creation and composition, not only and not even primarily consumption and interpretation, are becoming more the norm (cf. Hill & Vasudevan, 2008). In the edited collections that we reviewed, scholars noted inequalities regarding access to such tools and other accoutrements of being cosmopolitan in a global world, principally symbolic and literal mobility. Concomitantly, they acknowledged with angst their research focus on more privileged youth, often in Western but sometimes too in developing and transforming societies, for whom access and mobility are not at issue. However, the ascendancy of the digital in a global world and the connectivity and geographic and semiotic reach of the Internet are, at the end of the day, taken in the youth cultures literature as givens. There are increasing if uneven numbers of examples, too, of youth in developing, transforming, and non-Western societies who achieve and put to advantage access to digital tools. The central questions become, then—apart from how we might further improve access and equity in regard to the distribution and circulation of tools in new media age (cf. Moje et al., 2008)—the following: How do global youth employ the tools, and toward what ends? What are the implications and complications of their uses for youths' consciousness about self and other, for their literacies, and for their social and economic futures?

Partly because the Internet can reduce distance and increase reach—enabling global flows, to use the common metaphor—those who study technology and literacy recognized earlier than most the value of taking a global perspective on digitally enabled practices of interconnection. Lam's (2000) study of a Chinese American student is a case in point. This teenager used the Internet to create a website about a Japanese pop singer and developed a social network of interlocutors around the world who were interested in communicating about the same; along the way, he significantly improved his English, although he had not been able to make such progress in school. More broadly, Lam's work on literacy learning in transnational digital contexts signals the importance of the Internet as a site for communication across diasporas as well as skill acquisition. Schneider (2005) similarly examined the identity formation of a youthful immigrant but conducted a "reception case history" over a period of years, taking her disciplinary starting point from film studies. Schneider's particular purpose was to explain why Jackie Chan films held such sway as a role model for this young person, who was a Tamil immigrant from Sri Lanka living in Switzerland in the mid-1990s with foster parents.

This young person began watching Chan's movies on TV and proceeded with typical fan activities such as collecting and archiving newspaper articles and promotional materials, compiling lists of films, imitating the star's poses in photographs. He later made brief movies himself, including Jackie Chan trailers and then "Schlegli" films, or "beat-em-up" (Schneider, 2005, p. 145) movies, in Chan fashion. Like the young man in Lam's study, he independently engaged with writing as a part of his fan activities, and he likewise struggled with writing in school. It is important that Schneider demonstrates how Jackie Chan represents not only an Asian male superstar (cf. Soep, 2005) but also a cosmopolitan who is globally successful. In Schneider's words, Chan represented "a necessary symbolic resource for the negotiation of questions of belonging and diaspora identity, and of the conflicts that come with them" (p. 154). What a wealth of information such a study can provide educators about the desires, proclivities, abilities, and the "motor forces of creation" (Muñoz & Marín, 2006, p. 132) that propel their students, who are often generally and simplistically summarized as "at risk" in their increasingly globalized home and school contexts.

Creating, Reclaiming, and Reconfiguring Desirable Spaces

The Internet is daily claimed by global youth as a powerful space for interaction, consumption, play, creativity, and learning. Indeed, a sensitivity to space, place, and landscape (Mitchell, 2002)—actual, digital, metaphorical and mixtures thereof— runs through global youth studies, and it has indeed invigorated social science research during the past decade, resulting in an emphasis on the spatial as well as the temporal and the social (cf. Leander & Sheehy, 2004; Massey, 1998b; Nayak, 2003; Scourfield, Dicks, Drakeford, & Davies, 2006; Skelton & Valentine, 19988; Soja, 1996). We suggest that a mapping of how youth and others, in the context of glob- alization, its constraints, and its affordances, are creating, reclaiming, and reconfig- uring desirable spaces for interaction, consumption, play, creativity, learning, and work is a necessary and important project in pushing forward an equity agenda. As a modest beginning, our review has alerted us to shifting and sliding dimensions in relation to youth and space—what is private, what is public; what is safe and what is dangerous; what is accessible, what is off limits, and where one can dare to trans- gress; where one can be visible, where invisibility is required, and where there is needed a masquerade; where performance and play come to the fore, and where par- ticipation and learning are possible and productive.

Holden (2006) demonstrated that in Japan, where young people have limited space, time, and finances and space is at a premium, mobile phones "provide an insular world of undisturbed thought and invisible social interactivity beyond the confines of an overly-constricted Japanese society" (p. 83). Soep (2005) unveiled the imaginative work of a group of adolescent boys (African American, Filipino American, and Chinese American) who used inexpensive VCRs and camcorders, their free time, and a mother's basement to "introduce into their domestic space global narratives—about immigra- tion, world politics, organized crime across national borders" (p. 176)—that is, to make a movie, pass time, and stay "clean." Nuttall (2008) detailed a postmodern cityscape called the "Zone," an upscale district in Johannesburg and home to Y Culture, described above. A public space, it is also an exclusive one that does not welcome the poor. Yet it is one of the city's "relatively few up-market open spaces where some manner of the unexpected is possible" and where "a young person (or anyone else) walking around the Zone circulates within an imagined Africa much larger than Johannesburg alone" (p. 156). Hansen (2008) took the cities of Recife, Hanoi, and Lusaka and their youth as a can- vas, insisting on the beneficial and necessary juxtaposition of urban and youth studies and investigating their reciprocal importance to each other.

Present and Absent Trajectories

Spaces, places, and landscapes are not only traversed internally but also moved across and through over time, a temporality and movement that should have special importance for youth, traditionally represented as progressing toward an age- determined adulthood that is accompanied by schooling, work, and familial transitions.

However, if there is anything plain and simple that a global view of youth can tell us, or even a nuanced view of youth in the United States, it is that the old patterns of age and prospects have been forever altered. Most young people in our global age cannot look forward to following traditional work, marriage, and family patterns, and their economic futures are uncertain also in the West where, granted, opportunities, resources, and possibilities nonetheless remain significantly greater in comparison to the rest of the world. In the words of Hansen (2008), "Regardless of how youth is defined, limited life opportunities and poor wage-labor prospects are challenging the age and gender ideals that used to guide the social organization of households and families in both the West and the developing world" (p. 9). If not silent on the absence of rewarding trajectories through school and into work and adulthood, most of the global youth literature that we have reviewed mentions these in passing, on its way toward vibrant descriptions of popular cultural sites, aesthetically primed participation, and the agentive production of hybrid cultural forms.

Notable exceptions to this work are Hansen's (2008) examination of the effects of globalization on the lived experience and future prospects of youth in three "developing countries," Nayak's (2003) ethnography of young White men's construction of masculine identities in northeastern England in the context of global change and economic restructuring, and Jeffrey and Dyson's (2008) edited collection of 13 detailed portraits of individual young people around the world and the everyday, daunting challenges they face, including homelessness, joblessness, and religious persecution. Another exception is Soep's (2005) study of boys' self-taught production of movies during their leisure time. It speaks to their longing (like Randy's) to practice the aesthetic labor they hope someday to be paid for and also how unlikely such occupational desires are to be fulfilled. Soep writes, "The reality is that few will land well-compensated, emotionally rewarding, and nonexploitative (on some level) positions in any field, let alone the global entertainment industry" (p. 191; cf. Tannock, 2000). There is a similar and related absence of accounts of the power and promise of schooling as preparation for living in a global world and developing cosmopolitan sensibilities.

This literature is uniformly glum about and almost dismissive of the relevance of schooling as usual for the future trajectories of youth in general and vulnerable youth especially. Some accounts illustrate how easily and unreflectively educators can proceed with conventional assumptions and curricula, marching out of step with young people's histories, identities, and desires for the future. Singh and Doherty (2008), for example, juxtaposed interviews with educators and their international students in Australian higher education, who were mainly of Chinese heritage from Southeast Asia and who comprised an impressive 23% of the total student population. The teachers, who found themselves increasingly part-time and at the economic mercy of multiple employers, made unhelpful and reductive moral judgments about these international students, viewing their motivations cynically and with disappointment. Singh and Doherty lay blame at the feet of an "institutionalized pedagogy that builds its common-sense categories solely from concepts of 'culture,' 'cultural difference,' and fixed cultural identities" (p. 116; cf. Sarroub, 2005).

In her foreword to Dolby's (2001) ethnography of a Durban high school, McCarthy (2001) makes clear the educational significance for researchers and educators in the West of not only Dolby's ethnography and what it reveals about the dynamic relationship of race and culture in South Africa but also scholarship on globalization in general. McCarthy's commentary is worth quoting at length:

Put directly, contemporary curriculum thinkers and practitioners cannot any longer afford to look askance at critical developments associated with globalization now transforming social and cultural life outside and inside schools around the globe. These developments have enormous implications for pedagogical practice and the educational preparation of school youth. . . . The great task of teachers and educators as we enter the new millennium is to address these new patterns of racial reconfiguration, cultural rearticulation, hybridity, and multiplicity now invading educational institutions in the new era of globalization. Against the tide of these developments, curriculum thinkers, particularly in the United States, have tended to draw down a bright line of distinction between the established school curriculum and the teeming world of multiplicity, hybridity and plurality that now flourishes in the everyday lives of school youth beyond the school. (p. 3)

We are likewise convinced, and we hope our review will persuade readers, of how critical it is for schools and educational practice to be informed by a global youth studies, a scholarship that we also argue should itself be engaged with the challenging landscape of school and curricular reform as well as the desires and needs on the part of global youth for satisfying and sustaining work and careers, even as solutions to school and work reform seem out of reach.

CONCLUSION: EQUITABLE SOLUTIONS FOR GLOBAL YOUTH

In a compelling book on media in our global world, Silverstone (2007) theorizes the potential of media to be a moral public space, a "mediapolis" where we see and are seen, where our worlds are represented, and where we have both a right to "hospitality," and thereby to be welcomed and to speak, and an obligation to be hospitable, to listen, and to hear. Silverstone argues that global media, both mass media and personal media, now position us to engage with the "other" as we and the rest of the world experience the "mediated images of strangers" that "increasingly define what constitutes the world" (p. 4). Silverstone believes that, to an extent, this experience can reverse the "customary taken-for-granted nature of media representation, in which we in the West do the defining, and in which you are, and I am not, the other" (p. 3); this perhaps will be an outcome of the social networking exchange in Laxmi's school, introduced at the beginning of our review. Like Appiah (2005, 2006) and Benhabib (2002), Silverstone wrestles with seemingly divisive global and local diversity and plurality, as they are juxtaposed with the necessity of interdependence. "Does difference," he asks, "condemn humanity either to indifference or to a fundamental refusal of its value" (p. 13)? Or can we adopt "cosmopolitanism" as an ethic, whereby we "recognize not just the stranger as other, but the other in oneself" (p. 14)? He continues, "Cosmopolitanism implies and requires, therefore, both reflexivity and toleration. In political terms it demands justice and liberty. In social terms, hospitality. And in media terms, it requires . . . an obligation to listen" (p. 14). We think of Randy's meditation on Darfur.

Silverstone's work resonates with several themes of this chapter. Most straightforwardly, it underlines the important place of media in processes of globalization, elaborating theoretically what the global youth we have introduced understand experientially: the positive and negative dimensions and potential of the role of media in connectivity and representation. Second, he reminds us once more of the interconnectedness of our world, despite its divisions, an interconnectedness, he insists, that is made possible by and experienced through media. Last, and most evocative in this context, he bravely asserts that media must be ethically constituted:

Insofar as they provide the symbolic connection and disconnection that we have to the other, the other who is the distant other, distant geographically, historically, sociologically, then the media are becoming the crucial environments in which a morality appropriate to the increasingly interrelated but still horrendously divided and conflictual world might be found, and indeed expected. (p. 8)

We similarly consider what might constitute ethical research and practice when our focus is equity and youth—youth at risk but youth, as we have seen, of vast promise—in a global world. One basic answer is that scholarship and activism around youth, risk, and equity must, *perforce,* be globally aware, positioning youth to learn, communicate, and participate and to do so across geographical, ideological, semiotic, cultural, and linguistic difference and boundaries.

The examples assembled below illustrate different possibilities for more equitable school and life experiences for youth such as Laxmi, José, and Randy, and a range of projects and types of involvement on the part of researchers and educators. The vicissitudes and challenges of globalization have forced some places—a school in Sweden, for example—to forge new educational pathways for their students. The potentialities of new technologies have opened up spaces for other programs—a teaching network in rural India, an after-school program in Louisiana, an interdisciplinary research program in Mumbai—to offer youth and their teachers new paths for academic and personal exploration and growth. We find that the five programs we highlight below, each of which Appadurai (2000) might term a "grassroots globalization effort," attempt to address some of the negative accompaniments of globalization: displacement, poverty, lack of educational opportunity, and the trauma that sometimes accompanies immigration.

Tensta Gymnasium: Local and Global Schooling

We learned about the Tensta Gymnasium from Marcelo Suàrez-Orozco and Carolyn Sattin (2007). This Stockholm school serves "children of displaced peoples from nearly every troubled spot on earth" (p. 14) and has worked to meet the needs of its students in innovative, but not impossible-to-duplicate ways. As Wikan (2007) notes, countries such as Sweden, Norway, and Denmark, whose languages are not spoken elsewhere yet which are increasingly multiethnic and multilingual, face huge and particular globalization-related challenges. Teachers and administrators at Tensta worked with their counterparts at their sister city, the Ross School in New York, to

overhaul their curriculum and entire ethos (see http://www.ross.org/podium/
default.aspx?t=36398). Suàrez-Orozco and Sattin (2007), and others (Crul, 2007;
Süssmuth, 2007; Wikan, 2007), document the changes at Tensta over time; they suggest that it serves as a model for schools in global cities because it encompasses

increasing diversity; increasing complexity; premiums placed on collaboration and interdisciplinary work,
taking multiple perspectives on problems, and moving across language and cultural boundaries; and the
sophisticated use of state-of-the-art technologies to enhance student engagement. (p. 17)

Writing about the integration of immigrant youth, Crul (2007) reminds us that
schools such as Tensta—with large immigrant populations and (at the start of this
documentation) low test scores and falling enrollment—do not become model
schools for large cities with more funds alone. "To turn the tide," Crul writes, "a
whole new concept of learning must be considered and carefully implemented"
(p. 227). He argues that increased teacher–student contact and interaction time are
central to the success of both the school and its students, as teachers are more easily
able to make interventions and tailor programs to students' needs when they have
more time to spend with students on meaningful activities (in direct contrast to the
working and learning conditions at José's school).

Digital Study Hall: Local Teaching, Global Network

Kanta, a teacher in an informal rural learning center in a remote village in northern India, stood in the tiny alcove of her two-room house. A dozen or so adolescent
girls sat crowded at her feet, having put aside their "chikan" embroidery, the vocational training their parents had sent them to receive, while a bevy of younger children peered in and pushed for a prime spot at the door. All awaited the start of the
video lesson, a digital story called "The Lion and the Tiger," which they listened to
and then read in English with Kanta's mediation, translating the unfamiliar words
into Hindi and back again. This remarkable scene comes courtesy of Digital Study
Hall (http://dsh.cs.washington.edu/), a teacher development project whose central
hub is physically located in Lucknow, Utter Pradesh, India, but whose spokes extend
to other parts of the country and more recently the world. In this project, urban and
rural teachers learn subject matter and pedagogy from digitized videos of good teaching. These videos are created in the classrooms of more experienced teachers, such as
those who teach at Laxmi's urban private school, and are mediated by local teachers
on site, with all teachers—and sometimes students standing in for teachers—learning
about practice (Sahni et al., 2008).

The use of inexpensive and readily available digital video technologies, combined
with an expansive notion of teaching, texts, and literacy, linked to a network of like-
minded teachers, trainers, and information and communications technology professionals, enables teachers such as Kanta, who have no formal training, to both learn
and teach a group of children whom the world has forgotten. The migration of people
and the movement of texts and images around the world are phenomena that some
consider the quintessential feature of our digital and global age (Appadurai, 1996).

Teachers such as Kanta and the youth she instructs have historically been shut out of these movements, confined and constrained geographically, socially, and educationally. However, the Digital Study Hall project provides evidence that it is possible to reconfigure flows of information, tools, people, and texts, creating a band of geospatial opportunity within which the educational and social spaces of inhabitants of remote villages can be improved, allowing them hopeful access to some of the advantages of a digital information age.

In one sense, this is a very local project, culturally attuned and informed by local knowledge and customs, but it is situated in a global network that extends to the edges of India and beyond, in terms of its users, funders, and human resources, especially its volunteers, who come principally from the United States. In addition, the literacy pedagogy—whole language, child centered—is nonlocal, and the ideas presented to teachers by teachers expand local ideas about what it means to teach and learn. We see this work as an integration of global literacies and local needs in so-called non-integrated gap areas, especially rural villages. These children and their teachers desire educational advancement, and the project itself is a melding of new technologies and a global perspective with the needs and life plans of the local population.

Hurricane Katrina Evacuees: Youth Writing Themselves Into Their Social Worlds

In this third example, we turn to work inspired by California-based UC Links researchers (e.g., Cole, 2006; O. Vasquez, 2003) and teachers in an after-school program for New Orleans youth displaced by Hurricane Katrina. This is one of a growing number of projects in which written and/or visual narratives serve as tools with which participants craft agentive selves (cf. Hull & Zacher, 2007). In the 2 years after the hurricane, UC Links set up an after-school program in one of the evacuee camps in Baton Rouge. The camp, "built" out of FEMA trailers, was home to an indeterminate number of children and youth who attended school and the after-school program sporadically. Local university students came to work with the youth, who attended to create digital stories about topics of their choosing. The goals of the project were twofold: "students used the virtual world of digital storytelling to negotiate their sense of displacement and to begin to re-define both their sense of place in a disordered world and their sense of themselves as emerging 'experts' in that world" (Avila, Underwood, & Woodbridge, 2008, p. 8; also see Avila, 2008).

We have included it here not only because of the use of digital technologies with youth who would not otherwise have access to them but also because the digital movie products, many visible online at http://www.storyagainstsilence.org, "enabled these students to write themselves back into their own lives and social worlds" (Avila et al., 2008, p. 9). Although Hurricane Katrina was a climatic event, the effects it produced in the United States are similar to the effects of some processes of globalization (i.e., civil war, immigration) on youth in the United States and in many other countries (see Taylor & Yamasaki, 2006). In this sense, a project that works with children in need, and offers ways for them to express themselves, acquire new skills, and perhaps recontextualize themselves in new futures, is a useful one indeed.

PUKAR: Documentation as Intervention and Research

In Mumbai, Arjun Appadurai, Carol A. Breckenridge, and their colleagues have created PUKAR, which both means "to call" in Hindi and is an acronym for "Partners in Urban Knowledge Action and Research" (see http://www.pukar.org.in). The overarching goal of PUKAR is "to bring together youth and globalization in a forum for cross-disciplinary debate oriented to extend beyond the upper middle-classes of the city" (Appadurai, 2006b, p. 173). Those who donate time to PUKAR—it is an extremely grassroots project, with no government funding, no NGO connections, and no university ties—do so with the desire to bring "the capacity to research within the reach of ordinary citizens, especially college-age youth" (p. 175). Lately, concerned with the accessibility and utility of research as well as the ways that knowledge is both "more valuable and more ephemeral" (p. 168) in a globalized world (also see Appadurai, 2001, 2006a), PUKAR has attempted to bring the "right to research," which is generally seen as the purview of more highly educated academics and professionals, to city youth.

One of the goals of PUKAR is an insistence that research in "the arts, humanities, film media should not be separate from research on the economy, infrastructure, and planning" (Appadurai, 2006b, p. 174). This ethos is combined with efforts to develop the ability to see how the city and its future are "embedded in global processes" (ibid.) in Mumbai citizens. According to the PUKAR website, a related goal is "to democratize research and broaden access to knowledge among disenfranchised or weakly institutionalized groups and to create a space from which their non-traditional and non-expert knowledge can contribute to local, national and global debates about their own futures" (http://www.pukar.org.in/aboutus.htm). The projects of these "barefoot researchers" (A. Appadurai, personal communication, September 2008) are based on research methods taught by Rahul Srivastava that Appadurai (2006b) characterizes as "documentation as intervention" (p. 174). Ten to fifteen "junior fellows" and up to 300 Mumbai youth are trained each year in these methods through the Youth Fellowship program (http://www.pukar.org.in/fellowship .htm). Thus, PUKAR directly addresses a growing knowledge gap—what Appadurai terms the "gap between the globalization of knowledge and the knowledge of globalization" (p. 175)—through active, experimental local partnerships that, according to PUKAR's own reports, afford Mumbai youth a more agentive sense of their relationship to their global city.

Brown Paper Studio

Run by a group of student volunteers from a local university and begun by a Fulbright scholar from the United States (Judyie Al-Bilali; see Al-Bilali, 2006), a group of youth meet weekly in a voluntary after-school program that contributes to the "arts and culture" component of the new South African curriculum. The school's endorsement of the Brown Paper Studio, as it is called, is partly informed by the fact that schools such as this, Glendale High, in Mitchell's Plain, a township created by the apartheid policy of forced removals in the 1970s, have no teaching capacity or infrastructure to implement the arts and culture aspect of the new outcomes-based curriculum. The aim of Brown Paper Studio, whose name comes from the practice of having brown paper sheets on the walls for participants to write on, is to use cultural engagement and creativity to promote cross-cultural engagement and understanding among youth who are severely at risk.

Many of these youth are from Mitchell's Plain, a township originally designated for "colored" or "mixed race" South Africans; because of political changes since 1995, refugees and Xhosa speakers have also moved in. Other attendees in search of ways to improve their English are from nearby historically designated Black townships. However, all of them are, like Laxmi, José, and Randy, young people variously "at risk." In fact, the Mitchell's Plain area is notorious in Cape Town for its high levels of poverty, alcoholism, gangsterism, and crime. Cape Town is also the South African city with the highest levels of violence perpetrated both against and by youth (Ward, Flisher, Zissis, Muller, & Lombard, 2001).

One recent product of the studio was a youth-authored play, titled *Only a Name*. In writing this particular play, youth participants chose to explore tensions between groups perceived as "other" long before the "outbreak" of xenophobia across the country (Flockemann, 2008). Indeed, the "others" referred to in the play were their own South African classmates, foregrounding the divisions between South African Black communities within the same classroom. The play developed through workshops and was often the subject of heated debates in which the youth were able to both perform and experience an approximation of Appiah's (2006) cosmopolitanism. The youths' involvement was via a rehearsal, rather than an enactment, of what Benhabib (2002) describes as a "deliberative democracy" sensitive to political and cultural differences, allowing these differences to be voiced, contested, and negotiated. The self-stylization involved in these performative enactments was not an end in itself; rather, it became the method through which the young people could enter into conversations with others and experiment with issues encountered in broader civic society, intimate relationships at home, their classroom, and the streets of Mitchell's Plain, all spheres in which they can still be defined as at risk.

Equitable Solutions and Futures?

A conundrum of this review is that it juxtaposes evidence of the creativity, agency, and bursting potential of youth growing up in a global world with the undeniable, severe, and intolerable material constraints associated with poverty and other inequalities as well as the dangers associated with ideological differences. So at one and the same time, our challenge is to acknowledge the ways that youth are indeed at risk in a global world and to refuse to allow reductive notions of risk to limit our visions of ability, curriculum, schooling, and life trajectories. We believe the above examples of research, program development, and teaching, often intertwined, accomplish these double aims. In the search for educational experiences, programs, institutions, and practices that will make a difference in the lived experiences and life chances of global youth at risk, we acknowledge, with Luke (2008), that educational efforts alone are generally insufficient, needing to be joined to sociologically aware theorizing (e.g., Albright & Luke, 2007; Bourdieu, 1977), broader economic reform, and more comprehensive interventions (e.g., Tough, 2008). Yet within the realm of education, it is nonetheless crucial to consider what educational approaches, pedagogies, programs, and theories can best constitute equitable and powerful contexts for learning and identity formation in a global world and—like the efforts illustrated in the last section—do our best to help create them. Such work will do more than glamorize the creativity of youth who are so at risk that their agency alone cannot clear a path to successful school and work trajectories. It will also see past futures that can only be bleak, in which young people do not measure up, their worlds are hopelessly constrained, and they are viewed as merely at risk.

NOTES

[1] The names of people and places are pseudonyms.

[2] Sachs (2006) reminds us that poverty varies in its extremity; for example, most who are considered poor in the United States, although certainly disadvantaged here, do not suffer the same deprivation or face such severe struggles as do people who are poor in parts of Africa. The same is true, of course, when we consider youth labeled "at risk." There is a danger in asserting an equivalency between youth "at risk" here and elsewhere, as one of the reviewers of this article helpfully noted. Indeed, Laxmi's material circumstances are both better and worse than those of youth in different settings and societies. Creating a heightened awareness of this lack of equivalency is, in fact, one of the goals for our article, but at the same time we see benefits in examining the commonalities that connect youth who are growing up in a global world.

[3] We regularly refer in this article to the "West" and "Western," as do many of the researchers whose work we review. We acknowledge that, although we do not herein unpack and complicate these terms, there is a great need to do so in our own work as in much contemporary scholarship. For an example of how these terms can be helpfully interrogated in relation to language and literacy scholarship, see Bhattacharya (2008).

[4] As even its supporters acknowledge, the notion of cosmopolitanism is problematic in a number of ways, including its association with elitist and mainly Western traditions. For discussions of cosmopolitanism, see Beck (2006), Held (1995, 2003), Luke and Carrington (2002), and Silverstone (2006).

[5] For descriptions of localized critical literacy efforts in South Africa, including attempts to both foster and document multimodal literacies, see Stein (2000), Stein and Newfield (2002), and Stein and Slonminsky (2006).

[6] There is not a one-to-one mapping of the eight analytic categories to the sections that follow because some categories, such as identity formation, thread throughout.

[7] It remains to be seen whether what we have called an aesthetic turn reflects a change in the actual phenomena among the populations studied or a shift in the focus of the researchers themselves in terms of what piques an ethnographic imagination. We thank Allan Luke for this insight.

ACKNOWLEDGEMENTS

We thank the following colleagues and friends for their generous assistance in preparing this article: Marina Aminy, Arnetha Ball, Vivian Gadsden, Norton Grubb, Adrienne Herd, Lanette Jimerson, Joanne Larson, Allan Luke, Julia Menard-Warwick, Mihir Pandya, Urvashi Sahni, Loukia Sarroub, Shannon Stanton, and Mayssun Sukarieh.

REFERENCES

Abel, L. (2001). Challenges to reading teachers in multilingual settings in South Africa. In E. Arua (Ed.), *Reading for all in Africa: Building communities where literacies thrive* (pp. 123-127). Newark, DE: IRA.

ACER. (2003). *PISA test country map, 2006.* Retrieved July 31, 2008, from http://www.acer.edu.au/ozpisa/whatis.html

Al-Bilali, J. (2006). *Across the threshold: Sharing a big vision for art, education and human evolution* (Unpublished manuscript). Cape Town, South Africa: University of the Western Cape, CLIDE Research Project.

Albright, J., & Luke, A. (Eds.). (2007). *Pierre Bourdieu and literacy education.* Mahwah, NJ: Lawrence Erlbaum.

Alvermann, D. E. (2002). Effective literacy instruction for adolescents. *Journal of Literacy Research, 34,* 189–208.

Alvermann, D. E. (in press). Why bother theorizing adolescents' online literacies for classroom practice and research? *Journal of Adolescent & Adult Literacy.*

Alvermann, D. E., Hinchman, K. A., Moore, D. W., Phelps, S. F., & Waff, D. R. (Eds.). (1998). *Reconceptualizing the literacies in adolescents' lives.* Mahwah, NJ: Lawrence Erlbaum.

Alvermann, D. E., Young, J. P., Weaver, D., Hinchman, K. A., Moore, D. W., Phelps, S. F., et al. (1996). Middle and high school students' perceptions of how they experience text-based discussions: A multicase study. *Reading Research Quarterly, 31,* 244–267.

Amit-Talai, V., & Wulff, H. (Eds.). (1995). *Youth cultures: A cross-cultural perspective.* New York: Routledge.

Appadurai, A. (1996). *Modernity at large: Cultural dimensions of globalization.* Minneapolis: University of Minnesota Press.

Appadurai, A. (2000). Grassroots globalization and the research imagination. *Public Culture, 12*(1), 1–19.

Appadurai, A. (Ed.). (2001). *Globalization.* Durham, NC: Duke University Press.

Appadurai, A. (2006a). *Fear of small numbers: An essay on the geography of anger.* Durham, NC: Duke University Press.

Appadurai, A. (2006b). The right to research. *Globalisation, Societies, and Education, 4*(2), 167–177.

Appiah, K. A. (2005). *The ethics of identity.* Princeton, NJ: Princeton University Press.

Appiah, K. A. (2006). *Cosmopolitanism: Ethics in a world of strangers.* New York: Norton.

Apple, M. (2001). Afterword: The politics of labeling in a conservative age. In G. Hudak & P. Kihn (Eds.), *Labeling: Pedagogy and politics* (pp. 261–283). New York: Routledge.

Arua, E. (Ed.). (2001). *Reading for all in Africa: Building communities where literacies thrive.* Newark, DE: IRA.

Avila, J. (2008). A desire line to digital storytelling. *Teachers College Record.* Retrieved December 9, 2008, from http://www.tcrecord.org/content.asp?contentid=15463

Avila, J., Underwood, C., & Woodbridge, S. (2008). "I'm the expert now": Digital storytelling and transforming literacies among displaced children. In D. McInerney & A. D. Liem (Eds.), *Research on sociocultural influences on motivation and learning: Teaching and learning: International best practice,* pp. 349-376. Charlotte, NC: Information Age.

Bakhtin, M. (1981). *The dialogic imagination: Four essays by M. M. Bakhtin* (M. E. Holquist, Ed.; C. Emerson & M. Holquist, Trans.). Austin: University of Texas Press.

Bauman, R., & Briggs, C. L. (1990). Poetics and performance as critical perspectives on language and social life. *Annual Review of Anthropology, 19,* 59–88.

Beck, U. (1992). *Risk society: Towards a new modernity.* London: Sage. (Original work published 1986)

Beck, U. (2000). *What is globalization?* New York: Polity.

Beck, U. (2006). *Cosmopolitan vision.* Cambridge, UK: Polity.

Bekker, I. (2003). Using historical data to explain language attitudes: A South African case study. *AILA Review, 16,* 62–77.

Benhabib, S. (2002). *The claims of culture: Equality and diversity in the global era.* Princeton, NJ: Princeton University Press.

Benjamin, W. (2002). *The arcades project.* Cambridge, MA: Harvard University Press.

Best, S., & Kellner, D. (2003). Contemporary youth and the postmodern adventure. *Review of Education, Pedagogy, and Cultural Studies, 25,* 75–93.

Bhabha, Homi. (1994). *The location of culture.* London: Routledge.

Bhattacharya, U. (2008). *The West in literacy.* Unpublished manuscript.

Bloch, C. (2006). Theory and strategy of early literacy in contemporary Africa with special reference to South Africa (PRAESA Occasional Paper 25). Cape Town, South Africa: PRAESA.

Bottrell, D. (2007). Resistance, resilience and social identities: Reframing "problem youth" and the problem of schooling. *Journal of Youth Studies, 10*(5), 597–616.

Bourdieu, P. (1977). *Outline of a theory of practice.* Cambridge, UK: Cambridge University Press.

Brock-Utne, B., Desai, Z., & Qorro, M. (Eds.). (2004). *Researching the language of instruction in Tanzania and South Africa.* Cape Town, South Africa: African Minds.

Brozo, W., Shiel, G., & Topping, K. (2007). Engagement in reading: Lessons learned from three PISA countries. *Journal of Adolescent and Adult Literacy, 51*(4), 304–315.

Bucholtz, M. (2002). Youth and cultural practice. *Annual Review of Anthropology, 31,* 525–552.

Buenfil, R. N. (2000). Globalization and educational policies in Mexico, 1988–1994: A meeting of the universal and the particular. In N. Stromquist & K. Monkman (Eds.), *Globalization and education: Integration and contestation across cultures* (pp. 275–298). Oxford, UK: Rowman & Littlefield.

Burbules, N., & Torres, C. A. (Eds.). (2000). *Globalization and education: Critical perspectives.* New York: Routledge.

Butcher, M., & Thomas, M. (2006). Ingenious: Emerging hybrid youth cultures in western Sydney. In P. Nilan & C. Feixa (Eds.), *Global youth? Hybrid identities, plural worlds* (pp. 53–71). London: Routledge.

Canagarajah, S. A. (1999). *Resisting linguistic imperialism in English language teaching.* Oxford, UK: Oxford University Press.

Carnoy, M. (2007). *Cuba's academic advantage: Why students in Cuba do better in school.* Stanford, CA: Stanford University Press.

Cassidy, J., Garrett, S., & Barrera, E. (2008). What's hot in adolescent literacy 1997–2006. *Journal of Adolescent & Adult Literacy, 50*(1), 30–36.

Castells, M. (2000). *The rise of the network society.* Malden, MA: Blackwell.

Castells, M. (2004). *The network society: A cross-cultural perspective.* Cheltenham, UK: Edward Elgar.

Chavez, L. (1991). *Shadowed lives: Undocumented immigrants in American society.* New York: Harcourt Brace Jovanovich College Publishers.

Cole, M. (2006). *The Fifth Dimension: An after-school program built on diversity.* New York: Russell Sage.

Condry, I. (2001). Japanese hip-hop and the globalization of popular culture. In G. Gmelch & W. Zenner (Eds.), *Urban life: Readings in the anthropology of the city* (pp. 357–387). Prospect Heights, IL: Waveland.

Crul, M. (2007). The integration of immigrant youth. In M. Suàrez-Orozco (Ed.), *Learning in the global era: International perspectives on globalization and education* (pp. 213–231). Berkeley: University of California Press.

Crystal, D. (2003). *English as a global language.* Cambridge, UK: Cambridge University Press.

Cuban, L. (1989). The "at-risk" label and the problem of urban school reform. *Phi Delta Kappan, 70,* 780–784, 799–801.

Dallaire, C. (2006). "I am English too": Francophone youth hybridities in Canada. In P. Nilan & C. Feixa (Eds.), *Global youth? Hybrid identities, plural worlds* (pp. 32–52). London: Routledge.

Deschenes, S., Cuban, L., & Tyack, D. (2001). Mismatch: Historical perspectives on schools and students who don't fit them. *Teachers College Record, 103*(4), 525–547.

DiIulio, J., Jr. (1998). Introduction: Religion reduces deviance. In D. Larson & B. Johnson (Eds.), *Religion: The forgotten factor in cutting youth crime and saving at-risk urban youth* (Jeremiah Project Report No 2). Retrieved October 10, 2008, from http://www.manhattan-institute.org/html/jpr-98-2.htm

Dolby, N. E. (2001). *Constructing race: Youth, identity, and popular culture in South Africa.* Albany: State University of New York Press.

Dolby, N., & Rahman, A. (2008). Research in international education. *Review of Educational Research, 78*(3), 676–726.

Dolby, N., & Rizvi, F. (Eds.). (2008). *Youth moves: Identities and education in global perspective.* London: Routledge.

Durand, A. P. (2002). *Black, Blanc, Beur: Rap music and hip-hop culture in the Francophone world.* Lanham, MD: Scarecrow Press.

Dyers, C. (2004). Intervention and language attitudes: The effects of a development programme on the language attitudes of three groups of primary school teachers. In B. Brock-Utne, Z. Desai, & M. Qorro (Eds.), *Researching the language of instruction in Tanzania and South Africa* (pp. 202–220). Cape Town, South Africa: African Minds.

Edge, J. (2006). *(Re-)locating TESOL in an age of empire.* Houndmills, UK: Palgrave Macmillan.

Featherstone, M. (1998). The flâneur, the city and virtual public life. *Urban Studies, 35*(5–6), 909–925.

Finders, M. (1997). *Just girls: Hidden literacies and life in junior high.* New York: Teachers College Press.

Finn, J. L. (2001). Text and turbulence: Representing adolescence as pathology in the human services. *Childhood, 8*(2), 167–191.

Finnegan, R. (2002). *Communicating: The multiple modes of human interconnection.* London: Routledge.

Flockemann, M. (2008). Complicit Refugees and Cosmopolitans: Khaled Hosseini's The Kite Runner and Romesh Gunesekera's Reef in conversation with texts on xenophobia in South Africa. Paper presented at the 6th International Conference on New Directions in the Humanities, Istanbul, Turkey, 15-18 July 2008.

Flores, B., Cousin, P., & Diaz, E. (1991). Transforming deficit myths about learning, language, and culture. *Language Arts, 68*, 369–379.

Foucault, M. (2005). *The hermeneutics of the subject* (G. Burchell, Trans.). New York: Picador.

France, A. (2008). Risk factor analysis and the youth question. *Journal of Youth Studies, 11*(1), 1–15.

Gee, J., Hull, G., & Lankshear, C. (1996). *The new work order: Behind the language of the new capitalism.* Boulder, CO: Westview.

Giddens, Anthony. (1991). *Modernity and self-identity: Self and society in the late modern age.* Stanford, CA: Stanford University Press.

Grossberg, L. (1993). Cultural studies and/in new worlds. *Critical Studies in Mass Communication, 10*(1), 1–22.

Grubb, N. W., & Lazerson, M. (2006). The globalization of rhetoric and practice: The education gospel and vocationalism. In H. Lauder, P. Brown, J. Dillabough, & H. Halsey (Eds.), *Education, globalization and social change* (pp. 295–316). Oxford, UK: Oxford University Press.

Hall, S. (1997). Old and new identities, old and new ethnicities. In A. King (Ed.), *Culture, globalization, and the world-system*, pp. 41-68. Minneapolis, MN: University of Minnesota Press.

Hansen, K. T. (with Dalsgaard, A. L., Gough, K. V., Madsen, U. A., Valentin, K., & Wildermuth, N.). (2008). *Youth and the city in the global south*. Bloomington: Indiana University Press.

Hebdige, D. (1979). *Subculture: The meaning of style*. London: Methuen.

Held, D. (1995). *Democracy and the global order: From the modern state to cosmopolitan governance*. Stanford, CA: Stanford University Press.

Held, D. (2003). *Cosmopolitanism: A defense*. Cambridge, UK: Polity.

Hill, M. L., & Vasudevan, L. (Eds.). *Media, learning, and sites of possibility*. New York: Peter Lang.

Holden, T. J. M. (2006). The social life of Japan's adolechnic. In P. Nilan & C. Feixa (Eds.), *Global youth? Hybrid identities, plural worlds* (pp. 72–90). London: Routledge.

Hondagneu-Sotelo, P., & Avila, E. (1997). "I'm here, but I'm there": The meanings of Latina transnational motherhood. *Gender & Society, 11*(5), 548–571.

Hopper, R. (2005). What are teenagers reading? Adolescent fiction reading habits and reading choices. *Literacy, 39*(3), 113–120.

Hoppers, C. A. O. (2000). Globalization and the social construction of reality: Affirming or unmasking the "inevitable"? In N. Stromquist & K. Monkman (Eds.), *Globalization and education: Integration and contestation across cultures* (pp. 99–122). Oxford, UK: Rowman & Littlefield.

Hudak, G., & Kihn, P. (Eds.). (2001). *Labeling: Pedagogy and politics*. New York: Routledge.

Hull, G., & Katz, M. (2006). Crafting an agentive self: Case studies on digital storytelling. *Research in the Teaching of English, 41*(1), 43–81.

Hull, G., & Nelson, M. (2005). Locating the semiotic power of multimodality. *Written Communication, 22*(2), 224–262.

Hull, G., & Nelson, M. E. (in press). Literacy, media, and morality: Making the case for an aesthetic turn. In M. Prinsloo & M. Baynham (Eds.), *The future of literacy studies*. Houndmills, England: Palgrave Macmillan.

Hull, G., Rose, M., Fraser, K. L., & Castellano, M. (1991). Remediation as social construct: Perspectives from an analysis of classroom discourse. *College Composition and Communication, 42*(3), 299–329.

Hull, G., & Schultz, K. (Eds.). (2002). *School's out! Bridging out-of-school literacies with classroom practice*. New York: Teachers College Press.

Hull, G., & Zacher, J. (2007). Enacting identities: An ethnography of a job training program. *Identity: An International Journal of Theory and Research, 1*, 71–102.

Huq, R. (2006). European youth cultures in a post-colonial world: British Asian underground and French hip-hop music scenes. In P. Nilan & C. Feixa (Eds.), *Global youth? Hybrid identities, plural worlds* (pp. 14–31). London: Routledge.

Hursh, D. (2007). Assessing No Child Left Behind and the rise of neoliberal educational policies. *American Educational Research Journal, 44*(3), 493–518.

Ibrahim, A. (1999). Becoming Black: Rap and hip hop, race, gender, identity, and the politics of ESL learning. *TESOL Quarterly, 33*(3), 349–369.

Jeffrey, C., & Dyson, J. (Eds.). (2008). *Telling young lives: Portraits of global youth*. Philadelphia: Temple University Press.

Johnson, S., & Muhlhausen, D. (2005). North American transnational youth gangs: Breaking the chain of violence. *Trends in Organized Crime 9*(1), 38–54.

Katz, C. (2004). *Growing up global: Economic restructuring and children's everyday lives*. Minneapolis: University of Minnesota Press.

Kelly, J. (2008). Diasporan moves: African Canadian youth and identity formation. In N. Dolby & F. Rizvi (Eds.), *Youth moves: Identities and education in global perspective* (pp. 85–99). New York: Routledge.

Kelly, P. (2001). Youth at risk: Processes of individualization and responsibilisation in the risk society. *Discourse: Studies in the Cultural Politics of Education, 22*(1), 23–33.

Kenway, J., & Bullen, E. (2003). *Consuming children: Education–entertainment–advertising.* Buckingham, UK: Open University Press.

Kenway, J., & Bullen, E. (2008). The global corporate curriculum and the young cyberflaneur as global citizen. In N. Dolby & F. Rizvi (Eds.), *Youth moves: Identities and education in global perspective* (pp. 17–32). New York: Routledge.

Kincheloe, J. (1997). *Home Alone* and "Bad to the Bone": The advent of a postmodern childhood. In S. Steinberg & J. Kincheloe (Eds.), *Kinderculture: The corporate construction of childhood* (pp. 31–52). Boulder, CO: Westview.

Kirkland, D. (2007). The power of their text: Teaching hip hop in the secondary English classroom. In K. Keaton & P. R. Schmidt (Eds.), *Closing the gap: English educators address the tensions between teacher preparation and teaching writing in secondary schools* (pp. 129–145). Charlotte, NC: Information Age.

Knobel, M., & Lankshear, C. (2008). Remix: The art and craft of endless hybridization. *Journal of Adolescent & Adult Literacy, 52*(1), 22–33.

Koh, A. (2008). Disciplining "Generation M": The paradox of creating a "local" national identity in an era of "global" flows. In N. Dolby & F. Rizvi (Eds.), *Youth moves: Identities and education in global perspective* (pp. 193–206). New York: Routledge.

Kraidy, M. (2005). *Hybridity, or the cultural logic of globalization.* Philadelphia: Temple University Press.

Kumaravadivelu, B. (2006). Dangerous liaison: Globalization, empire, and TESOL. In J. Edge (Ed.), *(Re-)locating TESOL in an age of empire* (pp. 1–26). Houndmills, UK: Palgrave Macmillan.

LaChapelle, D. (2005). *Rize.* Los Angeles: David LaChapelle Studios.

Lam, E. (2000). L2 literacy and the design of the self: A case study of a teenager writing on the Internet. *TESOL Quarterly, 34*(3), 457–482.

Larson, D., & Johnson, B. (1998). *Religion: The forgotten factor in cutting youth crime and saving at-risk urban youth* (Jeremiah Project Report No. 2). Retrieved October 10, 2008, from http://www.manhattan-institute.org/html/jpr-98-2.htm

Lash, S. (1994). Reflexivity and its doubles: Structure, aesthetics, community. In U. Beck, A. Giddens, & S. Lash (Eds.), *Reflexive modernization: Politics, tradition and aesthetics in the modern social order* (pp. 110–173). Cambridge, UK: Polity.

Leander, K. M., & Sheehy, M. (Eds.). (2004). *Spatializing literacy research and practice.* New York: Peter Lang.

Luke, A. (2008). Race and language as capital in school: A sociological template for language education reform. In R. Kubota & A. Lin (Eds.), *Race, culture and identities in second language education.* London: Routledge.

Luke, A., & Carrington, V. (2002). Globalisation, literacy, curriculum practice. In M. Lewis, R. Fisher, & G. Brooks (Eds.), *Language and literacy in action* (pp. 231–250). London: Routledge.

Luke, A., & Luke, C. (2000). A situated perspective on cultural globalization. In N. C. Burbules & C. A. Torres (Eds.), *Globalization and education: Critical perspectives* (pp. 275–297). New York: Routledge.

Lukose, R. (2008). The children of liberalization: Youth agency and globalization in India. In N. Dolby & F. Rizvi (Eds.), *Youth moves: Identities and education in global perspective* (pp. 133–149). New York: Routledge.

Lukose, R. (2009). *Liberalization's children: Gender, youth and consumer citizenship in globalizing India.* Chapel Hill, NC: Duke University Press.

Maira, S., & Soep, E. (Eds.). (2005). *Youthscapes: The popular, the national, the global.* Philadelphia: University of Pennsylvania Press.

Martin, L. H., Gutman, H., & Hutton, P. H. (Eds.). (1987). *Technologies of the self: A seminar with Michel Foucault.* Amherst: University of Massachusetts Press.

Masland, T. (2004, April 5). South Africa: Generation born free. *Newsweek*, pp. 38–39.

Massey, D. (1998a). *Power-geometries and the politics of space-time* (Hettner Lecture Series). Heidelberg, Germany: University of Heidelberg, Department of Geography.

Massey, D. (1998b). The spatial construction of youth places. In T. Skelton & G. Valentine (Eds.), *Cool places: Geographies of youth cultures* (pp. 121–129). London: Routledge.

Mbembe, A. (2001). At the edge of the world: Boundaries, territoriality, and sovereignty in Africa. In A. Appadurai (Ed.), *Globalization* (pp. 22–51). Durham, NC: Duke University Press.

McCarthy, C. (2001). Foreword. In N. Dolby, *Constructing race: Youth, identity, and popular culture in South Africa* (pp. 1–4). Albany: State University of New York Press.

McKay, S. L. (2002). *Teaching English as an international language: Rethinking goals and approaches.* Oxford, UK: Oxford University Press.

McRobbie, A. (1991). *Feminism and youth culture: From "Jackie" to "Just Seventeen."* Boston: Unwin & Hyman.

McRobbie, A. (1993). Shut up and dance: Youth culture and the changing modes of femininity. *Cultural Studies, 7,* 402–426.

Meier, D., & Wood, G. (Eds.). (2004). *Many children left behind: How the No Child Left Behind Act is damaging our children and our schools.* Boston: Beacon.

Mitchell, W. J. T. (2002). Space, place, and landscape. In W. J. T. Mitchell (Ed.), *Landscape and power* (2nd ed., pp. vii–xii). Chicago: University of Chicago Press.

Moje, E. B. (2002). Re-framing adolescent literacy research for new times: Studying youth as a resource. *Reading Research and Instruction, 41,* 207–224.

Moje, E. B., Overby, M., Tysvaer, N., & Morris, K. (2008). The complex world of adolescent literacy: Myths, motivations, and mysteries. *Harvard Educational Review, 78*(1), 107–154.

Moore, T. (1991). The African-American church: A source of empowerment, mutual help, and social change. *Prevention in Human Services, 10,* 147–167.

Morrell, E. (2002). Toward a critical pedagogy of popular culture: Literacy development among urban youth. *Journal of Adolescent and Adult Literacy, 46*(1), 72–77.

Moss, B. (2001). From the pews to the classroom: Influences of the African American church on academic literacy. In J. Harris, A. Kamhi, & K. Polluck (Eds.), *Literacy in African American communities* (pp. 195–212). Mahwah, NJ: Lawrence Erlbaum.

Muñoz, G., & Marín, M. (2006). Music is the connection: Youth cultures in Colombia. In P. Nilan & C. Feixa (Eds.), *Global youth? Hybrid identities, plural worlds* (pp. 130–148). London: Routledge.

National Commission on Excellence in Education. (1983). *A nation at risk: The imperative for educational reform.* Washington, DC: Author.

Nayak, A. (2003). *Race, place and globalization: Youth cultures in a changing world.* Oxford, UK: Berg.

Nazario, S. (2007). *Enrique's journey.* New York: Random House.

Niang, A. (2006). Bboys: Hip-hop culture in Dakar, Sénégal. In P. Nilan & C. Feixa (Eds.), *Global youth? Hybrid identities, plural worlds* (pp. 167–185). London: Routledge.

Nilan, P. (2006). The reflexive youth culture of devout Muslim youth in Indonesia. In P. Nilan & C. Feixa (Eds.), *Global youth? Hybrid identities, plural worlds* (pp. 91–110). London: Routledge.

Nilan, P., & Feixa, C. (Eds.). (2006a). *Global youth? Hybrid identities, plural worlds.* London: Routledge.

Nilan, P., & Feixa, C. (2006b). Introduction: Youth hybridity and plural worlds. In P. Nilan & C. Feixa (Eds.), *Global youth? Hybrid identities, plural worlds* (pp. 1–13). London: Routledge.

Hull et al.: Youth, Risk, and Equity   **157**

No Child Left Behind Act of 2001, Pub. L. No. 107-110 (2002).

Nuttall, S. (2008). Youth cultures of consumption in Johannesburg. In N. Dolby & F. Rizvi (Eds.), *Youth moves: Identities and education in global perspective* (pp. 151–178). New York: Routledge.

Orozco, M. (2002). Globalization and migration: The impact of family remittances in Latin America. *Latina American Politics & Society, 44*(2), 41–66.

Osborn, D. (2006). African languages and information and communication technology: Literacy, access and the future. In J. Mugane (Ed.), *Selected proceedings of the 35th annual conference on African linguistics* (pp. 86–93). Somerville, MA: Cascadilla Proceedings Project.

Pennycook, A. (2003). Global Englishes, rip slyme, and performativity. *Journal of Sociolinguistics, 7*(4), 513–533.

Pennycook, A. (2007a). *Global English and transcultural flows.* London: Routledge.

Pennycook, A. (2007b). The myth of English as an international language. In S. Makoni & A. Pennycook (Eds.), *Disinventing and reconstituting languages* (pp. 90–115). Clevedon, UK: Multilingual Matters.

Petrova, Y. (2006). Global? local? multi-level identifications among contemporary skinheads in France. In P. Nilan & C. Feixa (Eds.), *Global youth? Hybrid identities, plural worlds* (pp. 186–204). London: Routledge.

Plüddemann, P., Braam, D., October, M., & Wababa, Z. (2004). *Dual-medium and parallel medium schooling in the Western Cape: From default to design* (PRAESA Occasional Paper 17). Cape Town, South Africa: PRAESA.

Rampton, B. (1999). Sociolinguistics and cultural studies: New ethnicities, liminality and interaction. *Social Semiotics, 9*(3), 355–373.

Rose, M. (1989). *Lives on the boundary: An account of the struggles and achievements of America's educationally underprepared.* New York: Penguin.

Rose, M. (1995). *Possible lives: The promise of public education in America.* New York: Penguin Books.

Ryan, J. (2005). Young people choose: Adolescents' text pleasures. *Australian Journal of Language and Literacy, 28*(1), 38–47.

Sachs, J. (2006). *The end of poverty: Economic possibilities for our time.* New York: Penguin.

Sahni, U. (in press). Finding "self," finding "home": Drama in education. *Canadian Theatre Review.*

Sahni, U., Gupta, R., Hull, G., Javid, P., Setia, T., Toyama, K., et al. (2008, March). *Using digital video in rural Indian schools: A study of teacher development and student achievement.* Paper presented at the annual meeting of the American Educational Research Association, New York.

Sarroub, L. K. (2002). In-betweenness: Religion and conflicting visions of literacy. *Reading Research Quarterly 37*(2), 130–148.

Sarroub, L. K. (2005). *All American Yemini girls: Being Muslim in a public school.* Philadelphia: University of Pennsylvania Press.

Sarroub, L. K. (2008). Living "glocally" with literacy success in the Midwest. *Theory Into Practice, 47*(1), 59–66.

Schleicher, A. (in press). Seeing school systems through the prism of PISA. In A. Luke, A. Woods, & K. Weir (Eds.), *Curriculum, syllabus design and equity: A primer and a model.* New York: Routledge.

Schneider, A. (2005). "Jackie Chan is nobody, and so am I": Juvenile fan culture and the construction of transnational male identity in the Tamil diaspora. In S. Maira & E. Soep (Eds.), *Youthscapes: The popular, the national, the global* (pp. 137–154). Philadelphia: University of Pennsylvania Press.

Schonert-Reichl, K. (2000, April). *Children and youth at risk: Some conceptual considerations.* Paper presented at the North Pan-Canadian Education Research Agenda Symposium, Ottawa, Ontario, Canada.

Scourfield, J., Dicks, B., Drakeford, M., & Davies, A. (Eds.). (2006). *Children, place, and identity: Nation and locality in middle childhood.* London: Routledge.

Sen, A. (2006). *Identity and violence: The illusion of destiny.* New York: Norton.

Shahabi, M. (2006). Youth subcultures in post-revolution Iran: An alternative reading. In P. Nilan & C. Feixa (Eds.), *Global youth? Hybrid identities, plural worlds* (pp. 111–129). London: Routledge.

Shepler, S. (2005). Globalizing child soldiers in Sierra Leone. In S. Maira & E. Soep (Eds.), *Youthscapes: The popular, the national, the global* (pp. 119–133). Philadelphia: University of Pennsylvania Press.

Shin, F. (2004). English language development standards and benchmarks: Policy issues and a call for more focused research. *Bilingual Research Journal, 28*(2), 253–266.

Silverstone, R. (2006). *Media and morality: On the rise of the mediapolis.* Cambridge, UK: Polity.

Singh, P., & Doherty, C. (2008). Mobile students in liquid modernity: Negotiating the politics of transnational identities. In N. Dolby & F. Rizvi (Ed.), *Youth moves: Identities and education in global perspective* (pp. 115-130). New York: Routledge.

Skelton, T., & Valentine, G. (Eds.). (1998). *Cool places: Geographies of youth cultures.* London: Routledge.

Soep, E. (2005). Making hard-core masculinity: Teenage boys playing house. In S. Maira & E. Soep (Eds.), *Youthscapes: The popular, the national, the global* (pp. 173–191). Philadelphia: University of Pennsylvania Press.

Soja, E. W. (1996). *Thirdspace: Journeys to Los Angeles and other real-and imagined-places.* Malden, MA: Blackwell.

Spady, J. G., Alim, H. S., & Meghelli, S. (2006). *Tha global cipha: Hip hop culture and consciousness.* Philadelphia: Black History Museum Press.

Spring, J. (2008). Research on globalization and education. *Review of Educational Research, 78*(2), 330–363.

Stanton, S. (2006). From novice to expert: Literacy practices of an urban church youth group. Berkeley, CA: Unpublished Doctoral Dissertation, UC Berkeley.

Stein, P. (2000). Rethinking resources: Multimodal pedagogies in the ESL classroom. *TESOL Quarterly, 34*(2), 333–336.

Stein, P., & Newfield, D. (2002). Shifting the gaze in South African classrooms: New pedagogies, new publics, new democracies. *International Journal of Learning, 9,* 3–11.

Stein, P., & Slonminsky, L. (2006). An eye on the text and an eye on the future: Multimodal literacy in three Johannesburg families. In K. Pahl & J. Rowsell (Eds.), *Travel notes from the new literacy studies: Instances of practice* (pp. 118–146). Clevedon, UK: Multilingual Matters.

Stiglitz, J. E. (2003). *Globalization and its discontents.* New York: Norton.

Stromquist, N. P. (2002). *Education in a globalized world: The connectivity of economic power, technology, and knowledge.* Lanham, MD: Rowman & Littlefield.

Stromquist, N. P., & Monkman, K. (Eds.). (2000). *Globalization and education: Integration and contestation across cultures.* Oxford, UK: Rowman & Littlefield.

Suàrez-Orozco, M. M. (Ed.). (2007). *Learning in the global era: International perspectives on globalization and education.* Berkeley: University of California Press.

Suàrez-Orozco, M., & Qin-Hilliard, D. B. (Eds.). (2004). *Globalization: Culture and education in the new millennium.* Berkeley: University of California Press.

Suàrez-Orozco, M., & Sattin, C. (2007). Introduction: Learning in the global era. In M. Suàrez-Orozco (Ed.), *Learning in the global era: International perspectives on globalization and education* (pp. 1–43). Berkeley: University of California Press.

Sukarieh, M., & Tannock, S. (2008). In the best interests of youth or neoliberalism? The World Bank and the New Global Youth Empowerment Project. *Journal of Youth Studies, 11*(3), 301–312.

Süssmuth, R. (2007). On the need for teaching intercultural skills: Challenges for education in a globalizing world. In M. Suàrez-Orozco (Ed.), *Learning in the global era: International perspectives on globalization and education* (pp. 195–212). Berkeley: University of California Press.

Swadener, B. B., & Lubeck, S. (Eds.). (1995). *Children and families "at promise."* Albany: State University of New York Press.

Tannock, S. (2000). *Youth at work: The unionized fast-food and grocery workplace.* Philadelphia: Temple University Press.

Taylor, D., & Yamasaki, T. (2006). Children, literacy and mass trauma: Teaching in times of catastrophic events and on going emergency situations. *Penn GSE Perspectives on Urban Education, 4*(2), 1-62.

Thaman, K. H. (2007). Education and globalization: A view from Oceania. In L. Hufford & T. Pedrajas (Eds.), *Educating for a worldview: Focus on globalizing curriculum and instruction* (pp. 1–14). Lanham, MD: University Press of America.

Tough, P. (2008). *Whatever it takes: Geoffrey Canada's quest to change Harlem and America.* New York: Houghton Mifflin.

Turner, G. (1996). *British cultural studies: An introduction* (2nd ed.). London: Routledge.

Valdivia, A. N. (2008). Popular culture and recognition: Narratives of youth and Latinidad. In N. Dolby & F. Rizvi (Ed.), *Youth moves: Identities and education in global perspective* (pp. 101–114). New York: Routledge.

Valencia, R. R., & Solorzano, D. G. (1997). Contemporary deficit thinking. In R. R. Valencia (Ed.), *The evolution of deficit thinking: Educational thought and practice* (pp. 160–219). London: Falmer.

Vasquez, G. A. G. (2005). Homies Unidos: International barrio warriors waging peace on two fronts. In S. Maira & E. Soep (Eds.), *Youthscapes: The popular, the national, the global* (pp. 103–118). Philadelphia: University of Pennsylvania Press.

Vasquez, O. (2003). *La clase mágica: Imagining optimal possibilities in a bilingual community of learners.* Mahwah, NJ: Lawrence Erlbaum.

Ward, C. L., Flisher, A. J., Zissis, C., Muller, M., & Lombard, C. (2001). Exposure to violence and its relationship to psychopathology in adolescents. *Injury Prevention, 7*, 297–301.

Watson, P., & Pienaar, M. (2007). A case study of the language in education complaints received by the CRL Commission: Multilingualism a far cry from implementation. *Southern African Linguistics and Applied Language Studies, 25*, 575–588.

Wikan, U. (2007). Rethinking honor in regard to human rights: An educational imperative in troubled times. In M. Suàrez-Orozco (Ed.), *Learning in the global era: International perspectives on globalization and education* (pp. 272–290). Berkeley: University of California Press.

Willis, P. (1977). *Learning to labour: How working class kids get working class jobs.* Farnborough, UK: Saxon House.

Willis, P. (1990). *Common culture: Symbolic work at play in the everyday cultures of the young.* Buckingham, UK: Open University Press.

World Bank. (2008). *The road not traveled: Education reform in the Middle East and North Africa.* Washington, DC: International Bank for Reconstruction and Development.

Xinhua. (2007, May 29). Wen: Give "left-behind" kids more love. *China Daily.* Retrieved on August 3, 2008, from http://chinadaily.com.cn/china/2007–05/29/content_882092.htm

Zacher, J. (2008). *Case studies of 3 English language learners in a highly structured language arts classroom: Achievement measures and ethnographic observational data.* Manuscript submitted for publication.

Zehm, S. (1973). *Educational misfits: A study of poor performers in the English class 1825–1925.* Unpublished doctoral dissertation, Stanford University, Stanford, CA.

Chapter 6

Gender Risks and Education: The Particular Classroom Challenges for Urban Low-Income African American Boys

DUANE E. THOMAS
HOWARD STEVENSON
University of Pennsylvania

A fundamental consideration in discourses on risk and schooling for primary and secondary school-age students focuses on gender inequalities in the classroom. Gender equity in education debates have raged for several decades and so remain an enduring concern of educators and researchers across the nation (Klein, Kramarae, & Richardson, 2007). Gender politics in classrooms, in teaching, and in teacher training have been accorded minimal to no attention by No Child Left Behind (NCLB) legislation and other educational policies. The blindness of NCLB, toward an approach best characterized by its "devil and/or god in the details," still sends parents, educators, and researchers battling over how much gender matters and how much these issues go unaddressed throughout the school day. A recent report by the American Association of University Women found no disadvantage toward boys in American education, and it discredited the myth that boys are receiving less attention and less schooling as compared to that of girls (Corbett, Hill, & St. Rose, 2008). This report was in response to a pendulum swing in the field from the earlier position that girls were disadvantaged, particularly in math and science skills development. Gender war debates have used individual studies to document disadvantage on both ends. However, a consistent review of the literature tends to point to one challenging reality—namely, that gender may be too broad a category in critically examining the more challenging problems of educational equity or in developing future training, programs, and policies to ameliorate educational risk for students in primary and secondary schools (Dee, 2005).

We take issue with a broad definition of *risk* within the context of gender because it tends to focus on a universalism that masks subgroups of students at greatest risk

Review of Research in Education
March 2009, Vol. 33, pp. 160-180
DOI: 10.3102/0091732X08327164
© 2009 AERA. http://rre.aera.net

for negative outcomes as they relate to education. We instead affirm an approach that appreciates the intersections of race, gender, and class but not one covered in a color-blind philosophy where particularities of oppression are denied. As discussed by Michele Fine and Peter Kuriloff (2006), this intersectionality offers a distinctive contribution to how notions of gender are forged and understood in particular settings, particularly with respect to how boys operate within and are affected by specific social spaces. However, educational research often overlooks the intersection between gender, class, and race in discourse on schooling experiences and achievement (Davis, 2003). We believe that a closer investigation of this intersectionality would lead us to the challenges confronting African American boys in inner-city schools. In addition, we oppose traditional conceptions of risk as a notion of exclusively individual-level variables. We believe that a concurrent analysis on contextual influences is critical and that classroom context is an important risk contributor that can promote, exacerbate, and/or maintain poor academic outcomes for urban low-income African American boys.

Our purpose for this chapter is to examine these realities and to summarize extant research on issues pertaining to gender risks and schooling, with attention given to the academic and classroom social challenges faced by African American boys attending primary and secondary schools serving economically disadvantaged urban neighborhoods. Drawing on recent empirical findings and discourse in education and the social sciences, we first review research on gender inequities in education. This includes an analysis of gender and racial disparities in classroom opportunity structures and school discipline procedures that place urban low-income African American males at great risk for poor academic outcomes. This is followed by a discussion of the ways in which social processes within classrooms—namely, interactions with teachers—converge in complex ways with general academic challenges to increase risk for adjustment difficulties across multiple domains of functioning. Next, we examine the emotional and cultural coping strategies used by African American male students to manage emotional, behavioral, and performance difficulties associated with inequitable teacher practices in education. Last, we make recommendations for future research and for interventions tailored to students most likely to experience negative academic and behavioral outcomes owing to disparities in education across lines of gender, race, and social class.

Let us first consider the possibility that in the field of education, we have yet to understand why gender is dichotomously defined. Given the growing biological evidence to the contrary, gender may be best understood along a continuum of expressions, and students who are transgendered and/or questioning their gender identities can be lost in the shuffle of polemic masculine and feminine arguments (Eyler & Wright, 1997; Knaak, 2004). Given the space to address the issues in this chapter and because matters concerning gender and sexual identity are addressed by authors in volume 31 of the *Review of Research in Education*, we are not going to engage those issues of gender risks and schooling. Instead, we would like to propose a better way to understand gender risks in K–12 education—namely, subgroup analyses on boys and girls that take into consideration the effects of race and class. We suggest that similar contextual analyses must be done for different gender, race, and class subgroups. As the most recent American Association of University Women report has acknowledged (Corbett et al., 2008), race and income may be better ways to make sense of the achievement gap challenges in education. To speak of gender as a larger rubric ignores the nuances of teacher–student relationships in which entrenched racial and class biases are more likely to explain the outcomes that we are seeing in lower-performing student groups. Race and class subgroups of boys and girls may better help us understand how gender politics play out in classrooms for primary and secondary school students. An understanding of these diverse inequities, as lying in either foreground or background positions (depending on the situational politics), may help in making sense of the politics and implications for educating boys and girls who are at risk for academic underachievement.

Hence, we propose here that a subgroup analysis is best to understand the gender risk issues in education; urban low-income African American male students are the main focus of this chapter. An important consideration is that across grade levels, teachers tend to have lower expectations for the abilities and performance of African American students; they provide them with fewer opportunities for exposure to science and mathematics role models; and they offer them less encouragement toward enrollment in advanced courses (Atwater, 2000; Entwisle, Alexander, & Olsen, 2007; Farkas, 2003; Oates, 2003). Moreover, there is the disproportionate overrepresentation of low-income African American males among serious school discipline procedures (Fenning & Rose, 2007; Noguera, 2003a; Skiba, Michael, Nardo, & Peterson, 2002).

Both of these are worthy issues to deconstruct in some meaningful way in discussion on gender risks and schooling. Just as significant are ways in which these students cope with such risks as a result of their gender orientation, as well as their race and social class status, which may exacerbate risks for academic failure and other classroom adjustment problems. When these issues are taken together, our focus here then becomes classroom social challenges with teachers that present barriers to equitable education for many children and youth, as a result of the confluence of racial, class, and gender categorizations, in which race is considered to be a more significant determinant of how boys and girls are differentially treated in schools.

GENDER INEQUITIES IN EDUCATION AND THE VULNERABILITY OF AFRICAN AMERICAN BOYS

Reviews of gender research, such as a recent one by Hyde and Lindberg (2007), have identified several themes to the gender wars. One of the most familiar is that teachers do not encourage math and science skills development for female students, relative to male students, and that this failure to promote these skills in girls explains higher-level male performance in math and science achievement. Another more recent theme centers on the feminizing classroom environments in which boys' behavioral and emotional expressions are overly punished and controlled (Younger,

Warrington & Williams, 1999). This argument is often used to explain disproportionate discipline applied to male students. Whereas these themes call attention to key factors that may impinge on the equitable instruction and management of students across gender lines and that may in turn shape educational policies and practices toward eradicating such inequities, there may be more to be desired with respect to analyses on gender risks in education.

A familiar finding in educational research is that Black students,[1] especially, African American boys, tend to perform more poorly in math and science than do students from other racial groups and that these disparities in achievement increase with grade level (Noguera, 2003b). In addition, whereas males may fare significantly worse than girls in this current zeitgeist of zero-tolerance school discipline policies and practices, the boys' punishment may differ depending on whether they are Black or White. Research has documented that racial disproportionalities in exclusionary discipline is common, with African American male students receiving punishments (e.g., suspensions and expulsions) harsher than those of their European American counterparts; in fact, those harsher consequences tend to be administered for less severe offenses (Skiba et al., 2002). These findings imply that racial bias is an important risk factor in considering gender inequities and that therein lies an enormously difficult set of circumstances facing African American boys, especially in America's schools. Although the math and science skills gap argument and the contextual misfit gap argument are prominent, we have an extremely convoluted set of issues that are not easily deconstructed or addressed through conventional gender debates; that is, there are other gender-based critiques to make.

Gender debates have been fueled by a growing awareness that stereotypes exist in the classroom that may inform the schooling practices of male and female students in ways that are often unconscious. The growing work of Claude Steele and Joshua Aronson (1995, 2000) has helped us to see that such stereotypes as "Boys are simply better in math than girls" are not benign but rather have viruslike qualities in their ability to infect one's self-efficacy beliefs and actions in the social arena of gender politics. Therefore, "If I believe that I am not capable of doing well in math and science, then why try?"[2] becomes a logical consequence for subgroups of students who are being typecast to fail academically. Ironically, the learning of these stereotypes about gender and math/science appears to be stimulated by key socializing agents, including parents and teachers, as well as mass media, with observable gender differences found as early as third grade and continuing through college (Smith & Hung, 2008). This finding is hardly surprising, given the widely publicized "brazen" views of the former Harvard president Lawrence Summers, who publically questioned the "intrinsic aptitude" of women for top-level math and science positions.

Gender inequity in education has consistently been explored from this perspective of generating parity between boys and girls in various school performance-based activities, namely, math and science (Adenika-Morrow, 1996). Still, as we survey the research on gender equity in education, low-income African American boys remain at the most risk, relative to other groups for disparities in education and with respect to being at a disadvantage in terms of academic outcomes. Several studies have shown that this subgroup of students receives lower grades in school and lower standardized tests scores when compared to those of their White and Asian counterparts (Jencks & Phillips, 1998; Osborne, 1999; Steele, 1997). In fact, research has revealed that in contrast to most other groups, where males commonly perform at higher levels in math- and science-related courses, African American males demonstrate significant underperformance, often with little attention to class (Noguera, 2003b; Pollard, 1993). For example, in seminal work on cultural and contextual influences on the academic performance of African American males, Noguera (2003b) notes that even class privilege and the material benefits that come with it fail to inoculate Black boys from low academic performance. According to Noguera, middle-class African American males lag significantly behind their White peers in grade point average and standardized test scores. Hence, across income levels, education-related gender disparities exist for African Americans, with males evidencing fewer gains across a spectrum of achievement indices. This finding is especially striking for those of low socioeconomic status (Wood, Kaplan, & McLoyd, 2007).

There are several other vulnerabilities that have come to define the experiences of low-income African American males. One of these is their higher dropout rates. Utilizing data from 50 states, the Schott Foundation report on the public education of African American boys revealed that more than half the boys in their sample did not graduate on time, with less than 30% of the boys graduating on time in Florida and Nevada (Jackson, 2008). In addition, several studies have documented the overrepresentation of African American students in remedial and special education classes and their underrepresentation in advanced placement and honors courses (Artiles, 2003; Irving & Hudley, 2005; Jackson, 2008; Noguera, 2003b; Pollard, 1993). In a literature review, Artiles (2003) documented research comparing special education placement patterns in various disability categories across racial groups. According to his analysis of earlier research (see Donovan & Cross, 2002), the risk index of placement in special education for African Americans was higher than that of all students being served in special education at the national level (13% versus 12%, respectively). When examining the disability category, African Americans were noted to be overrepresented in mental retardation, learning disability, emotional disability, and developmental delay programs. Structural discrimination was reported to be a critical precursor for the disproportionate placement of African American students in special education. When considering the confluence of gender with race, disparities in the educational placement of African American boys appear dourer. Indeed, although African American boys represent 9% of the public school population, they represent 20% of special education enrollment and only 4% of the honors or gifted placement (Jackson, 2008). Such findings suggest that whereas African American boys may benefit from certain privileges associated with being male in American society, this population may be distinctively subjugated to specific risks, which are revealed as clear inequities in their classroom experiences.

Along with the achievement gap, another challenge faced by educators and school service providers is inequities in school discipline practices. According to findings from a recent national survey of public school administrators, approximately 64% of respondents rated classroom discipline problems as a primary issue facing America's public schools, with peer victimization and acts of defiance toward teachers being identified as foremost problems (U.S. Department of Education, 2004). Such behaviors are a leading cause toward student identification for and referral to mental health services inside and outside the school setting, and they have been shown to exacerbate risk for academic underachievement (Frick et al., 1991; Hinshaw, 1992; Hinshaw & Lee, 2003). For these reasons, classroom disciplinary problems occupy a primary residence in discourses on risk factors that affect the social functioning and academic success of students in primary and secondary schools. However, a closer examination of research on gender inequity reveals that African American male students remain at the greatest risk for classroom behavior adjustment problems and concomitant academic underperformance across socioeconomic status levels (Ford & Harris, 1997; Noguera, 2003b). Nevertheless, research has persistently documented the distinct negative effects of socioeconomic disadvantage on child development across multiple domains of functioning (Bradley & Corwyn, 2002; Huston, McLoyd, & Coll, 1997; McLoyd, 1998); for African American males, it is a significant risk contributor impinging upon their academic performance, classroom behavior, and overall achievement from their initial entry to formal schooling to higher grade levels (Entwisle et al., 2007; Wood et al., 2007).

Although boys compose approximately 71% of all referrals for disciplinary procedures taken against students (Mid-Atlantic Equity Consortium, 2000), a closer analysis shows that African American boys represent a disproportionate percentage of boys overall who are subjected to exclusionary disciplinary actions. The overrepresentation of African American boys in school discipline referrals and exclusionary consequences has been well documented since the 1970s (Children's Defense Fund, 1975; Fenning & Rose, 2007; Gregory & Mosely, 2004; Noguera, 2003a; Skiba et al., 2002; Skiba & Reece, 2000). However, the gap in discipline between African American students and other student groups has gained much less attention than that of the achievement gap, which by comparison is widely discussed in the media (Gregory & Mosely, 2004). This fact notwithstanding, the disproportionate application of discipline policies to male students of color is culpable in compromising educational equity. As has been demonstrated in many school districts throughout the United States, African American male students are more likely than any other group to be suspended and expelled from school (Noguera, 2003a; Serwatka, Deering, & Grant, 1995; Skiba et al., 2002). Such disparities in school disciplinary practices have been shown to contribute to low academic achievement and behavior problems across groups of ethnic minority children and youth (U.S. Department of Education, 1999).

The increased numbers African American males being disciplined at school should not come as much of a surprise. School suspensions and other disciplinary actions in schools across the country have increased considerably. According to the U.S. Department of Education (1999), school suspensions from 1974 to 1999 increased from 1.7 million to 3.1 million. Similar trends currently remain, with this increase disproportionately affecting African American and Latino male students

(Skiba et al., 2002). On a national level, African American male students are suspended at approximately twice their proportion in the school population (Bay Area School Reform Collaborative, 2001); for instance, during the 1997 school year, African American children made up only 17% of the U.S. population, but 32% of those were suspended because of alleged disciplinary infractions in primary and secondary schools (U.S. Department of Education, 1999). Even among preschoolers, African American boys nationwide are expelled more than students from any other gender/racial group (Gilliam, 2005), suggesting that disproportionalities in school discipline procedures is a far-reaching and protracted issue. In explaining these phenomena, research examining the dynamics of race, gender, and schooling equity has consistently found that discipline practices at schools are not only biased but culturally loaded and unjust against children and youth of color, especially, boys (Neal, McCray, Webb-Johnson, & Bridgest, 2003; Skiba et al., 2002).

Disparities in achievement and school discipline practices create plausible academic setbacks that fail to promote the scholastic and social well-being of children and youth of color, particularly, boys. In examining the complex interplay between gender and variables within the social structure of schools that foster disproportionate challenges for African American male students, research has yielded, as Foster (2001) asserts, more questions unanswered than answered. However, a major factor theorized to increase exceptional risk for underachievement and behavioral adjustment difficulties in the classroom for African American males can be found within the social fabric of classrooms—namely, through interactions between this gender subgroup and their teachers.

NEGATIVE TEACHER EXPECTATIONS AND STUDENT OUTCOMES

Teachers' perceptions and expectations of student abilities and behavior are key determinants of student adaptation across multiple domains of academic and social functioning in schools (Ferguson, 1998; Jussim, Eccles, & Madon, 1996; Oates, 2003); relative to other teacher variables, such perceptions and expectations are linked to children's and youths' academic outcomes and behavior. In a study on this very topic, Oates (2003) investigated the effects of teachers' perceptions on the standardized test performance of African American and European American students, utilizing data from the National Educational Longitudinal Study (U.S. Department of Education, 1994), a nationally representative survey with student, parent, teacher, and other school staff components. As such, the investigator found that teachers' perceptions, based on the expectations and diligence appraisals of student assessments made in the 10th grade, affected students' performance on standardized tests taken in the 12th grade, as measured by the average of scores on item-response-theory tests of reading, mathematics, history/citizenship/geography, and science. Results showed signs that unfavorable teacher perceptions are consequential for the test performance of African American students, as compared to European American students, especially when their classroom work habits, behaviors, and future academic capabilities are judged by White teachers.

One can glean from Oates's work (2003) that teachers' dispositions toward their students can elevate or undermine the academic and social success of students, depending on whether these attitudes are positive or negative. For instance, research suggests that teachers who harbor negative impressions of their students' behaviors also negatively affect the degree of support they offer in classrooms and so create an ambience that fosters more strained teacher–student relations (Meehan, Hughes, & Cavell, 2003). Negative teacher perceptions have also been associated with teachers' use of inflexible and punitive classroom management strategies (Conduct Problems Prevention Research Group, 1999), unnecessary disciplinary and special education referrals (Roderick, 2003), and related actions, which can cumulatively stifle some students' adjustment to the social and behavioral demands of the classroom, give rise to academic troubles, and portend more serious behavioral consequences.

Whether intentional or not, teachers bring their preconceived beliefs to the classroom (Murrell, 1993, 2001; Sleeter 2004). Biases that are fortified in the media, in the judicial system, and perhaps in personal experiences are kept in mind as teachers assess the schoolwork and behavior of boys and girls; but teacher perceptions of African American boys and girls are uniquely different. Again, we think educational research that demonstrates inattention to these subgroup differences will also mask risk by spreading it across different underachieving subgroups. African American girls are oftentimes perceived in the classroom as being loud and brash rather than articulate and self-assured (Fordham, 1993). African American males are generally viewed as possessing characteristics incongruent with academic success (e.g., laziness), valuing athletics over academic accomplishments, and having a propensity toward aggression and violence (Hall, 2001; Wood et al., 2007).

Teachers' bias and expectancy effects on the academic and behavioral outcomes of African American children have been demonstrated in recent work. For instance, McKown and Weinstein (2008) examined the role of classroom context in moderating the relationship between child ethnicity and teacher expectations. Utilizing data on 1,872 elementary school-age children in 83 classrooms, they showed that in ethnically diverse classrooms where students reported high levels of differential teacher treatment, the teachers' expectations of the successful performance of European American and Asian American students were significantly higher (between 0.75 and 1.00 standard deviations) than the expectations of African American and Latino students with similar achievement records. The results also showed that teachers' expectations contributed significantly to the achievement gap between the students in their sample. In classrooms characterized by high levels of teacher bias, teacher expectancy accounted for upward of 0.38 standard deviations of the achievement gap between the students at the end of the school year, with the African American students being at the lower rungs of this gap.

Ann A. Ferguson's book *Bad Boys* (2001) is a telling account of how 11- and 12-year-old Black boys are criminalized and are expected by teachers (and other school staff) to manifest significant classroom disciplinary problems and at some point make contact with the criminal justice system. It is also a critical analysis of how schools and classroom experiences in particular can be complicit in the actualization of these projections. Across both genders, the expectation that teachers make regarding African American students' academic underperformance and failures in the social arena has sizable literature support spanning five decades (Atwater, 2000; Bennett, 1976; Clark, 1965; Keller, 1986; Kellow & Jones, 2008; Lewis & Kim, 2008; Murray, 1996; Oates, 2003; Plewis, 1997; Richman, Bovelsky, Koovand, Vacca, & West, 1997; Zirkel, 2005). This body of work illuminates how broad intersectionality analyses may miss the unique learning needs of African American boys and their particular vulnerability to misperceptions of their abilities and classroom behavior by educators.

These perceptions may be highly vulnerable to racialized gender stereotypes, which can predict the unfair practices and maltreatment exercised by teachers (Neal et al., 2003). This process appears especially salient for African American male students attending public schools, particularly when there is teacher–student racial incongruence (Oates, 2003). To illustrate, Casteel (1998) investigated disparities in the classroom treatment of African American and European American seventh graders, as demonstrated by European American teachers during 32 hours of instruction. Results revealed that the European American boys in the sample received the most favorable treatment by teachers and initiated the most student–teacher contact. Conversely, the teachers tended to interact less positively with the African American boys relative to the other students. This finding is an important concern, given that African Americans compose approximately 17% of public school enrollments nationwide but only 6% to 8% of the teachers (Dee, 2005; see also, Lynn, 2002; Murrell, 1993). Stereotypes of wrongdoing by African American boys have been demonstrated in recent studies. For instance, Neal and colleagues (2003) showed that White teachers perceived African American male students' movement styles and cultural expressions (e.g., stroll walk and neighborhood jargon) to be higher in aggression, and they perceived the male students themselves to be lower in academic achievement and more in need of special education services. Irrespective of the teacher's race, teachers often misinterpret culturally relevant movement and language styles as being aggressive and disrespectful: Moore (2002) revealed that although African American teachers recognized styling behaviors associated with African American males, they were less favorable toward these students when they engaged in culturally sanctioned behaviors.

Research on the perceptual distortion of low-income African American female students has also received attention but to a lesser extent than that of their male counterparts. In qualitative research of African American high school students, Fordham (1993) explored the idea of the invisible Black female. Fordham proposed that invisibility is expressed in environments where dominant Black female traits are seen as the embodiment of "nothingness," that is, without value. This racial/gender invisibility causes the most plausible path toward the successful attainment of womanhood to be dependent on the assimilation of White middle-class female characteristics—namely, being demure and helpful. Some might argue that this representation of White middle-class womanhood to be problematic as well. Such questions are similarly raised for generalized references to African American girls. Some African American girls engage in stereotypic displays of "loudness," which may have real functional value in their families and neighborhoods, to resist intrusive cultural values and preserve their genuine gender identities (Fordham, 1993). Unfortunately, these frank cultural expressions are in diametric opposition to perceptions of White feminine values of demureness and, according to Fordham, are viewed by teachers as defiance or aggression. She noted that academically successful girls instead choose to be silent "ghosts/phantoms" or imitators of characteristically male ways of being—the implication being that to be successful, some African American girls make calculated efforts to erase their gender identities. All in all, Fordham's work, as well as that of others examining linkages between teacher expectations and racial differences in academic outcomes, demonstrates that these disparities ultimately involve the inextricable and intricate interplay of gender, race, and class.

RISK-COPING STRATEGIES

Whereas teachers' perceptual bias and resulting discriminatory practices are important considerations in discourses on gender risks in schooling, an equally important concern includes strategies used by recipients of this maltreatment to cope with these challenges. In the case of African American boys, research has demonstrated that their ability to adapt successfully or succumb to racialized gender politics in classrooms is contingent on individual-level differences in anger expression strategies and sensitivity to rejection.

Anger Expression

Anger expression is an important phenomenological variable of interest in investigating contextual challenges and emotional coping among African American male youth (Stevenson, 2003; Stevenson, Herrero-Taylor, Cameron, & Davis, 2002). The expression of anger is a reality among African Americans who are frustrated with their racial status in life, and it is used in different ways to mediate the psychological effects of racial provocation (Stevenson et al., 2002). Two possible strategies that African Americans use include suppressing their anger and channeling their angry feelings into socially adaptive behaviors. Research has revealed that although African Americans experience racial provocation more often than other racial groups do, they often suppress or hold in their anger, lest retaliation if they express anger openly (e.g., loss of job, failing grades, suspension from school; Johnson & Greene, 1991). Other studies have shown that African American youth also tend to engage in some form of impression management to control their anger linked to racial discrimination (Franklin & Boyd-Franklin, 2000). For instance, African American males have been shown to utilize role-flexing—or the altering of one's speech, behavior, or appearance—to diminish the effects of negative stereotypes and gain more social acceptance (Franklin & Boyd-Franklin, 2000). An example of role-flexing would be hypervigilance to appear nonthreatening, such as speaking softly and using care not to express overt anger. The use of humor has also been found to be an adaptive strategy of African American youth for controlling their anger and effectively coping with day-to-day stressors. Steward and colleagues (1998) found that among African American urban high school students, student playfulness and class clowning were significantly related to the students' psychological adjustment, although such behaviors were maladaptive for their academic outcomes.

Conversely, some African American male students engage in more overt, acting-out expressions of anger in the face of classroom adversities. Research in this area has highlighted the utilization of hypermasculine coping styles by urban African American male youth to negotiate race-related stress and other perceived threats in schools and other contexts (Cassidy & Stevenson, 2005; Spencer, 1999; Spencer, Fegley, Harpalani, & Seaton, 2004; Swanson, Cunningham, & Spencer, 2003). Hypermasculinity is gender-intensified behavior utilized by males to evoke respect and thwart impositions from others, particularly when they feel as though they can not achieve it effectively through other orientations or courses of action (Swanson et al., 2003). African American male youth in risky urban environments make use of the hypermasculine coping strategy to ensure their personal safety and livelihood and to garner respect from their peers (Majors & Billson, 1992; Noguera, 2003a). This may manifest as a simple "cool pose" or as blustering conduct whereby the male creates the impression of invincibility or noncompliance but does not personally identify with aggressive attitudes and insubordinate behavior (Majors & Billson, 1992).

In certain circumstances, hypermasculinity might take the form of more outward displays of anger, such as noncompliance, insubordination, and direct physical aggression (Noguera, 2003a; Stevenson et al., 2002). In the school setting, this behavior may be a reaction to consistently unfair treatment by teachers and peers in the classroom and in other situations. In fact, teachers' perceptual bias has been associated with high levels of tension between African American male youth and their teachers in urban secondary schools and with the youths' strategic yet maladaptive use of aggression and other acting-out behaviors (Cassidy & Stevenson, 2005). Often, these reactions are feeble attempts to mollify social maltreatment and thus preserve feelings of self-worth and self-respect (Cassidy & Stevenson, 2005; Spencer, 1999; Stevenson et al., 2002).

Hypermasculinity can have numerous negative effects that lead to poor outcomes for African American male students (Neal et al., 2003; Spencer, 1999). In a tragic set of reciprocal reactions, these behaviors can reinforce stereotypic images harbored by teachers, further reduce teachers' expectations of the aptitude and behavioral intentions of African American male students, and prompt disciplinary referrals and/or special education recommendations (Neal et al., 2003). For instance, Spencer (1999) documented that hypermasculine behaviors are significantly and positively intercorrelated with negative teacher perceptions of school adjustment for African American male students. She also reported that although hypermasculinity may garner respect or increase acceptance, it has been associated with general unpopularity with peers.

Rejection Sensitivity

Another emotional coping factor concerns how emotionally vulnerable or sensitive African American male youth contend with rebuff social and interpersonal difficulties. There is evidence that children's early, prolonged, or acute rejection experiences with significant others can lead them to develop a heightened sensitivity to rejection (Downey, Lebolt, Rincón, & Freitas, 1998; Pietrzak, Downey, & Ayduk, 2005). According to Downey et al. (1998), what follows are expectations of rejection in situations involving others, a lowered threshold for perception of negativity, an increased propensity for personalizing negative cues, and intense affective reactions— all of which can lead to an anxious, hostile, and aggressive interpersonal style emerging during early adolescence. Similar processes have been reported for African American students who encounter rejection based on race (Mendoza-Denton, Downey, Purdie, & Pietrzak, 2002).

For boys and girls, rejection sensitivity might involve individual differences in their expectations and perceptions of and negative reactions to adversities in the classroom. Researchers have examined the extent to which African American boys in urban public schools respond to anticipated or perceived gender- and race-based rejection. For example, Cassidy and Stevenson (2005) found that measures of rejection sensitivity significantly and positively correlated with measures of anger and aggression among the Black adolescent males in their sample. Examining this variable across both genders, Rosenbloom and Way (2004) found racial discrimination by teachers and other high school staff to be an important factor contributing to the hostility of urban African American students toward other students. Both studies by these researchers suggest that rejection sensitivity is a potential instigant of behavior adjustment problems among African American boys.

Taken together, expressions of anger (overt, hypermasculine expressions of anger in particular) and rejection sensitivity are risky coping reactions, and they have been associated with elevated levels of conflict between African American boys and their teachers. Both coping styles have been shown to be maladaptive reactions to environmental stress, thereby promoting the development of aggression and other disciplinary problems in the classroom that in turn exacerbate negative attention from teachers and lead to poor academic adjustment outcomes. Racial socialization has been found to temper anger expression and rejection sensitivity in African American male youth (Cassidy & Stevenson, 2005; Stevenson, 1997).

RACIAL SOCIALIZATION AS A UNIQUE PROTECTIVE FACTOR FOR GENDER INEQUITIES IN EDUCATION

Racial socialization has emerged in scientific literature as a leading protective factor for African American children, and it refers to the developmental processes through which parents shape children's knowledge about their race and about relations between different ethnic groups (Hughes et al., 2006; McHale et al., 2006). In this process, children acquire behaviors, perceptions, values, and attitudes of their respective racial groups and come to take pride in and see themselves as members of such groups (Coard & Sellers, 2005; Stevenson, 1997). The process also involves adaptive and protective processes, preparation for the deleterious and promotive effects of racial discrimination, mainstream and bicultural coping, spiritual coping, and egalitarianism (McHale et al., 2006; Neblett, Phillip, Cogburn, & Sellers, 2006; Stevenson et al., 2002). Within school settings, racial socialization has been linked to the adjustment of African American students across multiple domains of functioning at different grade levels (Neblett et al., 2006; Phinney & Chavira, 1995; Stevenson et al., 2002; Thomas, Townsend, & Belgrave, 2003). For example, Thomas and colleagues (2003) found among African American students attending an urban, public elementary school, a significant positive association between students' endorsement of positive attitudes toward their racial group and their self-ratings of classroom behavior control and orientation toward school, including positive beliefs concerning grades and schooling in general. The researchers also found that indices of racial socialization were predictive of teacher ratings of classroom behavior problems among the young sample. Using an older sample of African American adolescents, Neblett et al. (2006) found that racial socialization variables (e.g., racial pride and egalitarianism) were unique predictors of various academic achievement outcomes, including academic curiosity, engagement and task persistence in classrooms, and self-reported grades. Investigating the coping responses of low-resource African American youth, Spencer, Fegley and Harpalani (2003) showed that cultural socialization, including the internalization of messages regarding the importance of religion/spirituality and racial pride, was important in the development of a healthy sense of self and a healthy sense of self in relation to others. This was especially the case among the adolescent boys in their sample.

More recently, we have investigated whether features of healthy racial socialization, including strong cultural identity formation and preparation for bias experiences, are essential and distinctly influential in keeping African American boys from engaging in overactive aggressive behaviors in the classroom (Thomas, Coard, Stevenson, Bentley, & Zamel, in press). This study was guided by the phenomenological variant of ecological systems theory (Spencer, 1995, 2006), a cyclic recursive model of human development for racially and ethnically diverse individuals that provides a heuristic device for examining youths' cultural experiences in various interrelated contexts, including classrooms. Spencer (2006) conceptualizes this theory as representing five components—net vulnerability, net stress engagement, reactive coping strategies, emergent identity, and life-stage specific outcomes—linked by bidirectional processes that offer a relevant framework for investigating the complex interplay of individual and contextual influences that may underlie classroom behavior adjustment for some African American male youth. With this framework in mind, we sought to understand the impact of racial socialization experiences and different modes of reactive emotional coping on teacher perceptions of classroom behavioral adjustment of urban African American adolescent males.

Results from the investigation showed racial socialization to be an important determinant for teacher perceptions of behavioral overactivity for African American male youth, generally and across different behaviors. With regard to the influence of racial socialization factors, the boys in the sample who demonstrated limited awareness of their African American cultural heritage were more likely to have their behaviors rated by teachers as being problematic. This suggests that the more the boys internalized messages from parents (and other relevant adults) about their cultural heritage, the less likely they were to react to stressful social situations and engage in behaviors in the classroom that would put them at risk for negative evaluations of their behavior. This finding substantiates results from earlier work, namely, that of Stevenson (1997), showing that African American male youth who embraced beliefs indicative of healthy racial socialization were better able to refrain from acting out with defiance and hostility in school than were those without this distinguishing characteristic. However, findings from Thomas et al. (in press) help to establish that racial socialization—above and beyond its influence on the way that African American boys manage their emotions and react to adverse situations in classrooms—affects the extent to which the boys' behaviors are interpreted positively or negatively by teachers in these settings. To the extent that differential treatment in classrooms differentially compromises and challenges the academic performance and associated behavioral adjustment of boys and girls (with African American boys experiencing unique risks for such outcomes), racial socialization may not only foster individual resilience but also offer a serum to counteract the effects of racialized gender politics operating in classrooms.

IMPLICATIONS FOR EDUCATIONAL RESEARCH AND PRACTICE

Gender risks in education, and the extent to which boys and girls experience differential treatment in classrooms, are complicated by race and class. If we follow the data, subgroup analyses point to urban low-income African American boys as the most at-risk group when using larger achievement-level and teacher–student relationship level data. Certainly, we are not arguing that White male or female students from low-income backgrounds are not at risk for underachievement and negative behavioral outcomes. We are arguing that context matters in defining the relevant risk issues for particular racial/gender subgroups. We have chosen one such subgroup, realizing that other subgroup research reviews are necessary.

The research highlighted in this review speaks to the need for increased attention in research studies to the interplay between and among individual emotional coping strategies, racial/gender socialization processes, and the behavior options chosen by African American male students. Future investigations on correlates of behavior adjustment for these students should continue to elucidate the momentous impact that classroom experiences can have on their functioning. In effect, student classroom experiences must include direct assessments of peer socialization processes and some index of disparities in teachers' expectations toward students from different cultural backgrounds. Unwarranted accusations of wrongdoing and social rebuffs by teachers have been implicated in the disproportionate referral of African American boys for severe disciplinary measures and emotional support services and in their strategic yet counteractive displays of aggression and hypermasculinity in the school setting (Cassidy & Stevenson, 2005; Stevenson et al., 2002). Given these potential consequences, the ability to detect classroom inequities and related social challenges would greatly contribute to explicating relationships between classroom environment effects and individual behavioral outcomes for students from different gender backgrounds.

The research summarized in this review has important implications regarding school-based practices—namely, in their capability of addressing inequitable practices in schooling. In considering the widening achievement gap and what Gregory and Mosely (2004) describe as the broadening discipline gap, interventions that challenge stereotyping that disproportionally hampers the academic success and psychosocial well-being of African American males are very important. Smith and Hung (2008) provide a useful approach to helping this subgroup of students and others who are on the receiving end of discriminatory practices in the classroom. They list six possible strategies: reduce the importance of the tasks in dispute, reduce the salience of the tasks in dispute, provide reasons for the underachievement, describe the task or test as being invulnerable to stereotype, view ability as a malleable entity rather than a fixed one, and access role models from one's gender or racial background who can perform the tasks well. There are many other strategies to combat the negative effects of internalizing stereotypes, and recent evidence by Nussbaum and Steele (2007) revealed that some students may not be permanently susceptible to stereotype threat and, rather, may disidentify only long enough to problem-solve the dilemmas of the task so that they can reenter the stressful task situation with more successful interactions.

Thus, interventions for reducing risks of educational underachievement for low-income African American male students during the primary and secondary school years may be improved by efforts with a dual focus on racial/cultural identification and sociocognitive problem solving. Racial socialization, as applied to the development of students' racial negotiation skills within the tension of classroom interactions with peers and teachers, may allow for students to take initiative in ways that other achievement gap strategies have failed to teach—namely, those that ignore the gender and racial dynamics in the classroom. In a pilot project entitled Can We Talk? Stevenson, Thomas, and Gadsden (2008) have developed an intervention with a cultural socialization curriculum that emphasizes the teaching, development, and assessment of social relations and emotional coping skills across different racial groups. For instance, strategies that emotionally prepare African American male students for classroom situations in which racial, gender, and academic achievement stereotypes are prevalent may influence how they respond to that unfair treatment. The potential in such a strategy rests in the teaching of cultural issues germane to the African American experience, which is layered with gender, race, and class disparities. Research has provided some evidence of the effectiveness of such interventions (Stevenson, 2003), but more work is necessary to identify the links to pro-social in-class academic agency and achievement outcomes that may come from racial socialization-based interventions.

Future school-based interventions involving African American boys in urban primary and secondary schools may also be strengthened by working with teachers to examine their perceptions and concomitant classroom management practices. Not unlike other professionals, teachers are not immune from being influenced by over-generalizations based on cultural differences. Whether their behavior is intentional or not, it may result in classroom interactions and practices that respond to cultural biases and preconceived notions about the cultural expressions and emotions displayed by Black male students in the classroom. We are deeply aware that teachers are equally stressed by the multiple cultural elephants in the classroom, where the burgeoning questions of race, class, gender, and difference undermine quality teacher–student relationships. These questions include "How fearful and worried am I in teaching Black boys?" and "Do I have the skills to successfully navigate the racial/gender and achievement tensions in the classroom?" However, there is promise in preparing and supporting teachers to answer these questions with responses that reflect challenge rather than threat so that they do not misinterpret the behavioral and emotional expressions of racial/gender subgroups of students as being reflective of internal dysfunction; rather, we hope that teachers will understand these expressions to be what research suggests they are: culturally scripted reactive coping styles to authority figures. Our overall point here is that there is an uneasy interaction of teacher perceptions and the cultural style expressions of African American male students. We suggest that if these expressions are understood, such understanding might well lead to positive teacher–student relationships, a factor consistently found to be central to students' behavioral adjustment and a worthy antivirus to the risk of the most challenging gender inequities that hamper educational achievement.

NOTES

[1]We use the term *Black* to refer to the diversity of people in the African diaspora and with respect to common usages in research focused on African Americans.

[2]In this statement, we are drawing on the comments of students in our research studies.

REFERENCES

Adenika-Morrow, T. J. (1996). A lifeline to science careers for African-American females. *Educational Leadership, 53*(8), 80–83.

Artiles, A. J. (2003). Special education's changing identity: Paradoxes and dilemmas in views of culture and space. *Harvard Educational Review, 73*, 164–202.

Atwater, M. M. (2000). Equity for Black Americans in precollege science. *Science Education, 84*, 154–179.

Bay Area School Reform Collaborative. (2001). The color of discipline: Understanding racial disparity in school discipline practices. *Equity Brief.* Retrieved July 9, 2008, from http://www.springboardschools.org/research/documents/EquityBriefJan01

Bennett, C. E. (1976). Student's race, social class, and academic history as determinants of teacher expectation of student performance. *Journal of Black Psychology, 3*(1), 71–86.

Bradley, R. H., & Corwyn, R. F. (2002). Socioeconomic status and child development. *Annual Review of Psychology, 53*, 371–399.

Cassidy, E. F., & Stevenson, H. C. (2005). They wear the mask: Hypervulnerability and hypermasculine aggression among African American males in an urban remedial disciplinary school. *Journal of Aggression, Maltreatment & Trauma, 11*(4), 53–74.

Casteel, C. A. (1998). Teacher–student interactions and race in integrated classrooms. *Journal of Educational Research, 92*(2), 115–120.

Children's Defense Fund (1975). *School suspensions: Are they helping children?* Cambridge, MA: Washington Research Project.

Clark, K. (1965). *Dark ghetto: Dilemmas of social power.* Washington, DC: Advancement Project. ED013264

Coard, S. I., & Sellers, R. M. (2005). African American families as contexts for racial socialization. In V. C. McLoyd, N. E. Hill, & K. A. Dodge (Eds.), *African American family life* (pp. 264–284). New York: Guilford.

Conduct Problems Prevention Research Group. (1999). Initial impact of the Fast Track prevention trail for conduct problems: II. Classroom effects. *Journal of Consulting and Clinical Psychology, 67*(5), 648–657.

Corbett, C., Hill, C., & St. Rose, A. (2008). *Where the girls are: The facts about gender equity in education.* Washington, DC: American Association of University Women Education Foundation.

Davis, J. E. (2003). Early schooling and academic achievement of African American males. *Urban Education, 38*(5), 515–537.

Dee, T. S. (2005). A teacher like me: Does race, ethnicity, or gender matter? *American Economic Review, 95*(2), 158–165.

Donovan, S., & Cross, C. (Eds.). (2002). *Minority students in special and gifted education.* Washington, DC: National Academy Press.

Downey, G., Lebolt, A., Rincón, C., & Freitas, A. L. (1998). Rejection sensitivity and children's interpersonal difficulties. *Child Development, 69,* 1072–1089.

Entwisle, D. R., Alexander, K. L., & Olsen, L. S. (2007). Early schooling: The handicap of being poor and male. *Sociology of Education, 80,* 114–138.

Eyler, A. E., & Wright, K. (1997). Gender identification and sexual orientation among genetic females with gender-blended self-perception in childhood and adolescence. *International Journal of Transgenderism, 1*(1). Retrieved October 12, 2008, from http://www.symposion.com/ijt/ijtc0102.htm

Farkas, G. (2003). Racial disparities and discrimination in education: What do we know, how do we know it, and what do we need to know? *Teachers College Record, 105*(6), 1119–1146.

Fenning, P., & Rose, J. (2007). Overrepresentation of African American students in exclusionary discipline: The role of school policy. *Urban Education, 42,* 536–559.

Ferguson, A. A. (2001). *Bad boys: Public schools in the making of Black masculinity.* Ann Arbor: University of Michigan Press.

Ferguson, R. F. (1998). Teachers' perceptions and expectations and the Black–White test score gap. In C. Jencks & M. Phillips (Eds.), *The Black–White test score* (pp. 273–317). Washington, DC: Brookings Institution.

Ford, D. Y., & Harris, J. J., III. (1997). A study of the racial identity and achievement of Black males and females. *Roeper Review, 20*(2), 105–110.

Fine, M. & Kuriloff, P. (2006). Forging and performing masculine identities within social spaces: Boys and men negotiating the crucible of dominant cultural representations at the intersection of class, race, ethnicity, and sexuality. *Men and Masculinities, 8,* 257-261.

Fordham, S. (1993). "Those loud Black girls": (Black) women, silence, and gender "passing" in the academy. *Anthropology and Education Quarterly, 24*(1), 3–32.

Foster, M. (2001). Education and socialization: A review of the literature. In W. H. Watkins, J. H. Lewis, & V. Chou (Eds.), *Race and education: The roles of history and society in education African American students* (pp. 220–224). Needham Heights, MA: Allyn & Bacon.

Franklin, A. J., & Boyd-Franklin, N. (2000). Invisibility syndrome: A clinical model of the effects of racism on African-American males. *American Journal of Orthopsychiatry, 70*(1), 33–41.

Frick, P. J., Kamphaus, R. W., Lahey, B. B., Christ, M. A., Hart, E. L., & Tannenbaum, T. E. (1991). Academic underachievement and the disruptive behavior disorders. *Journal of Consulting and Clinical Psychology, 59*, 289–294.

Gilliam, W. S. (2005). *Prekindergarteners left behind: Expulsion rates in state prekindergarten systems.* New Haven, CT: Yale University Child Study Center.

Gregory, A., & Mosely, P. M. (2004). The discipline gap: Teacher's views on the over-representation of African American students in the discipline system. *Equity and Excellence in Education, 37*, 18–30.

Hall, R. E. (2001). The ball curve: Calculated racism and the stereotype of African American men. *Journal of Black Studies, 32*(1), 104–119.

Hinshaw, S. P. (1992). Externalizing behavior problems and academic underachievement in childhood and adolescence: Causal relationships and underlying mechanisms. *Psychological Bulletin, 111*, 127–155.

Hinshaw, S. P., & Lee, S. S. (2003). Conduct and oppositional defiant disorders. In E. J. Mash & R. A. Barkley (Eds.). *Child psychopathology* (2nd ed., pp. 144–198). New York: Guilford Press.

Hughes, D. L., Johnson, D., Smith, E., Rodriguez, J., Stevenson, H. C., & Spicer, P. (2006). Parents' ethnic/racial socialization practices: A review of research and directions for future study. *Developmental Psychology, 42*(5), 747–770.

Huston, A., McLoyd, V. C., & Coll, C. G. (1997). Poverty and behavior: The case for multiple methods and levels of analysis. *Developmental Review, 17*(3), 376–393.

Hyde, J. A., & Lindberg, S. M. (2007). Facts and assumptions about the nature of gender differences and the implications for gender equity. In S. S. Klein, B. Richardson, D. A. Grayson, L. H. Fox, C. Kramarae, D. S. Pollard, & C. A. Dwyer (Eds.), *Handbook for achieving gender equity through education* (2nd ed., pp. 19–32). Mahwah, NJ: Lawrence Erlbaum.

Irving, M. A., & Hudley, C. (2005). Cultural mistrust, academic outcome expectations, and outcome values among African American adolescent men. *Urban Education, 40*(5), 476–496.

Jackson, J. H. (2008). *Given half a chance: The Schott 50-state report on public education and African American males.* Cambridge, MA: Schott Foundation for Public Education.

Jencks, C., & Phillips, M. (1998). The Black–White test score gap: An introduction. In C. Jencks & M. Phillips (Eds.), *The Black–White test score gap* (pp. 45–62). Washington, DC: Brookings Institute.

Johnson, E. H., & Greene, A. F. (1991). The relationship between suppressed anger and psychosocial distress in African American male adolescents. *Journal of Black Psychology, 18,* 47–65.

Jussim, L., Eccles, J., & Madon, S. (1996). Social perception, social stereotypes, and teacher expectations: Accuracy and the quest for the powerful self-fulfilling prophesy. *Advances in Experimental Social Psychology, 28*, 281–387.

Keller, H. R. (1986). In-school adaptive behavior: Assessment domains of behavior scales and child characteristics. *Journal of Psychoeducational Assessment, 4*(1), 1–12.

Kellow, J. T., & Jones, B. D. (2008). The effects of stereotypes on the achievement gap: Reexamining the academic performance of African American high school students. *Journal of Black Psychology, 34*(1), 94–120.

Klein, S. S., Kramarae, C., & Richardson, B. (2007). Examining the achievement of gender equity in and through education. In S. S. Klein, B. Richardson, D. A. Grayson, L. H. Fox, C. Kramarae, D. S. Pollard, & C. A. Dwyer (Eds.), *Handbook for achieving gender equity through education* (2nd ed., pp. 1–13). Mahwah, NJ: Lawrence Erlbaum.

Knaak, S. (2004). On the reconceptualizing of gender. Implications for research design. *Sociological Inquiry, 74*(3), 302–317.

Lewis, J. L., & Kim, E. (2008). A desire to learn: African American children's positive attitudes toward learning within school cultures of low expectations. *Teachers College Record, 110*(6), 1304–1329.

Lynn, M. (2002). Critical race theory and the perspectives of Black men teachers in the Los Angeles public schools. *Equity and Excellence in Education, 35*(2), 119–130.

Majors, R., & Billson, J. M. (1992). *Cool pose: The dilemmas of Black manhood in America.* New York: Maxwell Macmillan.

McHale, S. M., Crouter, A. C., Kim, J., Burton, L. M., Davis, K. D., Dotterer, A. M., et al. (2006). Mothers' and fathers' racial socialization in African American families: Implications for youth. *Child Development, 77*(5), 1387–1402.

McKown, C., & Weinstein, R. S. (2008). Teacher expectations, classroom context, and the achievement gap. *Journal of School Psychology, 46*(3), 235–261.

McLoyd, L. C. (1998). Socioeconomic disadvantage and child development. *American Psychologists, 53*(2), 185–204.

Meehan, B. T., Hughes, J. N., & Cavell, T. A. (2003). Teacher–student relationships as compensatory resources for aggressive children. *Child Development, 74*(4), 1145–1157.

Mendoza-Denton, R., Downey, G., Purdie, V. J., & Pietrzak, J. (2002). Sensitivity to status-based rejection: Implications for African American students' college experience. *Journal of Personality and Social Psychology, 83*(4), 896–918.

Mid-Atlantic Equity Consortium. (2000). *Update on Title IX: Achieving gender equity.* Retrieved July 28, 2008, from http://www.maec.org/titleixupdate.html

Moore, A. L. (2002). African-American early childhood teachers' decisions to refer African-American students. *International Journal of Qualitative Studies in Education, 15*(6), 631–652.

Murray, C. B. (1996). Estimating achievement performance: A confirmation bias. *Journal of Black Psychology, 22*(1), 67–85.

Murrell, P. (1993). Afrocentric immersion: Academic and personal development of African American males in public schools. In T. Perry & J. Fraser (Eds.), *Freedom's plow: Teaching in the multicultural classroom* (pp. 231–259). New York: Routledge.

Murrell, P. (2001). *The community teacher: A new framework for effective urban teaching.* New York: Teachers College Press.

Neal, L. V. I., McCray, A. D., Webb-Johnson, G., & Bridgest, S. T. (2003). The effects of African American movement styles on teachers' perceptions and reactions. *Journal of Special Education, 37*(1), 49–57.

Neblett, E. W., Phillip, C. L., Cogburn, C. D., & Sellers, R. M. (2006). African American adolescents' discrimination experiences and academic achievement: Racial socialization as a cultural compensatory and protective factor. *Journal of Black Psychology, 32*(2), 199–218.

Noguera, P. A. (2003a). Schools, prisons, and the social implications of punishment: Rethinking disciplinary practices. *Theory Into Practice, 42*(4), 341–351.

Noguera, P. A. (2003b). The trouble with Black boys: The role and influence of environmental and cultural factors on the academic performance of African American males. *Urban Education, 38*(4), 431–459.

Nussbaum, A. D., & Steele, C. M. (2007). Situational disengagement and persistence in the face of adversity. *Journal of Experimental Social Psychology, 43*(1), 127–134.

Oates, G. L. S. C. (2003). Teacher–student racial congruence, teacher perceptions, and test performance. *Social Science Quarterly, 84*(3), 508–525.

Osborne, J. W. (1999). Unraveling underachievement among African American boys from an identification with academics perspective. *Journal of Negro Education, 68*(4), 555–565.

Phinney, J. S., & Chavira, V. (1995). Parent ethnic socialization and adolescent coping with problems related to ethnicity. *Journal of Research on Adolescence, 5*(1), 31–53.

Pietrzak, J., Downey, G., & Ayduk, O. (2005). Rejection sensitivity as an interpersonal vulnerability. In M. W. Baldwin (Ed.), *Interpersonal cognition* (pp. 62–84). New York: Guilford Press.

Plewis, I. (1997). Inferences about teacher expectations from national assessment at Key Stage One. *British Journal of Educational Psychology, 67*(2), 235–247.

Pollard, D. S. (1993). Gender, achievement and African American students' perceptions of their school experience. *Educational Psychologist, 28*(4), 294–303.

Richman, C. L., Bovelsky, S., Kroovand, N., Vacca, J., & West, T. (1997). Racism 102: The classroom. *Journal of Black Psychology, 23*(4), 378–387.

Roderick, M. (2003). What's happening to the boys? Early high school experiences and school outcomes among African American male adolescents in Chicago. *Urban Education, 38*(5), 538–607.

Rosenbloom, S. R., & Way, N. (2004). Experiences of discrimination among African American, Asian American, and Latino Adolescents in an urban high school. *Youth & Society, 35*(4), 420–451.

Serwatka, T. S., Deering, S., & Grant, P. (1995). Disproportionate representation of African Americans in emotionally handicapped classes. *Journal of Black Studies, 25*(4), 492–506.

Skiba, R. J., Michael, R. S., Nardo, A. C., & Peterson, R. L. (2002). The color of discipline: Sources of racial and gender disproportionality in school punishment. *Urban Review, 34*(4), 317–342.

Skiba, R. J., & Reece, L. P. (2000). School discipline at a crossroads: From zero tolerance to early response. *Exceptional Children, 66*(3), 335–346.

Sleeter, C. (2004). How White teachers construct race. In C. McCarthy & W. Crichlow (Eds.), *Race, identity and representation in education* (pp. 157–171). New York: Routledge.

Smith, C. S., & Hung, L.-C. (2008). Stereotype threat: Effects on education. *Social Psychology of Education, 11*(3), 243–257.

Spencer, M. B. (1999). Social and cultural influences on school adjustment: The application of an identity-focused cultural ecological perspective. *Educational Psychologist, 34*(1), 43–57.

Spencer, M. B. (2006). Phenomenology and ecological systems theory: Development of diverse groups. In *Handbook of child psychology: Vol. 1. Theoretical models of human development* (6th ed., pp. 829–893) Hoboken, NJ: John Wiley.

Spencer, M. B., Fegley, S. G., & Harpalani, V. (2003). A theoretical and empirical examination of identity as coping: Linking coping resources to the self-processes of African American youth. *Applied Developmental Science, 7*(3), 181–188.

Spencer, M. B., Fegley, S. G., Harpalani, V., & Seaton, G. (2004). Understanding hypermasculinity in context: A theory-driven analysis of urban adolescent males' coping responses. *Research in Human Development, 1*(4), 229–257.

Steele, C. M. (1997). A threat in the air: How stereotypes shape intellectual identity and performance. *American Psychologist, 52*(6), 613–629.

Steele, C. M., & Aronson, J. (1995). Stereotype threat and the intellectual test performance of African Americans. *Journal of Personality and Social Psychology, 69*(5), 797–811.

Steele, C. M., & Aronson, J. (2000). *Stereotype threat and the intellectual test performance of African Americans.* New York: Psychology Press.

Stevenson, H. C. (1997). Managing anger: Protective, proactive, or adaptive racial socialization identity profiles and African-American manhood development. *Journal of Prevention and Intervention in the Community, 16*(1/2), 35–61.

Stevenson, H. C. (2003). *Playing with anger: Teaching coping skills to African American boys through athletics and culture.* Westport, CT: Praeger.

Stevenson, H. C., Herrero-Taylor, T., Cameron, R., & Davis, G. Y. (2002). Mitigating instigation: Cultural phenomenological influences of anger and fighting among "big-boned" and "baby-faced" African American youth. *Journal of Youth and Adolescence, 31*(6), 473–485.

Stevenson, H. C., Thomas, D. E., & Gadsden, V. (2008). *Can we talk? Promoting the academic engagement of high school students through racial socialization.* Unpublished manuscript.

Steward, R. J., Jo, H. I., Murray, D., Fitzgerald, W., Neil, D., Fear, F., et al. (1998). Psychological adjustment and coping styles of urban African American high school students. *Journal of Multicultural Counseling and Development, 26,* 70–82.

Swanson, D. P., Cunningham, M., & Spencer, M. B. (2003). Black males' structural conditions, achievement patterns, normative needs and "opportunities." *Urban Education, 38*(5), 608–633.

Thomas, D. E., Coard, S. I., Stevenson, H. C., Bentley, K., & Zamel, P. (in press). Racial and emotional factors predicting teachers' perceptions of classroom behavioral maladjustment for urban African American male youth. *Psychology in the Schools.*

Thomas, D. E., Townsend, T. G., & Belgrave, F. Z. (2003). The influence of cultural and racial identification on the psychosocial adjustment of inner-city African American children in school. *American Journal of Community Psychology, 32*(3/4), 217–228.

U.S. Department of Education. (1994). *National Education Longitudinal Study of 1988 (Base year—second follow-up)* [CD-ROM]. Washington, DC: National Center for Education Statistics.

U.S. Department of Education. (1999). *Projected student suspension rates values for the nation's public schools by race/ethnicity: Elementary and secondary school civil rights compliance reports.* Washington, DC: Office of Civil Rights.

U.S. Department of Education. (2004). *Crime and safety in America's public schools: Selected findings from the School Survey on Crime and Safety* (NCES Report No. 204-370). Washington, DC: National Center for Education Statistics.

Wood, D., Kaplan, R., & McLoyd, V. C. (2007). Gender differences in the educational expectations of urban, low-income African American youth: The role of parents and the school. *Journal of Youth and Adolescence, 36,* 417–427.

Younger, M., Warrington, M., & Williams, J. (1999). The gender gap and classroom interactions: Reality and rhetoric. *British Journal of Sociology of Education, 2,* 327–343.

Zirkel, S. (2005). Ongoing issues of racial and ethnic stigma in education 50 years after *Brown v. Board. Urban Review, 37*(2), 107–126.

Chapter 7

Negotiating Linguistic and Cultural Identities: Theorizing and Constructing Opportunities and Risks in Education

Jin Sook Lee
University of California, Santa Barbara

Kate T. Anderson
National Institute of Education, Singapore

The life chances of students are determined by their ability to interact critically with the discourses around them, while still avoiding the temptation to be seduced by the disempowering messages those discourses often contain. The discourse surrounding children teaches them who they are, what their place is in the world and what they need to do to become autonomous and valuable citizens. Language, critically acquired, is potentially empowering for people as they constantly build on previous encounters with the words in their unique search for meaning and value.

—Corson (2001, p. 14)

Present discourses in the media and social sciences research about accelerating global change increasingly locate individuals and their interactions across multiple boundaries: linguistic, cultural, ethnic, racial, economic, religious, political, national, and digital. The fluidity of both perceived and actual movements of persons and messages makes it necessary to reconsider how identities are conceptualized and framed as "mattering" in social interactions across different contexts. In educational contexts, questions of identity are especially critical because the development of educational practice and policies are grounded in different ways of understanding who learners are or should be. How students interpret and develop their identities in a given context is shaped by self-perceptions, desires, hopes, and expectations, as well as salient aspects of the social context, such as sociopolitical ideologies, histories, and structures that are often beyond the control of an individual (Sadowski, 2003). The various ideologies, power structures, and historical legacies associated with different forms of language use, cultures, and situations frame individuals' linguistic and

Review of Research in Education
March 2009, Vol. 33, pp. 181-211
DOI: 10.3102/0091732X08327090
© 2009 AERA. http://rre.aera.net

cultural practices as those of specific types of people (e.g., types of learners, types of speakers, learners with types of recognizable practices; Anderson, 2008).

As Corson (2001) comments in the opening quotation, students' social and academic opportunities are shaped by their ability to understand and identify themselves through language and other semiotic systems of meaning. Thus, the processes of identity negotiation for students can become a site of opportunity and struggle in local institutional spaces, as well as in cultural imaginaries through various grain sizes of linguistic and cultural reference (McDermott, 1993). In other words, identity can be understood as crossing multiple timescales and mediating micro- and macro-social processes based on how it is conceived by local social actors and by researchers—that is, how identity types are identified and constructed and how identity is enacted as a phenomenological practice across events, life spans, and institutions as a structural abstraction (Lemke, 2008).

The goal of this article is to examine different conceptions of identity and different processes of identity negotiation to make visible the implicit and explicit links between social practices and perceived risk, equity, and opportunities to learn for linguistically and culturally diverse students. We discuss analytic frameworks for the study of identity as a socially constructed, locally situated, and culturally reified construct, and we focus on how the empirical study of identity in educational contexts has contributed to different theoretical and practical uses of the term.

Over the past two decades, identity as a theoretical construct and an empirical focus has gained prominence in educational research. Many scholars believe that identity—whether understood as a way of belonging, as a category for policy making, or in myriad other ways—is intricately tied to the ways that we interact, learn, and teach (e.g., Ball & Ellis, 2007; Hall, 1996; Nasir, 2002; Norton, 1997; Sadowski, 2003). Although its use is approaching ubiquitousness in discourses about teaching and learning, the concept of identity and its impact on educational processes are not yet thoroughly understood.

To address our goals for this article, we begin by discussing the theoretical, epistemological, and methodological issues related to the broader concept of identity as a basis for understanding the negotiation of linguistic and cultural identities. As such, we focus on the negotiation processes of linguistically and culturally diverse students because their identities are often marked as being nonnormative or "other," in ways that provide salient insights into what is at stake when identity is connected to learning. We then review how linguistic and cultural identities are associated with the different ways in which minority status and risk have been socially constructed in the literature on identity and educational practice and performance. Following that, we engage in a review of empirical literature on the negotiation of linguistic and cultural identity as it relates to risk, minority status, and academic performance. This discussion highlights the persistent challenges associated with navigating categories and normativities, such as linguistic practices, race, class, gender, and ability, in the context of diversity and the attendant issues of access, equity, and risk that accompany perceived salient social differences. Finally, we present recommendations and considerations for future research and practice.

REVIEW OF CONCEPTUAL LITERATURE ON IDENTITY AND ITS NEGOTIATION

Definitions of Identity in Recent Educational Studies

There is no commonly agreed-upon definition of identity; however, many scholars have put forth definitions that may be useful for understanding social aspects of learning and discourses of school practice. Bryan Brown (2004) conceptualizes identity as a set of discursive domains that are evoked and constructed based on shared or negotiated assumptions, categories, and knowledge in classroom spaces. This conceptualization enables us to see the ways in which classroom interactions make available entry points into academic practices based on ability and desire to assimilate to, or take on, such ways of being (i.e., talking the talk and walking the walk, which for some students is a threat to their social standing). At a micro-interactional level, the negotiation of such discursive domains plays out in contestations and acceptances through various interactional resources (Brown, 2004; Noguera, 2003). Nasir and Saxe (2003) also speak to identity as a socially constructed process and artifact. They define identity as an affiliation that develops over time; that is, it is a resource for communicating aspects of positions and affiliations that develop as artifacts of local interaction. Viewed in this way, identity makes visible how local interaction (e.g., teacher–student interaction or peer interaction) is central in supporting or contesting certain types of identities and how these identities can become reified over time through persistent use and appeal to their relevance (Holland, Lachicotte, Skinner, & Cain, 1998; Holland & Lave, 2001; Wortham, 2006).

Bucholtz and Hall (2004, 2005) characterize identity as a product of symbolic systems arising from local and political relations of difference and legitimacy and as a tool for understanding local power relations and processes. Their perspective acknowledges the ways that different kinds of identities reflect different power relations, which may stem from larger sociopolitical relations and ideologies. Moreover, Norton (2000) defines identity as "how a person understands his or her relationship to the world, how that relationship is constructed across time and space, and how the person understands possibilities for the future" (p. 5). This view enables us to see how students' opportunities to participate in learning activities are affected not only by their investments in the learning process and by specific interactions, but also by discourses and ideologies of schooling. In her work with second-language learners, Norton highlights the agency and investment of the individual in negotiating her or his linguistic and cultural identities in ways that create or restrict opportunities to learn English. Norton's study demonstrated that students need to learn to negotiate identities in their different social worlds, in large part by developing linguistic and sociocultural competencies that afford them access to engaging in social opportunities for participation and to having that participation recognized by others.

However, an individual's agency to take up certain identities may be met with resistance from others. In a study of a 17-year-old Dominican American student and his negotiation of identity in a classroom, Bailey (2000) found that strategic uses of different language varieties allowed the student to highlight Dominican, American, and African American aspects of his Dominican American identity, depending on the situation. Yet, in his daily classroom interactions, the same student was simultaneously faced with "hegemonic forms of ascription" (p. 557), where others imposed labels and categories based on his appearance. Although Bailey's study highlights the idea that identities are constructed and negotiated in local contexts as well as within larger sociohistorical contexts, it makes visible how the identities that one may want to portray may be met with resistance and nonacceptance owing to the dominant forms of ascription that are culturally prevalent (for an earlier thorough discussion of the ways that identity is marked and negotiated dialectically through linguistic practice, cf. Le Page & Tabouret-Keller, 1985). Thus, such studies make visible how critical the negotiation process is in identity work as it relates to social relationships, learning environments, and self-development.

According to Gee (2000), the need to address the contemporary issues of access, networking, and mobility, all of which are intricately interconnected with identity negotiation processes, requires a finer conceptual understanding of identity. He defines identity as "being recognized as a certain 'kind of person' in a given context" (p. 99). Gee specifies four different but overlapping ways that individuals understand or make sense of identity:

> *nature identity:* a "natural" state of being, given from forces in nature (e.g., being biologically "Asian");
> *institution identity:* a position authorized within institutions (e.g., being a student or a teacher);
> *discourse identity:* an individual trait recognized in interactions (e.g., as a result of interaction, either passively or actively taken on); and
> *affinity identity:* a set of shared experience in practices of "affinity groups" (e.g., being a "tech geek").

Each of these interrelated perspectives enables us to understand how identities can be developed and maintained through dynamic and relevant social interactions. Furthermore, this typology of the ways that identities become recognized incorporates micro- and macro-social processes for identities' social realization, thus allowing the concept of identity to be understood along different dimensions—for example, collective, individual, assumed, ascribed, multiple, static, developmental, individual, relational, personal, institutional, biologically determined, and socially constructed, to name a few.

Yet, there has also been a good deal of criticism on how identity has been conceptualized and operationalized for scholarly use. For example, many treatments of identity have not been theoretically transparent in terms of their ontology and epistemology; therefore, they are limited in their usefulness (Sfard & Prusak, 2005). Bendle (2002) also points to the unreconciled ontological differences among scholars and across various disciplines as a source of analytic weakness in the use of identity as an analytic lens. Additionally, Rampton (in press) argues that identity is not a particularly useful analytic concept when dealing with interactional data; in the micro "here and now," we are interacting with particular others, not generalized cases of others: "Identity, in other words, tends to feature as a second- or third-order abstraction, a bridge back to social science literatures and public debate, one among a number of potential resources for answering 'so what?'" (p. 1). Implications for the study of identity cannot be easily realized methodologically owing to the use of inappropriate or insufficient methods (Omoniyi & White, 2006). These criticisms not only reflect the multifaceted and complex nature of the construct of identity but create room for further development of identity as a conceptual component of research on education, the ontological and epistemological discussions framing its use, and the methodologies by which it is operationalized.

Ontological Debates About the Nature of Identity

What has been termed the discursive turn (Harré, 2001), the crisis of late modernity (Giddens, 1991), and the information age (Castells, 2004) generally refers to a paradigm shift in how the "reality" of human communication and understanding has come to be characterized in social theory. This shift reflects epochal social changes in culture and systems of communication related to globalization, technological advances, new capitalism, and various *post*'s (e.g., postindustrial, poststate, postmodern) that characterize the last century. In their introduction to a recent volume on discourse and contested identities, Iedema and Caldas-Coulthard (2008) characterize the various fragmentations that trouble earlier notions of identity through rapidly changing communities, commitments, politics, and hierarchies. Thus, the supposed grounding of one's identity is less about how and where you belong and more about how transitions across contexts in the here and now render identities as boundary objects that index salient kinds of identities through behavior over time. Though far from over, this paradigm shift brings to light two heuristics that can be characterized as being ontologically distinct in their theoretical assumptions about the nature of mind and society—essentialist views of identity and social constructionist views of identity.[1]

Essentialist views are often associated with the cognitive revolution of the 1950s and 1960s; with psychological definitions of identity (e.g., Erikson, 1968); and with structuralist/mentalist constructions of the nature and development of the self (i.e., that there exists a unified or coherent sense of self internal to an individual). Essentialist views assume that identity is relatively stable and grounded in shared, self-evidently meaningful experiences that are unproblematically accepted (Rouse, 1995). As a result, such essentializing trends obscure the heterogeneity of individuals in identity discourses (Lemke, 2008).

Criticisms of the essentialist/Eriksonian/psychological approach hail largely from those sympathetic to social constructionist views of identity, which generally characterize identity as a process embodied in social practice and not as a given or a product (deFina, Schiffrin, & Bamberg, 2006). Identity is a fluid, socially constituted achievement that is multiply constructed across micro-social (individual) and macro-social (cultural/institutional) timescales (Bhabha, 1990, 1994; Chuang, 2004;

Grossberg, 1996; Hall, 1989, 1990, 1996; Lemke, 2008; McCarthey & Moje, 2002; Nasir & Saxe, 2003; Rampton, in press). Social constructionist views are associated with the discursive revolution of the 1980s and 1990s; with the anthropological approaches to identity that grew out of George Herbert Mead's earlier work (e.g., 1934) in symbolic interactionism in the early 20th century; with Vygotsky's sociocultural work (e.g., 1978) on how meaning is achieved through symbolic, socially constituted resources; and with sociocultural views of selves that are reflexively situated in social and cultural contexts (Holland & Lachicotte, 2007; Holland et al., 1998). In fact, social constructionism can be defined in terms of what it is not (i.e., anti-essentialist; Fenton, 1999). Furthermore, as the aforementioned global reconfigurations continue to offer new ways for people at the intersections of fragmenting social structures and relationships to articulate their identities (as well as offer new ways for analysts to conceptualize them), how people position themselves will differ, depending on the interactions that they have (Davies & Harré, 1990) and from context to context (Hall, 2000).

Whereas describing the theoretical differences between these two views of identity as a dichotomy is convenient for the sake of discussion, these theoretical camps are by no means airtight or even agreed on in some respects. However, a general understanding of essentialist and social constructionist views of identity places them at opposite ends of an ontological continuum, with identity being (a) fixed, internal, and in direct correlation with measurable characteristics at the essentialist end and (b) fluid, social, and variably related to contestable and constructed categories and contexts at the social constructionist end. As with any ontological discussion, attendant ideologies influence how the object of study is specified, relative to what one is looking for, how, and to what analytic ends, and how such ideologies are or are not taken into account in analysis, which we now discuss further.

Ideological Considerations

The acknowledgment of ideological influences on how identity is construed and studied is often excluded from essentialist treatments of identity, where the stability of self is unproblematically assumed to exist and be studiable. Social constructionist views, however, provide a critical lens to understand identity. Writ large, such views position the nexus of identity construction in social interaction. A subset of these views, poststructuralist approaches to identity, further highlight the ideological components to identity discourses (both public and academic) concerning interfaces between and among power, social structure, agency, and the immediate and longer-scale practices and events therein that compose the negotiation of available identity categories (Pavlenko & Blackledge, 2004; Rampton, in press). Poststructuralist views position ideological connections within the larger sociopolitical discourse, unlike essentialist treatments, which form an implicit ideological link between categories or actions (e.g., racial label and language practices) and identity, without acknowledging the value-laden-ness of this connection (Bucholtz & Hall, 2004). When discussing issues of risk and opportunity, as is the charge of this volume, educational researchers who are concerned with the social negotiation of identities are increasingly considering issues of language ideology (e.g., Corson, 1993; Hornberger, 1988); the deconstruction of received categories, such as race, gender, nationality, social class, and sexual orientation (e.g., Cavanagh, 2008; Kumashiro, 2001; Moya & Hames-Garcia, 2000; Orellana & Bowman, 2003; Pavlenko & Blackledge, 2004); multiple and new literacies (e.g., Jewitt, 2008; Luke, 1999; Street, 2003); globalization (e.g., Burbules & Torres, 2000; Castells, 2004); and other agency- and power-related issues in the examination of identity.

The complexity of social processes in the study of identity has led to other subfields of social constructionist orientations that attempt to capture the fluidity of identity constructions. For example, hybridity theory enables an understanding of how integrations and interactions based on mutual or forced influence, convergence, and mixing between cultures, language, and peoples disrupt understandings of identities, boundaries, and worldviews (e.g., Bhabha, 1990, 1994; Gilroy, 1993; Hall, 1996). It provides a framework to understand the experiences and identity work of multilingual/multicultural persons who may cross multiple linguistic and cultural borders in their daily interactions. Hybridity is also associated with third spaces wherein the negotiation between identities can occur (Bhabha, 1994, 1996) and the "in-between-ness," or interconnectedness, that characterizes hybridity affords exploration of identities' fluidity and intentionality (Bhabha, 1996; Turner, 1990). With the ambivalence and contradictions that are inherent when the familiar and foreign clash, the third space offers a fertile ground for translation and negotiation of identities to happen. However, as Lemke (2008) points out, the notion of hybridity can reify categories as cultural ideals, even when individuals are positioned as crossing them, so long as the categories being crossed are presupposed. We live across categories consistently, Lemke contends, and the notion of identity as being multiple requires consideration of how identity is a construct that mediates embodied phenomena (e.g., relationships, affiliations, and lifetimes) and characterized kinds or categories (e.g., enduring structures and semiotic abstractions). This contention leads us to consider some of the epistemological issues surrounding the study of identity negotiation.

Epistemological Divides in the Treatment of Identity

We now turn to epistemological considerations that such ontological debates about the nature and reality of identity raise regarding the construction, development, and negotiation of identities across the institutional landscape of formal public education in the United States. There is a general implication that we draw from the somewhat dichotomous relationship between essentialist and social constructionist views of identity—namely, that how one defines the nature of identity affects the way that one chooses to study it and the techniques one uses to study it, with the definition encapsulating where it lies (in the self or in interaction), how it develops (cognitively or socially), and how is it mediated (psychic struggle or cultural power differentiation).

When identity is assumed to be a fixed, mental, individualist construct, the contexts of its examination will differ from when it is seen as a dynamic, social, interactional achievement. For example, one salient difference in the ways that identity is discussed across these two paradigms is captured in the verbs used to describe the formation of identity. According to essentialist studies, identity is ascribed in practice or discovered through research; according to social constructionist studies, identity is constructed, contested, rescripted, and generally interpreted through research and interaction.

This being said, ontological commitments are not always clearly stated as drivers of epistemological tenets. Put simply, beliefs about the nature of identity should dictate how it is studied; yet, the relationship between beliefs about reality (ontology) and the study of identity (epistemology) is sometimes underdiscussed or undertheorized, especially when normative approaches to identity research take precedence (McCarthey & Moje, 2002). Despite the recent surge of empirical studies that examine the fluid, dynamic, and multiple negotiations of identities, many of the received ways of going about examining or discussing identity are still enmeshed in an essentialist paradigm that obscures crucial elements of identity's social and discursive situatedness (Pavlenko & Blackledge, 2004). DeFina, Schiffrin, and Bamberg (2006) list four perspectives that characterize discursive approaches to identity. These perspectives speak to bridges between the ontological and epistemological debates discussed thus far and to possible methodological considerations (discussed in the next section):

social constructionist views of identity as a process embodied in social practice: examination of social action for repertoires and resources for identity construction and negotiation;

anti-essentialist rejection of self as a stable core: examination of social systems of activity and personal agency therein;

membership and categories: analysis of how identity is performed and embodied through interpretation and enactment of categories (and how those are constructed locally and more broadly); and

indexicality: analysis of discourse across levels of social life (e.g., micro, macro), because linguistic signs point to extralinguistic reality and social context.

The first two points have been discussed in terms of ontological issues. It is the latter two points—categories and micro- and macro-social processes—that we address in the next section.

Methodological Considerations in the Study of Identity

In this section, we summarize two primary methodological considerations that accompany the ongoing debates about the reality and potential examination of identities in educational contexts. First, we discuss the intended and unintended usage of categories. Then, we examine the methodological need for looking across both micro- and macro-social processes in the consideration of how identities develop and are shaped. This examination includes a discussion of agency and social structure.

Categories and Identity Work

Bucholtz and Hall (2004) claim that identity *is* categories and that the categories that are imposed on us are as important as the perceptions that we have of ourselves. Identity categories are useful in practice because they are convenient and somewhat interpretable, but they should not be unproblematically taken as defining or appropriate (Fenton, 1999). That is, identity categories become problematic when they are essentialized as absolute truths about persons and when they impose limitations on potential actions or conceptions. When labels such as *English learner, learning disabled, underachiever,* and *gifted* are consistently used across contexts and in institutional discourses, the terms become tools to shape students' identities. In this way, schools play a significant role in reproducing the social inequalities among different individuals and groups.

Furthermore, as Berard (2005) suggests, strict adherence to fixed categories and labels obscures the social contexts in which these categories become relevant. For instance, the fixed categories used in surveys to capture the race and ethnicity of informants can be limiting in that the assumptions of homogeneity across racial categories no longer reflect well the demographics of changing populations and changing notions of what defines populations (e.g., shifting meanings of macro-social categories and how they are theoretically linked to micro-social realities; Glick & White, 2003; S. J. Lee, 1996; Liu, Tai, & Fan, in press). Orellana and Bowman (2003) problematize the common uses of general descriptive categories in educational research (e.g., "working-class Mexican American"). They argue that the use of such categories without further descriptions assumes that these categories hold the same social meaning to the participants, researchers, and consumers of the research, thereby reinforcing stereotyped and static notions of identities for different persons.

Social constructionist accounts do not methodologically position identity in a one-to-one relationship with different behaviors or features, nor do they assume the relevance of preexisting analytic categories, such as race, class, and gender (Fenton, 1999). Instead, identity is seen as being constructed out of difference and politics (Bucholtz & Hall, 2004). Seeing identity as a social construct and not an inherent fact relies on how categories of difference come to matter across time and context and how they are lived through persons, be they in action, communication, appearance, achievement, location, or affiliation. Without salient difference (i.e., difference that is implicitly or explicitly treated as being relevant in interaction, category ascription, and policy) or markedness (Myers-Scotton, 1998), certain aspects of identity fade into transparency and cease to be useful in those contexts. For example, the salience of clown-ness in a room full of clowns is likely to be diminished when they are engaged in a "cut-throat" chess tournament; or, the salience of Whiteness or speaking English can be invisible when taken to be the "norm" for racial/linguistic identity. Thus, identity does not fall out from its defining categories; rather, it is a product of social action that creates the categories by which it is later defined (Holland & Lachicotte, 2007). According to this dialectic, identities are negotiated in face-to-face interaction, but their significance is understood in terms of what those actions mean, according to sociocultural/historical practices that are more encompassing than those interactions themselves (Brown, Reveles, & Kelly, 2005).

Lemke (2008) states that politics and discourses of identity (surrounding how it is experienced and analyzed) tend to reinforce the status quo through categories' ideological baggage: Identity types are overly simplified; identity performances are largely reduced to a small set of recognizable or conceivable options; and categories emphasize invariance. He suggests that we consider identity as an analytic tool separately from identity as phenomenological experience, with the former being an abstraction that stands outside time and comprises categories and with the latter being an empirical, narratable, dynamic experience comprising affective actions across different timescales. Lemke argues that current analytic categories fall short because of our current lack of analytic tools for integrating the former semiotic resources with gradations that account for the lived flow of the latter. This notion of identity as being enacted in the moment and understood across events and life spans speaks to the next issue that we discuss: micro- and macro-social processes.

Micro- and Macro-Considerations in Identity Work

The dialectic of micro- and macro-social processes is crucial to conceiving of identity as an artifact and a process and not just a reified object of study (Calabrese Barton et al., 2008; Erickson, 2004; Iedema & Caldas-Couthard, 2008; Lemke, 2008). Although identity is often seen as being shaped by some combination of social interactions and social structure, it in turn shapes both of these. Thus, "individuals do not carve out an identity from the inside out or from the outside in, as it were, rather their environments impose constraints whilst they act on those environments, continuously altering and recreating them" (Block, 2007, p. 866). When identity is viewed as a process enmeshed in interaction, it comprises not only individual interactions at the micro-social level but also larger cultural imaginaries (Holland & Lachicotte, 2007), discourses, activity systems, communities of practice (Gee, 2000; Wenger, 1998), and sociopolitical meanings that coalesce through semiotic systems of symbolic interaction (Bucholtz & Hall, 2004; Mead, 1934; Vygotsky, 1978). This relationship results in a need to examine environmental constraints and affordances (e.g., the type of funding that schools receive based on student demographics, the tracking system that students enter into at school, and the available categories for students) as well as local interactional and discursive constraints and affordances (e.g., teachers' linguistic practices, formulations of goals and expectations, and patterns of interactions and relationships between teachers and students across institutions).

Gee's aforementioned discussion (2000) of the ways that identities are recognized appeals to levels of micro- and macro-social genesis of "kinds" of persons—that is, kinds seen as being natural via social imaginaries, kinds positioned as being real through institutions, kinds discursively produced via interaction, and kinds constituted by affiliation that has recognized social meaning. All these kinds of identities draw meaning from a complex of interaction and distributed knowledge among community members, social discourse genres, and institutional force. These multiple kinds of identities reinforce the layeredness of a person's identity across different timescales, ranging from micro-interactional (i.e., positioning in local interactions) to meso-interactional (i.e., shifting social meanings through participation) to macro-sociological (i.e., sociohistorically situated meanings; Nasir & Saxe, 2003).

Rampton (in press) offers a possible analytic solution to understanding how identities are negotiated across social processes. He suggests approaching such negotiations as reflexive stylized moments where salient shifts in persons' linguistic behavior link individuals to institutions and communities. This occurs through their stability and resonance, which develops by means of habitual use in and across persons. In this way, Rampton sees identity as a bridge to circulating discourses about what types of people there are and how they are identified and valued—a bridge that can be crossed when situated encounters between particular others index more general issues that analysts can interpret as salient points of struggle or negotiation.

Since identities shape and are shaped by social constructions across multiple timescales and spaces, meanings and consequences of certain identity choices are locally situated as well as less locally constrained, owing to what are seen as feasible choices for personal action and affiliation. In the next section, we examine how minority status and risk are also socially constructed and imposed on linguistically and culturally diverse students in local interactions and cultural imaginations, which carry both intended and unintended social and academic consequences.

MINORITY STATUS AND RISK AS SOCIAL CONSTRUCTIONS

Ascriptions of being a minority, or linguistically/culturally "other," and the values associated with these categories are not truths about individuals but are socially and locally constructed assumptions or beliefs. Unfortunately, *at-risk* and *minority* labels often bring about connotations of ethnic and linguistic deficiencies. Everyday uses of labels suggest their false neutrality. In educational literature and public discourse, the referent *linguistically and culturally diverse learners* is often used interchangeably with *immigrants* and *English-language learners,* and it is commonly associated with being socioeconomically challenged, low-achieving, culturally deprived, and at risk (Callahan, 2005; Ladson-Billings, 1999). Ladson-Billings (1999) notes how "being at risk became synonymous with being a person of color" (p. 218), pointing out the subtle but damaging change in the ways that difference, disadvantage, and diversity are used to construct positions of inferiority. These associations are rooted in what Ruiz (1984) calls the "language as a problem" orientation. This perspective is reflected, for example, in models of bilingual education that view English-language learners as having a deficiency that must be overcome. The *English-language learner* label potentially limits the ways that those positioned under its guise are considered by teachers and larger educational institutions in terms of ability and need. The label often overshadows the complex and rich sociocultural histories of students' identities and instead only makes salient their learning practices and abilities in relation to speaking or not speaking English. Ruiz calls for a shift away from compensatory, deficit-driven discourses and perspectives to promote a discourse in which linguistic and cultural diversity is viewed as a resource.

Although a combination of inadequate resources, inappropriate assessments, low expectations, and unfair tracking systems seem to position minority students at risk of academic failure (e.g., Callahan, 2005; Gee, 2007; Goodlad, 1984; Kozol, 1991; Oakes, 1985), the reason for low achievement has been predominantly located within individual learners rather than within the social, discursive, institutional, systemic, and ideological constraints that foster these kinds of outcomes (Callahan, 2005; Carter & Goodwin, 1994; Corson, 2001; Fordham & Ogbu, 1986; Garcia, 1993; Glick & White, 2003; McCarthey & Moje 2002; Moll & Gonzalez, 1994; Ogbu & Simmons, 1998; Olmedo, 2003; Ramirez & Carpenter, 2005). To account for the disproportionate presence of certain individuals and certain groups of individuals in remedial classes and in the categories of premature school leavers and low achievers, scholars have put forth various explanations, ranging from biological claims that certain racial groups are genetically inferior to Whites (Fredrickson, 1971; Gould, 1981), to sociological accounts that discuss the cultural backgrounds of non-White, non-middle-class students as being deprived (Bloom, 1964; Hunt, 1961), thereby positioning cultural differences in relation to an implied normative status quo. More recently, scholars have noted the long history and damaging effects of positioning students with special needs as being deficient or deprived based on perceived differences in their physical and/or learning needs (Artiles, 2003; Artiles, Harris-Murri, & Rostenberg, 2006; Coutinho & Oswald, 2000). Through such comparisons, difference is viewed as a deficiency and a disadvantage (see Carter & Goodwin, 1994; Nieto, 2002 for further discussion).

Over the past three decades, changes in research, social theory, and in some cases, educational policy have led to conceptions of linguistic, cultural, class, and racial differences, not as deprivation, but simply as marked difference and at times even a resource (e.g., Gonzalez, Moll, & Amanti, 2005). This shift has promoted greater recognition and tolerance of difference, and it has given rise to multicultural and culturally responsive pedagogies (Ball, 2002; Carter & Goodwin, 1994; Ladson-Billings, 1992). Yet, despite the fact that understandings of linguistic and cultural differences have broadened in some ways, educational practices and policies are based on ideologies that drive instruction and curricula to help compensate for the "deficiencies," or cultural gaps, experienced by those children (Allington, 1991; Boyd, 1991, Corson, 2001; Nieto, 2002; Noguera, 2001). Even multicultural approaches can lead to deficit discourses when the well-intentioned goals of English-language learning position students as requiring access into mainstream culture. The available categories and their values create a binary between norm/mainstream and "other," rather than a more inclusive approach that promotes the maintenance of one's own heritage language and culture (J. S. Lee & Suarez, in press). Such normative ascriptive practices thus implicate difference as marked and a problem, as opposed to a resource in its own right.

Researchers have long been interested in identifying the significant factors that put certain people at risk. For example, Pallas, Natriello, and McDill (1989) identified five key indicators that predict academic risk: minority racial/ethnic group "identity," poverty, single-parent family, poorly educated mother, and non-English-language background. According to this view, all immigrant children from a non-White, non-English-speaking, non-middle-class background are predicted to be "at risk." Moreover, these risk factors are fueled by sociocultural biases and by histories of value judgments about different languages, cultures, and persons. The appeal to such value-laden factors becomes problematic when categories are accepted as facts about students and families, based on generalized and largely fictionalized "kinds," as opposed to particular individuals' lived actions. Despite the fact that there are many linguistic and cultural minority students who do academically succeed within such conditions, the salience of these "risk" factors often shapes responses to and expectations of the abilities of students who come from these backgrounds. For example, teachers who expect problems from students because they are from a particular cultural and linguistic minority background are likely to interpret students' actions differently and expect low performance (Callahan 2005; Oakes, 1985; Rosenthal & Jacobson, 1968). These penchants often lead to tracking practices that limit access to academic courses and to learning environments that foster academic development and socialization, thereby putting some students at risk for failure (Anyon, 1995; Callahan, 2005; Duran, 1987; Oakes, 1985).

Carter and Goodwin (1994) cite such risk as an imposition by schools, claiming that "much of the risk, however, emanates from the schools themselves and is not inherent in children themselves" (p. 317). Being at risk is therefore not locatable within individual people or the traits associated with them, but it is a socially constructed phenomenon (Cummins, 1986). Whether it is perceived differences in skin color, style of language use, or cultural beliefs and practices, being labeled a "minority" makes available certain kinds of identities for ascription in institutional settings that may position youth to accept lowered expectations. For example, students who are socially constructed as needing compensatory educational services, such as remedial reading or math and instruction in English as a second language, are often "pulled out" from regular classroom instruction. However, what was intended to help children could in reality impinge on their opportunities to learn because it stigmatizes them and makes assumed aspects of their identities and needs highly visible to peers in the classroom (in addition to pulling them away from what other children would be learning for instruction that is generally less rigorous). This practice may work to increase the gap between these students' and mainstream students' opportunities to learn (Callahan, 2005; Kirst & Jung, 1982). However, these characterizations by no means apply to all students, because many may have the tools and opportunity to resist such expectations and their effects.

In summary, minority and risk status are social realities only in that they are constructed through the interplay between face-to-face interactions and more widely circulating discourses. Risk factors are not immalleable; many cultural and linguistic minority students have resiliency (Trueba, 2001) and can maximize their potential if perceived differences can be capitalized on rather than emphasized as deficits and problems. Until we make problematic and so raise critical awareness of the ways in which cultural and linguistic minority students' identities are variably positioned and negotiated (i.e., the ways in which cultural and linguistic minority students resist the casting of their identities, negotiate them, or reposition them), these students will continue to perform and be positioned in ways that perpetuate achievement gaps.

REVIEW OF EMPIRICAL STUDIES ON IDENTITY AND ACADEMIC PERFORMANCE

The relationship between identity and academic performance has been considered a critical one in education (see Ball & Ellis, 2007; Nasir, 2002; Nasir & Saxe, 2003; Sadowski, 2003). Some studies have suggested that certain conditions often lead minority students to disengage with school (Fordham & Ogbu, 1986; Graham, Taylor, & Hudley, 1998; National Research Council, 2003; Olmedo, 2003; Valenzuela, 1999), whereas others have documented how instructional practices that create spaces for students to build strong identities in schools can result in enhanced learning and achievement for minority students (Bartlett, 2007; Mehan, Hubbard, & Villanueva, 1994; Palmer, 2008). Although there have been large-scale survey and assessment studies that have used cultural and structural factors, such as race, socioeconomic status, ethnicity, and immigration-generation level, as representative characteristics of students who are lagging behind or performing well (e.g., Bali & Alvarez, 2004; Brooks-Gunn & Duncan, 1997; Callahan, 2005; Liu et al., in press; Padilla & Gonzalez, 2001; Ramirez & Carpenter, 2005), these quantitative studies do not tell us how these local factors and conditions shape the academic experiences and identities of individual learners nor how those conditions can be improved. Rather, such studies are important in identifying larger patterns and directing our attention to broader issues in understanding student achievement. In this section, we focus instead on studies that have examined processes of how identities have been or may be negotiated to lead to different conceptions of cultural and academic "performance" and to different outcomes of such performances.

We synthesize the findings from some empirical studies that have examined different paths to identity construction and their documented consequences on learning experiences or outcomes. We focus on three different paths—assimilation, opposition, and straddling—given that they represent some of the more commonly documented ways that youth negotiate their identities.[2] We review how certain ascribed labels, and the identities they imply, can shape minority students' opportunities to learn and their achievement, as well as how circulating discourses and interactional processes can shape students' identity work and learning. We do not purport that this is a comprehensive review of the literature, but rather a summary of an important subset of studies that have demonstrated different kinds of relationships among cultural and linguistic minority students' learning practices, outcomes, and related conceptions of identity.

Assimilating Identities and Academic Performance

Educational institutions reproduce social hierarchies that advantage those who have access to the ways and norms of the dominant group and that marginalize those who do not (Corson, 2001; Cummins, 2000; Lemke, 2008). The pressures to conform to the dominant language and cultural patterns in educational settings have reinforced normative ideals of what identifications and dispositions are necessary in order to succeed within formal learning contexts. However, the decision to assimilate to these norms entails accepting the nuanced ideological values and characteristics associated with often implicit norms. In this way, the disenfranchised tend to adhere to the norms of the dominant groups by nature of the perceived opportunities for formulating identities (Lemke, 2008).

Cultural and linguistic minority students who choose to conform to the norms of the dominant group are likely to gain the social resources needed to succeed academically (Bartlett, 2007; Carter, 2005; Martinez-Roldan & Malave, 2004; Ogbu & Simmons, 1998). However, complete assimilation seems to come with a price (J. S. Lee & Suarez, in press). Studies show that assimilation can come at the expense of a strong sense of ethnic identity, ingroup membership with co-ethnic peers, and lost learning opportunities (Gandara, 1995; Ogbu & Simmons, 1998). Carter (2005) suggests that some students who have racial and ethnic heritages that are constructed as "minority" choose to assimilate to mainstream schooling practices and ways of being even though doing so risks possible rejection by co-ethnic peers. Students in Carter's study sought the affirmation and support of teachers to negotiate their academic lives in ways that aligned with the norms and expectations of the school, thereby leading to high academic achievement. Ogbu and Simmons (1998) point out, however, that minority students—particularly, those from nonvoluntary immigrant backgrounds—may see assimilation into dominant schooling norms as a form of "cop-out," and those that fully assimilate are sometimes seen as traitors by their co-ethnic peers.

Related to learning opportunities, Bartlett's study (2007) of a female immigrant student at a bilingual high school describes how the student adopted recognized features of a successful "school identity," which afforded her opportunities to learn by engaging more with other "successful" students. However, her assimilative "good student" enactments also restricted her opportunities because she opted not to ask important questions that could enhance learning opportunities, for fear that she would reveal her lack of knowledge of things that "good" students are expected to know. Unfortunately, to have a chance to succeed academically, the student needed to pass up crucial opportunities to learn, which could have increased her chances of being at risk.

However, the process of taking up a conformist identity (Davidson, 1996) or assimilationist identity does not depend solely on the agency of the individual student. Minority students may be faced with hegemonic forms of ascription (Bailey, 2000), which are imposed upon them and thus affect their learning experiences and outcomes. For example, some studies have shown that even when students assimilate to what they see as unmarked ways of being—that is, "mainstream," which we recognize as a relational and value-laden construct and not a naturalized one—negative stereotypes about their academic competence (based on preconceived notions of their ability) can lead to their disengagement from school (Davis, 2003; Major, Spencer, Schmader, Wolfe, & Crocker, 1997; Osborne, 1997; Steele, 1997). Therefore, the nuanced relationship between students' identities and academic performance is complicated by factors that are oftentimes beyond the control of individual students.

Oppositional Identities and Academic Performance

Although researchers have suggested that oppositional identities increase risk for academic failure (Fordham & Ogbu, 1986; Valenzuela, 1999), this claim is by no means necessarily the case. For example, Foley (1991) and Davidson (1996) both found that accommodation to "mainstream" identities is not the sole route to academic success, and they concluded that those who oppose accommodating to mainstream expectations find alternative ways to succeed academically. Carter (2005) also challenged the view that oppositional identities toward White and middle-class culture foster attitudes and values that inhibit academic achievement. That is, if students' cultural alignments lead them to challenge compliance with the dominant cultural rules that denote being a "good student," it does not necessarily follow that there are not other ways to be a "good student." Carter suggests that ethno-racial cultural identities (in this case, youth whom she identified as "Black" and "Latino") serve to provide students with a sense of belonging, distinction, and support for how to cope with inequality. She concludes that cultural minority youths' enacted oppositional identities are "practices of distinction" that serve as a challenge to the mainstream identity rather than as a reaction or a submission to oppressive dominant forces.

In addition, studies have shown the critical nature and value of peer support among minority students where they purposefully elect an oppositional identity to fit in with peers who have a shared ethnic heritage. Fordham and Ogbu (1986) describe the effects of fictive kinships, which refer to a sense of collective identity or brotherhood/sisterhood among members of the same ethnic group—in this case, as they pertain to African American students' behavior and schooling. They found that many African American students took up oppositional identities to escape the "burden of acting White," which was associated with characteristics such as high academic achievement and disloyalty to one's group. Similarly, Gandara (1995) found that college-bound Latino students used a denial strategy regarding their academic achievement because they believed that it was not "cool" to look as if they cared about academics among their friends. Moreover, Gilbert and Yerrick (2001), in an ethnographic study of rural lower-achieving underrepresented minority students in the South, found that students elected oppositional identities toward the mainstream culture to place more emphasis on their shared ethnic history with their peers. They made sense of their place in school by understanding that it was difficult for them to break away from preconceived assumptions about their abilities, which were deeply rooted in sociopolitical histories. Thus, it made more sense for the students to place greater emphasis on building a stronger ingroup network than to try to work against preconceived assumptions. The authors argue for finding alternate ways to redefine school success that can embrace a variety of linguistic and ethnic perspectives, as opposed to simply implementing a de-tracking practice, which cannot easily work when cultural artifacts and beliefs are still in place that reinforce inequitable structures.

Not only are oppositional identities relevant to minority students, but they can also be taken up by any student who resists certain ascriptions and expectations placed on her or him. However, because of our focus here on risk as it disproportionately affects those who are labeled cultural or linguistic minorities, we have directed our attention to the ethnic minority student population as an example to show how oppositional identities are not necessarily a result of students' lack of socialization to or understanding of the cultural norms and expectations. Rather, such identities are a purposeful expression of students' agency and will to express themselves in ways salient to them, given the categories and choices availed by the local and institutional contexts (or through categories of their own making). The problem therefore seems to lie in how minority students' expressions of their identities are interpreted against the norms of the mainstream (e.g., deficient rather than legitimate), thereby tying in with our earlier discussion about the ideological loading of many available identity categories. In other words, the focus needs to be not on working to change the identities of students but on understanding and expanding the ways that different types of persons, activities, and values, as well as ways of talking and interacting, are constructed and seen as being relevant, thus leading to the circulation of scholarly and educational discourses that are more accepting of different linguistic and cultural identities.

Straddling Identities and Academic Performance

The adoption of assimilating and oppositional lenses on identity negotiation frame students as needing to make an either–or choice between the norms of the school and the ethnic or dominant group. However, it is quite possible that students can straddle such divisive categories and negotiate the tensions that can arise from perceived differences in the home, peer, school, and wider society.

Studies have documented that minority students who learn to maintain their ethnic identity while actively engaging in school practices, thereby accommodating without assimilating, can then experience academic success (e.g., Gibson, 1988; C. Suárez-Orozco, M. Suárez-Orozco, & Todorova, 2007). In her ethnographic study of Sikh American high school students in Northern California, Gibson (1988) found that these linguistic and cultural minority students were highly successful in their academic endeavors. The students learned how to enact norms and expectations of the mainstream school culture, yet they upheld their linguistic and cultural heritage, drawing on the resources within their co-ethnic community as a form of support. Carter (2005) calls these kinds of individuals *cultural straddlers*, and Davidson (1996) *transculturals*, because they utilize dominant cultural capital when necessary but are able to leverage language use and other action to signify their group membership with peers who may share the same ethnic history. Straddlers thus negotiate their identities in ways that enable them to be socially successful with their co-ethnic peers as well as juggle cultural norms and practices to navigate their understanding of teachers' expectations and what counts as performing "well" in school. These cultural straddlers may seek the affirmation of teachers, but they include peers in their considerations. In this vein, Delpit (1995) has charged schools with the responsibility of teaching all children "codes of power" to make available the language and knowledge that marginalized youth need in order to decode the system.

Furthermore, Mehan et al. (1994) found that Latino and African American students who participated in a de-tracking program developed not only academically situated identities that were recognized according to mainstream expectations but also an ability to critique such aspects of identity while affirming their culturally situated identities. These students managed multiple, seemingly contradictory facets of identity, thereby highlighting different aspects of their identities at school and with friends after school. The authors documented that these students were able to see academic achievement as being within their reach and gain critical cultural affirmation of their identities. As the authors suggest, the students effectively utilized strategies that enabled them to cross racial, ethnic, class, gender, and linguistic boundaries, also known as *border crossing* (Rampton, 2005). One such border-crossing strategy that is taken up in research to illuminate the dynamics of race, class, and cultural/identity politics is the use of language crossing. For example, Rampton (2005) shows how the purposeful use of Panjabi by youth of Anglo and Afro-Caribbean descent, as well as the use of Jamaican Creole by Anglo and Punjabi youth in Britain, has different functions and meanings across contexts and social relationships wherein crossing occurs. For instance, Asians using Jamaican Creole can be interpreted as enacting the identity of a troublemaker in order to be accepted by the resistant peer group, whereas such crossing in front of adults may signal something different. Crossing is therefore a means to invoke and play upon stereotypes that might exist, as well as to promote solidarity within mixed-race peer groups. Thus, we are able to see and understand how linguistically and culturally diverse students, through language use, can develop the ability to negotiate identities that are strategically valuable to them in their moment-to-moment local contexts.

Ball (2002) asserts that many students from culturally diverse backgrounds are confronted daily with demands to choose between salient aspects of their cultural identities and those of the mainstream culture. They are often in a position to make forced choices between projecting a strong ethnic identity versus a strong academic identity (Nasir & Saxe, 2003), a choice that is constructed within institutional and classroom settings (Mehan et al., 1994). In a study with African American college students, Steele and Aronson (1995) found that learners accepted the idea of fluid identities and were so able to conceive of themselves in such a way that enabled them to blend different aspects of their cultural identities. This skill gave them the option of not having to choose between assimilation to the mainstream and their own cultural maintenance.

Although these studies highlight the benefits and feasibility of developing academic as well as linguistically and culturally framed identities, they do not discuss in depth how different facets of identities intermesh. When alluding to multiple identities, one could infer that these identities are distinctly separate from one another; yet in reality it is probably the case that the intersections of the multiple facets of identities work to influence one another so that blended or even blurred identities are the outcomes (Ochs, 1993). Just as bilinguals are not two monolinguals in one speaker (Cook, 1992) but rather a composite of two or more linguistic and cultural systems, the negotiation of linguistically or culturally marked aspects of identities is constituted in the social discursive construction of salient kinds of individuals along linguistic and/or cultural lines. This construction of marked types leads to making certain categories available for ascription, uptake, resistance, or general negotiation. Discursive approaches to identity lend themselves to examining the complex processes of identity negotiation.

Going Beyond Straddling

By examining the flow and interactional details of classroom discourse among participants, Gutiérrez, Rymes, and Larson (1995) illustrate how "who gets to learn" and "what is learned" are closely related to the kinds of social relationships constructed in classrooms. The authors show how identity is interwoven and intimately connected to historically constructed power relations that exist within and between spheres of cultural practice. They present the concept of third space within which counterhegemonic activity or contestation of dominant discourses can occur for students and teachers. It is in this third space where identities and learning can be negotiated in ways that affirm students' personal knowledge and skills as resources upon which to build.

Validating and utilizing points of difference fosters participation and classroom communities that are open and flexible to student behaviors, which is critical in negotiating identities. Gutiérrez, Baquedano-López, and Tejeda (2000) offer a theoretical perspective on understanding diversity as a method for organizing and structuring learning. The authors demonstrate that by using all forms of language available to all the members in the class in ways that do not privilege one language or register over another, students take ownership of their learning and are empowered to learn in ways they know (see also C. D. Lee, 2006). Similarly, Rymes and Anderson (2004) explore the relationship between the ways in which different cultures are talked about (e.g., about Costa Rica) and the different linguistic practices that are enacted in a second-grade classroom (e.g., Spanish, the teacher's "school" English, and African American students' vernacular style of English). The authors suggest that the interactional effects of (a) the explicit recognition of cultural difference and celebration of Spanish as a resource and (b) the implicit disenfranchisement of linguistic difference in terms of using African American English present quite different opportunities and positions of power among students with different cultural and linguistic backgrounds.

The balancing of power, whether between students, languages, or ideologies, is a critical component in the creation of classrooms that offer spaces for minority students to develop positive academic identities, as well as a methodological focus for analyzing how identities are ascribed in classrooms and research accounts. Palmer (2008) examines the discourse patterns in a second-grade dual-immersion classroom to understand how the teacher deliberately exposes students to alternative discourses that she hopes will lead them to construct positive identities as learners. Even when the teacher in this setting tried to engage students in alternative discourses about positive academic identities, it proved difficult to avoid the influence of dominant discourses and ideologies. Furthermore, as Duff (2002) found, despite the teacher's apparently well-intentioned practices to support students in making cultural connections based on their personal experiences, students did not necessarily take up the identity positions that were made available to them. Specifically, the Chinese students in her study (who were learners of English as a second language) placed much more value on the social, cultural, and linguistic solidarity that the large Chinese community in the school provided them than they did acceptance by their local peers. According to Duff, we need to understand better "the extent to which students actually want to display their identities and personal knowledge in class or to conform to dominant, normative local sociolinguistic behaviors" (p. 313).

Although teachers can be powerful agents of change, they are not the sole source of agency, power, or opportunity in the lives of students. However, just as students have agency, so do teachers, particularly in their control over what goes on in their classrooms and the degree to which they can foster change within their institutional constraints. As teachers themselves struggle daily with issues of negotiating different identities that represent their different spheres of influence, the fundamental question becomes, what can teachers do to thoughtfully engage all students to create more equitable learning environments that view different linguistic and cultural identities as resources?

One way to do so is by positioning students as knowledge seekers, which works to expand the linguistic and cultural repertoires of minority students regarding how they see themselves fitting into the classroom culture. Cornelius and Herrenkohl (2004) found that "giving students higher positions of power in both the social and disciplinary realms of the classroom promotes the kinds of conversations in classrooms that help students challenge and refine their previous conceptions around the subject matter" (p. 490). Their study of a sixth-grade science classroom illustrates how creating opportunities for participation that give authority and power to students is crucial for successful learning. It also points to how such practices open up possibilities for students to negotiate identities as successful learners and participants in these science classrooms. Whereas positioning of this sort clearly has connections to teachers' and students' actions in the classroom, it relates to more broadly constituted social norms for teacher and student positions and the ideologies framing them as social actors in educational institutions, which provide resources for identity negotiation that transcend the immediate here and now (Rampton, in press).

Creating classroom conditions that enable students to negotiate their linguistic and cultural identities in ways that lead to positive academic outcomes includes not only creating third spaces that support identity negotiations in empowering ways and recognizing and validating multiple models of language use (Duff, 2002; Gutiérrez et al., 1995, 2000; Hornberger, 1990; Iddings & Katz, 2007; Rymes & Anderson, 2004), but also understanding that the goals of tasks and instruction influence the relationship between identity negotiation and learning. For example, Hornberger (1990) argued for creating a repertoire of alternative learning contexts. She notes that one solution cannot work for all students, because they have differing needs and learning styles. For example, developing meaningful and relevant goals situated in students' local concerns helps to build student motivation (Hornberger, 1990). Furthermore, Nasir (2002) examined the relationship between goals, identities, and learning to understand how race, culture, and schooling intersect for minority students in the United States. She found that changes in identity were related to shifts in practice-linked goals and learning. As community members' goals and practices shift, they come to learn new skills and knowledge that facilitate new modes of participation and increased avenues to imagining and enacting agentive aspects of identities relative to their communities. Thus, Nasir was able to show that the creation of new identities involved the construction of new goals that required learning new ways of interacting, knowing, and being.

One of the foundations of both Nasir's approach (2002) and many other educational researchers who are aiming to increase opportunities to learn and understand ways to be in classrooms (e.g., Beach, 2003; Green & Lee, 2006; Hickey & Anderson, 2007; C. D. Lee, 2007; Moss, Pullin, Gee, Haertel, & Young, 2008) is a sociocultural stance on the nature of learning as participation in practices, where learning is understood as students' becoming kinds of learners and developing ways of knowing within certain cultural contexts (e.g., Cole, 1996; Delpit, 1995; Gadsden, 1993; Gee, 1996; Greeno & Middle School Mathematics Through Applications Project Group, 1998; Lave & Wenger, 1991; Nasir, 2002; Rogoff, 1998; Wenger, 1998). According to a sociocultural perspective, the learning process is necessarily social and contextual; it is composed of relations, and it is mediated by participation in value-laden community practices (e.g., histories of privilege dominate schooling practices in many cases). One does not learn in a vacuum, and this maxim includes not only classroom interactions and tools but also the discourses and ideologies shaping the institutions, available positions, and values attributed to recognizable kinds of persons and interactions. A sociocultural view of learning aligns well with a social constructionist view of identity in that both consider the multiple social contexts by which meaning and action are understood and enacted by students, teachers, and researchers. Each takes crucially intertwined aspects of social life as its object of study with a slightly different focus, foregrounding either the learning process or the study of identity but never to the exclusion of the other. In other words, from a sociocultural perspective on learning, it is through developing recognized ways of being that learning occurs, and from a social constructionist perspective on identity, learning requires construction, recognition, and negotiation of identities. In the next section, we elaborate how ontological, epistemological, and methodological components of studying identity, as enacted in classrooms and as construed by researchers, highlight how increased opportunities to learn for students who are traditionally marginalized can be realized in practice and understood in theory.

Working Toward a Complex of Analytic Identity Potentials

As discussed above, the U.S. educational system often constructs points of divergence from the mainstream as being problematic for learning and teaching, as opposed to being celebrated resources (Nieto, 2002). Our review of research on identity and academic achievement illustrates some of the complex and multifaceted approaches to identity development and how forced choices and unproblematized binaries between mainstream, ideologically prioritized academic identities and those of students who are seen as falling outside of these bounds are an issue in practice and in research. Furthermore, identities are not necessarily constructed in opposition to one another. Rather, students can develop multiple and sometimes contradictory facets of identities, which can become significant resources for learning (Carter, 2005; Cummins, 2000; Moya, 2002; Nieto, 2002).

Points of difference that are seen as factors leading to academic achievement gaps should not be considered threats to academic learning processes but rather as enriching sources of learning opportunities. Moya (2002) argues for mobilizing identities in classrooms, which requires that teachers view their students as complex individuals that move beyond simple categories of the kinds of learners whom they are. However, we need the theoretical and pedagogical language in order to to understand and make room for these identity potentials for students. This is not easy to accomplish, given that many groups have had a long history of marginalization and oppression and have been given limited choices in how they can identify or be identified. With the given structures and accumulated histories and imaginaries of kinds of people, interactions, achievements, and abilities, how do we understand students' and teachers' ways of negotiating identity? What kinds of identities can be negotiated by whom, for whom, and with what kind of outcome under what conditions?

As Ball (1998) states, "successful learning environments allow participants to see themselves as responsible contributors" (p. 243) to a social context in which they can question authoritative discourses, be positioned as experts, respond freely, and learn through experience. Environments that foster inclusion, respect, and empowerment are likely to provide students with the freedom and the skills to explore facets of their identities and form new identifications based on their needs and not on existing restrictive labels (Raible & Nieto, 2003). We argue that these themes of choice and flexibility are critical for youth.

However, an important question to ask is, why is choice not always available and how can this be changed? Although identities have been defined in recent decades as being fluid and multiple, further empirical research is needed on the processes that constitute their multiplicity, in terms of local–interactional and social–structural processes as well as the critical confluence of experiences across timescales (Erickson, 1987, 2004; Lemke, 2000, 2008). Sociocultural views of learning and social constructionist views of identity direct attention to the underpinning ontologies about how we as people learn to be and how we as researchers organize our object of study.

We echo this sentiment and suggest that a path to better understanding and fostering more equitable learning opportunities can begin with research that addresses the creation of openings rather than the reification of staid categories and their ascription. If learning can be understood as a process of being (e.g., learning physics is more about learning to be like a physicist than learning facts that constitute a canon of physics; Bruner, 1960) and one of becoming (J. S. Lee, Hill-Bonnet, & Gillispie, 2008; Packer & Goicoechea, 2000), then attending to those aspects of classroom life can shed light on how identity functions "on the ground" and so may supersede identity as an analytic category that we overlay onto interaction, perhaps sometimes too soon in the research process (Rampton, in press). Wenger (1998) speaks of learning as the braiding of practice and identity. Yet, how identity functions in various local situations, how it is construed and valued, and how researchers attribute its importance to theory development can be further unpacked (e.g., Is it more expansive than an array of factors influencing performance? Is it the result of interaction? Is it a manifestation of performance that is only fleeting in interaction?).

We humbly call for approaching the messy work of studying identity from the vantage point of sociocultural theory and for examining different angles of the confluence where people and their learning converge across multiple grain sizes and through various overlapping processes (e.g., participation at the micro-level, expectations and institutional structures at the meso-level, and ideologies and policies at the macro-level). Accepting the ideological challenges to changing discourses of schooling and who learners are or should be requires that we start from within our own variegated camps. Promoting research on identity and opportunity that fosters new ontological and epistemological discourses among researchers is one way to understand identity and learning differently, which as this review suggests, some scholars have already begun. Since identity was first discussed in the 1950s, many changes in research and in the U.S. population and its politics have taken place; far fewer changes have taken place in the educational system. To drive more changes in educational practice, we must be reflective in our ontological commitments and follow through to different ways of doing research (Green & Lee, 2006; Packer & Goicoechea, 2000).

REMAINING QUESTIONS AND FUTURE DIRECTIONS

With the burgeoning of conceptual literature and empirical studies over the past few decades on the relationships between identity and learning, there is much that we have begun to understand and even more that we will need to continue to investigate as the needs, relevant contexts, and social worlds of students continue to change. In this final section, we pose some further questions about the negotiation of linguistic and cultural identities as they relate to risk, access, equity, and schooling.

Identity was first a topic of study as a static label ascribed to others and self. As identity work came to be understood as a process of negotiation—foregrounding the concept that identities are local, situated, and ongoing processes—questions were raised regarding what counts as identity and which identities come into play in shifting contexts of communication. For example, consider the following portrait: A woman is of Mexican and Chinese ancestry; she was born in France, and she immigrated to the United States at a young age; she holds American citizenship and speaks only English; she received remedial math instruction in middle school but scored perfectly on the SAT math section; she is a professor; she is also a mother, a wife, a sister, and a daughter; finally, she practices Chinese cultural customs—what identities would or could this person have? The complexities and multifaceted nature of identities are reflected in this example, thereby showing that there cannot be just one identity for any individual. This leads us to explore questions of which identities matter, in which contexts, with what consequences, and as defined by whom. In particular, in schools where youth are necessarily exposed to the norms, values, and the hegemonic ideologies of society (Ghosh, Mickelson, & Anyon, 2007), we need thicker descriptions of how students are sorted as certain kinds of people and where they learn to make choices about their identities. Thus, we need more in-depth study of everyday lives in schools that illustrate the nuanced contexts and consequences of identity negotiation for learning in their complex environments, and we need the development of theoretical constructions of identity and methodological platforms to do so.

By conducting process-oriented longitudinal studies, we will be able to understand more clearly how identities shift across space, time, and people and how negotiations are accomplished (Calabrese Barton et al., 2008; Wortham, 2006). We still have a long way to go in imagining a broader range of identity potentials for linguistically and culturally diverse students in these current times of unprecedented new technologies, new cultural constructs, new media, and cultural fusions. However, a starting point is to continue working toward an analytic framework to understand and speak to an educational model that values the cultural and linguistic identities of all students in ways that treat difference not as a cause of risk but as a resource and as sites of opportunities for the negotiation of linguistic and cultural identity potentials.

NOTES

We would like to thank Nancy Hornberger and Ben Rampton for their insights as our developmental reviewers, Judith Green for her guidance on earlier drafts, Jesse Gillispie for her help scouring the literature, and the editors of this volume for their invaluable feedback and support throughout the writing of this manuscript. All remaining shortcomings are our own.

[1]We use the umbrella term *social constructionist views of identity* to broadly characterize a number of approaches to the study of mind, learning, identity, and society, all of which take into account some aspects of the sociocultural and historical contexts and processes that inform the theorization of identity. This includes social developmental approaches, cultural historical activity theory, and linguistic anthropological and ethnographic approaches, to name a few. For the purpose of this article, we focus on this heuristic, and the family of approaches under its purvey, in terms of its ontological distinctiveness from the equally broad umbrella of "essentialist" approaches, rather than attempt to attend to all the parameters and limitations in the study of identities.

[2]These three pathways of identity negotiation are similarly profiled in Prudence Carter's book *Keepin' It Real* (2005). Carter uses *cultural mainstreamers, noncompliant believers,* and *cultural straddlers* to discuss differences in educational beliefs and racial and ethnic ideologies experienced by low-income African American and Latino students.

REFERENCES

Allington, R. L. (1991). Effective literacy instruction for at-risk children. In M. S. Knapp & P. M. Shields (Eds.), *Better schooling for the children of poverty* (pp. 9–30). Berkeley, CA: McCutchan.

Anderson, K. T. (2008). Justifying race talk: Indexicality and the social construction of race and linguistic value. *Journal of Linguistic Anthropology, 18,* 108–129.

Anyon, J. (1995). Race, social class, and educational reform in an inner city school. *Teachers College Record, 97,* 69–94.

Artiles, A. (2003). Special education's changing identity: Paradoxes and dilemmas in views of culture and space. *Harvard Educational Review, 73,* 164–204.

Artiles, A., Harris-Murri, N., & Rostenberg, D. (2006). Inclusion as social justice: Critical notes on discourses, assumptions, and the road ahead. *Theory Into Practice, 45,* 260–268.

Bailey, B. (2000). Language and negotiation of ethnic/racial identity among Dominican Americans. *Language in Society, 29,* 555–582.

Bali, V. A., & Alvarez, R. M. (2004). The race gap in student achievement scores: Longitudinal evidence from a racially diverse school district. *Policy Studies Journal, 32,* 393–415.

Ball, A. F. (1998). Evaluating the writing of culturally and linguistically diverse students: The case of the African American vernacular English speaker. In C. R. Cooper & L. Odell (Eds.), *Evaluating writing: The role of teachers' knowledge about text, learning, and culture* (pp. 225–248). Urbana, IL: National Council of Teachers of English.

Ball, A. F. (2002). Three decades of research on classroom life: Illuminating the classroom communicative lives of America's at-risk students. *Review of Research in Education, 26,* 71–111.

Ball, A. F., & Ellis, P. A. (2007). Identity and the writing of culturally and linguistically diverse students. In C. Bazerman (Ed.), *Handbook of research on writing* (pp. 495–509). Mahwah, NJ: Lawrence Erlbaum.

Bartlett, L. (2007). Bilingual literacies, social identification, and educational trajectories. *Linguistics and Education, 18,* 215–231.

Beach, K. (2003). Learning in complex social situations meets information processing and mental representation: Some consequences for educational assessment. *Measurement: Interdisciplinary Research and Perspectives, 3,* 149–177.

Bendle, M. (2002). The crisis of identity in high modernity. *British Journal of Sociology, 53,* 1–18.

Berard, T. J. (2005). On multiple identities and educational contexts: Remarks on the study of inequalities and discrimination. *Journal of Language, Identity, and Education, 4,* 67–76.

Bhabha, H. (1990). The third space: An interview with Homi Bhabha. In J. Rutherford (Ed.), *Identity: Community, culture, difference* (pp. 207–221). London: Lawrence & Wishart.

Bhabha, H. (1994). *The location of culture.* London: Routledge.

Bhabha, H. (1996). Culture's in-between. In S. Hall & P. du Gay (Eds.), *Questions of cultural identity* (pp. 53–60). London: Sage.

Block, D. (2007). The rise of identity in SAL research, post Firth and Wagner. *Modern Language Journal, 91,* 863–876.

Bloom, B. S. (1964). *Stability and change in human characteristics.* New York: Wiley.

Boyd, W. L. (1991). What makes ghetto schools succeed or fail? *Teachers College Record, 92,* 331–362.

Brooks-Gunn, J., & Duncan, G. J. (1997). The effects of poverty on children. *Future of Children, 7,* 55–71.

Brown, B. (2004). Discursive identity: Assimilation into the culture of science and its implications for minority students. *Journal of Research in Science Teaching, 41,* 810–834.

Brown, B., Reveles, J., & Kelly, G. (2005). Scientific literacy and discursive identity: A theo-retical framework for understanding science learning. *Science Education, 8,* 779–802.

Bruner, J. (1960). *The process of education.* Cambridge, MA: Harvard University Press.

Bucholtz, M., & Hall, K. (2004). Language and identity. In A. Duranti (Ed.), *A companion to linguistic anthropology* (pp. 369–394). Malden, MA: Blackwell.

Bucholtz, M., & Hall, K. (2005). Identity and interaction: A sociocultural linguistic approach. *Discourse Studies, 7,* 585–614.

Burbules, N., & Torres, C. (Eds.). (2000). *Globalization and education: Critical perspectives.* London: Routledge.

Calabrese Barton, A., Carlone, H., Cook, M., Wong, J., Sandoval, W., & Brickhouse, N. (2008). Seeing and supporting identity development in science education. In P. Kirschner, F. Prins, V. Jonker, & G. Kanselaar (Eds.), *Proceedings of the Eighth International Conference of the Learning Sciences: International Perspectives in the Learning Sciences: Cre8ing a Learning World, Part 3* (pp. 214–220). Utrecht, Netherlands: International Society of the Learning Sciences.

Callahan, R. (2005). Tracking and high school English learners: Limiting opportunity to learn. *American Educational Research Journal, 42,* 305–328.

Carter, P. (2005). *Keepin' it real.* London: Oxford University Press.

Carter, R., & Goodwin, A. L. (1994). Racial identity and education. *Review of Research in Education, 20,* 291–336.

Castells, M. (2004). *The power of identity.* Malden, MA: Blackwell.

Cavanagh, S. L. (2008). Sex in the lesbian teacher's closet: The hybrid proliferation of queers in school. *Discourse: Studies in the Cultural Politics of Education, 29,* 387–399.

Chuang, R. (2004). Theoretical perspectives: Fluidity and complexity of cultural and ethnic identity. In M. Fong & R. Chuang (Eds.), *Communicating ethnic and cultural identity* (pp. 51–68). Lanham, MD: Rowman & Littlefield.

Cole, M. (1996). *Cultural psychology: A once and future discipline.* Cambridge, MA: Harvard University Press.

Cook, V. J. (1992). Evidence for multi-competence. *Language Learning, 42,* 557–591.

Cornelius, L. L., & Herrenkohl, L. R. (2004). Power in the classroom: How the classroom environment shapes students' relationships with each other and with concepts. *Cognition and Instruction, 22,* 467–498.

Corson, D. (1993). *Language, minority education, and gender: Linking social justice and power.* Clevedon, UK: Multilingual Matters.

Corson, D. (2001). *Language diversity and education.* Mahwah, NJ: Lawrence Erlbaum.

Coutinho, M., & Oswald, D. (2000). Disproportional representation in special education: A synthesis and recommendation. *Journal of Child Family Studies, 9,* 135–156.

Cummins, J. (1986). Empowering minority students: A framework for intervention. *Harvard Educational Review, 56,* 18–36.

Cummins, J. (2000). *Language, pedagogy and power.* Clevedon, UK: Multilingual Matters.

Davidson, A. (1996). *Making and molding identities in schools: Student narratives on race, gen-der, and academic engagement.* Albany: State University of New York Press.

Davies, B., & Harré, R. (1990). Positioning: The discursive production of selves. *Journal for the Theory of Social Behavior, 20,* 43–63.

Davis, J. E. (2003). Early schooling and academic achievement of African American males. *Urban Education, 38,* 515–537.

deFina, A., Schiffrin, B., & Bamberg, M. (2006). Introduction. In A. deFina, B. Schiffrin, & M. Bamberg (Eds.), *Discourse and identity* (pp. 1–26). New York: Cambridge University Press.

Delpit, L. (1995). *Other people's children: Cultural conflict in the classroom.* New York: Free Press.

Duff, P. (2002). The discursive co-construction of knowledge, identity and difference: An ethnography of communication in the high school mainstream. *Applied Linguistics, 23,* 289–322.

Duran, R. (1987). Factors affecting development of second language literacy. In S. Goldman & H. Trueba (Eds.), *Becoming literate in English as a second language* (pp. 114–129). Norwood, NJ: Ablex.

Erickson, F. (1987). Transformation and school success: The politics and culture of educational achievement. *Anthropology and Education Quarterly, 18,* 335–356.

Erickson, F. (2004). *Talk and social theory: Ecologies of speaking and listening in everyday life.* Malden, MA: Polity Press.

Erikson, E. (1968). *Identity: Youth and crisis.* New York: Norton.

Fenton, S. (1999). *Ethnicity: Racism, class and culture.* Lanham, MD: Rowman & Littlefield.

Foley, D. (1991). Revisiting anthropological explanations of school failure. *Anthropology and Education Quarterly, 22,* 60–86.

Fordham, S., & Ogbu, J. U. (1986). Black students' school success: Coping with the "burden of acting White." *Urban Review, 18,* 176–206.

Fredrickson, G. M. (1971). *The Black image in the White mind: The debate on Afro-American character and destiny.* New York: Harper & Row.

Gadsden, V. (1993). Literacy, education, and identity among African-Americans. *Urban Education, 27,* 352–369.

Gandara, P. (1995). *Over the ivy walls: The educational mobility of low-income Chicanos.* Albany: State University of New York Press.

Garcia, E. E. (1993). Language, culture, and education. *Review of Research in Education, 19,* 51–98.

Gee, J. P. (1996). *Social linguistics and literacies: Ideologies in discourse.* London: Routledge.

Gee, J. P. (2000). Identity as an analytic lens for research in education. *Review of Research in Education, 25,* 99–125.

Gee, J. P. (2007). Reflections on assessment from a sociocultural-situated perspective. *Yearbook of the National Society for the Study of Education: Evidence and Decision Making, 106*(1), 362–375.

Ghosh, R., Mickelson, R., & Anyon, J. (2007). Introduction to the special issue on new perspectives on youth development and social identity in the 21st century. *Teachers College Record, 109,* 275–284.

Gibson, M. (1988). *Accommodation without assimilation.* Ithaca, NY: Cornell University Press.

Giddens, A. (1991). *Modernity and self-identity: Self and society in the late modern age.* Malden, MA: Polity Press.

Gilbert, A., & Yerrick, R. (2001). Same school, separate worlds: A sociocultural study of identity, resistance, and negotiation in a rural, lower track science classroom. *Journal of Research in Science Teaching, 38,* 574–598.

Gilroy, P. (1993). *The Black Atlantic: Modernity and double consciousness.* Cambridge, MA: Harvard University Press.

Glick, J., & White, M. (2003). The academic trajectories of immigrant youths: Analysis within and across cohorts. *Demography, 40,* 759–783.

Gonzalez, N., Moll, L. C., & Amanti, C. (2005). *Funds of knowledge: Theorizing practices in households and classrooms.* Mahwah, NJ: Lawrence Erlbaum.

Goodlad, J. I. (1984). *A place called school.* New York: McGraw-Hill.

Gould, S. J. (1981). *The mismeasure of man.* New York: Norton.

Graham, S., Taylor, A., & Hudley, C. (1998). Exploring achievement values among ethnic minority early adolescents. *Journal of Educational Psychology, 90,* 606–620.

Green, J., & Lee, C. D. (2006). Making visible the invisible logic of inquiry: Uncovering multiple challenges. *Reading Research Quarterly, 41,* 140–150.

Greeno, J., & The Middle School Mathematics Through Applications Project Group. (1998). The situativity of knowing, learning, and research. *American Psychologist, 53,* 5–26.

Grossberg, L. (1996). Identity and cultural studies: Is that all there is? In S. Hall & P. du Gay (Eds.), *Questions of cultural identity* (pp. 87–92). London: Sage.

Gutiérrez, K., Baquedano-López, P., & Tejeda, C. (2000). Rethinking diversity: Hybridity and hybrid language practices in the third space. *Mind, Culture, and Activity, 6,* 286–303.

Gutiérrez, K., Rymes, B., & Larson, J. (1995). Script, counterscript, and underlife in the classroom: James Brown versus *Brown v. Board of Education. Harvard Educational Review, 65,* 445–471.

Hall, S. (1989). Cultural identity and cinematic representation. *Framework, 36,* 68–81.

Hall, S. (1990). Cultural identity and diaspora. In J. Rutherford (Ed.), *Identity: Community, culture, difference* (pp. 222–237). London: Lawrence and Wishart.

Hall, S. (1996). Introduction: Who needs identity? In S. Hall & P. du Gay (Eds.), *Questions of cultural identity* (pp. 1–17). London: Sage.

Hall, S. (2000). Foreword. In D. A. Yon (Ed.), *Elusive culture: Schooling, race, and identity in global times* (pp. ix–xii). Albany: State University of New York Press.

Harré, R. (2001). The discursive turn in social psychology. In D. Schiffrin, D. Tannen, & H. E. Hamilton (Eds.), *Handbook of discourse analysis* (pp. 688–706). Malden, MA: Blackwell.

Hickey, D. T., & Anderson, K. T. (2007). Situative approaches to student assessment: Contextualizing evidence to support practice. *Yearbook of the National Society for the Study of Education: Evidence and Decision Making, 106*(1), 264–287.

Holland, D., & Lachicotte, W. (2007). Vygotsky, Mead and the new sociocultural studies of identity. In H. Daniels, M. Cole, & J. Wertsch (Eds.), *The Cambridge companion to Vygotsky* (pp. 101–135). New York: Cambridge University Press.

Holland, D., Lachicotte, W., Skinner, D., & Cain, C. (1998). *Identity and agency in cultural worlds.* Cambridge, MA: Harvard University Press.

Holland, D., & Lave, J. (Eds.). (2001). *History in person: Enduring struggles, contentious practice, intimate identities.* Santa Fe, NM: School of American Research.

Hornberger, N. H. (1988). Language ideology in Quechua communities of Puno, Peru. *Anthropological Linguistics, 30,* 214–235.

Hornberger, N. H. (1990). Creating successful learning environments for bilingual literacy. *Teachers College Record, 92,* 212–229.

Hunt, J. M. (1961). *Intelligence and experience.* New York: Ronald Press.

Iddings, A., & Katz, L. (2007). Integrating home and school identities of recent-immigrant Hispanic English language learners through classroom practices. *Journal of Language, Identity, and Education, 6,* 299–314.

Iedema, R., & Caldas-Couthard, C. R. (2008). Introduction. In C. R. Caldas-Couthard & R. Iedema (Eds.), *Identity trouble: Critical discourse and contested identities* (pp. 1–14). London: Palgrave McMillan.

Jewitt, C. (2008). Multimodality and literacy in school classrooms. *Review of Research in Education, 32,* 241–267.

Kirst, M., & Jung, R. (1982). The utility of a longitudinal approach in assessing implementation: A 13 year review of Title 1, ESEA. In W. Willing (Ed.), *Studying implementation: Methodological and administrative issues* (pp. 119–148). Berkeley, CA: Chatham House.

Kozol, J. (1991). *Savage inequalities: Children in American schools.* New York: Crown.

Kumashiro, K. (Ed.). (2001). *Troubling intersections of race and sexuality: Queer students of color and anti-oppressive education.* Lanham, MD: Rowman & Littlefield.

Ladson-Billings, G. (1992). Culturally relevant teaching: The key to making multicultural education work. In C. A. Grant (Ed.), *Research and multicultural education* (pp. 106–121). London: Falmer.

Ladson-Billings, G. (1999). Preparing teachers for diverse student populations: A critical race theory perspective. *Review of Research in Education, 24,* 211–248.

Lave, J., & Wenger, E. (1991). *Situated learning: Legitimate peripheral participation.* New York: Cambridge University Press.

Lee, C. D. (2006). Every good-bye ain't gone: Analyzing the cultural underpinnings of class-room talk. *International Journal of Qualitative Studies in Education, 19*, 305–327.

Lee, C. D. (2007). *Culture, literacy, and learning: Taking bloom in the midst of the whirlwind.* New York: Teachers College Press.

Lee, J. S., Hill-Bonnet, L., & Gillispie, J. (2008). Learning in two languages: Interactional spaces for becoming bilingual speakers. *International Journal of Bilingual Education and Bilingualism, 11*, 75–94.

Lee, J. S., & Suarez, D. (in press). A synthesis of the roles of heritage languages in the lives of immigrant children. In T. Wiley, J. S. Lee, & R. Rumberger (Eds.), *The education of language minority students in the United States.* Clevedon, UK: Multilingual Matters.

Lee, S. J. (1996). *Unraveling the "model minority" stereotype: Listening to Asian American youth.* New York: Teachers College Press.

Lemke, J. (2000). Across the scales of time: Artifacts, activities, and meanings in ecosocial systems. *Mind, Culture, and Activity, 7*, 273–290.

Lemke, J. (2008). Identity, development and desire: Critical questions. In C. R. Caldas-Couthard & R. Iedema (Eds.), *Identity trouble: Critical discourse and contested identities* (pp. 17–42). London: Palgrave McMillan.

Le Page, R., & Tabouret-Keller, A. (1985). *Acts of identity: Creole-based approaches to language and ethnicity.* New York: Cambridge University Press.

Liu, C., Tai, R., & Fan, X. (in press). Immigration, race, and higher education outcome. In T. Wiley, J. S. Lee, & R. Rumberger (Eds.), *The education of language minority students in the United States.* Clevedon, UK: Multilingual Matters.

Luke, C. (1999). Media and cultural studies in Australia. *Journal of Adolescent and Adult Literacy, 42*, 622–626.

Major, B., Spencer, S., Schmader, T., Wolfe, C., & Crocker, J. (1997). Coping with negative stereotypes about intellectual performance: The role of psychological disengagement. *Personality and Social Psychology Bulletin, 24*, 34–50.

Martinez-Roldan, C. M., & Malave, G. (2004). Language ideologies: Mediating literacy and identity in bilingual contexts. *Journal of Early Childhood Literacy, 4*, 155–180.

McCarthey, S. J., & Moje, E. B. (2002). Identity matters. *Reading Research Quarterly, 37*, 228–238.

McDermott, R. (1993). The acquisition of a child by a learning disability. In J. Lave & S. Chaiklin (Eds.), *Understanding practice: Perspectives on activity and context* (pp. 269–305). New York: Cambridge University Press.

Mead, G. (1934). *Mind, self, and society.* Chicago: University of Chicago Press.

Mehan, H., Hubbard, L., & Villanueva, I. (1994). Forming academic identities: Accommodation without assimilation among involuntary minorities. *Anthropology and Education Quarterly, 25*, 91–117.

Moll, L., & Gonzalez, N. (1994). Lessons from research with language minority children. *Journal of Reading Behavior, 26*, 439–454.

Moss, P., Pullin, D. C., Gee, J. P., Haertel, E. H., & Young, L. J. (Eds.). (2008). *Assessment, equity, and opportunity to learn.* New York: Cambridge University Press.

Moya, P. M. L. (2002). *Learning from experience: Minority identities, multicultural struggles.* Berkeley: University of California Press.

Moya, P. M. L., & Hames-Garcia, M. (Eds.). (2000). *Reclaiming identity: Realist theory and the predicament of postmodernism.* Berkeley: University of California Press.

Myers-Scotton, C. (Ed.). (1998). *Codes and consequences: Choosing linguistic varieties.* London: Oxford University Press.

Nasir, N. S. (2002). Identity, goals, and learning: Mathematics in cultural practice. *Mathematical Thinking and Learning, 4*, 213–247.

Nasir, N. S., & Saxe, G. (2003). Ethnic and academic identities: A cultural practice perspective on emerging tensions and their management in the lives of minority students. *Educational Researcher, 32*(5), 14–18.

National Research Council. (2003). *Engaging schools: Fostering high school students' motivation to learn.* Washington, DC: National Academies Press.

Nieto, S. (2002). *Language, culture and teaching.* Mahwah, NJ: Lawrence Erlbaum.

Noguera, P. (2001). Racial politics and the elusive quest for excellence and equity in education. *Education and Urban Society, 34,* 18–41.

Noguera, P. (2003). *City schools and the American dream: Reclaiming the promise of public education.* New York: Teachers College Press.

Norton, B. (1997). Language, identity, and the ownership of English. *TESOL Quarterly, 31,* 409–429.

Norton, B. (2000). *Identity and language learning: Gender, ethnicity, and educational change.* Harlow, UK: Longman/Pearson Education.

Oakes, J. (1985). *Keeping track: How schools structure inequality.* New Haven, CT: Yale University Press.

Ochs, E. (1993). Constructing social identity: A language socialization perspective. *Research on Language and Social Interaction, 26,* 287–306.

Ogbu, J. U., & Simmons, H. D. (1998). Voluntary and involuntary minorities: A cultural ecological theory of school performance with some implications for education. *Anthropology and Education Quarterly, 29,* 155–188.

Olmedo, I. M. (2003). Accommodation and resistance: Latinas' struggle for their children's education. *Anthropology and Education Quarterly, 34,* 373–395.

Omoniyi, T., & White, G. (2006). Introduction. In T. Omoniyi & G. White (Eds.), *The sociolinguistics of identity* (pp. 1–10). London: Continuum.

Orellana, M., & Bowman, P. (2003). Cultural diversity research on learning and development: Conceptual, methodological, and strategic considerations. *Educational Researcher, 32*(5), 26–32.

Osborne, J. (1997). Race and academic disidentification. *Journal of Educational Psychology, 89,* 728–735.

Packer, M. J., & Goicoechea, J. (2000). Sociocultural and constructivist theories of learning: Ontology, not just epistemology. *Educational Psychologist, 35,* 227–241.

Padilla, A., & Gonzalez, R. (2001). Academic performance of immigrant and U.S. born Mexican heritage students. *American Educational Research Journal, 38,* 727–742.

Pallas, A., Natriello, G., & McDill, E. (1989). The changing nature of the disadvantaged population: Current dimensions and future trends. *Educational Researcher, 18*(5), 16–22.

Palmer, D. (2008). Building and destroying students' academic identities: The power of discourse in a two-way immersion classroom. *International Journal of Qualitative Studies in Education, 1,* 1–24.

Pavlenko, A., & Blackledge, A. (2004). Introduction: New theoretical approaches to the study of negotiation of identities in multicultural contexts. In A. Pavlenko & A. Blackedge (Eds.), *Negotiation of identities in multilingual contexts* (pp. 1–33). Clevedon, UK: Multilingual Matters.

Raible, J., & Nieto, S. (2003). Beyond categories: The complex identities of adolescents. In M. Sadowski. (Ed.), *Adolescents at school: Perspectives on youth, identity and education* (pp. 145–162). Cambridge, MA: Harvard University Press

Ramirez, A., & Carpenter, D. (2005). Challenging assumptions about the achievement gap. *Phi Delta Kappan, 86,* 599–603.

Rampton, B. (2005). *Crossing: Language and ethnicity among adolescents* (2nd ed.). Manchester, UK: St. Jerome Press.

Rampton, B. (in press). Linguistic ethnography, interactional sociolinguistics and the study of identities. In C. Coffin, T. Lillis, & K. O'Halloran (Eds.), *Investigating language in action: Tools for analysis.* Milton Keynes, UK: Open University.

Rogoff, B. (1998). Cognition as a collaborative process. In D. Kuhn & R. S. Siegler (Eds.), *Handbook of child psychology: Vol. 2. Cognition, perception, and language* (pp. 679–744). New York: Wiley.

Rosenthal, R., & Jacobson, L. (1968). *Pygmalion in the classroom*. New York: Holt, Rinehart & Winston.

Rouse, R. (1995). Questions of identity: Personhood and collectivity in transnational migration to the United States. *Critique of Anthropology, 15,* 351–380.

Ruiz, R. (1984). Orientation in language planning. *NABE Journal, 8*(2), 15–32.

Rymes, B., & Anderson, K. T. (2004). Second language acquisition for all: Understanding the interactional dynamics of a classroom in which Spanish and AAE are spoken. *Research in the Teaching of English, 39,* 107–135.

Sadowski, M. (2003). *Adolescents at school: Perspectives on youth, identity, and education*. Cambridge, MA: Harvard University Press.

Sfard, A., & Prusak, A. (2005). Telling identities: In search of an analytic tool for investigating learning as a culturally shaped activity. *Educational Researcher, 34*(4), 14–22.

Steele, C. M. (1997). A threat in the air: How stereotypes shape intellectual identity and performance. *American Psychologist, 52,* 613–629.

Steele, C. M., & Aronson, J. (1995). Stereotype threat and the intellectual test performance of African Americans. *Journal of Personality and Social Psychology, 69,* 797–811.

Street, B. (2003). What's "new" in New Literacy studies? Critical approaches to literacy in theory and practice. *Current Issues in Comparative Education, 5,* 77–91.

Suárez-Orozco, C., Suárez-Orozco, M., & Todorova, I. (2007). *Learning a new land: Immigrant students in American society*. Cambridge, MA: Harvard University Press.

Trueba, E. T. (2001). Language and identity among Mexicans in the United States: The secret of resiliency and successful adaptation. *Studies in the Linguistic Sciences, 31,* 61–76.

Turner, V. (1990). Liminality and community. In J. C. Alexander & S. Seidman (Eds.), *Culture and society: Contemporary debates* (pp. 147–154). New York: Cambridge University Press.

Valenzuela, A. (1999). *Subtractive schooling: U.S.-Mexican youth and the politics of caring*. Albany: State University of New York Press.

Vygotsky, L. S. (1978). *Mind in society*. Cambridge, MA: Harvard University Press.

Wenger, E. (1998). *Communities of practice*. New York: Cambridge University Press.

Wortham, S. (2006). *Learning identity: The joint emergence of social identification and academic learning*. New York: Cambridge University Press.

Chapter 8

Re-mediating Literacy: Culture, Difference, and Learning for Students From Nondominant Communities

Kris D. Gutiérrez
P. Zitlali Morales
Danny C. Martinez
University of California, Los Angeles

In this chapter, we examine notions of educational risk in the context of literacy theories and research. Deficit notions about the cognitive potential of individuals from nondominant[1] communities have persisted in social science inquiry, particularly where literacy is concerned. The intellectual trails of current conflicting ideas about literacy can be traced in part to theories about the role of literacy in society. For example, the great divide theories of literacy, sustained by a view of culture as social evolution and progress (Cole, 2005), attributed significant differences to the cognitive and cultural development of literate and nonliterate people and their communities (Goody, 1977, 1986, 1987; Goody & Watt, 1963; Havelock, 1963; Ong, 1982).[2] This literacy thesis held that there were "categorical differences in cognition and language as consequences of literacy" (Reder & Davila, 2005, p. 171)—differences marked by stark dualities used to characterize literate and nonliterate communities: writing versus orality, modern versus traditional, and educated versus uneducated, for example (Collins, 1995, p. 75). As Reder and Davila (2005) have noted, "literacy was presumed to have broad and ubiquitous consequences in such areas as: abstract versus context-dependent uses and genre of language; logical, critical, and scientific versus irrational modes of thought; analytical history versus myth; and so forth" (p. 171). These theories of literacy were challenged for their wide-ranging dichotomies that perpetuated the hierarchical differences between "types of societies, modes of thought, and uses of language" (p. 171) and reductive notions of culture and thought (Cole & Scribner, 1974, 1977).

Review of Research in Education
March 2009, Vol. 33, pp. 212-245
DOI: 10.3102/0091732X08328267
© 2009 AERA. http://rre.aera.net

By the 1980s, the notion of the divide was challenged, and new work represented the link between literacy and orality as a continuum (see Coulmans & Ehlich, 1983). As Brian Street (1993) observed, the shift was more theoretical; that is, researchers held to views of literacy, as distinguished from orality and its consequences. Here, the metaphor of a divide or a continuum suggests a deficit in people whose literacy practices differ from those of dominant groups and are considered to be normative; such metaphors perpetuate what Street calls *autonomous models of literacy*, organized around the assumption that literacy will have effects on other social and cognitive practices (p. 77). Of relevance to present views of difference and diversity, these dichotomies have helped to frame the way that we view and study the literacies of nondominant communities, their members, and their practices.

In contrast to the ubiquitous autonomous model, models such as the ideological model advanced by new literacy studies (Street, 1984) reflect a culturally sensitive account of literacy that rejects static and homogeneous views of the literacy practices of cultural communities. In contrast to views of literacy as a "technical and neutral [and autonomous] skill" (Street, 2003, p. 2), an ideological model posits that literacy is always embedded in social practices, where the consequences of learning a literacy are dependent on its context of development. Viewing literacy as a social practice exposes the long-standing belief that introducing literacy to the poor, "culturally deprived," and "illiterate" communities (p. 1) will enhance their cognitive skills and so improve the economic conditions that created the illiteracy in the first place. In this chapter, we examine the flaws in dominant stereotypes regarding literacy; the views linked to autonomous conceptions of literacy; and the deficit discourses, theories, and methods of inquiry that have accompanied such models. We conclude by revisiting arguments against narrow perspectives and by urging critical arguments around re-mediating literacy.

A FUNCTIONAL SYSTEMS APPROACH TO THE CONSEQUENCES OF LITERACY

The literacy thesis and notions about the broad consequences of the effects of literacy are aligned with general notions of the expansive consequences of schooling, challenged decades ago by Sylvia Scribner and Michael Cole (1973). Through cross-cultural research, Scribner and Cole rejected extant methods of inquiry that could render only deficit views of the communities under scrutiny. Scribner and Cole maintained that the methods and problems of school could not be attributed to the problems and technologies of everyday life or the home; rather, the focus should be on rethinking the social organization of education and its effects: "Searching for specific 'incapacities' and 'deficiencies' are socially mischievous detours" (p. 558). There are differences in the way that the capacities of individuals and their communities are brought to bear in various problem-solving situations; what is needed, then, is a functional analysis of the phenomenon under study at several levels of social organization (p. 558). Drawing on cross-cultural research that documents how different educational experiences give rise to different functional learning systems (Bruner, 1964, 1966;

Greenfield & Bruner, 1966, 1969; Luria, 1971), Scribner and Cole, used the concept of the "functional learning system . . . to identify the varying ways basic capacities are integrated and brought into play for the purposes at hand" (p. 553). In literacy, this research highlighted the importance of studying literacy in the context of its use.

In examining the consequences of literacy and intellectual skills, Scribner and Cole (1973, 1981) were interested in whether differences in the social organization of education promote differences in the organization of learning and thinking skills in the individual (p. 553). To distinguish dominant conceptions of literacy from others, these researchers employed the metaphors of "literacy as development" and "literacy as practice" (p. 449) to examine the nature of evidence considered crucial for developing hypotheses about literacy and in the procedures for relating evidence to theory. The object of this work was to advance an approach to literacy that "moves beyond generalities to a consideration of the organization and use of literacy in different social contexts" (p. 450).

This cross-cultural work was instrumental in challenging notions about the affordances of literacy skills across settings and about the extant methods of studying literacy in nondominant communities. Scribner and Cole (1978) combined experimental psychological methods with ethnography to develop robust explanations regarding the practices and uses of literacy by the Vai people in Liberia focusing on what the researchers referred to as *literacy practices*—a unit of analysis to capture the sociocultural basis of literacy across the various activity systems of Vai life. A focus on practice was central to capturing the socially mediated nature of literacy in situ and the role of sociocultural history in the development of literacies. Scribner and Cole's functional analysis of Vai practices revealed that "schooling and the acquisition of literacy are separate activities" and led the researchers to reconsider the nature of literacy and its intellectual effects (p. 448). They argued that their functional analysis emerging from the Vai research could be useful for educational research in the United States. An emerging key principle to be employed suggests that different literacy practices should be analyzed independently, given that particular skills are promoted by particular literacy practices. Hence, it is essential to learn, as much as possible, how the individual and the community practice literacy. A second, related principle suggests that writing and reading activities in learning environments should be tailored to desired outcomes (Scribner & Cole, 1978).

Conceiving of literacy as a social practice has gained significant currency; this view has been extended in research across literacy, education, and anthropological literatures, with qualitative and discourse analytic methods at the methodological forefront. For example, cross-cultural literacy studies organized around a cultural–historical perspective provided alternative conceptions of literacy and methods of study that called into question the deficit paradigms used to define the language and literacy practices of cultural communities (Greenfield, 1972; Heath, 1983; Ochs, 1988; Schieffelin & Ochs, 1986). In educational contexts, the linguistic turn in social science research brought about a realignment in educational research; that is, it introduced new criteria and models for classroom research that allowed for more "contextual explanations of literacy as a social practice" (Luke, 1992, p. 107). Despite this shift, researchers from this tradition have remained largely acritical and have ignored how local and contextual issues relate to larger social issues—"the complex fabric of texts and discourses through which social representation and reproduction is effected" (Luke, 1992, p. 108). This omission leaves open the possibility of essentializing the literacy practices of individuals and communities.

In response to autonomous and acritical models of literacy that dominated the field up to the 1980s, new literacy studies research (Gee, 1991; Street, 1984, 2003) has focused on producing more complex understandings of literacy, particularly in terms of power relations and the social nature of literacy activity, through ethnographies of literacy that document the situated literacy practices that constitute everyday life in particular ecologies (Barton, 2001; Barton & Hamilton, 1998; Barton, Hamilton, & Ivanic 2000; Street, 1984, 1993).

This social view of literacy requires detailed, in-depth accounts of the actual practices of people in different cultural settings, to understand meanings of literacies across cultures and context (Street, 1993, p. 1). Situating people's literacy practices in local and broader historical contexts provides complexity to and understanding of how repertoires of literacy practice come into being and so necessarily challenge approaches to studying literacy as an "autonomous" skill. For Street (1993), autonomous models of literacy "assume the technology of literacy itself had 'impact.'" Instead, "it is the social construction of such technologies and their instantiation in specific social context that creates such 'impact'" (p. 1). By linking local literacy practices with distal influences and practices, new literacy studies address the problem of viewing global and dominant literacies as being static, unchanging, and immune to the influences of local practices or the processes of hybridization resulting from local–global contact. For example, Kulick and Stroud's (1993) study of the appropriation of new literacy practices brought by missionaries to New Guinea found that people take hold of the new practices and so adapt them to local situations. According to Street (2003), these "local–global encounters around literacy, then, are always a new hybrid rather than a single essentialized version of the other" (p. 80): Furthermore,

it is these hybrid literacy practices that [new literacy studies] focuses upon rather than either romanticizing the local or conceding the dominant privileging of the supposed "global." In terms of practical applications, it is the recognition of this hybridity that lies at the heart of an [new literacy studies] approach to literacy acquisition regarding, for instance, the relationship between local literacy practices and those of the school. (p. 80)

The lens of hybridity has been central in capturing the consequences of intercultural exchange, including border crossing and boundary crossing experienced by students from nondominant communities. Increased transnational migration, new diasporic communities, and the proliferation of media technologies have resulted in a variety of intercultural activities in which a range of linguistic practices become available to members of nondominant communities (Gutiérrez, 2008b). The resulting "linguistic bricolage" (Pavlenko & Blackledge, 2004, p. 32) reflects the ways that the local and the global are always implicated in the everyday linguistic practices of nondominant students, thus challenging narrow and essentialized notions of students' linguistic repertoires. Documenting the hybrid language practices[3] that students employ in school settings also calls into question dichotomous views of home and school, everyday and school-based literacies, and formal and informal practices that are not very useful in understanding students' literacy repertoires or the role that language plays in learning processes (Gutiérrez, 2008a; Gutiérrez, 2008b; Gutiérrez, Baquedano-Lopez, & Tejeda, 1999; Gutiérrez & Lee, in press; Gutiérrez, Rymes, & Larson, 1995; Lee, 2007, 2008).

It is against this backdrop of cultural–historical views of literacy (Cole, 1996; Engeström, 1987; Rogoff, 2003) that we examine how conceptions of literacy, risk, diversity, and difference have helped shape approaches to addressing differential performance in literacy learning for students from nondominant communities. We also note how approaches to mediating students' literacy skills are imbued with discourses of difference and deficit views that undergird interventions for students "at risk." Such approaches are organized around varying views of how to remedy students' literacy skills, including "fixing" individual students and their home literacy practices to help ensure their success in school.

We explore how these deficit discourses and approaches to remediation have played an important role in education and, specifically, how inexperienced readers and writers and the instruction they receive have been defined. We then describe approaches that are oriented toward more expansive views of literacy learning, particularly to members of nondominant communities. Finally, we move to a discussion of how difference and risk have been conceived in educational research to show how the history of their use is implicated in literacy studies.

THE DISCOURSES OF DIFFERENCE AND DIVERSITY

Luis Moll (2001) has written that the most common educational response to diversity has been to eliminate it and to practice, what Joel Spring (1997) terms, *deculturalization*. Or, as Michael Cole (1998) has put it, there are two ways to deal with diversity: make it go away or make use of it as a resource. Seeing diversity as a resource requires rethinking notions of culture and cultural communities and understanding what is truly cultural about what people do. Culture is "the artifact-saturated medium of human life" (p. 294). Cole and a growing number of researchers employ a cultural–historical activity theoretical (CHAT) approach to organize new forms of educational activity in which diversity is a resource and heterogeneity is a design principle. Understanding the organizing principles of a CHAT, then, is instructive to this review, and Cole has highlighted the key principles of such an approach:

1. The basic premise of a CHAT approach is that human beings have the need and ability to mediate their interactions with each other and the nonhuman world through culture.

2. Culture is conceived of as human being's "social inheritance." This social inheritance is embodied in artifacts, aspects of the environment that have been transformed by their participation in the successful goal-directed activities of prior generations. They have acquired value.

3. Artifacts, the constituents of culture, are simultaneously material and ideal/symbolic. They are materialized in the form of objects, words, rituals, and other cultural practices that mediate human life. Culture is exteriorized mind; mind is interiorized culture.

4. The "effective environments" of mental life are taken to be the different practices or forms of activity the person engages in. Humans are created in joint, mediated activity.

5. Consequently, it is by analyzing what people do in culturally organized activity, people-acting through mediational means in a context, that one comes to understand the process of being human. Mediation of action through culture in social interaction is the essential precondition for normal human development.

6. Because cultural mediation is a process occurring over time, a CHAT perspective emphasizes that it must be studied over time [and scale]. An implication of this view is that all human beings are fundamentally hybrids of the phylogenetic and the cultural.

7. In addition to focusing researchers on time and change, a CHAT perspective requires them to focus on the social/spatial ecology of the activities they study—the relation of activities to their institutional arrangements.

8. A CHAT perspective places a special emphasis on the principle of multivoicedness, the principle that every form of human interaction contains within it many different selves, arranged in multiple, overlapping, and often-contradictory ways. The contradictions, experienced by us as conflicts, are a major source of change. It is diversity all the way down.

9. The acid test of the theory is its success in guiding the construction of new, more humane forms of activity. (pp. 291–292)

This instrumental view of culture and its emphasis on the social and cultural organization of human activity have been fundamental to the study of people's practice and so have implications for how to design robust educational ecologies where diversity is viewed as a resource for expansive learning (Engeström, 1987). As Cole (1998) has observed,

it is these patterned ways of co-confronting life with one's social group that serve as the "units of selection" by which parts of the vast pool of cultural knowledge are made a part of the conduct of current actions. These units are what I have referred to as *activities*, or as *cultural practices*. (p. 274)

Using cultural practices as a unit of analysis challenges approaches in which culture is based on genetics or deficit notions that view the practices of particular communities as being homogeneous, unchanging, and deviant from what is considered normative. One salient example is the culture of poverty—a metaphor influenced by Oscar Lewis (1966)—which attributed shortcomings of individuals and groups to deficits in their cultures (Foley, 1997).

Human difference has been historically addressed as being problematic in society, whereby at times the very approaches designed to support students serve to reaffirm difference (Minow, 1990). The difference framework involves marshalling deficit-driven notions in which some populations of students are described as suffering from cultural deprivation, living in a culture of poverty (Lewis, 1966), or being part of the underclass—constructs that suggest a fixed or comparative norm. Such theories are rooted in deficit thinking, a view that posits that students who fail in school do so because of internal deficits or deficiencies rather than external attributions of school failure (Valencia, 1997, p. 2; Valencia & Solorzano, 1997). Drawing on Bernstein's work, Hess and Shipman (1965) advanced the notion of linguistic deprivation to describe the language practices of working-class children.

Such discourses about children and youth "at risk" are often organized around medical or pathological orientations that perpetuate negative or stereotypical assumptions about students who come to be known as the problem rather than a population of people who are experiencing problems in the educational system. In a stratified society, differences are never just differences; they are always understood, defined, and ranked according to dominant cultural norms, values, and practices (Gutiérrez & Orellana, 2006, p. 506). One such strategy has been described as "blaming the victim," a practice in which policy and programs intend to change people rather than the systems in which people participate. Understanding social problems in terms of individual deficiencies results in programs designed to correct deficiencies, and according to Ryan (1971), "the formula for action becomes extraordinarily simple: change the victim" (p. 3). More than 30 years after Ryan's analysis and despite some recognition of the structural failures of schools, new explanations for school failure still attribute it to individuals and so intertwine notions of innate or class and cultural deficiencies (Dabney, 1980, pp. 8–9).

CULTURAL MISMATCH THEORY

Cultural frameworks, such as cultural mismatch theory and cultural deprivation theory (see J. Baratz & Baratz, 1970; S. Baratz & Baratz, 1970), have endured as explanations for the persistent underachievement of nondominant groups, and they have bolstered ideologies that conflate race/ethnicity with culture and social class to highlight the nonalignment in the cultural practices of home and school. Cultural mismatch theory locates its explanation of the underperformance or underachievement of nondominant students in the nonalignment of the cultural practices of the home and school. The implicit comparison in mismatch explanations between home and school is problematic in a number of ways. First, comparisons within this framework presume a static monolithic family and cultural community in which there is little variance in the ways and extent to which individuals and groups participate in the valued practices of the community. The focus is on culture, the noun, in which what is cultural about people's practices is presumed by virtue of their membership in a cultural community rather than by their history of involvement in everyday practices. Without accounting for both the regularity and the variance in cultural communities, it is difficult to account for change or understand that change in the individual involves change in the practices in which the individual participates (Gutiérrez & Rogoff, 2003).

Further, grounding comparisons about student achievement and potential in analytical processes that rely on dichotomizing home and school, formal and informal learning, and school-based and everyday knowledge makes it more difficult to document students' repertoires of practice developed across the practices that constitute everyday life. The concept of repertoires of practice employed here is best understood as people's ways of engaging in activities stemming from participation in a range of cultural practices. This requires a shift in perspective from the discontinuities of home and school, for example, to documenting people's history of involvement in practices of the cultural community. Cultural differences from this perspective are attributed to the variation in individuals' involvement in common or shared practices of the particular cultural ecology (Gutiérrez & Correa-Chavez, 2006; Rogoff, 2003).

In educational contexts, Henry Trueba (1988) was instrumental in challenging culturally based explanations of minority students' academic achievement. In response to Ogbu's (1978) taxonomy of minority groups as "autonomous," "immigrant," or "castelike," Trueba's work advanced a framework that argued against the commonly used dichotomies—for example, macro versus micro, ethnographic and applied versus theoretical (pp. 270–271). For Trueba, Ogbu's study lacked sufficient empirical evidence for the scale of the claims being made. Ogbu's grand theory of the underachievement of minority populations required an overgeneralization about distinct student populations; the resulting analysis was reductive, and it was organized around classifications that did not account for the significant variance in cultural communities. Accordingly, Ogbu's theory lacked explanatory power regarding the success of many minority students.

In contrast to positing simplistic assimilationist frameworks that contribute to uncomplicated renderings of people and their communities, Trueba's (1988) work emphasized the centrality of the cultural community and context-specific influences. Sociohistorical theory was advanced as the conceptual lens for understanding and explaining successful learning activities and individuals' participation therein. From a Vygotskian perspective, "academic failure or success of children is not a personal attribute of any child, nor a collective characteristic of any ethnic group, but a social phenomenon linked to historical and social conditions" (p. 282).

Trueba (2002) argued that immigrants necessarily develop multiple identities to negotiate new environments and their demands. Moreover, this flexibility to cross borders and boundaries and to address oppressive practices and economic constraints can be understood as a form of cultural capital, or cultural wealth (Yosso, 2005), including the double consciousness about which Du Bois (1903/1989) wrote.

Trueba (1990) highlighted the role of culture in understanding students' literacy abilities, in his studies of the literacy acquisition of Latino students in two California communities: San Diego and Ventura-Oxnard. Of importance to Trueba, assessing students' competence required observing their participation in literacy practices across a range of tasks and boundaries "in a larger social, psychological and historical context" (p. 2). Documenting the ethnography of communication and participation revealed abilities, identities, and forms of competence that were otherwise often invisible:

Failure is not individual, so much as it is a failure of the sociocultural system which denies the child an opportunity for social intercourse, and thus for cognitive development. "Academic failure" is a sociocultural phenomenon fully understandable only in its macrohistorical, economic, and political contexts. (p. 5)

Although Trueba argued that children should participate in socioculturally appropriate contexts, his sociocultural approach helped to avoid generalized treatment of cultural communities that essentialized their members and their practices; instead, Trueba looked to the ways that "failure" is not an individual accomplishment.

To be sure, balancing the need to account for both the regularity and variance in culture and avoiding generalizations has been challenging; making culture a trait of the individual or normalizing a cultural community against a dominant norm often has become the default explanation. This is particularly the case for students who do not fit the mold of what American schools consider "normal" (Deschenes, Cuban, & Tyack, 2001) and who are defined as underachieving, having defects in intellect or character, differences in cultural background, or practices that contribute to students' underperformance; from this perspective, the causes of student 'failure' can be located in the "mind and language of the individual" (Cuban and Tyack, 1988, p. 315), not in the ways learning and instruction are organized in institutional settings.

The attribution of failure to students' individual traits has facilitated the practice of labeling students as "at risk" or "low achievers" (Cuban & Tyack, 1988; Hull, Rose, Fraser, & Castellano, 1991). As Stanley Zehm (1973) reported, a student who had difficulty in school in the early 19th century was known as being a "dunce," "shirker," or "loafer" or being "stupid," "depraved," incorrigible," or "vicious." Of consequence, these labels attribute identities and thus suggest plans of intervention because "contained in a name, either explicitly or implicitly, is both an explanation and a prescription [that reveal] a set of religious and moral convictions that placed responsibility for behavior and achievement in the sovereign individual" (Cuban & Tyack, 1988, p. 4, as cited in Hull et al., 1991, pp. 311–312).

RETHINKING DIFFERENCE

The social movements of the 1960s resulted in some shift in the discourse, from individual to societal failure, although the resulting economic explanations still relied on deficit, if not pathological, renderings of the cognitive abilities of nondominant and working-class cultures (Cuban & Tyack, 1988, p. 312). Rose (2004) deftly addresses the politics of intelligence in *The Mind at Work*, where the issue of how views of intelligence are "classed" is elaborated in studies of the cognitive demands of everyday work. Drawing on interdisciplinary approaches to study knowledge at work in a range of skilled labor professions, Rose detailed intelligence, learning, reasoning, problem solving, and the strategic use of skills in blue-collar and skilled work. In doing so, Rose took apart notions of intelligence that made implicit judgments about working-class jobs. He developed rich accounts regarding the range of cognitive skills and strategies employed—from the importance of memory in waitressing, to the complex mathematical and diagnostic skills used by carpenters, electricians, plumbers, and hair stylists. In documenting the intelligence of working-class, skilled workers, Rose revealed the limitations of previous understandings of cognition in work, and through this analysis, he pushed us to think about the definition of intelligence that best befits a democracy.

Valencia and Pearl (1997) took a prognosticatory approach to examine the sustainability of deficit explanations and cultural deficiency arguments regarding the academic performance and potential of students from nondominant communities. Their analyses relied on sociodemographic realities and trends; the consequences attributed to the end of school desegregation; the ways that the economy, politics, and education intermingle; and, as a result, an increasing anti-deficit-thinking discourse. Given the current sociodemographic trends, deficit thinking "is likely to gain momentum and currency" (p. 245) because high-poverty schools are likely to remain primary sites of educational research and intervention but with relatively limited change.

This is the case in the field of literacy, where deficit notions persist in the discourses, orienting frameworks, policies, and approaches that propose educational interventions supported by ideologies that depend on labeling and classifying students along a number of dimensions—principally by mental ability. A hallmark characteristic of interventions for students from nondominant communities in underresourced schools places the onus of change on the individual student (Artiles, 1998). Consider, for example, a language-development program created and offered more than 40 years ago designed to address the "linguistic deprivation" of poor African American students (Bereiter & Engelman, 1966). This program emphasized rote and unchallenging verbal stimulation to address students' "nonstandard" language practices. Reductive literacy practices are increasingly commonplace in school districts with large numbers of English learners. One prevalent practice involves adopting curricula designed for special-needs students or for young students with demonstrated low abilities, as an intervention for students for whom English is not the home language. For example, in one large district with a sizable number of English learners, a reading intervention program entitled High Point (Schifini, Short, & Tinajero, 2001), intended for use with struggling readers in lower grades, is used for high school English learners despite its intended use (Martínez, Moreno, Morales, & Hopkins, 2008).

American schools are driven by a preoccupation with identifying children in terms of categories that the schools themselves have constructed for them. What conceptions of learning and learners are at work in current programs for students from nondominant communities? What to do and how to instructionally intervene have been central empirical questions in regard to students whose literacy practices deviate from normative views of literacy. The research and practice in special education have tended to reveal particular assumptions about human development and learning where notions of variability in those domains are arranged in normal distributions and where points in such distributions come with particular identities (e.g., average, at risk, disabled, remedial, gifted). This perspective highlights the view that risk is a probabilistic notion about future performance, a stark contrast to Cazden's (1981) instructive notion of performance before competence in zones of possibility. We turn briefly to the field of special education—where this preoccupation with risk has been particularly evident—to help us rethink how difference is negotiated.

Artiles's (1998) analysis of the deficit framework at work in the disproportionate representation of ethnic and linguistic minority students in special education points to the field's inattention to the sociohistorical contexts of development of these students; historically, attention has focused on comparing and holding members of nondominant communities against a normative view that can render them only "different." As noted by Minow (1990, as cited in Artiles, 1998), *difference* is a comparative term that highlights what students from nondominant communities are not. Here, "sameness is sine qua non for equality" (Artiles, 1998, p. 32), or, in Minow's words (1990, as cited in Artiles, 1998), "to be equal one must be the same, [and] to be different is to be unequal or even deviant" (p. 32).

For Artiles (1998), notions of difference are undergirded by a set of assumptions and practices that sustain the normative backdrop against which students are measured. One assumption is that difference resides within the individual; that is, difference is a trait of the individual. Such assumptions are perpetuated in part by the culturally bound perspective of researchers who are neither self-conscious nor transparent about how their sociocultural experiences contribute to how they understand and instantiate difference in the research process (Arzubiaga, Artiles, King, & Harris-Murri, 2008). At the same time, there is a tendency in research to ignore or minimize the standpoint of the person who is the object of scrutiny and investigation. Following Rogoff (1995), one means to disrupt the practices-of-difference analysis is to attend to the multiple and mutually constitutive frames of development: the individual, the interpersonal, and the institutional. In this way, the interrelationship between the individual and the cultural practices is made evident.

As McDermott, Goldman, and Varenne (2006) have argued, the practice of labeling and classifying students is deeply implicated in special education in the United States; it is a practice that has helped shape how educational researchers view students with disabilities and those with nonstandard practices. Understanding students' practices and abilities in relation to their contexts of development counters the tendency to locate disability solely within individuals. The identity labels associated with disability become more complex and problematic when "the ambiguities of racial, ethnic, and linguistic labels and the competitive and politically consequential agendas for which the labels are made relevant, and the ties between [learning disabled] and minority status become intertwined" (p. 12).

McDermott and colleagues (2006) conducted a micro-analytic study of how the cultural practices of schools bestow labels on students that belie their actual skills. Their cultural approach

takes individuals seriously by focusing on their environments and rarely allows a single person to bear the undue burden of being targeted, accused, labeled, explained, worried about, remediated, or even rehabilitated without an account of the conditions in which he or she lives. (p. 13)

Although this cultural approach does not directly address the learning disability, it does account for the affordances and constraints of the discursive practices and social arrangements among people that result from the categories and contexts of learning disability. In this study, "doing school"—that is, doing the valued and recognized practices of schooling institutions—became a measure of success in ways that obfuscated the expertise and more appropriate measures of the schooling competence of two Latino students and one African American student. "Doing school" involves a kind of procedural display in which students learn how to display pseudo-learning without demonstrating competence of subject matter knowledge (Bloome, Puro, & Theodorou, 1989). "Doing school" becomes an increasingly valued practice in educational efforts for students whose home language practices are marked in learning activities and where English, the unmarked language, is normative (Gutiérrez, 2008b).

How difference and disability are viewed, studied, and interpreted is relevant to the focus of this chapter insofar as it points to the need to counter the tendency to categorize and label students in ways that delimit the possibility of participating in learning arrangements and curricular opportunities, developing identities, and becoming full members of robust and equitable learning ecologies. It calls into question quick-fix approaches organized around generic forms of support and generalized understandings of intelligence and competence (Rose, 2004). It also calls for a more accurate assessment of the skills and practices of students who might otherwise be regarded as being underskilled. From this perspective, attention shifts to how the social organization of American classrooms first arranges for children to look like failures and then attributes their lack of success to racial, gender, language, or community membership.

Trent, Artiles, and Englert (1998) advance a similar argument about special education's long history of overrelying on deficit notions to develop models of instruction and intervention for special education students. These models have included "child saving" and social control theories that promote the classification and segregation of students: programs for immigrants, English learners, and economically underresourced students—in other words, the continued segregation of children "on the basis of race, ethnicity, and socioeconomic status" (p. 283). Similar to McDermott and colleagues (2006), Trent and colleagues argue that the presumption of children's learning disabilities allows people to systematically ignore or miss what children can actually accomplish beyond the boundaries defined by tests, labels, or a priori categories.

As such, social constructivist and sociocultural approaches to understanding and responding to disability are proposed as an alternative to behaviorist and cognitive models of disability, in which the unit of analysis is often narrowly concentrated on the individual, with the concomitant focus on deficits. Here, a sociocultural approach challenges long-standing views that disability is located within individuals; it instead redirects the focus on developing situated notions of competence, ability, risk, disability, and difference as being culturally mediated.

A more ecological and situated understanding of learning shifts to a different set of approaches, focusing on apprenticeship in applied settings, access to empowering modes of discourse, guided instruction that leads to self-regulated learning, and understanding learning in cultural–historical contexts. As Trent and colleagues (1998) suggest, this contextualized approach to special education was evident in literacy programs for children with mild disabilities, organized around the principles listed above—notably, reciprocal teaching in literacy instruction (see Palincsar, 1984, 1986; Palincsar & Brown, 1989) and the Early Literacy Project (see Englert & Mariage, 1996; Englert, Tarrant, Mariage, & Oxer, 1994, as cited from Trent et al., 1998). Rather than emphasize deficit areas and remedial approaches to address those deficiencies, such programs organized learning in ways that employed what students knew, to support the development of language and reading comprehension.

GENRES OF DIFFERENCE AND
THE LANGUAGE OF EXCLUSION

Paraphrasing McDermott and colleagues (2006), culture is both enabling and constraining. This means that people must continually negotiate the affordances and constraints of the cultural practices of the ecology: those socially inherited, as well as those newly formed. Discourses and ideologies play important mediating and consequential roles in cultural activity, including schooling. Claims about the success and failure of students from nondominant communities are too often advanced without careful examination of the intellectual history of the constructs or descriptors employed, their history of use, or the consequences of their use on the target population. Consider the concepts of cultural mismatch, cultural deprivation, and cultural deficit advanced earlier in this chapter.

Rigorous, accurate, and useful empirical work involves a kind of theoretical integrity in which there is a principled congruence of constructs, methods, and orienting frameworks to explain a phenomenon. Gutiérrez and Orellana (2006) address the commonplace approaches to conceptualizing and reporting research about students from nondominant communities (specifically, English learners)—that is, approaches that unwittingly create or reinforce deficit views of students and their communities. The authors point to a new genre that has emerged in the reporting of research that has come to characterize studies of difference, risk, and nondominant student populations. One salient characteristic of this genre involves the ways in which the "problem" of nondominant students is typically framed as a comparison with a "mainstream" norm. For example, the home literacy practices of English learners are often compared with school-based practices in ways that can inadvertently construct home practices in terms of deficit. The point of the comparison may be to contrast abilities, home practices, attitudes, or school achievement.

The issue here is that the constructs and descriptors that researchers use may reveal a set of assumptions about normativity that necessarily involves an implicit comparison of nondominant and dominant (normative) communities, even when no empirical comparison has been conducted. From this perspective, instructional interventions are designed to "fix" what is broken or misaligned.

These notions of risk and difference have contributed to what Rose (1985) calls the language of exclusion—a discourse that helps to exclude from the academic community students who are in need of "repair," as well as helps to sustain an ideology of remediation that carries with it "the etymological wisps and traces of disease. (p. 193)

To extend the metaphor, the ideology of remediation places students "in scholastic quarantine until their disease can be diagnosed and remedied" (p. 193). We explore how this ideology is indexed in educational practices.

TRADITIONAL RESPONSES TO DIFFERENCE: THE IDEOLOGY AND PRACTICE OF REMEDIATION

The ideology of remediation is instantiated in practices organized around beliefs about literacy and learning. In our work (Gutiérrez, Hunter, & Arzubiaga, 2009), we have examined approaches to remediation for students from nondominant communities, many of whom are immigrants and English learners. In the aggregate, students from nondominant communities have been socialized to and through their participation in remedial courses, in which they develop unproductive and weak strategies for literacy learning. In general, their literacy instruction is organized around individually accomplished tasks with generic or minimal assistance, narrow forms of assessment, "homogeneous" grouping, and an overemphasis on basic skills with little connection to content or the practices of literacy—in short, an overemphasis on the technical dimensions of literacy. In the cases of California, Arizona, and Massachusetts, remedial instruction is delivered in a language other than the home language. In these states, we see how various ideologies of difference are indexed in pedagogies, practices, and assumptions about students from nondominant communities who require new and additional forms of assistance to "do school." This ideology of remediation has potent policy implications; as Rose (1989) suggests, "to be remedial is to be substandard, inadequate, and, because of the origins of the term, the inadequacy is metaphorically connected to disease and mental defect" (p. 171).

The discourse of remediation has had a sustained presence in education literature, emerging as early as the 1930s, when it first appeared in publications for teachers and educators (Breneman & Harlow, 1998; Rose, 1985). In the domain of literacy, Rose (1985) notes,

We still talk of writers as suffering from specifiable, locatable defects, deficits, and handicaps that can be localized, circumscribed, and remedied. Such talk reveals an atomistic, mechanistic-medical model of language that few contemporary students of the use of language, from educators to literary theorists, would support. (p. 351)

Our biases and assumptions about difference are culturally organized; thus, our proclivity to identify and label students who perform poorly or differently, to assign them to particular treatments, to assess them in particular ways, and to make a diagnosis about their future performance in schools and often beyond reveals habits of mind that index our nation's history with difference—primarily, race and class differences.

Our nation's preoccupation with difference and its inclination to fix perceived deficiencies helps to explain our focus in this review on the concept of remediation—a central construct used in the literature, concerned with students in need of additional support in learning situations. The term *remediation*, derivative of the Latin *rememdium*, is rooted in the discourse of medicine to describe the educational treatment that will "remedy" or "cure" students of the ailments that contribute to poor academic achievement, and it includes efforts to correct character flaws, improve intellectual prowess, and enhance cultural or social deficiencies (Gutiérrez et al., 2009; Hull et al., 1991). From this perspective, remedial education must be understood in its historical context and as an instantiation of how educational and social ideologies are mutually informing (Golby & Gulliver, 1985).

Throughout our educational history, students who have not been successful in school have been categorized and labeled as being incapable of learning; they have been retained, placed in special classes, tracked into low-ability classes, and often expelled from school (Oakes, 1985). Even the seminal report *A Nation at Risk* (U.S. National Commission on Excellence in Education, 1983) showed little awareness that schools, as currently organized, are much better calibrated to serve privileged groups than groups placed on the margin (Deschenes et al., 2001, p. 527). More recent reform efforts tend to perpetuate the same outcome for students from nondominant communities:

Despite the beliefs of the standards movement, though, there will always be a number of children who do not or cannot accomplish what their schools expect them to accomplish. In this way, the standards movement has and will have something in common with every American educational movement of the past century and a half: students who perform poorly and who fail. (p. 526)

Students who cannot meet the standards make up what Deschenes and colleagues (2001) consider the current "mismatch" group, distributed across one of four profiles prevalent in schools:

1. Students who do poorly in school have character defects or are responsible for their own performance.

2. Families from certain cultural backgrounds prepare children poorly for school and give them little support for achievement. . . .

3. The structure of the school system is insufficiently differentiated to fit the range of abilities and different destinies in life of its heterogeneous student body.

4. Children often fail academically because the culture of the school is so different from the cultural backgrounds of the communities they serve. (pp. 535–537)

Reform efforts such as the standards-based reforms require students to do more and to do it longer, or to repeat a year of school, rather than question or challenge what actually contributes to student failure in the first place. According to Deschenes and colleagues, schools must learn to adapt, address inequities (educational and social), and engage in significant transformation.

MOVING FROM REMEDIATION TO RE-MEDIATION

Remediation remains a central strategy in addressing the academic needs of students who differ from the dominant norm. In many of the current practices under No Child Left Behind (2001), remedial instruction is the default assistance strategy and the preferred pedagogical arrangement across the educational pipeline. Moreover, in an effort to provide alternative forms of instruction to mitigate underachievement, many remediation programs employed moralistic or deficit-oriented perspectives to justify their need and implementation. For example, Grimm (1996) noted that when "underprepared" students showed up in college, centers were created to "offer these unfamiliar students one last chance to remove the traces of their educational and cultural backgrounds" (p. 530). Such perspectives promote narrow notions of student ability and disregard students' repertoires of practice (Gutiérrez & Rogoff, 2003) as assets to successful learning (for a comprehensive overview, see Hull et al., 1991; Rose, 1985). Of consequence, these perspectives have made it more difficult to hold K–12 institutions accountable for the role in sustaining negative images of students as potential failures.

Cultural approaches informed by sociocultural views of learning and development have provided new approaches to extending students' literacy repertoires. In contrast to the traditional "remedial" approaches to instruction previously addressed, the notion of re-mediation—with its focus on the sociohistorical influences on students' learning and the context of their development—involves a more robust notion of learning and thus disrupts the ideology of pathology linked with most approaches to remediation. Instead of emphasizing basic skills—problems of the individual—re-mediation involves a reorganization of the entire ecology for learning and "a shift in the way that mediating devices regulate coordination with the environment" (Cole & Griffin, 1983, p. 70). Development here involves a "systems reorganization" in which designing for deep learning requires a "social systems reorganization" (p. 73) where multiple forms of mediation are in play. The concept of re-mediation constitutes a framework for the development of rich learning ecologies in which all students can expand their repertoires of practice through the conscious and strategic use of a range of theoretical and material tools.

To illustrate this concept, Cole and Griffin (1983) detail how a learning environment for elementary school students who struggle with reading was reorganized to produce improved reading results. In school settings, the comprehension activities frequently practiced by students too often prevent them from acquiring a deep understanding of the text and from engaging in literate practices. For example, one common comprehension activity (the central activity in the reading process) involves asking students to demonstrate their understanding of a text by selecting words from the text and then matching them to the question.

However, in an approach to increasing student comprehension, Cole and Griffin (1983) developed a script for a new practice—"Question Asking Reading"—in which students formulated their own questions about texts, as opposed to simply answering questions generated by someone else. In their study, Cole and Griffin placed students into small groups, assigned roles, and provided with scripts, with individual tasks listed on cards for completion. Through this process, students were able to understand the texts in more robust ways—including those that were more in alignment with the forms of comprehension valued in school. Here, the development of a functional system for teaching reading was created to re-mediate the local practices of one learning environment, as well as the history of practices organized for children's failure (Cole, 1998).

Of significance, the approach for helping students to develop productive reading strategies was not to focus on basic skills—that is, a progression from the simple (letters and sounds) to the more complex (meaning making); instead, teaching reading effectively involved emphasis on the activity of reading itself, where the individual skills associated with reading were already part of the activity. In short, learning was organized so that individuals could participate in the social practices of reading in joint activity with others, where multiple forms of assistance were readily available (Gutiérrez et al., 2009).

RE-MEDIATING WRITING

In the domain of writing, there is comparable antecedent work that has helped push back remedial interventions for students who are unfamiliar with academic discourse and writing genres. Rose (1985, 1988, 1989); Hull et al. (1991), and Hull and Rose (1989, 1990) produced a seminal body of work that sparked a critical conversation about writing pedagogies organized around exclusionary, deficit, and narrow discourses of literacy and literacy learners and around those of intelligence. Despite a number of important studies that called for new ways to think about writing and writers (Bartholomae, 1985; Bartholomae & Petrosky, 1986; Coe & Gutiérrez, 1981; Perl, 1979; Shaughnessy, 1977), we examine this body of work because it is among the first to reflect and bring a sociocultural analysis to rhetoric and composition studies, with a focus on the effects of remedial instruction on writers' development. These writing-specific studies help to illustrate the limits of remedial education and to signal the problems of broader deficit approaches to addressing the range of literacy needs of students. As part of their new approach, Rose and Hull worked to bring together a cognitive and social model to their analysis, rather than rely solely on literary studies to examine writing development.

In "The Politics of Remediation," Rose (1989) opened a conversation about students who are in the process of extending their writing repertoires to include academic writing. By reframing student identities as "literate people straining at the boundaries of their ability, trying to move into the unfamiliar, to approximate a kind of writing they can't yet command" (p. 188), Rose reframed commonplace conceptions of writers who are new to the conventions of academic discourses, genres, and practices. And nowhere would the clash between these conventions and students' vernacular and everyday practices be more evident than in the writing tutorial centers where Rose studied students who were struggling with the new tools of the academy, where he helped them write their way into the university (Bartholomae, 1985).

Such work is not neutral; in fact, it is work that is often at odds with the ideals and practices of the academy. Remedial work has never been regarded as being a part of the work of the university but rather a necessary and marginalized enterprise (see also Gutiérrez et al., 2009; North 1998; Street & Lea, 2006). At the university level—where the intellectual class structure privileges a certain cognitive work (e.g., research)—providing students with assistance such as tutoring is devalued or marginalized (Rose, 1989). To address the structural inequities in the education of students with different and emergent literacy repertoires, Rose (1989) contextualized his study in a policy analysis that examined the ways that knowledge is structured at the university and how students are prepared to participate within that disciplinary structure. Rose noted that claims of students' failure to write academically lack historical perspective and fail to address the role that institutions play in perpetuating students' participation in remedial writing programs. Such claims that blame the victim tend to draw on three kinds of evidence to advance the "problem" of remedial writing students: declines in students' local and national test scores, increasing enrollment in remedial programs and classes, and evaluations by university professors.

Building on this theme of exposing the consequences of remedial programs, Rose (1985) call for a reconsideration of the concept and practices of remediation and the need for new approaches that capture the complex cognitive and social processes that produce writing. In contrast to text-based analyses that do not account for cognitive and social factors or that have difficulty detecting the sources of error, Rose's proposed social–cognitive approach employed fine-grained analysis, process tracing, retrospective interviews, and observation of students' writing in situ to help document their writing history. They argued that with methods that help to make visible a logic in students' writing, instructors can develop new understandings of students' writing, of their potential, and of the appropriate pedagogical intervention. This approach was crucial in this historical period because

the theoretical and pedagogical model that was available for "corrective teaching" led educators to view writing problems within a medical–remedial paradigm. Thus they set out to diagnose as precisely as possible the errors (defects) in a student's paper—which they saw as symptomatic of equally isolable defects in the student's linguistic capacity—and devise drills and exercises to remedy them. (p. 352)

As the enrollment of nontraditional students in 4-year institutions increased, institutions more so relied on writing courses and tutorials to provide assistance to students who were attempting to master the conventions of academic writing. Hull and Rose's studies (1989, 1990) of remedial writing instruction provided close analysis of the ways that classroom practices help to construct student identities as remedial students; it also offered a study of how institutions are complicit in perpetuating the ideologies and practices that are instantiated in remedial approaches in the academy. In "'This Wooden Shack Place,'" Hull and Rose (1990) examined how a college student's classroom literacy practices are shaped by one's sociocultural background and individual history and the social organization of a writing conference between instructor and student. We learn how attention to the student's linguistic and sociocultural repertoire provides not only valuable insight into his or her inter-pretations of text bu also effective and responsive pedagogical approaches.

In a subsequent empirical work, Hull et al. (1991) elaborate the discussion of remediation as a social construct—that is, the product of perceptions and beliefs about literacy and learning—and they call for new methods that provide a fine-grained analysis against a cultural–historical backdrop to understand students' writ-ing practices and challenge narrow notions of intelligence. To connect these local classroom practices with larger systemic structures and ideologies, the researchers embed their case study of one student in a remedial college-level writing class within a broader history of American education where low-achieving students are consid-ered to be "lesser in character and fundamental ability" (p. 311). This work docu-ments how dominant discourses of remediation and teachers' unfamiliarity with nondominant discourses can contribute to the social construction of remediation and to views of students' thinking as being deficient—particularly, that of students whose repertoire does not include knowledge of traditional classroom discourse pat-terns, including the ubiquitous recitation script (Mehan, 1979).

CULTURAL MODELING

More recent approaches, organized around cultural–historical principles of learn-ing and development (Cole & Engeström, 1993), include interpretive approaches such as cultural modeling (Lee, 1995, 1997, 2000, 2007) and the Funds of Knowledge project (González, Moll, & Amanti, 2005; Moll, Amanti, Neff, & González, 1992). Researchers across disciplines responded to the importance of attending to culture in understanding students' learning while recognizing the ten-dency in previous research to conflate race/ethnicity with culture in ways that reduced culture to a trait of individuals by virtue of their membership in particular communities—notably, nondominant communities. Despite clear links to earlier cultural mismatch approaches, the cultural modeling framework resolves the prob-lems emerging in the cultural mismatch model and in related models through its use of a dynamic and processual notion of culture. Unlike approaches that rely on cul-tural explanations of difference, cultural modeling not only attempts to bridge home and school, as well as nondominant and dominant cultural practices; it also explores genuine connections that students can make with school-based learning. Specifically, studies within this framework examine how culture is implicated in everyday and school-based practices and knowledge domains.

Approaches that intended to challenge deficit notions regarding the literacy prac-tices of cultural communities often unintentionally produced narrow notions of culture and the practices of the communities under study (Gutiérrez & Rogoff, 2003). Furthermore, the deep lack of understanding regarding how to make sense of the "cultural displays of knowledge" from youth engaged in everyday practices has produced what Lee (2007) argues is a "pervasive culture of low expectations, to deficit models of student capacities, and to a myriad of misunderstandings within classrooms" (p. 25). In the field of literacy, cultural modeling has helped make visible and reframed students' literacy practices and "repositions what might be historically viewed as vernacular practices as intellectually rich" (pp. 26–27).

The most extensive body of work within this approach is the Cultural Modeling Project, developed by Carol Lee (1995, 1997, 2000, 2007). This model relies on ethnographic and linguistic anthropological traditions to develop grounded theories about the range of practices in which students participate across the various contexts of their everyday lives and the resulting expertise. Documenting students' everyday practices provides the opportunity to map such practices onto disciplinary modes of reasoning, analyze disciplinary modes of reasoning, and then map them onto academic processes and discourses. As such, the Cultural Modeling Project "is a framework for the design of learning environments that examines what youth know from everyday settings to support specific subject matter learning" (Lee, 2007, p. 15). Finding commonalities in modes of reasoning across contexts also serves to challenge deficit notions of students' repertoires developed across nonschool settings.

In this framework, students' repertoires of practice are viewed as being integral to their learning. In her work, Lee (2007) reorganizes African American students' learning of complex literacy tropes by leveraging analogous vernacular practices with subject-matter-specific practices within school. Lee's analytical framework illustrates how the rhetorical practices of speakers of African American English, such as those evident in the act of signifying (Smitherman, 2000), are also found in the figurative language of canonical literary texts. Thus, cultural modeling and its methods of study offer a productive approach to understanding the connections between everyday and school-based practices and between everyday and school-based discourses (Lee, 1995, 1997, 2000, 2007).

One important tenet of a cultural modeling framework involves what Lee (2007) refers to as a "cultural repertoires of practice" perspective on culture, drawing on the work of Gutiérrez and Rogoff (2003); Nasir, Rosebery, Warren, and Lee (2006); and Rogoff, Paradise, Arauz, Correa-Chavez, and Angelillo (2003). For Lee, students—including those from African American and other nondominant communities—"bring important cultural resources from their home and community experiences" (p. 10). Cultural modeling sheds light on the sophisticated tacit knowledge of youth by drawing on "cultural data sets" in classroom learning—that is, artifacts with which students themselves are expert. Through an analysis of these cultural data sets, students are socialized into academic discourse as they learn more about their familiar tools and practices, as well as about unfamiliar and even alienating canonical texts.

Antecedents of the cultural modeling framework are found in the concept of funds of knowledge, developed by Luis Moll and Norma González (González et al., 2005; Moll et al., 1992). By focusing on the range of social practices in which families engage, González, Moll, and colleagues developed an approach that documents the knowledge in practice that is part of household daily routines—that is, the social practices that families arrange for everyday life. Documenting quotidian activity also makes visible the household relations of exchange across settings and social networks. In doing so, the funds-of-knowledge analytical lens helps to redefine the kind of toolkit that students from Latino households have available to them—the linguistic, sociocultural, and emergent forms of disciplinary knowledge that become resources for learning across settings and practices.

A funds-of-knowledge framework provides opportunity for educators to examine their assumptions about the available expertise in the homes and practices of Latino families and to rethink explanations for student performance built around views of home–school dichotomies and mismatched practices of home and school. Using ethnography to identify the local funds of knowledge and social networks of exchange, teachers involved in the project become engaged in practices in which they make links between what they learn in homes and what they know in school contexts. Through participation in these practices, new forms of interaction between families and teachers have the potential to recognize and extend students' repertoires of practice and design new forms of learning activity that rely in part on a broader set of tools and practices to support literacy learning. Working within this framework, Civil (2006) developed a mathematics curriculum based on families' funds of knowledge in mathematical learning—that is, using the mathematical knowledge at work in families' practices.

Despite parallels between the two frameworks, Lee (2007) distinguishes several major differences. The first stems from the fact that a cultural modeling approach highlights the students' repertoires of practice rather than those of adults or those emerging from family networks. Second, cultural modeling focuses on the "demands" of context- or domain-specific skills, such as narrative writing in English-classroom contexts (Lee, 2007), paraphrasing across various subject matter contexts (Orellana & Reynolds, 2008), and mathematics learning (Nasir, 2000). Across both frameworks, though, "the challenge is to select highly generative cultural data sets and not to trivialize making connections between everyday knowledge and school based knowledge" (Lee, 2007, p. 35).

A cultural modeling approach then privileges the language practices of students in spaces that have historically devalued the linguistic and cultural repertoires of practice often deemed deficient or unrelated to academic achievement. For example, Lee (2007) found that when students were provided with cultural data sets that exemplified complex and dynamic figurative language—as well as interpretive problems, such as symbolism, irony, satire, and unreliable narration (e.g., rap lyrics, music videos, poetry, and canonical African American literary texts)—they developed deeper understandings of their tacit knowledge of signifying practices, including their function, range, and potential. Expertise in analyzing tacit knowledge facilitated students' potential to analyze canonical texts.

Other literacy researchers have employed a cultural modeling framework in cross-cultural studies of children's and youth's language practices. Arnetha Ball (1992, 1995, 2002; Ball & Farr, 2003), for example, has documented cultural preferences in expository writing among African American adolescent speakers of African American English. Ball examined the organizational patterns of conversational and written expository discourse of African Americans during informal contexts, and she utilized these patterns as resources to understand and produce expository writing in formal conversations and written contexts. In related work, *Exchanging Writing,*

Exchanging Cultures (Freedman, 1994) revealed how cultures of teaching and learning, in inner-city schools serving large numbers of students from nondominant groups, are organized differently at both the school level and the classroom level in different countries. This research showed that our "usual" ways of organizing teaching and learning are not necessary. For example, "mixed ability" was normal in U.K. secondary schools but unusual in U.S. schools. Similarly, teaching in the United Kingdom was characterized by its focus on developing curriculum informed by deep understandings of students and their development; in contrast, students' learning in inner-city schools was dependent on curricular changes. A noteworthy and fundamental distinction at the curricular level was that students in the United Kingdom had the opportunity to explore one another's cultures through the medium of writing exchanges, in which they reflected on their own cultural contexts and language practices. Studying these cultural practices of cross-cultural schooling environments provides useful insight into how to re-mediate students' learning in U.S. contexts.

Drawing on the cultural modeling tradition, Marjorie Orellana and Jennifer Reynolds (2008) studied the everyday linguistic practices of immigrant Latino/ Latina students to document the repertoires of practice of such youth who translate, or "para-phrase," for adults in their families. Beginning with ethnographic research to find analogous modes of reasoning within communities, these researchers found that children of Mexican immigrants often translate documents that require a "para-phrasing" of highly rigorous text; of significance, the researchers identified analogues between translating (or "para-phrasing") complex household or business interactions with the task of paraphrasing (or meaning making) in classroom activities. These students demonstrate their linguistic dexterity in their ability to perform paraphrasing tasks, despite believing that they cannot do so in school settings. In contrast to those whose work focuses on learning in a specific discipline, Orellana and Reynolds explore connections that can be made across content areas.

In related work, Martínez, Orellana, Pacheco, and Carbone (2008) drew on the cultural modeling tradition, as well as the funds-of-knowledge framework (Moll et al., 1992), to construct a curriculum informed by Mexican immigrant students' repertoires of practice in general and translation practices in particular. This empirical work relied on qualitative approaches to document generative ways of mapping students' "paraphrasing" skills onto academic processes—most notably, writing (Martinez et al., 2008, pp. 423–424). In this study, students first engaged in a series of writing tasks; then, they were asked to reflect on the context-specific nature of their writing practices and to draw on their knowledge regarding the ways that they would speak to each respective audience. One important goal of this work involved helping students to recognize how translation is a valuable skill both inside and outside the classroom. To make this point explicit, the research team (including the teacher) asked students to reenact scenarios for different audiences and to write to different audiences. Each audience was designated to represent peers, family members, and school faculty members, to demonstrate that students have access to various linguistic resources. The authors note that a key step in this process is to clearly and explicitly communicate to students that it is acceptable to draw on their full linguistic repertoires. Once students understand that teachers value the skills they possess, teachers can work with them to leverage and extend those skills. (Martinez et al., p. 430)

Within a cultural modeling frame, hybrid language and literacy practices are normative and so help to support a learning ecology in which students routinely draw on their linguistic toolkit to learn (Gutiérrez et al., 1999; Manyak, 2001). As Orellana and Reynolds (2008) note, leveraging students' practices neither romanticizes nor minimizes the potential that their linguistic repertoires can have across a range of tasks, activities, and contexts. Cultural modeling also allows for the emergence of hybrid language and literacy practices and thus creates space for students to draw on the full repertoire of their linguistic and cognitive skills (Gutiérrez et al., 1999; Manyak, 2001).

Other researchers have employed a cultural modeling framework across a range of disciplinary areas to document expertise not otherwise captured in studies of non-dominant students' mathematical and science learning. In particular, Nasir's work (2000, 2005) demonstrated how the cultural displays of African American youth playing dominoes and basketball can be used to understand the mathematical concepts of averages and algorithms in school-based settings. Researchers at the Chéche Konen project at TERC (Rosebery, Warren, & Conant, 1992; Warren, Ballenger, Ogonowski, Rosebery, & Hudicourt-Barnes, 2001) documented how the Haitian Creole argumentative structure facilitated learning in the science classroom.

Across all these projects, students' repertoires of practice served as robust units of analysis for understanding ways to design productive learning environments that supported subject matter learning. These studies highlight the importance of understanding the cultural displays of knowledge that emerge in everyday practices (Lee, 2007). Evident in the cultural modeling approach is an explicit stance toward challenging long-standing narratives and practices that diminish the educational possibilities for students from nondominant communities, through its use of robust measures to document students' linguistic toolkits more accurately and more comprehensively.

DESIGNING FOR EXPANSIVE LEARNING

Engeström (2001) proposed the theory of expansive learning, within the framework of cultural–historical activity theory, as a new approach to re-mediating previous theories of learning and their intervention projects. In particular, this activity theoretical approach is used to analyze and design learning ecologies in which new forms of collective activity can occur. To illustrate how expansive learning addresses the fundamental questions of any theory of learning, Engeström combined these first-order questions with the fundamental premises of an activity theoretical approach: activity systems as the unit of analysis, the multivoicedness of activity systems, historicity, the central role of contradictions as sources of change and development in the activity system, and the possibility of expansive cycles in activity systems (pp. 136–137) necessary to promote expansive forms of learning. Researchers taking an activity theoretical approach should ask,

1. Who are the subjects of learning, how are they defined and located?

2. Why do they learn, what makes them make the effort?

3. What do they learn, what are the contents and outcomes of learning? And

4. How do they learn, what are the key actions or processes of learning? (p. 133)

Within this framework, expansive learning is defined as a historically new type of learning that emerges as participants struggle through developmental transformations in their activity systems, moving across collective zones of proximal development (Engeström, 1999, p. 3). These developmental transformations can be understood "as the construction and resolution of successively evolving contradictions in the activity system" (p. 7).

Engeström, Virkkunen, Helle, Pihlaja, and Poikela (1996), colleagues at the Center for Activity Theory and Developmental Work Research, have written that the Change Laboratory (Engeström & Engeström, 1986) is a method in which practitioners can develop new work practices through its intensive and deep transformations. Although the laboratory has been used as a primary intervention for developmental work research, we include it here because it has influenced the educational interventions of scholars across a number of countries who are interested in re-mediating students' learning activity, including their developing more expansive forms of literacy.

The basic design of the Change Laboratory interventionist project is organized around Vygotsky's method of dual stimulation (see van der Veer & Valsiner, 1991). A fundamental notion at work here is that the experimental task is always reinterpreted and reconstructed by the participant by "means of his or her internalized 'psychological instruments' that cannot be strictly controlled from the outside" (Engeström et al., 1986, p. 5). As Engeström and colleagues observe,

rather than giving the child just a task, ignoring her interpretation and reconstruction of the task, and observing how she manages, Vygotsky and his colleagues typically gave the child also potentially useful mediating artifacts—tools and signs. With them, the nature of the task could be radically changed. The potential capabilities and emerging new psychological formations of the child might be revealed. Thus, dual stimulation may also be characterized as *re-mediational design*. (p. 5)

In this work, change laboratories create "temporary activity systems that are set up within existing organizations (e.g., hospitals, schools, factories, and banks)" (Cole & Engeström, 2007, p. 504). For example, using the change laboratory methodology, Teräs (2007) developed a culture laboratory to examine interculturality and hybridity in immigrants' education and training in a Finnish vocational education and training context.

Luria (1932) reported early work that employed Vygotsky's method of dual stimulation. In one illustrative example, Vygotsky worked with an adult man, who was suffering from Parkinson's disease, to re-mediate his ambulatory skills by introducing small pieces of paper—the means of which he was able to walk across a floor. By introducing a new mediating tool, the patient was helped "to overcome the symptoms of his disease by getting him to reorganize the mental processes he used in walking" (Luria, 2006, p. 129). This method was then widely used in designing methods for re-mediating the behavior of adults with brain damage and that of mentally retarded children (Amano, 1999; Luria, 1979, as cited in Cole & Engeström, 2007).

Interventionist projects organized around a cultural–historical activity theoretical approach such as the Change Laboratory described above, around formative–experimental research (Cole & Engeström, 2007), and around social design experiments (Vossoughi & Gutiérrez, 2008) center attention on a systems reorganization. Formative experiments are designed to coincide with the "time course of the 'formative' (developmental) processes under examination" (Cole & Engeström, 2007, p. 493). Similarly, social design experiments, organized around equity-oriented principles and expansive forms of learning, are oriented toward transformative ends through mutual relations of exchange among participants. Grounded in a humanist approach to research and a cultural–historical approach to learning and development (Cole, 1996; Cole & Engeström, 1993), this interventionist research is concerned with social consequences and transformative potential (Vossoughi & Gutiérrez, 2008). Social design experiments are open systems that are subject to revision, disruptions, and contradictions and are co-designed with researchers and the target community (Engeström, 2004).

This process entails a transformation in the social organization of learning, the social relationships, the forms and uses of artifacts, and the kinds of available assistance to ratchet up the possibilities for expansive learning. In the United States, these projects are situated in an activity theoretical tradition of human development to argue for a fundamental change in the way that instruction is organized that serves students who are struggling with academic work and in the educational and social inequities that they face.

In our work in literacy (Gutiérrez, 2008a; Gutiérrez et al., 2009), we elaborate the concept of re-mediation introduced by Cole and Griffin (1983) and Engeström's (2001) concept of expansive learning to redefine the object of re-mediating activity (Cole & Engeström, 1993) as meaningful learning in robust ecologies, as opposed to "fixing" the individual. Here, re-mediation of the learning ecology involves the reorganization of the activity system, including the social organization of learning, the social relationships, the division of labor, and the artifacts in use. The intercultural and hybrid nature of human activity, including classrooms and other learning environments, makes polycultural strategies and solutions an effective means to respond to diversity. Cole (1998) suggests that "In recognition that multiple cultures are present in every classroom, and that whenever culture-using creatures interact, they create between them a hybrid subculture, appropriate to the culture it mediates" (p. 300).

One hybrid collective activity system, termed *third spaces* (Gutiérrez, 2008a; Gutiérrez et al., 1995), emphasizes heterogeneity as an organizing principle—heterogeneity in the language practices; in age, grade, sex, gender, and race/ethnicity;

and in the tools, the forms of assistance, and the social organization and distribution of people with varying familiarity with reading and writing in the academy. These social design experiments (Vossoughi & Gutiérrez, 2008) are organized around expansive forms of learning, powerful literacies, and hybrid language practices that result from the intercultural exchange and boundary crossing involved in students' everyday lives. Mediational artifacts such as syncretic texts, designed to exploit the existing hybridity, help to create particular social environments of development in which students begin to reimagine who they are and what they might be able to accomplish, academically and beyond.

We highlight the syncretic literacy practice as one productive mediational artifact used to extend students' literacy repertoires. By design, the syncretic text draws on several seemingly contradictory or inharmonious conventions and practices—namely, a familiar cultural practice or a vernacular form of language with written texts that demand attention to the conventions of the academy and the editorial assistance of peers and instructors. The basic rule of re-mediation here involves an expansive, hybrid, and additive approach to difference and diversity, in which the social rules of participation and learning and the division of labor are re-mediated by a social imagination oriented toward new forms of collective activity and new uses of the technologies of reading and writing. These hybrid polycultural spaces are also exemplified in the Fifth Dimension project (a tertiary artifact; Cole, 1996; Vásquez, 2003) and in Change Laboratories (Engeström, 1998; Engeström, in press).

RE-MEDIATING INQUIRY: CONCLUDING COMMENTS

We conclude this review by returning to the discussion with which we began this chapter. Narrow notions of student ability and literacy learning are linked in important ways to beliefs about culture and cultural communities. They are also linked to the methods of inquiry employed to define and measure student competence. The long-standing practice of using one method to assess learning and achievement has made it increasingly difficult to identify and document students' repertoires of practice or view their linguistic toolkits as assets to learning (Erickson & Gutiérrez, 2002). This issue has been extensively addressed in previous research, and it was substantively elaborated in the work produced by the Laboratory for Comparative Human Cognition over the past decades (Cole, Engeström, & Vásquez, 1997).

In 1982, Michael Cole, Lois Hood, and Ray McDermott published a groundbreaking paper about the ecological invalidity of making inferences from laboratory-based observations, tasks, and tests to intellectual behavior observed and documented in the practices of everyday life. One significant observation advanced in this work emphasized the essential importance of addressing the dynamically organized influence of individuals on their environment as being fundamental to the organization of people's behavior (Cole et al., 1982). In this work, Cole and colleagues did not question the merit of cognitive theories and their use in laboratory settings or with experimental design; instead, their point was to demonstrate that theories and models emerging from laboratory or contrived settings should not be used to make predictions about human activity outside the laboratory. Cole et al. (1982) and others (Erickson & Gutiérrez, 2002; Scribner, 1976, 1985) have suggested that understanding and analyzing human behavior must begin with rich description of an everyday practice where the phenomenon under study can be observed in some systematic way.

The consequences—especially in relation to matters of race and ethnicity in cross-cultural research—have significance to dilemmas found in research today. In speaking to the nature and origin of cultural differences, Cole et al. (1982) note the ways that deficit thinking and the penchant for remediating the "unschooled" are complicated if not sustained in experimental/cognitive laboratory-based efforts and texts:

Even with allowances for selection of artifacts and careful efforts to equate stimulus familiarity, motivation and comprehension of instructions, differences between schooled and unschooled populations were of sufficient magnitude to suggest that schooled subjects employed more powerful, flexible, and efficient ways of remembering and thinking than their unschooled counterparts. (p. 370)

This work called for the necessity of using ecologically valid tasks and tools that were representative of the ways that people actually engage the intellectual tasks and challenges of their everyday lives. It focused on developing research practices that systematically examine the "cognitive ecology" of the people studied "to discover the general sets of everyday circumstances associated with improved, experimentally controlled performance without barriers" (p. 371). The guidelines derived from their work and theoretical orientations highlight important theoretical and methodological considerations that have salience in studies concerned with addressing risk, difference, ability, and literacy learning in school settings. Their work remains instructive to literacy research with students from nondominant communities.

In sum, this review signals the need for a radical transformation in the ways that we conceive people's literacy practices and how we extend the repertoires they develop across the practices of everyday life. Researchers have looked to cultural–historical approaches that rely on (a) "theory–practice methodology" (Cole & Engeström, 2007, p. 495) to design formative interventions, cultural modeling systems, and social design experiments and (b) social practice views of literacy to re-mediate current educational activity for students from nondominant communities. Learning across these related traditions involve amplifying students' cultural repertoires (Cole & Griffin, 1980), as opposed to relying on the default scripts of risk, difference, and deficiency—approaches that systematically fail to re-mediate educational activity in ways that make teachers and students active agents in learning processes.

NOTES

[1]We use the term *nondominant* rather than terms such as *minority, students of color,* and so on, given that the central issue is the power relations between those who are in power and those who, despite their growing census numbers, are not.

[2]Reder and Davila (2005, p. 171) summarize the link between the societal-level great divide theories (Levi-Strauss, 1962) and the great divide theories in literacy.

[3]*Hybrid language practices* refers to the strategic use of the complete linguistic toolkit in the service of learning.

REFERENCES

Amano, K. (1999). Improvement of schoolchildren's reading and writing ability through the formation of linguistic awareness. In Y. Engeström, R. Mietinen, & R.-L. Punamäki (Eds.), *Perspectives on activity theory* (pp. 183–205). Cambridge, UK: Cambridge University Press.

Artiles, A. J. (1998). The dilemma of difference: Enriching the disproportionality discourse with theory and context. *The Journal of Special Education, 32*(1), 32–36.

Arzubiaga, A., Artiles, A. J., King, K., & Harris-Murri, N. (2008). Beyond research on cultural minorities: Challenges and implications of research as situated cultural practice. *Exceptional Children, 74,* 309–327.

Ball, A. F. (1992). Cultural preferences and the expository writing of African-American adolescents. *Written Communication, 9*(4), 501–532.

Ball, A. F. (1995). Text design patterns in the writing of urban African-American students: Teaching to the strengths of students in multicultural settings. *Urban Education, 30,* 253–289.

Ball, A. F. (2002). Chapter 3: Three decades of research on classroom life: Illuminating the classroom communicative lives of America's at-risk students. *Review of Research in Education, 26,* 71–111.

Ball, A. F., & Farr, M. (2003). Language varieties, culture and teaching the English language arts. In J. Flood, D. Lapp, J. Squire, & J. Jensen (Eds.), *Handbook of research on teaching the English language arts* (2nd ed., pp. 435–445). Mahwah, NJ: Lawrence Erlbaum.

Baratz, J., & Baratz, S. (1970). Early childhood intervention: The social scientific basis of institutionalized racism. *Harvard Educational Review, 39,* 29–50.

Baratz, S., & Baratz, J. (1970). Negro ghetto children and urban education: A cultural solution. *Social Education, 33,* 401–405.

Bartholomae, D. (1985). Inventing the university. In M. Rose (Ed.), *When a writer can't write: Studies in writer's block and other composing process problems* (pp. 134–165). New York: Guilford.

Bartholomae, D., & Petrosky, A. (Eds.). (1986). *Facts, artifacts, and counterfacts.* Upper Montclair, NJ: Boynton/Cook.

Barton, D. (2001). Directions for literacy research: Analysing language and social practices in a textually mediated world. *Language and Education, 15* (2/3), 92–104.

Barton, D., & Hamilton, M. (1998). *Local literacies: Reading and writing in one community.* London: Routledge.

Barton, D., Hamilton, M., & Ivanic, R. (Eds.) (2000). *Situated literacies: Reading and writing in context.* London: Routledge.

Bereiter, C., & Engelman, S. (1966). *Teaching disadvantaged children in the preschool.* New York: Prentice Hall.

Bloome, D., Puro, P., & Theodorou, E. (1989). Procedural display and classroom lessons. *Curriuculum Inquiry, 19*(3), 265–291.

Breneman, D. W., & Harlow, W. N. (1998). Remedial education: Costs and consequences. Remediation in Higher Education Symposium. *Thomas B. Fordham Foundation Report, 2*(9), 1–57.

Bruner, J. (1964). The course of cognitive growth. *American Psychologist, 19,* 1–15.

Bruner, J., Oliver, R., & Greenfield, P. (Eds.). *Studies in cognitive growth.* New York: Wiley.

Cazden, C. B. (1981). Performance before competence: Assistance to child discourse in the zone of proximal development. *The Quarterly Newsletter of the Laboratory of Comparative Human Cognition, 3*(1), 5–8.

Civil, M. (2006). Building on community knowledge: An avenue to equity in mathematics education. In N. Nasir & P. Cobb (Eds.), *Improving access to mathematics: Diversity and equity in the classroom* (pp. 105–117). New York: Teachers College Press.

Coe, R. M., & Gutiérrez, K. (1981). Using problem-solving procedures and process analysis to help student with writing problems. *College Composition and Communication, 32*(3), 262–271.

Cole, M. (1996). *Cultural psychology: A once and future discipline.* Cambridge, MA: Belknap Press of Harvard University Press.

Cole, M. (1998). Can cultural psychology help us think about diversity? *Mind, Culture, and Activity, 5*(4), 291–304.

Cole, M. (2005). Cross-cultural and historical perspectives on the developmental consequences of education. *Human Development, 48,* 195–216.

Cole, M., & Engeström, Y. (1993). A cultural–historical approach to distributed cognition. In G. Salomon (Ed.), *Distributed cognitions: Psychology and educational considerations* (pp. 1–46). Cambridge, UK: Cambridge University Press.

Cole, M., & Engeström, Y. (2007). Cultural–historical approaches to designing for development. In J. Valsiner & A. Rosa (Eds.), *The Cambridge handbook of sociocultural psychology* (pp. 484–507). Cambridge, UK: Cambridge University Press.

Cole, M., Engeström, Y., & Vásquez, O. A. (1997). *Mind, culture, and activity: Seminal papers from the Laboratory of Comparative Human Cognition.* Cambridge, UK: Cambridge University Press.

Cole, M., & Griffin, P. (1980). Cultural amplifiers reconsidered. In D. R. Olson (Ed.), *The social foundations of language and thought* (pp. 343–364). New York: Norton.

Cole, M., & Griffin, P. (1983). A socio-historical approach to re-mediation. *The Quarterly Newsletter of the Laboratory of Comparative Human Cognition, 5*(4), 69–74.

Cole, M., Hood, L., & McDermott, R. (1982). Ecological niche picking. In U. Neisser (Ed.), *Memory observed* (pp. 365–373). San Francisco: Freeman.

Cole, M., & Scribner, S. (1974). *Culture and thought: A psychological introduction.* New York: Wiley.

Cole, M., & Scribner, S. (1977). Developmental theories applied to cross-cultural cognitive research. *Annuals of the New York Academy of Sciences, 285,* 366–373.

Collins, J. (1995). Literacy and literacies. *Annual Review of Anthropology, 24,* 75–93.

Coulmans, F., & Ehlich, K. (Eds.). (1983). *Writing in focus.* New York: Mouton.

Cuban, L., & Tyack, D. B. (1988, November). *"Dunces," "shirkers," and "forgotten children": Historical descriptions and cures for low achievers.* Paper presented at the Conference for Accelerating the Education of At-Risk Students, Stanford University.

Dabney, M. G. (1980, April). *The gifted black adolescent: Focus upon the creative positives.* Paper presented at the Annual International Convention of the Council for Exceptional Children, Philadelphia. (ERIC Document Reproduction Service No. ED189767)

Deschenes, S., Cuban, L., & Tyack, D. B. (2001). Mismatch: Historical perspectives on schools and students who don't fit them. *Teachers College Record, 103*(4), 525–547.

Du Bois, W. E. B. (1989). *The souls of Black folks.* New York: Bantam. (Original work published 1903)

Engeström, Y. (1987). *Learning by expanding: An activity–theoretical approach to development research.* Helsinki, Finland: Orienta-Konsultit Oy.

Engeström, Y. (1998). Activity theory and individual and social transformation. In Engeström, Y., Miettinen, R., & Punamaki, R.-L. (Eds.), *Perspectives on activity theory* (pp. 19-38). Cambridge, UK: Cambridge University Press.

Engeström, Y. (1999). Learning by expanding: Ten years after. In Lernen durch Expansion (German edition), Introduction to *Learning by expanding.* Marbury, BdWi-Verlag. (Reinhe Internationale Studien zur Tatigkeitstheorie, Bd. 5; translated by Falk Seeger.)

Engeström, Y. (2001). Expansive learning at work: Toward an activity theoretical reconceptualization. *Journal of Education and Work, 14*(1), 133–156.

Engeström, Y. (2004). New forms of learning in co-configuration work. *Journal of Workplace Learning, 16,* 11–21.

Engeström, Y. (in press). A future of activity theory: A rough draft. In A. Sannino, H. Daniels, & K. Gutiérrez (Eds.), *Learning by expanding with activity theory.* Cambridge, UK: Cambridge University Press.

Engeström, Y., & Engeström, R. (1986). Developmental work research: The approach and an application in cleaning work. *Nordisk Pedagogik, 6*(1), 2–15.

Engeström, Y., Virkkunen, J., Helle, M., Pihlaja, J., & Poikela, R. (1996). The Change Laboratory as a tool for transforming work. *Lifelong Learning in Europe, 1*(2), 10–17.

Englert, C. S., & Mariage, T. V. (1996). A sociocultural perspective: Teaching ways-of-thinking and ways-of-talking in a literacy community. *Learning Disabilities Research and Practice, 11,* 157–167.

Englert, C. S., Tarrant, K. L., Mariage, T. V., & Oxer, T. (1994). Lesson talk as the work of reading groups: The effectiveness of two interventions. *Journal of Learning Disabilities, 27,* 165–185.

Erickson, F., & Gutiérrez, K. D. (2002). Culture, rigor, and science in educational research. *Educational Researcher, 31*(8), 21–24.

Foley, D. E. (1997). Deficit thinking models based on culture: The anthropological protest. In R. R. Valencia (Ed.), *The evolution of deficit thinking: Educational thought and practice* (pp. 113–131). Bristol, PA: Taylor and Francis.

Freedman, S. W. (1994). *Exchanging writing, exchanging cultures: Lessons in school reform from the United States and Great Britain.* Cambridge, MA: Harvard University Press.

Gee, J. (1991). *Sociolinguistics: Ideology and discourses.* London: Falmer Press.

Golby, M., & Gulliver, J. R. (1985). Whose remedies, whose ills? A critical review of remedial education. In C. J. Smith (Ed.), *New directions in remedial education* (pp. 7–19). London: Falmer Press.

González, N., Moll, L. C., & Amanti, C. (Eds.). (2005). *Funds of knowledge: Theorizing practice in households, communities, and classrooms.* Mahwah, NJ: Lawrence Erlbaum.

Goody, J. (1977). *The domestication of the savage mind.* Cambridge, UK: Cambridge University Press.

Goody, J. (1986). *The logic of writing and the organization of society.* Cambridge, UK: Cambridge University Press.

Goody, J. (1987). *The interface between the oral and the written.* Cambridge, UK: Cambridge University Press.

Goody, J., & Watt, I. (1963). The consequences of literacy. *Comparative Studies in Society and History, 5*(3), 304–345.

Greenfield, P. (1972). Oral or written language: The consequences for cognitive development in Africa, the United States, and England. *Language and Speech, 15,* 169–178.

Greenfield, P. M., & Bruner, J. S. (1966). Culture and cognitive growth. *International Journal of Psychology, 1*(2), 89–107.

Greenfield, P. M., & Bruner, J. S. (1969). Culture and cognitive growth. In D. A. Goslin (Ed.), *Handbook of socialization theory and research* (pp. 633–657). New York: Rand McNally.

Grimm, M. N. (1996). Rearticulating the work of the writing center. *College Composition and Communication, 47*(4), 523–548.

Gutiérrez, K. (2007a). Commentary on a sociocritical approach to literacy. In C. Lewis, P. Enciso, & E. Moje (Eds.), *Identity, agency, and power: Reframing sociocultural research on literacy* (pp. 115–120). Mahwah, NJ: Lawrence Erlbaum.

Gutiérrez, K. (2007b). Historicizing literacy. In M. Blackburn & C. Clark (Eds.), *Literacy research for political action* (pp. ix–xiii). New York: Lang.

Gutiérrez, K. (2008a). Developing a sociocritical literacy in the third space. *Reading Research Quarterly, 43*(2), 148–164.

Gutiérrez, K. (2008b, May). *When non-dominant languages are unmarked: Using students' linguistic repertoires of practice to learn.* Plenary talk at the annual meeting of the Center for Language Interaction and Culture, University of California, Los Angeles.

Gutiérrez, K., Baquedano-Lopez, P., & Tejeda, C. (1999). Rethinking diversity: Hybridity and hybrid language practices in the third space. *Mind, Culture, and Activity, 6*(4), 286–303.

Gutiérrez, K., & Correa-Chavez, M. (2006). What to do about culture? *Lifelong Learning in Europe, 3,* 152–159.

Gutiérrez, K., Hunter, J. D., & Arzubiaga, A. (2009). Re-mediating the university: Learning through sociocritical literacies. Pedagogies: *An International Journal, 4,* 1–23.

Gutiérrez, K., & Lee, C. (in press). Robust informal learning environments for youth from non-dominant groups and implications for literacy learning in formal schooling. In L. Morrow, R. Rueda, & D. Lapp (Eds.), *Handbook of research on literacy instruction: Issues of diversity, policy, and equity.* New York: Guilford.

Gutiérrez, K., & Orellana, M. (2006). The problem of English learners: Constructing genres of difference. *Research in the Teaching of English, 40*(4), 502–507.

Gutiérrez, K., & Rogoff, B. (2003). Cultural ways of learning: Individual traits and repertoires of practice. *Educational Researcher, 32*(5), 19–25.

Gutiérrez, K., Rymes, B., & Larson, J. (1995). Script, counterscript, and underlife in the classroom: James Brown versus *Brown v. Board of Education. Harvard Educational Review, 65*(3), 445–471.

Havelock, E. (1963). *Preface to Plato.* Cambridge, MA: Harvard University Press.

Heath, S. B. (1983). *Ways with words: Language, life and work in communities and classrooms.* Cambridge, UK: Cambridge University Press.

Hess, R. D., & Shipman, V. C. (1965). Early experience and the socialization of cognitive modes in children. *Child Development, 35,* 869–886.

Hull, G., & Rose, M. (1989). Rethinking remediation: Toward a social–cognitive understanding of problematic reading and writing. *Written Communication, 6*(2), 139–154.

Hull, G., & Rose, M. (1990). "This wooden shack place": The logic of an unconventional reading. *College Composition and Communication, 41*(3), 287–298.

Hull, G., Rose, M., Fraser, K. L., & Castellano, M. (1991). Remediation as social construct: Perspectives from an analysis of classroom discourse. *College Composition and Communication, 42*(3), 299–329.

Kulick, D., & Stroud, C. (1993). Conceptions and uses of literacy in a Papua New Guinean village. In B. Street (Ed.), *Cross-cultural approaches to literacy* (pp. 30–61). Cambridge, UK: Cambridge University Press.

Lee, C. D. (1995). A culturally based cognitive apprenticeship: Teaching African American high school students skills in literary interpretation. *Reading Research Quarterly, 30,* 608–630.

Lee, C. D. (1997). Bridging home and school literacies: Models for culturally responsive teaching, a case for African American English. In J. Flood, S. B. Heath, & D. Lapp (Eds.), *Handbook of research on teaching literacy through the communicative and visual arts* (pp. 334–345). New York: Macmillan.

Lee, C. D. (2000). Signifying in the zone of proximal development. In C. D. Lee & P. Smagorinsky (Eds.), *Vygotskian perspectives of literacy research: Constructing meaning through collaborative inquiry* (pp. 253–284). Cambridge, UK: Cambridge University Press.

Lee, C. D. (2007). *Culture, literacy, and learning: Taking bloom in the midst of the whirlwind.* New York: Teachers College Press.

Lee, C. D. (2008). 2008 Wallace Foundation Distinguished Lecture: The centrality of culture to the scientific study of learning and development: How an ecological framework in education research facilitates civic responsibility. *Educational Researcher, 37,* 267–279.

Levi-Strauss, C. (1962). *The savage mind.* Chicago: University of Chicago Press.

Lewis, O. (1966). The culture of poverty. *Scientific American, 215*(4), 19–25.

Luke, A. (1992). The body literate: Discourse and inscription in early literate training. *Linguistics and Education, 4,* 107–129.

Luria, A. R. (1932). *The nature of human conflicts.* New York: Liveright.

Luria, A. R. (1971). Toward the problem of the historical nature of psychological processes. *International Journal of Psychology, 6,* 259–272.

Luria, A. R. (2006). Disturbances of brain functions. In M. Cole, K. Levitin, & A. Luria (Eds.), *The autobiography of Alexander Luria: A dialogue with the making of mind*. Mahwah, NJ: Lawrence Erlbaum.

Manyak, P. C. (2001). Participation, hybridity, and carnival: A situated analysis of a dynamic literacy practice in a primary-grade English immersion class. *Journal of Literacy Research, 33*(3), 423–465.

Martínez, D. C., Moreno, D., Morales, P. Z., & Hopkins, M. B. (2008, May). *Structured English immersion in LAUSD secondary classrooms: One size fits all as a restrictive language policy*. Presentation at the annual conference of the University of California Linguistic Minority Research Institute, Sacramento, CA.

Martínez, R., Orellana, M. F., Pacheco, M., & Carbone, P. (2008). Found in translation: Connecting translating experiences to academic writing. *Language Arts, 85*(6), 421–431.

McDermott, R., Goldman, S., & Varenne, H. (2006). The cultural work of learning disabilities. *Educational Researcher, 35*(6), 12–17.

Mehan, H. (1979). *Learning lessons: Social organization in the classroom*. Cambridge, MA: Harvard University Press.

Minow, M. (1990). *Making all the difference: Inclusion, exclusion, and American law*. Ithaca, NY: Cornell University Press.

Moll, L. C. (2001). The diversity of schooling: A cultural–historical approach. In M. de la Luz Reyes & J. J. Halcón (Eds.), *The best for our children: Critical perspectives on literacy for Latino children* (pp. 13–28). New York: Teachers College Press.

Moll, L. C., Amanti, C., Neff, D., & Gonzalez, N. (1992). Funds of knowledge for teaching: Using a qualitative approach to connect homes to classrooms. *Theory Into Practice, 31*(2), 132–141.

Nasir, N. S. (2000). "Points ain't everything": Emergent goals and averages and percent understandings in the play of basketball among African-American students. *Anthropology & Education Quarterly, 31*(3), 283–305.

Nasir, N. S. (2005). Individual cognitive structuring and the sociocultural context: Strategy shifts in the game of dominoes. *Journal of the Learning Sciences, 14*(1), 5–34.

Nasir, N., Rosebery, A. S., Warren, B., & Lee, C. D. (2006). Learning as a cultural process: Achieving equity through diversity. In K. Sawyer (Ed.), *Handbook of the learning sciences* (pp. 489–504). Cambridge, UK: Cambridge University Press.

No Child Left Behind Act of 2001, Pub. L. No. 107-110.

North, S. (1998). The idea of a writing center. *College English, 46*, 433–446.

Oakes, J. (1985). *Keeping track: How schools structure inequality*. New Haven, CT: Yale University Press.

Ochs, E. (1988). *Culture and language development: Language acquisition and language socialization in a Samoan village*. Cambridge, UK: Cambridge University Press.

Ogbu, J. U. (1978). *Minority education and caste: The American system in cross-cultural perspective*. New York: Academic Press.

Ong, W. J. (1982). *Orality and literacy*. London: Methuen.

Orellana, M. F., & Reynolds, J. (2008). Cultural modeling: Leveraging bilingual skills for school paraphrasing tasks. *Reading Research Quarterly, 43*(1), 48–65.

Palincsar, A. S. (1984, April). *Reciprocal teaching: Working with the zone of proximal development*. Paper presented at the annual meeting of the American Educational Research Association, New Orleans, LA.

Palincsar, A. S. (1986). The role of dialogue in providing scaffolded instruction. *Educational Psychologist, 21*, 73–98.

Palincsar, A. S., & Brown, A. L. (1989). Classroom dialogues to promote self-regulated comprehension. In J. Brophy (Ed.), *Advances in research on teaching* (Vol. 1, pp. 35–71). Greenwich, CT: JAI Press.

Pavlenko, A., & Blackledge, A. (Eds.). (2004). *Negotiation of identities in multilingual contexts* (Vol. 45). Clevedon, UK: Multilingual Matters.

Perl, S. (1979). The composing processes of unskilled college writers. *Research in the Teaching of English, 13*(4), 317–336.

Reder, S., & Davila, E. (2005). Context and literacy practices. *Annual Review of Applied Linguistics, 25,* 170–187.

Rogoff, B. (1995). Observing sociocultural activity on three planes: Participatory appropriation, guided participation, and apprenticeship. In J. V. Wertsch, P. D. Rio & A. Alvarez (Eds.), *Sociocultural studies of the mind* (pp. 139–164). Cambridge, UK: Cambridge University Press.

Rogoff, B. (2003). *The cultural nature of human development.* Oxford, UK: Oxford University Press.

Rogoff, B., Paradise, R., Arauz, R. M., Correa-Chavez, M., & Angelillo, C. (2003). Firsthand learning through intent participation. *Annual Review of Psychology, 54*(1), 175–203.

Rose, M. (1985). The language of exclusion: Writing instruction at the university. *College English, 47*(4), 341–359.

Rose, M. (1988). Narrowing the mind and page: Remedial writers and cognitive reductionism. *College Composition and Communication, 39*(3), 267-302.

Rose, M. (1989). The politics of remediation. In *Lives on the boundary: The struggles and achievements of America's underprepared* (pp. 167–204). New York: Free Press.

Rose, M. (2004). *The mind at work: Valuing the intelligence of the American worker.* New York: Viking.

Rosebery, A. S., Warren, B., & Conant, F. R. (1992). Appropriating scientific discourse: Findings from language minority classrooms. *Journal of the Learning Sciences, 2*(1), 61–94.

Ryan, W. (1971). *Blaming the victim.* New York: Random House.

Schieffelin, B., & Ochs, E. (Eds.). (1986). *Language socialization across cultures.* Cambridge, UK: Cambridge University Press.

Schifini, A., Short, D., & Tinajero, J. V. (2001). *High point: Success in language, literature, content.* Carmel, CA: Hampton-Brown.

Scribner, S. (1976). Situating the experiment in cross-cultural research. In K. F. Riegel & J. A. Meacham (Eds.), *The developing individual in a changing world: Historical and cultural issues* (pp. 310-321). The Hague, Netherlands: Mouton.

Scribner, S. (1985). Vygotsky's uses of history. In J. V. Wertsch (Ed.), *Culture, communication, and cognition: Vygotskian perspectives* (pp. 119–145). Cambridge, UK: Cambridge University Press.

Scribner, S., & Cole, M. (1973). Cognitive consequences of formal and informal education. *Science, 182*(4112), 553–559.

Scribner, S., & Cole, M. (1978). Literacy without schooling: Testing for intellectual effects. *Harvard Educational Review, 29*(2), 448-461.

Scribner, S., & Cole, M. (1981). *The psychology of literacy.* Cambridge, MA: Harvard University Press.

Shaughnessy, M. (1977). *Errors and expectations: A guide for the teacher of basic writers.* Oxford, UK: Oxford University Press.

Smitherman, G. (2000). *Talkin that talk: Language, culture, and education in African America.* New York: Routledge.

Spring, J. (1997). *The American school.* New York: McGraw-Hill.

Street, B. V. (1984). *Literacy in theory and practice.* Cambridge, UK: Cambridge University Press.

Street, B. V. (1993). *Cross-cultural approaches to literacy.* Cambridge, UK: Cambridge University Press.

Street, B. V. (2003). What's "new" in new literacy studies? Critical approaches to literacy in theory and practice. *Current Issues in Comparative Education, 5*(2), 1–14.

Street, B. V. (2004). Academic literacies and the "new orders": Implications for research and practice in student writing in higher education. *LATISS: Learning and Teaching in the Social Sciences, 1*(1), 9–20.

Street, B. V., & Lea, M. (2006). The "academic literacies" model: Theory and applications. *Theory Into Practice 45*(4), 368–377.

Teräs, M. (2007). *Intercultural learning and hybridity in the culture laboratory.* Unpublished doctoral thesis, University of Helsinki, Finland.

Trent, S. C., Artiles, A. J., & Englert, C. S. (1998). From deficit thinking to social constructivism: A review of theory, research, and practice in special education. *Review of Research in Education, 23,* 277–307.

Trueba, H. T. (1988). Culturally based explanations of minority students' academic achievement. *Anthropology & Education Quarterly, 19*(3), 270–287.

Trueba, H. T. (1990). The role of culture in literacy acquisition: An interdisciplinary approach to qualitative research. *International Journal of Qualitative Studies in Education, 3*(1), 1–13.

Trueba, H. T. (2002). Multiple ethnic, racial, and cultural identities in action: From marginality to a new cultural capital in modern society. *Journal of Latinos and Education, 1*(1), 7–28.

U.S. National Commission on Excellence in Education. (1983). *A nation at risk: The imperative for educational reform.* Washington, DC: Author.

Valencia, R. R. (1997). Conceptualizing the notion of deficit thinking. In R. R. Valencia (Ed.), *The evolution of deficit thinking: Educational thought and practice* (pp. 1–12). London: Falmer Press.

Valencia, R. R., & Pearl, A. (1997). Epilogue: The future of deficit thinking in educational thought and practice. In R. R. Valencia (Ed.), *The evolution of deficit thinking: Educational thought and practice* (pp. 242–256). London: Falmer Press.

Valencia, R. R., & Solorzano, D. G. (1997). Contemporary deficit thinking. In R. R. Valencia (Ed.), *The evolution of deficit thinking: Educational thought and practice* (pp. 160–210). London: Falmer Press.

Van der Veer, R., & Valsiner, J. (1991). *Understanding Vygotsky: A quest for synthesis.* Cambridge: Blackwell.

Vásquez, O. (2003). *La clase mágica: Imagining optimal possibilities in a bilingual community of learners.* Mahwah, NJ: Lawrence Erlbaum.

Vossoughi, S., & Gutiérrez, K. (2008). *"Lifting off the ground to return anew": Documenting and designing for equity and transformation through social design experiments.* Unpublished manuscript, Center for the Study of Urban Literacies, University of California, Los Angeles.

Warren, B., Ballenger, C., Ogonowski, M., Rosebery, A. S., & Hudicourt-Barnes, J. (2001). Rethinking diversity in learning science: The logic of everyday sense-making. *Journal of Research in Science Teaching, 38,* 529–552.

Yosso, T. J. (2005). Whose culture has capital? A critical race theory discussion of community cultural wealth. *Race Ethnicity and Education, 8*(1), 69–91.

Zehm, S. J. (1973). *Educational misfits: A study of poor performers in the English class 1825–1925.* Unpublished dissertation, Stanford University, Stanford, CA.

Chapter 9

The Education of Children in Im/migrant Families

ANGELA E. ARZUBIAGA
SILVIA C. NOGUERÓN
AMANDA L. SULLIVAN
Arizona State University

This chapter examines research on the education of children in immigrant families, focusing on the ways the children and the families have been constructed
in public arenas and conceptualized and classified in research discussions. Throughout
the chapter, we use the term *im/migrant* to denote those who have been labeled
immigrant, migrant, and *refugee,* including the undocumented. Although the distinction between each of these terms is critical—because they carry social and legal
implications—it is important to note that the terms are not always mutually exclusive or permanent.[1] Immigrants move to a country to seek permanent residence and
migrants move to find itinerant work. However, migrants may change their initial
intent to return to their home country and immigrants may also change their intent
to stay. In addition, families include members who fall within different immigration
categories such as siblings who are citizens and who are undocumented. Nonetheless,
what children of im/migrant families share is the risk of becoming educationally
underserved, being socially neglected, and being identified as problematic. Their
families are likely to live apart from each other for extended periods, they are
more likely to be mistakenly labeled and placed in special education, and their
educational paths are burdened with difficulties such as the fear of their parents'
deportation.

The numbers of im/migrant children in schools have increased throughout the
world. The principal receiving areas are North America, Western Europe, the Persian
Gulf, Asia and the Pacific, and the Southern Cone of South America (Massey,
1999). In the United States, one out of every four children younger than the age of
8 lives in a family where at least one parent is an immigrant (Foundation for Child
Development, 2007). Approximately 93% of children of immigrants were born in

Review of Research in Education
March 2009, Vol. 33, pp. 246-271
DOI: 10.3102/0091732X08328243
© 2009 AERA. http://rre.aera.net

the United States and are therefore citizens. Asian groups account for nearly one quarter of these children, and Latin American groups account for almost one half of the country's total immigrant population; among Latin American groups, Mexicans comprise the largest group of immigrants (Hernandez, Denton, & Macartney, 2007; Schmidley, 2001). Im/migrant families in the United States are settling in traditional ports of entry, gateway cities, and nontraditional urban, suburban, and rural areas.

The topic and range of issues associated with children in im/migrant families are embedded in broader immigration issues of the 21st century that have a force of their own, referred to by Stuart Hall as the *unstoppable mélange of histories and cultures* (MacCabe, 2007). This mélange, brought about with the mobilization of people, presents a host of concerns increasingly studied from multidisciplinary and multi-leveled perspectives. Of particular importance to the study of young children of im/migrant families is that people from unevenly developed societies live within the same countries. Of greater relevance is that these countries'[2] policies and laws increasingly exclude and/or control immigrants[3] (Suvin, 2007) while at the same time include economic and financial globalization measures that have set forth the mobilization, across national borders, of the very people they marginalize or exclude. People most clearly affected by these policies or the lack of these inclusion policies are im/migrants responding to the push and pull forces of economic globalization. They are particularly affected because their settlement in the countries that receive them is associated with the precondition of membership in the underclass.

Not all children of im/migrant families, however, receive the same treatment. Divergent paths of mobility have been explained by segmented assimilation theory (A. Portes & Zhou, 1993; Zhou, 1997). The theory suggests that persistent ethnic differences across generations have challenged traditional assimilation theory, which argued for the eventual integration of im/migrants to *mainstream*. A group's premigration status, including class, parental educational levels, income, and the structural and sociocultural features of the contexts of reception, account for the type of mobility pathways children are afforded (Cornfield & Arzubiaga, 2004; A. Portes & MacLeod, 1999; A. Portes & Rumbaut, 2001). Migration from Cuba, for example, during the fall of Batista drove upper- and middle-class families to migrate to the United States. In the United States, they were received as welcomed exiles. The experiences of the Cuban children who arrived in the 1960s and their adaptation cannot be generalized to other groups or compared to the experiences of the majority of today's new im/migrants. Fix and Zimmermann (1997) argued that U.S. immigration policies are policies of exclusion; that is, they fail to incorporate what is known about how immigrant families have adapted to life in the United States or their contributions to different areas of the country, such as to the labor force. Rather, these policies contribute to im/migrants' interests not being fully incorporated in societal discourses, deepen social divides, and support notions of im/migrants as second-class citizens.

Consequently, the discourses and (mis)representations of im/migrant families in public discussions extend often to questions about im/migrant families' roles in the education of children. Because the family is the primary social and learning space for young children, im/migrant families are subject for scrutiny. However, the im/migrant *family* often becomes just a backdrop or afterthought to the politics of inclusion or exclusion playing out in public debates. Citizenship, and its associated privileges, becomes part of the discourses and the justification for exclusionary views. At the extreme are media depictions of immigrants in metaphors such as "animals" or "as debased people" or "parasites or disease" (Santa Ana, 1999). Meanwhile, significant concerns, which should be at the foreground of these discourses, fall to the wayside. Substantial matters, such as the consequences of exclusion, which children of im/migrant families live with on a day-to-day basis, are often ignored.

The remainder of this chapter is divided into five sections. We first present some of the pressing issues that inform and shape the discussion on immigration, children, and families. Next, we review the research literature by focusing on the construction of the im/migrant family and child. We then challenge images in research and popular discourses on children of im/migrant families and education. In the fourth section, we examine issues facing children of im/migrant families within expanding contexts, including issues raised across disciplines. We close the chapter with final considerations.

PRESSING ISSUES IN IM/MIGRATION, CHILDREN, AND FAMILIES: BACKGROUND AND CONTEXT

The social stratification of people is inherent in immigration debates. In the case of Mexicans in the United States, current debates about building a wall to prevent immigration from Mexico fail to acknowledge the descendants of the inhabitants from territories incorporated by the United States and to address the presence of the estimated 12 million (Passel, Capps, & Fix, in 2004, estimated it at 9.3 million) undocumented persons who have already built a life for their families.[4] De Genova (2002) argued that undocumented migrations have been constituted not to exclude people physically but to include them socially under imposed conditions of enforced, protracted vulnerability.

Discussions about immigration and immigrant families assume a special tone when they focus on children. The vulnerability of the children of im/migrants is not typically considered when their potential contribution to social security is taken into account. Public discourses about immigration take on a different character when children in immigrant families' needs are mapped against the aging populations of traditional superpowers. For example, in the United States, the implication is that immigrants will help to pay for the mounting social security of a population ready to retire. At the same time, given immigrants' higher birth rates, they will produce workers for nations that show an increasing decline in births (McLoyd, 1998). However, it is not certain that the children of im/migrants will be afforded educational opportunities that allow rupture from social inclusion under conditions of enforced protracted vulnerability. Whether these workers or the children of im/migrants will be able to meet the technological demands of the future and be prepared to compete in new economies becomes a question, as long as investment in the education of the children of im/migrants is contested. The debates are fraught with contradictions such as those surrounding the language of instruction. Claims that English Only is ultimately in the best interest of the child stand in contrast to the education provided in elite schools that offers students the opportunity to become fluent in languages other than English. In countries where English is not the dominant language, children learn English, along with other languages.

These debates have implications for the role of im/migrant families and the changing demographics of the student body in schools. In the United States, one in five or 20% of school-aged children have im/migrant parents, and projections suggest that this number will increase significantly in the next decades (Chapa & De la Rosa, 2004; Hernandez et al., 2007). One of the paradoxes is that as the new economies are increasingly diverse and deterritorialized, there is an increasing demand for cultural competencies. Yet, public debates often reflect concerns about how im/migrant children are making schools worse off by draining resources, slowing other students' learning, and preventing districts from meeting education standards (e.g., see Bodfield, 2008, and comments made by the article's readers).

Families from many im/migrant groups are marginalized and become representative of what is wrong with society, as different national/cultural/ethnic groups are demonized (Balibar, 1990) and/or ascribed negative stereotypes (McDermott & Varenne, 1995). A myriad of social problems is projected onto these demonized im/migrant groups. At the same time, the groups fulfill a scapegoat role for communities. Some have argued that the difference between U.S. immigration in the 20th and immigration in the 21st century is that today's im/migrants are predominantly *people of color* from Asia and Latin America whereas yesterday's immigrants were European, moving into a country dominated by people of European ancestry (A. Portes, 1997; Massey, 1999; M. Suárez-Orozco, 2001). In addition to their status as outsiders, they are subject to biases ascribed to race.

The academic discourses and public discussions that have emerged over time are fueled by concerns about "the achievement gap" between students from nondominant groups[5] and the dominant group. The achievement gap refers to disparities in test scores between nondominant groups and dominant groups. In the United States, the concern focuses on the lower achievement of African Americans and Hispanics or Latinos. The preponderance of studies on the achievement gap from several fields examines the gap along racial and ethnic lines. The academic prospects for the children of immigrants are thought to be grim because the majority of recent im/migrants in the United States are Hispanics or from nondominant groups that are classified as low achievers.

The focus on the achievement gap between groups has been eloquently turned around by the notion of an *educational debt* (Ladson-Billings, 2006). Ladson-Billings (2006) directed us to examine the political, financial, and other structural inequities related to the schooling of students classified as low achievers. She proposed economic investment to change the inequity of the education of historically exploited and disenfranchised groups as a financial, moral, and ethical debt. Turning attention away from students' test scores and ethnic or racial groups' scholastic achievement, she made evident how thinking surrounding the achievement gap has been much like a Maginot Line—or the tendency to concentrate on the wrong front (Gillan, 2002). The notion of an educational debt relates to the children of im/migrants as they are less likely to have access to high-quality day care or preschool (Magnuson, Lahaie, & Waldfogel, 2006) and are more likely to be poor and to attend segregated schools where financial investments are low in comparison to the schools of the dominant group (Kohler & Lazarín, 2007; Orfield & Lee, 2006).

Pointing to inequities as a legacy of longstanding exploitations, Ladson-Billings (2006) made the case for an educational debt by noting African Americans' contribution to the economy of the United States during slavery and the labor contributions of Mexicans. Whether this ethical or moral obligation can be accepted and responsibility for it assumed remains to be decided in the public arena. However, debates over educational opportunity—namely, commitment to equal availability, accessibility, and adequacy of education—rarely take into account the needs of children of im/migrants (Ruiz de Velasco, Fix, & Clewell, 2000). The question as to whether the United States has a financial, moral, or ethical obligation to improve the inequities related to the education of im/migrant children is not as important as the notion that it can no longer afford to ignore them.

In another vein, the academic discourse related to the scholastic achievement of children from nondominant groups, in particular children of im/migrants, has been attributed to schools' limited use of the learning practices or funds of knowledge (N. González, Moll, & Amanti, 2005) of groups other than the dominant group. Despite the unstoppable mélange of histories and cultures, schools still privilege and officially recognize a limited body of student knowledge. Banks and his colleagues (2007) emphasized learning as a lifelong endeavor and drove home this point by underscoring that formal schooling barely represents 18.5% of a high school graduate's learning during a lifetime. Scholars are now challenging assumptions and practices around what counts as learning and whose knowledge counts while considering the knowledge of marginalized groups, including im/migrants (Green & Luke, 2006; Kelly, Luke, & Green, 2008; Lam, 2006). Whose knowledge counts is tied to notions of who belongs or what belongs in schools. A focus on *learning from* marginalized and disenfranchised groups requires a shift away from the legacy of deficit theories along racial, ethnic, and class lines that have shaped, in the past, research on diverse populations (Arzubiaga, Artiles, King, & Murri, 2008).

The im/migrant child and family have been a victim of narrow foci about whose knowledge counts and how to make use of the knowledge that students bring to school. Im/migrants are particularly vulnerable to such portrayals because of sedentarist assumptions associated with place that lead to defining displacement (and, therefore, the displaced im/migrant) not as a sociopolitical context but as an inner pathological condition of the displaced (Malkki, 1992). Sedentarist assumptions refer to equating country or a demarcated territory to culture and the consequent conflation or naturalization of country as equal to culture, language, race, and identity. These views pathologize im/migrants for not having what they lost with their migration. In this sense, children in im/migrant families are *at risk* or *resilient* when they make it and worthy of study as outside the norm.

THE EDUCATION OF CHILDREN IN IMMIGRANT FAMILIES: THEMES FROM THE RESEARCH LITERATURE

Research on the education of young children of im/migrants is of particular relevance because of its implications for children's future educational trajectories. Although research on higher education and the college pipeline has examined issues related to the education of im/migrant youth, there has been less attention focused on younger children. In recognition of this gap in research, the Foundation for Child Development created a New American Children Initiative that aims to build a knowledge base about the well-being of young children living in immigrant families. The following is a review of literature on young children of im/migrant families that presents different conceptualizations of the issues and that takes into consideration that *immigration, family,* and *children* are terms that rely on political and social constructions. The purpose of focusing on these conceptualizations and classifications is to examine the cultural nature of research in this area. Bowker and Star (1999) reminded us of the importance of examining conceptualizations and classification systems and the likelihood that classifications translate into infrastructure and become entrenched. The processes are of naturalization of the political category, such as when the term *migrant worker* renders invisible the family that may accompany the itinerant farm worker; in this sense, the classification creates layers of invisibility.

We have limited this review to studies appearing in peer-reviewed and data-based articles. They were selected because they examined some aspect of the education of children—preschool through eighth grade—in im/migrant families. In addition, they make reference to family or parents, have been published between 1997 and 2007, and have been conducted in the United States. Theoretical and/or literature review papers were not included in the analysis, although they were used to inform our work. Articles were gathered through a comprehensive search, based on aforementioned criteria, via a range of electronic search engines. The search yielded several hundred articles that the authors reviewed. Based on their review, 32 articles were selected. Of the studies, 12 relied exclusively on qualitative methods, whereas 2 employed mixed methods. The remaining 17 studies were composed of quantitative analyses. The sample sizes ranged from 1 to almost 18,000. In particular, 7 of the articles selected featured analyses of national databases, such as the National Education Longitudinal Study of 1988 (NELS) and the Early Childhood Longitudinal Survey–Kindergarten Cohort (ECLS-K; e.g., Hao & Bonstead-Bruns, 1998; Magnuson et al., 2006).

Pan-Ethnic, Country, Race, Ethnicity, and Inequity

Of the articles reviewed, 22% used pan-ethnic (i.e., various ethnicities in one term) categories to describe cultural lines (e.g., Bhattacharya, 2000). The most common category used was Asian, although 1 study also used European as a category. In addition, 14 articles (44%) used country categories to study the population or participants (e.g., Korean, Mexican, and Nicaraguan; e.g., see A. Portes & MacLeod, 1999; Feliciano, 2006). Clearly, such classifications mask multiple layers of difference within groups. Country, race, or ethnicity is not equal to language and to culture. A call for studies that can disaggregate the groups and consider their diversity and adaptability to the wide range of contexts of reception such as nontraditional settlement areas is in order.

Almost half of the articles included *race* or *ethnicity* as variables, and many authors used the terms interchangeably. However, less than one third of the articles that classified participants by race or ethnicity provided a rationale for the use of the classification. Only one author (Aldous, 2006) defined ethnicity, and only three provided a rationale for the use of such categories (Aldous, 2006; Glick & Hohmann-Marriott, 2007; Kao & Rutherford, 2007). The articles within an anthropological framework were more likely to place ethnicity and race within a sociocultural context. Only six studies explained how they determined race or ethnicity. Of these, five relied on parent or student self-report (e.g., Crosnoe, 2007; Dorner, Orellana, & Li-Grining, 2007; P. Portes, 1999); the remaining study used census reporting. Because few studies clearly defined the classifications used, it is not surprising that almost one half conflated race with ethnicity.

The conflation of race and ethnicity and the generalized practice of not explaining how participants were classified within these categories is cause for concern. However, what needs more attention, given the widespread use of these categories, is an examination of rationales for their usage. Researchers need to include explicit rationales for the usage of such classifications. This will lead us to more careful consideration and use of such categories. A lack of rationales for usage of these classifications can lead to erroneous causal inferences such as "Hispanic ethnicity is the cause of underachievement." Use of an ethnic or racial category when it is tied to the inequities groups experience makes sense for im/migrant groups.

Moreover, although issues around inequity, disinvestment, and marginalization are common denominators for the majority of new immigrants, only eight articles considered or discussed these issues. Articles that recognized social inequity determined it to be an underlying feature of the lives of im/migrants (e.g., Aspiazu, Bauer, & Spillett, 1998). This omission in the literature points to a need for greater focus on inequity, disinvestment, and marginalization given that the majority of the new im/migrants tend to be marginalized and affected by inequity and disinvestment.

Social Constructions of the Children in Im/migrant Families

Within the majority of articles in which educational achievement was the focus, achievement was defined as standardized math or reading scores (e.g., Glick & Hohmann-Marriott, 2007; Hao & Bonstead-Bruns, 1998). Only one study included assessment in both English and the students' native language (Bowler, Smith, Schwarzer, Perez-Arce, & Kreutzer, 2002). Two other studies (Dorner et al.,

2007; Glick & Hohmann-Marriott, 2007) relied on school grades. Only one study defined education and achievement more broadly so as to include parents' funds of knowledge and the learning experiences that take place at home (Pérez Carreón, Drake, & Barton, 2005). Only one author examined children's beliefs and perceptions about education (Bhattacharya, 2000).

More than one third of the studies used the traditional generational classification system to describe immigrant status (Louie, 2005; Rumbaut, 2004), as first- and second-generation participants. However, some studies placed first- and second-generation students into one "immigrant" category (e.g., Crosnoe, 2005, 2006) in order to make comparisons with a nonimmigrant or "native" category. Two studies (A. Portes & MacLeod, 1999; Glick & Hohmann-Marriott, 2007) referred to the 1.5 generation, which applies to those who arrived to the United States at an early age. The remaining studies (almost 20%) compared different generations of immigrants (see Chiswick & DebBurman, 2006; Kao & Rutherford, 2007), and others focused on one particular generation across different nationalities (e.g., Feliciano, 2006).

One core of studies (31%) did not rely on the traditional generational categorization when describing their populations. For example, Hao and Bonstead-Bruns (1998) and Magnuson and her colleagues (2006) compared native-born versus immigrant children. Other studies referred to the students as "children of immigrant parents," specifying the parents' origin. For example, Bowler et al. (2002) used "children of Mexican immigrants," and Sanchez and Orellana (2006) described their participants as "children of Mexican parents." Two studies based on the same sample (García Coll et al., 2002; Szalacha, Marks, Lamarre, & García Coll, 2005) differentiated immigrant communities from refugee communities.

Throughout several of the articles, im/migrant children's English proficiency was made problematic (e.g., Bhattacharya, 2000; McLaughlin, Liljestrom, Lim, & Meyers, 2002; Romanowski, 2003), and children were described as entering school with fewer requisite skills than their native peers (Magnuson et al., 2006). Among migrant children specifically, this *undereducation* was attributed to the group's highly mobile lifestyle (Romanowski, 2003). Poverty and poor quality schooling were also identified as factors that undermined the success of im/migrant students (Roopnarine, Krishnakumar, Metindogan, & Evans, 2006).

Several studies (25%) specifically referred to students' language differences as deficits and focused on the implications of these deficits for their academic trajectories (25%). A few studies examined the lack of English language proficiency (Bhattacharya, 2000; Riggs & Greenberg, 2004) and of children's involvement at an early age in institutionalized day care (Crosnoe, 2007; Magnuson et al., 2006). Still, other studies addressed the deficit or lack of alignment in social capital or parenting styles and emphasized issues of poverty and hardships (e.g., Kao & Rutherford, 2007; Roopnarine et al., 2006). Hao and Bonstead-Bruns (1998) specifically noted that Mexican background could be *harmful* in terms of educational expectations, but balanced this assertion by recognizing benefits of home language retention for Mexican students.

A few studies portrayed children in a positive light and emphasized the strength and flexibility displayed in children's ability to navigate cultures and languages. For example, Sanchez and Orellana (2006) studied children's roles as translators and mediators during parent and teacher conferences; Dorner and her colleagues (2007) examined students' role as language brokers and recognized language brokering as a practice that was favorably associated with academic achievement. Szalacha and her colleagues (2005) described academic pathways of two immigrant and one refugee community; a large percentage of trajectories were labeled as *positive,* and a few were defined as *negative.*

Social Constructions of Im/migrant Families

Research studies on im/migrant families are largely concerned with the families' abilities to educate and raise their children. A recurring theme in these studies focuses on parent involvement. However, parent involvement was often narrowly defined in terms of parents' direct contact with school; framed in terms of classroom volunteering or attendance at Parent Teacher Organization (PTO) meetings, school board meetings, or parent teacher conferences (Kao & Rutherford, 2007; L. Lopez, Sanchez, & Hamilton, 2000); and emphasizing parent-child support activities such as homework assistance (Aldous, 2006). The studies often referred to the low levels of such involvement within immigrant families (Bhattacharya, 2000; Glick & Hohmann-Marriott, 2007). They noted that several parents preferred indirect contact, apparently because of parents' discomfort with their limited proficiency in English (Glick & Hohmann-Marriott, 2007); however, others emphasized the power dynamics in communications between school personnel and families (Pérez Carreón et al., 2005).

Pérez Carreón and colleagues (2005) and G. Lopez, Scribner, and Mahitivanichcha (2001) noted that such restricted definitions of parent involvement ignore many meaningful activities and give little attention to the experiences of im/migrant parents. These authors instead offered a multidimensional perspective on parent involvement and engagement in their children's educational experiences that allowed for a range of activities both in and out of school that ultimately supported their children's academic growth. Pérez Carreón and colleagues highlighted parents' efforts to negotiate inequitable spaces in school and the multifaceted nature of presence in both formal and informal spaces.

Throughout the studies, differences in family engagement were both explicitly and implicitly linked to perceived differences in the value placed on education. Such values were positioned as both risk and protective factors. Im/migrant parents of Asian descent were viewed as prioritizing education and as immigrating to seek better educational and economic opportunities for themselves and their children (Bhattacharya, 2000). In addition, the social structure of Asian im/migrant communities was perceived as supporting acculturation relative to the American educational systems (Zhou & Kim, 2006).

Parents' high aspirations and value of education, regardless of direct involvement with school activities or academic tasks, were found to be related to higher achievement (Aldous, 2006). Roopnarine and colleagues (2006) emphasized the importance that Caribbean families placed on education. Bhattacharya (2000) also emphasized the value Asian families placed on schooling as a feature that promoted higher achievement despite limited contact with school. Some also noted that Mexican parents held educators in high esteem and valued education as a means to improve economic status (L. Lopez et al., 2000). While authors in these studies recognized that most immigrant groups value education, others (Hao & Bonstead-Bruns, 1998; Zhou & Kim, 2006) suggested that Chinese and Korean im/migrants' success was specifically due to such values and the structural features of their communities. They attributed the lower achievement of other groups to their lack of value for education and lack of social capital. For example, Hao and Bonstead-Bruns (1998) proposed that "Chinese background is beneficial for children's achievement, but Mexican background is harmful" (p. 175), due to the groups' divergent expectations. Asian cultures were described as placing greater emphasis on education, ambition, and persistence and described as providers of better role models and community-based educational opportunities.

Both Mexicans and Koreans were described as showing deference to teachers (McLaughlin et. al., 2002; Sohn & Wang, 2006; Souto-Manning, 2007). McLaughlin and colleagues (2002) noted school was perceived as the teachers' domain for Latino parents. Caribbean parents, however, acted as strong advocates for their children and frequently initiated contact, in addition to supporting a range of educational activities for their children (Roopnarine et al., 2006).

It is important to note that in a time when deficit frameworks are being questioned, most of the articles (64%) described im/migrant families along deficit lines. The arguments focused on what was described as a lack of social and cultural capital. For example, lack of understanding of the American school system was repeatedly noted as an obstacle for immigrant families (McLaughlin et al., 2002; Schaller, Rocha, & Barshinger, 2007; Sohn & Wang, 2006). Parents were characterized as in need of guidance (Schaller et al., 2007) because they lacked an understanding of school culture, the implicit social rules that permeate schools, their rights within educational systems, and the organization of educational systems (Pérez Carreón et al., 2005).

The importance of socioeconomic status (SES) in providing access to cultural, social, and financial capital, including access to good neighborhoods and schools, and support from ethnic entrepreneurs, was also emphasized, with lower SES constructed as a detriment to children's school outcomes (Zhou & Kim, 2006). Lower-class status was used to explain, in part, the segregation of children of im/migrants into "problematic sectors of the educational system" (Crosnoe, 2005, p. 295) and was identified as a primary cause of im/migrant students' low school readiness (Crosnoe, 2007). Social, economic, and educational "instability" of parents was positioned as creating a host of difficulties, including isolation, stress, and environmental disadvantages. Economic resources were identified as necessary to support learning (Magnuson et al., 2006) such that the low income of many im/migrant families was perceived as a risk.

Not surprisingly, two other issues identified as problematic were limited English proficiency (Bhattacharya, 2000; McLaughlin et al., 2002) and parents' educational levels (Aspiazu et al., 1998; Magnuson et al., 2006; Schaller et al., 2007). Language proficiency in English, or lack thereof, was described as a barrier for Asian and Latino im/migrant parents alike. In particular, Korean mothers were described as seeking indirect means of contact and showing reluctance to become involved in schools because of hesitancy to speak directly to educators (Sohn & Wang, 2006). In addition, these authors highlighted how cultural differences had an impact on relationships between teachers and parents. Korean mothers did not perceive themselves as equal partners and were hesitant to express disagreement with teachers. Other studies noted that language differences prevented parents from helping with schoolwork, which limited their possibilities of helping their children with school tasks in general (Aspiazu et al., 1998).

Few authors (36%) positioned im/migrant families as educators; rather, families were positioned as in need of education. Research in line with the family as educator model described families' values and their efforts to support children's school achievement. However, within this small group, only a couple described education more broadly than a focus on standardized test scores. These articles emphasized the importance of the families' role in shaping children's educational experiences and knowledge development more in line with a learning from families perspective. Learning was described as a continuous practice that involved family literacy activities (e.g., Roopnarine et al., 2006) as well as other tasks not considered traditionally academic or part of sanctioned official knowledge (Pérez Carreón et al., 2005).

IM/MIGRANT FAMILIES AND THEIR CHILDREN: CHALLENGING IMAGES IN RESEARCH AND POPULAR DISCOURSES

In the review thus far, we have discussed empirical findings from research studies in education primarily. These studies, as we noted, are relatively few. However, there are ongoing discussions—in scholarly, research, practice, policy, and popular arenas. This section discusses some of the driving themes in the conceptualization of the im/migrant family and their children. The themes on the family suggest they are elaborations on the question: Can the im/migrant family contribute to the education of their children? The themes on children often appear to address the question: Can children of im/migrant families be more similar to children of White middle-class U.S. *Americans*?

Can the Im/migrant Family Contribute to the Education of Their Children?

Characteristics of the *family* revolve around interrelated political, ideological, and economic definitions. From a political perspective, it can be argued that the family remains as one of the main institutions whose charge is to prepare and educate the future citizens of the nation. Historically however, im/migrants families' role in this endeavor has been questioned and not considered worthy of debate (e.g., Rogoff,

2003). For example, immigrants tested upon entrance to Ellis Island during the early 20th century were found to be of lower intelligence, based on IQ scores, and therefore less capable of educating their children. Consequently, it was the duty of the state to provide an education for im/migrant children. Today, im/migrant children are tested as part of the requirements of legislation such as No Child Left Behind and are found lacking, despite the questionable comparability of test results (Abedi & Dietel, 2004).

However, differences in regard to the contexts of reception, or the structural and sociocultural features of where im/migrants settle, add to the complexity related to whether the education of im/migrant children is even on the table in discussions on the well-being of children. In areas of the United States where immigration is a recent phenomenon, such as the Southeast and rural Midwest, until recently, im/migrant families were rendered invisible. Studies on immigration were mostly about labor and economics without consideration of the families, including the children accompanying the new labor force (Villenas, 2002). The *New Latino Diaspora* studies[6] have emerged to account for this gap in the field (Wortham, Murillo, & Hamann, 2002). Concerns about the expenses children of im/migrants represent contribute to how families are conceptualized along economic dimensions. Murillo (2002) pointed to the binary of immigrants as takers versus givers and the irony of conceptualizing exploited im/migrant laborers as such. Instead, these educational anthropology studies depict the im/migrant family as agents of cultural continuity, change, improvisation, and contestation as they adapt to difficult, discriminatory practices and policies.

Such discriminatory practices bring to the foreground the issues related to immigrant families and the tensions surrounding their presence as new im/migrants. "A family or a crowd?" asked an article in *The New York Times* (Caldwell, 2006) in regard to the growing number of homes occupied by im/migrant families. In Manassas, Virginia, attempts were made to restrict occupancy of houses to only *nuclear families* in response to the surge in im/migrant *households*.

Whereas *family* and *household* are defined culturally, it is important to consider the distinction between the two terms (Netting, Wilk, & Arnould, 1984). A critical feature of family is kinship that does not locate members as necessarily living together. Household, on the other hand, incorporates individuals who participate in tasks and shared activities common in the unit where they live. Household has been a relevant unit of analysis in the study of im/migrants' funds of knowledge (N. González et al., 2005). Study of the im/migrant household is important because it affords information about available kinship networks and the knowledge these provide to families. The funds of knowledge framework stresses the participation of children in the maintenance of the household and its networks and focuses on the broad and diverse knowledge associated with household functioning.

Several factors contribute to current conceptualizations of im/migrant families, as can be seen in demographic and socioeconomic indicators used to describe them. Im/migrant families are more likely to be constituted by people who are paid low wages (Capps, Fix, Passel, Ost, & Pérez-López, 2003), hold several jobs, have been affected by limited access to formal schooling, and who live in a household with many members (Larsen, 2004). Almost 40% of households with a foreign-born head of household from Central America, which includes Mexico, included at least five people or more (Larsen, 2004). In contrast, native-born households with five or more members were only 12.5% of households in the United States. Furthermore, only 9.8% of households with a foreign-born member from Europe had five or more people. However, these figures fail as a proxy for a more comprehensive understanding of the im/migrant family. As Waters (1997) suggested, there is no singular immigrant family experience.

These descriptors go hand in hand with deficit conceptualizations of the im/migrant family because they hearken back to culture of poverty arguments (Lewis, 1959). The culture of poverty argument is that some families lack the resources—material and human—to support its members' social advancement due to the value systems developed in response to their financial circumstances. In culture of poverty arguments, deficit views are often reserved for families with heads of household with low incomes, low formal educational attainment, and working in unskilled or menial service jobs. However, in the United States, certain groups, and therefore certain families, are stereotyped—if not stigmatized—with the deficit views imposed on them regardless of variability in the education and employment of their members. For example, Mexican nationality, Hispanic or Latina/o ethnicity, and the ascribed color brown of the immigrant majority become interchangeable classifications that go hand in hand with the deficit views.

It is the case that some cities have a longer history with receiving large numbers of immigrants. These gateway communities or traditional ports of entry such as Los Angeles and New York have a longer tradition of working with im/migrant families in schools, although even in these sites, the achievement of children is considered a problem. The proportion of the total population of immigrant families and the diversity of these larger metropolitan areas is greater than in many other communities, which makes for different contexts of reception. In Los Angeles, for example, almost 60% of families have at least one im/migrant member.

Despite the long tradition and the larger numbers of im/migrant children and families in these communities, im/migrants are not exempt from discriminatory practices and policies in the contexts of reception and the inequities produced by the lack of investment in their education. Zhou (1992; Zhou & Kim, 2006) and Light and Bonacich (1988) found that the presence of co-ethnics and ethnic enclaves offer certain buffers to the biases ascribed to race for Chinese and Korean children. Academic discourses about the im/migrant families' role in the education of children, however, have often fallen within themes that associate children with disadvantages. The immigrant parent is conceptualized as uninvolved in school, in need of social and cultural capital (following the concept as defined by Coleman, 1988), and unable to provide children with an appropriate education.

Research that counters such deficit views of im/migrant families highlights scholarly work on learning from nondominant groups (Green & Luke, 2006; Kelly et al.,

2008). Learning from nondominant groups' perspectives focus on the wealth of *knowledges* and *knowledge-making practices* of cultural and linguistic groups who have been at the margins. These approaches recognize the changing nature of knowledge and the roles people play in the construction of knowledges. In contrast to officially sanctioned knowledge that forms part of school curricula, the learning from non-dominant group perspective addresses knowledge that transcends fossilized discipli-nary knowledge. For instance, rather than being seen as a problem for children to overcome, the family is viewed as actively involved in strategies and devices to respond to the daily challenges of living; their practices are seen as constituting knowledge (N. González et al., 2005). Reyes, Alexandra, and Azuara (2007) offered another example of the learning from nondominant groups' perspective; they pre-sent the family as knowledge or language constructor in biliteracy practices within the home. The family in this manner is viewed as educator versus being in need of education. Attention to families' different repertoires of practice contributes to understanding the diverse forms of learning and teaching that occur in daily inter-actions (Gutiérrez & Rogoff, 2003; Rogoff, 2003). Ethnographic work also contests deficit perspectives, with families being depicted as organizing their resources to ben-efit their children (Arzubiaga, Ceja, & Artiles, 2000; Arzubiaga, Rueda, & Monzó, 2002; Menard-Warwick, 2007; Sanchez & Orellana, 2006).

However, the immigrant family is also often represented along cultural lines in a con-flation of pan-ethnic (e.g., Asian, Latino; Louie, 2005) or country (e.g., Chinese, Mexican) categories with cultural practices. In this manner, Asian im/migrants are rep-resented placing value on effort in school (e.g., Bhattacharya, 2000). In contrast, Hispanics are represented as having poor social capital throughout different generations (e.g., Kao & Rutheford, 2007).

Can Children of Im/migrant Families Be More Similar to Children of White Middle-Class U.S. Americans?

Conceptualizations of im/migrant children in public discourses fall along similar perspectives as those used to describe their families. The concerns, however, also reflect that in the United States, the emphasis is on the politics of language education (Arzubiaga & Adair, in press). Johnson (2005), for example, examined newspaper articles related to language policies (e.g., Proposition 203 in Arizona) and found metaphors describing language minority students as "victims" when not learning the English language and "invaders" in reference to their growing numbers in classrooms.

Academic and policy discourses that address the education of im/migrant chil-dren focus on their ability to learn English. Since the Bilingual Education Act of 1968, immigrant students have been labeled in ways that emphasize their lack of ability to master English. Initially, they were referred to in the legislation as *Limited-English-Speaking Ability* (LESA) students and later as *Limited English Proficient* (LEP) students (J. González, 2008). Other labels such as *non-nons* were used to refer to immigrant children whose oral native language skills were classified as nonexistent when measured with standardized tests (MacSwan, Rolstad, & Glass, 2002). Policy and certain strands of research have influenced each other in the use and interpretation of these descriptors. The label *English Language Learners* (ELLs) emerged as an alternative to the deficit perspective that Limited English Proficient suggested.

Generational status is also taken into account when classifying children of im/migrant families. Louie (2005) explained how the classic terminology has defined as first generation those who are foreign born; second generation as the children of immigrants born in the United States; and third generation as children and parents born in the United States. Rumbaut's[7] (2004) redefinition took into consideration the life stages during which migration occurred; it includes the 1.75 generation of those who arrive during their early childhood, the 1.5 generation for those who arrived between the ages of 6 and 12, and the 1.25 generation for those who migrated between the ages 13 and 17.[8]

The *model minority* paradigm also contributes to the conceptualization of the im/migrant child. In another example of the conflation of ethnic category with cultural practices, students within the pan-ethnic Asian category were referred to in vernacular as a model minority. These students were high achievers despite their families' demographic indicators. Disaggregation of the pan-ethnic Asian group has demonstrated, however, how this model did not work for Laotians. The model minority thesis (challenged by, among others, Lee, 1994; Takaki, 1989) has contributed to the portrait of the im/migrant child and has served to mark how im/migrant children who are not Asian fall short. Moreover, the model minority concept can be understood as evidence that some im/migrants make it without investment; are, therefore by implication, more deserving; and perhaps are even of a better stock. Notions of a model minority can lead to what Stuart Hall (MacCabe, 2007) called *cultural racism*, which Hall suggested carries a trace of biological racism.

In a similar vein, young children have been represented in relationship to the cultural frameworks with which they enter school. Li (2004) contended that cultural frameworks have an effect even early on in regard to children's predisposition to learn. For children of Chinese descent, learning was reinforced by emulating high achievers and involved practice and effort. American children, in contrast, were found to attribute peer negative reactions toward high achievers. In other words, for Americans the issue was competition and self-worth whereas for Chinese children it was the development of inner abilities. This line of research supports Varenne's (1987) argument in relation to American individualism. Varenne noted that American individualism is not an issue of not being Americans—just the norm against which everyone is compared.

In contrast, academic discourses more in line with a learning from perspective have signaled im/migrant children's practices as language brokers or their role as cultural and language mediators (e.g., Dorner et al., 2007; Sanchez & Orellana, 2006). Loss of authority in the parent-child relationship (C. Suárez-Orozco & Suárez-Orozco, 2001), however, has been construed as a collateral consequence of brokering practices. In addition, children's role in migratory processes and transnational networks has begun to receive attention (Orellana, Thorne, Chee, & Lam, 2001). Whereas public media perspectives at times depict the child as victim, these studies point to children's strengths. Nonetheless, a focus on strengths needs to go hand in hand with an understanding of the obstacles children of im/migrant families face over the course of their academic pathways. These obstacles are serious and often fall outside the scope of dominant groups' academic pathways. They include, for example, losses, family divisions, and prolonged periods of separation from family. Passel et al. (2004) estimated that 1.6 million children are undocumented and that approximately 3 million children have parents who are undocumented. These children may also face, in addition to the issues mentioned previously, psychological stress from illegal entry, fear of deportation, limited access to health care, their parents' ineligibility to drivers licenses and bank accounts, and their or family members' limited prospects of access to work, scholarships, and financial aid for schooling. In addition, there are reports of young children detained as they attempt to reunite with their family, which presents another problematic dimension to the conceptualization of the child.[9] These issues often have grave consequences in relation to the education of im/migrant children. Study of children of im/migrants requires interdisciplinary perspectives.

Issues Being Raised Across Disciplines

The study of young children in immigrant families and their education must be informed by and build upon interdisciplinary perspectives. Anthropology, developmental psychology, education, and sociology, among other fields, have made contributions to the study of immigrant families; however, until recently the focus has been on adolescents. Nonetheless, the views and approaches they offer provide a wealth of perspectives upon which to build an area of inquiry on children of im/migrant families.

An important, often contested concern about the children of im/migrants is the deterioration noticed over time in their educational achievement and health status. Fuligni (1997) found foreign-born adolescents who came to the United States at later ages evidenced fewer problem behaviors and better physical health than those who immigrated at younger ages. The second generation has been known as the one that maximizes the opportunities afforded in the new land. Their families' "culture of optimism" and "ideologies of opportunity" may serve as buffers or protective factors (M. Suárez-Orozco & Suárez-Orozco, 2003). On the other hand, later generations are not expected to do as well; their achievement scores and health indicators are projected to fall to the level of their co-ethnic groups. C. Suárez-Orozco and Suárez-Orozco (2001) argued that these later generations' experiences mirror the images society holds to them. If this is the case, following a cohort of young immigrant children over time to understand their identity formation could contribute to much-needed data on the factors that influence their schooling. However, further scrutiny of the lower achievement of third and successive im/migrant generations is warranted. We need to determine if the second generation is doing well in their new settlement areas. Moreover, given the different contexts of reception, can we predict similar success?

In a similar vein, the achievement and health decline over time of im/migrants might suggest that their adaptation patterns are in line with that of involuntary groups. According to Ogbu, groups brought into U.S. society involuntarily develop secondary cultural differences and oppositional frames of reference in response to community forces embedded in prolonged discriminatory practices.[10] However, the literature (e.g., Arzubiaga et al., 2002) suggests there is also a range of variability in achievement indicators for the descendents of im/migrant families. Nonetheless, Waters (1997) argued that im/migrants' ethos and social capital can erode due to several forces in American society, such as isolation of nuclear families and work hours. From her perspective, families are undermined as a result of these forces, including disinvestment in schools. Her proposal on the erosion of immigrants' ethos over time might also explain the divergence in achievement and adaptation between second and later generations of immigrants.

Work on the achievement gap has had a strong influence on how nondominant groups' education is studied. Until recently, studies were predominantly comparisons of groups based on ethnicity conflated with race. The approaches fell within models that separated the material conditions of families, schools, and communities and their attitudes and behaviors, or individual attributes, including motivation of students (Rumberger & Arellano, 2007). Obviously, these models fall short from an *investment*-in-education perspective (Ladson-Billings, 2006) given their focus on outcome measures. However, they are also problematic because of the variability across models and the limitations of the definitions used to inform them. Motivation, for example, is explained as time on task in one study and student-teacher evaluations in another; the causes of underachievement are located within the individual. In contrast, motivation from a sociocultural perspective is not within an individual; rather, motivation is socially and culturally situated (Rueda, MacGillivray, Monzó, & Arzubiaga, 2001).

Sociological approaches have contributed structural perspectives to the study of im/migrant families and education. As Zhou and her colleagues (Zhou, 1997; Zhou & Kim, 2006) explained, the structural perspective contends that cultural values and behavior patterns can be conducive to upward social mobility when they interact with structural factors, including advantageous class status with which a particular group arrived and a favorable opportunity structure in the host society. Furthermore, they elaborated, ethnicity cannot be simplified into a proxy for culture because it encompasses not only values and behavioral patterns but also group-specific social structures that may be contingent upon circumstances prior to and after immigration.

Discussions on diversity have exhorted the developmental field to consider multiple childhood pathways. In line with this thinking, García Coll and her colleagues (1996, 2002) helped propel the child development field to approach the study of minority groups with an integrative model. They proposed contextual forces, such as poverty, racism, and discrimination, need to be taken into account in the study of children. As García Coll and her colleagues suggested, the focus needs to move to what or how nondominant groups exercise culture, for example, in their pursuit of education and in contrast to views that focus on parental detachment at school.

The role of cultural beliefs in im/migrants' adaptations also has been a focus of study. Fuligni (1997; Fulgini, Yip, & Tseng, 2002), building on a developmental psychology perspective, examined adolescents' cultural beliefs, such as obligation to the family, in relation to school adjustment, family relations, and psychological well-being. He also argued for a departure from cross-sectional studies of groups and a focus on longitudinal studies of immigrants.

UNDERSTANDING ISSUES FACING CHILDREN OF IM/MIGRANT FAMILIES: EXPANDING CONTEXTS

This section extends the discussion of the literature in terms of different spatial contexts in which to consider children of im/migrant families, particularly young children. A number of the studies reviewed for this chapter suggest that the lack of conclusiveness in their findings may be attributed to a failure to capture certain features of children's care, experiences, and well-being. For example, Crosnoe (2007) noted that the quality of day care was important to consider but it was not discernible from the Early Childhood Longitudinal Study–Kindergarten Cohort database. The ECLS-K is a nationally representative sample of kindergarteners. One third of the empirical studies examined large databases that have intrinsic limitations in the variables. Moreover, disaggregation was not possible, and there was loss in the definitions or conceptualizations used. Beyond expanding the focus of studies to include both sending and receiving countries, nontraditional settlement areas, and institutional contexts, such as preschool, day care, elementary, and parish schools, there needs to be a shift in the classifications and conceptualizations of the im/migrant child and family.

As research on im/migrant children moves forward, there is a need to examine the issues in ways that do not pathologize the im/migrant child and family for lacking the same capital of dominant native groups or for what, arguably, their family lost with migration. Although prevalent in research paradigms, classifications by country, race, or ethnicity are not equal to language and to culture. Im/migrants create their own pathways and are forging their futures. As mentioned previously, children's role in transnational networks has received some attention; however, transnationalism[11] as a cultural pathway available to children needs further study. It has been argued that transnationalism plays a greater role for recent or first-generation im/migrants (Gil & Vega, 1996; A. Portes, Escobar, & Arana, 2008), although new technologies and expanded access to these technologies continue to change the way transnationalism affects im/migrants' lives. In the same manner that transnationalism pushes us to consider im/migrants' contexts beyond those of their physical boundaries, we need to study both sending and receiving contexts of reception avoiding compartmentalized approaches. Missing from the literature were more studies that provided links between sending and receiving countries such as premigration cultural frameworks and im/migrant families' prior sociocultural realities.

The definition of the im/migrant family needs further elaboration. The studies reviewed generally did not define the family; at most, a few studies described families as nuclear, parents, primary caregivers, or two-parent households; few studies included other members of the household; and few mentioned families in sending countries. Broader understandings of the family will need to take into account that the family generally is dependent on several layers of society and thus its conceptualization and classification is subject to change. Families are embedded in layers of influence that shape them. Just as the individual cannot be understood out of context, we need to understand families in context and provide a space for the role of the state and its institutions. Im/migrant families are particularly vulnerable to the role and policies enacted by nation states and public institutions. Research on the im/migrant family needs to be informed by the policies that restrict or afford educational rights and access. Separating groups by the policies under which they are living such as immigration and language policies would provide important understandings about the developmental pathways of children of im/migrant families. The ongoing study, Children Crossing Borders, which focuses on the preschool of im/migrants in five countries, holds promise to shed light in this area (Tobin, Arzubiaga, & Mantovani, 2007). The research examines how parents and teachers construct notions about who belongs and whose practices are favored. It considers the inherent tensions, within each country, in supporting diversity on one hand and creating unity and national identity on the other.

CLOSING CONSIDERATIONS AND CONCLUSION

An interdisciplinary, comparative, and longitudinal perspective is needed for research on and with children of im/migrant families. Research needs to take into account that immigration is not static but a complex interplay of time, context, and people. Changes in time, context, or people without considering their interplay render comparisons across groups problematic. However, within the unstoppable mélange of histories and cultures, notions about who is entitled and whose knowledge counts need to be at the foreground. These issues are crucial for the education of children of im/migrants and should be part of research and practice agendas on children and their families. Studies that move discourses away from deficit views will provide better understandings about the education of im/migrant children. The promising line of research that intends to account for other ways of learning and for the representation of knowledge from groups whose knowledge is usually not officially sanctioned needs to be further developed in regard to young children of im/migrants. Families can then be framed as educators instead of in need of education.

In particular, research on Rosaldo's *cultural citizenship* holds promise to further the appreciation of im/migrants' everyday practices (see Flores & Benmayor, 1997). This work moves citizenship debates to a broader construction of citizenship. It is in line with learning from perspectives as it unpackages how nondominant groups' values and rights organize individual and collective identities and can include the knowledge-making practices of parents and children.

Much is to be gained from learning about immigrant families' repertoires of practice. The multitude of ways im/migrants approach and solve the vicissitudes' of daily living, within a variety of contexts of reception, comprise areas of research waiting to be explored. These areas are important because what families are doing or their repertoires of practice constitute children's primary social and learning spaces. They represent a rich array of adaptations, and hybrid practices product of a mélange of histories and cultures. In light of the diversity, there needs to be an increase in ecological approaches to the study of children's developmental pathways. For example, ecological and cultural (Weisner, 2002) understandings on how families organize their lives within specific contexts of reception can afford us ways of understanding the wide range of experiences children live. Families' organizations are arranged within the constraints and affordances of the ecologies of where they live but are based on family members' ingenuity and histories. These organizations provide children with practices and activities that constitute their developmental pathways.

There is also need for more mindfulness and explanations related to the use of categories such as race and ethnicity. Use of these without deliberate examination can inadvertently perpetuate the marking, the racialization of problems, and the exclusion of nondominant groups. These categories should be connected to notions such as disinvestment in communities of color. Rather than a focus on what families lack and how children fall short, research needs to consider how communities might have a long-term investment approach toward the education of young children of im/migrants.

NOTES

[1]The terms at times designate individuals in categories that represent parts of immigration processes and/or their associated legal status. Immigration processes can fall along a continuum—undocumented, permanent resident, citizen—but not all im/migrants necessarily follow the same immigration trajectories.

[2]Since the end of the Cold War, this pattern of exclusion is increasingly prevalent. During the Cold War, these same countries, for example, were geared toward welcoming the Cold War refugees and allowing their resettlement as permanent exiles.

[3]U.S. immigration policy claims goals of family reunification but fails in coherence and resource allocation (Fix & Zimmermann, 1997). Attempts in the past few years to pass a nationwide legislation have not been approved. States have been left to deal with these groups on their own terms. The undocumented include not only those who have crossed without documentation to the United States but also those whose visas expire and stay.

[4]In fact, as D. S. Massey, Durand, and Malone (2002) contended, the presence of this unprecedented number of undocumented people is in part due to the measures of the Immigration Reform and Control Act (IRCA) of 1986, which interrupted the cycle of circular migration and led people to settlement migration. The restrictions imposed by IRCA made people stay. Although IRCA was intended to control migration and promote economic development, it is also responsible for the settlement of an unprecedented number of undocumented persons.

[5]*Nondominant* refers to a group's hegemonic position and not to its actual numbers in population (Gutiérrez, Hunter, & Arzubiaga, in press).

[6]Enrique Murillo and Sofia Villenas were the first to refer to the increasing numbers of Latinos migrating to nontraditional areas as the *New Latino Diaspora*. The New Latino Diaspora studies focus on the educational experiences of the newcomers, the politics of identity, and the mediating institutions—primarily schools—where these are constructed.

[7]However, Rumbaut (2004) questioned the validity of the act of "lumping" or "splitting" adults and children through these generational groups when studying issues of adaptation. Rumbaut argued how the terms *first* and *second generation* assume the socialization of individuals in another country or in the United States, with disregard to their age of arrival in the United States.

[8]Rumbaut (2004) stressed that in different types of migration, multiple entries to the country may take place. He mentioned that in national data sources, such information is not taken into account. For transnational students who navigate different educational systems when moving back and forth, broad assumptions made about each type of generational label may have some shortcomings.

[9]The Detained Immigrant and Refugee Initiative (Florence Immigrant & Refugee Rights Project, 2008) provided the following information. U.S. immigration authorities detain several thousand children annually, and the numbers of detained children in Arizona has skyrocketed. More than 1,000 children were expected to pass through Arizona detention facilities in 2005. Approximately 160 juveniles are detained each day in Phoenix and unknown numbers of immigrant children are held at Border Patrol stations awaiting transfer. Children typically come from Central America, Brazil, and Ecuador, but others come from China, Poland, Sri Lanka, and other countries. Mexican children are turned around and so do not make it to shelters in the United States, which makes them vulnerable. Children in detention are 15 to 17 years old, but there have been 1-year-olds detained, and children between the ages of 5 and 10 are detained regularly. The Office of Refugee Resettlement will release a child to be reunified with undocumented family members but must notify Immigration. This discourages families from coming forward.

[10]For Ogbu, refugees who are often involuntarily brought to the United States would eventually take on the values and beliefs of their host communities. In this sense they would be more like his *immigrant* classification in regard to their adaptation patterns (Luciak, 2004).

[11]A. Portes, Escobar, and Arana (2008) noted in its contemporary usage, and as applied to immigrant populations, *transnationalism* was introduced by social anthropologists who first noted the intense interaction between places of origin and destination and the impact such activities had in communities at both ends of the migration stream.

ACKNOWLEDGMENTS

We are grateful to Norma González (University of Arizona), Robert Rueda (University of Southern California), and the *RRE* editors for their feedback in earlier versions of this chapter.

REFERENCES

Abedi, J., & Dietel, R. (2004). Challenges in the No Child Left Behind Act for English-language learners. *Phi Delta Kappan, 85*, 782–785.

Aldous, J. (2006). Family, ethnicity, and immigrant youth's educational achievements. *Journal of Family Issues, 27*, 1633–1667.

Arzubiaga, A., & Adair, J. (in press). Misrepresentations of language and culture, language and culture as proxies for marginalization: Debunking the arguments. In E. Murillo (Ed.), *Handbook of Latinos and education*. Mahwah, NJ: Lawrence Erlbaum.

Arzubiaga, A., Artiles, A., King, K., & Murri, N. (2008). Beyond culturally responsive research: Challenges and implications of research as situated cultural practice. *Exceptional Children, 74*, 309–327.

Arzubiaga, A., Ceja, M., & Artiles, A. J. (2000). Transcending deficit thinking about Latinos' parenting styles: Toward an ecocultural view of family life. In C. Tejeda, C. Martinez, & Z. Leonardo (Eds.), *Charting new terrains of Chicana(o)/Latina(o) education* (pp. 93–106). Cresskil, NJ: Hampton Press.

Arzubiaga, A., Rueda, R., & Monzó, L. (2002). Family matters related to the reading engagement of Latino children. *Journal of Latinos and Education, 1*, 231–243.

Aspiazu, G. G., Bauer, S. C., & Spillett, M. (1998). Improving academic performance of Hispanic youth: A community education model. *Bilingual Research Journal, 22*, 127–147.

Balibar, E. (1990). Paradoxes of universality. In D. T. Goldberg (Ed.), *Anatomy of racism* (pp. 283–294). Minneapolis: University of Minnesota Press.

Banks, J., Au, K., Ball, A., Bell, P., Gordon, E., Gutiérrez, K., et al. (2007). *Learning in and out of school in diverse environments: Life-long, life-wide, life deep.* Retrieved June 5, 2008, from http://life-slc.org/wp-content/up/2007/05/Banks-et-al-LIFE-Diversity-Report.pdf

Bhattacharya, G. (2000). The school adjustment of South Asian immigrant children in the United States. *Adolescence, 35,* 77–85.

Bodfield, R. (2008, October 1). 28% of AZ schools are short of US standards. *Arizona Daily Star.* Retrieved October 21, 2008, from http://www.azstarnet.com/sn/metro/260212.php

Bowker, G., & Star, S. L. (1999). *Sorting things out: Classification and its consequences.* Cambridge, MA: MIT Press.

Bowler, R. M., Smith, M., Schwarzer, R., Perez-Arce, P., & Kreutzer, R. (2002). Neuropsychological and academic characteristics of Mexican-American children: A longitudinal field study. *Applied Psychology: An International Review, 51,* 458–478.

Caldwell, C. (2006, February 26). A family or a crowd? *The New York Times.* Retrieved June 15, 2006, from http://www.nytimes.com/2006/02/26/magazine/26wwln_lead.html?ex=1298610000&en=4419abb98a33d377&ei=5090&partner=rssuserland&emc=rss

Capps, R., Fix, M., Passel, J., Ost, J., & Pérez-López, D. (2003). *A profile of the low-wage immigrant force.* Retrieved June 3, 2008, from http://www.urban.org/url.cfm?ID=310880

Chapa, J., & De la Rosa, B. (2004). Latino population growth, socioeconomic and demographic characteristics, and implications for educational attainment. *Education and Urban Society, 36,* 130–149.

Chiswick, B., & DebBurman, N. (2006). Pre-school enrollment: An analysis by immigrant generation. *Social Science Research, 35,* 60–87.

Coleman, J. (1988). Social capital in the creation of human capital. *American Journal of Sociology, 94,* S95–S120.

Cornfield, D. B., & Arzubiaga, A. (2004). Immigrants and education in the U.S. interior: Integrating and segmenting tendencies in Nashville, Tennessee. *Peabody Journal of Education, 79,* 157–179.

Crosnoe, R. (2005). Double disadvantage or signs of resilience? The elementary school contexts of children from Mexican immigrant families. *American Educational Research Journal, 42,* 269–303.

Crosnoe, R. (2006). Health and the education of children from racial/ethnic minority and immigrant families. *Journal of Health and Social Behavior, 47,* 77–93.

Crosnoe, R. (2007). Early child care and the school readiness of children from Mexican immigrant families. *International Migration Review, 41,* 152–181.

De Genova, N. P. (2002) Migrant "illegality" and deportability in everyday life. *Annual Review of Anthropology, 31,* 419–447.

Dorner, L. M., Orellana, M. F., & Li-Grining, C. (2007). "I helped my mom," and it helped me: Translating the skills of language brokers in improved standardized test scores. *American Journal of Education, 113,* 451–478.

Feliciano, C. (2006). Beyond the family: The influence of premigration group status on the educational expectations of immigrants' children. *Sociology of Education, 79,* 281–303.

Fix, M., & Zimmermann, W. (1997). *Welfare reform: A new immigrant policy for the United States.* Retrieved December 3, 2008, from http://www.urban.org/publications/407532.html

Florence Immigration & Refugee Rights Project. (2008). *Detained immigrant and refugee children's initiative.* Retrieved July 13, 2008, from http://www.firrp.org/children.asp

Flores, W. V., & Benmayor, R. (Eds.). (1997). *Latino cultural citizenship: Claiming identity, space, and rights.* Boston: Beacon.

Foundation for Child Development. (2007). *All our children? The health and education of children of immigrants: 2007 annual report.* Retrieved December 3, 2008, from http://www.fcd-us.org/resources/resources_show.htm?doc_id=561788

Fuligni, A. (1997). The academic achievement of adolescents from immigrant families: The roles of family background, attitudes, and behavior. *Child Development, 68*, 351–363.

Fuligni, A. J., Yip, T., & Tseng, V. (2002). The impact of family obligation on the daily behavior and psychological well being of Chinese American adolescents. *Child Development, 73*, 306–318.

García Coll, C., Akiba, D., Palacios, N., Bailey, B., Silver, R., DiMartino, L., et al. (2002). Parental involvement in children's education: Lessons from three immigrant groups. *Parenting: Science and Practice, 2*, 303–324.

García Coll, C., Lamberty, G., Jenkins, R., McAdoo, H. P., Crnic, K., Wasik, B. H., & García, H. V. (1996). An integrative model for the study of developmental competencies in minority children. *Child Development, 67*, 1891-1914.

Gil, A. G., & Vega, W. A. (1996). Two different worlds: Acculturation stress and adaptation among Cuban and Nicaraguan families. *Journal of Social and Personal Relationships, 13*, 435–456.

Gillan, J. (2002). Focusing on the wrong front: Historical displacement, the Maginot Line, and "the bluest eye." *African American Review, 36*, 283–298.

Glick, J. E., & Hohmann-Marriott, B. (2007). Academic performance of young children in immigrant families: The significance of race, ethnicity, and national origins. *International Migration Review, 41*, 371–402.

González, J. (2008). Labeling bilingual education clients: LESA, LEP and ELL. In J. González (Ed.), *Encyclopedia of bilingual education* (Vol. 1, pp. 415–417). Thousand Oaks, CA: Sage.

González, N., Moll, L., & Amanti, C. (2005). *Funds of knowledge: Theorizing practices in households, communities and classrooms.* Mahwah, NJ: Lawrence Erlbaum.

Green, J., & Luke, A. (2006). Rethinking learning: What counts as learning and what learning counts. *Review of Research in Education, 30*, xi-xvi.

Gutiérrez, K., & Rogoff, B. (2003). Cultural ways of learning: Individual traits or repertoires of practice. *Educational Researcher, 32*(5), 19–25.

Gutiérrez, K. D., Hunter, J., & Arzubiaga, A. E. (in press). Re-mediating the university: Learning through sociocritical literacies. *Pedagogies.*

Hao, L., & Bonstead-Bruns, M. (1998). Parent-child differences in educational expectations and the academic achievement of immigrant and native students. *Sociology of Education, 71*, 175–198.

Hernandez, D., Denton, N., & Macartney, S. (2007). *Children in immigrant families: The U.S. and 50 states: National origins, language, and early education.* Retrieved October 21, 2008, from http://mumford.albany.edu/children/img/Research_brief_1.pdf

Johnson, E. (2005). Proposition 203: A critical metaphor analysis. *Bilingual Education Journal, 29*, 69–84.

Kao, G., & Rutherford, L. T. (2007). Does social capital still matter? Immigrant minority disadvantage in school-specific social capital and its effects on academic achievement. *Sociological Perspectives, 50*, 27–52.

Kelly, G., Luke, A., & Green, J. (2008). What counts as knowledge in educational settings: Disciplinary knowledge, assessment and curriculum. *Review of Research in Education, 32*, vii-x.

Kohler, A., & Lazarín, M. (2007). *Hispanic education in the United States* (Statistical Brief No. 8). Washington, DC: National Council of La Raza.

Ladson-Billings, G. (2006). From the achievement gap to the education debt: Understanding achievement in U.S. Schools. *Educational Researcher, 35*(7), 3–12.

Lam, W. S. E. (2006). Culture and learning in the context of globalization: Research directions. *Review of Research in Education, 30*, 213–237.

Larsen, L. J. (2004). *The foreign-born population in the United States: 2003* (Current Population Reports). Washington, DC: U.S. Census Bureau.

Lee, S. J. (1994). Behind the model-minority stereotype: Voices of high-and low-achieving Asian American students. *Anthropology & Education Quarterly, 25*, 413–429.

Lewis, O. (1959). *Five families: Mexican case studies in the culture of poverty*. New York: Basic Books.

Li, J. (2004). Learning as a task and a virtue: U.S. and Chinese preschoolers explain learning. *Developmental Psychology, 40*, 595–605.

Light, I., & Bonacich, E. (1988). *Immigrant entrepreneurs: Koreans in Los Angeles*. Berkeley: University of California Press.

Lopez, G., Scribner, J., & Mahitivanichcha, K. (2001). Redefining parental involvement: Lessons from high-performing migrant-impacted schools. *American Educational Research Journal, 38*, 253–288.

Lopez, L., Sanchez, V., & Hamilton, M. (2000). Immigrant and native-born Mexican-American parents' involvement in a public school: A preliminary study. *Psychological Reports, 86*, 521–525.

Louie, V. (2005). Immigrant newcomer populations, ESEA, and the pipeline to college: Current considerations and future lines of inquiry. *Review of Research in Education, 29*, 69–105.

Luciak, M. (2004). Minority status and schooling: John U. Ogbu's theory and the schooling of ethnic minorities in Europe. *Intercultural Education, 15*, 359–368.

MacCabe, C. (2007). An interview with Stuart Hall. *Critical Quarterly, 50*, 12–42.

MacSwan, J., Rolstad, K., & Glass, G. V. (2002). Do some school-age children have no language? Some problems of construct validity in the Pre-LAS Español. *Bilingual Research Journal, 26*, 213–238.

Magnuson, K., Lahaie, C., & Waldfogel, J. (2006). Preschool and school readiness of children of immigrants. *Social Science Quarterly, 87*, 1241–1262.

Malkki, L. (1992). National geographic: The rooting of peoples and the territorialization of national identity among scholars and refugees. *Cultural Anthropology, 7*, 24–44.

Massey, D. (1999). International migration at the dawn of the twenty-first century: The role of the state. *Population and Development Review, 25*, 303–322.

Massey, D. S., Durand, J., & Malone, N. (2002). *Beyond smoke and mirrors: Mexican immigration in an age of economic integration*. New York: Russell Sage.

McDermott, R., & Varenne, H. (1995). Culture "as" disability. *Anthropology & Education Quarterly, 26*, 324–348.

McLaughlin, J., Liljestrom, A., Lim, J. H., & Meyers, D. (2002). LEARN: A community study about Latino immigrants and education. *Education and Urban Society, 34*, 212–232.

McLoyd, V. C. (1998). Changing demographics in the American population: Implications for research on minority children and adolescents. In V. C. McLoyd & L. D. Steinberg (Eds.), *Studying minority adolescents: Conceptual, methodological, and theoretical issues* (pp. 3–28). Mahwah, NJ: Lawrence Erlbaum.

Menard-Warwick, J. (2007). Biliteracy and schooling in an extended-family Nicaraguan immigrant household: The sociohistorical construction of parental involvement. *Anthropology and Education Quarterly, 38*, 119–137.

Murillo, E. G., Jr. (2002). How does it feel to be a problem?: "Disciplining" the transnational subject in the American South. In S. Wortham, E. G. Murillo, Jr., & E. T. Hamann (Eds.), *Education in the new Latino Diaspora* (pp. 215–240). Westport, CT: Greenwood.

Netting, R. McC., Wilk, R., & Arnould, E. (1984). Introduction. In R. McC. Netting, R. R. Wilk, & E. J Arnould (Eds.), *Households: Comparative and historical studies of the domestic group* (pp. xiii–xxxviii). Berkeley: University of California Press.

Orellana, M. F., Thorne, B., Chee, A., & Lam, W. S. E. (2001). Transnational childhoods: The participation of children in processes of family migration. *Social Problems, 48*, 572–591.

Orfield, G., & Lee, C. (2006). *Racial transformation and the changing nature of segregation*. Cambridge, MA: The Civil Rights Project, Harvard University.

Passel, J., Capps, R., & Fix, M. (2004). *Undocumented immigrants: facts and figures*. Unpublished manuscript, Urban Institute, Washington, DC.

Pérez Carreón, G., Drake, C., & Barton, A. C. (2005). The importance of presence: Immigrant parents' school engagement experiences. *American Educational Research Journal, 42*, 465–498.

Portes, A. (1997). Immigration theory for a new century: Some problems and opportunities. *International Migration Review, 31*, 799–825.

Portes, A., Escobar, C., & Arana, R. (2008). Bridging the gap: Transnational and ethnic organizations in the political incorporation of immigrants in the United States. *Ethnic and Racial Studies, 31*, 1056–1090.

Portes, A., & MacLeod, D. (1999). Educating the second generation: Determinants of academic achievement among children of immigrants in the United States. *Journal of Ethnic & Migration Studies, 25*, 373–396.

Portes, A., & Rumbaut, R. (2001). *Legacies: The story of the immigrant second generation.* Berkeley: University of California Press.

Portes, A., & Zhou, M. (1993). The new second generation: Segmented assimilation and its variants. *Annals of the American Academy of Political and Social Science, 530*, 74–96.

Portes, P. (1999). Social and psychological factors in the academic achievement of children of immigrants: A cultural history puzzle. *American Educational Research Journal, 36*, 489–507.

Reyes, I., Alexandra, D., & Azuara, P. (2007). Literacy practices in Mexican immigrant homes. *Cultura y Educación, 19*, 464–474.

Riggs, N. R., & Greenberg, M. T. (2004). Moderators in the academic development of migrant Latino children attending after-school programs. *Journal of Applied Developmental Psychology, 25*, 349–367.

Rogoff, B. (2003). *The cultural nature of human development.* New York: Oxford University Press.

Romanowski, M. (2003). Meeting the unique needs of the children of migrant farm workers. *The Clearing House, 77*, 27–33.

Roopnarine, J. L., Krishnakumar, A., Metindogan, A., & Evans, M. (2006). Links between parenting styles, parent-child academic interaction, parent-school interaction, and early academic skills and social behaviors in young children of English-speaking Caribbean immigrants. *Early Childhood Research Quarterly, 21*, 238–252.

Rueda, R., MacGillivray, L., Monzó, L., & Arzubiaga, A. (2001). Engaged reading: A multi-level approach to considering sociocultural factors with diverse learners. In D. McInerny & S. VanEtten (Eds.), *Research on sociocultural influences on motivation and learning* (pp. 233–264). Greenwich, CT: Information Age Publishing, Inc.

Ruiz de Velasco, J., Fix, M., & Clewell, B. C. (2000). *Overlooked and underserved: Immigrant Students in U.S. Schools.* Washington, DC: Urban Institute.

Rumbaut, R. (2004). Ages, life stages, and generational cohorts: Decomposing the immigrant first and second generations in the United States. *International Migration Review, 38*, 1160–1205.

Rumberger, R., & Arellano, B. (2007). Understanding and addressing achievement gaps during the first four years of school in the United States. In R. Teese, S. Lamb, & M. Duru-Bellat (Eds.), *International studies in educational inequality: Theory and policy* (Vol. 3, pp. 129–149). New York: Springer.

Sanchez, I. G., & Orellana, M. F. (2006). The construction of moral and social identity in immigrant children's narratives-in-translation. *Linguistics and Education, 17*, 209–239.

Santa Ana, O. (1999). "Like an animal I was treated": Anti-immigrant metaphor in US public discourse. *Discourse & Society, 10*, 191–224.

Schaller, A., Rocha, L. O., & Barshinger, D. (2007). Maternal attitudes and parent education: How immigrant mothers support their child's education despite their own low levels of education. *Early Childhood Education Journal, 34*, 351–356.

Schmidley, A. D. (2001). *Profile of the foreign-born population in the United States: 2000.* Retrieved October 17, 2008, from http://www.census.gov/prod/2002pubs/p23-206.pdf

Sohn, S., & Wang, X. C. (2006). Immigrant parents' involvement in American schools: Perspectives from Korean mothers. *Early Childhood Education Journal, 34*, 125–132.

Souto-Manning, M. (2007). Immigrant families and children (re)develop identities in a new context. *Early Childhood Education Journal, 34*, 399–405.

Suárez-Orozco, C., & Suárez-Orozco, M. M. (2001). *Children of immigration*. Cambridge, MA: Harvard University Press.

Suárez-Orozco, M. M. (2001). Globalization, immigration, and education: The research agenda. *Harvard Educational Review, 71*, 345–365.

Suárez-Orozco, M. M., & Suárez-Orozco, C. (2003, May). *Rethinking immigration*. Invited keynote address at the Dealing With Difference Summer Institute, Macomb, Illinois, Western Illinois University.

Suvin, D. (2007). Immigration in Europe today: Apartheid or civil cohabitation. *Critical Quarterly, 50*, 206–233.

Szalacha, L. A., Marks, A. K., Lamarre, M., & García Coll, C. (2005). Academic pathways and children of immigrant families. *Research in Human Development, 2*, 179–211.

Takaki, R. (1989). *Strangers from a different shore: A history of Asian Americans*. Boston: Little, Brown.

Tobin, J., Arzubiaga, A., & Mantovani, S. (2007). Entering into Dialogue with immigrant parents. *Early Childhood Matters, 108*, 34–38.

Varenne, H. (1987). Talk and real talk: The voices of silence and the voices of power in American family life. *Cultural Anthropology, 2*, 369–394.

Villenas, S. (2002). Reinventing education in New Latino communities: Pedagogies of change and continuity in North Carolina. In S. Wortham, E. G. Murillo, Jr., & E. T. Hamann (Eds.), *Education in the new Latino Diaspora* (pp. 17–36). Westport, CT: Greenwood.

Waters, M. (1997). Immigrant families at risk: Factors that undermine chances for success. In A. Booth, A. C. Crouter, & N. Landale (Eds.), *Immigration and the family: Research and policy on U.S. immigrants* (pp. 79–87). Mahwah, NJ: Lawrence Erlbaum.

Weisner, T. S. (2002). Ecocultural understanding of children's developmental pathways. *Human Development, 45*, 275–281.

Wortham, S., Murillo Jr., E., & Hamann, E. T. (Eds.). (2002). *Education in the New Latino Diaspora: Policy and the politics of identity*. Westport, CT: Greenwood.

Zhou, M. (1992). *Chinatown: The socioeconomic potential of an urban enclave*. Philadelphia: Temple University Press.

Zhou, M. (1997). Segmented assimilation: Issues, controversies, and recent research on the new second generation. *International Migration Review, 31*, 825–858.

Zhou, M., & Kim, S. (2006). Community forces, social capital, and educational achievement: The case of supplementary education in the Chinese and Korean Immigrant communities. *Harvard Educational Review, 76*, 1–29.

Chapter 10

Linguistic Diversity, Access, and Risk

JOHN BAUGH

Washington University, St. Louis

Rarely do we view educational risk from a linguistic perspective. There are note-worthy exceptions, among them Valdés (1996) and Zentella (1997). However, of the educational literature devoted to risk, the vast majority attends to the array of attributes and circumstances that perpetuate cycles of poverty (Williams, 1970). The aim of this discussion is to examine educational risk, paying particular attention to the possible existence of a "linguistic stereotype threat." If such a threat does exist, it is very possible or even likely that linguistic stereotyping inhibits the academic achievement of many students who lack fluency in the dominant linguistic norms of their local speech communities. From a linguistic point of view, students in any speech community tend to fit within three general categories, including

1. native speakers of the dominant local language(s) = DL(s),
2. native speakers of nonstandard dialects of the dominant local language(s) = NSDL(s), and
3. those for whom the dominant local language(s) is/(are) not native = NNDL(s).

Beyond personal linguistic circumstances, people have different access to the very learning opportunities that accentuate academic vulnerabilities (or advantages) for diverse students anywhere in the world.

I am mindful that a great deal of the research available on this topic is U.S.-centric. As a result, most of the illustrations provided here are drawn from educational circumstances in the United States. However, I would like to reassure readers that to the fullest extent possible, I will try to identify instances wherein globally, matters of linguistic diversity, in combination with differing access to educational resources, can have a profound impact on the likelihood that students will obtain a competent

Review of Research in Education
March 2009, Vol. 33, pp. 272-282
DOI: 10.3102/0091732X08327188
© 2009 AERA. http://rre.aera.net

and competitive education, that is, one that prepares them to pursue higher education or a profession that utilizes their academic preparation successfully.

Children throughout the world do not have equal access to education. Those without access to education are at extreme risk; *risk* by definition is a situation involving exposure to danger. A child who is deprived of an education has greater potential to be exposed to danger than his or her better-educated counterparts. Even if children have an opportunity to attend a school, the relative quality of the education they receive does, in most instances, correspond closely with the wealth of the children's parents and the corresponding education or lack thereof of the child's mother (Olson, 2005). Children of the poor are at greater educational risk than the children of the wealthy, but to what extent, if any, are these risks the result of undetected linguistic considerations?

This chapter reviews long-standing issues that influence students' academic and social experiences in school as well as more contemporary debates that respond to (mis)understandings of linguistic styles of Black people and larger issues of race. Few issues have contributed more to students' risk in U.S. classrooms, schools, and society than the spoken language and linguistic varieties of Black students. I begin with an overview of the limitations of legislation intended to increase educational access for students in the United States to attend to the range of linguistic histories and varieties represented in the U.S. student population. Next, I argue against racial classification as a defining feature, followed by an extended discussion of racial classification and labeling in the United States and South Africa. I then turn my attention to the ways that risk is constructed through linguistic stereotype threats, followed by a section that offers a heuristic model that measures the existence of a linguistic stereotype threat. My next section brings together the arguments around linguistic risk in the preceding sections of the chapter to address the salient issues of educational risk and is followed by a conclusion.

LEGAL FOUNDATIONS AND LINGUISTIC DIVERSITY

Having devoted most of my research to the linguistic circumstances affecting Black people in the U.S. and other parts of the world, I have given considerable thought to matters of race as they intersect with access to educational opportunities, or the lack thereof. The landmark *Brown v. Board of Education* (1954) ruling, for example, is racially grounded. As a linguist, however, I am keenly aware that racial groups, irrespective of how they are defined, do not neatly intersect with language or dialect groupings. In other words, people of any given race can and do have very different linguistic experiences. Consider, for example, linguistic diversity among African Americans. At first blush, this may appear to be a simple matter, perhaps one that could be classified in terms of those who self-identify as "Black Americans" or "African Americans." Barack Obama's rising visibility provides a useful illustration. Clearly, he is an African American; however, neither of his parents is a slave descendant. By contrast, Michelle Obama, formerly Michelle Robinson, is a direct descendant of Africans who were once enslaved in the United States.

Brown v. Board of Education (1954) is the landmark Supreme Court ruling that concentrates on racial segregation and equal access to educational facilities for students from any racial background, but the ruling itself is not directly devoted to the special linguistic circumstances of Black students or other students who qualify as NSDL. By contrast, *Lau v. Nichols* (1974) concentrated directly on the educational plight of American students who do not speak English natively. In that case, the court ruled in favor of Lau, a Chinese student who spoke no English. The Supreme Court ruled as follows:

The failure of the San Francisco school system to provide English language instruction to approximately 1,800 students of Chinese ancestry who do not speak English, or to provide them with other adequate instructional procedures, denies them a meaningful opportunity to participate in the public educational program and thus violates § 601 of the Civil Rights Act of 1964, which bans discrimination based "on the ground of race, color, or national origin," in "any program or activity receiving Federal financial assistance," and the implementing regulations of the Department of Health, Education, and Welfare. (*Lau. v. Nichols*, 1974).

Although the *Lau v. Nichols* (1974) ruling deals centrally with language, it does not fully address the linguistic circumstances of U.S. slave descendants. Therefore, it is not easy to determine the extent to which *Brown v. Board of Education* (1954) pertains to the special linguistic circumstances of students who are not only U.S. slave descendants but who also speak nonstandard varieties of African American Vernacular English. Part of the risk confronting NSDL and NNDL students in American schools includes frequent misdiagnosis and/or misclassification. Policies that sort students on the basis of race are cumbersome and especially so when educators strive to find effective ways to educate all students regardless of their background.

BEYOND RACIAL CLASSIFICATION: CASTELIKE GROUPINGS

Rather than accentuate the *Brown v. Board of Education* (1954) trend toward overstating racial or "color" considerations, I believe John Ogbu's (1978, 1992) castelike classifications of U.S. citizens have the potential to refine efforts to enhance educational prospects for less fortunate students.

Ogbu's observations, which illustrate that educational outcomes may have less to do with race than with one's ancestry, do not rely on racial classifications. Instead, he focuses on alternative paths to U.S. citizenship. While Ogbu was completing his classical studies, he pondered his own plight as a Black American, albeit one who was born in Nigeria and who learned English as a second language. He knew that his journey to U.S. citizenship differed from that of typical U.S. slave descendants who were the object of relief in the *Brown v. Board of Education* (1954) ruling. During an era when so much of educational research focused on racial disparities in testing (Jensen, 1969; Labov, 1972), Ogbu was mindful of his own educational success and aspirations as a Black man who had not, to his own knowledge, been ensnared by racist obstacles. Indeed, he noted that he counted a number of White Americans among his strongest supporters (personal communication). Ogbu therefore concluded that racism was not the critical factor in explanations of low Black academic performance.

The ensuing result of his scholarly training and international research comparisons led Ogbu to draw analogies between India and the United States. More precisely, he argued that U.S. citizens are composed of three distinct heritage categories: voluntary immigrants, involuntary immigrants, and autonomous immigrants (cf. Ogbu, 1978, 1992). When individuals identify themselves as members of one or more racial groups, the way they do so is generally to trace (in)voluntary heritage paths to their ancestors. Indeed, you, the reader, can illustrate this point. First, are you a U.S. citizen? If not, you may wish to apply Ogbu's castelike classifications to your place of birth. For U.S. citizens, this exercise is fairly straightforward: Did you or your ancestors migrate to the United States, or are your ancestors Native Americans (including natives of Alaska and Hawaii)? For those U.S. citizens whose ancestors immigrated to the United States, the ensuing questions correspond to their "voluntary" or "involuntary" immigrant status. Whereas some educational risk analyses concentrate on racial differences, Ogbu's castelike categories call attention to diversity within any racial group.

RACIAL CLASSIFICATION AND LABELING: SOUTH AFRICA AND THE UNITED STATES

A brief linguistic exercise further illustrates the point. Please consider the four Black politicians presented in Figure 1. Although all four politicians are Black, only three are African American. Of the three who are African American, only two are slave descendants, and Condoleezza Rice is the only one who is a U.S. slave descendant. Were race used alone to calculate their educational risk as "Black students," a great deal of their diversity would be overlooked—all four politicians would simply be "Black." We can therefore see how Ogbu's observations regarding diversity within a racial group are significant. Barack Obama's ancestors were voluntary U.S. immigrants, and although Colin Powell's parents voluntarily emigrated to the United States from Jamaica, their African ancestors were once enslaved there. Again, it is only Condoleezza Rice that retraces her ancestry to Africans who were enslaved in the United States. Ogbu's castelike classifications offer important cultural distinctions among people who share the same race. Gates (1994) offers similar observations, albeit without explicit reference to Ogbu's categories.

Figure 1 also has important linguistic relevance, if only anecdotally, because each of the four political figures above is a gifted, eloquent speaker. Although each commands fluency in Standard English, they and their ancestors reflect a broad range of linguistic experience. Nelson Mandela learned English as a second language. Secretary Powell and Secretary Rice are African Americans whose respective command of Standard American English is incontrovertible; however, it is also incontrovertible that their enslaved ancestors did not share their command of literate Standard English. By striking contrast, Barack Obama does not share the linguistic legacy of U.S. slave descendants.

Why, then, are these observations relevant to a discussion concerned with educational risk? From a purely pragmatic perspective, it would appear that mastery of

	Black	African American	Slave Descendent	U.S. Slave Descendent
Nelson Mandela	Yes	No	No	No
Barack Obama	Yes	Yes	No	No
Colin Powell	Yes	Yes	Yes	No
Condoleeza Rice	Yes	Yes	Yes	Yes

FIGURE 1   Ancestry of Black Politicians

Standard English in both the United States and South Africa has direct correlations with one's prospects to obtain one of the highest executive appointments in either country. The danger or risk for those who lack fluency in the dominant linguistic norms may not be self-evident at first glance, particularly in cultures where folk notions of "eloquence" are culturally relative. In addition, those who are raised in households where the dominant (e.g., standard) linguistic norms are native will have less linguistic risk than will children who are raised in circumstances where non-dominant dialects or languages prevail.

Comparing the United States with South Africa is intentional; both societies had overt policies of racial discrimination in the past, along with national stereotypes that attribute/d low intelligence to Blacks who do/did not speak English properly. However, the South African situation illustrates that the majority population need not speak the dominant language. Unlike the United States, South Africa's White population remains the minority group, yet English is one of the dominant languages.

Rather than devote my attention to linguistic circumstances other than that of the African American community, I commend readers to the excellent volumes by Ferguson and Heath (1981), and more recently, by Finegan and Rickford (2004); they provide a vast array of the linguistic circumstances that have evolved in the United States, where Standard American English—although not classified as an official language—is of greatest utility to anyone seeking to conduct professional business of any kind within the United States. Clearly, students who live in homes where nondominant languages or dialects are native will be at a considerable disadvantage, if not "risk," regarding a high-quality, competitive education that can provide full and open access to all professional possibilities.

Viewed in terms of language, anyone who is not fluent in one or more varieties of American English is likely to be at a disadvantage, with noteworthy exceptions. For example, some dialects, such as educated varieties of British English, tend to be highly valued by many Americans. Some consider a French accent to sound alluring or exotic. Other dialects, by contrast, are often devalued and rarely escape scorn or ridicule, especially outside of the group of speakers who speak stigmatized languages or dialects. This proved to be the case during the Ebonics controversy of 1996, where Black American dialects were castigated and greatly misunderstood (Adger, Christian, & Taylor, 1999; Baugh, 2000; Rickford & Rickford, 2000; Smitherman, 2000).

FORMULATING RISK THROUGH POTENTIAL LINGUISTIC STEREOTYPE THREATS

Thus far, we have considered linguistic and anthropological dimensions of educational risk that are devoid of racial consideration. However, when the legal implications of *Brown v. Board of Education* (1954) are taken into consideration, along with racial controversies regarding affirmative action and the allocation of educational resources, it is important to consider research where racial dimensions of risk have been explored. In this regard, Claude Steele's (1992, 1997) studies of "stereotype threat" have been explicit in their experimental control of race as a research variable. Moreover, because Steele's analyses utilize standardized tests, his studies expose long-standing racially charged controversies regarding African American educational achievement or the glaring lack thereof (Herrnstein & Murray, 1996; Jensen, 1969; Labov, 1972). High-stakes standardized tests continue to be used throughout the United States and other countries for gatekeeping purposes, and students who are less fluent in their usage of academic discourse are clearly at risk. Although Steele's studies do not focus specifically on language, many of his African American subjects would—under Ogbu's classifications—be considered the descendants of involuntary immigrants, whereas the vast majority of Steele's White subjects represent the American posterity of voluntary immigrants, most of whose ancestors immigrated from Europe.

There are many scholars who have produced important and exciting research about African American language and culture (e.g., Alim, 2004; Ball, 2006; Goodwin, 1990; Green, 2002; Jacobs-Huey, 2006; Labov, 1972; Lanehart, 2002; Lee, 1993; Morgan, 2002; Rickford, 1999; Rickford & Rickford, 2000; Smitherman, 2000; Spears, 1997); readers who are unfamiliar with vernacular African American language and culture would benefit tremendously from familiarity with these insightful studies. By contrast, there are relatively few psychological studies that integrate linguistic diversity into their experimental design. As long as "race" (e.g., Black, Brown, or White) is used as a social science or educational variable, differences such as those described by Ogbu (1978, 1992) and Gates (1994) will escape critical detection.

This discussion presumes general familiarity with Steele's formulation of stereotype threat, where college students who are members of minority groups taking high-stakes standardized tests perform less well than Whites. His studies are extensive and far more complicated than suggested by my abbreviated account. However, Steele (1992) did divide his subjects by race. Steele's (1992) studies provide an excellent illustration of the potential for research in which Ogbu's categories and/or a student's linguistic background could be taken into account. Gates (2004) observed, for example, that many African American students are now the children of recent Black immigrants to the United States. As such, their heritage, like that of Barack Obama, does not trace its lineage to Africans who were enslaved in America.

Barack Obama's political ascendancy illustrates many of the cultural and linguistic dimensions of educational risk that grow directly from Ogbu's important observations; namely, as the child of voluntary immigrants who also happened to live in Hawaii, Obama received an education that is atypical when compared to that of African Americans who trace their ancestry to involuntary immigrants. Indeed, *Brown v. Board of Education* (1954), which is written in racial terms, should, for the sake of accuracy, be reexamined with more precise foci on students who are the descendants of U.S. slaves. In much the same manner that some children are born into wealthy families that provide a substantial boost at birth, others are born into poverty, which in some communities, is amplified by a legacy of historical racial disparities and the allocation of inferior resources and facilities to U.S. slave descendants.

Ward Connerly (2000) and Shelby Steele (1990), whose writings have received considerable attention in the popular press, have independently called for the dismantling of affirmative action for Blacks or anyone, based on racial classification. Shelby Steele's plea to eliminate race-based affirmative action is, allegedly, in pursuit of Dr. King's dream that every American be judged based on his or her content of character, that is, without racial consideration whatsoever. Ward Connerly (2000) echoes this sentiment during his travels from state to state to initiate ballot measures that would allow voters to eliminate all state-funded "race-based" affirmative action. Ironically, both Steele (i.e., Shelby) and Connerly are iconic examples of the very racial preferences they decry; if either of them were not African American, their opinions would readily be dismissed on ideological grounds. However, as Black men, they are often given credibility, if not considered to be very courageous, for bucking the trend of the vast majority of African Americans, who strongly believe that African Americans, as a people, have yet to overcome fully.

A HEURISTIC MODEL OF LINGUISTIC STEREOTYPE THREAT

I believe Claude Steele's analyses can be further refined to include diversity within racial groups, and I have modified Ogbu's original classifications to illustrate the point. If you are a U.S. citizen, please consider your own family history. How did you or your ancestors become U.S. citizens? Was it by birth or through voluntary immigration?[1] If you are an immigrant, did you learn English as a second language, and did you feel any linguistic disadvantages in school due to your lack of English fluency? If English is your mother tongue, how would your describe your own speech? Does it reflect the region where you live or your social background? Clearly, your answers to these questions will differ considerably from that of other readers, but were we to consider your heritage based on your racial background alone, we would not have an accurate portrait of any potential language-related educational risk or advantage that you may possess.

In an attempt to offer new diagnostics that can support this process, Figure 2 contains nine categories that compare and contrast a person's castelike heritage with differences in native language acquisition.

	Voluntary Immigrants	Involuntary Immigrants	Indigenous Ancestors
Dominant language(s) native	A	B	C
Nonstandard dominant language(s)	D	E	F
Dominant language(s) are not native	G	H	I

**FIGURE 2　Castelike Heritage Combined With
Native Language Acquisition**

Because the illustrative educational circumstances are not unique to the United States, Figure 2 presents a heuristic model that could be used to measure the existence of a linguistic stereotype threat that may result from differences in linguistic experience and exposure. In light of Claude Steele's (1992) findings that Black college students suffer from standardized test anxiety, future evaluations could consider linguistic diversity within a racial group. For example, Gates (2004) observed that many of today's Black students are—in Ogbu's terms—African American children of voluntary immigrants whose parents moved to the United States of their own volition (often to provide a brighter future for themselves and their children). These African Americans represent voluntary immigrants who might not suffer the lingering linguistic consequences of slavery but who may face different linguistic barriers. For example, African Americans who have emigrated from Haiti are likely to have more linguistic difficulty in America than are immigrants from Jamaica, who, in all likelihood, speak and understand English; both are Black, but their educational risk could vary considerably, as might their corresponding linguistic stereotype threat.

The Black political figures previously introduced further illustrate the point. Barack Obama falls into Category A; his parents were voluntary immigrants, and he grew up attending an affluent school in Hawaii where he had extensive exposure to Standard American English. Nelson Mandela, by contrast, has royal African ancestry. As such, he traces his ancestry to the indigenous people of Africa, yet he was born speaking a language other than English. Of all of the Black political figures presented here, President Mandela faced the greatest linguistic risk; he would be classified in Category I. As the child of Jamaican immigrants who was born in Harlem and grew up in the South Bronx, Colin Powell was exposed to a wide variety of speech styles. His biography suggests that he, too, may be classified in Category A, unless his childhood language usage began in Category D, that is, if he adopted any nonstandard speech usage during his youth. Condoleezza Rice spent her childhood in segregated Birmingham, Alabama. However, she is the daughter of highly educated African Americans who placed great importance on education and personal achievement. As such, Secretary Rice's linguistic heritage is best characterized by Category B; that is, she is among that population of U.S. slave descendants who have native Standard American English fluency. For the purpose of this discussion, it may be useful to ponder the future plight of diverse students based on their relative linguistic stereotype threat.

RELEVANCE TO EDUCATIONAL RISK

The primary reason for illustrating the linguistic heritage of prominent Blacks is to affirm diversity within any racial group and, by so doing, to call attention to important linguistic differences that exist among people who share the same racial background. To what extent, if any, do students suffer from a linguistic stereotype threat? The strongest legal foundation regarding these risks is embodied in the *Lau v. Nichols* (1974) case. That landmark ruling calls specific attention to the plight of students in categories G, H, and I, namely, students who are enrolled in U.S. schools but whose mother tongue is not English.

Many students who lack fluency in dominant discourse norms may suffer from alternative forms of linguistic stereotype threats, and this might easily compound their educational risk. More precisely, there is a long-standing history of linguistic disadvantages in the United States for English language learners or students who speak nonstandard English dialects. When teachers, parents, and others who are involved in children's education harbor false linguistic stereotypes, they may—often inadvertently—overlook or devalue the intellectual potential of students who are not facile users of academic discourse.

Last, although we have alluded to some of the legal dimensions of educational risk embodied in the *Brown v. Board of Education* (1954) and *Lau v. Nichols* (1974) rulings, we are not able in this chapter to devote sufficient attention to the important risk facing deaf students throughout the United States and elsewhere who are subjected to antiquated policies that fail to recognize their special educational needs. Those who are fluent (and native) users of sign language may learn English as a second language, yet their educational needs are rarely treated as being akin to that of others who learn English as a second language. Rather, due to legal classifications, deaf children who use sign language are provided with educational programs through the Individuals with Disabilities Education Act (i.e., IDEA). However, as long as policies for deaf students are not accurate or well informed, they may forestall the very educational advances they seek to profess.

CONCLUSION

As long as educational policies do not give linguistic diversity greater attention, they are likely to miss the important dimensions of diversity that defy simplistic racial classification. This discussion owes much to the innovative scholarship of others and, most notably, the efforts of John Ogbu, who wrestled with matters of race within the confines of rigorous social science inquiry. Similarly, Claude Steele's efforts to account for racially salient differences in standardized testing achievement among college students provide a solid empirical foundation on which to build a diagnostic infrastructure that can account for the combination of linguistic and heritage characteristics that may constitute neglected educational dangers for students who, through no fault of their own, live in circumstances where they are not fluent users of the dominant linguistic norms. Nelson Mandela is the best example provided here of someone who has overcome nearly insurmountable racial, educational, linguistic, political, and economic obstacles despite living through South African apartheid and decades of imprisonment. His ensuing efforts to pursue peaceful democracy while promoting racial harmony throughout the world were boldly illustrated through South Africa's Truth and Reconciliation Commission (Gibson, 2004).

It is perhaps most fitting to close in tribute to the uplifting studies of all who have contributed to this volume through their collective effort to overcome the remaining educational perils and pitfalls that still stand as unresolved impediments to our desired vision of truly equal educational opportunities for all children, wherever they may be.

ACKNOWLEDGMENTS

I am grateful to the Ford Foundation for its generous support for my analyses of linguistic profiling and their policy relevance. This chapter has benefited greatly from the vision, advice, and insights of Vivian Gadsden, Stephanie Biermann, H. Samy Alim, Morgan Marchbanks, Marjorie Goodwin, and John Rickford. I have not consistently followed their advice, and all limitations herein are my own.

NOTES

[1]Technically, becoming a citizen other than by birth is through naturalization, not immigration, which often does not result in naturalization and citizenship.

[2]The Individuals With Disabilities Education Act (IDEA) is a federal law enacted in 1990 and reauthorized in 1997. It is designed to protect the rights of students with disabilities by ensuring that everyone receives a free and appropriate public education (FAPE) regardless of ability. Furthermore, IDEA strives not only to grant equal access to students with disabilities but also to provide additional special education services and procedural safeguards.

REFERENCES

Adger, C., Christian, D., & Taylor, O. (Eds.). (1999). *Making the connection: Language and academic achievement among African American students. Proceedings of a conference of the Coalition on Language Diversity in Education.* Washington, DC: Center for Applied Linguistics; McHenry, IL: Delta Systems Co.

Alim, H. S. (2004). *You know my steez: An ethnographic and sociolinguistic study of styleshifting in a Black American speech community.* Publication of the American Dialect Society (No. 89). Durham, NC: Duke University Press.

Ball, A. (2006). *Multicultural strategies for education and social change: Carriers of the torch in the United States and South Africa.* New York: Teachers College Press.

Baugh, J. (2000). *Beyond Ebonics: Linguistic pride and racial prejudice.* New York: Oxford University Press.

Brown v. Board of Education, 347 U.S. 483 (1954).

Connerly, W. (2000). *Creating equal: My fight against race preferences.* San Francisco: Encounter Books.

Ferguson, C., & Heath, S. B. (Eds.). (1981). *Language in the USA.* New York: Cambridge University Press.

Finegan, E., & Rickford, J. (Eds.). (2004). *Language in the USA: Themes for the twenty-first century.* New York: Cambridge University Press.

Gates, H. L. (1994). *Colored people: A memoir.* New York: Knopf.

Gates, H. L. (2004). *America behind the color line: Dialogues with African Americans.* New York: Warner Books.

Gibson, J. (2004). *Overcoming apartheid: Can truth reconcile a divided nation?* New York: Russell Sage.

Goodwin, M. H. (1990). *He-said-she-said: Talk as social organization among Black children.* Bloomington: Indiana University Press.

Green, L. J. (2002). *African American English: A linguistic introduction.* New York: Cambridge University Press.

Herrnstein, R., & Murray, C. (1996). *The bell curve: Intelligence and class structure in American life.* New York: Simon & Schuster.

Individuals With Disabilities Education Act of 1990, 20 U.S.C. § 1400 *et seq.*

Individuals With Disabilities Education Act Amendments of 1997, 20 U.S.C. § 1400 *et seq.*

Jacobs-Huey, L. (2006). *From the kitchen to the parlor: Language and becoming in African American women's hair care.* Oxford, UK: Oxford University Press.

Jensen, A. (1969). How much can we boost IQ? *Harvard Educational Review, 39*(1), 1–123.

Labov, W. (1972). *Language in the inner city: Studies in the Black English vernacular.* Philadelphia: University of Pennsylvania Press.

Lanehart, S. (2002). *Sista, speak! Black women kinfolk talk about language and literacy.* Austin: University of Texas Press.

Lau v. Nichols, 414 U.S. 563 (1974).

Lee, C. D (1993). *Signifying as a scaffold for literary interpretation: The pedagogical implications of an African American discourse genre.* Urbana, IL: National Council of Teachers of English.

Morgan, M. (2002). *Language, discourse and power in African American culture.* New York: Cambridge University Press.

Ogbu, J. (1978). *Minority education and caste: The American system in cross-cultural perspective.* New York: Academic Press.

Ogbu, J. (1992). Understanding multicultural education. *Educational Researcher, 21,* 5–14, 24.

Olson, L. (2005). Early childhood education: Investing in quality makes sense. *Essential Information for Educational Policy, 3*(2), 1–4. Washington, DC: American Educational Research Association.

Rickford, A. (1999). *I can fly: Teaching reading and narrative comprehension to African American and other ethnic minority students.* Lanham, MD: University Press of America.

Rickford, J. R., & Rickford, R. J. (2000). *Spoken soul: The story of Black English.* New York: John Wiley.

Smitherman, G. (2000). *Talkin that talk: Language, culture, and education in African America.* New York: Routledge.

Spears, A. (Ed.). (1997). *Race and ideology: Language, symbolism, and popular culture.* Detroit, MI: Wayne State University Press.

Steele, C. (1997). A threat in the air: How stereotypes shape intellectual identity and performance. *American Psychologist, 52*(6), 613–629.

Steele, C. (1992, April). Race and schooling of Black Americans. *The Atlantic Monthly, 269*(4), 68–78.

Steele, S. (1990). *The content of our character: A new vision of race in America.* New York: St. Martin's.

Valdés, G. (1996). *Con respeto: Bridging the distances between culturally diverse families and schools: An ethnographic portrait.* New York: Teachers College Press.

Williams, F. (Ed.). (1970). *Language and poverty. Perspectives on a theme.* Chicago: Markham.

Zentella, A. C. (1997). *Growing up bilingual: Puerto Rican children in New York.* Malden, MA: Blackwell, 1997.

Chapter 11

Consequences of Physical Health and Mental Illness Risks for Academic Achievement in Grades K–12

Sean Joe[1]
Emanique Joe
Larry L. Rowley
University of Michigan

Educational research, practice, and institutions regularly highlight the significance of factors outside of schooling that affect children's engagement and participation in classroom learning. However, they are less likely to intervene in issues that are described as nonacademic despite their clear relevance to students' academic experiences. The health of children and families is one such issue with implications for the quality of children's school experiences, treatment in school, and academic achievement. A focus on health concerns both identifiable risk factors (e.g., obesity) as well as less easily identified risks (e.g., eating disorders) that may serve as obstacles to children's engagement and challenge efforts to increase preventive health and health maintenance measures.

In this review, we are concerned with risk(s) to children that results from educational and health disparities. We are similarly concerned with the intersection of these disparities and social inequalities that are embedded in them to students' academic achievement. The incidence and prevalence of these risks are often greater for children from ethnic minority groups; however, the problems that result from high-risk behaviors affect children across ethnic groups and income levels. Children who suffer from poor health early in their lives are placed in a precarious position of having descending academic trajectories and socioeconomic success that continue into their adulthood (Case, Fertig, & Paxson, 2005; Palloni, 2006; Palloni & Milesi, 2006). The preponderance of educational research on disparities in academic achievement tends to focus on familial and socioeconomic conditions (i.e., parental educational attainment, income, poverty status, and single-family household), student behaviors

Review of Research in Education
March 2009, Vol. 33, pp. 283-309
DOI: 10.3102/0091732X08327355
© 2009 AERA. http://rre.aera.net

and youth experiences (i.e., student motivation and effort for learning, drug use, alcohol, and crime), and the conditions of schools and educational practices (i.e., instructional resources, school dropout, and segregation) (Grissmer, Flanagan, & Williamson, 1998; Wasserman, McReynolds, Ko, Katz, & Carpenter, 2005). More recently, research has begun to attend to children's early health experiences, their role in children's academic achievement, and the subsequent social inequalities that children will face as adults (Needham, Crosnoe, & Muller, 2004; Palloni, 2006).

Increased attention by schools to students' health risks stands in the face of educational policies that do not take on these issues of children's health as a primary focus of legislation or implementation. No Child Left Behind (NCLB), despite its emphasis on accountability for student performance via a standards-based approach to children's academic achievement, has been relatively neglectful of issues related to children's physical and mental health and the implications for their academic achievement. Although NCLB contains provisions to advance health services within schools, the law has made it extremely difficult for educators and health professionals to understand the practical and legal interface between this educational policy and the school health movement. However, even if the legislation or other educational policies required a more rigorous effort on health, there are vast differences in the availability of social and economic resources to schools that limit their ability to address children's health concerns. Given the association between children's health and their academic performance, policy initiatives and interventions could successfully target education institutions as a conduit for addressing students' nonacademic experiences, including cultural and social experiences, and the ways these are translated in school settings by students and educators alike (Ma, 2000; Millstein, 1988).

Academic achievement among American children and adolescents has critical consequences for adult health and socioeconomic status (Kramer, Allen, & Gergen, 1995; Needham et al., 2004; Palloni, 2006), and academic achievement gaps remain a central educational policy concern for the nation. In general, the terms *academic achievement gap* or *academic disparities* refer to differences (e.g., in race, gender, and class) in academic performance using national average standardized test scores and graduation rates (Ladson-Billings, 2006). Prior research indicates that academic disparities are seen as early as kindergarten, particularly among racial and ethnic minorities, who enter school lagging behind academically (Entwisle & Alexander, 1993; Lewit & Schuurmann Baker, 1995). Such disparities are one of several factors that led to the creation of federal programs such as Head Start, Healthy Start, Early Head Start, and a range of similar programs designed for children from low-income homes and communities. The racial differences in academic performance between ethnic minority and White students continue to widen over the educational life course and are evident in the higher high school dropout rates, lower advanced placement examinations, and lower college admittance among ethnic minorities (Campbell, Hombo, & Mazzeo, 2000; Ladson-Billings, 2006; J. Lee, 2002).

Growing concerns regarding the physical and mental health of children and adolescents in the United States have garnered increased public health and policy attention, but the implications for academic achievement are less understood. Well-established in existing research are the reverse relationships, namely how disparities in physical and mental health status and health risk behaviors are structured—at least in part—by educational attainment and other indicators of social status (Kessler, Foster, Saunders, & Stang, 1995; Palloni, 2006). Whether childhood health conditions are predictors of academic performance, including academic failure, is a question receiving slow but increasing attention (Field, Diego, & Sanders, 2001; Thies, 1999). The new scientific interest is bolstered by research showing that there are strong associations between the physical and mental health status of children and their long-term adult social status (Case et al., 2005; Kessler et al., 1995).

Our review is based largely on work that draws heavily from quasi-experimental research primarily, given that much of research on children's health has used epidemiological and experimental frameworks. However, the review also aims to ground the issues from these studies in a more expansive analysis of the cultural and social experiences and histories of children in school, speaking to the ways that existing educational, health, and social welfare structures support or fail them in their school lives. For example, empirical evidence points to race, ethnicity, and other known social correlates of academic performance as affecting some children more critically than others. Because Black children are more likely to live in poverty and also face worse health conditions than their White peers, it is likely that early health conditions might have stronger developmental effects for them (Palloni & Milesi, 2006). We review the research for evidence of differential effects of health on academic performance by race, ethnicity, and socioeconomic status.

This review is organized in the following manner. First, we focus on health problems and health risk behaviors, particularly chronic illnesses, and then we address health risk behaviors and their influence on academic performance. In the next section, we examine lingering issues of physical and mental health in research and in practice, followed by a consideration of the possibilities for academic achievement and the improvement of children's health. We conclude with a discussion of the importance of schools as sites for addressing health problems of children and families.

HEALTH AND RISK BEHAVIORS: CONTEXT AND ISSUES

Early-life health is garnering increased attention from researchers and policymakers because of the role it plays in the intergenerational transmission of socioeconomic status (Palloni & Milesi, 2006). A growing number of studies have linked childhood and adolescent health status to later mortality, general health status, earnings and employment, and educational achievement and attainment (Crosnoe, 2006b; Palloni & Milesi, 2006). Research studies suggest that those children who experience physical illness are often affected through their adulthood either directly, through the illness itself, or indirectly via their restricted educational attainment and social status (Kuh & Wadsworth, 1993).

The relationship between health and education is often examined from the point of view of how educational attainment determines access to health care, general health, and well-being. Less clear are the mechanisms through which early health might affect educational achievement. Although the possible causal pathways are many, for this review we examine health conditions that would influence children's abilities to perform academically, namely their school enrollment, rates of absenteeism, cognitive abilities, dropout, or capacity to focus on classroom instruction or do homework. A recent report by the Centers for Disease Control and Prevention reveals that, in 2006, 5% of school-aged children 5–17 years of age missed 11 or more days of school in the past 12 months because of illness or injury (Bloom & Cohen, 2007). In addition, 8.6% of school-aged children had limited ability to perform activities usual for their age group because of a physical, mental, or emotional problem. Children's health can also significantly siphon schools' resources, affect educational policy decisions, and increase strain on students and their families in ways that adversely affect students' achievement trajectories.

This review focuses on select health conditions. It is impossible to discuss every possible contribution of every physical health condition and health risk behavior on children's achievement. Therefore, we focus on the health conditions that are most common and that are more likely to have an impact on a broader swath of American children through the potential causal pathways described above. For example, research suggests that children's academic achievement is adversely affected by injuries and illnesses because of children's having higher rates of absenteeism or through lack of sleep, discomfort, or pain that limits children's ability to remain focused on school tasks (Fowler, Davenport, & Garg, 1992).

It is also important to make the distinction between physical health conditions and health risk behaviors. *Health risk behaviors* refers to behavioral maladaptations that occur despite negative or positive environmental influences. These are behaviors that place children and adolescents at risk for the onset of a potentially mortal or functionally debilitating physical illness (e.g., HIV/AIDS, heart disease, lung cancer, emphysema, kidney failure; Institute of Medicine, 2001). Specifically, *risk* refers to the probability of a future event, given a specific condition or set of conditions. For example, although adolescent females are five times more likely to attempt suicide than males, boys are more likely to die by suicide than females (Gould, Greenberg, Velting, & Shaffer, 2003). Health risk behaviors also should be considered along a hazard continuum whereby they are risk factors, that is, markers, correlates, or, in the best cases, the causes of physical illness (Institute of Medicine, 2001). For this review, we will focus on health risk behaviors that research shows are common among school-aged children and that contribute to the leading causes of death and disability among adults and youth. Health risk behaviors usually are established during childhood, persist into adulthood, are interrelated, and are preventable (Institute of Medicine, 2001). These behaviors are not only associated with causing serious health conditions but they also contribute to a range of educational and social problems that disrupt the lives of students, including failure to complete high school, unemployment, and crime (Crosnoe, 2006a; Daniels, 2006).

HEALTH CONDITIONS AND ACADEMIC ACHIEVEMENT: FOUR EXAMPLES

This section of the review examines research on four health conditions that are considered to be among the most pressing for school-aged children and adolescents: (a) obesity, (b) nutrition and physical activity, (c) asthma, and (d) epilepsy and sleep disturbance. We offer a summary of the prevalence of each here and a short discussion under each subheading of the implications for children's academic achievement and for the role of schools in supporting children experiencing these health problems. Some of the issues can be addressed directly through improved school practices and others can be addressed by schools indirectly through enhanced efforts around health and well-being and through attention to students who are experiencing difficulties due to health problems.

Obesity

The United States has the highest prevalence of obesity among the developed nations, and a large percentage of those who are obese are children and adolescents (Ahn, Juon, & Gittelsohn, 2008; Baskin, Ard, Franklin, & Allison, 2005; National Center for Health Statistics, 2006; Ogden et al., 2006). The increased public health concern regarding the national prevalence of obesity in the past 30 years is attributed largely to the fact that obesity places individuals at an increased risk of serious health conditions (i.e., diabetes, hypertension, cardiovascular disease; Institute of Medicine, 2001). The terms *obesity* and *overweight* are often used interchangeably in the literature and are measured most typically using body mass index. Body mass index is defined as weight divided by height. Obesity in adolescents (ages 13–17) is defined as body mass index greater than 25 or the 85th percentile (Taras & Potts-Datema, 2005). Childhood obesity is one of the nation's most serious health problems. Not only has the number of obese children tripled in the past three decades, but by 1999–2002 those children who were obese tended to be heavier than obese children in the past (Anderson & Butcher, 2006). Obesity in children and adolescents places them at risk of experiencing serious health conditions earlier in their lives and has long-term negative implications for their well-being.

According to the latest estimates, there are approximately 12.5 million (17.1%) overweight children and adolescents in the United States (National Center for Health Statistics, 2006; Ogden et al., 2006). Obesity patterns vary by race, gender, and other social factors. Compared to their White peers, ethnic minority (e.g., Mexican American and Black) and low-income children have significantly higher obesity rates (Anderson & Butcher, 2006). Among all children, obesity rates increased, but the rise was highest among African American children (Anderson & Butcher, 2006; Kumanyika & Grier, 2006). Such racial, ethnic, and socioeconomic differences in the rate of overweight or obese children are partially explained by group differences in dieting and exercise behaviors (Delva, Johnston, & O'Malley, 2006).

Many of the problems around children's inactivity and failure to exercise have been attributed as well to the inability of children in high-crime communities to feel safe in their neighborhoods, limiting their access to playgrounds and play with friends except in a sheltered setting with restricted spaces for physical activity (Burdette & Whitaker, 2005; Cohen et al., 2003; Gómez, Johnson, Selva, & Sallis, 2004). There are also gender differences in rates of overweight or obese children. From 1999 to 2004, there was a significant increase in the prevalence of overweight girls (13.8% in 1999 to 16.0% in 2004). The increase was similar for boys, from 14.0% in 1999 to 18.2% in 2004 (Ogden et al., 2006; Sweeting, 2008). These data contribute to greater public health concern that these children's life chances are threatened, given the increased risk that they may come to suffer from elevated blood pressure and cholesterol-related illnesses, Type II diabetes, asthma, depression, and anxiety (U.S. Department of Health and Human Services, 2000).

The increased prevalence of obesity among children and adolescents in the United States compared to children growing up in the past is attributed to several issues. For example, today's children are living a more sedentary lifestyle; have reduced physical activity in schools; are consuming diets poor in nutritional value (i.e., fast foods and sweetened beverages) in and out of school; and are growing up in a technological age of high computer and Internet usage, television viewing, and video-game playing (Anderson & Butcher, 2006; Juster, Ono, & Stafford, 2004). In the past 20 years, young Americans between the ages of 6 and 17 have seen an increase in time spent in school (up to 6 or 7 hours a day), yet many are spending less time involved in sports and physical activities during the week days. A recent report estimates that from 1980 to 2003, for youth in some age groups, the amount of time devoted to physical activity dropped approximately 31%, from 6.5 hours to 4.5 hours per week (Juster et al., 2004). In short, studies strongly suggest that being overweight and obese affect children's physical, social, and intellectual development (Anderson & Butcher, 2006; Sabia, 2007).

Although the research literature is equivocal about the mechanism by which obesity influences academic achievement, there is evidence of a direct association between them (Sabia, 2007; Taras & Potts-Datema, 2005). A study involving 11,192 kindergartners found disparities in academic achievement associated with being overweight. Datar, Sturm, and Magnabosco (2004) found that overweight children had significantly lower math and reading test scores at the beginning of the year than did their healthy-weight peers and that these differences persisted into first grade. In a study of adolescents, Sabia (2007) found among White females, aged 14–17, that a difference in weight of 50 to 60 pounds (approximately two standard deviations) is associated with an 8–10% difference in grade-point averages. Prior research also reveals that children with weight problems are twice as likely to be in special education and remedial classes and to report impaired school functioning (Schwimmer, Burwinkle, & Varni, 2003; Tershakovec, Weller, & Gallagher, 1994). In addition, obese and overweight children and adolescents are more likely to have mental health conditions (e.g., depression, low self-esteem, anxiety disorders), which may serve as the mediating factors for an overweight child's poor performance in school (Taras & Potts-Datema, 2005). However, despite the link between being overweight and poor academic achievement, obesity should be considered a marker for lower academic performance and not the cause itself (Story, Kaphingst, & French, 2006).

Nutrition and Physical Activity

The basic understanding of the physiology of weight gain is unequivocal in that weight is gained when the energy intake surpasses energy outlay. However, less clear are the determinants of the increase in childhood obesity. Implicit in our understanding of the physiology of weight gain and well supported by empirical research is that the combination of diet and physical activity has a clear impact on obesity (Anderson & Butcher, 2006). Evidence of a link between factors of poor nutrition and physical inactivity among children suggests that those children who have limited access to enough food to meet their basic needs are more likely to be obese than are other children (Currie, 2005). Beyond the impact that diet and physical activity have on obesity, we consider these two health behaviors here in our review for two reasons. First, given the amount of time children spend in school, diet and physical activity are two health behaviors that schools can clearly influence. For instance, school meal programs have been known to improve school-aged children's diets significantly by providing them with increased consumption of nutritional foods (Gleason & Suitor, 2001). Moreover, these diet and physical activities have their own independent impact on differences in student achievement. Prior studies have shown that children participating in the school breakfast programs have increases in daily attendance, class participation, academic test scores, and decreases in tardiness (Florence, Asbridge, & Veugelers, 2008). This evidence reveals that efforts to improve nutrition and increase physical activity in school may have the twin benefits of reducing obesity and improving the academic performance of all children, whether they are at risk of obesity or not (Story et al., 2006).

The discussion about the relationship between diet and academic performance centers on nutrition and whether the diets of children and adolescents in schools are appropriate. Despite the possibilities that schools hold for helping children engage in healthier eating habits, schools may be part of the problem. As a recent popular report has shown, students' access to à la carte items (e.g., French fries) in addition to their access to vending machines, snack bars, and stores within schools contribute to students' school diets being high in fat and sugar and of little nutritional value (Kann, Brener, & Wechsler, 2007). Poor diet is characterized by the intake of fat and refined sugars and an inadequate intake of fruits, vegetables, and grains (Florence et al., 2008). Nevertheless, it appears that children who suffer from poor nutrition during their early developmental years and those who are overweight are at risk of not performing well in school (Brown & Pollitt, 1996; Datar et al., 2004). Diminished nutrition as a result of either hunger or poor diet interferes with cognitive function and is associated with lower academic achievement. For example, poor nutrition and related iron deficiency is linked to shortened attention span, irritability, fatigue, and difficulty with concentration (Parker, 1989). The reason hunger and poor diet are related to disparities in student achievement is that undernourished children are more likely to have decreased attendance and attention spans and poorer academic performance in contrast to well-nourished children (Florence et al., 2008; Rampersaud, Pereira, Girard, Adams, & Metzl, 2005).

Relatively few studies have begun to elucidate the relationship between physical activity and academic achievement among children and adolescents. However, the emerging empirical literature provides data that demonstrate the importance of physical activity programs in helping school-aged children develop social skills, improve mental health, and reduce risk-taking behaviors (Taras, 2005). Evidence also indicates that short-term cognitive benefits of physical activity—that is, during the school day—adequately compensate for time spent away from other academic areas (Taras, 2005). Despite such evidence and the adoption by states and local districts of policies stating that schools will teach physical education, many school districts are not providing or requiring students to engage in adequate levels of physical activity. Nationally, only 8% of elementary schools and 6% of middle schools and high schools meet the recommended 150 minutes and 225 minutes per week in physical activities, respectively (Burgeson, Wechsler, Brener, Young, & Spain, 2001; Lee, Burgeson, Fulton, & Spain, 2007).

Although caution should be used when interpreting the results of research, data suggest that there is an association between obesity, malnourishment, or less physical activity in children and their poor academic performances (Daniels, 2006; Florence et al., 2008; Sabia, 2007; Taras, 2005). However, because these conditions are linked to poor academic performance, one should not assume that they cause poor performance among children and adolescents. As mentioned in the previous section of this chapter, research indicates that low academic achievement among students is also attributed to a range of social factors (e.g., socioeconomic status and parents' educational attainment) and that these physical conditions should be considered as markers for poor academic performance and not the cause (Story et al., 2006). In addition, whether children are overweight is also associated with their having externalizing and internalizing behavioral problems that are known to affect academic performance (Judge & Jahns, 2007). Such findings could be attributed to a new array of challenges that overweight children experience as they approach adolescence, such as identity formation and interconnectedness in their social relationships (Daniels, 2006; Sabia, 2007; Story et al., 2006). The prevalence of overweight and obese children gives schools a mandate and opportunity to support students in developing and maintaining healthy behaviors, particularly schools serving children and families from underrepsented groups and in low-income urban and rural communities. However, because of the current financial crises facing many schools in this country, school districts often opt either to reduce the frequency of students' physical education programs or to eliminate them completely. Given the recent research that suggests that increased physical activity in children is associated with their academic, behavioral, and social outcomes (Story et al., 2006; Taras, 2005), the elimination of physical education programs within schools is potentially harmful for children.

Asthma

Children who are considered asthmatic are those who suffer from episodes of inflammation of their airways, which restricts their breathing and is typically exhibited through wheezing. According to national estimates, 13% of children who are under the age of 18 have been diagnosed with asthma (Bloom, Cohen, Vickerie, & Wondimu, 2003). As is generally seen with chronic health conditions of children in the general population, ethnic minority children and those from low-income families have higher rates of being diagnosed with asthma (Bloom, 2003; Newacheck & Halfon, 2000). For example, in the United States the prevalence rates for children with asthma is higher for Black (15.7%) than for White (12.2%) people, but interestingly it is lowest for Hispanic people (11.2%) (Bloom et al., 2003). Among Black children, 7.7% had an attack in the past 12 months, compared to 5.7% for Whites and 4% for Hispanics. Additionally, when compared to their more affluent peers (12%), poor children are more likely to have been diagnosed with asthma (16%). Furthermore, many children (especially those with severe asthma) do not grow out of asthma, but they continue to experience symptoms during adulthood.

As a chronic illness, asthma is the leading cause of children's emergency room visits, hospitalization, and school absenteeism (Currie, 2005). Depending on the severity of their asthmatic episodes, children often need to miss school entirely or to be dismissed early for doctors' visits or for required medical treatments. One would assume that school absenteeism would influence children's academic performance. However, research suggests that, in general, asthma is not necessarily a precursor to poorer educational attainment or academic performance among children (Anderson, Bailey, Cooper, Palmer, & West, 1983; Gutstadt et al., 1989; Roder, Kroonenberg, & Boekaerts, 2003; Silverstein et al., 2001). Those studies that have found an association between asthma and low academic performance have typically relied on subjective measures of parents' concerns for their children's performance or parents' ratings of children's learning problems (Fowler et al., 1992; Wjst et al., 1996). Also, given the existing differences in prevalence rates for asthma by social class and race or ethnicity, a small amount of research suggests that, after controlling for demographic factors, poor asthmatic children have lower academic performance when compared to their more affluent peers (Fowler et al., 1992; Gutstadt et al., 1989).

What these and other data suggest is that despite the apparent increases in asthma among poor children the problems do not appear to have a direct relationship to children's performance in school. The urgency for attention to children with asthma, therefore, centers on questions about the measures that schools and medical institutions will take to reduce a problem that threatens children's well-being. Health professionals in schools must be particularly aware of children who suffer from asthma, and they along with school administrators and teachers can take up the issues related to this problem in their daily interactions with students.

Epilepsy and Sleep Disturbance

Although epilepsy and disruptive sleep apnea are low-frequency health problems, we mention them here because they are serious, and many children and adolescents have disrupted academic experiences because of them. Epilepsy is a neurological condition that produces brief disturbances in the normal electrical functions of the brain. The brain experiences intermittent bursts of electrical energy that are much more intense than its normal functioning; this affects one's consciousness, bodily movements, or sensations for a short time and is exhibited by epileptic seizures (Bailet & Turk, 2000). When seizures continue to occur for unknown reasons or because of an underlying problem that cannot be corrected, the condition is known as *epilepsy*. Although no definite cause of epilepsy can be found, it is thought that the condition occurs as a result of various conditions that affect a person's brain such as brain injuries, infections, or illnesses (e.g., meningitis) and certain genetic disorders.

Children with epilepsy have been shown to be at greater risk for lags in academic achievement and behavioral problems in school, although the nature of the problems of academic achievement has not been examined carefully (Breslau, 1985; Fowler, Johnson, & Atkinson, 1985; Howe, Feinstein, Reiss, Molock, & Berger, 1993; Mitchell, Chavez, Lee, & Guzman, 1991). The factors that appear to place children at a higher risk of having academic problems include the age at onset and severity and frequency of the seizures. In a relevant study, Bailet and Turk (2000) found that children with epilepsy had high rates of grade retention and placement in special education compared with their sibling control group who did not have epilepsy. These differences in grade retention and special education placement persisted over time. However, we have relatively little data to determine the distribution of students with epilepsy by ethnic or racial group identification, socioeconomic classes, or gender. The limitations of the data leave several questions unanswered: for example, whether students from certain ethnic groups were overrepresented among those referred to special education; whether these students were indeed low achievers or were uncomfortable in the classroom, making others uncomfortable; and whether their assignment to special education classes was appropriate.

Finally, sleep apnea poses a threat to the academic performance of many school-age children. Whereas some children sleep in school because they have stayed up too late, others may be exhausted because of sleep disruption, reducing their ability to engage in classroom work. As a result of sleep disruption, students are at risk of daytime sleepiness, particularly among those who are overweight. A recent study estimates that one third of severely overweight young patients had symptoms associated with obstructive sleep apnea and 5% had severe obstructive sleep apnea (Daniels, 2006). Sleep apnea is not likely to cause children or adolescents to be absent for extended periods of time. However, this condition is serious in that it disrupts students' concentration and, thus, hampers their ability to engage fully in the learning process or to complete assignments (Needham et al., 2004).

HEALTH RISK BEHAVIORS AND ACADEMIC PERFORMANCE

Equally as important as these acute and chronic health conditions are those behaviors in which adolescents engage that place them at risk for the onset of a potentially mortal or functionally debilitating physical illness (e.g., HIV/AIDS, heart disease, lung cancer, emphysema, kidney failure). Existing research substantiates a relationship between health risk behaviors and adolescents' academic performance and school dropout, yet it is unclear how the effect occurs across developmental periods (Currie, 2005; Fowler et al., 1985). However, the potential adverse consequence of such behaviors on adolescents' well-being is an important consideration for their schooling. The following section provides a discussion of those health risk behaviors that are more common among adolescents and summarizes how they are associated with educational outcomes: alcohol and tobacco use and abuse, substance use and abuse, and teenage pregnancy. We present the epidemiology of these behaviors and conclude with a summary of all of them as not to be redundant, given the amount of comorbidity among these behaviors (Bennett & Kemper, 1994) and the frequency with which they hold a similar association with academic performance.

During adolescence, many young people experiment with a number of substances, including cigarettes, alcohol, prescription and over-the-counter medicines, and illegal drugs. Substance use refers to a drug or other chemicals whose use leads to effects that are detrimental to an individual's physical and mental health or the welfare of others. Adolescents' use of substances is considered a health risk because engaging in associated behaviors places children and adolescents at risk for future adverse health outcomes (Blum, 1987; Ozer, Brindis, Millstein, Knopf, & Irwin, 1998). A considerable amount of attention has been paid to the factors that appear to place youth at higher risk of alcohol and substance abuse. Of these factors, peer influence is strongly associated with adolescents' engagement in high-risk behaviors. For instance, teens who have friends who are smokers are more likely to smoke themselves (Kobus, 2003). Also, those children who have been physically or sexually abused are much more likely to engage in high-risk behaviors such as substance use (Bennett & Kemper, 1994; Simantov, Schoen, & Klein, 2000). However, there are several protective factors that reduce the risk of adolescents engaging in high-risk behaviors. These protective factors include parent support (i.e., emotional support and sense of closeness), parents' high expectations for their children's academic achievement, self-perception, engagement in extracurricular activities, and sense of connectedness to school (Crocker & Knight, 2005; Resnick et al., 1997; Simantov et al., 2000; Willis, Vaccaro, & McNamara, 1992).

Alcohol Use and Abuse

Adolescents' initial use of alcohol often occurs early, and alcohol is used by more young people in the United States than tobacco or illicit drugs (U.S. Department of Health and Human Services, 2007). A recent national survey of the prevalence rate of alcohol use among adolescents indicates that 75% of youth (under the age of 21) have had at least one drink of alcohol before reaching adulthood. In addition, 23.8% of these youths have their first drink of alcohol before reaching the age of 13 (Centers for Disease Control and Prevention, 2008). There are also differences in prevalence rates for alcohol use among adolescents, with White (47.3%) and Hispanic adolescents (47.6%) engaging in current alcohol use at higher rates than Black adolescents (34.5%).

There has been increasing public concern regarding adolescents' alcohol use and increasing attention to the problems of drinking on college campuses (Committee on Substance Abuse, 2001; Hingson, Heeren, Winter, & Wechsler, 2005). This is partially attributed to fears that adolescents and young adults become addicted to alcohol more rapidly than do adults who drink, especially those under the age of 15 (Grant & Dawson, 1997). Another cause for concern is that alcohol abuse places adolescents at a higher risk of developing serious physical health issues (e.g., liver disease, cancer, cardiovascular disease, and neurological damage) as well as psychiatric problems (Naimi et al., 2003) at an earlier age. Furthermore, alcohol use is largely responsible for an overall yearly increase in the number of accidents and unintentional injuries, and it also results in the greatest number of deaths for those younger than 21 years of age (R. N. Anderson, 2002; National Highway Traffic Safety Administration, 2005).

Tobacco Use and Abuse

Although there has been a slight reduction in the number of adolescents who smoke cigarettes in the past decade, cigarette smoking is still a prevalent risk behavior and serious health issue among adolescents in the United States (National Institute on Drug Abuse, 2007). Concerns about cigarette smoking and other forms of tobacco consumption by adolescents generally focus on the risks for future health problem such as respiratory aliments (e.g., emphysema), lung cancer, and cardiovascular disease. According to a recent nationwide survey, 50.3% of adolescents have tried smoking cigarettes before reaching adulthood (Centers for Disease Control and Prevention, 2008), and 25.7% of adolescents reported current cigarette, smokeless tobacco, or cigar use (Centers for Disease Control and Prevention, 2008). Additionally, of those adolescents who use various forms of tobacco, it appears that typically the prevalence rates are higher among males than females and among White than Black and Hispanic adolescents.

Drug Use and Abuse

Marijuana is the most commonly used illicit drug among adolescents in the United States (Substance Abuse and Mental Health Services Administration, 2007). Often considered to be the gateway drug, young people who smoke marijuana are more likely to move on to harder drugs (e.g., cocaine; Degenhardt et al., 2008). Health risks associated with smoking marijuana are similar to the respiratory symptoms exhibited by tobacco use, including coughing, phlegm production, chronic bronchitis, shortness of breath, and wheezing. Also, the long-term use of marijuana may increase the risk of developing chronic cough, bronchitis, and emphysema as well as cancer of the head, neck, and lungs (Centers for Disease Control and Prevention, 2008).

In addition, there are many other illicit drugs commonly used by adolescents such as cocaine, ecstasy, methamphetamines, heroin, and hallucinogenic drugs. Results from a national study suggest that teen use for the majority of these illicit drugs has steadily declined over the past 5 years (Centers for Disease Control and Prevention, 2008). However, there has also been a nationwide increase of teens abusing prescription and over-the-counter drugs. In fact, with the exception of marijuana, young people aged 12 to 17 abuse prescription drugs more than any illicit drug (e.g., cocaine, methamphetamines, and heroin) combined. The prescription drugs most commonly abused by teens are powerful narcotics prescribed to treat pain; antidepressants, sedatives (e.g., sleeping pills), or antianxiety drugs; and stimulants (e.g., Ritalin medication for treatment of attention deficit hyperactivity disorder). Increasing numbers of adolescents are also abusing over-the-counter drugs, primarily cough and cold remedies that contain dextromethorphan, a cough suppressant. The hidden danger of prescription and over-the-counter medications is that they are either free or inexpensive. Until recently, many young people have had wide access to these substances; however, there has been increased effort to reduce their access, as stores have increasingly required identification to obtain the medications. Also, it is often falsely believed that these legal drugs are safer than illicit drugs like cocaine or heroin. However, teens' misuse of over-the-counter and prescription drugs can cause serious health effects, addiction, and in some instances even death (Substance Abuse and Mental Health Services Administration, 2007).

Teenage Pregnancy

Many young people in the United States begin having sexual intercourse during their teenage years; in fact, the United States remains higher than any other developed nation in pregnancy among those under the age of 20. The younger the age of first sexual intercourse, the greater the risk of unwanted pregnancy and sexually transmitted diseases (Lammers, Ireland, Resnick, & Blum, 2000). Those who begin having sex at young ages may be exposed to the risk of sexually transmitted diseases earlier and for a longer time and are less likely to use contraception. Although there is increased usage of contraceptives by adolescents, nonuse of contraceptives leads to approximately 50% of adolescent pregnancies within the first 6 months of sexual intercourse (Haffner & Haffner, 1998). In the United States for 2006, a total of 435,427 infants were born to mothers aged 15 to 19 (Centers for Disease Control and Prevention, 2007)—41.9 births per 1,000 females up from 40.5 in the previous year (Child Trends, 2008).

Additionally, a disproportionate number of adolescents who become early parents are ethnic minorities and from poor and low-income families. The prevalence rates indicate that in 2005 the birth rate per 1,000 women (aged 15 to 19) for Blacks was 60.9, for Hispanics was 81.5, and for Whites was 26.0 (Child Trends, 2008). Furthermore, research indicates that although 38% of adolescents in this country are from poor and low-income families, as many as 83% of adolescents who give birth, along with 61% who have abortions, are from poor and low-income families (Klein, 2005). Although several factors may contribute to adolescent pregnancy, data suggest that social factors place adolescents at risk for becoming early parents, such as age at first intercourse, family structure, low self-esteem, academic and behavioral problems, low educational attainment, lack of career aspirations and goals, prior pregnancies, and whether the adolescent was raised by a teen parent (Domenico & Jones, 2007; Kaufman, 1996; McCullough & Scherman, 1991; Woodard, Fergusson, & Horwood, 2001; Xie, Cairns, & Cairns, 2001).

Teen pregnancy has become a significant health issue largely because of the various adverse consequences on the well-being of adolescents and their children, both prepregnancy and postpregnancy. Research suggests that adolescent mothers under the age of 17, when compared to older mothers, are at an increased risk of having acute medical problems such as pregnancy-induced hypertension, anemia, and sexually transmitted diseases (Forrest, 1993; Klein, 2005; Satin et al., 1994). The emotional well-being of teen mothers is also of concern, given that research has shown these young mothers to be at an increased risk for maternal depression (Knoche, Givens, & Sheridan, 2007).

However, not only do teen mothers experience health problems but they engage in high-risk behaviors (e.g., smoking and drug use) and seek prenatal care at inadequate rates, which contributes to poor birth outcomes for adolescents (East & Felice, 1996). For example, adolescents are at an increased risk of having low birth weight and premature babies because of inconsistent prenatal care. Furthermore, evidence suggests that premature births are related to early death, serious long-term health problems, and future problems in psychosocial development of premature children (Centers for Disease Control and Prevention, 2007). Additionally, those children born to adolescent mothers are more likely to suffer from adverse developmental outcomes, emotional and/or behavioral disorders, learning problems, and language delays (Haffner & Haffner, 1998), which have a direct bearing on children's academic and developmental trajectories.

LINGERING ISSUES OF PHYSICAL AND MENTAL HEALTH

Because existing research does not establish causal connections between adolescent high-risk behaviors and academic performance, it is unclear how existing mechanisms of individual health-risk behaviors influence specific areas of student achievement. However, when compared to their peers, adolescents who do not engage in behaviors such as cigarette smoking, marijuana use, or alcohol use receive higher academic grades than their classmates do (Bryant, Schulenberg, O'Malley, Bachman, & Johnston, 2003; Centers for Disease Control and Prevention, 2003). Research further indicates that underachievement of those adolescents who engage in high-risk behaviors could indicate negative school experiences (Hawkins, Catalano, & Miller, 1992; Petraitis, Flay, & Miller, 1995), such as problems with low academic achievement, behavioral issues within the classroom, truancy, or lack of motivation for schoolwork. Although schools may not be directly responsible for students' behaviors, they can be a safe space for students who are struggling with these issues as they formulate and revise their identities (Gadsden, Jacobs, Bickerstaff, Park, & Kane, 2008). Specifically, children with negative school experiences are more likely than are their peers with positive school experiences to use alcohol and smoke cigarettes and marijuana (Bryant, Schulenberg, Bachman, O'Malley, & Johnston, 2000; Bryant & Zimmerman, 2002). Furthermore, when adolescents have high levels of school interest, they exhibit more effort at school and feel a certain bond with their school, making them less likely to engage in tobacco or alcohol use (Bryant et al., 2003). Further research should specify the nature of the relationship between substance use and achievement and the ways that schools as community institutions can provide support.

In addition to the issues described here, there are several lingering problems of both understanding the scope of health issues affecting children's participation in school and providing the necessary instructional support without labeling students. One issue that is relevant to children's overall health is their mental health, which is often discussed separately from health but in fact has been found to be a significant factor in physical health maintenance and well-being. A second concern focuses on special needs that have been identified for increasing numbers of children, across ethnic groups and income levels, and which may require special preparation by teachers and/or result in classroom disruption. Labeled as behavior disorders, these are behaviors that are described as being disruptive to instruction and classroom functioning. However, the concept also has been used to describe behaviors that do not affect classroom activity—self-destructive behavior that affects an individual child but that has increased in disproportional significance to other problems over a relatively short time. We discuss three of these disorders that are thought to be most common among children and youth: attention deficit hyperactivity disorder (ADHD), conduct disorders, and eating disorders that may be concealed but affect the well-being of children and their ability to achieve in school.

ADHD

It is estimated that between 3 and 5% of children in the United States, or approximately 2 million children, have ADHD (National Institute of Health, 1996). ADHD can occur among children as early as their preschool years and often represents itself in inattention, hyperactivity, and impulsivity behaviors. For example, children with ADHD have difficulty controlling their behavior and/or paying attention, which may adversely affect their schooling. Therefore, it is critical that children suspected of having ADHD promptly receive an appropriate diagnosis by a well-qualified professional. Unfortunately, ADHD diagnostic criteria are not unequivocal, which often makes it difficult to distinguish between developmental normalcy among children who may present these symptoms (i.e., inattentiveness, hyperactivity, and impulsivity) at a low level and indication of another disorder. In addition, those more at risk for going undiagnosed and/or less likely to receive treatment for ADHD are boys and children from ethnic minority backgrounds, although these children, even when their problems are ADHD, are likely to be identified as learning disabled (Bussing, 1998; Bussing, Zima, & Belim, 1998; Massetti et al., 2008; Simonoff, Pickles, Wood, Gringras, & Chadwick, 2007; Zarin, Suarez, Pincus, Kupersanin, & Zito, 1998). Prior research has found that poor academic achievement among children is associated with ADHD (DuPaul, McGoey, Eckert, & Vanbrakle, 2001; Massetti et al., 2008). However, little is known about the nature of academic deficits experienced by children who have this behavioral disorder (Massetti et al., 2008).

Conduct Disorder

Conduct disorder, also known as a *disruptive behavior disorder*, affects 1 to 4% of 9- to 17-year-old children, depending on how the disorder is defined (U.S. Department of Health and Human Services, 1999). Of the young people affected by conduct disorder, boys are overrepresented, and behavior disorder increases in prevalence as children age (Maughan, Rowe, Messer, Goodman, & Meltzer, 2004). Many factors may contribute to a child's developing conduct disorder, including brain damage, child abuse, genetic vulnerability, school failure, and traumatic life experiences (Renk, 2008).

Typically, conduct disorder causes children and adolescents to act out their feelings or impulses in destructive ways; thus it can result in disruptive school behavior. Marmorstein and Iacono (2001) conducted a study with twin adolescent girls with conduct disorder, and results suggest that conduct disorder is related to significant difficulties in functioning and school adjustment. They found that adolescents with conduct disorders tend to have an increased number of negative school-related events such as suspension and failure of classes. Many children and adolescents with this behavior disorder have difficulty following rules and behaving in a socially acceptable way. They are often viewed by other children, adults, and social agencies as bad or delinquent rather than mentally ill.

Eating Disorders

Eating disorders as well as awareness of eating disorders have become increasingly prevalent (Austin et al., 2005; Walsh et al., 2005). Over the past 25 years, awareness of eating disorders among adolescent girls in Westernized countries has increased significantly. Females are much more likely than males are to develop an eating disorder. In fact, only an estimated 5% to 15% of people with anorexia or bulimia and an estimated 35% of those with binge-eating disorder are male (Andersen, 1995; Spitzer et al., 1993). Additionally, adolescents who suffer from eating disorders are more likely to have higher rates of distorted body images (Smolak, 2004). Increased public concern regarding eating disorders among adolescents is primarily because of the increased risk of morbidity and mortality and to those physical problems associated with eating disorders (i.e., anemia, hair and bone loss, tooth decay; Reijonen, Pratt, Patel, & Greydanus, 2003).

The two common eating disorders this section focuses on are anorexia nervosa and bulimia nervosa. In their lifetimes, an estimated 0.5% to 3.7% of females suffer from anorexia, and an estimated 1.1% to 4.2% suffer from bulimia (American Psychiatric Association Work Group on Eating Disorders, 2000). Anorexia is a life-threatening condition that commonly begins in adolescence (National Institutes of Health, 1999). One in every 100 to 200 adolescent girls and a much smaller number of boys suffer from anorexia (National Institutes of Health, 1999). Anorexia is characterized by adolescents' refusal to maintain their body weight at or above a minimally normal weight for age and height. Anorexic youth are often underweight but have an intense fear of gaining weight or becoming fat. On the other hand, reported rates of bulimia vary from 1 to 3 of every 100 young people (National Institutes of Health, 1999). In addition, bulimia affects approximately 1 in 5 teenage females within the United States (Pipher, 1994). Young people with bulimia nervosa have frequent episodes of binging in which they eat huge amounts of food in one sitting. Because of their extreme concern of preventing weight gain, bulimics engage in the following behaviors: self-induced vomiting, use of drugs such as laxatives and enemas, or obsessive exercise.

The association between eating disorders and the academic performance of young people is not entirely clear. It is understood that eating disturbances have acute detrimental effects on adolescents' performance on a range of cognitive tasks (Green & Rogers, 1995a, 1995b; Wing, Vazquez, & Ryan, 1995). As discussed previously, there is an association between diminished nutrition (as a result of either hunger or poor diet) and children's cognitive function, often resulting in lower academic achievement. As an indicator of the association between eating disturbance and negative body image, a recent study of undergraduate students found that higher levels of body dissatisfaction and eating disturbance among young people was associated with higher levels of interferences in their academic performance (Yanover & Thompson, 2008). Although focused on college students, this study gives us an indication of where eating problems may lead. With increasing rates of adolescents suffering from this behavior disorder, education research could benefit from examining the various ways in which anorexia and bulimia may influence children's and adolescents' school-related behaviors or their academic performance and achievement.

CONSIDERATIONS AND POSSIBILITIES FOR ACADEMIC ACHIEVEMENT WITH AN EYE TOWARD CHILDREN'S HEALTH

In this review, our goal was to provide an overview of existing literature that goes beyond the scope of traditional discussions of factors associated with the achievement gap commonly addressed in education research. A fundamental premise of this review is not only that disparity in academic achievement is beset with social inequalities but that health problems may predict differences in achievement among children and adolescents. Such problems often result from these social inequalities and, in fact, the failures around health insurance and access to health care for poor and working families in the United States further exacerbate these social inequalities. As discussed in this review, certain physical illnesses are particularly disruptive for various aspects of children's and adolescents' school lives and often result in limited cognitive abilities, excessive absenteeism, inability to remain focused and complete schoolwork and school-related tasks in a timely manner, and disruptive behaviors or depressive moods. Each of these factors may influence perceptions of students by their teachers and increase their chances of academic failure and, thus, school dropout. Such school disruption poses serious consequences not only for young people's postsecondary education but for their later employment opportunities and personal and family lives (Palloni, 2006). Early onset of physical and mental illness has significant consequences and must be included as a part of future educational research.

The interface between the achievement goals and health of school-aged children and adolescents is an emerging, though still poorly conceptualized, area. Empirical research has consistently found associations between physical illnesses and high-risk behaviors and children's and adolescents' academic trajectories; however, these findings have not resulted in any substantial political efforts or interventions to address health issues for children and families. This review highlights the need for research on the intersections of these problems and for practice that has increased capacity to support the learning of children who may be experiencing or be affected by certain health problems. At present, schools address issues of health with varying levels of effort. In some cases, this may take the form of a course that may focus on a range of issues from health problems prevention to abstinence; in others, it may include seminars and policies specially designed to increase faculty and school awareness. In addition, partnerships between universities and schools have resulted in increased attention to health; among these, the University of Pennsylvania has been involved in collaborative work with local, urban elementary and high schools to improve community health. Such discussions may mean a different focus on health and different and increased collaborations between and among educators, health professionals, and social workers, all of whom have a stake in ensuring the best circumstances for children to learn but each of whom represents different foci in their primary work.

A next step in education research on health and academic performance is to attend to the complex nature of the nexus between and among health, school experiences, and academic achievement: high comorbidity and association with many of the same risk factors. The high comorbidity among mental and physical health conditions suggests that single-indicator research (i.e., research that focuses on one measure of health) does not provide the knowledge base to develop interventions that can adequately result in more holistic developmental trajectories for children and adolescents. Therefore, the multifaceted nature of health conditions demands more complex empirical analyses that consider the comorbidity, common variance related to similar risk factors, and bidirectionality of the relationship of children's health and their academic achievement. Another casual pathway that must also be considered is when one social factor (e.g., adolescents' sense of neighborhood safety) may be more associated with children's academic performance and may eventually lead to subsequent involvement in high-risk behaviors that result in health problems, whereas another social factor (e.g., limited access to nutritious foods) may be more associated with children's health but may be a precursor to poor academic performance. Research advanced along these lines will require that nonschool factors be examined and non-school settings be considered as targets of educational interventions and public policy strategies.

Additionally, there is increasing evidence that there are ecological factors that affect all children and adolescents and their engagement in health risk behaviors. Just as children from low-income households and ethnic minority groups experience high risk for many health problems, young people from rural communities and others from affluent families are often overlooked in empirical research. Yet they are potentially more susceptible to symptoms of depression and experimenting with illicit substances. Specifically, when compared to their peers in urban areas, rural youth engage in higher levels of alcohol and drug abuse (Van Gundy, 2006). In fact, in 2003 about 50% of rural children surveyed (12 to 17 years of age) believed that drugs were highly accessible to them (Van Gundy, 2006). In addition, research by Luthar and Latendresse (2005) suggests that children from families of high socio-economic statuses are especially vulnerable to depressive symptoms, anxiety, and substance use. Given the association between high-risk behaviors among youth and underachievement, education research should further investigate these ecological differences among young people in this country and what role health plays.

We urge more rigorous research that directly examines the impact of physical illness on academic performance, as evidenced by the fact that current research on health and academic outcomes does not focus enough on children and adolescents, particularly ethnic minority children. Furthermore, current research has not established a causal connection between children's and adolescents' health issues, high-risk behaviors, and their overall academic achievement. This is partially a result of the methodologies used in existing research where most studies are cross-sectional and retrospective in design. Therefore, the temporal order of relationship between these factors is unclear. What is becoming more obvious is the bidirectional relationship between certain health conditions and children's academic performance. To illustrate this point, a vicious cycle exists between obesity and low grades among students, which creates a downward spiral toward worsening physical and mental health and failing grades. In such a situation, it is difficult to determine whether students' obesity caused low grades or vice versa. Future research must attend to the temporal organizations of these processes.

Over the past decade, research has shown that young people who suffer from poor health experience adverse consequences not only in terms of their well-being but in their academic performance. This review suggests that it is critical to study educational and health trajectories in tandem (or pathways over time). If child and adolescent health problems threaten students' trajectories through the school systems, then the negative long-term association between educational attainment and adult health may be partially attributed to these early health problems among children (Needham et al., 2004).

Lastly, the quasi-experimental work on the issues of health and schooling would be well complemented by ethnographic and qualitative studies. Some studies in medicine and public health (e.g., National Longitudinal Study of Adolescent Health—Add Health) collect qualitative data as part of a mixed-methods approach. Such studies will provide a better sense of how the issues of health unfold within communities, how students understand the problems that they experience or for which they may be genetically at risk (e.g., high blood pressure), how they cope in the context of school and home, and what factors in and out of school might support them best.

SCHOOLS AS A CONDUIT OF CHANGE

Children spend a significant amount of time in schools, giving the school environment enormous potential to provide information and resources or to operate as a link to community-based interventions in efforts to address children's physical and mental well-being. As mentioned in the introduction and throughout this review, health has traditionally not been a part of the formal mission of the educational system or research, yet there are examples of the effectiveness of school-based health-focused initiatives (e.g., public vaccinations, emotional counseling) that benefit children's early health. In addressing the health of children and youth, schools could effectively use their frequent contact with parents and food service to stress the importance of nutrition and physical activity. For example, in addition to providing nutritious meals once or twice per day to many children and educating children on nutrition, schools also have the opportunity to inform parents about the importance of diet and physical activity on children's academic performance.

Health issues affect not only the students themselves who may manifest the problems but also parents, family members, and community members who suffer by being restricted from providing children with the safe and stimulating environments in which to grow. Add to that the limited knowledge of schools, school administrators, and educators to recognize and respond to the physical and mental health issues of students, and these problems children experience are exacerbated. These compounding issues raise interesting problems regarding child and adolescent well-being. Educational and health institutions have the ability to work toward addressing these problems and to contribute to slowly unfolding but much-needed research, practice, and policy to ensure the well-being of children in and out of school.

NOTE

[1]All authors contributed equally to the preparation of this chapter. Correspondence should be addressed to Sean Joe, School of Social Work, University of Michigan, 1080 South University Ave., Ann Arbor, MI 48109; e-mail: sjoe@umich.edu.

REFERENCES

Ahn, M. K., Juon, H. S., & Gittelsohn, J. (2008). Association of race/ethnicity, socioeconomic status, acculturation, and environmental factors with risk of overweight among adolescents in California. *Preventing Chronic Disease, 5*(3), 1–10.

American Psychiatric Association Work Group on Eating Disorders. (2000). Practice guide-line for the treatment of patients with eating disorders. *American Journal of Psychiatry, 157*(Suppl. 1), 1–39.

Andersen, A. E. (1995). Eating disorders in males. In K. D. Brownell & C. G. Fairburn (Eds.), *Eating disorders and obesity: A comprehensive handbook* (pp. 177–187). New York: Guilford.

Anderson, H., Bailey, P., Cooper, J., Palmer, J., & West, S. (1983). Morbidity and school absence caused by asthma and wheezing illness. *Archives of Disease in Childhood, 58,* 777–784.

Anderson, P. M., & Butcher, K. F. (2006). Childhood obesity: Trends and potential causes. *The Future of Children, 16*(1), 19–45.

Anderson, R. N. (2002). *Deaths: Leading causes for 2000* (No. 16). Hyattsville, MD: National Center for Health Statistics, Centers for Disease Control and Prevention.

Austin, S. B., Field, A. E., Wiecha, J., Peterson, K. E., & Gortmaker, S. L. (2005). The impact of a school-based obesity prevention trial on disordered weight-control behaviors in early adolescent girls. *Archives of Pediatric Adolescent Medicine, 159*(3), 225-230.

Bailet, L. L., & Turk, W. R. (2000). The impact of childhood epilepsy on neurocognitive and behavioral performance: A prospective longitudinal study. *Epilepsia, 41,* 426–431.

Baskin, M. L., Ard, J., Franklin, F., & Allison, D. B. (2005). Prevalence of obesity in the United States. *Obesity Reviews, 6*(1), 5–7.

Bennett, E. M., & Kemper, K. J. (1994). Is abuse during childhood a risk factor for devel-oping substance abuse problems as an adult? *Journal of Developmental and Behavioral Pediatrics, 15,* 426–429.

Bloom, B., & Cohen, R. A. (2007). *Summary health statistics for U.S. children: National health interview survey, 2006.* Retrieved July 30, 2008, from http://www.cdc.gov/nchs/data/series/sr_10/sr10_234.pdf

Bloom, B., Cohen, R. A., Vickerie, J. L., & Wondimu, E. A. (2003). *Summary health statistics for U.S. children: National health interview survey, 2001.* Hyattsville, MD: National Center for Health Statistics, Centers for Disease Control and Prevention.

Bloom, B. (2003). *Summary health statistics for U.S. children: National health interview survey, 2001.* Hyattsville, MD: National Center for Health Statistics, Centers for Disease Control and Prevention.

Blum, R. W. (1987). Contemporary threats to adolescent health in the United States. *Journal of American Medical Association, 257,* 3390–3395.

Breslau, N. (1985). Psychiatric disorder in children with physical disabilities. *Journal of the American Academy of Child & Adolescent Psychiatry, 24,* 87–94.

Brown, L., & Pollitt, E. (1996). Malnutrition, poverty, and intellectual development. *Scientific American, 274,* 38–43.

Bryant, A. L., Schulenberg, J. E., Bachman, J. G., O'Malley, P. M., & Johnston, L. D. (2000). Understanding the links among school misbehavior, academic achievement, and cigarette use: A national panel study of adolescents. *Prevention Science, 1,* 71–87.

Bryant, A. L., Schulenberg, J. E., O'Malley, P. M., Bachman, J., G., & Johnston, L. D. (2003). How academic achievement, attitudes, and behaviors relate to the course of substance use during adolescence: A 6-year, multiwave national longitudinal study. *Journal of Research on Adolescence, 13,* 361–397.

Bryant, A. L., & Zimmerman, M. A. (2002). Examining the effects of academic beliefs and behaviors on changes in substance use among urban adolescents. *Journal of Educational Psychology, 94,* 621–637.

Burdette, H. L., & Whitaker, R. C. (2005). A national study of neighborhood safety, outdoor play, television viewing, and obesity in preschool children. *Pediatrics, 116,* 657–662.

Burgeson, C. R., Wechsler, H., Brener, N. D., Young, J. C., & Spain, C. G. (2001). Physical education and activity: Results from the School Health Policies and Programs Study 2000. *Journal of School Health, 71*, 279–293.

Bussing, R. (1998). Children in special education programs: attention deficit hyperactivity disorder, use of services, and unmet needs. *Journal of the American Public Health Association, 88*, 880–886.

Bussing, R., Zima, B. T., & Belim, T. R. (1998). Differential access to care for children with ADHD in special education programs. *Psychiatric Services, 49*, 1226–1229.

Campbell, J. R., Hombo, C. M., & Mazzeo, J. (2000). *NAEP 1999 trends in academic progress: Three decades of student performance*. Washington, DC: U.S. Department of Education.

Case, A., Fertig, A., & Paxson, C. (2005). The lasting impact of childhood health and circumstance. *Journal of Health Economics, 24*, 365–389.

Centers for Disease Control and Prevention. (2003). *Alcohol and other drug use and academic achievement*. Retrieved September 5, 2008, from www.cdc.gov/HealthyYouth/health_and_academics/pdf/alcohol_other_drug.pdf

Centers for Disease Control and Prevention. (2007). *Teen pregnancy*. Retrieved October 22, 2008, from http://www.cdc.gov/reproductivehealth/AdolescentReproHealth/PDF/TeenPreg-FS.pdf

Centers for Disease Control and Prevention. (2008). Youth risk behavior surveillance—United States, 2007. *Morbidity and Mortality Weekly Report: Surveillance Summaries, 57*(4), 1–136.

Child Trends. (2008). *Facts at a glance: A fact sheet reporting national, state-level, and city-level trends in teen childbearing*. Retrieved August 31, 2008, from www.childtrends.org/ Files/ Child_Trends-06_26_2007_FG_2007FactsAtAGlance.pdf

Cohen, D. A., Mason, K., Bedimo, A., Scribner, R., Basolo, V., & Farley, T. A. (2003). Neighborhood physical conditions and health. *American Journal of Public Health, 93*, 467–471.

Committee on Substance Abuse. (2001). Alcohol use and abuse: A pediatric concern. *Pediatrics, 108*, 185–189.

Crocker, J., & Knight, K. M. (2005). Contingencies of self-worth. *Current Directions in Psychological Science, 14*, 200–203.

Crosnoe, R. (2006a). The connection between academic failure and adolescent drinking in secondary school. *Sociology of Education, 79*(1), 44–60.

Crosnoe, R. (2006b). Health and the education of children from racial/ethnic minority and immigrant families. *Journal of Health and Social Behavior, 47*(1), 77–93.

Currie, J. (2005). Health disparities and gaps in school readiness. *The Future of Children, 15*(1), 117–138.

Daniels, S. R. (2006). The consequences of childhood overweight and obesity. *The Future of Children, 16*(1), 47–67.

Datar, A., Sturm, R., & Magnabosco, J. L. (2004). Childhood overweight and academic performance: National study of kindergartners and first-graders. *Obesity Research, 12*(1), 58–68.

Degenhardt, L., Chiu, W. T., Conway, K., Dierker, L., Glantz, M., Kalaydjian, A., et al. (2008). Does the "gateway" matter? Associations between the order of drug use initiation and the development of drug dependence in the National Comorbidity Study replication. *Psychological Medicine, 9*, 1–11.

Delva, J., Johnston, L. D., & O'Malley, P. M. (2006). The epidemiology of overweight and related lifestyle behaviors: Racial/ethnic and socioeconomic status differences among American youth. *American Journal of Preventative Medicine, 33*(Suppl. 4), S178–S186.

Domenico, D. M., & Jones, K. H. (2007). Career aspirations of pregnant and parenting adolescents. *Journal of Family and Consumer Sciences Education, 25*(1), 24–33.

DuPaul, G. J., McGoey, K. E., Eckert, T. L., & Vanbrakle, J. (2001). Preschool children with attention-deficit/hyperactivity disorder: Impairments in behavioral, social, and school functioning. *Journal of the American Academy of Child & Adolescent Psychiatry, 40,* 508–515.

East, P. L., & Felice, M. D. (1996). *Adolescent pregnancy and parenting: Findings from a racially diverse sample.* Mahwah, NJ: Erlbaum.

Entwisle, D. R., & Alexander, K. L. (1993). Entry into school: The beginning school transition and educational stratification in the United States. *Annual Review of Sociology, 19,* 401–423.

Field, T., Diego, M., & Sanders, C. (2001). Adolescent depression and risk factors. *Adolescence, 36*(143), 491–498.

Florence, M. D., Asbridge, M., & Veugelers, P. J. (2008). Diet quality and academic performance. *Journal of School Health, 78,* 209–215, 239–241.

Forrest, J. D. (1993). Timing of reproductive life stages. *Obstetrics and Gynecology, 82*(1), 105–111.

Fowler, M. G., Davenport, M. G., & Garg, R. (1992). School functioning of U.S. children with asthma. *Pediatrics, 90,* 939–944.

Fowler, M. G., Johnson, M. P., & Atkinson, S. S. (1985). School achievement and absence in children with chronic health conditions. *Journal of Pediatrics, 106,* 683–687.

Gadsden, V., Jacobs, C., Bickerstaff, S., Park, J., & Kane, S. (2008, March). *Health and education: Addressing risk and community health disparities through interdisciplinarity.* Paper presented at the annual meeting of the American Educational Research Association, New York.

Gleason, P., & Suitor, C. (2001). *Food for thought: Children's diets in the 1990s.* Princeton, NJ: Mathematica Policy Research.

Gómez, J. E., Johnson, B. A., Selva, M., & Sallis, J. F. (2004). Violent crime and outdoor physical activity among inner-city youth. *Preventive Medicine, 39,* 876–881.

Gould, M. S., Greenberg, T., Velting, D. M., & Shaffer, D. (2003). Youth suicide risk and preventive interventions: A review of the past 10 years. *Journal of the American Academy of Child and Adolescent Psychiatry, 42,* 386–405.

Grant, B. F., & Dawson, D. A. (1997). Age at onset of alcohol use and its association with DSM-IV alcohol abuse and dependence: results from the national longitudinal alcohol epidemiologic survey. *Journal of Substance Abuse, 9,* 103–110.

Green, M. W., & Rogers, P. J. (1995a). Impaired cognitive functioning during spontaneous dieting. *Psychological Medicine, 25,* 1003–1010.

Green, M. W., & Rogers, P. J. (1995b). Impairments in working memory associated with spontaneous dieting behavior. *Psychological Medicine, 28,* 1063–1070.

Grissmer, D., Flanagan, A., & Williamson, S. (1998). *Why did the Black-White score gap narrow in the 1970s and 1980s?* Washington, DC: Brookings Institute.

Gutstadt, L., Gillette, J., Mrazek, D., Fukuhara, J., LaBrecque, J., & Strunk, R. (1989). Determinants of school performance in children with chronic asthma. *American Journal of Diseases of Childhood, 143,* 471–475.

Haffner, D. W., & Haffner. (1998). Facing facts—Sexual health for American adolescents. *Journal of Adolescent Health, 22,* 453.

Hawkins, J. D., Catalano, R. F., & Miller, J. Y. (1992). Risk and protective factors for alcohol and other drug problems in adolescence and early adulthood: Implications for substance abuse prevention. *Psychological Bulletin, 112,* 64–105.

Hingson, R., Heeren, T., Winter, M., & Wechsler, H. (2005). Magnitude of alcohol-related mortality and morbidity among U.S. college students ages 18–24: Changes from 1998–2001. *Annual Review of Public Health, 26,* 259–279.

Howe, G. W., Feinstein, C., Reiss, D., Molock, S., & Berger, K. (1993). Adolescent adjustment to chronic physical disorder: Comparing neurological and non-neurological conditions. *Journal of Child Psychology and Psychiatry, 34,* 1153–1171.

Institute of Medicine. (2001). *Health and behavior: The interplay of biological, behavioral and societal influences.* Washington, DC: National Academy Press.

Judge, S., & Jahns, L. (2007). Association with overweight with academic performance and social and behavioral problems: An update from the early childhood longitudinal study. *Journal of School Health, 77,* 672–678.

Juster, F. T., Ono, H., & Stafford, F. P. (2004). *Changing times of American youth: 1981–2003.* Ann Arbor: Institute for Social Research, University of Michigan.

Kann, L., Brener, N. D., & Wechsler, H. (2007). Overview and summary: School health policies and programs study 2006. *Journal of School Health, 77,* 385–397.

Kaufman, J. (1996). Teenage parents and their offspring. *Annals of the New York Academy of Sciences, 789*(1 psychobiology), 17.

Kessler, R. C., Foster, C. L., Saunders, W. B., & Stang, P. E. (1995). Social consequences of psychiatric disorders, I: Educational attainment. *American Journal of Psychiatry, 152,* 1026–1032.

Klein, J. D. (2005). Adolescent pregnancy: Current trends and issues. *Pediatrics, 116*(1), 281.

Knoche, L. L., Givens, J. E., & Sheridan, S. M. (2007). Risk and protective factors for children of adolescents: Maternal depression and parental sense of competence. *Journal of Child and Family Studies, 16,* 684–695.

Kobus, K. (2003). Peers and adolescent smoking. *Addiction, 98*(Suppl. 1), 37–55.

Kramer, R. A., Allen, L., & Gergen, P. J. (1995). Health and social characteristics and children's cognitive functioning: Results from a national cohort. *American Journal of Public Health, 85,* 312–318.

Kuh, D. J., & Wadsworth, M. E. (1993). Physical health status at 36 years in a British national birth cohort. *Social Science and Medicine, 37,* 905–916.

Kumanyika, S., & Grier, S. (2006). Targeting interventions for ethnic minorities and low-income populations. *The Future of Children, 16*(1), 187–207.

Ladson-Billings, G. (2006). From the achievement gap to the education debt: Understanding achievement in U.S. schools. *Educational Researcher, 35*(7), 3–12.

Lammers, C., Ireland, M., Resnick, M., & Blum, R. (2000). Influences on adolescents' decision to postpone onset of sexual intercourse: A survival analysis of virginity among youths aged 13 to 18 years. *Journal of Adolescent Health, 26,* 42–48.

Lee, J. (2002). Racial and ethnic achievement gap trends: Reversing the progress toward equity? *Educational Researcher, 31*(1), 3–12.

Lee, S. M., Burgeson, C. R., Fulton, J. E., & Spain, C. G. (2007). Physical education and physical activity: Results from the school health policies and programs study 2006. *Journal of School Health, 77,* 435–463.

Lewit, E. M., & Schuurmann Baker, L. (1995). School readiness. *The Future of Children, 5*(2), 128–139.

Luthar, S. S., & Latendresse, S. J. (2005). Children of the affluent: Challenges to well-being. *Current Directions in Psychological Science, 14,* 49–53.

Ma, X. (2000). Health outcomes of elementary school students in New Brunswick: The education perspective. *Evaluation Review, 24,* 435–456.

Marmorstein, N. R., & Iacono, W. G. (2001). An investigation of female adolescent twins with both major depression and conduct disorder. *Journal of the American Academy of Child and Adolescent Psychiatry, 40,* 299–306.

Massetti, G. M., Lahey, B. B., Pelham, W. E., Loney, J., Ehrhardt, A., Lee, S. S., et al. (2008). Academic achievement over 8 years among children who met modified criteria for attention deficit hyperactivity disorder at 4–6 years of age. *Journal of Abnormal Child Psychology, 36,* 399–410.

Maughan, B., Rowe, R., Messer, J., Goodman, R., & Meltzer, H. (2004). Conduct disorder and oppositional defiant disorder in a national sample: Developmental epidemiology. *Journal of Child Psychology and Psychiatry, 45,* 609–621.

McCullough, M., & Scherman, A. (1991). Adolescent pregnancy: Contributing factors and strategies for prevention. *Adolescence, 26,* 809–817.

Millstein, S. G. (1988). *The potential of school-linked centers to promote adolescent health and development.* Unpublished manuscript.

Mitchell, W. G., Chavez, J. M., Lee, H., & Guzman, B. L. (1991). Academic underachievement in children with epilepsy. *Journal of Child Neurology, 6,* 65–72.

Naimi, T., Brewer, R., Mokdad, A., Denny, C., Serdula, M., & Marks, J. (2003). Binge drinking among U.S. adults. *Journal of American Medical Association, 289,* 70–75.

National Center for Health Statistics. (2006). *Obesity still a major problem.* Retrieved October 29, 2008, from http://www.cdc.gov/nchs/pressroom/06facts/obesity03_04.htm

National Highway Traffic Safety Administration. (2005). *Traffic safety facts: Speeding* [DOI HS 810 629]. Washington, DC: Author.

National Institute of Health. (1996). *Attention deficit hyperactivity disorder.* Retrieved October 29, 2008, from http://www.nimh.nih.gov/health/publications/adhd/nimhadhdpub.pdf

National Institutes of Health. (1999). Brief notes on the mental health of children and adolescents. *Children's mental health facts: Children and adolescents with mental, emotional, and behavioral disorders.* Retrieved December 1, 2008, from http://mentalhealth.samhsa.gov/publications/allpubs/CA-0006/default.asp

National Institute on Drug Abuse. (2007). *NIDA survey shows a decline in smoking and illicit drug use among eighth graders.* Retrieved September 4, 2008, from http://www.drugabuse .gov/pdf/news/NR1211.pdf

Needham, B. L., Crosnoe, R., & Muller, C. (2004). Academic failure in secondary school: The inter-related role of health problems and educational context. *Social Problems, 51,* 569–586.

Newacheck, P. W., & Halfon, N. (2000). Prevalence, impact, and trends in childhood disability due to asthma. *Archives of Pediatrics & Adolescent Medicine, 154,* 287–293.

Ogden, C. L., Carroll, M. D., Curtin, L. R., Macdowell, M. A., Tabak, C. J., & Flegal, K. M. (2006). Prevalence of overweight and obesity in the United States: Associations with neighborhood characteristics. *American Journal of Preventative Medicine, 33*(Suppl. 4), S240–S245.

Ozer, E. M., Brindis, C. D., Millstein, S. G., Knopf, D. K., & Irwin, C. E. (1998). *America's adolescents: Are they healthy?* San Francisco: National Adolescent Health Information Center, University of California.

Palloni, A. (2006). Reproducing inequalities: Luck, wallets, and the enduring effects of childhood health. *Demography, 43,* 587–615.

Palloni, A., & Milesi, C. (2006). Economic achievement, inequalities and health disparities: The intervening role of early health status. *Research in Social Stratification and Mobility, 24,* 21–40.

Parker, L. (1989). *The relationship between nutrition and learning: A school employee's guide to information and action.* Washington, DC: National Education Association.

Petraitis, J., Flay, B. R., & Miller, T. Q. (1995). Reviewing theories of adolescent substance use: Organizing pieces in the puzzle. *Psychological Bulletin, 117,* 67–86.

Pipher, M. (1994). *Reviving Ophelia: Saving the selves of adolescent girls.* New York: Penguin.

Rampersaud, G. C., Pereira, M. A., Girard, B. L., Adams, J., & Metzl, J. D. (2005). Breakfast habits, nutritional status, body weight, and academic performance in children and adolescents. *Journal of the American Dietetic Association, 105,* 743–762.

Reijonen, J. H., Pratt, H. D., Patel, D. R., & Greydanus, D. E. (2003). Eating disorders in the adolescent population: An overview. *Journal of Adolescent Research, 18,* 209–222.

Renk, K. (2008). Disorders of conduct in young children: Developmental considerations, diagnoses, and other characteristics. *Developmental Review, 28,* 316–341.

Resnick, M. D., Bearman, P. S., Blum, R. W., Bauman, K. E., Harris, K. M., Jones, J., et al. (1997). Protecting adolescents from harm: Findings from the National Longitudinal Study on Adolescent Health. *Journal of the American Medical Association, 278,* 823–832.

Roder, I., Kroonenberg, P. M., & Boekaerts, M. (2003). Psychosocial functioning and stress-processing of children with asthma in the school context: Differences and similarities with children without asthma. *Journal of Asthma, 40,* 777–787.

Sabia, J. J. (2007). The effect of body weight on adolescent academic performance. *Southern Economic Journal, 73,* 871.

Satin, A. J., Leveno, K. J., Sherman, M. L., Reedy, N. J., Lowe, T. W., & McIntire, D. D. (1994). Maternal youth and pregnancy outcomes: Middle school versus high school age groups compared with women beyond the teen years. *American Journal of Obstetrics and Gynecology, 171,* 184–187.

Schwimmer, J. B., Burwinkle, T. M., & Varni, J. W. (2003). Health-related quality of life of severely obese children and adolescents. *Journal of the American Medical Association, 289,* 1813–1819.

Silverstein, M., Mair, J., Katusic, S., Wollan, P., O'Connell, E., & Yunginger, J. (2001). School attendance and school performance: A population-based study of children with asthma. *Journal of Pediatrics, 139,* 278–283.

Simantov, E., Schoen, C., & Klein, J. D. (2000). Health compromising behaviors: Why do adolescents smoke or drink? Identifying underlying risk and protective factors. *Archives of Pediatrics and Adolescent Medicine, 154,* 1025–1033.

Simonoff, E., Pickles, A., Wood, N., Gringras, P., & Chadwick, O. (2007). ADHD symptoms in children with mild intellectual disability. *Journal of the American Academy of Child & Adolescent Psychiatry, 46,* 591.

Smolak, L. (2004). Body image in children and adolescents: Where do we go from here? *Body Image, 1,* 15–28.

Spitzer, R. L., Yanovski, S., Wadden, T., Wing, R., Marcus, M. D., Stunkard, A., et al. (1993). Binge eating disorder: Its further validation in a multisite study. *International Journal of Eating Disorders, 13,* 137–153.

Story, M., Kaphingst, K. M., & French, S. (2006). The role of schools in obesity prevention. *The Future of Children, 16*(1), 109.

Substance Abuse and Mental Health Services Administration. (2007). *Results from the 2006 national survey on drug use and health: National findings.* Rockville, MD: Author.

Sweeting, H. N. (2008). Gendered dimensions of obesity in childhood and adolescence. *Nutrition Journal, 7,* 1.

Taras, H. (2005). Physical activity and student performance at school. *Journal of School Health, 75,* 214–218.

Taras, H., & Potts-Datema, W. (2005). Obesity and student performance at school. *Journal of School Health, 75,* 291–295.

Tershakovec, A. M., Weller, S. C., & Gallagher, P. R. (1994). Obesity, school performance and behaviour of Black, urban elementary school children. *International Journal of Obesity and Related Metabolic Disorders, 18,* 323–327.

Thies, K. M. (1999). Identifying the educational implications of chronic illness in school children. *Journal of School Health, 69,* 392–397

U.S. Department of Health and Human Services. (1999). *Mental health: A report of the surgeon general.* Rockville, MD: U.S. Department of Health and Human Services, Substance Abuse and Mental Health Services Administration, Center for Mental Health Services, National Institutes of Health, National Institute of Mental Health.

U.S. Department of Health and Human Services. (2000). *Healthy people 2010: Understanding and improving health*. Retrieved October 29, 2008, from http://www.healthypeople.gov/Document/tableofcontents.htm#uih/uih_2htm#obj

U.S. Department of Health and Human Services. (2007). *The Surgeon General's call to action to prevent and reduce underage drinking*. Rockville, MD: Author.

Van Gundy, K. (2006). Substance abuse in rural small town America. *Reports on Rural America, 1*, 1–38.

Walsh, B., Bulik, C., Fairburn, C., Halmi, K., Herzog, D., & Golden, N. E. A. (Eds.). (2005). *Treating and preventing adolescent mental health disorders: What we know and what we don't know: A research agenda for improving the mental health of our youth*. New York, NY: Oxford University Press.

Wasserman, G. A., McReynolds, L. S., Ko, S. J., Katz, L. M., & Carpenter, J. R. (2005). Gender differences in psychiatric disorders at juvenile probation intake. *American Journal of Public Health, 95*, 131–137.

Willis, T. A., Vaccaro, D., & McNamara, G. (1992). The role of life events, family support, and competence in adolescent substance use: A test of vulnerability and protective factors. *American Journal of Community Psychology, 20*, 349–374.

Wing, R. R., Vazquez, J. A., & Ryan, C. M. (1995). Cognitive effects of ketogenic weight-reducing diets. *International Journal of Obesity, 19*, 811–816.

Wjst, M., Roell G., Dold S., Wulff A., Reitmeir P., Fritzsch C., et al. (1996). Psychosocial characteristics of asthma. *Journal of Clinical Epidemiology, 49*, 461–466.

Woodard, L., Fergusson, D. M., & Horwood, L. J. (2001). Risk factors and life processes associated with teenage pregnancy: Results of a prospective study from birth to 20 years. *Journal of Marriage and Family, 63*, 1170–1184.

Xie, H., Cairns, B. D., & Cairns, R. B. (2001). Predicting teen motherhood and teen fatherhood: Individual characteristics and peer affiliations. *Social Development, 10*, 488–511.

Yanover, T. J., & Thompson, K. (2008). Eating problems, body image disturbances, and academic achievement: Preliminary evaluation of the eating and body image disturbances academic interference scale. *International Journal of Eating Disorders, 41*, 184–187.

Zarin, D. A., Suarez, A. P., Pincus, H. A., Kupersanin, E. B., & Zito, J. M. (1998). Clinical and treatment characteristics of children with attention-deficit/hyperactivity disorder in psychiatric practice. *Journal of the American Academy of Child and Adolescent Psychiatry, 37*, 1262–1270.

Chapter 12

The Social Production of Adolescent Risk and the Promise of Adolescent Literacies

LALITHA VASUDEVAN
Teachers College, Columbia University

GERALD CAMPANO
Indiana University

Within the past decade, adolescents have become an increasingly scrutinized age group in the United States and abroad (Maira & Soep, 2005; Nayak, 2003; Nilan & Feixa, 2006; Phelan, Davidson, & Yu, 1998; Vadeboncoeur & Patel Stevens, 2005). They are often the focus of attention across disciplines when references are made to youth, although the concept, youth, encompasses a much broader age range and range of experiences than adolescence alone. The stereotypical image of youth and of adolescence by extension—as a boisterous embodiment of the "unruly" stage of life between childhood and adulthood (G. S. Hall, 1904)—has long dominated discussions about definitions of and subsequent policy regarding adolescents (Skelton & Valentine, 1998). The advent of compulsory schooling (Varenne & McDermott, 1998) and the establishment of the Juvenile Court (Platt, 1977) have influenced further discourses about adolescents, which quickly became steeped in containment, control, punishment, and remediation. These narratives persist and are reflected in the practices and policies of schools, afterschool programs, youth development organizations, the criminal justice system, and many other institutions that youth negotiate on a daily basis.

This chapter focuses on a particular subset of educational issues, the literacies of adolescents, which in the past 10 years have become the focus of critique and concern in educational research, practice, and policy (Jetton & Dole, 2004; Patel Stevens, 2008; Vacca, 1998). Academic journals have devoted whole issues to the topic (e.g., special issue of *Harvard Educational Review*, Spring 2008—"Adolescent

Review of Research in Education
March 2009, Vol. 33, pp. 310-353
DOI: 10.3102/0091732X08330003
© 2009 AERA. http://rre.aera.net

Literacy") and related subjects (e.g., special issue of *Discourse*, 2005—"Digital Childhood and Youth: New Texts, New Literacies"). This increased attention is due, in part, to a previous dearth of research focused on the literacy experiences of young people who fell outside the designations of early childhood and adult. A simple search for the words *adolescents* and *literacy* on Google Scholar, limited to the years between 1900 and 1950, for example, yields about 50 hits. The same search for just the year 2007 generates more than 3,000 results. Far from being a scientific analysis of research about adolescents' literacy, this simple snapshot signals a significant upward trend in research related to adolescents and literacy, which for years was framed in relationship to issues surrounding adult literacy (see Davidson & Koppenhaver, 1993). This connection to adult literacy, seen, for example, in publications such as the *Journal of Adolescent and Adult Literacy*, reflects a definition of adolescents as being in transition—from child to adult—with little focus on the space that they occupy in their own right, not simply as refugees from childhood or expectant travelers to adulthood.

In addition to concerns about adolescent literacies, there has been considerable discussion and concern about the quality of schooling to which many adolescents, particularly those who are economically marginalized and identify as ethnic minorities, are exposed and how such schooling fails to prepare them for life after high school, either in the workplace or in institutions of higher education (Ginwright, 2004; Noguera, 2003a). Dropout rates among these same populations of adolescents remain high and emphasize the exodus of high school students as early as the ninth and tenth grade (Neild, Stoner-Eby, & Furstenberg, 2008). Compounding this reality are additional factors, including the limited literacy support for adolescents in middle and high school settings, overcrowded and underresourced classrooms, and outdated classroom texts.

One compelling response to the apparent concerns comes from the literacy research community. Recognizing the challenges faced by many adolescents in living and learning literacy, several researchers in the past 20 years (e.g., Fisher, 2007; Morrell, 2004a, 2004b; Taylor, 1991) have aimed to shift the focus of attention away from individual performance and deficit toward an understanding of the sociocultural factors and structural forces that inform literacy learning. For example, Morrell (2006) advocates for research that is "'critical,' 'participatory,' and 'action-oriented' [and] fundamentally questions who has the right to engage in research by positioning students, community members, and K–12 literacy teachers as legitimate and integral participants in the research process" (p. 3). He embraces the idea of youth, in particular, as knowers about their own literacies and seeks out and generates knowledge about literacy that is not tethered to preexisting frames of deficit (e.g., "struggling reader"). Instead, Morrell (2006) implicitly responds to Moje's (2002) call to action to conduct literacy research through which researchers might aim to learn with and from youth and youth cultures. Thus, Morrell (2006) frames inquiry about gaps in achievement by focusing on adolescents' literacy assets and abilities and proffers pedagogical approaches to supporting adolescents' literacy learning that are grounded in the belief that adolescents are already literate in a variety of cultural domains (e.g., popular culture and virtual worlds) (see also Morrell, 2004a, 2004b, 2008).

At the heart of Morrell's work and that of other scholars is that literacy is not a neutral set of skills but a social practice that must be understood in context and with attention to power dynamics (also see Bartlett, 2007; Bloome, Carter, Christian, Otto, & Shuart-Faris, 2005; Bloome & Green, 1991; Gee, 1996, 2000; Lewis, Enciso, & Moje, 2007; Freebody & Luke, 1990; Morrell, 2002, 2004a, 2004b, 2008; Street, 1984). This work examines the social and cultural contexts in which literacy is learned, used, shared, and revised and the social practices. Such ethnographic and qualitative research, emerging as early as the 1980s, has led scholars to broaden definitions of literacy beyond conventional "schooled" reading and writing and to consider critically how students engage in and use cultural and social practices and how they enact these practices in the daily acts of learning and schooling (see Camitta, 1993; Heath, 1983). More recently, a new wave of research (e.g., Black, 2005; Fecho, 2003; Fisher, 2003; Moje, 2000) has begun to take on these issues with a heightened sense not only of sociocultural contexts but also of the generational shifts and new cultural practices that have emerged among adolescents within the past 10 to 15 years.

In this chapter, we provide a selective review of issues drawn from research literature and policy reports that have collectively shaped current perceptions about the literate lives of adolescents; some of this work has been appropriated by the public media, and for this reason, we address some of the resulting public perceptions. The vast majority of these texts reproduce risk-laden discourses that we examine closely. However, we also examine a range of emerging scholarship that offers more nuanced and multidimensional insights about adolescents' literacies. Throughout the review, we focus on the ways that risk is embedded in the identification of adolescents as low literate and the ways that the concept of adolescent literacies has garnered negative attention in some contexts. We argue against these negative depictions and propose a more expansive conceptualization built on sociocultural perspectives. Moreover, we document examples of adolescents taking up reading, writing, speaking, and other semiotic modes in ways that are intimately tied to their understandings of themselves in relationship to the world. This body of scholarship has extended early work by scholars such as Davidson and Koppenhaver (1993) by exploring out-of-school contexts, raising critical issues that speak to contemporary realities facing adolescents and youth, and providing rich examples of innovative classrooms in which adolescents are not seen as lacking but, to the contrary, are portrayed as creative and socially engaged knowledge producers (e.g., Alvermann, 2002a, 2002b; Alvermann, Hinchman, Moore, Phelps, & Waff, 2006; Fecho, 2003; Gustavson, 2007; O'Brien, 2001, 2003; Ware, 2008).

Whereas sociocultural studies of adolescent literacies are interested in exploring adolescents' social, cultural, and intellectual worlds, literacy policies and standardized curricula often are mired in discourses of student deficit and, sometimes, by implication, family and community pathology, as described by Gutierrez (2001). This divergence highlights a gap between research and policy, as manifested in the different paradigms, epistemologies, and pedagogies that frame discussions of literacy across schooling contexts. The lens of the testing paradigm, regularly used by policymakers to make determinations and write public narratives, positions adolescents in ways that are not necessarily advantageous for their educational trajectories.

In certain cases, some groups of adolescent learners (e.g., African American and Latino students from low-resourced homes) may be presented as "lacking" academic skills, while others who are also underserved by the educational system (e.g., Cambodian American, Native American, the descendants of Filipino migrant workers, and poor Whites) are invisible in larger policy discussions. These representations, while appearing to give deserved attention to African American and Latino students, actually give a kind of currency to the other groups, thereby underemphasizing the participation of minoritized youth in largely low-quality, underserved schools. This public narrative of crisis about adolescents' literacies has garnered significant media attention, which locates the blame on inadequate teaching, unsupportive families, and a general culture of moral decline among adolescents themselves.

Throughout this chapter, we use a sociocultural lens to examine the issues of adolescent risk and literacy. We understand literacy to be socially constructed and mediated by the social and cultural contexts in which meaning making occurs. This stance is informed by Vygotsky's (1978) theorizing about the interdependence of cultural practices and social conditions of learning and resonates with more current applications of this theoretical framework to the study of literacy (e.g., Gee, 1991, 1996; Lewis et al., 2007; Pérez & McCarty, 2004). We focus on the experiences of adolescents whose literacy practices do not align with the expectations of literacy in school. Because these adolescents are often reading, writing, and remaking their identities across contexts, we challenge explanations that locate risk within students and families and instead examine the conditions and discourses that produce risk, among them inequitable school funding, poverty, and institutional labeling. In other words, we aim to present a narrative of possibility while addressing the existing problems and strengths in current discourses.

This chapter is divided into four sections. In the next section, we focus on the broad dimensions of youth and risk, examining the social production of risk. We then examine how institutionalized labels and policies seemingly designed to attend to risk unwittingly reinforce such labels, paradoxically placing students at risk. Next, we outline the contributions and counternarratives of adolescent literacy research that challenge assumptions about literacy deficit and student inadequacy and explore the evolving terrain of adolescent literacies. Following this review of adolescent literacy research, we present an overview of emerging research that challenges the *risk* label and in which educators who have cultivated a decidedly antideterministic stance in their literacy curricula are discussed. In the conclusion, we focus on educators who are working together with adolescents to create alternative spaces characterized by possibility, imagination, and hopefulness and offer closing commentary.

MULTIPLE DISCOURSES ON YOUTH, LITERACY, AND RISK

A range of discourses focus on youth, the problems they face, and the approaches to supporting them. At the level of public news and conversation, youth are often the scapegoats of accusatory discourses that invert causality. Rather than understanding how students are placed at risk through forms of structural violence (e.g., poverty, school tracking, and severely underresourced and over-crowded schools) as well as direct violence (e.g., racial profiling and hate crimes), they are blamed for the very conditions that oppress them and are often accorded an inflated and superstitious form of destructive power. In other words, a student may be thought to be "ruining the class" for everyone else, without anyone giving attention to his or her marginalization in school; a group of friends may be described as "jeopardizing the climate of a school," rather than the school being described as placing them under surveillance as deviants; a reluctant learner may be viewed as defying "scientifically proven instruction," rather than presented as someone who is resisting low expectations; a child may be said to be acting "out of control," rather than understood as responding rationally to a school environment that is chaotic and inhospitable.

As the literary critic and theologian Rene Girard (1986) has theorized, the scape-goating mechanism is often employed to promote social cohesion and uniformity at the expense of victims. The victims are arbitrary—they have not caused the problems—and are often chosen because they have ambiguous social status, as both insiders and outsiders within the community. The practices of (what we have termed here) scapegoating are perhaps no more evident today than in the current discourse surrounding immigration, where the pejorative nominalization, "illegals," dehumanizes many who are already dehumanized by the economic system. With valences of the "parasite" and the "criminal," the racially coded term *illegals* revives and rein-scribes previous forms of scapegoating, such as the pernicious stereotype of the "wel-fare queen." It also erases the very geopolitical dynamics, neoliberal economic policies, and histories of conquest and colonization that have displaced populations and caused worldwide migratory flows. In these and other examples, the "right to education" (*Universal Declaration of Human Rights*, n.d., Article 26) remains a par-tially realized mandate. This is especially applicable to adolescents embroiled in the criminal justice system, itself seen as a site of inequity (Mickelson, 2000; Schwartz, 2001). A "dangerous symbiosis" (Wacquant, 2001) between urban schools and jails has emerged; at once lost and hypervisible in the midst of this growing symbiosis are the youth whose actions have become increasingly criminalized (Polakow, 2000). Infractions that were once handled within the classroom or school walls are now referred to the police, whose presence is especially palpable in many urban schools.

Amid all of the efforts to control and contain, the education of adjudicated youth—who are ushered through court appearances, multiple schools, and educational programs—is at best sporadic; at worst, school policies and practices (e.g., drop out, push out, and limited efforts toward engagement) contribute to the incarceration of boys and young minoritized males and increasing numbers of girls and women (American Bar Association & National Bar Association, 2001), particularly in urban areas. Both the growing "prison industrial complex" and its educational manifestation, the "school-to-prison pipeline," are monikers that refer to the escalating numbers of legislative and policy actions taken toward the disciplining and containment of youth (Giroux, 2001; Wald & Losen, 2003). Like the discourse of immigration, the discourses of incarceration become associated with particular groups of people, who in turn are placed at heightened risk of discriminatory practices, physical harm, and inequitable access to education. In this section, we examine three discourses that present issues facing youth: risk, child-saving, and delinquency; adolescent literacy, panic, and the call to action; and adolescents, race, and gender.

The Discourse of Risk, Child Saving, and Delinquency

Current practices of scapegoating have their roots in reform efforts that originated in the United States more than a century ago. The focus of these efforts was the remediation of communities and individuals who did not conform to the reformers' cultural ideal of "Americanism." The social policies that emerged during this era targeted immigrant communities, poor families, and adolescents in particular, all of whom were concentrated in urban areas that were expanding as a result of rapid postindustrialization growth. Leading the charge in the 19th century were the "child savers," whose legacy of remediation and delinquency discourses are alive today. The name for "progressive reformers" comprising primarily middle-class White women, child savers brought a sense of urgency to child protection and came to be designated as reformers. In their version of reform, children were seen as victims of neglect but not poverty or other factors that imperil children; the mothers of the children were seen as needing advice about appropriate childrearing and cultural norms rather than child support services (Finkelstein, 2000).

The efforts of the child savers, while seemingly benign, catalyzed the establishment of the modern juvenile justice system, which resulted in the increased incarceration of youth for extended periods of time and which, as Platt (1977) suggests, subjected incarcerated youth to "long hours of labor and militaristic discipline and the inculcation of middle-class values and lower-class skills" (p. 176). However, as Platt also describes in his study of the child-saving movement, the remedies of the child savers seemed to aggravate the problem, rather than protect children from moral and physical danger. Platt writes, "[T]he juvenile court system brought attention to and thus 'invented' new categories of youthful deviance, particularly behavior in which the actor was seen as his own 'victim'" (p. 145). As a result, youth who were identified as "delinquents" were detained in institutions at a higher rate based on the rationale that "their reformation was more likely if they were removed from 'immoral' parents and a 'vicious' environment" (p. 145). Although the reference to delinquency has declined (as has the use of the term *illiteracy*) in the past 20 years, different forms of "delinquency" discourses persist. Traces of "delinquency" categories—such as "deviant," "troublesome youth," "troublemakers," "truant," and "antisocial"—are often aligned with cultural deficit theories, which position minority cultural values as dysfunctional and leading to low educational and occupational attainment (see Foley, 1997; Solorzano & Yosso, 2001).

Delinquency and deficit discourses situate risk as an inherent trait of children and communities, rather than identifying social conditions that create risk. They create a moral panic, characterized by widespread feelings of fear about the predicted actions and failure of certain individuals. Rather than making the risk transparent, however, moral panic typically obscures the real risk that adolescents and their families experience: underfunded schools, high rates of unemployment, and an increased state of surveillance (Lipman, 1998; Valenzuela, 1999). Osei-Kofi (2005) reminds us that "more than 12 million children live in poverty; over 9 million children have no health insurance; and 13 million children and over 20 million adults live in households where hunger or food insecurity is a part of every day" (p. 367). Osei-Kofi suggests that although a crisis of access, discrimination, and inequity affecting the lives of many adolescents exists, the moral panic about adolescents remains distanced from any real analysis of social inequality. Consequently, actions taken in response often result in blunt "remedies," such as the development of scripted curricula and symbolic violence (Bourdieu & Passeron, 1977) in the form of retention, disciplinary measures, extensive placement in special education, and tracking.

Adolescent Literacy, the Sense of Panic, and the Call to Action

High dropout rates in the United States, "particularly for students of color, [suggest] the urgency to maintain a focus on literacy learning and retaining students in their adolescent years" (Schultz & Fecho, 2005, p. 678). How we respond to the urgency matters. We examined several reports and have selected to review a few that have received significant attention in the past few years, as they have set a tone for policies and practices related to the ways institutions support the literacy of adolescents.

One example is the 2004 *Reading at Risk* report commissioned by the National Endowment for the Arts, which was based on the results from the literature section of an interview survey administered in 2002 to 17,135 adults over the age of 18 to ascertain the current state of "art and literature consumption" (p. ix) in which respondents were asked about their attendance at cultural events and artistic performances, the arts programs they watched, and the literature they read throughout a 12-month period. *Reading at Risk* focused on survey responses related to reading literature, listening to readings or recordings of literature, and creative writing activities. Of particular relevance to our review about risk and the literacies of adolescents are the following findings, which we have condensed from the longer list of 10 key findings found in the report:

- Literary reading—across age groups, gender, and ethnicities and education levels— is in a state of decline.
- Literary decline is steepest among younger age groups (18 to 24 and 25 to 34 years old).
- "The decline in literary reading foreshadows an erosion in cultural and civic participation" (p. xii).
- "The decline in reading correlates with increased participation in a variety of electronic media, including the Internet, video games, and portable digital devices" (p. xii).

Respondents were asked about the number of books they had read in a 1-year period, excluding books read for work or school. They were also asked about their literary reading, which was defined as the consumption of novels, short stories, plays, or poetry. In *Reading at Risk*, the literary consumption habits of respondents were used to draw conclusions about broader categories like "civic engagement" and "cultural life," and the report suggests a decline in these areas as well. Although the report points to important data about the state of adolescent literacy, its definition of the frequent reader draws on a particular profile that may result in a labeling of students from certain groups (e.g., Hispanic women and men, African American men, and young people) and that is entrenched in conceptions of literacy as limited to reading and writing print alone.

Several national initiatives, such as the Advancing Literacy Initiative of the Carnegie Corporation and Adolescent Literacy Research Network of National Institute of Child Health and Human Development, also contribute to the narrative of national concern regarding the state of adolescents' reading. The report *Adolescent Literacy and the Achievement Gap: What Do We Know and Where Do We Go From Here?* was commissioned by the Advancing Literacy Initiative and also refers to "certain groups" of adolescents—African American and Latino students whose first or home language is not English or who live in poverty—who continue to perform significantly below expectation on standardized measures of reading and writing in upper elementary and high school (Snow & Biancarosa, 2003, p. 2). Here, the authors maintain a discursive focus on the performance of "certain groups" rather than question the use of high-stakes measures as determinants of students' educational status and achievement; they pursue their analysis in spite of their own admission that "many students, in particular minority group members, are dropping out of high school in anticipation of not receiving diplomas" (p. 2). The assertion of expected reading difficulty is explained by pointing to socioeconomic factors—such as dangerous neighborhoods and lack of access to educational resources, health, and nutrition—as well as sociocultural factors. In this explanation, culture is framed as a hindrance not only to literacy proficiency, which is reduced to reading comprehension, but also to academic achievement overall. Home literacies and family discourses are set as far removed from the expectations and norms of school and framed as a challenge to overcome. There is no discussion, for example, of engaging adolescents' "native-language stories" as part of classroom life (see C. Lee, 2007) or through innovative uses of the arts (see Gadsden, 2008), nor is there recognition of the benefits of building adolescents' existing literacies, practices, or knowledge base.

Two additional reports from the Advancing Literacy Initiative are worth noting, although they differ slightly in their analyses of the problem. *Reading Next: A Vision for Action and Research in Middle and High School Literacy* (Biancarosa & Snow, 2006) begins with the following subtitles: "A Literacy Crisis" and "Cause for Alarm." The reader is immediately informed of the number of students who drop out of high school, lack literacy skills, and score "below reading level" according to the National Assessment of Education Progress (NAEP). In suggesting that there is "a need to improve adolescent literacy" (p. 9) and that "enough is already known about adolescent literacy" (p. 10), the report promotes a specific view of literacy as merely reading and presupposes that we know everything we need to know about adolescents' literate lives. The action proposed by the report comes in the form of 15 key elements of effective adolescent literacy programs, and educators are encouraged to find the "optimal mix" of interventions to suit the needs of their students to improve reading comprehension. Although calling for literacy support in the form of instruction aimed specifically at adolescents who are struggling, the guiding principles advocated for by *Reading Next* may inadvertently reproduce the myth that literacy learning ceases in elementary school and may denote reading instruction as a set of "best practices" that can be implemented across contexts with minimal regard to the particular identities, knowledge, and experiences of students, teachers, or communities. Enough may already be known, but the question of what counts as "enough" persists (see Gadsden, 2008).

A second report, *Writing Next: Effective Strategies to Improve Writing of Adolescents in Middle and High Schools* (Graham & Perin, 2007), defines the scope of the writing problem in the context of NAEP writing proficiency goals and indicates the failure of students in Grades 4, 9, and 12 to meet these goals. Prepared with an eye toward students' postsecondary options, the report suggests that youth who have difficulty with writing will experience direct consequences in their ability to find a job and be successful in their higher educational endeavors. *Writing quality* is defined within the parameters of essays written with appropriate use of idea development, examples, and supporting details. The report draws on a meta-analysis of experimental and quasi-experimental research on adolescent writing instruction and presents 11 key elements of effective pedagogy in writing instruction with adolescents. The authors of the report rightfully point to the lack of research on effective writing instruction for low-income, urban, low-achieving adolescent writers. We would also add that not enough is known about the many ways that adolescent learners are engaged in "literate" practice (Johnston, 1999; Langer, 2004, 2008) in and out of school and that the definition of *writing* would benefit from broadening to include knowledge about writing as a socially situated practice (Camitta, 1993; Dyson, 1997; Emig, 1971; Jewitt, 2002).

The reports issued by the Carnegie Corporation as well as other research and policy briefs about adolescent literacy (e.g., Alliance for Excellent Education, 2004) are appropriately intended to call attention to the needs of an understudied and underserved group; however, they do not urge us to consider youth whose scores on measures of reading and writing are less than "proficient" as literate. Rather, they offer suggestions for instructional practices that are designed to engage, motivate, and more effectively acclimate adolescents too often described as unmotivated and resistant into the existing school structures. Debates within professional organizations also have garnered the attention of the news media, with headlines correlating the "decline of reading" with declining test scores (Rich, 2007, 2008), even as the National Council on Teachers of English (NCTE), the International Reading Association, and the National Reading Conference have issued position statements, research reviews, and policy briefs that are reflective of a broader and evolving understanding of the literacies of adolescents (Alvermann, 2002b; Moore, Bean, Birdyshaw, & Rycik, 1999; NCTE, 2004). Despite widespread recognition of the changing nature of literacies (e.g., NCTE, 2007; Rich, 2008), school curricula and assessment often describe literacy as simple and mechanistic skills, and as Street (2002) suggests, they "fail to do justice to the richness and complexity of actual literacy practices" in adolescents' lives (p. 52).

We agree that there is more we need to know about "effective adolescent literacy instruction" (Snow & Biancarosa, 2003, p. 31), but knowing about teaching adolescents entails knowing more about the ways they use language and literacy in their lives. Correlations drawn between the social conditions of adolescents' lives and their performance on school measures of literacy attainment must be interrogated beyond causal explanations. In addition to asking "What are the most promising instructional programs focused on improving adolescent literacy outcomes?" "Are they indeed effective in improving literacy?" and "Which works best with subgroups of struggling readers?" (Snow & Biancarosa, 2003), researchers, practitioners, and policymakers should also raise questions about the range and variation of ways in which adolescents are engaging in literacy across multiple contexts, including school, home, and community; the diverse modes of communication through which adolescents are expressing themselves and communicating their ideas; and adolescents' engagement with and access to new literacies and technologies. As Patel Stevens (2008) writes, "the invocation of crisis across [many] policy documents is one framed by ideas of competence but, more fundamentally, is one of time" (p. 72), and a "national achievement crisis" is invoked and national responses to supporting adolescents' literacies are painted with the brush of crisis remediation.

Adolescents, Race, and Gender

The sense of urgency and the studies that were discussed in the previous section, in making their case, refer to issues of race, class, and gender. Several recent research projects have also addressed these issues, although with different purposes and results. Studies such as the Opportunity Gap Project reveal the institutional and structural forces that impose obstacles "to opportunity and the advancement of [youth's] goals" (Fine et al., 2004, p. 1). This shift in perspective recasts the achievement gap script, from an emphasis on the inadequate achievement of students to the inequitably distributed resources in a socially stratified education system. Fine et al. (2004), who included urban and suburban youth, surveyed 4,474 students from across 15 districts in the New York/New Jersey metropolitan region who attended racially integrated high schools to investigate youth perspectives on issues of educational equity. Their findings draw attention to students' perceptions of the social justice dimensions of adolescent achievement in schools. For example, youth across demographic groups had high academic aspirations. However, African American and Latino students were particularly aware of the limitations of their academic preparation (e.g., for standardized measures such as the PSAT and SAT and high-stakes testing) and of their options (e.g., financial issues). The data from this study suggest that the question is not simply whether students resist learning or lack investment in schooling but rather how we adjust differential supports and expectations to ensure access for all students.

Moral panic about youth is often based on essentialized notions of who "at-risk" adolescents are and how they learn. Several researchers focus specifically on what contributes to adolescent students' identities and how the literacy practices of adolescents are marginalized in schools and engender stereotypes along lines of class, race, and gender. Fordham's (1993) ethnographic study of the disciplining and silencing of young Black women in an urban high school documents the reductive dehumanizing by school officials of their identities to the phrase "loud Black girls." She writes that most of the "academically successful girls" at the school where she conducted her study adopted a code of silence, where they practiced being seen and not heard. Other young women in her study refused to accept the notion that the only way to achieve in school was to participate in an oversimplified binary: embodying markers of "White femininity" or adopting the rhetorical style of men. For refusing to be socialized into silence, the latter group paid a high educational price, and Fordham concludes that "'those loud Black girls' are doomed not necessarily because they cannot handle the academy's subject matter, but because they resist 'active participation in [their] own exclusion'" (p. 10). Although Fordham does not focus explicitly on the young women's literacies, her research reveals the real costs of standardized communicative practices that are not limited to test performance or school-based assessments. The literacy practices of the young women were indicted through the use of racialized and gendered markers, which were made into pejoratives by school officials. By not adopting the acceptable communicative forms, the young women's very existence—when *Black* and *girl* were conjoined with the word *loud*—became a liability.

Finders's (1997) research extends our discussion of school's governance over girls' literacies. She examines how two social networks of middle school girls—the Social Queens and the Tough Cookies—used writing to construct their identities and focuses on the implications of literacy acts for female adolescents navigating the dominant school culture. Within the confines of the school curriculum, Finders notes how one social group participated in alternative forms of literacy, such as passing notes or writing bathroom graffiti, to affirm their gendered and peer group identities. She also focuses on a second set of girls who did not self-identify as a group but were nonetheless ascribed outsider status because of their shared socioeconomic background and marginality within the "popular girl" school culture. These girls used literacy as a means of privileging independence rather than group identity and resisted participation in literacy activities that made them vulnerable. Finders locates the practices of both groups within the framework of official school notions of writing and of adolescence and argues that teachers' characterizations of the girls' identities as students were filtered through preconceived ideas about what it means for adolescents to be engaged in the classroom.

In these examples, the ways in which the young women expressed themselves were discordant with institutional expectations of femininity, broadly, and acceptable forms of communication, more specifically. Their literacy practices did not reflect a degradation of their moral character, as the labels that were ascribed to them might suggest, but rather helped them navigate the complex world of middle and high school. Many of the students code switched to negotiate their relationships with various peer groups and with teachers and schools that (mis)read their behaviors as delinquent.

Recent discourses about adolescent boys also echo a narrative of moral panic, engendering critiques from the scholarly community (Duncan, 2005; Gordon, 1999) as well as the popular press (e.g., Eckholm, 2006; Herbert, 2007). Researchers argue that data, such as arrest statistics (Mauer, 2003) and high school graduation rates (Stillwell & Hoffman, 2008), are interpreted through essentialist lenses, wherein structural inequalities are obscured behind a language of blame and vilification. Black boys, in particular, are placed at greater risk of being "labeled as less intelligent, to be punished severely for minor offenses, to be excluded from educational opportunities such as advanced classes, and to be relegated to special education" (Hull, Kenney, Marple, & Forsman-Schneider, 2006, p. 4; see also Noguera, 2003b). These patterns of punishment and remediation of certain children serve to reinforce stereotypes about intellectual capacity and ability, through which "implicit and explicit messages about racial and gender identities are conveyed" (Noguera, 2008, p. 30).

This research points to how students are placed at risk by an educational system that prefigures the criminal justice system through heavy-handed discipline and punishment, especially for racial minorities (Fenning & Rose, 2007; Skiba, Michael, Nardo, & Peterson, 2002). The issue, however, is not simply negative labels or stereotypes; ostensibly positive stereotypes are equally pernicious, such as the model minority (S. Lee, 1996) or the "quiet Asian boy" (Lei, 2003), which are defined against other ethnic generalizations. These seemingly positive labels do a disservice to Asian students themselves, many of whom remain underserved in schools.

Studies that disrupt the pathologizing of youth raise the question of how best to support students who are placed at risk by the educational system (e.g., Fine et al., 2004). One of the most popular prescriptions involves creating curricula that often reify essentialized identities, including a number of approaches that intend to support the literacies of students who are viewed as especially vulnerable in the system, such as adolescent boys (Newkirk, 2002; Scieszka, 2005; Smith & Wilhelm, 2002; Sullivan, 2003). The advocates of these boys argue for the inclusion of more diverse texts (e.g., popular culture reading) that have "real guy appeal" (Sullivan, 2003) and ones that are chosen by adolescent boys themselves. Expanding the reading curriculum to be more inclusive of boys' identities and multiple modes of expression is laudable. However, pedagogical approaches must be empirically tested to make any strong statement about whether and how boys may learn differently than girls. To date, there is little empirical evidence. The panic about boys, literacy, and schooling might be redirected to consider the gender oppression that both boys and girls experience when they do not conform to school expectations and the ways that these gender identities are complicated by racial and class ascriptions. As an alternative, literacy curricula may invite young men to become partners in challenging heteronormative and homophobic assumptions and cultivate feminist masculinities. Engaging students in this way would entail a critical literacy curriculum that acknowledges the role of power in schooling. So long as the cycle of moral panic and quick fix remedies continues, adolescents will remain at risk, and there will persist a "pedagogical divide that limits the learning opportunities" (Cummins, 2007, p. 564) of adolescents who are already vulnerable in the school system.

LITERACY RISK IN POLICIES AND PRACTICES

The tension that Delpit (1995) articulated more than a decade ago still exists: How can schools effectively teach and meet the needs of all children in a way that accommodates cultural diversity but does not sacrifice consistent and equitable access to discourses of cultural power? Additionally, we ask, "How can literacy researchers identify student needs without creating labels that instrumentally sort youth?"

The proliferation of labeling in American schools has garnered ample critique (e.g., Hudak & Kihn, 2001), particularly in light of increased high-stakes testing and an era of accountability as measurement (Darling-Hammond, 2006). Labels and classifications, by themselves, may not be harmful. S. Hall (1996) notes that it is human nature to classify the social and cultural worlds in which we live. However, when labels create an exclusive norm for human behavior and reinforce an ideology of (in)ability, there invariably will be hierarchy. For example, designations like *bluebirds* and *mountaineers*, which may be used by a classroom teacher to distinguish among reading groups in her classroom, are easily decoded by children as being indicative of reading aptitude and internalized as an indication of general intellect. Thus, a seemingly innocuous organizational structure becomes a means of educational reproduction, especially if the opportunities for children in each group are predetermined based on assumptions and quantifications of ability.

Solorzano, Ceja, and Yosso (2000) discuss how the enactments of these labels at the pedagogical level, such as differential expectations for achievement based on some aspect of adolescents' identity (e.g., race, ethnicity, class), are often a product of teachers' (mis)perceptions about students based on labels and test scores and can have a profound impact on school performance (see also R. Ferguson, 2003). In their study of how African American college students experience the racial climate of their predominantly White college campus, the authors describe various types of racial micro-aggressions, "or unconscious and subtle forms of racism" (p. 60), that were embedded in the students' accounts. Solorzano et al. (2000) analyzed the narratives that the participating students shared during guided focus group discussions. The students reported patterns of dismissive counseling (e.g., students talked out of pursuing premed coursework), feeling invisible or hypervisible during classroom discussions, and deficit assumptions that they attributed to race (e.g., being accused of cheating on an exam that resulted in a high score) (for a related discussion of Native American college students' experiences of marginalization and surveillance while attending elite universities, see Brayboy, 2004). These students' experiences in a college environment are foreshadowed in the labeling and sorting practices and policies of K–12 schooling, which result in explicit actions such as tracking, as well as implicit attitudes and assumptions, such as those echoed by the college students (Ladson-Billings & Tate, 1995; Solorzano & Yosso, 2001; Villenas & Deyhle, 1999).

Although we tend to associate designations like the *bluebirds* with elementary education, increasingly middle and high schools are attempting to replicate these models of ability grouping. The *struggling reader* (and by extension, the *struggling writer*) is another label that emerges from institutional discourses of risk. Alvermann (2002b) wrestles with this idea of a struggling reader, suggesting that the term itself is contested and is interpreted differently, depending on who interprets, where it is interpreted, and with what expectations and results. For example, she notes that the term is as likely to be used to refer to youth with clinically diagnosed reading disabilities as it is to "those who are English language learners (ELLs), [identified as] 'at risk,' underachieving, unmotivated, disenchanted, or generally unsuccessful in school literacy tasks that involve print-based texts" (p. 195). As she suggests, the labels provide little information about the reader and serve, often, as a cultural and social marker for adolescents who are not performing at desired levels of reading achievement. McDermott and Varenne (1995) identify schools' practices of labeling as a reification of a "culture as disability" perspective. That is, translated in work with adolescents, people and institutions contribute to the construction of adolescents being seen as "at risk" or "illiterate." The ways that spaces such as schools are organized can afford or constrain the positions one can inhabit (Alvermann, 2002b, p. 196).

Labels such as *at risk* and *struggling reader* can limit adolescents who are defined or seen as literate beings (Moje, Young, Readence, & Moore, 2000). The identities that youth claim for themselves can in fact be a point from which to resist the negative effects of institutional labels. Research continues to illustrate adolescents' rich literate traditions and practices inside and outside of school (Chandler-Olcott & Mahar, 2003; Schultz, 1996). Hull and Schultz (2001), who provide an in-depth review of significant literacy research that has occurred in out-of-school settings and that has informed recent literacy theory, demonstrate that people are engaged in literacy practices across home, school, and community contexts. In an edited volume focused on bridging what they see as a gap between out-of-school literacies and classroom practices, Hull and Schultz (2002) urge against the dichotomizing of adolescents' literacies, a practice that results when artificial in- and out-of-school literacy boundaries are enforced.

In many cases, however, students have to suppress or distance themselves from their own forms of personal and cultural expression to advance in school. For example, Blackburn (2002/2003, 2003) describes the experiences of Justine, a young woman who spent time at a youth-run center for lesbian, gay, bisexual, transgender, and questioning (LGBTQ) youths. Justine, who self-identifies as "an African American lesbian writer" (p. 315), lived through implicit and explicit heterosexism and homophobia throughout her schooling experiences and through her poetry challenged these biases. Through her writing, Justine claimed an activist identity; however, she "dichotomiz(ed) her personal and academic writing" (p. 322), finding no space for this political work in school.

Justine's marginalization did not only occur at the linguistic level; it was not only her writing that did not align with school. Anzaldua (1987) might describe Justine's "ethnic identity [as being] twin skin to linguistic identity" (p. 11); in other words, she is her language. Like Justine, other young men and women, whose literacies appear to have no space in schools, find their educational opportunities and life chances limited. The consequences of institutional language and literacy policies are severe, as evident after the passage of Proposition 227, which eliminated bilingual education in California and constrained teachers to the use of highly prescriptive reading programs (Gutierrez, 2001; Zacher, 2007). Not only do such programs "strip teachers of their agency and expertise," but "the deskilling of teachers further serves to normalize teachers and their teaching practices toward a new language ideology" (Gutierrez, 2001, p. 115). Such an ideology views the nonschool language and literacies of adolescents not as "funds of knowledge" (Moll, 1992) to be nurtured but as deficits to be corrected. Thus, English-only policies sacrifice the literate and biliterate development of many adolescents and further "devalue and exclude" youth, some of whom inhabit subject positions that are already precarious within the institutional gaze.

Despite institutional constraints, Justine had the benefit of the LGBTQ center, where she could grow as a writer and not be defined against a norm to which she did not subscribe. Wissman (2007) created a similar space with young women as they worked together in a poetry and photography elective class at an urban public high school. As Wissman notes, "urban public schools are often contexts in which students are beset with silencing, surveillance, decontextualized curricula, and low expectations" (p. 341). Within their group, Wissman's inquiry community, who called themselves "the Sistahs," engaged in topics that had relevance to their immediate lives and interests but were at odds with the school's expectations. Wissman recounts, for example, how the students' request to attend a demonstration in protest of the Iraq war was met with skepticism and cynicism by the administration, which felt that students were feigning interest in politics to leave school early, rather than taking seriously their civic engagement. The young women, who had consistently displayed their artistic, intellectual, and literacy prowess as part of the Sistahs, felt dismissed and misjudged by the administration.

In ideologies of labeling, identity markers such as clothing, skin color, and ways of speaking often represent degrees of deviation from an imagined ideal and are translated into stigmas, where an arbitrary difference becomes misrecognized as student inferiority or deficit. For example, ELLs are often designated to be at a lower level of reading and writing because they are tested in their second language. Reading levels are even used to forecast the growth of prisons. Franzak (2006) notes that "[b]ecause marginalized adolescent readers are initially identified as such within the school context, the underlying structure and values of school literacy are built into definitions of struggling readers" (p. 219). What are supposedly neutral evaluations of a student's skills are really social assessments of their identities.

Approaches to addressing the achievement gap, and particularly the persistent disparities in adolescents' performance on school-based measures of literacy, have largely placed an emphasis on categorizing and remediating students through standardized measures mandated by the NAEP and the No Child Left Behind (NCLB) legislation. Lipman (2006) describes NCLB as a "system of centralized regulation of schools through high-stakes accountability" (p. 101) that places curricular authority in outside administrators and policymakers, while devaluing the local knowledge of adolescents (Moje, 2002), parents (Tuzzolo & Hewitt, 2006/2007), and teachers (Cochran-Smith & Lytle, 2006; Schultz & Fecho, 2005). These policies homogenize classroom experiences and foster conformity, while simultaneously sorting students along a normal curve.

Consider, for example, the young Black boys whom A. A. Ferguson (2000) studied. A. A. Ferguson's ethnography traces the use of the label *troublemaker* in the schooling experiences of Black boys as part of a process she terms *adultification*, referring to the ways that actions and behaviors of boys, many as young as 11 and 12 years old, preempt any opportunity for them and how adults identify them as headed for jail (see also Burton, 2007, for a differently constructed analysis of adultification and Gadsden & Fuhrman, 2007, for a brief discussion in reference to Hurricane Katrina). A. A. Ferguson documented the criminalization of the boys' very identities, which only served to place the boys at risk in how the school treated them. Certain behaviors became coded as deviant: walking in the hallway without a pass, tardiness, truancy, talking out of turn, missed homework, or even practicing forms of youth vernacular.

But there is also another way of looking at adolescents. Instead of changing the child to fit a (often White middle-class) norm, the school itself can work to accommodate the robust diversity of 21st-century classrooms by thinking more expansively about literacy and what constitutes youth intellectual and cultural expression. Our understandings about the emerging literacies landscapes can potentially have a profound impact on how we re-imagine the literate identities of adolescents. Too often, emerging practices such as the creation of virtual world avatars or the innovative production of media are reappropriated within assessment-driven curricula (e.g., the use of digital devices and capabilities to essentially replace paper in skill and drill software "games" and the like). As a result of this "pedagogization" (Street,

1995), not only are adolescents' literate identities reduced to easily classifiable labels based largely on test performance, but also an entire body of literature that attends to the multiple, social, and multimodal understandings of literacies remains on the periphery of mainstream teaching, learning, and professional development.

The expansive sense of self that many youth are experiencing in their out-of-school lives is being constricted or homogenized in schools. This is where the real risk lies. On one hand, adolescents are increasingly finding a range of outlets for intellectual and creative expression and acquiring literacy practices that enable them to have a greater sense of who they are as well as who they may become. On the other hand, literacy pedagogies in school—still beholden to rigid and autonomous models of literacy (Street, 1984), in which literacy is reduced to discrete, learnable skills—result in putting students in narrow categories that often deny their full potential. In the yawning gap between these two worlds, invariably many adolescents will become alienated and disenchanted with schooling. Ethan Yazzie-Mintz (2007), who asked students themselves how they feel about school through a national High School Survey of Student Engagement, found the following results: 65% reported that they are engaged by "individual reading" either "not at all" or "a little," and 69% reported being engaged by "writing projects" either "not at all" or "a little." When looking at boys only, those numbers were even higher: 70% of boys surveyed reported being engaged "not at all" or "a little" by "individual reading," and 74% of boys reported being engaged by "writing projects" either "not at all" or "a little." By the time students—especially boys—get to high school, the majority of them are not being engaged by school literacy curricula that view reading and writing narrowly. This reality highlights the urgency to interrupt deficit constructions of students and learn from them about what is not working in schools and how we can honor the full array of adolescent literacy practices.

ADOLESCENT LITERACIES: REMAKING RISKY TERRAIN

The terrain of adolescent literacy has been taken up by literacy researchers, not as a site of remediation and concern but rather as reflective of rich literacy traditions in the lives of youth. In the introduction to this chapter, we commented on the relative lack of research about adolescents' literacies. However, increasingly, literacy researchers are beginning to locate their work within the contexts adolescents inhabit, including out-of-school spaces such as community centers, parks, afterschool programs, sports teams, and a range of online and virtual spaces. This trend can be seen as a response to the increased discourse of panic about adolescents, such as the research on secondary literacy (e.g., Moje, Dillon, & O'Brien, 2000) and content area literacy (e.g., Bean, Readence, & Baldwin, 2008; Moje et al., 2004; Patel Stevens, 2002). Another focus in recent literacy research on adolescents concerns the evolving digital landscape and its mutually constitutive relationship with the communicative and meaning-making practices of adolescents, in particular (e.g., Chandler-Olcott & Mahar, 2003; Hill & Vasudevan, 2008; Lankshear & Knobel,

2006). Finally, a third strand of adolescent literacy research grows out of understandings about identities and culture that emerge through observations about how adolescents navigate their social and cultural worlds and explores the significance of popular culture (e.g., Morrell, 2002) and hip hop culture (e.g., Hill, 2009; Richardson & Lewis, 2000) in the lives of youth.

These strands are not mutually exclusive. As we emphasize in this section, many researchers are contributing to our understandings of the field through multiple purposes for their research—for example, bridging hip hop and academic literacies, exploring identity performances across virtual worlds, or researching literate identities across educational spaces. Much of this work has been informed by sociocultural theory and also draws on critical, social, and activist-oriented frameworks. We begin this section with a brief discussion of the sociocultural perspectives underpinning recent literacy research. Although not all of the recent literacy research adopting this lens has focused on adolescents, we draw on this wide body of work, which also explores the literacies of children and adults, here to provide a context for our current understandings and inform our scholarship about the range of literacies that adolescents, in particular, are engaging with and performing. In addition, we acknowledge critical work that appeared in the 1980s (e.g., Bloome & Green, 1991; Heath, 1983; Taylor & Dorsey-Gaines, 1988) and early 1990s (Dyson, 1997; Freebody & Luke, 1990; Gadsden, 1993, 1995; C. Lee, 1992; Taylor, 1996) that focused on a range of populations and contexts, offered new analyses regarding the role of contexts, and contributed to epistemological shifts about literacy, learning, culture, and identity.

Sociocultural perspectives on the study of literacy refocus attention away from deficit orientations by attempting "to account for . . . a wide range of mediators in human literacy learning and practice" (Lewis et al., 2007, p. 3). Researchers who draw on sociocultural theories recognize that "literacy is less a state of being and more an ongoing, continual" (Bartlett, 2007, p. 53) endeavor that is best understood as practices situated in social and cultural contexts. These perspectives have been highlighted in studies that provide descriptions of how people of all ages, including adolescents, use language and literacy in their everyday lives across multiple settings. Heath's (1983) examination of varying reading and writing events within working-class communities in North Carolina and Street's (1984) investigation of literacy practices across home, community, and school boundaries in Iran catalyzed what Gee (1999) subsequently identified as the "social turn" in research. This "turn" shifts the gaze of research "away from a focus on individuals and their 'private' minds and towards interaction and social practice" (Gee, 1999, p. 1). Therefore, a person who reads poetry displayed on placards in a crowded subway car is engaged in a different sort of practice than someone who is performing poetry, which he or she has written, for a full audience. Such variation in the uses of literacy practices is reflected in the idea of "multiple literacies" or the different meanings literacies have in different contexts (Street, 1995). Studies of literacy practices and identities in the past 10 years (e.g., Hull & Schultz, 2002; Mahiri, 2004; Moje, 2000; New London Group, 1996) further reflect this "social turn" by stressing the importance of looking beyond institutional walls and beyond the use of print on paper (e.g., Jewitt & Kress, 2003) for understandings of how our literacy practices and identities are shaped, enacted, and represented in diverse ways.

Among the main contributions of this body of research are numerous accounts that describe how a privileged group's "ways with words" often becomes universalized as an ideal standard for human behavior (Cook-Gumperz, 1986; Freebody & Luke, 1990; Heath, 1983; Maybin, 1994). In addition, an ideological definition of literacy challenges the widely accepted belief that the literacy of school—commonly referred to as "traditional" or "standard" literacy—is neutral or composed solely of discrete and "learnable" skills. Insistence on "schooled literacy" as the dominant form of literacy (Cook-Gumperz, 1986) positions nonschooled forms of literacy as not only nondominant but also inferior to the practices and discourses of school. Such a dichotomous view of literacies sustains a belief that demonstrable literacy proficiency, on school-based standardized measures, is attainable if the child/adult/community would just work hard enough (e.g., Taylor, 1996; Taylor & Dorsey-Gaines, 1988).

Studies inquiring into the literate lives of adolescents, which employ sociocultural perspectives, present a robust counternarrative to the prevalent image of the disaffected, disengaged youth. In an emerging body of work, adolescents are portrayed as poets (Jocson, 2006; Kinloch, 2005), popular culture pedagogues (Hagood, 2008; Morrell, 2004b), filmmakers (Goodman, 2003), multimodal composers and storytellers (DeJaynes, 2008; Hull & Nelson, 2005; Pleasants, 2008; Ranker, 2008; Schmier, 2008), and masters of musical improvisation (Meacham, 2001). In these studies, adolescents' literacies are viewed through the lenses of multimodality, multiliteracies, and critical literacy; analyzed with critical theories (feminist, poststructural, and critical race); and investigated through the use of diverse methodologies (e.g., participatory action research, ethnography, and practitioner inquiry) (Blackburn & Clark, 2007; Leander & Rowe, 2006; Mahiri, 2004; Mahiri & Sablo, 1996; Morrell, 2004a, 2004b; Nichols, 2008). As this research demonstrates, "new media literacies . . . [are used] to redefine and reposition [adolescent] learners as capable and innovative" (O'Brien, 2001, para. 2) and convey possibilities for transforming adolescents' experiences within educational spaces. These possibilities are presented in the accounts of adolescents engaging in creative literacy practices as they explore new (virtual) worlds (Thomas, 2005, 2007), produce innovative self-representations (Wissman, 2008) and media texts (Staples, 2008), and navigate online social spaces (Leander & McKim, 2003). A simple fact reverberates soundly from these studies: Literacies are in a state of transformation. Several recently published volumes have addressed the dimensions and implications of this evolving terrain of literacies (Jewitt, 2006; Leu, Coiro, Knobel, & Lankshear, 2008; McKenna, Labbo, Kieffer, & Reinking, 2006; Pahl & Rowsell, 2006), and some have focused particularly on the myriad aspects of literacies in the lives of youth (e.g., Alvermann et al., 2006; Christenbury, Bomer, & Smagorinsky, 2008; McPherson, 2007; Noguera, Ginwright, & Cammarota, 2006).

Nowhere is the transformation of literacies more evident than in the lives of adolescents, and no area is more closely linked to adolescents and adolescent literacy than media and technologies. The current digital landscape is one of increased social collaboration, characterized by social networking sites (e.g., Facebook, Myspace), video sharing sites (e.g., youtube.com, TeacherTube.com), virtual worlds (e.g., Second Life, Whyville), multifunction mobile phones, and an exponentially growing number of blogs and wikis. With all of this new "technical stuff" comes new "ethos stuff," which refers to the ways in which these new digital capabilities are used to create increasingly participatory, distributive, and collaborative literacy spaces (Lankshear & Knobel, 2008) like the ones noted earlier. Wikis, which are collaboratively editable Web pages, promote increased democratic participation in the production of knowledge, as evidenced in the ongoing phenomenon of Wikipedia.com, an online encyclopedia that relies on the collective knowledge of its contributors to populate and edit entries. Similarly, blogs, which function as interactive online journals, reflect a participatory culture that mediates knowledge production across space and time (Jenkins, 2006; Leander & Vasudevan, in press; Myers & Beach, 2004). This new digital landscape is commonly referred to as Web 2.0 and is generative of products that reflect innovations in communication technologies, which beget new literacies and communicative practices (Leu, Kinzer, Coiro, & Cammack, 2004) and new educational spaces (Kleifgen & Kinzer, in press). These spaces are largely populated by adolescents, who push the boundaries of communication and representation; they navigate, consume, and also help create these spaces through their participation as designers, contributors, and respondents. As a result of their role in transforming the digital communicative landscape, there is a growing narrative about youth as digital pioneers (Alvermann, 2002a; Boyd, 2008; Ito, 2005). However, as we have documented earlier, the language of innovation and discovery does not permeate the labels most frequently used to describe the youth on whom we have been focused in this review. Below, we highlight several studies that recognize adolescents as innovative, creative, and literate beings whose identities are not reducible to categories of risk but rather illustrative of literate possibilities.

Rethinking the Context of Literacy Learning

We think it is important to recognize that the emergence of recent studies that inform our understandings of literacy (e.g., Black, 2005; Fisher, 2006, 2008; Gustavson, 2007; Guzzetti & Gamboa, 2004; Kinloch, 2007; Knobel, 1999; Mahiri, 2004; Moje, 2000; Schultz, 2002; Thomas, 2005, 2007), like the seminal work of anthropologists and sociolinguists who provided a strong foundation for its scholarly descendents, are largely located in out-of-school settings (Hull & Nelson, 2005; Hull & Schultz, 2001). Recent theorizing about the spatial dimensions of literacies builds on sociocultural studies of literacy and, particularly in this moment of digital and posttypographic communicative practices, suggests a rethinking of the meaning of context (Leander & Sheehy, 2004). That is, the space of literacies is not necessarily linked to any one location or modality, and the context for literacy practices may exist across multiple time spaces (Leander & McKim, 2003). Many youth, for instance, are remaking their identities through their use of new technologies, media, and digital spaces where they engage in transglobal cultural exchange. Lam's (2006) study of immigrant students' online literacy practices pushes us to "re-think our nation-centric views of immigrant students' adaptation and their language and literacy development" (p. 171). In her study of Chinese working-class adolescent girls, Lam spent 8 months shadowing the girls' language and literacy use in school spaces, home spaces, and their Internet use. She focused on their participation in a chatroom in which the girls were "able to cross these socially constructed boundaries" established in their school experiences and use the "hybrid language produced" in their chatroom discourse to "disrupt the monolingual coherence of the English code" (p. 182). Lam asserts that

as immigrant students traverse different timespaces in their daily lives, it is important to note how their identity formation and socialization in the use of language(s) are defined not only by the imagined community of the nation state (Anderson, 1983/1991) but also by various imagined communities on a global scale (Appadurai, 1996). (p. 174)

Adolescents' literacies are practiced through the engagement of multiple modalities (e.g., pen, keyboard, and camera) across multiple spaces (a piece of paper, an online chatroom, and a friend's bedroom). Like Lam, Jacobs (2007) found that the literacies of Lisa, a young White woman at the center of her study of instant messaging (IMing), could not be fully understood solely through an analysis of her IM transcript nor through observing her IMing alone. In the case of Lisa, this online literacy practice existed as multiple simultaneous chats and in conversation with a phone call with a friend. Meaning is found across these discursive spaces and within the range of literacies in which she was engaged—for example, discussing homework, exchanging love notes with her boyfriend, and talking with a friend about an upcoming exam. The context of her literacy practices is both temporally and spatially hybrid. Within the same span of time and physical location of her bedroom, Lisa, like many other adolescents, engaged in multiple forms of communication through the use of multiple modalities (IMing, word processing, and the telephone). Yet for many adolescents, there is little intellectual synergy between their literacy learning in school and their literate identities outside of school.

The application of spatial theories, which recognize spaces as being actively produced through socially dynamic interactions, to literacy studies engenders new definitions of context in our research into the complex literacy landscapes of adolescents. Some researchers are asking different questions and employing new methodologies, which reflect an understanding of how context and the literacies that emerge from within are not neutral but rather are mutually constitutive of one another (e.g., Lewis & Fabos, 2005; O'Brien, 2006; for a discussion about ethnography in online spaces, see Hine, 2000; Leander & Rowe, 2006). The girls in Lam's and Jacobs's studies practiced their literacy across online and offline spaces and across the sites of home and school. In the process, they cultivated new literate identities as well as a range of communicative practices. The literacies of adolescents, therefore, exist in and across multiple contexts. Digital technologies make it possible to pedagogically revision existing sites of education so that they are more inclusive of diverse literate identities and practices. As the examples in this section illustrate, technologies not only are tools for learning but serve as spaces for new literacies (Vasudevan, 2008).

For Allie Feng, a female Chinese American junior in high school, digital story-telling afforded her the opportunity to redefine a context for her hybrid ethnic identity (Skinner & Hagood, 2008). She created a digital story of her transcontinental journeys between China and the United States, which contained photographs of places that held significance for her. In producing this artifact, Allie "construct[ed] identities that were important to her" and allowed her to "reflect upon her identities across space" (p. 27). Additionally, the space of digital story-telling allowed Allie to combine what the authors call "foundational literacies"—referring to practices associated with the writing process—with digital literacies to give "a multilayered representation of Allie's new literacies skills and practices that reflect the social literacy practices of her life and that relate specifically to her cultural identities" (p. 29).

Kinloch (2007, in press) draws on theories of postmodern geography and critical pedagogy to analyze the cultural production of Quentin and Kavon, two African American teenagers with whom she was engaged in participatory research. Specifically, she illustrates how these two young men using mapping, photography, and video interviews documented art forms in Harlem, being attentive to visible signs of decline and the ways that the community was reconceptualizing art. Together, Kinloch and her youth participants documented stories of change and engaged in sustained critique of the gentrification they saw taking hold in their Harlem neighborhood. Kinloch illustrates the ways in which the youth used various forms of documentation to engage in the productive struggle to reconfigure the cultural spaces in their neighborhoods, particularly through a visual revisioning of "Harlem as art." In addition to providing the insightful accounts of these two young men, Kinloch's research also demonstrates literacy engagement that is grounded in activism and social change at personal and public levels. Like June Jordan, whose transformative Poetry for the People (P4P) collaborative workshop opened up spaces for critical inquiry and activism through poetry and performance (Muller, Jordan, & P4P, 1995), Kinloch draws on participatory action approaches to engage youth as meaning makers about their literate identities and the literate spaces they inhabit and create, through the engagement of multiple modes of inquiry and representation.

These examples, as well as recent theorizing about the spatiality of literacies, present just cause to extend how we think about context. For many adolescents, whose cultural affiliations place them at the margins of resilience discourses and at the center of remediation scripts, the institutional contexts in which they practice their literacies must be reconfigured. And despite increased "pedagogization" (Street, 1995) of out-of-school time and the restrictions placed on the creativity of these spaces (Gadsden, 2008), a rich patchwork of literate life continues to flourish in adolescent-populated spaces. Adolescent literacy, as reflected in these studies, is understood as not a phrase mired in crisis but rather an indicator of creativity, innovation, exploration, and possibility.

Transformative Adolescent Literacies Within the School Walls

Although there is reason to be concerned about the lack of creativity afforded by some current curricular and instructional climates, there is also some evidence of transformative practices and projects occurring within classrooms and schools. Like Kinloch, whose work we described earlier, Jocson (2006, 2008) also demonstrates the literacy transformation that occurs for many adolescents. She, too, draws inspiration from the legacy of June Jordan in her work with youth and different forms of poetry, including spoken word and digital visual poetry. In one study, she describes the experiences of Damon, a 17-year-old biracial high school senior (Black and Filipino) whose participation in P4P in school led to the production of poetry as personal transformation. Jocson (2006) notes the unique placement of this program within the high school English classroom, whereas other P4P sites are located outside of school. Jocson (2006) wrote of Damon that his poetry explorations addressed

complex social, cultural, and political issues related to forms of present-day racism and notions of race and culture . . . [and that] his work exemplified what some marginalized urban youth face as they confront realities in their homes, schools, and neighborhoods. (p. 706)

Jocson's findings resonate with those of others (e.g., Hoechsmann & Low, 2008; Wissman, 2008) who have observed the power of literate traditions other than schooled reading and writing to create meaningful spaces for adolescent literacy learning and literate identity development within the classroom.

Similarly, in her work with adolescents at a New York City high school, Fisher (2007) shares the stories of the young men and women, and their dedicated teachers, who composed the Power Writers, a unique program in a Bronx high school where the literacies of adolescents were viewed as a space of possibility and transformation. Joseph Ubiles, a high school teacher and facilitator of the Power Writers, along with the youth participants of the project, who came from diverse ethnic and racial backgrounds, came together to engage in deep critical inquiry, language exploration, and personal reflection. Fisher writes, "Power Writing was more than a class. It was a job, a sacred space, a home, a functional—or sometimes 'dysfunctional,' as one student wrote in a poem—family" (p. 3). The teacher, Joe, adds to the student's observation and describes Power Writing as an "'open mic' for the 'truth'" (p. 3). Students are engaged in writing, reading each other's work, and actively listening to one another to provide critical, thoughtful, and generative feedback. The young men and women who were a part of the program came to understand and enact different ways of being and becoming literate. Likewise, Fisher urges educators to recognize that "young people are yearning to be chosen and to be claimed" as part of something bigger and "help young people develop the tools to transform this yearning into words and actions that chart the future they desire and deserve" (p. 101). Although this project occurs at the margins of the school day—before and after school—the work permeates the temporal and spatial boundaries of school.

The effort to bridge in- and out-of-school literacies (Hull & Schultz, 2002) continues to gain momentum, as reflected in research that seeks to build on the literacies of adolescents to support literacy learning in school. Some researchers who employ pedagogical practices in their research have explored the terrain of popular culture with youth. Morrell and Duncan-Andrade (2002, 2005) have advocated for the critical engagement of popular culture texts as bridges to school-sanctioned texts and literacies. They push against definitions of urban adolescents as "nonacademic" or "semiliterate" and draw on critical pedagogy and sociocultural lenses in their work with high school students. Like Kinloch (2007), Morrell and Duncan-Andrade (2005) advocate for the creation of multiple opportunities for youth to express themselves through modes other than solely linguistic, including photography and music, to make connections with school cultures. Morrell (2002), inspired by critical theorists, views popular culture "as a site of struggle between the subordinate and the dominant groups in society" and as "a terrain of exchange between" mass culture and people's culture (p. 73). Morrell and others (e.g., Alim, 2007; Hill, 2009; Kirkland, 2007, 2008) explicate the significance of hip hop language and culture, in particular, for the learning experiences of linguistically marginalized youth. These are young people whose literate identities are jeopardized because of their perceived distance from in-school literacy expectations. Some youth-focused researchers, including those noted above, interrogate the deficit assumptions associated with literacies that are sometimes dismissed as "nonschool," including those associated with hip hop and popular culture tropes (Dimitriadis, 2001; Johnson, 2008). These assumptions place adolescents at risk of being misread and mislabeled and ultimately miseducated. When the everyday, cultural affiliations and resources that youth bring into educational spaces are engaged productively, however, educators are better poised to develop students' critical and analytic skills, engage in social commentary, and design and complete projects with immediate significance to their communities (Morrell, 2006).

Staples (2008) also invites the reader to re-imagine classroom spaces by describing the popular culture negotiations she engaged in with African American urban adolescents within the space of an afterschool program, Youth Leadership (YL). Together, Staples and the youth she taught and with whom she learned were focused on critical readings of media—print media, Internet artifacts, film, and television— as they re-authored themselves through various practices of naming and renaming. The youth carried with them the school-identified labels of *struggling* and *disengaged reader* into YL's critical media space. However, in the course of 2 years and through the exploration of a multitude of media artifacts, Staples and the young men and women with whom she worked codevised a pedagogical framework for reading, rereading, and re-authoring the narratives they encountered in popular culture media texts. In one instance, while watching the movie *Hustle & Flow*, the group conversation turned to the negative portrayals of Black masculinity in the film.

Staples writes that the group used the critical media framework they had developed to not only read the film in multiple ways. They also looked closely at the visual landscape (e.g., facial gestures, characteristics), asked questions, recorded reflections, and in the process not only renamed the main character using terms that emerged from these practices but also engaged in re-authoring their own identities. Staples urges educators to open up spaces for adolescents to connect in new ways with popular culture texts with which they are familiar. By making the familiar strange, adolescents engage in meaningful literacy learning and also reassert the power to shed institutional labels and name themselves.

Other researchers anchor their work within the theoretical frame of multiple literacies to rethink the space of school (O'Brien, 1998; Rubinstein-Avila, 2003). For instance, Carter (2006) draws on an understanding of multiple literacies to examine the agency and in-group solidarity of African American young women in a high school English classroom. Although the students were positioned as disengaged and underperforming by the teacher, Carter demonstrates how their use of nonverbal modes of interaction conveyed a counterargument to the Eurocentric assumptions embedded in what the teacher modeled as ideal learning. The power of Carter's work is that it illustrates the importance of our theoretical paradigms for resisting deficit constructions of students. Through the lens of Black feminist epistemologies, students can be more fruitfully and accurately understood as interpretive agents who can collaboratively discern power dynamics. One implication of Carter's work is teachers must have the humility to learn from the theoretical and critical work of students who are historically excluded from the traditional curriculum. Similarly, T. Hall and Damico (2007) discuss how a multiple literacies perspective can be a pedagogical approach as well as an analytical tool. They demonstrate the ways African American youth draw on their rich discursive and literary traditions in the context of student video productions. They argue for the possibilities of creating educational arrangements in new literacies and technologies that affirm students' cultural ways of knowing.

Adolescent Literacies and Activism

Much of the recent research on adolescent literacies has a pronounced emphasis on activism and the belief that an important part of knowing about the world involves knowing how to change it (e.g., Blackburn & Clark, 2007; Duncan-Andrade & Morrell, 2008; Noguera et al., 2006). This activist research stance has entailed a theoretical paradigm shift, a departure away from postmodern or poststructuralist conceptions of language toward more critical realist orientations. Although helpful in calling attention to power dynamics and disrupting singular conceptions of "truth," some aspects of postmodernism, such as its dogmatic skepticism about objectivity and privileging of indeterminacy, have been ill suited for projects of transformation. Realists agree that people's experiences and perspectives are invariably social constructions, mediated by culture and discourse, but believe that this need not lead to a debilitating relativism that undermines epistemic claims about better and worse social and educational arrangements (Mohanty, 1997, p. 211). There are features of the world that can be described more or less accurately or with more or less social distortion. Activist literacy researchers strive to articulate a progressive agenda that identifies social injustice and proposes norms for more equitable alternatives.

Realist theory has diverse intellectual lineages (including neo-Marxism, anarchism, Freirian critical pedagogy, African American and African Diaspora epistemologies, and transnational feminisms) and perhaps has been most thoroughly and eloquently theorized by members of the Future of Minority Studies Project (FMS), an interdisciplinary think tank of scholars interested in articulating and enacting a vision of social justice (Alcoff & Mohanty, 2006; Mohanty, 1997; Moya, 2001; Moya & Hames-Garcia, 2000). The FMS scholars have argued that people's experiences and identities are causally related to features of the world, are not mere epiphenomena as some postmodernists might suggest, and thus can be reliable sources of knowledge (Mohanty, 1997, p. 203). In particular, individuals who occupy historically marginalized social locations have potentially privileged epistemic access to the world, "a special advantage with respect to possessing or acquiring knowledge about how fundamental aspects of our society operate to sustain matrices of power" (Moya, 2001, p. 479). Although this shift to realism may not be explicitly articulated as such in educational research, we believe many of its theoretical assumptions underlie much current activist work in adolescent literacies. Many activist literacy educators are interested in going beyond analyzing how social actors are trapped in ideologies and discourses of which they are not fully aware and instead view students (and teachers) as organic intellectuals (Gramsci, 1971) and historically situated agents who have the capacities to interpret their experiences and act toward change.

Considering literacy more broadly necessitates creating alternative spaces and pedagogies for students to mobilize their identities and engage in incisive social critique based on their own experiences. Literacy becomes a vehicle for students to use "subjective experience" to "criticize and rewrite dominant and oppressive narratives" (Alcoff & Mohanty, 2006, pp. 4–5). Many of these approaches are also examples of prefigurative pedagogy (Campano, 2007, in press). In the act of critique, educators and students are also prefiguring other educational possibilities with different values: for example, ones that emphasize cooperation and care over individuation and competition. As Audre Lorde (1984) famously stated, "the Master's tools will never dismantle the master's house" (p. 112). Adolescent literacies provide new tools to (re)imagine and enact more just educational arrangements. The process of moving away from a dogmatic skepticism toward real notions of "better" and "worse" has played a central role in helping researchers forward a progressive agenda and think about how social and political organizing may be a part of their methodologies. However, the caution for activist-oriented research is to retain a sense of humility and self-criticism, what realists refer to as a fallibalistic attention to precision and error, so as not to bend the stick too far back in the other direction of reifying certainty and standardizing new, albeit equally dogmatic, educational orthodoxies.

CULTIVATING AN ANTIDETERMINISTIC STANCE:
ADOLESCENT LITERACY IN SCHOOL CONTEXTS

It is in the spirit of questioning the status quo approach to literacy that we share what Campano (in press) has learned from his work with educators and teachers at the Boys Academy, a public, gendered elementary school in Northwestern Indiana that focuses on literacy and engagement, attempting to both challenge and transcend stereotypes that urban males do not like to read or write. During a family night at the Boys Academy, the principal suggested that everyone present knew the obstacles that the boys were going to face in their lives. There was no need to recount them in detail. The more important task, he argued, is to provide students the requisite skills to negotiate an often unjust world and for educators to create a nurturing, supportive, and intellectually demanding learning environment: in short, a resilient system. One implication of her words is that the teachers and community members are hardly naïve or unconscious. They are fully aware of issues of power and inequity, including the criminal (in)justice system, which threatens so many young lives. However, they would rather place their emphasis on working for positive change and putting language and literacy in the service of emancipation, a legacy that has deep roots in the African American human rights movements. This is decidedly an antideterministic stance, a belief that "another world is possible" and that literacy practices are part of the human labor to create that new world.

At a ribbon-cutting ceremony to celebrate a partnership between Indiana University and the Boys Academy, a district superintendent introduced the opening of a "Writers House" at the school with the following comments: "We envision the Writers House as a place where the students can develop their creative genius." Her remarks were soon given credence by several of the sixth grade student leaders who recited incredible verse about their neighborhoods, families, and legacies inspired by George Ella Lyons's *Where I'm From*, a poem made popular in schools by the teacher researcher and critical educator Linda Christensen (2000). In a grassroots reform effort, the committed faculty at the school, many themselves from the community, decided to refurbish an old classroom into a Writers House, where the students could both create and go public with their literary, artistic, and creative forms of cultural expression. The walls of the Writers House are adorned with images of famous African American authors. Books line the shelves, from canonical literature to more contemporary works of young adult fiction, graphic novels, and biographies. There is a computer station and several centers that highlight the writing process. Set prominently in the center of the room is a stage, where the students can perform drama, recite spoken-word poetry, rehearse powerful oratory, and use words to connect with a range of audiences, including family members, community supporters, and outside visitors.

The simple yet elegant phrase "a place . . . to develop creative genius" remains a radical premise that speaks "truth to power" in today's educational climate, which too often labels and sorts students along lines of ability. Part of what gives the phrase its radical import is its universality, that it is necessarily abstract and acontextual. In other words, irrespective of a student's test score, life circumstances, zip code, or any other contingency too often used to categorize experience, each and every student has the fundamental capacity to ingeniously create and engage in profound intellectual inquiry. Each student can employ literacy to fashion identities and theorize the world in an ongoing process of becoming.

These potentials will invariably take different forms and will be mediated by the rich and enriching diversity of 21st-century classrooms, but the capacity itself is, and should be, taken as a given. Although this may seem obvious, one needs to just examine current educational policies to realize the degree to which we are enamored with labeling and sorting students according to rigid notions of ability. Like most schools, the Boys Academy is not inured from these pressures. The administration, faculty, and students are held accountable to a series of quantitative measures. The Writers House, however, also points to a countervailing force, the desire to construct and foster less alienating, alternative educational arrangements and practices more conducive to student flourishing and self-determination. The reconfigured classroom is figuratively and literally a new world being born in the shell of the old.

The Writers House represents the unleashing of students' creative genius through uses of a larger understanding of literacy set against the backdrop of a narrowing notion of literacy operating in America's schools. For the boys in the Writers House, spoken word poetry became just one vehicle for them to link their particular family, neighborhood, and cultural experiences to larger social issues. The teachers' work with the students is comprehensive in nature. It includes, but is not limited to, implementing more culturally engaged literature; weaving the arts, such as drama, into the literacy curriculum; working with a native archeologist to think about how data from digs may be used to help students research and conceptualize issues like colonization and gender roles; inviting the students to conduct inquiry into issues that have immediate relevance to their own lives, such as economic abandonment and inequality; working with area writers and poets to introduce the school to local literary traditions; and mentoring the students to create their own nonfiction and informational texts derived from original research. The venue of the Writers House helps to make learning a social phenomenon where teachers feel empowered to create a rigorous, intellectually engaging community of meaning. It is an example of what Lytle (2006) calls

expanded notions of practice . . . a deep belief in teachers as leaders in their own classrooms, as makers of knowledge about teaching and learning, and a parallel conviction that the walls of the classroom do not delimit their commitments and responsibilities as educators. (p. 261)

As Hull and Katz (2006) observe, "moments of agency are sparsely illustrated in the literature, and the discourse of 'possibility' is often tentative about its own hopeful assertions" (p. 43). The story of EJ, whom Vasudevan (in press) met while he was a participant in an alternative to incarceration program (ATIP) in New York City, provides one illustration of agency made possible, ironically enough, through his participation in a program for court-involved youth. EJ is an 18-year-old youth of Honduran descent, who identifies as Hispanic American. He spent most of the last 6 years out of school and most of the last 3 years involved with the juvenile justice system. He lives with his mother and older brother in an apartment building that spans a city block and worked for a time in the kitchen of an upscale restaurant in the center of town. EJ's education is a marbled composition that consists of his life experiences, his involvement as a student at the school for youth living in a group home where he spent nearly 2 years, and his laudable and engaged participation in ATIP. During the course of his young life, EJ has been identified by many labels—*angry, dropout, delinquent, disappointment*—but the label he has given himself is most telling: *writer.* It is this last label that he has most recently embraced through his involvement in ATIP's theater program and the one that is being nurtured by the teachers and staff at the program who are committed to supporting his goal of pursuing a college education. Like educators we read about elsewhere (Fisher, 2007; Ladson-Billings, 1995; C. Lee, 2007), EJ's teachers afforded him multiple modes of participation within and outside of the classroom and did not treat his history as determinant of his future.

EJ's narrative, like that of many young people living and growing up in urban neighborhoods, is fraught with contradictions that could earn him the label of *at risk.* He will not have completed a traditional high school path, although he has earned his high school equivalency diploma; he is in the process of reestablishing a relationship with his family after being away from the home for nearly 2 years; he is working a minimum-wage job and has extensive household, personal, and extracurricular expenses; and he continues to live in the same geographic location where he was arrested twice, even as he strives to imagine life beyond correctional control. Scenarios such as this are the focus of much of the research literature landscape situated at the intersection of literacy, culture, and risk in the lives of adolescents (e.g., Dwyer & Wyn, 2001). The story less told is one that addresses not only daily struggles but also the everyday and lived achievements of adolescents whose cultural and literate lives are routinely maligned in institutional practices and the public discourse.

Such work often occurs in the extra moments teachers at ATIP take to inquire about the lives of youth to know them as more than "participants" or "court-involved youth" and in the ongoing and reflexive curriculum development that extends academic programming to include media and arts electives and college preparation support (classes as well as counseling). For EJ, the impact of ATIP's approach has been profound. After completing the first cycle of the theater project and receiving rave reviews for his character portrayals as well as his leadership in the group, EJ was hired as an intern to help facilitate the experiences of participants involved in the second cycle of the project. He sees himself as a college student enrolled at a 4-year institution in the near future and has ample support from ATIP teachers who continue to maintain relationships with many of the alumni. Adolescents, like EJ, and adults, like his teachers and counselors at ATIP, can engage in antideterministic acts that pave a new path of hope, possibility, and intellectual inquiry—acts that do not ignore the entrenched discourses of risk but rather work against them by providing youth with opportunities for renaming (Staples, 2008), critical inquiry (Morrell, 2004a), and imagining new futures for themselves (Fisher, 2007).

CLOSING THOUGHTS: PEDAGOGIES OF HOPE

The idea that hope alone will transform the world, and action under-taken in that kind of naïveté, is an excellent route to hopelessness, pessimism, and fatalism. But the attempt to do without hope, in the struggle to improve the world, as if that struggle could be reduced to calculated acts alone, or a purely scientific approach, is a frivolous illusion. To attempt to do without hope, which is based on the need for truth as an ethical quality of the struggle, is tantamount to denying that struggle is one of the mainstays. (Freire & Freire, 2004, p. 2)

In *Pedagogy of Hope: Reliving Pedagogy of the Oppressed*, Freire and Freire (2004) make a simple claim: "Hope, as an ontological need, demands an anchoring in practice" (p. 2). Although we have spent much of this review delineating the ways in which risk is socially and culturally constructed and institutionalized, our goal was not to suggest a hopeless trajectory for adolescents. Rather, we find hope that the narrative of "adolescent risk" is being rewritten in spaces like the Boys Academy, ATIP, and several others we discuss later and others that exist in a larger world, the borders of which we have yet to discover. There exist sites of possibility (Vasudevan & Hill, 2008) where spaces of and for inquiry are being re-imagined. Although adolescents continue to be placed and perceived as "at risk," there are also spaces where educational arrangements function democratically and literacies are flourishing.

Digital Underground Storytelling for Youth (DUSTY, n.d.) is an afterschool program for middle and high school students founded as a university and community collaboration, where youth develop their facility with a range of media technologies and software to produce digital stories. Glynda Hull and her colleagues have demonstrated the powerful literacy, identity, and pedagogical work that has emerged from this space (Hull & James, 2007; Hull & Nelson, 2005; Hull & Zacher, 2004), whose mission is grounded in urgency as well as possibility:

At the current moment and in the foreseeable future, the only places that most urban youth will, (1) get access to cutting edge technologies and (2) have opportunities and instruction for using those technologies meaningfully, will be after-school programs. The best of such programs don't replicate school and offer computers just for drill and practice or Internet surfing or word-processing; rather, they use new technologies to allow youth to communicate about their communities and themselves using to full advantage the power of multi-media, which is the literacy of the future. (DUSTY, n.d.)

Like DUSTY, YouthRadio views adolescents as not only literate but also as knowers whose insights are important for the very act of education, in and out of school. The diverse team of youth and adult collaborators at YouthRadio work together to produce radio documentaries on topics including family, health, education, society, and relationships. Like the ethos of DUSTY, the mission of YouthRadio is simultaneously simple and profound:

To promote young people's intellectual, creative and professional growth through training and access to media and to produce the highest quality original media for local and national outlets. (YouthRadio, n.d.)

In a space of "engaged pedagogy" (hooks, 1994), "rather than expect(ing) only students to learn and change, teachers also are transformed," and when "teachers offer their own narratives or interpretations, they cease to function as 'all-knowing silent interrogators'" (Soep & Chavez, 2005, p. 417).

Simon (2005) describes the work of Life Learning Academy, a high school for juvenile justice–involved youth founded as a part of a citywide reform effort in conjunction with the Delancey Street Foundation, a self-help rehabilitation organization for former drug addicts and offenders. The school's establishment is indicative of its ideological foundation: The students literally built an alternative school space from the ground up, working with architects, teachers, and volunteers to design and build their own classrooms. At Life Learning Academy, students engage in inquiry-based, interdisciplinary curricula they coconstruct with their teachers, including a working café that functions as a platform for weaving cross-curricular learning in subjects like economics, the humanities, and the arts. The participatory and resource-oriented approach of the school provides an opening for students who had been subject to inequitable conditions and criminalization, and had struggled academically, to take charge of their own learning. In this way, students who had previously been constructed as institutional failures are able to build more empowering academic identities.

Adolescents engaged in activist collectives provide not only a counternarrative that resists pathologizing images of youth but also a new trajectory that views, investigates, and engages the lives of adolescents through different lenses. The young people involved in the Film Inquiry Research and Media Education embody the engagement of new lenses quite literally, as they produce "varriomentaries," or documentaries produced by "marginalized and oppressed youth" (Film, Inquiry, Research and Media Education, n.d.), that document and offer critique on a wide range of issues: border protection legislation, illegal dumping of waste and toxins, schooling inequality in the United States, and dangers of migration. Similarly, Honeyford (2008) describes how middle school Latina/o students in Indiana claim a voice and identity in the community as cultural citizens by agitating for change and making the local library more accessible to the Spanish-speaking populations.

Pedagogies of hope are not limited to spaces focused on media and new literacies. They are found in spaces that engage adolescents as partners in literacy inquiry (Staples, 2008), provide adolescents with multiple modes through which to enter the educational process (Jewitt, 2006), promote the arts as a way to express social critique (Kinloch, 2007), and are generative of pedagogies that are responsive to and actively engage adolescents' multiple subjectivities (Blackburn, 2003; Campano, 2007; Jones, 2006). Teaching is "a marathon and not a sprint," and effective pedagogy "is about using the inequities of the system not as an excuse for leaving, but as a condition against which you set your purpose everyday" (Fecho, 2003, p. 3). If we are to effectively redress the injustices committed by persistent inequities, we need more educators who understand that "we need not cave into social arrangements that are unjust; we can write against them" (Ladson-Billings, 2003, p. 203).

Much of the research on adolescents and risk has focused on resiliency and the "resilient student." We have intentionally distanced ourselves from this literature because we believe it places the onus of responsibility on the individual student rather than on the ethical prerogative to create resilient educational arrangements that will support adolescents as they cope with life's vicissitudes and profound injustices. One of the messages of EJ's story is not that he lacks resiliency but much more that a young person with such intellectual and imaginative capacity has been so utterly failed by the education system. And EJ is not alone. According to the activist movement Critical Resistance, there are about 6.5 million people "under some form of supervision within the criminal justice system" (Critical Resistance, n.d., para. 5). School-aged children, in particular, are affected directly in two penetrating ways—first as a result of their own imprisonment and second as a result of their experiences when parents who would normally be responsible for their well-being are themselves imprisoned (Gadsden, 2003, Miller, 2006). They are disproportionately people of color, and women are one of the fastest growing prison populations, up by almost 400% since 1980 (Bureau of Justice Statistics, 1995). We are constantly reminded about the role (mis)education plays in this catastrophe. When asked about high school, one of Campano's former elementary students directly commented, "It's like a prison in here."

It is obviously not enough to highlight the way power operates to sustain inequality. We have to move beyond analysis. As Leonardo (2004) has commented with respect to critical social theory more generally, critical educators "must not stop at a language of critique. In order to provide students with a sustainable education, educators are encouraged to forge a language of transcendence, what Giroux (1983) calls a 'language of hope'" (p. 15). We might also add that we have to move beyond merely language, to putting action and theorizing in a dialectical, mutually informing relationship. A more hopeful direction is to learn from and with teachers, researchers, and teacher researchers who are working with adolescents regularly and are not content with just unearthing patterns but more with breaking them to liberate the fuller potentials of students. As we have learned from such committed educators such as the teachers and administrators at the Boy's Academy, this collective project needs to be comprehensive in nature. There is no one pedagogical approach or thinker that will provide all the answers. At the very least, it will involve cooperative work on several levels. In classrooms, teachers need to support students with "empowering" discourses and pedagogies (Ball, 2000). Or as Vivian Gadsden (Personal Communication, April 19, 1999) reminds us, we need to "teach all students with the expectation that they will surpass our own accomplishments." At the school and district level, we should encourage the creation of alternative learning spaces where students may truly display their prodigious creative and intellectual gifts and cultivate their own critical perspectives. Sometimes these spaces will be sexy and cutting edge, such as ones that involve new technologies and popular culture, and sometimes they may appear more mundane or traditional, such as drama worlds or literature discussion groups. What they should all share is a commitment to providing students with opportunities to engage in processes of educational self-determination and self-definition, the opposite, for example, of the role that tracking plays in sorting and remediating students. Finally, the work needs to occur outside the classroom. We should never lose sight of how poverty, the prison industrial complex, lack of health care, and educational underfunding place adolescents at risk, and ideally, we should create literacy curricula that invites future generations to both challenge and work to change these historically and socially produced realities. By viewing diverse adolescent identities as positive theoretical constructs that provide epistemological insights for educational transformation, the new literature on adolescents' literacies holds promise for rethinking education to be more equitable and empowering for all adolescents.

ACKNOWLEDGEMENTS

We thank the editors of this volume of *Review of Research in Education* for the invitation to contribute our voices to the important conversation about risk, equity, and school. We are especially indebted to Vivian Gadsden for her guidance and invaluable feedback throughout the process of writing this review. We appreciate the support and input that Maria Ghiso, Tiffany DeJaynes, and Kristine Rodriguez provided at different points along this writing journey. Finally, we also want to thank our reviewers, Bob Fecho and Arlette Willis, for their thoughtful and critical comments on earlier drafts of this chapter.

REFERENCES

Alcoff, L., & Mohanty, S. (2006). Reconsidering identity politics: An introduction. In L. Alcoff, M. Hames-Garcia, S. Mohanty, & P. Moya (Eds.), *Identity politics reconsidered* (pp. 1–9). New York: Palgrave Macmillan.

Alim, H. S. (2007). Critical hip-hop language pedagogies: Combat, consciousness, and the cultural politics of communication. *Journal of Language, Identity, and Education, 6*(2), 161–176.

Alliance for Excellent Education. (2004). *Reading for the 21st century: Adolescent literacy teaching and learning strategies* (issue brief). Washington, DC: Author. Retrieved August 11, 2008, from www.a114ed.org/files/Reading_21stCentury.pdf

Alvermann, D. (Ed.). (2002a). *Adolescents and literacies in a digital world.* New York: Peter Lang.

Alvermann, D. (2002b). Effective literacy instruction for adolescents. *Journal of Literacy Research, 34*(2), 189–208.

Alvermann, D., Hinchman, K., Moore, D. W., Phelps, S., & Waff, D. (2006). *Reconceptualizing the literacies in adolescents' lives* (2nd ed.). Mahwah, NJ: Lawrence Erlbaum.

American Bar Association & National Bar Association. (2001). *Justice by gender: The lack of appropriate prevention, diversion, and treatment alternatives for girls in the justice system.* Washington, DC: Author.

Anzaldua, G. (1987). *Borderlands/la frontera: The new mestiza.* San Francisco: Aunt Lute Books.

Ball, A. F. (2000). Empowering pedagogies that enhance the learning of multicultural students. *Teachers College Record, 102*(6), 1006–1034.

Bartlett, L. (2007). Literacy, speech and shame: The cultural politics of literacy and language in Brazil. *International Journal of Qualitative Studies in Education, 20*(5), 547–563.

Bean, T. W., Readence, J. E., & Baldwin, R. S. (2008). *Content area literacy: An integrated approach* (9th ed.). Dubuque, IA: Kendall/Hunt.

Biancarosa, G., & Snow, C. E. (2006). *Reading next—A vision for action and research in middle and high school literacy: A report to Carnegie Corporation of New York* (2nd ed.). Washington, DC: Alliance for Excellent Education.

Black, R. W. (2005). Access and affiliation: The literacy and composition practices of English-language learners in an online fanfiction community. *Journal of Adolescent and Adult Literacy, 49*(2), 118–128.

Blackburn, M. (2002/2003). Disrupting the (hetero)normative: Exploring literacy performances and identity work with queer youth. *Journal of Adolescent and Adult Literacy, 46*(4), 312–324.

Blackburn, M. (2003). Exploring literacy performances and power dynamics at the loft: Queer youth reading the world and the word. *Research in the Teaching of English, 37*(4), 467–490.

Blackburn, M., & Clark, C. (2007). *Literacy research for political action and social change.* New York: Peter Lang.

Bloome, D., Carter, S. P., Christian, B. M., Otto, S., & Shuart-Faris, N. (2005). *Discourse analysis & the study of classroom language & literacy events: A microethnographic perspective.* Mahwah, NJ: Lawrence Erlbaum.

Bloome, D., & Green, J. L. (1991). Educational contexts of literacy. *Annual Review of Applied Linguistics, 12*, 49–70.

Bourdieu, P., & Passeron, J. C. (1977). *Reproduction in education, society and culture.* London: Sage.

Boyd, D. (2008). Why youth (heart) social network sites: The role of networked publics in teenage social life. In D. Buckingham (Ed.), *Youth, identity, and digital media* (pp. 119–142). Cambridge, MA: MIT Press.

Brayboy, B. M. J. (2004). Hiding in the ivy: American Indian students and visibility in elite educational settings. *Harvard Educational Review, 74*(2), 125–152.

Bureau of Justice Statistics. (1995). *State and federal correctional facilities census, 1995.* Washington, DC: U.S. Department of Justice.

Burton, L. (2007). Childhood adultification in economically disadvantaged families: A conceptual model. *Family Relations, 56*(4), 329–345.

Camitta, M. (1993). Vernacular writing: Varieties of literacy among Philadelphia high school students. In B. Street (Ed.), *Cross-cultural approaches to literacy* (pp. 228–246). Cambridge, UK: Cambridge University Press.

Campano, G. (2007). *Immigrant students and literacy: Reading, writing, and remembering.* New York: Teachers College Press.

Campano, G. (in press). Teacher research as a collective struggle for humanization. In M. Cochran-Smith & S. L. Lytle (Eds.), *Inquiry as stance: Practitioner knowledge and learning.* New York: Teachers College Press.

Carter, S. P. (2006). "She would've still made that face expression": The use of multiple literacies by two African American young women. *Theory Into Practice, 45*(4), 352–358.

Chandler-Olcott, K., & Mahar, D. (2003). "Tech-savviness" meets multiliteracies: Exploring adolescent girls' technology-mediated literacy practices. *Reading Research Quarterly, 38*(3), 356–385.

Christenbury, L., Bomer, R., & Smagorinsky, P. (2008). *Handbook of adolescent literacy research.* New York: Guilford.

Christensen, L. (2000). *Reading, writing, and rising up: Teaching about social justice and the power of the written word.* Chicago: Joyce Foundation.

Cochran-Smith, M., & Lytle, S. (2006). Troubling images of teaching in No Child Left Behind. *Harvard Educational Review, 73*(4), 668–697.

Cook-Gumperz, J. (1986). *The social construction of literacy.* Cambridge, UK: Cambridge University Press.

Critical Resistance. (n.d.). *What is the prison industrial complex?* Retrieved September 29, 2008, from http://criticalresist.live.radicaldesigns.org/article.php?preview=1&cache=0&id=58

Cummins, J. (2007). Pedagogies for the poor? Realigning reading instruction for low-income students with scientifically based reading research. *Educational Researcher, 36*(9), 564–572.

Darling-Hammond, L. (2006). Securing the right to learn: Policy and practice for powerful teaching and learning. *Educational Researcher, 35*(7), 13–24.

Davidson, J., & Koppenhaver, D. (1993). *Adolescent literacy: What works and why* (2nd ed.). New York: Garland.

DeJaynes, T. (2008, March). *Understanding the multimedia composing processes of youth.* Paper presented at the Annual Meeting of the American Educational Research Association, New York.

Delpit, L. (1995). *Other people's children: Cultural conflict in the classroom.* New York: Norton.

Digital Underground Storytelling for Youth. (n.d.). *Mission statement.* Available at http://www.oaklanddusty.org/

Dimitriadis, G. (2001). "In the clique": Popular culture, constructions of place, and the everyday lives of urban youth. *Anthropology and Education Quarterly, 32*(1), 29–51.

Duncan, G. A. (2005). Critical race ethnography in education: Narrative, inequality and the problem of epistemology. *Race Ethnicity and Education, 8*(1), 93–114.

Duncan-Andrade, J., & Morrell, E. (2008). *The art of critical pedagogy: Possibilities for moving from theory to practice in urban schools.* New York: Peter Lang.

Dwyer, P., & Wyn, J. (2001). *Youth, education and risk: Facing the future.* London: Routledge.

Dyson, A. H. (1997). *Writing superheroes: Contemporary childhood, popular culture, and classroom literacy* (Language and Literacy Series). New York: Teachers College Press.

Eckholm, E. (2006, March 20). Plight deepens for Black men, studies warn. *The New York Times,* Retrieved December 6, 2008, from http://www.nytimes.com/2006/03/20/national/20blackmen.html?pagewanted=print

Emig, J. (1971). *The composing processes of twelfth graders.* Urbana, IL: National Council of Teachers of English.

Fecho, B. (2003). *"Is this English?" Race, language, and culture in the classroom.* New York: Teachers College Press.

Fenning, P., & Rose, J. (2007). Overrepresentation of African American students in exclusionary discipline: The role of school policy. *Urban Education, 42*(6), 536–559.

Ferguson, A. A. (2000). *Bad boys: Public schools in the making of Black masculinity.* Ann Arbor: University of Michigan Press.

Ferguson, R. (2003). Teachers' perceptions and expectations and the Black-White test score gap. *Urban Education, 38*(4), 460–507.

Film, Inquiry, Research and Media Education. (n.d.). *Film, Inquiry, Research and Media Education.* Available at http://www.firmeproductions.com/

Finders, M. (1997). *Just girls: Hidden literacies and life in junior high.* New York: Teachers College Press.

Fine, M., Bloom, J., Burns, A., Chajet, L., Guishard, M., Perkins-Munn, T., et al. (2004). *Echoes of Brown: The faultlines of racial justice and public education.* New York: The Graduate Center, City University of New York.

Finkelstein, B. (2000). A crucible of contradictions: Historical roots of violence against children. In V. Polakow (Ed.), *The public assault on America's children: Poverty, violence, and juvenile injustice* (pp. 21–41). New York: Teachers College Press.

Fisher, M. T. (2003). Open mics and open minds: Spoken word poetry in African Diaspora participatory literacy communities. *Harvard Educational Review, 73*(3), 362–389.

Fisher, M. T. (2006). Earning "dual degrees": Black bookstores as alternative knowledge spaces. *Anthropology and Education Quarterly, 37*(1), 83–99.

Fisher, M. T. (2007). *Writing in rhythm: Spoken word poetry in urban classrooms.* New York: Teachers College Press.

Fisher, M. T. (2008). *Black literate lives: Historical and contemporary perspectives.* New York: Routledge.

Foley, D. (1997). Deficit thinking models based on culture: The anthropological protest. In R. R. Valencia (Ed.), *The evolution of deficit thinking: Educational thought and practice* (pp. 113–131). New York: Routledge.

Fordham, S. (1993). "Those loud Black girls": (Black) women, silence, and gender "passing" in the academy. *Anthropology and Education Quarterly, 24*(1), 3–32.

Franzak, J. K. (2006). "Zoom": A review of the literature on marginalized adolescent readers, literacy theory, and policy implications. *Review of Educational Research, 76*(2), 209–248.

Freebody, P., & Luke, A. (1990). Literacies programs: Debates and demands in cultural context. *Prospect: Australian Journal of TESOL, 5*(7), 7–16.

Freire, P., & Freire, A. M. A. (2004). *Pedagogy of hope: Reliving pedagogy of the oppressed.* New York: Continuum International Publishing Group.

Gadsden, V. (Ed.) (2003). *Heading Home: Offender Reintegration into the Family.* American Community Corrections Association and International Community Corrections Association.

Gadsden, V. L. (1993). Literacy, education, and identity among African-Americans: The communal nature of learning. *Urban Education, 27*(4), 352–369.

Gadsden, V. L. (1995). Literacy and poverty: Intergenerational issues within African American families. In H. Fitzgerald, B. Lester, & B. Zuckerman (Eds.), *Children of poverty* (pp. 85–119). New York: Garland.

Gadsden, V. L. (2008). The arts and education: Knowledge generation, pedagogy, and the discourse of learning. *Review of Research in Education, 32*(1), 29–61.

Gadsden, V. L., & Fuhrman, S. (2007). Reflections on educational equity in post-Katrina New Orleans. In S. P. Robinson & M. C. Brown (Eds.), *The children Hurricane Katrina left behind: Schooling context, professional preparation, and community politics* (pp. 73-88). New York: Peter Lang.

Gee, J. (1991). Socio-cultural approaches to literacy (literacies). *Annual Review of Applied Linguistics, 12,* 31–48.

Gee, J. (1996). *Social linguistics and literacies: Ideology in discourses* (2nd ed.). London; Bristol, PA: Taylor & Francis.

Gee, J. (1999). The new literacy studies and the "social turn." Retrieved August 8, 2008, from http://www.schools.ash.org.au/litweb/page300.html

Gee, J. P. (2000). Teenagers in new times: A new literacy studies perspective. *Journal of Adolescent and Adult Literacy, 43*(5), 412–420.

Ginwright, S. A. (2004). *Black in school: Afrocentric reform, urban youth & the promise of hip-hop culture.* New York: Teachers College Press.

Girard, R. (1986). *The scapegoat.* Baltimore: Johns Hopkins University Press.

Giroux, H. A. (2001). Mis/education and zero tolerance: Disposable youth and the politics of domestic militarization. *Boundary, 28*(3), 61–94.

Goodman, S. (2003). *Teaching youth media: A critical guide to literacy, video production, & social change* (The Series on School Reform). New York: Teachers College Press.

Gordon, E. (1999). Foreword: The experiences of African American males in school and society. In V. C. Polite & J. E. Davis (Eds.), *African American males in school and society: Practices and policies for effective education* (pp. ix–xiii). New York: Teachers College Press.

Graham, S., & Perin, D. (2007). *Writing next: Effective strategies to improve writing of adolescents in middle and high schools—A report to Carnegie Corporation of New York.* Washington, DC: Alliance for Excellent Education.

Gramsci, A. (1971). *Selections for the prison notebooks* (G. N. Smith & Q. Hoare, Trans.). New York: International Publishers.

Gustavson, L. (2007). *Youth learning on their own terms: Creative practices and classroom teaching.* New York: Routledge.

Gutierrez, K. (2001). Smoke and mirrors: Language policy and educational reform. In J. Larson (Ed.), *Literacy as snake oil: Beyond the quick fix* (pp. 111–122). New York: Peter Lang.

Guzzetti, B. J., & Gamboa, M. (2004). Zines for social justice: Adolescent girls writing on their own. *Reading Research Quarterly, 39*(4), 408–436.

Hagood, M. C. (2008). Intersections of popular culture, identities, and new literacies research. In J. Coiro, M. Knobel, C. Lankshear, & D. Leu (Eds.), *Handbook of research on new literacies* (pp. 531–551). New York: Lawrence Erlbaum.

Hall, G. S. (1904). *Adolescence*. New York: D. Appleton and Company.

Hall, S. (Writer). (1996). *Stuart Hall—RACE: The floating signifier* (S. Jhally, Producer). Northampton, MA: Media Education Foundation.

Hall, T., & Damico, J. (2007). Black youth employ African American vernacular English in creating digital texts. *The Journal of Negro Education, 76*(1), 80–88.

Heath, S. B. (1983). *Ways with words: Language, life, and work in communities and classrooms*. Cambridge, UK: Cambridge University Press.

Herbert, B. (2007, June 9). School to prison pipeline. *The New York Times*.

Hill, M. L. (2009). Wounded healing: Forming a storytelling community in hip-hop lit [electronic version]. *Teachers College Record, 111*. Retrieved October 19, 2008, from http://www.tcrecord.org/Content.asp?contentid=15215

Hill, M. L., & Vasudevan, L. (Eds.). (2008). *Media, learning, and sites of possibility*. New York: Peter Lang.

Hine, C. (2000). *Virtual ethnography*. Thousand Oaks, CA: Sage.

Hoechsmann, M., & Low, B. E. (2008). *Reading youth writing: "New" literacies, cultural studies & education*. New York: Peter Lang.

Honeyford, M. (2008, April). *Citizens in the middle: A study of bilingual immigrant students translating change*. Paper presented at the annual conference of the American Educational Research Association, New York.

hooks, b. (1994). *Teaching to transgress: Education as the practice of freedom*. New York: Routledge.

Hudak, G. M., & Kihn, P. (2001). *Labeling: Pedagogy and politics*. London: Routledge.

Hull, G., & James, M. A. (2007). Geographies of hope: A study of urban landscapes and a university-community collaborative. In P. O'Neil (Ed.), *Blurring boundaries: Developing writers, researchers, and teachers: A tribute to William L. Smith* (pp. 250–289). Kresskill, NJ: Hampton Press.

Hull, G., & Katz, M. L. (2006). Crafting an agentive self: Case studies of digital storytelling. *Research in the Teaching of English, 41*(1), 43–81.

Hull, G. A., Kenney, N. L., Marple, S., & Forsman-Schneider, A. (2006). *Many versions of masculine: An exploration of boys' identity formation through digital storytelling in an after-school program*. New York: The Robert Bowne Foundation.

Hull, G., & Nelson, M. E. (2005). Locating the semiotic power of multimodality. *Written Communication, 22*(2), 224–261.

Hull, G., & Schultz, K. (2001). Literacy and learning out of school: A review of theory and research. *Review of Educational Research, 71*(4), 575–611.

Hull, G., & Schultz, K. (2002). *School's out! Bridging out-of-school literacies with classroom practice*. New York: Teachers College Press.

Hull, G., & Zacher, J. (2004). What is an after-school worth? Developing literacy and identity in school. *Voices in Urban Education, 3*, 36–44.

Ito, M. (2005). Mobile phones, Japanese youth, and the re-placement of social contact. In R. Ling & P. Pedersen (Eds.), *Mobile communications: Re-negotiation of the social sphere* (pp. 131–148). New York: Springer-Verlag.

Jacobs, G. (2007). Locating the local: Developing methodology for problematizing the construction of context. In M. Blackburn & C. T. Clark (Eds.), *Literacy research for political action and social change* (pp. 53–75). New York: Peter Lang.

Jenkins, H. (2006). *Confronting the challenges of participatory culture: Media education for the 21st century*. Chicago: The MacArthur Foundation.

Jetton, T. L., & Dole, J. A. (2004). *Adolescent literacy research and practice*. New York: Guilford.

Jewitt, C. (2002). The move from page to screen: The multimodal reshaping of school English. *Visual Communication, 1*(2), 171–195.

Jewitt, C. (2006). *Technology, literacy and learning: A multimodal approach*. London; New York: Routledge.

Jewitt, C., & Kress, G. R. (2003). *Multimodal literacy*. New York: Peter Lang.

Jocson, K. M. (2006). "There's a better word": Urban youth rewriting their social worlds through poetry. *Journal of Adolescent and Adult Literacy, 49*(8), 700–707.

Jocson, K. M. (2008). *Youth poets: Empowering literacies in and out of schools*. New York: Peter Lang.

Johnson, E. (2008, November). *Suits, earrings and literacy: Performing race and success in the high school English classroom*. Paper presented at the Annual Meeting of the American Anthropological Association, San Francisco.

Johnston, P. (1999). *Unpacking literate "achievement."* Retrieved October 29, 2008, from http://cela.albany.edu/reports/Johnstonunpacking12007.pdf

Jones, S. (2006). *Girls, social class, and literacy: What teachers can do to make a difference*. Portsmouth, NH: Heinemann.

Kinloch, V. F. (2005). Poetry, literacy, and creativity: Fostering effective learning strategies in an urban classroom. *English Education, 37*(2), 96–114.

Kinloch, V. F. (2007). Youth representations of community, art, and struggle in Harlem. *New Directions for Adult and Continuing Education, 116*, 37–49.

Kinloch, V. F. (in press). *Black spaces as cultural institutions: Place, race, and youth narratives of community*. New York: Teachers College Press.

Kirkland, D. (2007). The power of their text: Teaching hip hop in the secondary English classroom. In K. Keaton & P. R. Schmidt (Eds.), *Closing the gap: English educators address the tensions between teacher preparation and teaching writing in secondary schools* (Language, Literacy, and Learning Series for Information Age Publishing, pp. 129–145). Charlotte, NC: Information Age Publishing.

Kirkland, D. (2008). "The rose that grew from concrete": Hip hop and the new English education. *The English Journal, 97*(5), 69–75.

Kleifgen, J. & Kinzer, C. K. (in press). Alternative spaces for education with and through technology. In H. Varenne & E. Gordon (Eds.). *Comprehensive education explorations, possibilities, challenges*. Lewiston, NY: Ewin Mellen Press.

Knobel, M. (1999). *Everyday literacies: Students, discourse, and social practice*. New York: Peter Lang.

Ladson-Billings, G. (1995). Toward a theory of culturally relevant pedagogy. *American Educational Research Journal, 32*(3), 465–491.

Ladson-Billings, G. (2003). It's your world, I'm just trying to explain it: Understanding our epistemological and methodological challenges. *Qualitative Inquiry, 1*(9), 5–12.

Ladson-Billings, G., & Tate, W. (1995). Toward a critical race theory of education. *Teachers College Record, 97*(1), 47–68.

Lam, W. S. E. (2006). Re-envisioning language, literacy, and the immigrant subject in new mediascapes. *Pedagogies: An International Journal, 1*(3), 171–195.

Langer, J. (2004, May). *Developing the literate mind*. Speech delivered at the International Reading Association, Newark, DE. Retrieved October 29, 2008, from http://www.albany.edu/cela/researcher/langer/IRA_Develop.pdf

Langer, J. (2008). Contexts for adolescent literacy. In L. Christenbury, R. Bomer, & P. Smagorinsky (Eds.), *Handbook of adolescent literacy research* (pp. 49–64). New York: Guilford.

Lankshear, C., & Knobel, M. (2006). *New literacies: Everyday practices and classroom learning* (2nd ed.). Maidenhead, NY: Open University Press.

Lankshear, C., & Knobel, M. (2008). *Digital literacies: Concepts, policies and practices*. New York: Peter Lang.

Leander, K. M., & McKim, K. K. (2003). Tracing the everyday "sitings" of adolescents on the Internet: A strategic adaptation of ethnography across online and offline spaces. *Education, Communication & Information, 3*(2), 211–240.

Leander, K. M., & Rowe, D. W. (2006). Mapping literacy spaces in motion: A Rhizomatic analysis of a classroom literacy performance. *Reading Research Quarterly, 41*(4), 428–460.

Leander, K. M., & Sheehy, M. (2004). *Spatializing literacy research and practice.* New York: Peter Lang.

Leander, K., & Vasudevan, L. (in press). Multimodality and mobile culture. In C. Jewitt (Ed.), *Handbook of multimodal analysis.* London: Routledge.

Lee, C. (1992). Literacy, cultural diversity, and instruction. *Education and Urban Society, 24*(2), 279–291.

Lee, C. (2007). *Culture, literacy & learning: Taking bloom in the midst of the whirlwind.* New York: Teachers College Press.

Lee, S. (1996). *Unraveling the "model minority stereotype": Listening to Asian American youth.* New York: Teachers College Press.

Lei, J. L. (2003). (Un)Necessary toughness?: Those "loud Black girls" and those "quiet Asian boys." *Anthropology and Education Quarterly, 34*(2), 158-181.

Leonardo, Z. (2004). Critical social theory and transformative knowledge: The functions of criticism in quality education. *Educational Researcher, 33*(6), 11–18.

Leu, D., Coiro, J., Knobel, M., & Lankshear, C. (2008). *Handbook of research on new literacies.* New York: Lawrence Erlbaum/Taylor & Francis Group.

Leu, D., Kinzer, C. K., Coiro, J., & Cammack, D. (2004). Toward a theory of new literacies emerging from the Internet and other information and communication technologies. In R. B. Ruddell & N. J. Unrau (Eds.), *Theoretical models and processes of reading* (5th ed., pp. 1568–1611). Newark, DE: International Reading Association.

Lewis, C., Enciso, P., & Moje, E. B. (2007). *Reframing sociocultural research on literacy: Identity, agency, and power.* Mahwah, NJ: Lawrence Erlbaum.

Lewis, C., & Fabos, B. (2005). Instant messaging, literacies, and social identities. *Reading Research Quarterly, 40*(4), 470–501.

Lipman, P. (1998). *Race, class, and power in school restructuring* (SUNY Series, Restructuring and School Change). Albany: State University of New York.

Lipman, P. (2006). "This is America" 2005: The political economy of education reform against the public interest. In G. Ladson-Billings & W. F. Tate (Eds.), *Education research in the public interest: Social justice, action, and policy* (pp. 98–118). New York: Teachers College Press.

Lorde, A. (1984). *Sister outsider: Essays and speeches.* Trumansburg, NY: Crossing Press.

Lytle, S. (2006). The literacies of teaching urban adolescents in *these times.* In D. Alvermann, K. Hinchman, D. W. Moore, S. F. Phelps, & D. R. Waff (Eds.), *Reconceptualizing the literacies in adolescent's lives* (2nd ed., pp. 257–278). Mahwah, NJ: Lawrence Erlbaum.

Mahiri, J. (2004). *What they don't learn in school: Literacy in the lives of urban youth.* New York: Peter Lang.

Mahiri, J., & Sablo, S. (1996). Writing for their lives: The non-school literacy of California's urban African American youth. *Journal of Negro Education, 65*(2), 164–180.

Maira, S., & Soep, E. (2005). *Youthscapes: The popular, the national, the global.* Philadelphia: University of Pennsylvania Press.

Mauer, M. (2003). The crisis of the young African American male and the criminal justice system. In O. Harris & R. R. Miller (Eds.), *Impacts of incarceration on the African American family* (pp. 199–218). New Brunswick, NJ: Transaction Publishers.

Maybin, J. (Ed.). (1994). *Language and literacy in social practice.* London: Multilingual Matters.

McDermott, R., & Varenne, H. (1995). Culture as disability. *Anthropology and Education Quarterly, 26*(3), 324–348.

McKenna, M. C., Labbo, L., Kieffer, R. D., & Reinking, D. (2006). *International handbook of literacy and technology* (Volume II). Mahwah, NJ: Lawrence Erlbaum.

McPherson, T. (Ed.). (2007). *Digital youth, innovation, and the unexpected.* Cambridge, MA: MIT Press.

Meacham, S. (2001). Vygotsky and the blues: Re-reading cultural connections and conceptual development. *Theory Into Practice, 40*(3), 190–197.

Mickelson, R. (2000). Learning to read in cages: A metaphor for race and class disparities in opportunities to learn? *Teachers College Record.* Retrieved November 16, 2008, from http://www.tcrecord.org/content.asp?contentid=10484

Miller, K. (2006). The Impact of Parental Incarceration on Children: An Emerging Need for Effective Interventions. *Child and Adolescent Social Work Journal, 23*(4), 472-486.

Mohanty, S. (1997). *Literary theory and the claims of history: Postmodernism, objectivity, multicultural politics.* Ithaca, NY: Cornell University Press.

Moje, E. B. (2000). "To be part of the story": The literacy practices of "gangsta" adolescents. *Teachers College Record, 102*(3), 652–690.

Moje, E. B. (2002). But where are the youth? On the value of integrating youth culture into literacy theory. *Educational Theory, 52*(1), 97–120.

Moje, E. B., Ciechanowski, K. M., Kramer, K., Ellis, L., Carrillo, R., & Collazo, T. (2004). Working toward third space in content area literacy: An examination of everyday funds of knowledge and discourse. *Reading Research Quarterly, 39*(1), 38–70.

Moje, E. B., Dillon, D. R., & O'Brien, D. (2000). Reexamining roles of learner, text, and context in secondary literacy. *Journal of Educational Research, 93*(3), 165–180.

Moje, E. B., Young, J. P., Readence, J. E., & Moore, D. W. (2000). Reinventing adolescent literacy for new times: Perennial and millennial issues. *Journal of Adolescent and Adult Literacy, 43*(5), 400–410.

Moll, L. C. (1992). Funds of knowledge for teaching: Using a qualitative approach to connect homes and classrooms. *Theory Into Practice, 31*(1), 132–141.

Moore, D. W., Bean, T. W., Birdyshaw, D., & Rycik, J. A. (1999). *Adolescent literacy: A position statement for the Commission on Adolescent Literacy of the International Reading Association.* Newark, DE: International Reading Association.

Morrell, E. (2002). Toward a critical pedagogy of popular culture: Literacy development among urban youth. *Journal of Adolescent and Adult Literacy, 46*(1), 72–77.

Morrell, E. (2004a). *Becoming critical researchers: Literacy and empowerment for urban youth.* New York: Peter Lang.

Morrell, E. (2004b). *Linking literacy and popular culture: Finding connections for lifelong learning.* Norwood, MA: Christopher-Gordon Publishers.

Morrell, E. (2006). Critical participatory action research and the literacy achievement of ethnic minority groups. *National Reading Conference Yearbook, 55*, 1–18.

Morrell, E. (2008). *Critical literacy and urban youth: Pedagogies of access, dissent, and liberation.* New York: Routledge.

Morrell, E., & Duncan-Andrade, J. M. R. (2002). Promoting academic literacy with urban youth through engaging hip-hop culture. *English Journal, 91*(6), 88–92.

Morrell, E., & Duncan-Andrade, J. (2005). Popular culture and critical media pedagogy in secondary literacy classrooms. *International Journal of Learning, 12*, 1–11.

Moya, P. (2001). *Learning from experience: Minority identities, multicultural struggles.* Berkeley: University of California Press.

Moya, P., & Hames-Garcia, M. (Eds.). (2000). *Reclaiming identity: Realist theory and the predicament of postmodernism.* Berkeley: University of California Press.

Muller, L., Jordan, J., & Poetry for the People. (1995). *June Jordan's Poetry for the People: A revolutionary blueprint.* New York: Routledge.

Myers, J., & Beach, R. (2004). Constructing critical literacy practices through technology tools and inquiry. *Contemporary Issues in Technology and Teacher Education, 4*(3), 257–268.

National Council of Teachers of English. (2004). *A call to action: What we know about adolescent literacy and ways to support teachers in meeting students' needs.* Urbana, IL: Author.

Retrieved October 29, 2008, from http://www.ncte.org/about/over/positions/category/read/118622.htm

National Council of Teachers of English. (2007). *Adolescent literacy: A policy research brief.* Urbana, IL: Author. Retrieved October 29, 2008, from www.ncte.org/library/files/Publications/News paper/Chron0907ResearchBrief.pdf

National Endowment for the Arts. (2004). *Reading at risk: A survey of literary reading in America* (Research Division Report #46). Washington, DC: Author.

Nayak, A. (2003). *Race, place and globalization: Youth cultures in a changing world* (1st ed.). New York: Berg.

Neild, R. C., Stoner-Eby, S., & Furstenberg, F. (2008). Connecting entrance and departure: The transition to ninth grade and high school dropout. *Education and Urban Society, 40*(5), 543–569.

Newkirk, T. (2002). *Misreading masculinity: Boys, literacy, and popular culture.* Portsmouth, NH: Heinemann.

New London Group. (1996). A pedagogy of multiliteracies: Designing social futures. *Harvard Educational Review, 66*(1), 60–92.

Nichols, R. (2008). "Kind of like emerging from the shadows": Adolescent girls as multiliteracy pedagogues. In M. L. Hill & L. Vasudevan (Eds.), *Media, learning, and sites of possibility* (pp. 119–156). New York: Peter Lang.

Nilan, P., & Feixa, C. (2006). *Global youth? Hybrid identities, plural worlds.* London; New York: Routledge.

Noguera, P. (2003a). *City schools and the American dream: Reclaiming the promise of public education.* New York: Teachers College Press.

Noguera, P. (2003b). The trouble with Black boys: The role and influence of environmental and cultural factors on the academic performance of African American males. *Urban Education, 38*(4), 431–459.

Noguera, P. (2008). *The trouble with Black boys: Essays on race, equity, and the future of public education* (1st ed.). San Francisco: Jossey-Bass.

Noguera, P., Ginwright, S. A., & Cammarota, J. (2006). *Beyond resistance! Youth activism and community change: New democratic possibilities for practice and policy for America's youth.* New York: Routledge.

O'Brien, D. (2001). "At-risk" adolescents: Redefining competence through the multiliteracies of intermediality, visual arts, and representation. *Reading Online, 4*(11).

O'Brien, D. (2003). Juxtaposing traditional and intermedial literacies to redefine the competence of struggling adolescents. *Reading Online, 6*(7).

O'Brien, D. G. (1998). Multiple literacies in a high school program for "at-risk" adolescents. In D. E. Alvermann, K. A. Hinchman, D. W. Moore, S. F. Phelps, & D. R. Waff (Eds.), *Reconceptualizing the literacies in adolescents' lives* (pp. 27-49). Mahwah, NJ: Erlbaum.

O'Brien, D. G. (2006). Struggling adolescents' engagement in multimediating: Countering the institutional construction of incompetence. In D. E. Alvermann, K. A. Hinchman, D. W. Moore, S. F. Phelps, & D. R. Waff (Eds.), *Reconceptualizing the literacies in adolescents' lives* (2nd ed., pp. 29–46). Mahwah, NJ: Lawrence Erlbaum.

Osei-Kofi, N. (2005). Pathologizing the poor: A framework for understanding Ruby Payne's work. *Equity & Excellence in Education, 38,* 367–375.

Pahl, K., & Rowsell, J. (2006). *Travel notes from the new literacy studies: Instances of practice.* Clevedon, UK; Buffalo, NY: Multilingual Matters.

Patel Stevens, L. (2002). Making the road by walking: The transition from content area literacy to adolescent literacy. *Reading Research and Instruction, 41*(3), 267–278.

Patel Stevens, L. (2008). Adolescent literacy policy: (Re)framing policy analysis. *Journal of Adolescent and Adult Literacy, 52*(1), 70–73.

Pérez, B., & McCarty, T. L. (2004). *Sociocultural contexts of language and literacy* (2nd ed.). Mahwah, NJ: Lawrence Erlbaum.

Phelan, P., Davidson, A. L., & Yu, H. C. (1998). *Adolescents' worlds: Negotiating family, peers, and school.* New York: Teachers College Press.

Platt, A. M. (1977). *The child savers: The invention of delinquency* (2nd ed.). Chicago: University of Chicago Press.

Pleasants, H. (2008). Negotiating identity projects: Exploring the digital storytelling experiences of three African American girls. In M. L. Hill & L. Vasudevan (Eds.), *Media, learning, and sites of possibility* (pp. 205–233). New York: Peter Lang.

Polakow, V. (2000). *The public assault on America's children: Poverty, violence, and juvenile injustice.* New York: Teachers College Press.

Ranker, J. (2008). Making meaning on the screen: Digital video production about the Dominican Republic. *Journal of Adolescent and Adult Literacy, 51*(5), 410–422.

Rich, M. (2007, November 19). Study links drop in test scores to a decline in time spent reading. *The New York Times.* Retrieved December 6, 2008, from http://www.nytimes.com/2007/11/19/arts/19nea.html

Rich, M. (2008, July 27). Literacy debate: Online, R U really reading? *The New York Times.* Retrieved December 6, 2008, from http://www.nytimes.com/2008/07/27/books/27reading.html

Richardson, E. B., & Lewis, S. (2000). "Flippin the script"/"blowin up the spot": Puttin' hip-hop online in (African) American and South Africa. In G. E. Hawisher & C. L. Selfe (Eds.), *Global literacies and the world-wide web* (pp. 251–276). New York: Routledge.

Rubinstein-Avila, E. (2003). Conversing with Miguel: An adolescent English language learner struggling with later literacy development. *Journal of Adolescent and Adult Literacy, 47*, 290–302.

Schultz, K. (1996). Between school and work: The literacies of urban adolescent females. *Anthropology and Education Quarterly, 27*(4), 517–544.

Schultz, K. (2002). Looking across space and time: Reconceptualizing literacy learning in and out of school. *Research in the Teaching of English, 36*(3), 356–390.

Schultz, K., & Fecho, B. (2005). Literacies in adolescence: An analysis of policies from the United States and Queensland, Australia. In N. Bascia, A. Cumming, A. Datnow, K. Leithwood, & D. Livington (Eds.), *International handbook for educational policy* (pp. 677–694). Dordrecht, the Netherlands: Kluwer Academic Publishers.

Schmier, S. (2008, March). *Spatial design: Shaping social spaces for possibilities through the design of multimodal texts.* Paper presented at the Annual Meeting of the American Educational Research Association, New York.

Schwartz, R. G. (2001). Juvenile justice and positive youth development. In P. L. Benson & K. J. Pittman (Eds.), *Trends in youth development: Visions, realities, and challenges* (pp. 231–267). New York: Springer.

Scieszka, J. (2005). *Guys read.* Retrieved September 29, 2008, from http://www.guysread.com/

Simon, R. (2005). Bridging life and learning through inquiry and improvisation: Literacy practices at a model high school. In B. V. Street (Ed.), *Literacies across educational contexts.* Philadelphia: Caslon Press.

Skelton, T., & Valentine, G. (1998). *Cool places: Geographies of youth cultures.* London; New York: Routledge.

Skiba, R. J., Michael, R. S., Nardo, A. C., & Peterson, R. L. (2002). The color of discipline: Sources of racial and gender disproportionality in school punishment. *Urban Review, 34*(4), 317–342.

Skinner, E., & Hagood, M. C. (2008). Developing literate identities with English language learners through digital storytelling. *The Reading Matrix, 8*(2), 12–38.

Smith, M. W., & Wilhelm, J. D. (2002). *"Reading don't fix no Chevys": Literacy in the lives of young men.* Portsmouth, NH: Heinemann.

Snow, C. E., & Biancarosa, G. (2003). *Adolescent literacy and the achievement gap: What do we know and where do we go from here?* New York: Carnegie Corporation of New York.

Soep, E., & Chavez, V. (2005). Youth radio and the pedagogy of collegiality. *Harvard Educational Review, 75*(4), 409–434.

Solorzano, D., Ceja, M., & Yosso, T. (2000). Critical race theory, racial microaggressions, and campus racial climate: The experiences of African American college students. *Journal of Negro Education, 69*(1–2), 60–73.

Solorzano, D. G., & Yosso, T. J. (2001). From racial stereotyping and deficit discourse toward a critical race theory in teacher education. *Multicultural Education, 9*(1), 2–8.

Staples, J. M. (2008). "Hustle & Flow": A critical student and teacher-generated framework for re-authoring a representation of Black masculinity. *Educational Action Research, 16*(3), 377–390.

Stillwell, R., & Hoffman, L. (2008). *Public school graduates and dropouts from the common core of data: School year 2005–06* (NCES 2008–353rev). Washington, DC: National Center for Education Statistics, Institute of Education Sciences, U.S. Department of Education. Retrieved October 19, 2008, from http://nces.ed.gov/pubsearch/pubsinfo.asp?pubid=2008353rev

Street, B. V. (1984). *Literacy in theory and practice.* Cambridge, UK; New York: Cambridge University Press.

Street, B. V. (1995). *Social literacies: Critical approaches to literacy in development, ethnography, and education.* London; New York: Longman.

Street, B. V. (2002). Understanding literacy issues in contemporary multiethnic schooling contexts, with particular reference to EAL pupils. In C. Leung (Ed.), *Language and additional/second language issues for school education* (pp. 49–58). Watford, UK: National Association for Language Development in the Curriculum.

Sullivan, M. (2003). *Connecting boys with books: What libraries can do.* Chicago: American Library Association.

Taylor, D. (1991). *Learning denied.* Portsmouth, NH: Heinemann.

Taylor, D. (1996). *Toxic literacies: Exposing the injustice of bureaucratic texts.* Portsmouth, NH: Heinemann.

Taylor, D., & Dorsey-Gaines, C. (1988). *Growing up literate: Learning from inner-city families.* Portsmouth, NH: Heinemann.

Thomas, A. (2005). Children online: Learning in a virtual community of practice. *E-Learning, 2*(1), 27–38.

Thomas, A. (2007). *Youth online: Identity and literacy in the digital age.* New York: Peter Lang.

Tuzzolo, E., & Hewitt, D. T. (2006/2007). Rebuilding inequity: The re-emergence of the school-to-prison pipeline in New Orleans. *High School Journal, 90*(2), 59–68.

Universal declaration of human rights. (n.d.). Retrieved July 19, 2008, from http://www.un.org/Overview/rights.html

Vacca, R. T. (1998). Let's not marginalize adolescent literacy (literacy issues in focus). *Journal of Adolescent and Adult Literacy, 41*(8), 604–609.

Vadeboncoeur, J. A., & Patel Stevens, L. (2005). *Reconstructing the "adolescent": Sign, symbol, and body.* New York: Peter Lang.

Valenzuela, A. (1999). *Subtractive schooling: U.S.-Mexican youth and the politics of caring* (SUNY Series, The Social Context of Education). Albany: State University of New York.

Varenne, H., & McDermott, R. (1998). *Successful failure: The school America builds.* Boulder, CO: Westview Press.

Vasudevan, L. (2008). Media and adolescent literacies. *NewLits.Org.* Retrieved October 22, 2008, from: http://www.newlits.org/index.php?title=Main_Page

Vasudevan, L. (in press). Performing new geographies of teaching and learning. *English Education.*

Vasudevan, L., & Hill, M. L. (2008). Moving beyond dichotomies of media engagement in education: An introduction. In M. L. Hill & L. Vasudevan (Eds.), *Media, learning, and sites of possibility* (pp. 1–12). New York: Peter Lang.

Villenas, S., & Deyhle, D. (1999). Critical race theory and ethnographies challenging the stereotypes: Latino families, schooling, resilience and resistance. *Curriculum Inquiry, 29*(4), 413–445.

Vygotsky, L. (1978). *Mind in society*. Cambridge, MA: Harvard University Press.

Wacquant, L. (2001). Deadly symbiosis: When ghetto and prison meet and mesh. *Punishment & Society, 3*(1), 95–133.

Wald, J., & Losen, D. J. (2003). Defining and redirecting a school-to-prison pipeline. *New Directions for Youth Development, 99*, 9–15.

Ware, P. D. (2008). In and after school: Teaching language learners using multimedia literacy. *Pedagogies: An International Journal, 3*(1), 37–51.

Wissman, K. (2007). "Making a way": Young women using literacy and language to resist the politics of silencing. *Journal of Adolescent and Adult Literacy, 51*(4), 340–349.

Wissman, K. (2008). "This is what I see": (Re)envisioning photography as a social practice. In M. L. Hill & L. Vasudvan (Eds.), *Media, learning, and sites of possibility* (pp. 13–45). New York: Peter Lang.

Yazzie-Mintz, E. (2007). *High School Survey of Student Engagement, Spring 2007*. Center for Evaluation & Education Policy, Indiana University, Bloomington.

YouthRadio. (n.d.). *Goal four: Launch research and development opportunities*. Retrieved December 6, 2008, from http://www.youthradio.org/about/goal-4

Zacher, J. C. (2007). Talking about difference and defining social relations with labels. *Language Arts, 85*(2), 115–124.

About the Editors

Vivian L. Gadsden is the William T. Carter Professor of Education and Child Development in the Graduate School of Education and Affiliated Faculty in the Center for Africana Studies at the University of Pennsylvania. Dr. Gadsden's research and publications span interests in cultural and social factors affecting learning and literacy across the life-course and within families, particularly those at the greatest risk for academic, health, and social vulnerability and intergenerational poverty and educational access. Her publications include journal articles, booklength volumes, and federally commissioned reports on these issues as well as questions of race, equity, and difference. Her current research studies, including an NICHD study of early childhood, a study on children of incarcerated parents, and a study on health and educational disparities, examine the intergenerational and cross-cultural nature of learning and identity formation among children, issues of persistence and resilience, and youth cultures. Her conceptual framework, family cultures, focuses on the interconnectedness between families' political, cultural, and social histories and racialized identities. At Penn, she is the Principal Investigator and Director of the National Center on Fathers and Families. Dr. Gadsden has served on panels of the National Academy of Sciences; White House initiatives on families and education; multiple federal, state, and local initiatives; and international/cross-cultural research and policy initiatives. In 2003–2006, she served as Vice President of Division G and established the Social Context of Education Research Project, involving 22 AERA/ Division G early career scholars and mentors. In 2007, she was a Resident Fellow at the Spencer Foundation.

Alfredo J. Artiles is Professor of Special Education and Transborder Chicana/o Latina/o Studies at Arizona State University. His research examines disability identification practices as a window into schools' cultural constructions of difference. His research also focuses on teacher learning for social justice. His publications include three edited books and numerous manuscripts in journals such as *Harvard Educational Review, Teachers College Record, Educational Researcher, Review of Research in Education, Exceptional Children*, and *Journal of Special Education*. Dr. Artiles is Editor (with Terry Wiley) of the *International Multilingual Research Journal* (Taylor & Francis), and edits (with Elizabeth Kozleski) the book series *Disability, Culture, &*

Review of Research in Education
March 2009, Vol. 33, pp. 354-355
DOI: 10.3102/0091732X08331314
© 2009 AERA. http://rre.aera.net

Equity (Teachers College Press). He was a Spencer Foundation/NAE Postdoctoral Fellow and a 2008-09 Resident Fellow at the Center for Advanced Study in the Behavioral Sciences (Stanford University). He is principal investigator of the National Center for Culturally Responsive Educational Systems, the Equity Alliance at ASU, and two doctoral training grants. Current research includes a comparison of 13 countries' equity dilemmas that emerge during the implementation of inclusive education models. Dr. Artiles has been an advisor/consultant to organizations/projects such as Harvard's and UCLA's Civil Rights Projects, the Annenberg Institute for School Reform (Brown University), the Council for Exceptional Children, the Southern Poverty Law Center, and the Joseph P. Kennedy Jr. Foundation. Dr. Artiles is Vice President Elect of AERA's Division G, Social Contexts of Education.

James Earl Davis is Professor in the Department of Educational Leadership and Policy Studies at Temple University and affiliate faculty in African American Studies and Women Studies. His research generally focuses on educational policy, urban school reform, and the intersection of race, class and gender. His recent scholarship has engaged questions about the academic and social experiences of African American boys and young men placed at risk for underachievement and school disengagement, with particular attention to the role of identity constructions and gender conformity. His work has appeared in numerous journals, edited volumes and policy reports, including *Gender & Society, Evaluation Review, Peabody Journal of Education,* Educational Researcher, and *American Journal of Evaluation.* He is coauthor of *African American Males in School and Society: Policies and Practices for Effective Education* (with Vernon Polite) and *Black Sons to Mothers: Compliments, Critiques, and Challenges for Cultural Workers in Education* (with M. Christopher Brown). A former Spencer Postdoctoral Fellow, he has been a Visiting Scholar at the Institute for Research on Women and Gender at the University of Michigan and in the Center for Education Research at the University of Wisconsin-Madison. He recently served as the Visiting John W. Porter Distinguished Chair in Urban Education at Eastern Michigan University. His research has been funded by the Spencer Foundation, the National Science Foundation, Marcus Foundation, and the U.S. Center for Substance Abuse Prevention.

About the Contributors

Kate Anderson is an Assistant Professor in the Learning Sciences Lab at the National Institute of Education in Singapore. She received her Ph.D. in Linguistics and an Interdisciplinary Qualitative Studies Graduate Certificate from the University of Georgia where she focused on exploring different methodological approaches to discourse on race and language as well as the role of discourse and ideology on students' opportunities to learn. Her work examines students' positional identity through post-structural approaches to discourse, ideology, and opportunity to learn. Her research enlists interactive digital media to explore multimodality, positioning, and semiotic mediation of participation in designing digital storytelling workshops. By working with youth who are disenfranchised or marginalized to develop literacy practices on their own terms with implications for curricular design, her scholarly work aims to bridge formal and informal learning in Singapore. She is a member of AERA Division G's Social Context of Education Research Group.

Angela Arzubiaga is an Assistant Professor in the Division of Psychology in Education at Arizona State University. She received her Ph.D. from University of California at Los Angeles. She has also received the University of California President's Postdoctoral Fellowship and an International Society for the Study of Behavioral Development award. Her research focuses on the education of children of immigrants, eco-cultural and sociocultural perspectives on family life and home-institution connections, and immigrant families' adaptations. She is a Spencer and Bernard Van Leer investigator on the Children of Immigrants in US Preschool: Parent and Teacher Perspectives and the Children Crossing Borders studies.

John Baugh is the Director of African and African American Studies and Professor of Psychology, both in Arts and Sciences at Washington University in St. Louis. He is the inaugural holder of an Arts and Sciences endowed professorship named in honor of prominent civil rights attorney and emerita trustee Margaret Bush Wilson. In addition, he holds appointments in the Departments of Anthropology, Education and English, all in Arts and Sciences. Baugh, author of *Beyond Ebonics: Linguistic Pride and Racial Prejudice*, a significant piece of work on the Ebonics controversy, is a renowned linguistics expert.

Review of Research in Education
March 2009, Vol. 33, pp. 356-363
DOI: 10.3102/0091732X08331152
© 2009 AERA. http://rre.aera.net

Gerald Campano is an Assistant Professor at Indiana University, Bloomington. He has been a full-time classroom teacher in Houston, Texas, Puerto Rico, and California's Central Valley and has worked with adult English language learners in North Philadelphia. His research interests and publications address immigrant identities in the context of schooling, urban education, Filipina American studies, and teacher research. Campano is a Carnegie Scholar and the author of *Immigrant Students and Literacy: Reading, Writing, and Remembering* (2007). He holds a Ph.D. in education (reading/writing/literacy) from the University of Pennsylvania.

Lijun Chen is a researcher at Chapin Hall Center for Children at the University of Chicago. His research interests include statistical modeling and analysis of longitudinal and survival data for children in foster care. He has published in *Social Service Review* and participated in the preparation and writing of research reports on children in child welfare. His recent analyses focus on foster care contract agency performance evaluation and the development of children in foster care.

Kris Gutiérrez is a Professor in the Graduate School of Education & Information Studies at the University of California, Los Angeles and serves as the Director of the Center for the Study of Urban Literacies, as well as the Director of the Education Studies Minor. Professor Gutierrez' research focuses on studying the literacy practices of urban schools. In particular, her research concerns itself with the social and cognitive consequences of literacy practices in formal and non-formal learning contexts. Across her work, she examines the relationship between literacy, culture and human development. Professor Gutierrez was the 2005 recipient of the AERA Division C Sylvia Scribner Award and was a Fellow at the Center for Advanced Studies in the Behavioral Sciences, 2006–07.

Liesel Hibbert is an Associate Professor in the English Department at the University of the Western Cape in South Africa. She received her Ph.D. from the University of Cape Town in 2000. Her research traces youth development in an economically marginal community and school in Mitchell's Plain outside Cape Town. The focus in this study is on multilingualism, multiliteracies, identity formation, and agency in a theatre training project. Some of her recent publications are: "Representations/(re)contextualisations of Traditional Repertoires in Parliamentary Discourse in South Africa" in *Mannheimer Beitraege: Identities in Migration Contexts* (2006); "Globalization, the African Renaissance and the Role of English" in the *International Journal of the Sociology of Language* (2004); "Changing language practices in South Africa" in *South African Linguistics and Applied Language Studies Journal* (2003); and "Comparing Black South African English and African American Vernacular English" in *English Today* (2002).

Lori Diane Hill is an Assistant Professor in the School of Education and the Center for Afro-american and African Studies at the University of Michigan. She holds a Ph.D. in sociology from the University of Chicago. Her research interests include urban education, stratification and inequality, youth social networks and social capital, and organizational analysis. Her work focuses on the educational attainment processes of youth of color and examines how education policies, school practices and social resources within families cooperatively shape the social mobility trajectories of students in urban contexts in the U.S. and South Africa. Her current research focuses on the educational experiences of Black youth in South Africa and considers emerging patterns of educational inequality as they relate to the intergenerational transmission of ideologies about race and education.

Glynda Hull is a Professor of English Education at New York University. She studies literacy, broadly conceived; urban school-university partnerships; out-of-school and workplace literacies; and most recently, multi-media, multi-modal composing and internet-enabled social networking. Her projects are carried out in different contexts—classrooms, workplaces, community settings—and engage participants across the age range: college students, Silicon Valley assembly workers, children, youth, adults from urban communities, and "global" youth in several countries. Hull's books include *Changing Work, Changing Workers: Critical Perspectives on Language, Literacy, and Skill* (SUNY Press); *The New Work Order: Education and Literacy in the New Capitalism* (Allen & Unwin; with James Gee and Colin Lankshear); and *School's Out! Bridging Out-of-School Literacies with Classroom Practice* (Teachers College with Katherine Schultz). She teaches graduate and undergraduate courses on literacy, media, and teacher education, and received the Distinguished Teaching Award at the University of California, Berkeley.

Emanique Joe is currently a Postdoctoral Research Fellow at the University of Michigan in the School of Education. Her academic affiliations are with the Combined Program in Education and Psychology and Department of Educational Studies, and she also is a Fellow at the Center for the Study of Black Youth in Context. Dr. Joe's research focuses on ethnic minority parents' influence (i.e., via their beliefs and parenting behavior) on their children's school readiness and early academic success. Dr. Joe is also interested in evidence-based educational policy and programs that seek to improve family and school partnerships. With a professional background in social work, she has worked with low-income families on issues related to welfare reform policy and the availability of quality child care and has facilitated parent leadership classes around early childhood education advocacy issues. Dr. Joe is a member of the Emerging Scholars Interdisciplinary Network.

Sean Joe holds a joint position as Assistant Professor in the School of Social Work and the Department of Psychiatry at the University of Michigan Medical Center. He is also a Faculty Associate with the Program for Research on Black Americans at the University's Institute for Social Research. Dr. Joe is a recognized authority on suicidal behavior among African Americans. His current research projects focus on Black adolescents' mental health service use patterns; the role of religion in Black suicidal behavior (NIMH), salivary biomarkers for suicidal behavior; and development of father-focused, family-based interventions to prevent urban African American adolescent males from engaging in multiple forms of self-destructive behaviors (e.g., suicidal behavior). Dr. Joe is co-chair of the Emerging Scholars Interdisciplinary Network Research Study Group on African American Suicide, a national interdisciplinary group of researchers committed to advancing research in this area, and serves on the board of directors of the Suicide Prevention Action Network, the scientific advisory board of the National Organization of People of Color Against Suicide, and the editorial board of *Advancing Suicide Prevention,* a policy magazine.

Carol D. Lee is Professor of Education and Social Policy in the Learning Sciences Program at Northwestern University. She is President-Elect of the American Educational Research Association, a member of the National Academy of Education, and a former fellow at the Center for Advanced Study in the Behavioral Sciences. Professor Lee is the author of three books including the most recent *Culture, Literacy and Learning: Taking Bloom in the Midst of the Whirlwind* and co-editor of *Vygotskian Perspectives on Literacy Research,* along with numerous other scholarly publications. Her research focuses on ecological influences on learning and development, including the Cultural Modeling Framework for the design of instruction that scaffolds knowledge constructed from youth's everyday experience to support discipline-specific learning. She is a co-founder of four schools in Chicago, including three charter schools, serving as chairman of the Board of Directors of the Betty Shabazz International Charter Schools.

Jin Sook Lee is an Assistant Professor at the Gevirtz Graduate School of Education at the University of California, Santa Barbara. She received her doctorate in education from Stanford University. Her research interests focus on the cultural, sociopolitical, and sociopsychological factors that influence the language learning processes of immigrant children. Her research projects examine the role of heritage language learning in the development of cultural identity and the development of dual language competence among young immigrant children. She serves on the editorial board of the *International Multilingual Research Journal* and *Language Arts* and is co-editing a book, entitled *The Education of Language Minority Students in the United States* (Multilingual Matters), with Terrence Wiley and Russ Rumberger. She is a recent recipient of the Foundation for Child Development Young Scholars Program Award and is a member of AERA Division G's Social Context of Education Research Group.

Danny C. Martinez is a doctoral student in the Division of Urban Schooling at the University of California, Los Angeles, Graduate School of Education & Information Studies. His research interests center on exploring how nondominant students' language practices can be used as a resource for learning in classrooms. Through a critical language awareness framework, he hopes to explore how students' home languages can become an integral part of the development of academic language and literacy skills. He believes his future research can inform pre-service and current teachers to value, nurture, and preserve the languages of nondominant youth. Prior to entering the doctoral program, Martinez taught middle and high school ESL and English in San Francisco and Los Angeles.

Ray McDermott is a Professor in Education and Anthropology at Stanford University. He takes a broad interest in the analysis of human communication, the organization of school success and failure, and the history and use of various literacies around the world. His work includes studies of inner-city public schools, after-school classrooms, and the function of information technologies in different cultures. At present, he is working on the intellectual history of ideas like genius, intelligence, race, and capital.

P. Zitlali Morales is a doctoral student in the Urban Schooling program at the Graduate School of Education & Information Studies at UCLA. Her research interests include education policy, language ideologies, bilingual education, and achievement of English language learners. Morales previously worked as a School Partnership Director for Partners In School Innovation, a reform organization in the San Francisco Bay Area. Her dissertation focuses on the academic identity development of linguistic minority students in a Spanish-English dual immersion program in the Los Angeles area.

Silvia Noguerón is a Ph.D. student in the Division of Curriculum and Instruction, Mary Lou Fulton College of Education at Arizona State University. She is specializing in the areas of language and literacy. Her research interests include the education of transnational students and their families, especially in terms of access to English language learning and digital literacy practices. Her previous publications include contributions to the *Encyclopedia of Bilingual Education* (J. González, Ed., 2008).

Carla O'Connor is an Associate Professor of Education at the University of Michigan. Her disciplinary emphasis is sociology of education and she has expertise in the areas of African American achievement, urban education, and ethnographic methods. Her work includes examinations of how Black identity is differentially constructed across multiple contexts and informs achievement outcomes; how Black people's perceptions of opportunity vary within and across social space and influence academic orientation; and how Black educational resilience and vulnerability is structured by social, institutional, and historical forces. Dr. O'Connor's work has been published in the *American Educational Research Journal, Educational Researcher, Sociology of Education,* and *Ethnic and Racial Studies.* She co-edited (with Erin McNamara Horvat) the book, *Beyond Acting White: Reframing the Debate on Black Student Achievement.* She is a co-principal investigator for an NSF IRAD grant which established the Center for Black Youth in Context. She was named an Arthur F. Thurnau Professor, an honor given to tenured faculty with exceptional commitment to undergraduate teaching. Dr. O'Connor received her Ph.D. in Education from the University of Chicago. She also holds an M.A. in Education from the University of Chicago and a B.A. in English from Wesleyan University.

Jason Raley is a lecturer at the Gevirtz Graduate School of Education at the University of California, Santa Barbara. He received his doctorate in education from Stanford University. His research interests include teacher education, educational philosophy, educational equity, learning, anthropology, social interaction, and social relations.

Shanta R. Robinson is a doctoral student in Educational Foundations and Policy and a Rackham Merit Fellowship recipient at the University of Michigan. Her research interests focus on social justice education and theory, including issues of race, class, gender, and sexuality, with particular attention to policy development and pre-service teacher preparation. She has five years of public secondary school teaching experience. In addition, she has extensive experience in nonprofit management consulting and grant writing development, as well as diversity sensitivity workshop facilitation. She holds a M.A. from the University of North Carolina at Charlotte in Public Administration and a B.A. from the University of North Carolina at Asheville in Sociology and Education.

Larry L. Rowley is an Assistant Professor of Higher Education in the School of Education and Assistant Professor of Afroamerican and African Studies in the College of Literature, Science, and the Arts at the University of Michigan. He holds a Ph.D. in higher education and an M.Ed. in social foundations of education, both from the University of Virginia. Dr. Rowley's research applies theories of race, education and social development to empirical analyses of African Americans in communities and higher education institutions. His research has examined the public service mission and social functions of higher education, non-monetary benefits of undergraduate education, race and American academic/ intellectual hierarchies, and relationships between universities and black urban communities. He has published work on W. E. B. DuBois's contribution to sociology of knowledge in the American academy and implications for blacks in higher education as well as the importance of mentoring for black college students. Professor Rowley has published his work in *The Urban Review, Educational Researcher, Journal of Negro Education, African American Research Perspectives,* and *About Campus.*

Ingrid Seyer-Ochi is an Assistant Professor at the Graduate School of Education at the University of California, Berkeley. Her research and teaching interests focus on urban education; the history of education; families, neighborhoods, and community organizations as educative institutions; and the relationships among school and beyond-school learning contexts. Underlying all of her work is an interest in the experiences of socially-constructed and marginalized groups as they interact with multiple social service institutions across structured and segregated landscapes. Her book, *Smart on the Under, Wise to the Streets: Mapping the Landscapes of Urban Youth,* is forthcoming.

Cheryl Smithgall is a Research Fellow at Chapin Hall Center for Children at the University of Chicago. Her work focuses on the areas of child welfare, children's mental health, and education, and she employs quantitative, qualitative, and mixed-methods approaches. She is currently leading an evaluation of the Illinois Department of Child and Family Services' Integrated Assessment Program. Within the area of education, she is currently leading or contributing to a number of projects that inform Chicago Public Schools' efforts to design, implement, and assess interventions or initiatives aimed at improving behavioral and academic outcomes for all children. Past projects have included the National Evaluation of Family Preservation and

Reunification Services, the assessment of behavior problems and educational issues among children in out-of-home care, and a study of mental health needs and service utilization among children in their grandparents' care.

Howard Stevenson is an Associate Professor and chair of the Applied Psychology and Human Development Division in the University of Pennsylvannia's Graduate School of Education. His research and consultation work identify cultural strengths that exist within families and seek to integrate those strengths in interventions to improve the psychological adjustment of children and adolescents and families. Dr. Stevenson is conducting a classroom-based racial negotiation skills-building intervention for teachers and students, the goal of which is to reduce negative stress-related reactions in cross-racial student-teacher relationships. This project is called *Can We Talk? (CWT)*.

Amanda Sullivan is a doctoral candidate in the School Psychology program in the Mary Lou Fulton College of Education at Arizona State University. Her research addresses issues of diversity and equity in school psychology and special education, with attention to the ways in which systemic factors, educational policy, and professional practices shape the experiences of culturally and linguistically diverse students.

Duane Thomas is an Assistant Professor at the Graduate School of Education at the University of Pennsylvania. His research has focused on elucidating classroom effects on the early development of serious aggressive behavior problems for children. His research also examines sociocultural protective factors contributing to resiliency in urban African-American youth exposed to high levels of community violence and related environmental risks. Thomas' professional background includes providing a range of psychological services for children, youth, and families from diverse backgrounds and participating in large-scale community-based violence prevention research.

Lalitha M. Vasudevan is an Assistant Professor of Technology and Education at Teachers College, Columbia University. She completed her Ph.D. at the University of Pennsylvania. Vasudevan has worked with youth both in and out of school, as a teacher and as a researcher, and is interested in how youth craft stories and produce knowledge using different literacies, technologies, and media. She is studying education, literacy and media in the lives of court-involved youth using a multimedia storytelling methodology. Vasudevan's research has been published in the *Journal of Adolescent and Adult Literacy, E-Learning,* and *English Education,* and she is co-editor of the volume, *Media, Learning, and Sites of Possibility* (2008, Peter Lang).

Fred Wulczyn is a Research Fellow at Chapin Hall Center for Children at the University of Chicago. He is the recipient of the National Association of Public Child Welfare Administrators' Peter Forsyth Award for leadership in public child welfare. Wulczyn is lead author of *Beyond Common Sense: Child Welfare, Child Well-Being, and the Evidence for Policy Reform*, published by Aldine Transaction in 2005.

He is also co-author of *Child Protection: Using Research to Improve Policy and Practice*, published in 2007 by Brookings Institution Press. Wulczyn is also the director of the Center for State Foster Care and Adoption Data, which provides cutting-edge information technology to member agencies for use in performance measurement, was the architect of Chapin Hall's Multi-State Foster Care Data Archive, and constructed the original integrated longitudinal database on children's services in Illinois, now in use for over 20 years. Wulczyn received his Ph.D. from the School of Social Service Administration (Social Welfare Policy) at the University of Chicago.

Jessica Zacher is an Assistant Professor in Teacher Education and Liberal Studies at the California State University, Long Beach. She teaches courses on literacy and multicultural education. She received her Ph.D. from the University of California, Berkeley, Graduate School of Education in Language, Literacy, and Culture, in 2005. Zacher has published articles in journals such as *The Journal of Educational Foundations* (forthcoming), *Research in the Teaching of English* (2008), *Language Arts* (2007), *Identity: An International Journal of Theory and Research* (2007, with G. Hull), and others. She also has authored several book chapters, individually and with colleagues, in books such as *Bourdieu and Literacy Education*, Allan Luke & Jim Albright (Eds.), (2008); *Secondary School Reading and Writing: What Research Reveals for Classroom Practices*, A. Berger, L. Rush, & J. Eakle (Eds.), (2007, with K. Leander); and *Research on Sociocultural Influences on Motivation and Learning: Focus on Curriculum*, D. McInerney & S. Van Etten (Eds.), (2005). Zacher's ethnographic research project investigates the experiences of second language learners in a high-poverty urban school, focusing on both the mandated curriculum and students' out-of-school lives.